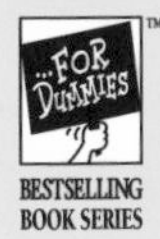

Windows® XP Timesaving Techniques™ For Dummies®, 2nd Edition

Cheat Sheet

Windows Media Player Shortcut Keys

This Key	*Does This*
F8	Turns off the sound
F9	Decreases the volume
F10	Increases the volume
Ctrl+P	Play/Pause
Ctrl+S	Stop
Ctrl+B	Back one track
Ctrl+F	Forward one track

Woody's Take on Burning Music

Format	*Sampling Rate*	*Hassle Factor*	*Music Quality*	*Songs on a 128MB Player*	*Comments*
MP3	64 Kbps	Low	Blech	60–70	Good enough for playing on blah computer speakers.
MP3	128 Kbps	Low	Very Good	30	Woody's Choice Award Winner.
AAC	64 Kbps	Medium	So-so	70-80	Not as good as WMA at 64 Kbps.
AAC	128 Kbps	Medium	Best of the bunch	30-35	Apple's AAC-to-WMA converter helps, particularly because so few AAC players exist (other than the iPod and variants, of course).
WMA	64 Kbps	High	So-so	70–80	Why not go up to 128 Kbps?
WMA	128 Kbps	High	Excellent	30–35	A decent choice if you only plan to play music on your PC, or you have a small music player that can handle WMA.

Camera Resolution and JPG File Sizes

This Resolution	*Produces JPEG Files About This Size*	*So This Many Pictures Fit on a 128MB Memory Card*	*These Shots Are Suitable For*	*And Take About This Long to Download*
2400 x 1800	1.6MB	80	High-quality enlargements	5 minutes
2048 x 1536	1.2MB	100	10 x 12 prints	4 minutes
1600 x 1200	0.8MB	160	8 x 10 prints	2.5 minutes
1280 x 960	0.5MB	250	5 x 7 prints	1.5 minutes
1024 x 768	0.4MB	300	4 x 6 prints	1 minute
800 x 600	0.2MB	500	Wallet-size prints	30 seconds
640 x 480	0.1MB	1000	Decent Web graphics	15 seconds

For Dummies®: Bestselling Book Series for Beginners

Windows® XP Timesaving Techniques™ For Dummies®, 2nd Edition

Searching with the Google Toolbar

The Google Toolbar is a great addition to Internet Explorer, because the Toolbar can help you zero in on the information you want — fast. See Technique 24 for downloading instructions and more quick tricks.

- **Google Menu:** The Google Menu on the far left lets you jump directly to various Google pages, such as the Advanced Search page.
- **Search Terms box:** Type the words that you want to find in this box, and then press Enter or click the Search Web button. Google searches the Web for what you ask.
- **Search Site:** This button is a great timesaver. Type the terms you want to find in the Search Terms box and then click Search Site. Google performs the search, restricting itself to the current Web site.
- **PageRank:** When you hover your mouse over the PageRank button — assuming you opted for the Advanced Google Toolbar — you see Google's assigned PageRank, on a scale from 0 to 10. A PageRank of 6 or higher generally means you're looking at a reliable page that many other sites refer to.
- **Highlight:** If you click the Highlight button, Internet Explorer highlights the words in the Search text box that appear in the Web page, each with a different color.

What You Need to Do Now to Protect Yourself

- **Buy, install, update, and religiously use a major antivirus package.** See Technique 49.
- **Force Windows to show you filename extensions.** Microsoft's decision to have Windows hide filename extensions — the letters at the end of a filename, such as `.doc` or `.vbs` — is a dangerous design mistake that you can fix (see Technique 20).
- **After you can see filename extensions, watch out for suspicious extensions in e-mail attachments.** If you receive a file with one of the doubtful extensions attached to an e-mail message (see the table of filename extensions in Technique 49), and you double-click the file, it runs immediately, with potentially disastrous results. This is the most common way for viruses to travel via e-mail.
- **Never open or run a file attached to an e-mail message until you**
  - Contact the person who sent you the message and verify that he or she specifically sent you the file.
  - Save the file on your hard drive, update your antivirus software's signature file, and run your antivirus software on the file.
- **Get Windows Firewall working right.** It may not be as easy as you think; and you should put a "fast lockdown" icon on your desktop (Technique 50).
- **Clobber scummy programs before they clobber you.** Ad-Aware, SpyBot-Search & Destroy, and Startup Monitor belong on every PC — and they're free (Techniques 11, 52, and 53).

Item 7883-9.
For more information about Wiley Publishing, call 1-800-762-2974.

For Dummies: Bestselling Book Series for Beginners

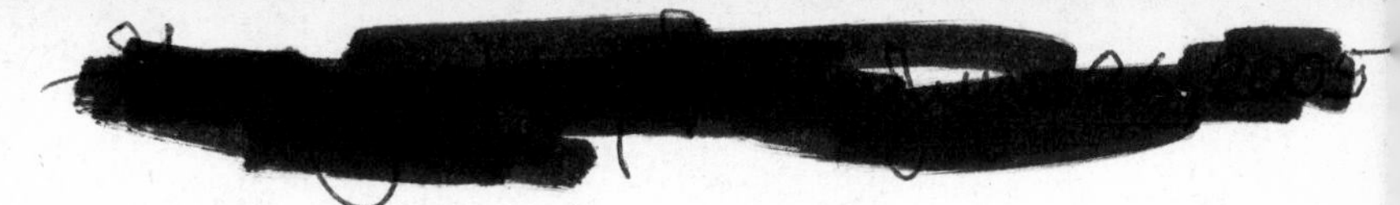

Windows® XP Timesaving Techniques™ FOR DUMMIES®

2ND EDITION

by Woody Leonhard

***Author of* Windows® XP All-in-One Desk Reference For Dummies®**

with Justin Leonhard

Wiley Publishing, Inc.

Windows® XP Timesaving Techniques™ For Dummies®, 2nd Edition

Published by
Wiley Publishing, Inc.
111 River Street
Hoboken, NJ 07030-5774

Published by Wiley Publishing, Inc., Indianapolis, Indiana

Published simultaneously in Canada

For general information on our other products and services, please contact our Customer Care Department within the U.S. at 800-762-2974, outside the U.S. at 317-572-3993, or fax 317-572-4002.

For technical support, please visit `www.wiley.com/techsupport`.

Wiley also publishes its books in a variety of electronic formats. Some content that appears in print may not be available in electronic books.

Library of Congress Control Number: 2004116452

ISBN: 0-7645-7883-9

Manufactured in the United States of America

10 9 8 7 6 5 4 3 2 1

2V/QU/QR/QV/IN

About the Authors

Woody Leonhard: Curmudgeon, critic, and perennial "Windows Victim," Woody Leonhard runs a fiercely independent Web site devoted to delivering the truth about Windows and Office, whether Microsoft likes it or not. With up-to-the-nanosecond news, observations, tips and help, `AskWoody.com` has become the premiere source of unbiased information for people who actually use the products.

In the past decade, Woody has written more than two dozen books, drawing an unprecedented six Computer Press Association awards and two American Business Press awards. Woody was one of the first Microsoft Consulting Partners and is a charter member of the Microsoft Solutions Provider organization. He's widely quoted — and reviled — on the Redmond campus.

Justin Leonhard: Lives with his dad in Phuket, Thailand. Justin contributed to *Windows XP All-in-One Desk Reference For Dummies*. He frequently helps Woody with various writing projects and keeps the office network going. Justin is an accomplished scuba diver, budding novelist, and the best video game player for miles. He was admitted to Mensa International at the age of 14.

Dedication

To Duangkhae Tongthueng (better known as "Add"), a truly amazing lady, who has helped me in so many ways.

Author's Acknowledgments

I would like to thank Phakdee Noosri, my researcher (better known as "Lek"), Web master, and assistant extraordinaire. Lek was born in Nakhorn Si Thammarat, in southern Thailand. He recently graduated with a degree in Computer Science at Prince of Songkla University, Phuket Campus. Lek is an avid photographer, camper, and swimmer. You can frequently find him swimming around Lampsing Beach — one of the most beautiful beaches in the world. You can see his handiwork at `AskWoody.com`.

I would also like to thank my wondrous agents, Claudette Moore and Debbie McKenna; Becky Huehls, who got all the hard work, including the nail-biting task of ensuring this book made it out on time; Steven Hayes, who approached me with a fascinating idea that ultimately turned into the first edition of this book; Rebecca Senninger for yeoman's work on the editing, and all the composition services people who have done an outstanding job with the unique layout that makes this book so easy to use.

Thanks, folks.

Publisher's Acknowledgments

We're proud of this book; please send us your comments through our online registration form located at www.dummies.com/register/.

Some of the people who helped bring this book to market include the following:

Acquisitions, Editorial, and Media Development

Project Editor: Rebecca Huehls

Senior Acquisitions Editor: Steve Hayes

Copy Editor: Rebecca Senninger

Technical Editor: Lee Musick

Editorial Manager: Leah P. Cameron

Media Development Manager: Laura VanWinkle

Media Development Supervisor: Richard Graves

Editorial Assistant: Amanda Foxworth

Cartoons: Rich Tennant (www.the5thwave.com)

Composition Services

Senior Project Coordinator: Nancee Reeves

Layout and Graphics: Amanda Carter, Lauren Goddard, Denny Hager, Stephanie D. Jumper, Melanee Prendergast, Jacque Roth, Heather Ryan

Proofreaders: Leeann Harney, Joe Niesen, Carl William Pierce, Christine Pingleton

Indexer: Rebecca R. Plunkett

Publishing and Editorial for Technology Dummies

Richard Swadley, Vice President and Executive Group Publisher

Andy Cummings, Vice President and Publisher

Mary Bednarek, Executive Acquisitions Director

Mary C. Corder, Editorial Director

Publishing for Consumer Dummies

Diane Graves Steele, Vice President and Publisher

Joyce Pepple, Acquisitions Director

Composition Services

Gerry Fahey, Vice President of Production Services

Debbie Stailey, Director of Composition Services

Contents at a Glance

Table of Contents

Introduction

Tell me if you've heard this one before: You're supposed to be at your son's school play in two hours. You're typing away on the computer, putting the finishing touches on a rush report, and all of a sudden Windows XP freezes tighter than a drum, taking your work along with it.

Blecch.

Whatever happened to the old-fashioned notion that PCs are supposed to save time, not waste it by the bushelful? What can average people do to make Windows work *for* them, not *against* them?

That's where this book comes in. This book isn't limited to dry "click this, press that" tips: *Windows XP Timesaving Techniques For Dummies* goes outside the traditional computer box to solve real-world problems that Windows XP users encounter every day.

About This Book

Microsoft says that Windows XP contains 50,000,000 lines of programming code. 400,000,000 PCs run Windows. Half of them use Windows XP, and roughly half of *them* run Service Pack 2. Heaven only knows how many people have used Windows. Nobody — absolutely nobody — understands more than a tiny part of Windows XP. Yet everybody — everybody outside of an ashram, anyway — has to come to grips with it.

Not an easy task, eh?

Windows XP Timesaving Techniques For Dummies concentrates on high-payoff techniques that save you time. These techniques make Windows work faster, more reliably, and more like the way you work, day in and day out. Use these techniques to spend less time spluttering and futzing with your machine.

Foolish Assumptions

I assume that you know how to use a computer and you can navigate Windows XP without fretting or asking a lot of questions. In fact, that's the first way this book saves you time: I don't cover old ground.

I assume that you're not scared to get under the hood, monkey around, and make changes to Windows XP — especially if those changes are going to make your computing life easier, more productive, and more hassle free in the long run.

I assume you're using Windows XP, and most of the techniques in this book apply to any version, particularly if you've installed Service Pack 2 or later (the security and wireless networking techniques assume that you use SP2). There are a few exceptions — some techniques apply only to Windows XP Home Edition or only Windows XP Professional Edition.

When a given technique only applies to a specific version of Windows XP, I'll be sure to give you some advanced warning. But you should be aware of the fact that a great schism is lurking here. Some people think that there's a big difference between Windows XP Home Edition and Windows XP Professional Edition, but the greatest gulf is the difference between running a peer-to-peer network (what Microsoft calls a *workgroup*) and a client-server network (a *domain* in Microsoft parlance).

When there's a difference in Windows XP between the way it acts in a peer-to-peer setting and the way it acts on a Big Corporate Network, I usually stick with the peer-to-peer approach, simply because that's usually the only configuration you have control over. If you have to wrestle with your network administrator, don't use this book as a blunt instrument, though. You can say, instead, "Hey, it says here that I can do that in piddling little Windows XP Home Edition; why can't I do it with Windows XP Professional Edition here at Flummox Corporation?"

You should assume that I'm not going to waste your time. I don't dillydally around, explaining *why* you may want to do something. Everything here has a common theme: Use these techniques to save time.

What's in This Book

To save you time, I organized this book into *techniques* — groups of related tasks that make you or your computer (or possibly both!) more efficient and effective. Some techniques are short 'n' sweet, tackle one specific topic, and get you in and out of the machine in record time. Other techniques are more involved and explore the pros and cons of various options.

Wherever an important ancillary topic, shorter tip, or loosely related timesaver may be of use, I include it. Watch for the icons. They can save you gobs of time. And don't be surprised if you bump into a tip or two that urges you to change the way you work, as opposed to simply making changes to your computer.

This book is laid out in a unique, easy-to-read two-column format full of figures and other visual cues that make it easier for you to scan and jump into a technique at the point most appropriate for your circumstances. Linear thinking is good. Nonlinear scanning is better.

Lay the book flat so you can see exactly what you're doing without flipping a bunch of pages (and tearing your hair out in the process).

You can read the book from front to back, or you can dive right into the technique of your choice. Either way works just fine. Anytime a concept is mentioned that isn't covered in depth in that technique, you'll find a cross-reference to another technique to find out more. If you're looking for something specific, check out either the table of contents or the index.

The Cheat Sheet at the beginning of the book lists my choices as the most important timesaving techniques. Tear it out, tape it to your monitor, pass it around to other folks at the office, and be sure to tell 'em Woody shares their pain.

All Gaul may have been divided into three parts, but this book needs eleven (a particularly, uh, galling admission). Here's what you'll find.

Part I: No-Bull Installation and Setup

If you haven't yet set up Windows XP, or if you're still in the process of getting adjusted to Service Pack 2, this is the place to start. In addition to advice that gets you up and running in no time, I cover the rarely discussed aspects of product registration, retrieving your product key, and installing a legitimate copy of Windows over the top of a pirate copy — without losing all your settings or wiping out your hard drive.

Part II: Making Windows Lean and Clean

Fine-tune Windows so that it helps you work faster. Here you can decide which desktop settings really make a difference and which ones don't. I also show you how to train Windows to respond to your needs. You find out how to transfer your old settings to a new PC, activate Passport without divulging your personal information, set up (or avoid) ClearType, "brand" your laptop computer to deter theft and identify you as its owner if it somehow gets lost, make your PC turn itself off when you shut down Windows, and how to switch users in the blink of an eye.

Part III: Convincing Windows to Work Your Way

You discover how to launch your most frequently used programs quickly — both on the Windows taskbar and by using hot keys, including hot keys that you build yourself.

I also show you how to take good care of your data. Discover quick file management techniques, such as renaming a group of files en masse, finding files quickly and effectively (and getting rid of Rover the Search Companion in the bargain), printing a list of files in a folder with a click, and much more.

Part IV: Making the Most of Internet and E-Mail

Take back control of the World Wide Timesink. You can find out about configuring and customizing Internet Explorer (including zapping pop-up, pop-over, and pop-under ads for good), controlling cookies to reduce spam, taking control of Windows/MSN Messenger so everybody and their brothers don't bother you when you're online, and keeping Outlook Express running like a dream. I help you set up Trillian, so you can run instant messaging with anyone, anytime. I also show you how to make the most of Google. And if you've got kids, this is the part where I show you how to protect them online.

Part V: Optimizing Your Musical Entertainment

A surprising number of pitfalls await the unfortunate. Here's how to avoid them. Get no-nonsense, person-to-person music gathering techniques; recommendations for buying music; and inside tips on ripping and burning. Customize Windows Media Player 10 and manipulate playlists, create your own music CDs, transfer music to players and other PCs, and tune in to WMP radio. Yes, the free radio is still there, if you know where to find it.

Part VI: Having Fun and Saving Time with Visual Media

Video and pictures take time to handle, but they're such fun. So here's how to *spend* less time while having more fun. Take snapshots and record videos with a Webcam, edit your home movies, manage digital pictures, and decrease picture download times. Ever wonder how to retrieve pictures that you accidentally deleted from your camera? The answer's here. You can also find techniques for printing pictures and using your scanner effectively.

Part VII: Ensuring Peak Network Performance

These days, everyone's networked, or so it seems. But how efficient is your network? Here you can find out how to get the most out of your peer-to-peer network, get home and small office network installation tips, find out the best way to share one Internet connection among several machines, and add (and configure) new network users.

If you're looking for help installing a wireless network, look no further. I take you through the fastest way to set up your network — and, far more importantly, secure it.

I also tell you the whole story — the *real* story — behind Windows XP Simple File Sharing. It isn't as simple (or as secure) as you think.

Part VIII: Fast Security Techniques

This part contains full behind-the-scenes coverage of the Windows Security Center, new in Service Pack 2. It gives you common-sense approaches to solving the rabidly hyped problem of computer security. Protect your PC from real viruses; conduct fast, easy, and safe online shopping transactions; and thwart intruders with a firewall. Best of all, I show you how to put an icon on your desktop that will "lock down" your system in a split-second. If you need to set up and monitor your security perimeter, look no further.

Part IX: Keeping Your PC Alive

An ounce of prevention is worth a ton of painful cures. Here you can discover how to run periodic maintenance automatically while you're off lounging somewhere (or meeting some insane deadline). I show you how to decide how much maintenance is enough and how to determine when to run maintenance checks so that your workflow isn't affected. And what about keeping Windows up to date? I show you why I don't trust Microsoft to update my PCs automatically. Decide which updates are critical and which ones can wait, get Remote Assistance and other forms of help, and make backups without a problem.

Part X: Fast (Nearly Painless) Disaster Recovery

Has Windows gone to Hades in a handbasket? *Again?* Here are the tricks you need to try in down-to-earth language. Find out how to survive (and permanently *stop)* the dreaded Blue Screen of Death. Find out how to get your PC to boot when it doesn't want to, restore your system to its pre-calamitous condition, and recover lost passwords. It ain't pretty, but sometimes you have to take the Windows bull by the horns.

Part XI: The Scary (Or Fun!) Stuff

Most of the techniques in the first ten parts are pretty straightforward. In Part XI, I take you deep into the belly of Windows XP. Find out how to make changes to the Registry without getting burned, and go through three of my favorite Registry tweaks that aren't covered by Microsoft's programs. I also show you how to use Program Compatibility Mode when you absolutely, positively have to get an old program to work.

Conventions Used in This Book

I try to keep the typographical conventions to a minimum:

- The first time a buzzword or concept appears in text, I italicize it and define it immediately so that you can easily find it again if you need to re-read the definition.
- When you see an arrow (⇨) in text, it means you should click, click, click to success. For example, "Choose Start⇨Control Panel⇨Add or Remove

Programs" means you should click Start, then click Control Panel, and then click Add or Remove Programs. Rocket science.

- When I want you to type something, I put the letters in bold. For example: Type **myfirstfilename1.doc** to name your new file.
- I set off Web addresses and e-mail IDs in monospace. For example, my e-mail address is `woody@AskWoody.com` (true fact), and my Web page is at `www.AskWoody.com` (another true fact).
- All filenames, paths, and just about anything you see on-screen are shown in monospace font, as well. For example, this bad boy, found in the Windows Registry, is set off like this: `HKEY_LOCAL_MACHINE\SOFTWARE\Microsoft\Windows NT\Current Version\WinLogons`
- I always, absolutely, adamantly include the filename extension — those letters (like `.doc` or `.vbs` or `.exe`) at the end of a filename — when talking about a specific file. Yeah, I know that Windows XP hides filename extensions unless you go into the program and change it (which I recommend in Technique 20).

Icons Used in This Book

While perusing this book, you'll notice some icons in the margins screaming for your attention. Each one has a purpose.

Here's how I call out the inside story — pointed facts that Microsoft might find embarrassing, school-of-hard-knocks advice, the kind of straight (sometimes politically incorrect) talk that shows you what's *really* happening. Hit my Web site, AskWoody.com, for the latest.

When time is of the essence, this icon emphasizes the point. More than a tip, but not quite a full technique, this icon points out a quick trick that can save you time — either now or later.

You don't need to memorize the stuff marked with this icon, but you should try to remember that this icon indicates something special that you need to know in future Windows XP endeavors.

When I'm jumping up and down on one foot with an idea so absolutely cool that I can't stand it any more — that's when I stick in a Tip icon. You can browse through any chapter and hit the very highest points by jumping from Tip to Tip.

Achtung! ¡Cuidado! Anyplace you see a Warning icon, you can be sure that I've been burnt — badly — in the past. Mind your fingers. These are really, really mean suckers.

Where to Go from Here

If you want your voice to be heard, you can contact the publisher of the *For Dummies* books by clicking the Contact Us link on the publisher's Web site at `www.dummies.com` or by sending snail mail to Wiley Publishing, Inc., 10475 Crosspoint Boulevard, Indianapolis, IN 46256.

You can contact Woody or Justin at `woody@AskWoody.com`. I can't answer all the questions I get — man, there ain't enough hours in the day! — but I take some of the best and post them on AskWoody.com frequently.

Speaking of AskWoody.com, drop by! I bet you'll be pleasantly surprised by the straight story, and coverage of important news items that you can't find anywhere else.

Confused about where to go next? Well, you can flip the page. Or you can flip a coin. Or you could hire a hundred monkeys and have them sit down at a hundred PCs and see how long it takes them to come up with the first technique.

Choices, choices . . .

Part I

No-Bull Installation and Setup

The 5th Wave
By Rich Tennant
Before installing Windows XP, Dwayne prepares to partition the hard drive.
©RICHTENNANT

Getting the Latest Version of Windows

Save Time By

- Getting the right version of Windows XP — the first time
- Updating Windows to the latest version
- Making the best installation decisions
- Bringing over all your old files and settings quickly — or maybe not

Appearances to the contrary, Windows XP hasn't taken over the earth. Three years after Microsoft unleashed Windows XP on an unsuspecting world, only half of the roughly 400,000,000 Windows machines alive were running XP. The other 200,000,000 were still chugging along with Windows 2000, or even <*shudder*> 98 or Me.

With the advent of Service Pack 2 and its considerable improvements in dozens of different areas, Microsoft is betting that more people will buy new computers, thereby acquiring Windows XP. If the Softies are lucky, many folks who just said "No" to the original Windows XP may be convinced to part with their hard-earned clams to upgrade their current machines to the "reloaded" Windows XP SP2.

If you're struggling with the question of whether to get Windows XP Home or part with the extra hundred bucks and go straight for Windows XP Professional, the first part of this technique pays for the book several times over — and saves you a bunch of time in the process.

If you have a new PC, or you've just installed Windows XP on an older PC, you need to wade through the arcana of Service Pack 2, and make a few key decisions with precious little unbiased advice. This technique points the way.

If you're faced with the chore of upgrading an older version of Windows to Windows XP, this technique includes a handful of school-of-hard-knocks recommendations that can save you hours (days!) of hassle. When is it safe to stick in the upgrade CD and let it have its way with your machine? When do you need to reformat the whole ^%$#@! hard drive before installing XP? Find the straight answers here.

Finally, in this technique, I take you behind the scenes with the Files and Settings Transfer Wizard, a remarkable Wizard if ever a Wiz there Wuz. Bet you didn't know that you can use it to transfer files when you switch computers at the office — even if you're moving to a computer that's been around forever — and save yourself a headache in the process.

Installing Service Pack 2

Windows XP Service Pack 2 may sound like a patch — it's called a *Service Pack*, after all — but in reality SP2 embodies a massive upgrade for Windows XP. No doubt you've heard lots of horror stories about upgrading to SP2, or buying a new machine with SP2 installed. Some of the horror stories are true — but most of them, fortunately, are way overblown, and there are ways (which I discuss in this technique) to minimize your chances of turning your PC into SP2 Road Kill. If you don't have SP2, you should get it, right now.

You gotta ask yourself one question...Do I feel lucky? Well, do ya, punk?

Oops. Wrong movie.

If you decide to upgrade to Service Pack 2, seriously consider wiping out your entire hard drive, reinstalling Windows XP, applying Service Pack 2, and then bringing back all your programs, data, and settings. It's a Herculean task, but your system runs better for it. If you're willing to install from scratch, and you have a day or two to spare, jump in this technique to the section called "Breezing through clean installs." Back up your data, install Windows XP, install SP2, and then follow along here in the section called "Setting up Service Pack 2". Then bring your programs and data back. Your PC will thank you for it.

If you just unpacked a new computer with Windows XP, or if you're brave enough to ignore the hype and upgrade to Windows XP Service Pack 2 in spite of your brother-in-law's podiatrist's secretary's nail stylist's recommendation, here's the best way to proceed:

1. **Make sure you aren't running SP2 already. Click Start, right-click My Computer, and choose Properties (see Figure 1-1).**

   If you see the phrase "Service Pack 2" (or anything later — perhaps "Service Pack 3"), you already have SP2 and can skip this section completely.

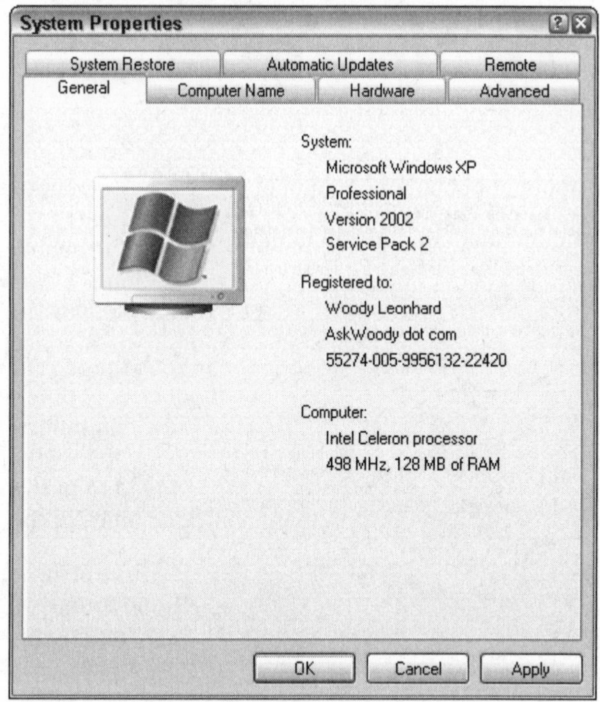

• Figure 1-1: Service Pack 2 identifies itself on the System Properties dialog box.

2. **Check your hardware manufacturer's Web site to make sure that your BIOS is up to date. While you're there, search the site for any specific recommendations about installing Windows XP Service Pack 2.**

   The BIOS is a small, crucial program that lets your computer communicate with the outside world. If you have an older edition of your computer's BIOS, it may work fine with the version of Windows that you're using now — and die when confronted with Service Pack 2.

Installing a new BIOS is almost always quick and painless, it's frequently free or almost free, and the latest BIOS may well make your PC run better. You should update your BIOS every couple of years anyway. Just be sure to follow your computer manufacturer's instructions precisely. If you've never updated a BIOS, or need a refresher course, check out www.howstuffworks.com/bios.htm.

3. **If you can't get the latest BIOS, at the very least you must protect yourself from a well-known bug in the SP2 installer that causes PCs to completely freeze in the middle of installation. If you can't get the BIOS, download and install the so-called Prescott C-0 Stepping Patch at** support.microsoft.com/?kbid=885626.

Microsoft screwed this one up big time. They discovered the bug after Service Pack 2 shipped. Instead of spending millions of dollars to reissue Service Pack 2, they decided to release a patch that has to be run *before* you install SP2.

4. **Follow Technique 52 to install and run Spybot-Search & Destroy. Then follow Technique 53 to install and run Ad-Aware.**

   Both of these steps are necessary to clean garbage out of your system before you install Service Pack 2. There's one specific piece of software — a, uh, "permission-based contextual marketing network" program called T.V. Media that throws the SP2 installer for loops.

5. **Follow Technique 60 and perform a complete backup of your system.**

   If you can run Norton Ghost, or some other program that makes a full mirror image of your hard drive, all the better.

6. **Make sure you're the only one logged on to your computer, and shut down all running programs.**

   If you have Fast User Switching enabled (see Technique 8), make sure all other users are logged off.

7. **Make sure you have Service Pack 2 ready.**

   Got the update CD? Great. That's all you need. If you can't find the CD at your local computer shoppe and don't want to order it from Microsoft (www.microsoft.com/athome/security/protect/cd/confirm.aspx; allow four to six weeks), it's easy to find online. If you have a fast Internet connection, go to www.microsoft.com/technet/prodtechnol/winxppro/maintain/winxpsp2.mspx, click the Download and Deploy Service Pack 2 to Multiple Computers link, and download the SP2 installation file — all 270MB of it. If you're limping along with a slow connection, or you want to follow the Microsoft Party Line, you can use Windows Update (see the next step).

Depending on which patches you already have installed, Windows Update may only download a portion of the full SP2 package. If there's any chance that you might want to re-run the SP2 installer, or if you want to have a copy of SP2 to give to a friend or co-worker, avoid Windows Update.

8. **Run the update.**

   Stick the CD in the drive and follow the instructions on-screen. Or double-click the WindowsXP-KB835935-SP2-ENU.exe file and run it. Or, choose Start➪All Programs➪Windows Update, and wade through a zillion questions to get SP2 Express Update going.

9. **When the installer finishes, restart your computer.**

   SP2 immediately asks for security information, which I discuss in the next section.

Setting Up Service Pack 2

Immediately upon installing Service Pack 2, or unpacking and plugging in a new computer with Service Pack 2, Windows XP demands answers to a few key security questions. Depending on your route to enlightenment... er, depending on the way you received Service Pack 2, the physical appearance of the questions may vary. But in the end, Windows XP only wants to know how to handle its Security Center settings (see Figure 1-2).

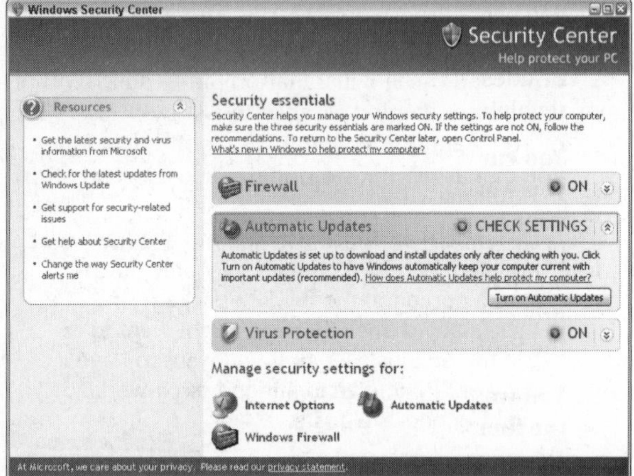

• **Figure 1-2: You establish key security settings during SP2 setup.**

If you've already gone through the initial setup and you want to rethink your answers to the key questions, you can bring up the Security Center by choosing Start⇨Control Panel and double-clicking Security Center.

My strong recommendations for the three Security Center settings:

- **Firewall:** Set to ON, signifying that Windows Firewall is turned on, unless you have a third-party firewall (such as Zone Alarm, which I cover in Technique 51).
- **Automatic Updates:** Set to notify you when updates are available, but not install until you give your permission.

This may be the most controversial recommendation in the entire book, but I believe it's in your best interests to control when (or, indeed, if) patches are installed, simply because Microsoft's record with botched patches has been so abysmal. You can do so by clicking the Automatic Updates icon at the bottom of the Security Center, and then selecting one of the two middle buttons in the Automatic Updates dialog box (see Figure 1-3). See Technique 55 for the gory details.

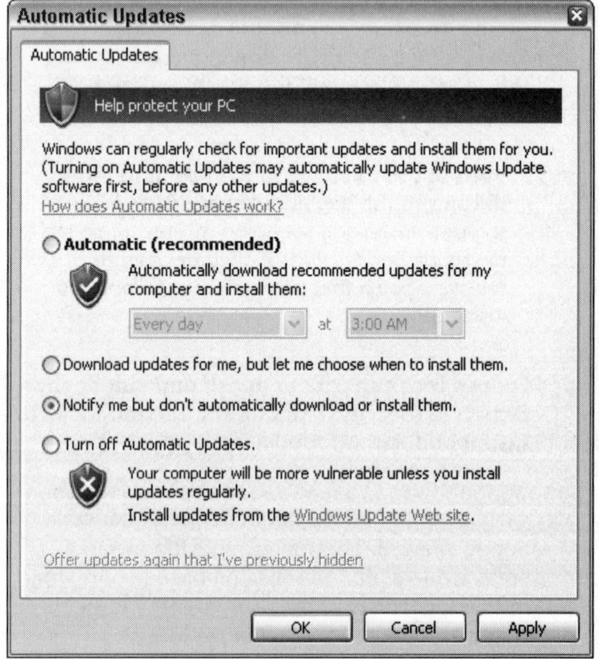

• **Figure 1-3: I tell Windows Update to notify me about updates, but leave the driving to me.**

- **Virus Protection:** May not show anything at all: Windows Security Center is notorious for not correctly identifying the status of antivirus protection. Regardless of what the Security Center says, you need to have one of the major antivirus packages installed, and update it daily.

When setup is complete, some of your programs may not work. See the next section for details.

Recovering from SP2 Problems

Most Service Pack 2 problems that I encounter fall into two broad categories:

- Hardware that doesn't work because new drivers are needed.
- Programs that don't work because of Windows Firewall settings.

Immediately after you install Service Pack 2, run through Technique 58 and make sure that all your drivers are up to date. If you have a program that doesn't work, look at Technique 50 for detailed information on poking through Windows Firewall.

With a bit of luck, you'll have Service Pack 2 up and running in no time.

Choosing Between XP Home and XP Professional

Everybody knows that Windows XP Professional is "better" than Windows XP Home, right? That's why XP Professional costs a hundred bucks more. But the simple fact is that most individual Windows users (that is, people who aren't connected to a Big Corporate Network) are better off with Windows XP Home.

There are some exceptions, however. Aren't there always?

Chances are very good that the company you bought your computer from advertises that it "recommends Windows XP Professional". You know why? Because Microsoft forced PC manufacturers to boldly post that phrase, as part of their licensing agreement: If Frodo Computer Co wanted to sell Windows XP, Frodo had to say "Frodo recommends Windows XP Professional", conspicuously, whether anybody at Frodo Inc gave two cat's whiskers about XP Pro or not. As this book went to press, Microsoft's, uh, creative marketing requirement was being contested in court.

Here are the cases when you must choose XP Professional:

- **You're connected to a Big Corporate Network (a *domain* in Microsoft-speak).** Your network administrator will almost undoubtedly insist that you use Windows XP Professional Edition. And you mustn't anger the network administrator. Besides, he or she has good reasons, mostly revolving around security. End of discussion.
- **You currently run Windows 2000 or NT 4, and you want to upgrade to XP without wiping out your hard drive.** You can install XP Home on a PC that currently runs Windows 2000 or NT, but you have to reformat the hard drive in the process. (See the next section for details.) With the Professional Edition, you can skip that step.
- **You want to set up a slave machine to use with the Remote Desktop feature.** The *Remote Desktop* feature (see Figure 1-4) allows XP Professional machines to act as slaves. You can take control over your slave PC using just about any computer that can connect to the slave over a network, and the slave behaves as if you were sitting right in front of it. This setup is great for retrieving files you left at home or printing a document at the office while you're on the road. Two important details
  - XP Professional must be running on the slave machine, but you can have any version of Windows on the master machine.
  - Both XP Home and XP Professional have a similar feature called *Remote Assistance* (see Technique 61), but someone has to be sitting at the slave machine to get Remote Assistance to work.

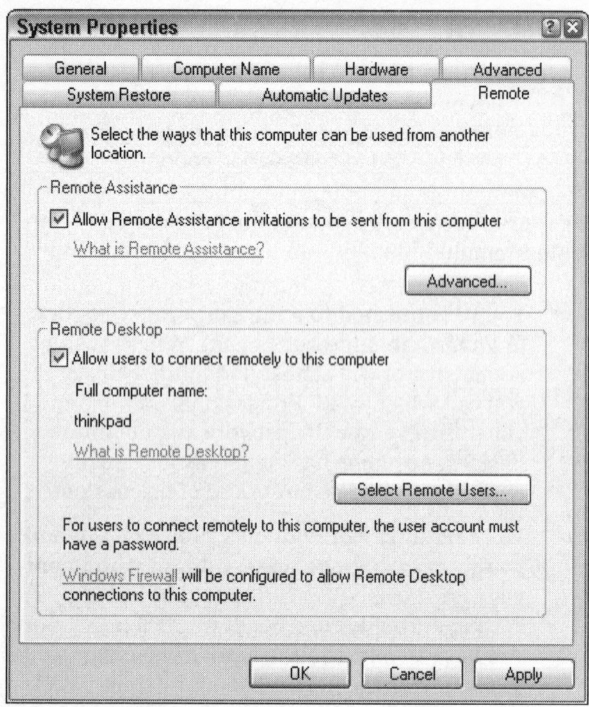

• Figure 1-4: XP Professional's Remote Desktop lets you take over and operate a PC from anywhere.

If you want to be able to access your PC as a slave, and someone will always be around the slave machine to click a few times when you make the connection, XP Home (with Remote Assistance) works just as well as XP Professional (with Remote Desktop).

- **You want to use specific kinds of exotic hardware, a handful of special-purpose software, or you need the extra security of NTFS file encryption.** Only XP Professional supports dual processor systems, or the 64-bit Itanium processor (in yer dreams). XP Home doesn't include the settings to run more than one monitor simultaneously, which is great for gamers and people with *biiiig* spreadsheets, but most video card manufacturers have multiple-monitor-capable drivers of their own.

- **You want to clump together two or more hard drives so that they look like a single hard drive (what the big-time geeks call *dynamic disks*), or to set up a mini-Web site.** XP Professional also supports a very secure form of file encryption, so that you can password-protect all your files.

- **You want to have Windows handle all your backups and restores.**

Microsoft really bungled this one. XP Home has a handy Backup capability, but restoring those backups is, ahem, less than dependable. (See Technique 60.) XP Professional contains a very versatile — but quite complex — backup/restore feature called ASR. If you're willing to do your own backups, possibly with a third-party utility, such as Norton Ghost for making full disk mirror copies (`www.symantec.com`), or ZipBackup (`www.zipbackup.com`) for backing up individual files or folders, XP Home is fine.

- **If you're using XP on a portable, and you want to automatically synchronize network files when you unplug the portable from the network, you probably want XP Professional.** For most people struggling with the idea of spending an extra hundred dollars on XP Professional, it boils down to one question: whether Offline Files (in XP Professional only and shown in Figure 1-5) works better than the older Briefcase (which is available in XP Home). The timesaving answer: If you have a lot of files that you frequently need to synchronize between your laptop and the network, XP Professional is worth the money.

Figure out where you stand with those seven issues, and you'll quickly discover whether you need to spend the extra money on XP Professional.

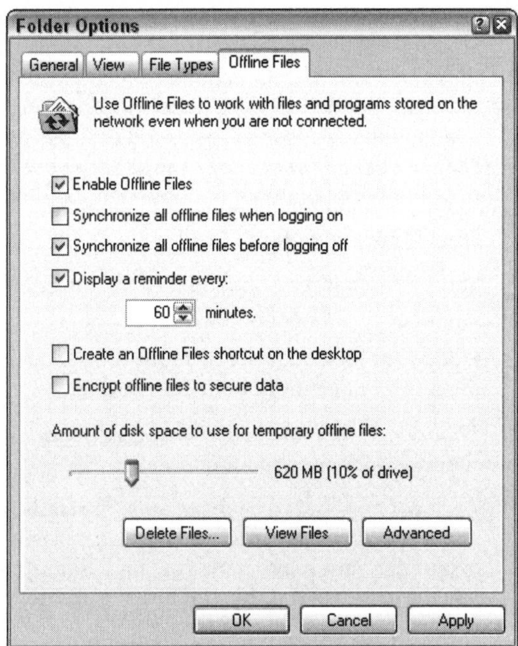

• **Figure 1-5: Offline Files synchronize themselves automatically.**

Get the upgrade?

If you're upgrading Windows from an earlier version, Microsoft gives you a price break. In fact, most of the boxes you see on store shelves are for the upgrade version of Windows XP. You don't need to have an older version of Windows running on the machine in question in order to take advantage of the upgrade. If no older version of Windows is hanging around — perhaps you deleted it in order to perform a clean install of Windows XP — all you need to do is insert an old Windows CD (Windows 95, 98, 98SE, Me, NT 4, or 2000) for a moment at one specific point early in the installation process. There's no check to see if the old version of Windows is registered properly — on this or any other machine. All the upgrade requires is that old CD.

Microsoft says that Windows 95 does not qualify for an upgrade to Windows XP, and you can't upgrade a Windows 95 PC to Windows XP, leaving all your files in place. But if you're willing to reformat the hard drive, the Windows 95 CD works just fine for verification during the installation.

Upgrading Quickly

If you're installing Windows XP on a machine that has another version of Windows running, the most important decision you make is whether to upgrade Windows on top of the current version or wipe out the hard drive entirely, reformat it, and start all over from scratch.

Make the wrong decision, and you'll regret it for months or years to come.

In my experience, people who have done a *clean install* — where they completely wipe out the hard drive and install Windows XP from scratch — have many fewer problems down the road than those who upgrade *in-place*.

The problem: A clean install takes more time now, but results in a much more stable copy of Windows. An in-place upgrade goes much faster now, but the resulting system may be less stable over the long term.

Even upgrading to Service Pack 2 goes much more cleanly and works far better if you wipe out the old copy of Windows prior to installing SP2.

You need to also make sure that any peripherals you own will work with Windows XP: You're in for a rude awakening if you have an old CD burner, for example, that doesn't coexist with Windows XP. Check the manufacturer's Web site for XP-specific drivers.

Multiboot systems

If you have two hard drives, or a lot of extra space in a second partition of one hard drive, you might want to consider installing two (or more) versions of Windows on the same machine. Windows XP works well in multiboot configurations: Every time you reboot the system, you have to pick which version of Windows you want to run. In some cases,

(continued)

you can share data between the two different versions of Windows, but you almost always want to install two copies of any software that you use. A good overview of the advantages and pitfalls is at `www.winxpfix.com/page5.htm` (scroll way down to the bottom of the page). Detailed instructions are at `www.blackviper.com/Articles/OS/Multiboot/multiboot1.htm`.

In-place upgrades in a snap

In my experience, *upgrading in-place* (which is to say, without wiping out your hard drive, deleting the old copy of Windows, and installing a completely new version) from Windows 2000 to XP Professional almost always goes quite well. Upgrading in-place from a fully functional Windows Me system to XP Home or XP Professional typically goes well, too. With other combinations, your chances for success aren't as great. Most frequently, old drivers can't make the leap to XP. Occasionally, the hardware itself isn't supported under XP — or not supported well enough.

If you decide to upgrade in-place, keep in mind that your options may be limited by your current version of Windows. Make sure that you're upgrading along one of the acceptable paths (see Table 1-1).

In addition to the permitted in-place upgrades I list in Table 1-1, Microsoft has a specially priced "step-up" pack if you decide to move from XP Home to XP Professional.

To perform an in-place upgrade, follow these steps:

1. **Make sure your PC is upgraded to the latest BIOS.**

   Don't skip this step. The BIOS is a program that runs deep inside your PC. Windows XP talks directly to the BIOS. If you aren't running the latest version of the BIOS, don't attempt to upgrade to Windows XP. I've seen more fatal Windows XP upgrade problems that could be attributed to problems with an outdated BIOS than all other problems combined.

   Contact your computer's manufacturer (or look at its Web site), and follow the instructions to download and install the latest BIOS. If you have never updated your BIOS, take a look at the instructions and, if you're intimidated, get help. Any local PC shop or user group has plenty of people who have experience updating BIOSs.

2. **Start your computer.**

   Make sure that it's connected to the Internet and to any other networks.

3. **Follow the instructions in Technique 60 to create a full snapshot of your hard drive.**

   That can save your tail if the upgrade goes to Hades in a Multimedia Handbasket.

4. **Turn off any antivirus programs, firewalls, and other background programs. Close any running programs, and make sure you save that novel you've been writing for the last ten years.**

   Your system can survive for a few minutes while you upgrade.

5. **Insert the upgrade CD (see Figure 1-6) and click Install Windows XP.**

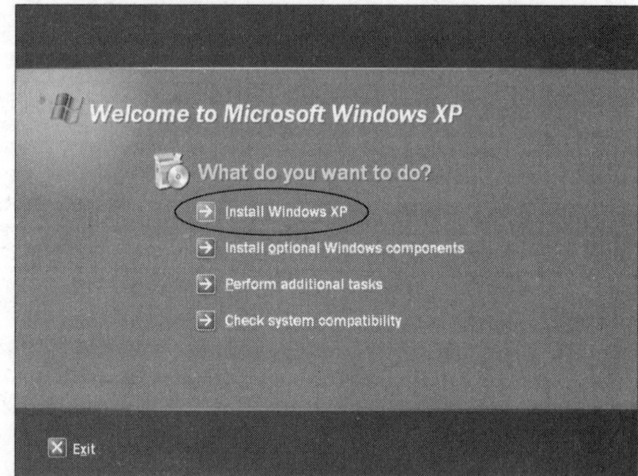

• **Figure 1-6: This way to install Windows XP.**

6. **Follow the instructions on-screen.**

   When the installer asks if you want to perform a Dynamic Update, do so. If you're connected to the Internet, Dynamic Update reaches out to

Table 1-1: Acceptable Windows XP In-Place Upgrade Paths

Upgrading From	Windows XP Home	Windows XP Professional	Other Info
Windows 3.*x*, 95, NT 3.*x*	No	No	You can use your old Windows 95 disk to verify installation if you're willing to reformat your drive.
Windows 98	Yes	Yes	Generally regarded as the most difficult upgrade path; lots of potential for problems with older hardware.
Windows 98 Second Edition (SE)	Yes	Yes	Most upgrades go well, but some fail miserably.
Windows Millennium Edition (Me)	Yes	Yes	If the upgrade goes well, the difference in stability will amaze you.
Windows NT Server	No	No	Windows XP is not a server.
Windows 2000 Server	No	No	
Windows NT 4	No	Yes	
Windows 2000	No	Yes	Windows 2000 has many settings and features that are available only in XP Professional.

Microsoft's big computers and pulls down the latest versions of all the software that you need. It takes a while longer to use Dynamic Update, but in the end, you get the most stable version of Windows XP available.

Windows starts and restarts itself a couple of times, and in the end, you get to run through a flashy (and not very informative) infomercial.

Breezing through clean installs

Performing a clean install takes quite a bit of up-front work:

1. **Write down all your settings:**

   - Telephone numbers, IDs, passwords, and mail settings (servers, Secure Password Authorization, and so on) for all your Internet service providers.

When you type a password into your computer, the characters appear as dots or stars. Unfortunately, if you've told Windows to keep track of your passwords, you may have, ahem, forgotten which passwords you used. There's an amazing, little, free utility called Snadboy Revelation (`www.snadboy.com`) that lets you peek behind the dots or stars that show onscreen. Download, install it, click the dots or stars, and presto! Revelation shows you the password that you forgot.

   - Web addresses, IDs, and passwords for all your favorite Web sites.
   - If you have a network, make sure you know its name. If you assigned a manual (static) IP address to your PC, make sure you get it, too. (See the sidebar, "Finding the name and IP address," elsewhere in this technique.)

2. **Upgrade your computer to the latest BIOS.**

   Don't skip this step. The BIOS is a program that runs deep inside your PC. Windows XP talks directly to the BIOS. Having the latest version of the BIOS before you even try to upgrade is important. I've seen more fatal Windows XP upgrade problems attributable to outdated BIOSs than all other problems combined. Contact your computer's manufacturer (or look on its Web site), and follow the instructions to download and install the latest BIOS. If you don't feel comfortable with the instructions, find someone to help you.

3. **Follow the instructions in Technique 60 to create a full snapshot of your hard drive — a nice idea in case the upgrade turns ugly.**

4. **Back up all your data files. All of them.**

   You can put the files on a second hard drive, copy them to a PC on your network, or burn the data to CD. You may want to use the Windows XP Files and Settings Transfer Wizard. See the next section for details.

5. **Make sure you have CDs for all your applications.**

   You have to reinstall them, too.

If you can't find the installation CD and registration key for an expensive program, such as Microsoft Office, seriously consider upgrading in-place. When you wipe out your hard drive in a clean install, you take all the programs along with it. You have to reinstall the programs, and if you can't find your registration key, you may need to buy a new copy of the program! (With Office, things aren't quite so dire — you can call and explain, and you usually get a key over the phone. But it's a real pain in the neck.)

6. **Tell your computer to boot from the CD.**

   The easiest way to verify that your PC is set up to boot from the CD is to put the Windows XP CD in your computer (don't install anything!) and then shut it down normally. When you restart the computer, the Windows Setup screen appears (see Figure 1-7).

   If the Windows Setup screen doesn't appear, you need to muck around with your computer's BIOS to change the *boot order* so that the computer boots your CD drive before booting your hard drive. Every machine is different; look at your computer's documentation (or hop onto the manufacturer's Web site) to see how to change the boot order.

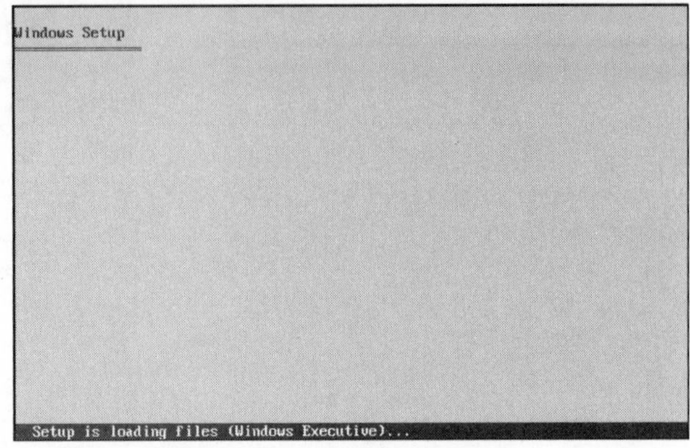

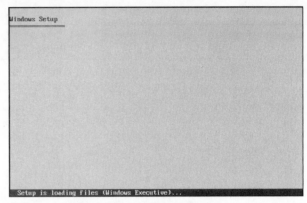

• **Figure 1-7: The Windows XP Setup screen.**

7. **With the Windows XP installation CD in the drive, start your computer.**

   Make sure the computer is plugged into your network, if you have one, and if it's supposed to dial the Internet directly, make sure the modem is connected to a working phone line.

Do not reformat your hard drive manually. It's much faster and less error-prone to reformat during the installation.

8. **Follow the Setup screens.**

   In the Welcome to Setup screen, press Enter to set up Windows XP. You have to agree to the End User License Agreement, and you may be asked to insert a CD to verify that you have an older version of Windows.

9. **When you get to the Setup screen that allows you to delete a partition, select the partition that contains the current version of Windows and press D (see Figure 1-8).**

This key step effectively erases all the data in that partition. It's the point of no return. The Windows XP setup routine asks you, ***twice***, if you're sure.

10. **Click Yes twice.**

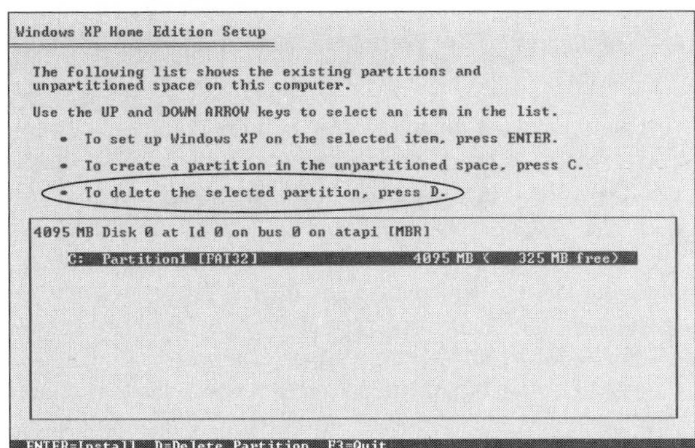
Windows XP Home Edition Setup
The following list shows the existing partitions and unpartitioned space on this computer.
Use the UP and DOWN ARROW keys to select an item in the list.
• To set up Windows XP on the selected item, press ENTER.
• To create a partition in the unpartitioned space, press C.
• To delete the selected partition, press D.
4095 MB Disk 0 at Id 0 on bus 0 on atapi [MBR]
C: Partition1 [FAT32] 4095 MB (325 MB free)
ENTER=Install D=Delete Partition F3=Quit

• **Figure 1-8: To perform a clean install, delete the partition that includes the current copy of Windows.**

11. Create a new partition (or partitions) to replace the old ones by pressing C.

See Figure 1-9.

This is the partition that will hold your fresh copy of Windows XP.

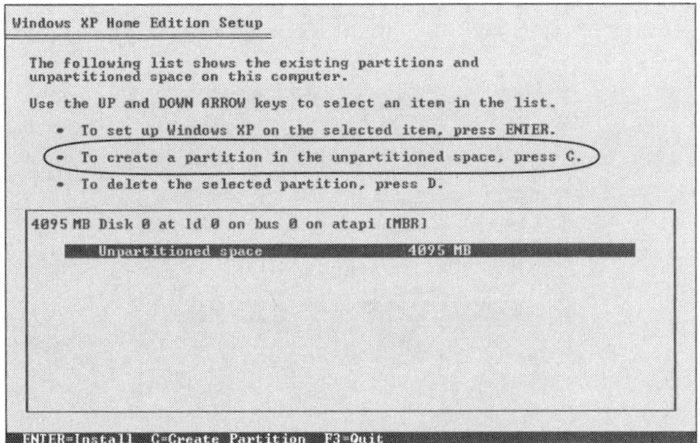
Windows XP Home Edition Setup
The following list shows the existing partitions and unpartitioned space on this computer.
Use the UP and DOWN ARROW keys to select an item in the list.
• To set up Windows XP on the selected item, press ENTER.
• To create a partition in the unpartitioned space, press C.
• To delete the selected partition, press D.
4095 MB Disk 0 at Id 0 on bus 0 on atapi [MBR]
Unpartitioned space 4095 MB
ENTER=Install C=Create Partition F3=Quit

• **Figure 1-9: Press C to create a new partition.**

12. Unless you have compelling reasons to the contrary, format the new partition with the Windows NT File System (NTFS) (see Figure 1-10).

With very few exceptions, the only good reason to use the older FAT32 type of formatting is if you have more than one operating system on this computer, and one of the other operating systems is DOS, Windows 95, or Windows 98/SE/Me. (Those older versions of Windows can't "see" data on an NTFS drive partition.)

Avoid the temptation to do a quick format. Now is the time to make sure your whole hard drive is in proper working order, and a quick format cuts too many corners.

13. At this point, you can go get a latte or figure out a workable scheme to end world hunger.

Windows doesn't need you for a half hour or so (depending on the size of the drive), and when you come back, the final questions you need to answer in order to complete the installation are mundane.

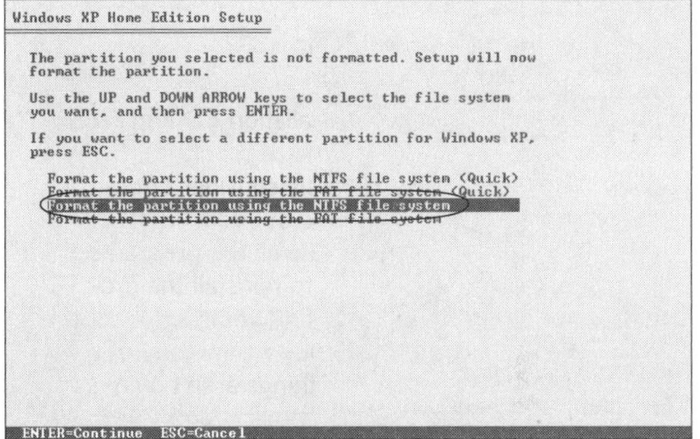
Windows XP Home Edition Setup
The partition you selected is not formatted. Setup will now format the partition.
Use the UP and DOWN ARROW keys to select the file system you want, and then press ENTER.
If you want to select a different partition for Windows XP, press ESC.
Format the partition using the NTFS file system (Quick)
Format the partition using the FAT file system (Quick)
Format the partition using the NTFS file system
Format the partition using the FAT file system
ENTER=Continue ESC=Cancel

• **Figure 1-10: Format the partition with NTFS.**

When Windows asks you to activate, don't bother. There's no advantage to activating right now. Read Technique 2 first.

As soon as you're up and running, Windows steps you through the process of reattaching your computer to your network (if you have one) and to the Internet.

Finding the name and IP address

If you're going to perform a clean install on a PC attached to a network, you need to know the network's name. It helps to use the same computer name, too, so that people

(continued)

who use the network can find things (such as printers) in the same location after the Windows XP upgrade. So you need to find and write down the network and computer name before you perform the install, so you can tell your PC its name when it comes back from being reformatted.

In Windows 98/SE/Me, choose Start➪Settings➪Control Panel➪Network➪Identification, and you see the info you need in the following window.

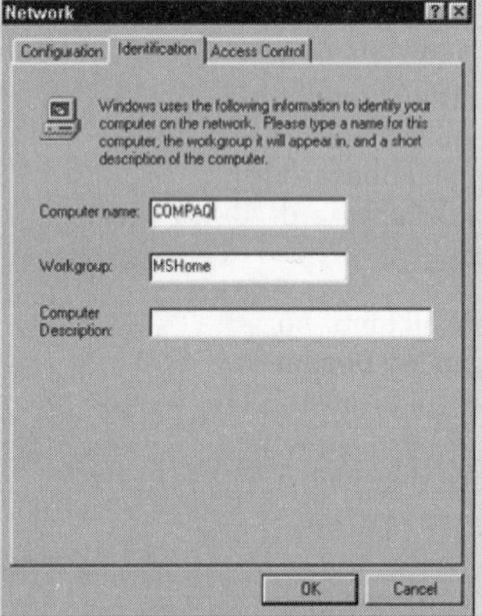

To find the network name in Windows 2000, choose Start➪Settings➪Control Panel➪System➪Network Identification, and a window like the following one appears with the network name.

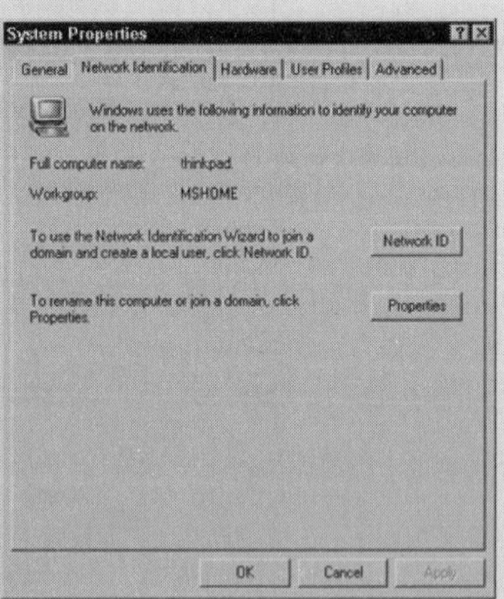

In both cases, the computer name appears in the Workgroup area of the same dialog box.

After you have the network name and the computer name, you're ready to track down your computer's IP address. Usually your network cards pick up their unique IP addresses dynamically from the network itself. (IP addresses are sets of four numbers, each between 0 and 255, which uniquely identify your computer on the network. They're usually written something like `192.168.0.1`.) In some cases, though, you have to set the IP address manually — for example, many high-speed Internet connections require you to set a static IP address by monkeying around inside Windows itself. If you've ever had to mess around with IP addresses, you know how much time it can take to get them right.

If you're going to perform a clean install of Windows XP, it's important that you figure out if you have a static IP address on the PC that's being upgraded, and if so, precisely what that IP address is. In Windows 98/SE/Me, choose Start➪Settings➪Control Panel➪Network (or Network and Dial-Up Connections). In Windows 98/SE/Me, you see a dialog box like the one shown in the following figure. Double-click the TCP/IP -> entry that lists your network connector, and then click the IP Address tab.

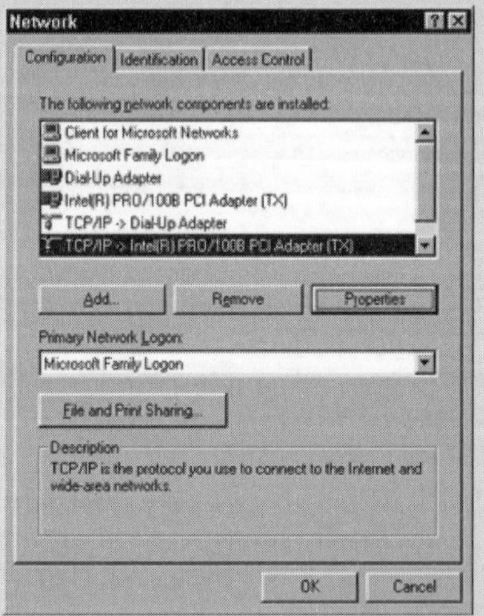

In Windows 2000, choose Start➪Settings➪Network and Dial-Up Connections. Right-click Local Area Connection and choose Properties. Then click Internet Protocol (TCP/IP) and click Properties.

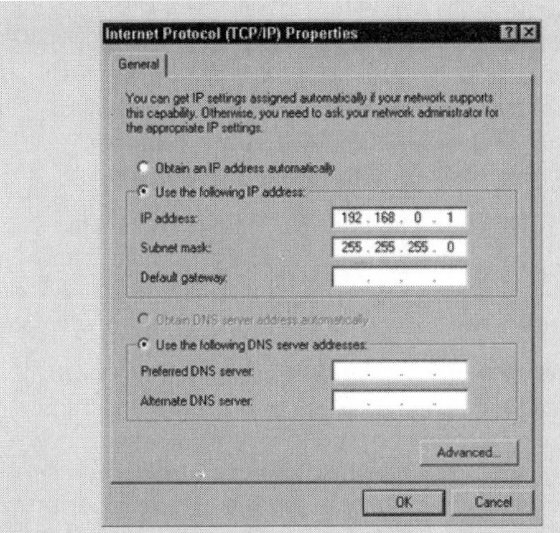

In Windows 98/SE/Me or 2000, if you have a manually assigned, static IP address, the Use the Following IP Address radio button is selected. Write down the address and all the other information in this dialog box. You need it to get Windows working after you perform the upgrade.

Transferring Files and Settings

Moving to a new system rates right up there on the tedium scale with root canals and rush hour. Fortunately, Windows XP has a wizard that can make things go faster — and maybe even a little better.

If you perform a clean install of Windows XP (described in the preceding section), you can use the Files and Settings Transfer Wizard to pull the data off your machine before upgrading it. When you're done upgrading, the same wizard puts the data on the fresh, new system. If you're fortunate enough to buy a new machine with Windows XP preinstalled, and if you can keep your old machine around for a day or two after the new one arrives, the Files and Settings Transfer Wizard has you working in no time.

The wizard also comes in handy when you simply want to transfer a lot of files or transfer certain program settings between machines.

Understanding what gets transferred

You can lose an enormous amount of time if you think something will come across when it won't! The Files and Settings Transfer Wizard lets you transfer files only, settings only, or both files and settings.

Settings includes all the Windows settings (your desktop, taskbar, screen saver, and the like), Internet Explorer and Outlook/Outlook Express settings, modem options and dial-up networking info, favorites, cookies, and the like. You also get the Registry entries brought over for all Microsoft products (including Office, of course), plus recent versions of applications from many other vendors (see the sidebar, "The wizard transfers non-Microsoft files, too").

Files include all fonts, sounds, Microsoft Office files, everything in My Documents and several other common folders, plus most (if not all) the files from recent versions of applications from many other vendors (see the sidebar, "The wizard transfers non-Microsoft files, too").

The Files and Settings Transfer Wizard does not, will not, and cannot transfer programs! You have to manually install the programs on the new PC, typically from their original CDs, before transferring their files and settings with the wizard.

The wizard transfers non-Microsoft files, too

Microsoft put a great deal of effort into creating a Files and Settings Transfer Wizard that works quite well with data from other products — even competing products. Among the big ones: Adobe Acrobat Reader, AOL and AOL Instant Messenger, Eudora Pro, ICQ, Lotus SmartSuite, MusicMatch Jukebox, Photoshop, Prodigy, Quicken, QuickTime, Real Jukebox, RealPlayer, WinZip, WordPerfect Office, and Yahoo! Messenger.

(continued)

Of course, Microsoft doesn't guarantee that the files and settings from competing products will come across intact. If a company changes the location of its Registry entries or the filename extensions on its files, the wizard doesn't have a clue. But by and large, it works quite well.

If you need a precise list of the versions of third-party programs that Microsoft has tested for the Files and Settings Transfer Wizard, look at `support.microsoft.com/?kbid=304903`. An obscure list is also located on many Windows XP computers, usually at `c:\Windows\System32\migapp.inf`.

You can transfer files and settings from systems running Windows 95, 98/SE/Me, NT 4, 2000, or XP onto any Windows XP machine. The Files and Settings Transfer Wizard doesn't transfer files from Windows NT Server or Windows 2000 Server machines.

The wizard does transfer settings and files to any Windows XP machine – even if it's been running for a long, long time. If you need to copy a bunch of files from one machine to another – perhaps you changed cubicles and need to get all your Microsoft Office files moved across – the wizard can save you a lot of time.

Choosing storage media for transferring your files

The Files and Settings Transfer Wizard works with a diverse array of storage media:

- **Diskettes:** Floppy disks (and lots of 'em) work in a pinch, particularly if you're transferring settings only, but if you're transferring any data at all, *fuhgeddaboutit*.
- **COM ports:** A direct PC-to-PC cable can be used to connect the 9-pin serial ports (COM ports) on two machines. This method is only marginally faster than diskettes. You have to use a specific kind of cable commonly called a *null modem* (I've also heard it called a *laplink cable* — one of the wires is crossed-over). No, you can't use your 25-pin serial ports. No, you can't use a USB or FireWire cable.
- **Removable drives/USB flash drives:** Removable drives (such as Zip drives) and USB flash drives work well. If you have a hard drive that you can transport by hook or by crook between the machines — perhaps with the aid of a screwdriver — that does quite well, too.
- **CD/RW:** You can burn the data to a CD. This approach generally isn't as fast as using removable drives or hard drives, and you may need to burn quite a few CDs, if you have a lot of files.
- **Network:** By far the best way is to have both machines connected to a network. If you're performing a clean upgrade on a networked machine, you can easily save your files and settings to some other PC on the network, perform the upgrade, and then retrieve the files and settings after the upgrade is done.

Transferring files and settings on a clean install

If you're performing a clean install and need to copy your data before wiping out your hard drive, this section is for you. It's also a good backup approach before you upgrade to Service Pack 2. In all other cases, starting on the receiving machine is easiest — skip to the next section, "Breezing through a transfer."

If you're performing a clean install of Windows XP (in other words, if you're deleting all your old data), the Files and Settings Transfer Wizard still works very well indeed. To get started, here's what you need to do:

1. **Before you install Windows XP (or upgrade to SP2), start Windows normally and insert the Windows XP CD.**
2. **A screen appears. Choose Perform Additional Tasks⇨Transfer Files and Settings, and then click Next.**
3. **Use the wizard to save your files and settings to another hard drive on the PC (one that you're not reformatting!), or use one of the other methods to get the data transferred off the machine.**

4. **After you finish the clean install, start with Step 1 in the section, "Breezing through a transfer," and retrieve the data from where it's stored.**

Breezing through a transfer

So you have the data from your old machine in hand (or on a disk) and you want to transfer it onto your new machine. Here's how:

1. **Install the latest version of the Files and Settings Transfer Wizard on the receiving machine.**

   The version that originally shipped with Windows XP has quite a few bugs. But the version in Service Pack 2 works much better. Run through Windows Update (Start⇨All Programs⇨Windows Update) to see if a newer version is available.

2. **If you want to pull data across for a specific program, make sure that program is installed on the receiving computer.**

   For example, if you want to have the Files and Settings Transfer Wizard bring across settings for Adobe Acrobat Reader, you need to ensure that Reader is installed on the receiving PC.

3. **Exit all running programs, and then choose Start⇨All Programs⇨Accessories⇨System Tools⇨Files and Settings Transfer Wizard.**

   The initial wizard splash screen appears. Click Next. The wizard asks which computer you're using (see Figure 1-11).

4. **Select the New Computer radio button and then click Next.**

   You have an opportunity to create a copy of the wizard on a disk.

5. **If you're using a newer version of the wizard than the one on your CD — and you probably are — select I Want to Create a Wizard Disk in the Following Drive to make a copy on a diskette, and then click Next (see Figure 1-12).**

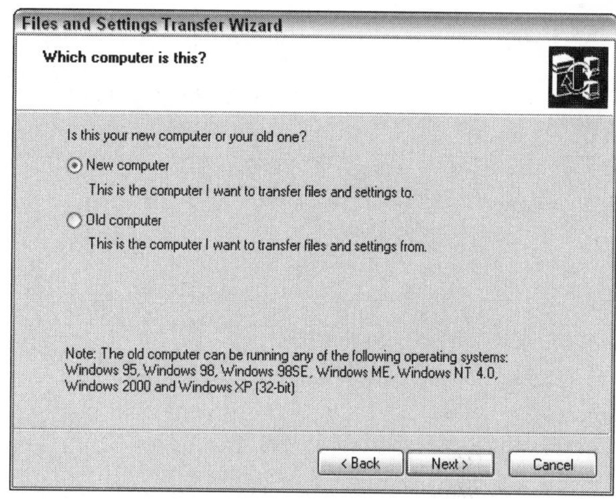

• **Figure 1-11: Identify the receiving computer.**

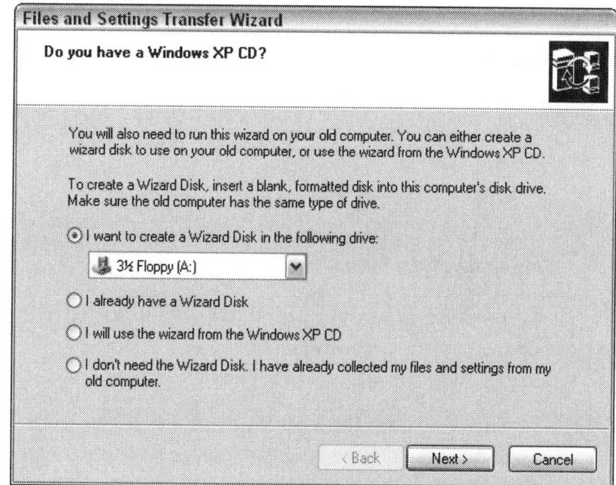

• **Figure 1-12: If you are working with the latest version of FSTW, make a copy on diskette instead of relying on the one that shipped with your CD.**

   The wizard then has you move over to the "sending" machine (see Figure 1-13).

6. **To use the Wizard Disk, insert it into the sending machine, choose File⇨Run, type** a:\fastwiz, **and press Enter.**

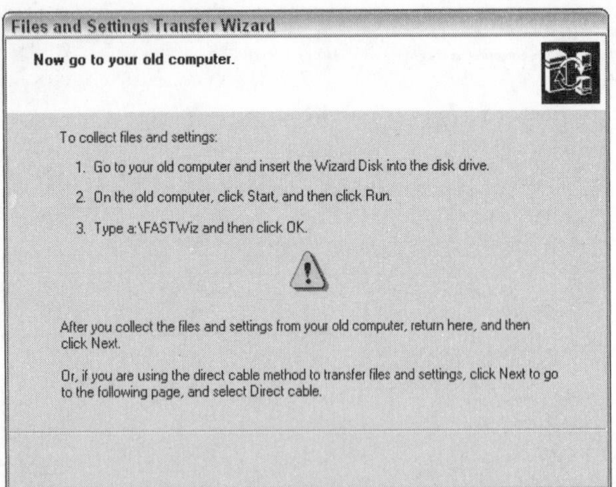

• **Figure 1-13: Time to retrieve the files from the sending machine.**

If you decide to use the version of the wizard on the Windows XP CD (instead of a version you downloaded), insert the XP CD into the CD drive of the sending PC. A screen appears. Choose Perform Additional Tasks➪Transfer Files and Settings. Then click Next.

7. **Pick the transfer medium (see Figure 1-14) and click Next.**

   The wizard is smart enough to scale back the amount of data it offers to transfer, if you're using a slower transfer method.

8. **When the What Do You Want to Transfer page appears, click Files or Settings or Both and then click Next.**

   If you want to specify precisely which settings, folders, and types of files get sent, don't hesitate to check the Let Me Select a Custom List of Files and Settings When I Click Next box. Pick the files you want, and click Next.

   The wizard warns you if you need to install any specific programs on the receiving machine.

9. **Before the transfer begins, if the two machines are connected directly, the wizard displays a password on the receiving machine and has you type it on the sending machine.**

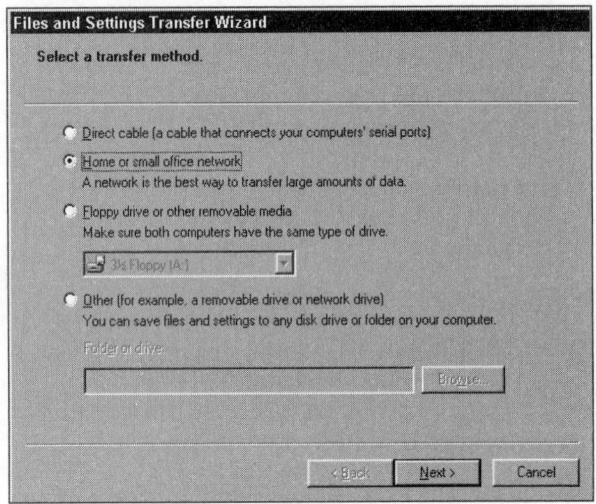

•**Figure 1-14: If it's available, your best choice is by network.**

Transferring a lot of big files can take hours, so be patient!

The Files and Settings Transfer Wizard is, hands down, the fastest way to get application data transferred from one machine to another.

The fastest way to shoot data from one machine to another is over the network. If you have the luxury of running both the old and the new machines in the same location, seriously consider setting up a simple network — for all sorts of good reasons. See Technique 45 for details.

Running the Activation Gauntlet

Save Time By

- Understanding the difference between activation and registration
- Reactivating Windows XP on a new computer quickly
- Being stingy with your personal information
- Staying off spam lists

Follow the steps in this technique to reduce spam, keep your private information private, and save time over and over again, every day, for as long as you run Windows XP.

Here's the key question: Just how much information do you need to give Microsoft when you activate your copy of Windows XP, when you register Windows XP, or when you sign up for a Passport or Hotmail account?

That question may sound a bit esoteric until you realize that Microsoft can use the information you provide to send you junk mail, both electronic and in meatspace. (*Meatspace* being that ever-shrinking corner of reality that hasn't yet been transformed to bits.) Microsoft will also "share" (I love that word) your personal information with "Passport Partners" (companies that pay a big fee to get this information from Microsoft). These partners aren't supposed to send you spam — but marketing promotional material? Who knows? Best to keep your name off any lists, no matter who maintains them, now or in the future.

In this technique, I tell you about another trick I bet you didn't know. If you buy and install Windows XP on a PC and then later decide to get rid of that PC, you can install the same copy of Windows XP on another PC, if you call Microsoft and ask the right way. Talk about saving time and money.

Understanding Activation, Registration, and Passport

Unlike any of its predecessors, Windows XP requires *activation* — the process whereby Microsoft irrevocably identifies a specific copy of Windows with one PC. Microsoft requires activation, quite simply, so that you can't install a copy of Windows XP on more than one computer: If you want to run Windows XP on a second PC, you have to buy another copy of the software or get a license to install multiple copies. Period.

It doesn't matter if the computers all belong to the same family, or if they're networked together, or if you use a portable and a desktop. Each computer has to have its own copy. One computer, One XP.

I get into the nitty-gritty of what activation and registration actually require in "Activating Windows XP the Right Way," the next section in this technique.

Registration, on the other hand, works much the same way as sending in a postcard to register a television or refrigerator. You fill out a form, send it to Microsoft, and never hear from anyone at Microsoft again.

Or do you?

And then there's Passport, Microsoft's giant database — quite likely the most extensive, most accurate collection of computer users' personal information in all the world. Windows XP bugs you incessantly to sign up for a Passport.

Do you want to?

Windows registration and getting a Passport can lead to enormous time sinks, and you pay the piper for a long time. Sure, filling out a form only takes a couple of minutes. But the time you spend dotting i's and crossing t's pales in comparison to the amount of time you spend wading through spam or worrying about the way Microsoft's "Partners" handle your personal info.

Activating Windows XP the Right Way

If you want to save time and pestering, it's vitally important that you understand where activation ends and registration begins. You *have* to activate Windows, but registering is entirely voluntary. Don't be confused or cowed into divulging information that'll soak up your time for years to come.

Understanding your activation options

When you're getting started with Windows XP, here's how to tell whether you need to activate your copy:

- If you bought a new computer with Windows XP preinstalled, your copy of Windows XP was probably activated at the factory. With a little luck, you'll never face the activation monster.
- Large companies — and even many small ones — sometimes buy volume licenses (VLs) for Windows and other Microsoft products. You can purchase a VL that covers as few as five copies (details at `www.microsoft.com/licensing`). VL copies of Windows XP have special product keys that don't require activation.
- On the other hand, if you buy a copy of Windows XP on a store shelf, the minute you install it, Windows Product Activation (WPA) kicks in. WPA asks you if you want to activate your copy (see Figure 2-1).

  If you select No, Remind Me to Activate Windows Every Few Days, you have 30 days to activate it.

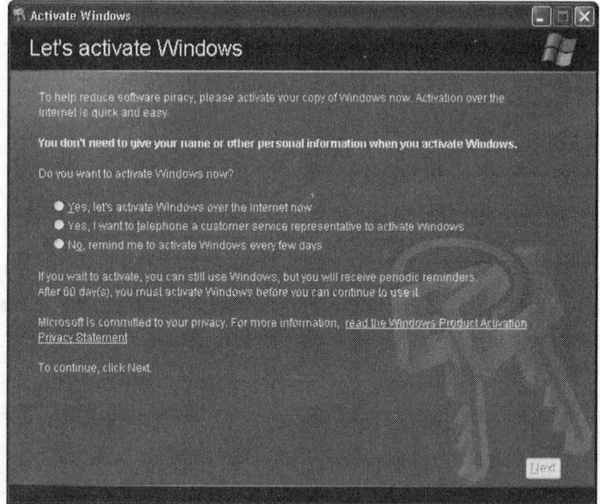

• Figure 2-1: Windows XP wants you to tell Microsoft precisely which computer goes with this copy of the software.

You can activate Windows XP over the telephone, but if you have an Internet connection that's working, I suggest using the much, much faster (and less error-prone) online activation process instead.

There is no reason to activate Windows XP immediately. In fact, you have every reason to hold off so that you can make sure the software works as it should on your PC.

Should you wish to activate Windows XP at a later date, you can always choose the Activate Windows entry at the top of the Start⇨All Programs menu (see Figure 2-2), or by choosing Start⇨All Programs⇨Accessories⇨System Tools⇨Activate Windows.

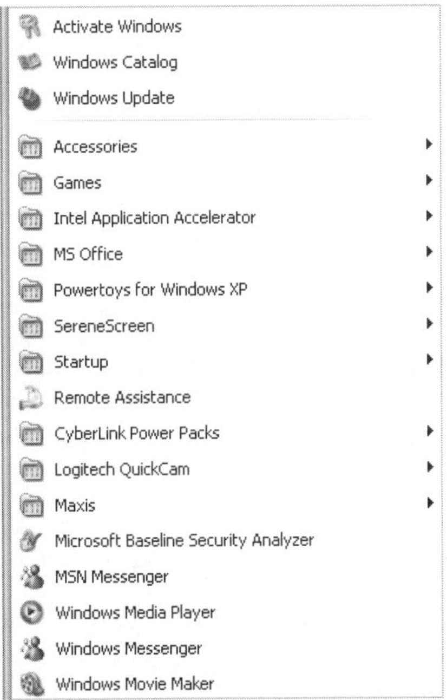

• **Figure 2-2: Activate Windows XP after you install it from the Start⇨All Programs menu.**

If you can't find the Activate Windows entry on your Start menu or in System Tools, not to worry — you're already activated!

That's activation. If you buy Windows XP off the shelf, you have to do it. No choice. More often than not, you have to reactivate your copy of Windows XP only if (or should I say *when?*) your primary hard drive gives up the ghost, or if you decide to reformat your hard drive and reinstall Windows entirely.

Installing an old copy of Windows XP on a new computer

Microsoft cuts you some slack with activation. For example, if you buy a copy of Windows XP, install it on one computer, and later decide to use that computer as a boat anchor (man, I've been tempted sometimes) — or if the computer is lost or stolen, or the hard drive dies and you decide to toss it in the trash — Microsoft usually lets you install your copy of Windows XP on a second machine.

If you want to use your copy of XP on a new computer, the trick is to install Windows XP on the new machine and, during activation, tell Windows that you want to activate by telephone (see Figure 2-3). Tell the person on the other end of the line precisely how and why your old machine is going to that big bit-and-byte bucket in the sky. Chances are very, very good that you get a new confirmation ID on the spot.

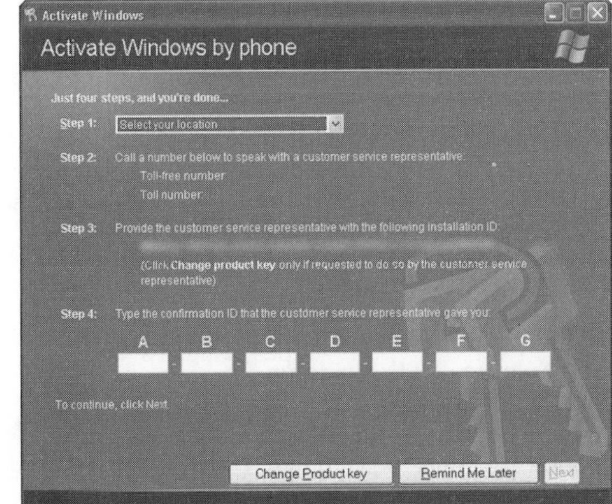

• **Figure 2-3: Activate by telephone if you have a good reason for switching XP to a new machine.**

You can find a very detailed, technical (and accurate!) description of product activation at www.microsoft.com/technet/prodtechnol/winxppro/evaluate/xpactiv.mspx.

Registering for Fun and Profit

If you activate Windows XP when you install it (see the preceding section), you're presented with the option of registering as well.

Registering Windows XP with Microsoft has lots of advantages — and they're all advantages for Microsoft. Details you offer are entered in Microsoft's *regbase* (short for *registration database*) and, once there, you can anticipate receiving no end of wonderful offers (note the bottom line in Figure 2-4).

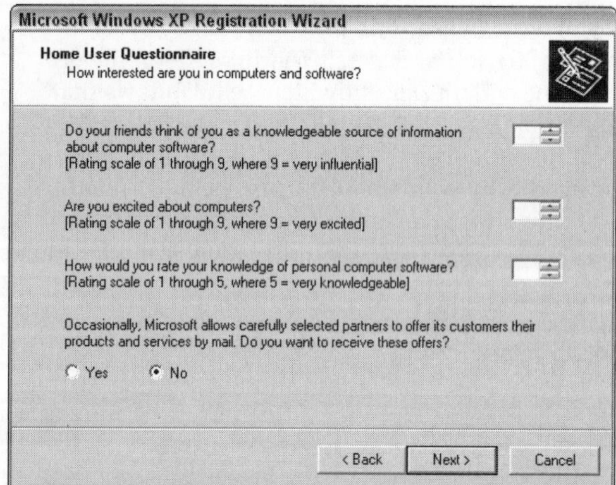

• Figure 2-4: With one click, you can give your personal information to Microsoft's "carefully selected partners."

On the other hand, you have absolutely nothing to gain by registering.

If you're tricked into registering while activating Windows XP, don't feel too bad. The first time I activated an early test copy of Windows XP, I registered, too.

The Microsoft Windows XP Registration Wizard states that registration helps you "Get the latest files and drivers through Windows Update" (yes, but Windows Update works for everybody — registered and unregistered users alike) and "Receive better customer support" (only because you're already in Microsoft's database).

Save yourself time now, and spam in the future. Don't register. Windows has the good sense not to ask you again.

Signing Up for Passport (And Hotmail)

Microsoft's creation of Passport was its attempt to put together a centralized database for all Internet users — a single sign-in ID and password that would authenticate you, no matter where you ventured on the Web.

In theory, you could enter all your information in one place (including, ahem, credit card numbers and lots of juicy, detailed personal information), and Microsoft would take care of authenticating you with Web sites (such as online merchants). Sign on to a participating Passport Web site with your Passport ID and password, and you could use your credit card with click-click-click ease.

After some hair-raising security breaches, an investigation by the Federal Trade Commission (www.usatoday.com/tech/columnist/2001/11/08/sinrod.htm), tough talk with the European Union, and a small dose of reality, Microsoft backed off. As currently constituted, Passport offers little more than a one-stop repository for information that Microsoft wants before it lets you use its products, including Messenger and Hotmail, or sign up for Microsoft newsletters.

Even though the Passport of today looks like the Ghost of Passport Past, sooner or later, you're going to want a Passport. Windows XP nags you mercilessly about it. There's no harm at all in caving in — if you know the tricks.

If you give Passport all your contact information, including your primary e-mail address, you can expect to be bombarded with spam and hassled for the rest of your online life.

Follow the instructions here closely to garner all the advantages of a Passport, without creating perpetual time sinks along the way.

If you want a Passport, start by setting up a new, free (can you say bogus?) Hotmail account, which you'll use only with and for Passport. Here's how:

1. **Log on to Hotmail (`www.hotmail.com`) and click New Account Sign Up (the precise wording on Hotmail's site changes from week to week, but a new account button is somewhere).**

   Apply for a new account, even if you already have one. Or two. Or ten.

2. **Fill out the requested personal information.**

   Creativity counts. (See Figure 2-5.)

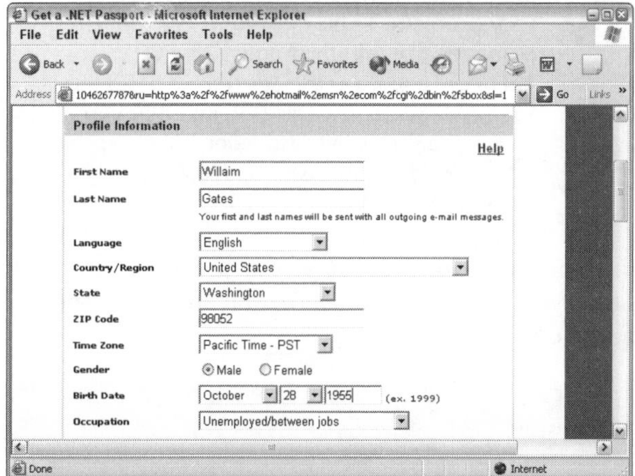

• **Figure 2-5: My favorite way to fill out the Hotmail registration information.**

3. **Continue with the rest of the form, but when Microsoft asks for an Alternate E-Mail Address (one that Hotmail can use to send you password reset instructions), think long and hard about what address you give out.**

4. **Be sure you read the 50-or-so pages of dense legalese describing your agreement with Microsoft, type in your (er, your account's) last name, and then click I Agree.**

   A dialog box appears, telling you that your registration is complete.

5. **Click Continue.**

   Although your Hotmail account and Passport account are already set up and activated, an upsell screen shown in Figure 2-6 appears, asking whether you want to pay good money for free e-mail.

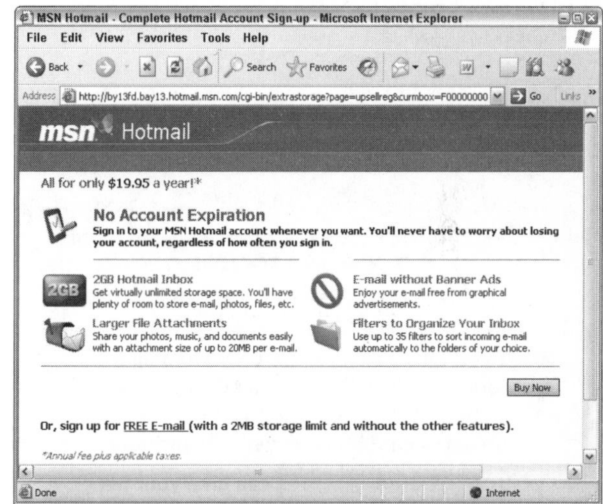

• **Figure 2-6: The Hotmail upsell screen tries to get you to pay for additional services, of dubious value.**

6. **Click the <u>FREE E-mail</u> link at the bottom.**

   No need to buy what's being offered.

   Microsoft hits you with two more full screens of advertisements.

7. Click Continue twice.

If you're tempted to click anything, be mindful that the information you offer can be used to hound you in the future.

You end up at Microsoft's, ahem, tasteful Hotmail welcome screen (see Figure 2-7).

You now have a clean Hotmail account that's associated with your new Passport.

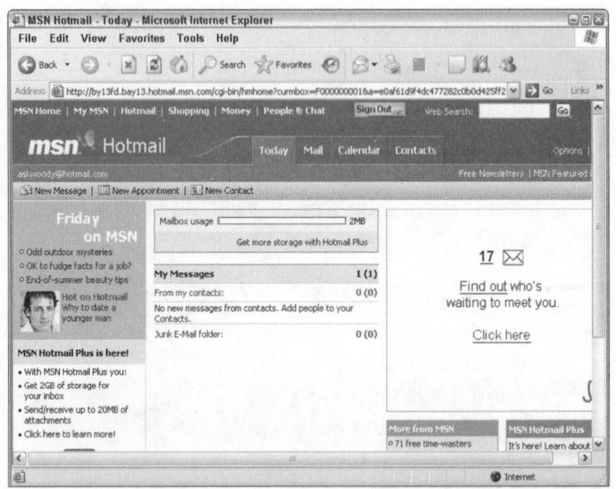

• Figure 2-7: Hotmail's main page has devolved to this. Gee, 17 envelopes are waiting to meet *me*. I feel so . . . special.

If you take care to share your Hotmail e-mail address only with close friends (including, notably, people you want to list as contacts in Trillian or MSN Messenger — your friends need your e-mail address to be able to send you messages), you should have few problems with spam.

Log into Hotmail once a month and clean out the junk. (You have to log on once a month or Microsoft deactivates your account.) That's all there is to it.

After you sign up for a Passport, Microsoft has your information, and you can't do much about it. Officially, you can close your Passport account (see `memberservices.passport.net/memberservice.srf?lc=1033&cbid=486`). But for all practical purposes, Microsoft is under no obligation to purge your personal information from its database.

Staying on Top of Privacy Issues

Spam, not viruses, and not worms, is rapidly becoming the number-one threat to Internet users. Junk e-mail. Spam. Who knew?

Microsoft has built many features into Windows XP that take information about you and your proclivities and send this information to the Microsoft Mother Ship in Redmond. The hooks in Windows XP — from blatant advertising in Windows Media Player, linked to Microsoft's `www.windowsmedia.com`, to the automatic error reporting that can send copies of files on your machine to Redmond — are a constant source of concern to many people.

And rightfully so.

Brian Livingston, one of my favorite authors, has a detailed discussion of some of the privacy problems in his *InfoWorld* "Window Manager" column for August 23, 2002 (`www.infoworld.com/articles/op/xml/02/08/26/020826opwinman.xml` — note that you have to register). We also follow privacy problems closely on the AskWoody Web site (`www.askwoody.com`).

If spam saps your productivity as much as it does mine, you owe it to yourself to stay informed and get involved.

I cover spam — and many related e-mail topics — in Technique 29.

Retrieving Your Product Key

Save Time By

- Reconstructing your Windows XP product key
- Verifying that you have a legit copy of Windows

You *know* you're supposed to hold onto the plastic jewel case or cardboard pack that your Windows XP CD came in, right?

If you bought your copy of Windows (as opposed to having it preinstalled on the PC), and you ever need to reinstall it, that 25-character product key (see Figure 3-1) is the only thing that stands between you and a $2,000 hunk of useless machinery. If you don't have your product key, you can't even start the installation.

What? You bought your PC with Windows XP preinstalled? Hey, don't act so smug. Are you sure you got a genuine copy of Windows XP? If you're running a bootleg Windows XP, Microsoft may refuse to let you apply security patches; Microsoft could even keep you off the Windows Update site. You might be prohibited from installing Service Pack 2 (see Technique 4). It doesn't matter if you're at fault or not; the restrictions apply automatically.

Stop whatever you're doing. Reading this technique only takes a few minutes, and it could save your tail some day.

• Figure 3-1: And you should never rip those tags off your mattresses, either.

Unlocking the Secrets of the Windows XP Product Key

Every copy of Windows XP ships with a product key, a 25-character string that looks something like T9TRD-9CTTR-V8X7W-R8888-6TPYR. If you bought your PC with Windows XP preinstalled, you might not realize that you have a product key, but you do.

When you install or reinstall Windows XP, one of the first steps in the installation process requires you to type that key (see Figure 3-2).

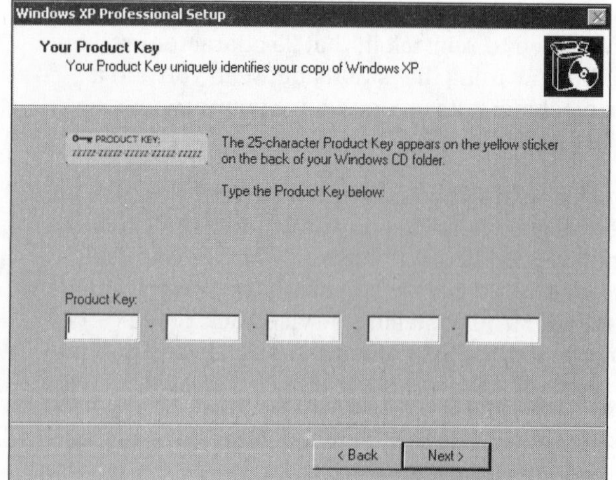

• **Figure 3-2: Windows XP doesn't install unless you can provide the 25-character product key.**

If you don't have the 25-character key, Windows XP doesn't install — period — even if you're reinstalling Windows. That's because your hard drive self-immolated ("This computer will self-destruct . . ."). If you don't have the key, expect to spend hours (or even days) on the phone with Microsoft trying to get it.

Locating the Key

Take a minute or two right now and make sure that you can find your product key:

If you have more than one copy of Windows XP, you'd better make sure that you know which machine goes with which product key!

- If you bought a new computer with Windows XP preinstalled, the Windows XP product key should be on a sticker that's permanently attached to the computer's chassis (the metal box that all the plastic hangs on). Look for a multicolored sticker proclaiming itself to be a Windows XP Certificate of Authenticity (see Figure 3-3).

• **Figure 3-3: The chassis sticker with your product key.**

- If you bought a copy of Windows XP, the product key is on a yellow sticker affixed to the plastic jewel case or cardboard folder that contains the Windows XP CD.
- If you (or your company) has a volume license (VL) for Windows XP, the product key came in the package with the VL.

What? You can't find the cardboard holder your copy of Windows XP came in? Has the chassis sticker succumbed to years of abrading by an amorous house pet? Do you have three copies of Windows XP, and can't remember which machine goes with what copy? Don't fret. You can get the product key back.

All joking aside, if you have any reason to believe that your copy of Windows XP is, ahem, less than genuine, follow the steps in the section, "Verifying Your Product Key," to make sure you don't have a pirate copy — even if you found the product key.

Reconstructing the Product Key

A tremendous single-purpose product called Magical Jelly Bean Keyfinder (no, I don't make this stuff up) reaches into your Windows Registry, assembles all the lost pieces, and re-creates your original Windows XP product key (see Figure 3-4).

• **Figure 3-4: Magical Jelly Bean Keyfinder reconstructs product keys, based on information buried in the Windows Registry.**

Keyfinder is a tiny program that doesn't take long to download and that runs in a snap. I strongly suggest you run it right now while you're thinking about it, and write down your product key some place where you won't lose it. Here's how:

1. **Go to** `www.magicaljellybean.com`**.**

   If you like Keyfinder, consider clicking the PayPal Donate button and sending a few shekels to Magical Jelly Bean Software.

2. **Click the link to the Keyfinder and then click the Download button that's closest to your location.**

   Internet Explorer starts downloading a Zip file.

3. **When IE asks if you want to open or save the file, click Open.**

4. **After the Zip file opens, double-click the** `keyfinder.exe` **file to run it.**

5. **If IE gives you a security warning, click Run.**

   Eventually, the Keyfinder program runs, producing the dialog box shown in Figure 3-4.

6. **Write down your registration key and then choose File⇨Exit to leave the program.**

I used to recommend a product called ViewKeyXP, but it doesn't work with systems running Windows XP Service Pack 2.

If Windows came preinstalled on your machine, there's a small chance that Keyfinder can't reconstruct the product key. If that's the case, make sure you understand how to reinstall the *original* copy of Windows XP — usually from a "panic" CD or "recovery" CD (see Figure 3-5) that came with the computer, or from a hidden partition on your hard drive.

• **Figure 3-5: A typical Dell recovery CD, which contains a version of Windows XP that only installs on the original PC.**

Verifying Your Product Key

Making sure that you're using a legitimate copy of Windows XP is important — and not just so that Microsoft gets the income it's due.

By verifying your key, you can avoid getting caught in a time-consuming crunch at some indeterminate point in the future.

Microsoft has no obligations to you if you're running a pirate copy of Windows XP, even if you were duped into buying one. In fact, the Softies have, at times, made life very difficult for people who use bootleg versions of Windows XP:

- Service Pack 1 (and, reportedly, Service Pack 2) refuses to install itself if it determines that you're using one of the most commonly ripped-off product keys, including the following volume license key, which has appeared on hundreds of thousands of pirated copies of Windows XP: `FCKGW-RHQQ2-YXRKT-8TG6W-?????`
- Microsoft has, from time to time, threatened to block access to the Windows Update site for PCs that use any of the commonly distributed "bad" product keys.

Microsoft is caught between a rock and a hard spot on this topic: Pirate copies of Windows get infected just as easily as legitimate copies. Restricting access to security patches only helps increase the number of exposed systems, and thus contributes to the spread of malware. While cool heads don't always prevail at Microsoft, it seems less and less likely that Redmond will take draconian steps in the future to withhold security patches from pirates.

Of course, companies are particularly at risk. The Business Software Alliance (`www.bsa.org`) commonly rakes in hundreds of thousands of dollars in penalties from companies that run bootleg software, and individuals are liable, as well.

If you want to save yourself a major headache in the future, take a few seconds to check the key. Here's how:

- **If you bought your PC with Windows XP preinstalled:** Compare the product key from Keyfinder with the one on the chassis sticker. (I talk about how to get and run Keyfinder in "Reconstructing the Product Key," earlier in this technique.)

  If the two keys don't match, Microsoft wants to hear about it. Start at `www.microsoft.com/piracy/YourPC.mspx` and follow the instructions for tracking down and reporting a bad Certificate of Authenticity. If your sticker really is bad, you got ripped off — and you can help fight against future rip-offs by reporting the offending party.
- **If you bought Windows XP at a store, compare the product key from Keyfinder with the yellow sticker on the CD's case (assuming you can find the case, of course):** If the keys don't match, you almost assuredly have the wrong CD case/cardboard folder. Hunting this one down is well worth your time, because an extra copy of Windows XP is floating around! Chances are very good you just switched around a couple of CD cases, but I know at least one person who discovered he had a long-forgotten legitimate, licensed copy of Windows XP sitting on his desk.
- **If you have any reason to believe that you were ripped off and bought a pirate copy of Windows XP, contact Microsoft immediately:** Microsoft takes this stuff seriously, because it loses billions of dollars a year to pirates. The easiest way to contact the right people is to send e-mail to `piracy@microsoft.com`. Don't be shy. People who sell you a bogus copy of Windows rip off Microsoft, of course — but they also take you to the cleaners.

Save yourself a lot of time — and headache — by permanently keeping your product key with your CD. Take out a permanent marker and print the product key on the top of your Windows XP CD. That's the side with the hologram (see Figure 3-6). Do it right now, and you'll never need to worry about it again.

• **Figure 3-6:** You can mark your Windows XP CD on the side that has the hologram.

Installing a Legal Copy of Windows XP over a Bootleg

Save Time By

- Identifying common pirate product keys
- Changing the product key without reinstalling Windows

So you followed the advice you found on the Internet and used a bootlegged product key to install an illegal copy of Windows, eh? Or perhaps you aren't quite sure if you have a bootleg copy or not. You went through the steps in the preceding technique, and you're kind of sitting on a fence, not yet certain if Fast Forward Fanny's Fawn Shop sold you a legit copy of Windows or not. Either way, the bottom line's clear: If you have a pirate version of Windows, you need to get legit, quick.

Copyright laws aside, Microsoft hints from time to time that, in the future, bootleg copies of Windows XP won't get access to Windows Update, or won't qualify for upgrades. Microsoft can change all of that any time they like, of course: If you're running pirate software, Microsoft has no obligation to provide any services at all for you — *even if you paid for the program.*

This technique shows you a few bona-fide pirate keys, and then takes you through two different methods of installing a genuine version of Windows over the top of a bootleg version. Yes, it is possible to "get legal" without completely reformatting your hard drive.

Nailing Pirate Product Keys

A very large percentage of all the pirate versions of Windows XP get installed with one of two specific pirated product keys.

Microsoft intentionally built Service Pack 2 so it would install on all quasi-functional versions of Windows XP, even pirate copies. There's a reason why. Bootleg versions of Windows XP get infected just as easily as the real thing — and infected Windows computers are bad for everybody. Microsoft decided (correctly, in my opinion) that it was better to fix every copy of Windows XP, regardless of pedigree, and use different methods to encourage folks to run legit versions of Windows XP. The fact that SP2 installed on your computer without a hitch is no guarantee that you have a legitimate copy of Windows XP.

You can tell if you have one of these mass market fakes by clicking Start, right-clicking My Computer, and choosing Properties (see Figure 4-1).

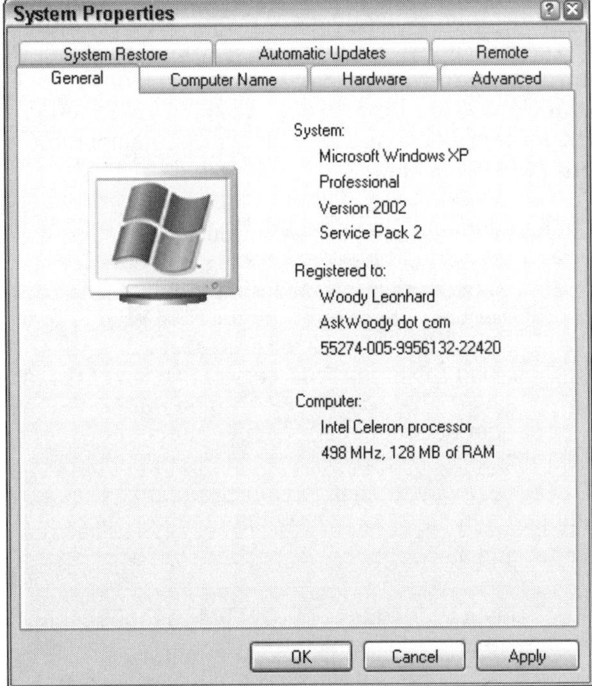

• **Figure 4-1: Your Windows XP Product ID is at the bottom of the Registered To section.**

If your copy of Windows XP was installed with either of the two widespread pirate product keys, your Product ID — that string of 20 digits at the bottom of the Registered To section — is one of the numbers shown in Table 4-1.

Table 4-1: Bogus WinXP Product IDs

?????-640-0000356-23???
?????-640-2001765-23???
?????-640-643718?-23???
?????-641-309376?-23???
?????-642-064580?-23???
?????-642-464364?-23???
?????-643-334701?-23???
?????-644-081772?-23???
?????-644-451265?-23???
?????-644-874896?-23???
?????-644-933704?-23???
?????-644-962396?-23???
?????-645-833254?-23???
?????-645-994962?-23???
?????-646-031843?-23???
?????-646-104081?-23???
?????-646-105103?-23???
?????-647-318838?-23???
?????-647-592029?-23???
?????-647-677834?-23???
?????-648-301691?-23???
?????-648-819992?-23???
?????-649-106765?-23???
?????-649-941392?-23???
?????-650-292312?-23???

? can be any single digit so, for example, 12345-640-0000356-23789 is bogus.

If your Product ID appears in the list shown in Table 4-1, two things are certain.

- **The bad news:** You have a pirate copy of Windows XP. You should buy a legitimate copy of Windows XP and use this technique to change your Product ID code so it's valid.
- **The good news:** You are probably running an unmodified copy of Windows XP. Some pirate copies of Windows XP have been whacked — the bits inside Windows have been changed — so much that you never know exactly what the program is doing. Versions with the bogus Product IDs in Table 4-1 generally aren't whacked.

I won't cry any crocodile tears about how the big, bad pirates are stealing revenue from defenseless little Microsoft. But the fact remains that if you run a pirate copy of Windows XP, you're doing something illegal, and you may get caught. If you get caught, the penalties can be severe. Even if you don't get caught, Microsoft can shut you off from important updates, or otherwise make your "Windows experience" a little less . . . seamless.

Recently "KeyGen" programs have been developed that spit out valid Windows XP product IDs by the zillions. I'm told that Microsoft has a way to tell if a specific product ID on a specific computer came from a KeyGen system. Whether the folks in Redmond will use that capability in some way in the future — most likely to limit access to the Windows Update site — remains to be seen.

Updating Your Key the Easy Way

If the Windows gods are smiling, you may be able to change your product ID in a few minutes, and carry on as if nothing has happened. In general, your chances of getting away with a quick change improve if

- **You're using a legitimate copy of Windows.** Sometimes companies change product IDs on perfectly valid systems to bring the computers into compliance with volume licensing requirements. Sounds strange, but true.
- **You have one of the product IDs listed in Table 4-1.** In that case, changing the product ID, coupled with an upgrade to Windows XP Service Pack 2 or later, results in a top-notch system.
- **You installed Windows XP with a bogus product ID.** If you, personally, installed Windows XP on a computer and you used a product ID of dubious lineage, chances are very good that the copy of Windows you're running works fine.

On the other hand, if you bought your computer with a bogus copy of Windows XP pre-installed, or if you got a "whacked" version of Windows XP that doesn't require any product ID at all, you may be in for some interesting times. Many different pirate versions of Windows XP are floating around with all sorts of weird whacks. Some reset the 60-day activation clock every time they're started. Others reset the system clock. At least one bypasses activation checking altogether.

If there's any chance that you have a whacked version of Windows XP, it's in your own best interests to follow the instructions in the next section, "Toughing It Out the Hard Way." That's the only way to ensure that you're running a fully functional copy of Windows XP, short of completely reformatting your hard drive.

The easiest way to change your product ID uses Magical Jelly Bean Keyfinder, which I discuss in Technique 3:

1. **Buy a legitimate copy of Windows.**

   If you're fixing a pirate copy of Windows Professional (identified as such in the dialog box shown in Figure 1-1), buy Windows Professional. If you're fixing a pirate copy of Windows Home, get Windows Home.

In theory, you're supposed to buy the "full" version — not the "upgrade" (which is much more readily available, and considerably cheaper) to Windows XP. In practice, I haven't heard of any problems fixing a pirate copy with an "upgrade" product ID. But you don't want an OEM product ID (OEM = Original Equipment Manufacturer). OEM copies of Windows are supposed to be installed by the folks who assemble PCs from scratch. I've had nothing but trouble with OEM Windows XP packages, except in a scorched-earth install accompanied by a reformat of the hard drive.

2. **Go to** `www.magicaljellybean.com`. **Click the link to Keyfinder, and then click one of the Download buttons.**

3. **When IE asks if you want to open or save the file, click Open.**

4. **Double-click** `keyfinder.exe` **to run it. If IE gives you a security warning, click Run.**

5. **Choose Options⇨Change Windows Key.**

   Keyfinder brings up the dialog box shown in Figure 4-2.

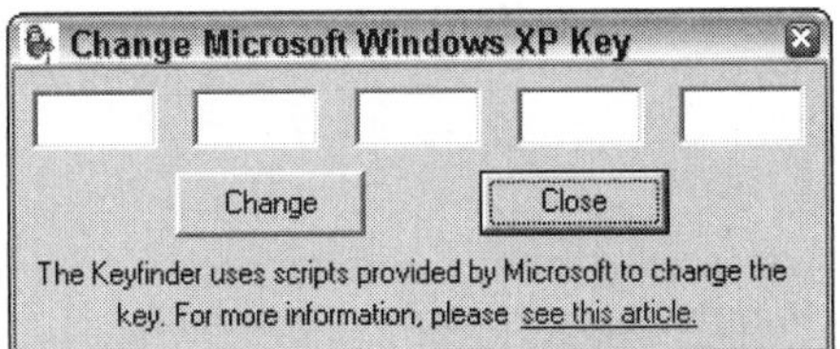

• Figure 4-2: Magical Jelly Bean Keyfinder does all the hard work in changing product IDs.

6. **Tear open the package that contains your new, legitimate version of Windows XP and look for the Product ID.**

   It's a 25-character string that looks something like T9TRD-9CTTR-V8X7W-R8888-6TPYR. You can usually find it on a bright orange sticker, either inside the package or on the plastic jewel case that contains the Windows CD.

7. **Type the new key in the Change Microsoft Windows XP Key dialog box and click Change.**

   If Keyfinder tells you that you don't have a valid key, you're going to have to change the key the hard way. See the next section.

8. **Choose File⇨Exit to get out of Keyfinder.**

9. **Choose Start⇨Turn Off Computer and Restart your PC.**

When Windows comes back, your new product ID is in force.

Toughing It Out the Hard Way

I've hit a few cases where Magical Jelly Bean Keyfinder doesn't work. I'm not sure exactly why, but some perfectly good-looking product IDs just don't pass muster.

If you find yourself ready to tear your hair out, and wondering why you're going through this much trouble to line Microsoft's coffers, be of good cheer. Another alternative isn't too difficult, but it is time-consuming. It involves a repair installation of Windows XP.

Before you try a repair installation, you might want to look at `support.microsoft.com/?kbid=328874` **and see if the first method listed there works for you. In my experience, if Jelly Bean Keyfinder doesn't do the trick, that Knowledge Base article won't either, but ya never know.**

Running a repair installation doesn't knock out any of your programs, delete any of your data, or change any of your settings. If you have whacked pieces of Windows flying around, it removes the bad parts of Windows and replaces them with good ones.

Here's how to perform a repair installation with a legitimate copy of Windows XP. It's confusing:

1. **Put your new, legitimate Windows XP CD in your CD drive and boot from the CD drive.**

   You may need to change a setting in the computer's BIOS, to allow your computer to boot from CD. You probably need to press a key while the computer is booting to get it to boot from CD. Check your computer manufacturer's Web site if you need help.

2. **This is where it starts to get confusing. Windows whirs along for a while, and sooner or later you see a screen that says**

   ```
   This portion of the Setup program prepares Microsoft Windows XP to run on your computer:
   ```

```
To setup Windows XP now, press ENTER.
To repair a Windows XP installation
   using Recovery Console, press R.
To quit Setup without installing
   Windows XP, press F3.
```

3. **Do NOT Choose "To repair a Windows XP installation . . ." Contrary to any known variant of multi-valued logic or rules of English syntax, you must press Enter.**

4. **Setup asks you to press F8 to accept the License Agreement. Do it.**

5. **Setup presents you with a list of Windows installations on the computer. You probably only have one. Highlight the bootleg Windows system, and press R to start the repair.**

   Windows pulls a whole bunch of files off the CD and reboots.

6. **Do NOT boot from the CD the second time.**

   Your PC no doubt offers to let you boot from CD the second time, but you want it to boot normally, from the hard drive. Usually, booting from the hard drive is easy — you simply do nothing and wait for a while, and your computer ignores the CD and boots directly from the hard drive. See, I told you it was confusing.

7. **This time when Windows boots, you want it to boot from your hard drive, using the files that the repair routine copied in the preceding step.**

   Setup acts like it's performing a full installation. DON'T PANIC. Your data and programs are safe.

8. **When asked for your product ID, be sure to enter the ID from the new, legitimate copy of Windows.**

   D'OH.

9. **Continue with a full, normal installation.**

   When Windows comes back up for air, everything is in place — and your new product ID is in full force.

Immediately after you come back, hit Windows Update (choose Start➪All Programs➪Windows Update) and get all the latest patches – including Service Pack 2, of course, if your old copy of Windows XP didn't have it.

Part II

Making Windows Lean and Clean

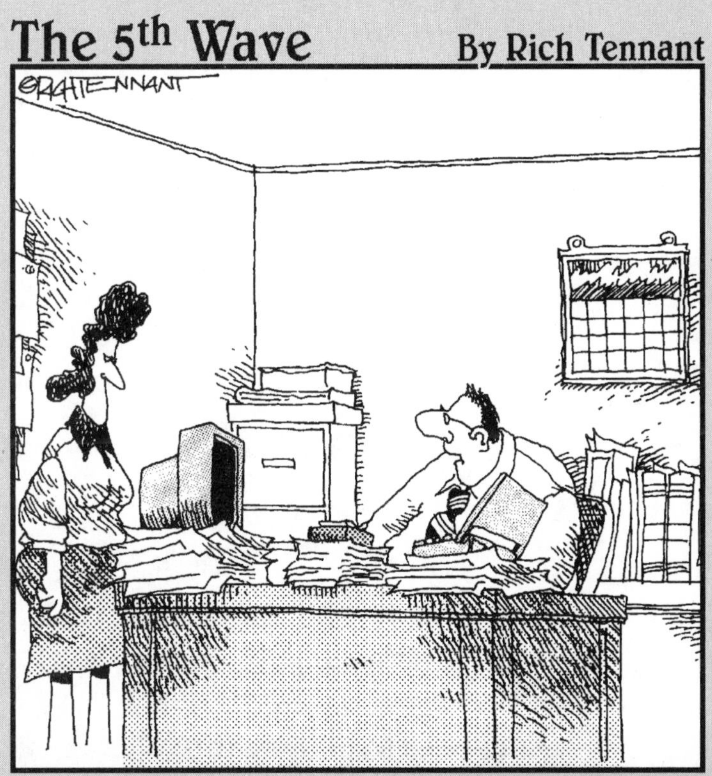

"The new technology has really helped me get organized. I keep my project reports under the PC, budgets under my laptop and memos under my pager."

Technique 5

Making Windows Work Faster

Save Time By

- Making Windows skip the logon screen
- Adding memory — but only if you need it
- Tweaking Windows in ways that really save time
- Running the best disk system optimizer

This technique includes the cream of the "speed up Windows" crop — rapid-fire steps you can take to get the most out of your Windows XP computer. You won't find any picayune obscure bit-blasting here. I recommend everyone with Windows XP take these steps to make his or her computer work faster — no advanced degree required.

Many of the detailed speed-up tricks you'll find on the Web (and even in some more, uh, reliable places) claim they'll boost your performance by leaps and bounds. All you have to do is check this box, change that Registry entry, run this little program, *buy* this little program, and your system will run *sooo* much faster. Lemme let you in on a little trade secret. Most techniques you find online (especially the ones you have to pay for) don't do squat. The best speed-up tweaks might increase your system performance slightly, but you'll never notice the difference. The worst ones crash your system.

Believe me, Microsoft has gone over Windows with a million fine-toothed combs. If any little twiddles would boost performance, they'd already be twiddled. And they built a couple of big twiddles into Windows already. This technique separates the speed-up wheat from the chaff. The speed-up techniques that really work involve big changes in the way your system does its job.

Bypassing the Logon Screen

Windows XP was built to perform in a variety of computing environments such as homes, offices, Big Corporate Networks, teensy-tiny laptops. A large percentage of Windows users always log on the same way every time they turn on their PCs, using the same ID and password.

If you always log on with the same ID and password, and you aren't too worried about somebody sitting down at your PC and pretending that they're you, you can easily have Windows perform the log on, and go straight to your desktop.

If you have any concerns about security at all, *don't* use this technique. Anyone who can turn on your computer will be automatically identified to the system (and the network) as you.

That said, realize that anyone who can physically touch your computer can use a number of tricks to break in and get anything they want anyway (check out `www.briansbuzz.com/w/030213` for an eye-opener).

To enable automatic logon the easy way, follow these steps:

1. **Download and install the TweakUI PowerToy (see the sidebar, "Using Windows XP PowerToys").**

   In fact, if you haven't already done so, download all the PowerToys and install them. You'll use most of them sooner or later.

2. **ChooseStart⇨All Programs⇨PowerToys for Windows XP⇨TweakUI.**

   The TweakUI About screen appears.

3. **On the left, choose Logon⇨Autologon**

   A window like the one shown in Figure 5-1 appears.

4. **Check the Log On Automatically at System Startup check box.**

5. **If your account has a password, click the Set Password button, type your password, and then click OK.**

6. **Click OK to exit TweakUI.**

7. **Shut down and restart your computer.**

   You are logged on immediately.

If you ever need to see the logon screen, perhaps to choose a different user, hold down the Shift key while Windows starts. You can also bring up the logon screen anytime by logging off (Start⇨Log Off⇨Log Off) or switching users (Start⇨Log Off⇨Switch User).

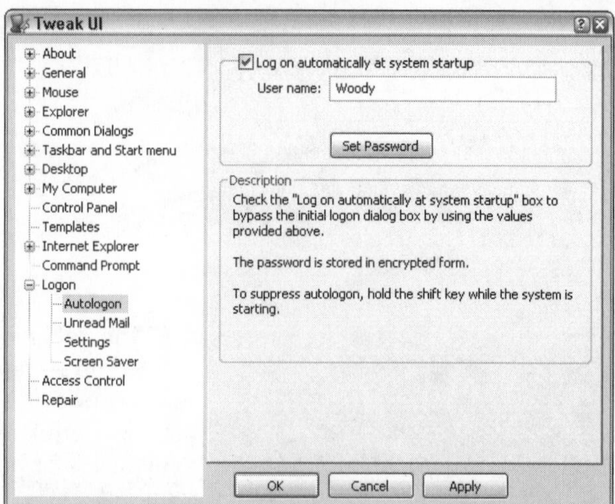

• **Figure 5-1: Use TweakUI for a fast, no-hassle automatic logon.**

As far as I'm concerned, bypassing the logon screen is the best high-payback way to speed up Windows booting.

Using Windows XP PowerToys

According to Windows legend, Windows developers wrote the PowerToys in their spare time — presumably between 1:00 and 1:30 a.m. on alternating Wednesdays. In fact, the PowerToys comprise an amazing collection of Windows utilities that many (present company included) believe should've been part of Windows itself. Microsoft has released PowerToys for every version of Windows since Windows 95. The Microsoft Official Party Line says that the PowerToys aren't supported by the company, even though they're created by the company, distributed by the company, recommended by the company . . . well, you get the picture. (In fact, Microsoft *does* support PowerToys from time to time, particularly when folks find bugs in them that interfere with other Microsoft products.)

If you can stand the thought of running (ooh, the *agony*) unsupported software on your machine, I urge you to download the PowerToys and keep them handy. I show you several ways to use them in this book. Go to the PowerToys Web site (`www.microsoft.com/windowsxp/downloads/powertoys/xppowertoys.mspx`), where you can find short descriptions of each toy, and download the toys as you need them. Better yet, bite the bullet, take a few minutes, and download the bunch. Each comes with a quick installer, so you can download and save the file and then double-click it to install.

Monitoring System Performance

If you've ever come face-to-face with the hourglass cursor, and watched and watched and watched as your system seemingly did absolutely nothing, there's a small utility that may make you feel better.

Stuck or *twisting* (as in twisting in the wind) hourglasses generally reflect one (or more) of the four following preoccupations that commonly bedevil PC users:

- Windows is out to lunch.
- Your system is waiting for some data to come to it over the network or Internet.
- Your system is trying to bring in a massive amount of data from a hard drive, CD, or diskette.
- Something has your computer's processor red-lined.

The first problem is a fact of life — like taxes, traffic, and bad hair days. I talk about the second and third problems (and their solutions) in various techniques throughout this book. (See Technique 23, for example.) You can monitor (and at least identify, if not solve) the last problem with a simple Windows utility called Task Manager.

To use the Task Manager, follow these steps:

1. **Bring up Task Manager by pressing Ctrl+Alt+Delete.**

   You probably see the Applications tab, from which you can stop applications that appear to be running amok (see Technique 11, for example).

   But that isn't why we're here.

2. **Click the Performance tab.**

   The Task Manager shows you a live running log of your computer's processor usage. (See Figure 5-2.)

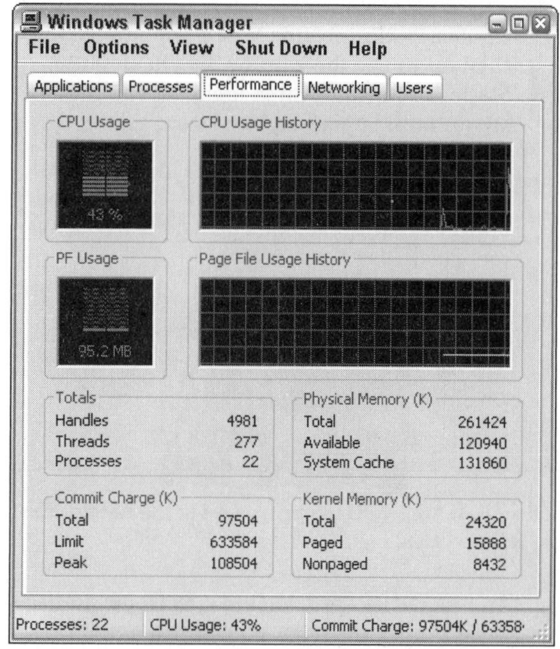

• Figure 5-2: Task Manager shows you both the current Central Processor Usage, and a rolling history log.

3. **Double-click the CPU Usage or CPU Usage History label.**

   In fact, you can double-click anywhere in the upper part of the dialog box. Task Manager turns into a very simple box that you can move anywhere on the desktop, or resize by dragging on the edges or corners (see Figure 5-3).

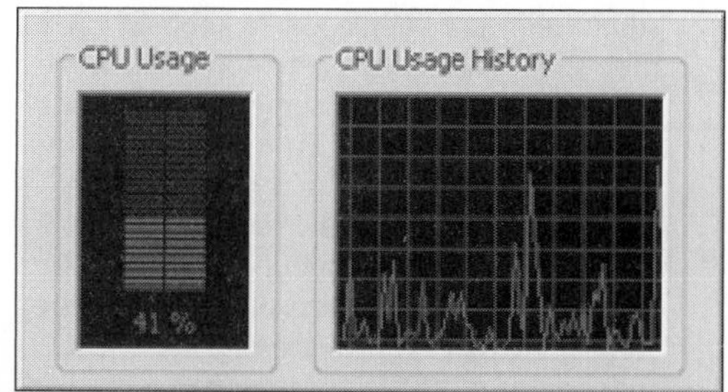

• Figure 5-3: Task Manager's stripped-down look.

4. Double-click this stripped-down box.

Task Manager returns to its normal size (refer to Figure 5-2).

5. Choose Options⇨Hide When Minimized, and then minimize the window by clicking the Minimize button (which looks like an underscore) in the upper-right corner.

When you minimize the Task Manager in this way, it doesn't appear on the taskbar, but it does appear in the notification area, next to the system clock (see Figure 5-4).

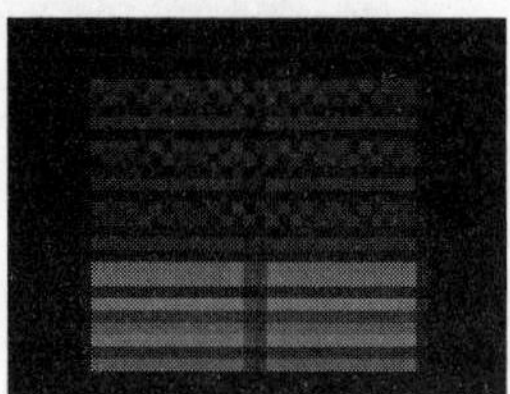

• **Figure 5-4: Your CPU usage appears in the notification area.**

6. To restore the Task Manager to its original size, double-click the icon in the notification area.

If you've ever wondered why that hourglass won't let go, this is a fast, easy, and free way to watch what's happening.

Usually, the Task Manager reports on CPU usage every two seconds. To increase the sampling rate to twice per second, choose View⇨Update Speed⇨High. To decrease it to once every four seconds, choose View⇨Update Speed⇨Low.

Although some people like to keep an eye on their CPU utilization, most people watch the bouncing lines to see if something has gone really haywire. If your CPU usage goes up to 100% when you start a program and stays there for more than a few seconds, something is probably wrong — a lot of overhead from old, unused add-ons, for example, or maybe a startup file that's grown too big. If the CPU usage pegs at 100% for more than a minute, the program itself could be suspect. Microsoft has released several faulty patches that drive applications up to 100% CPU utilization for extended periods of time. If you suspect a bad patch, get online and ask — AskWoody.com is always a good starting place. If your Page File usage swings up and stays up through a normal, everyday workload, you need more memory. See the next section, "Eliminating the #1 Bottleneck: Memory Drain" for details.

Does this tweak really make my computer faster?

Some people love to tweak their PCs. At some point tweaking turns into a hobby: Spending ten minutes working on a tweak that saves ten seconds per day isn't my idea of a good return on a timesaving investment. If you want to benchmark your machine, though, a good program is available on the Internet called *Passmark Performance Test*. After a 30-day free trial, it costs $24 for the full version. You can download it from `www.passmark.com`. My computer has a Performance Test V5 combined score of 315.4, which ain't bad for a 2.4 GHz Pentium 4. To see how that rating stacks up against other computers, I have to pay the registration fee, and then connect to the Passmark Web site. But if I'm only interested in testing speed-up results on a single machine, I can tweak and measure to my heart's content, for 30 days.

Benchmarking can tell you whether a particular change in your system speeds it up. (All too frequently, unverified "undiscovered tips" actually slow down the system!) I'll let you in on my own, personal benchmark, which has served me well for many years: *If I can't feel a difference, it doesn't matter*. Big performance increases come from the kinds of timesaving techniques I discuss here. Minor performance increases don't matter much and aren't worth your effort.

Eliminating the #1 Bottleneck: Memory Drain

If you read the magazines and the advertisements, you'll no doubt become convinced, sooner or later, that spending a few hundred bucks on this flammermajabber or that floohickey will make your system fly.

By and large, it's a crock. Hardware upgrades rarely do much to make your system run faster.

The exceptions (there are always exceptions)

- If you spend a lot of time playing high-end games or designing buildings, a faster display card may make your system run noticeably better.
- If you burn a lot of CDs, a faster CD-R or DVD-R drive might make a difference.

If you don't fit these criteria, chances are that instead of seeing much real timesaving improvement from a typical hardware upgrade, that blazing new gizmo will only accentuate the laggardly performance of another part of your system.

Two hardware upgrades that will never do you wrong are

- Getting a faster Internet connection
- Adding more memory

Broadband Internet connections fall into a productivity enhancing category all their own, and I discuss them extensively in this book.

When it comes to memory, the only real question is whether adding more memory will speed things up. Fortunately, you have an excellent tool at your disposal that answers this question. The Task Manager, which I discuss in the preceding section, tracks a couple of numbers that tell you when you need more memory:

1. **Open the Windows Task Manager by pressing Ctrl+Alt+Delete.**
2. **Click the Performance tab.**
3. **Watch the Page File Usage History graph and the Available Physical Memory amount as you perform normal daily tasks (see Figure 5-5).**

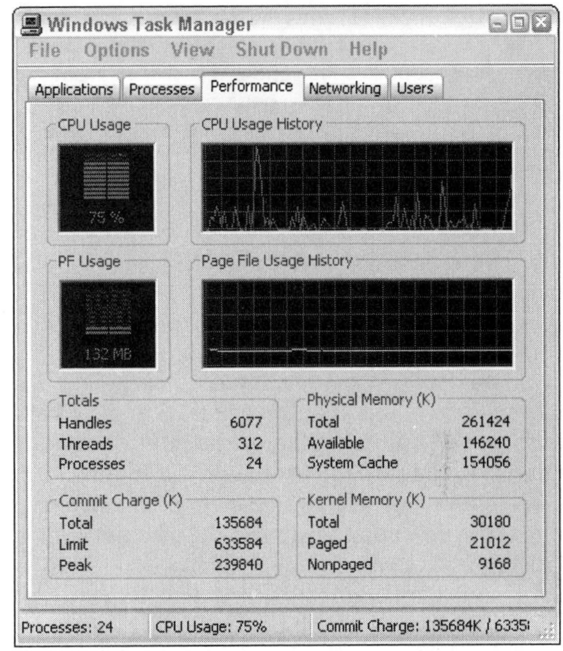

• **Figure 5-5: The Task Manager keeps track of how much memory your system uses.**

The Page File Usage History graph keeps track of how often Windows XP runs out of memory. If the line on the graph goes up to the top and stays there for any appreciable amount of time, you need more memory.

Similarly, the amount of Available Physical Memory shows how much memory Windows has available. If that number goes below 10,000, consistently, your system needs more memory, too.

Watch the Windows Task Manager to get the whole story and apply these quick rules for Windows XP:

- Everyone needs at least 128MB of memory.
- If you use Microsoft Office or another large application (such as Adobe Photoshop or Adobe PageMaker), you need at least 256MB of memory. 512MB wouldn't hurt, especially if you leave Outlook 2003 (in Office 2003) open all the time.
- If you frequently have many applications open at the same time, watch Task Manager and see if going beyond 512MB helps.

Unless you're handy with computer stuff, have the company that sells you the memory install it. That makes the vendor responsible, from beginning to end, to get it right. In the long run, this strategy can save you time if a problem occurs.

No-Nonsense Tweaking

Be careful what you tweak.

Permit me to illustrate. The Internet has plenty of places (as do books and magazines) that offer half-baked, speed-up tricks that end up interfering with your work, all for the sake of making Windows appear to run faster. If you've ever wiled away an hour or two rummaging around the Internet and playing with various dubious Windows speed-up tricks, you've no doubt stumbled onto the one that tells you to speed up the Start menu by changing a Registry setting called `HKEY_CURRENT_USER\Control Panel\Desktop\MenuShowDelay`. Yes, you can do it. Yes, it speeds up the Start menu. But you can accomplish the same thing by using an easier, faster, safer technique that is built into Windows itself. See the next section, "Using Windows' built-in tweaking tools."

Most people can't stand to have `MenuShowDelay` set to zero. It's almost impossible to choose Start➪Control Panel, among many others, if the other menus get in the way too fast!

If you've manually changed that key and want to change it back — perhaps so you can use the tweak in the next section — the original value is 400.

Using Windows' built-in tweaking tools

Windows XP brings together many of the performance tweaks you may have seen strewn throughout earlier versions of Windows, and sticks them in a place you aren't likely to stumble onto. All these involve minor changes to the way Windows appears — say, sliding menus, or shadows under menus — that involve a significant amount of overhead.

Adjusting some of these Performance settings can change your desktop; you have no way to change them back unless you back up your current desktop settings before you start tweaking.

Here's how to back up your current desktop settings:

1. **Right-click a blank spot on the desktop and choose Properties.**
2. **On the Themes tab, choose Save As.**

   You see the Save As dialog box.
3. **Give your current desktop settings a name by typing it into the File Name box. Click Save and then click OK.**

   That saves your current desktop settings as a Theme.
4. **Choose Start➪Control Panel➪Performance and Maintenance➪System➪Advanced.**

   You see the System Properties dialog box shown in Figure 5-6.
5. **In the Performance box, click the Settings button.**

   The Performance Options dialog box has all its options checked, for "best appearance."
6. **Uncheck the boxes on specific time-consuming effects that you don't want.**

   My personal choices for animations that I can live without (see Figure 5-7)

   - Fade or Slide Menus Into View
   - Fade or Slide ToolTips Into View
   - Show Shadows Under Menus
   - Smooth Edges of Screen Fonts
   - Use a Background Image for Each Folder Type
   - Use Visual Styles on Windows and Buttons

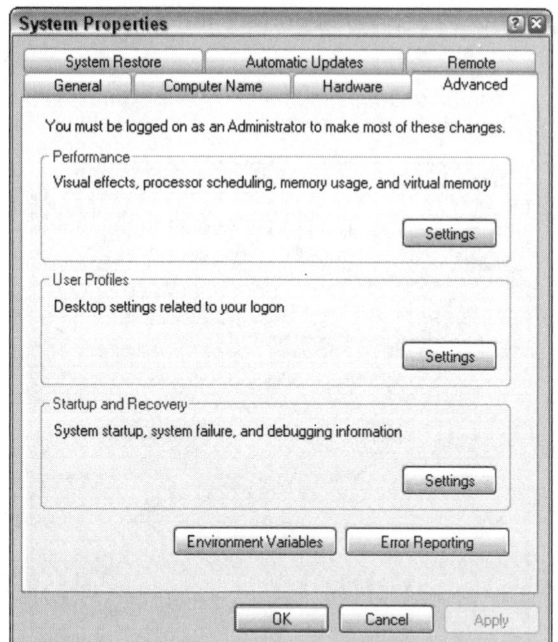

• **Figure 5-6: Performance tweaks lie buried beneath this dialog box.**

If you're a graphics designer, then the concept of font smoothing (or anti-aliasing) is probably pretty important to you. It works by adding various shades of gray pixels (or lower-intensity colored pixels, if the character isn't black) to the edges and corners of characters. If you're not a graphics designer, maybe you can live without it. Find details at `www.microsoft.com/typography/links/link9.htm` and be sure to look at Technique 7, which talks about ClearType.

Although you can choose to uncheck all the boxes (to do so quickly, click the Adjust For Best Performance radio button), you may find the resulting desktop, uh, Spartan.

7. **Click Apply or OK and your choices take effect.**

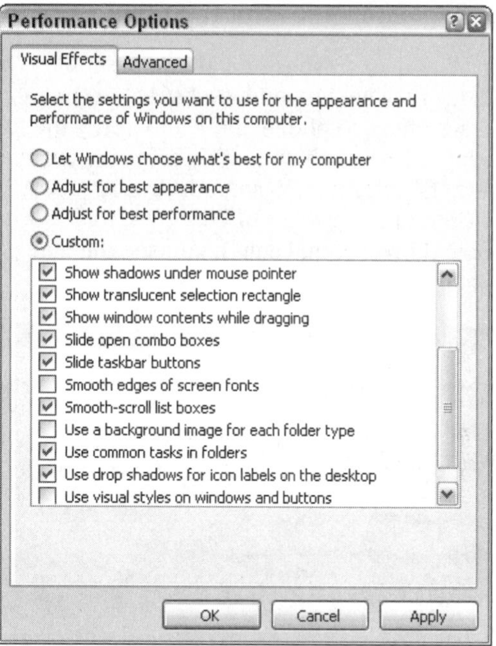

• **Figure 5-7: Each feature you can live without makes Windows work a tiny bit faster.**

Changing settings in this manner may clobber your desktop settings under certain circumstances. For example, Windows starts out set to Let Windows Choose What's Best For My Computer. You might want to try to Adjust for Best Performance. If you subsequently change your mind and move back to Let Windows Choose What's Best For My Computer, your desktop background color gets clobbered (no idea why; it looks like a bug in Windows). If any settings are changed without your say-so, you can restore your desktop using the Theme you saved:

1. **Right-click a blank spot on the desktop and choose Properties.**
2. **On the Themes tab, select the Theme that you saved in Step 2 in the preceding steps list.**
3. **Click Apply or OK, and your old desktop is restored.**

Disabling automatic error reporting

When Windows crashes or a Microsoft application heads for that big bit-and-byte bucket in the sky, Windows offers to phone home and notify the folks in Redmond about the untimely event. For example, if Internet Explorer does something it isn't supposed to do (in earlier versions of Windows, this was called a "General Protection Fault"), you see the dialog box shown in Figure 5-8.

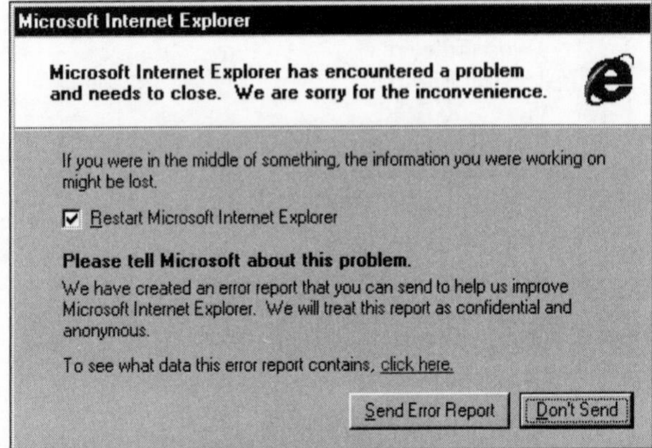

• Figure 5-8: Windows ever-so-politely asks if it's okay to send your data to the Mother Ship.

Although this process isn't terribly time consuming if you're permanently connected to a fast Internet line, it is always distracting and occasionally bothersome.

Many folks figure they don't want to send information (including snippets of "live" data, and potentially embarrassing bits) to Microsoft's computers, no matter how quick the process may be.

You can permanently turn off this feature:

1. **Choose Start⇨Control Panel⇨Performance and Maintenance⇨System⇨Advanced.**

   Once again, you see the System Properties dialog box (refer to Figure 5-6).

2. **Click the Error Reporting button in the lower-right corner.**

   Windows brings up the Error Reporting dialog box shown in Figure 5-9.

• Figure 5-9: Turn off error reporting permanently.

3. **Click Disable Error Reporting.**

   I recommend that you also leave a check mark in the But Notify Me When Critical Errors Occur box. If you do, an abbreviated dialog box appears that tells you when something unfortunate has happened, but no attempt is made to phone home.

Cleaning and defragging your hard drive

If you have a horrendously overused hard drive, with files being added and deleted with wild abandon, you might be able to speed things up by cleaning it (removing unneeded files) and then defragging it (sliding files around so they're in contiguous locations; see the sidebar, "Understanding disk fragmentation," for details).

This is one of those things, like cleaning behind your ears, that's perennially preached and rarely performed. For good reason. A full-fledged defrag on a really bad drive can take hours, and it's a rare system indeed that needs to be defragged more than twice a year. Still, it's good to check your system once in a while.

Understanding disk fragmentation

If you gloss over a few details, visualizing disk *fragmentation* is easy. Windows carves up a disk so it has lots of little spaces, like boxes. When Windows puts a file on the disk, it starts with the first open box, and pours the data from the file into the first box until it's full. Then Windows goes on to the next available box, fills it up, and so on.

When you delete a file, Windows goes back and marks the boxes that contain the file as "available," freeing them up for more data. None of the data is moved, however — the content in all the boxes stays put. Because new files are saved in the first available box, over time the boxes turn into a patchwork quilt, with files scattered all over the drive — fragmentation. Extensive fragmentation is bad because your PC must waste resources and time piecing together a file that's spread out all over the place.

When you defragment a hard drive, Windows rearranges the data so that each file is saved in a single block of mailboxes. With the files located contiguously, pulling data into the computer takes less time.

You can set up the Windows XP Scheduler to run Cleanup and Defrag automatically, while you sleep. I think you should run both of these utilities manually at least once, just so that you can see what is happening. After that, when you're comfortable with letting your computer do the heavy lifting for you, have Scheduler run both the utilities automatically. See Technique 56 for details.

Here's how to delete unnecessary files from your hard drive and then defragment it:

1. **Choose Start⇨My Computer.**
2. **Right-click the hard drive you want to optimize and then choose Properties.**

   The drive's Properties box appears, as shown in Figure 5-10.

3. **Click Disk Cleanup.**

   Windows XP scans your disk, looking for files that can be deleted.

Many people want to clean up the junk, but don't care about compressing rarely used files. Life's too short, and compressing and uncompressing files on the fly takes a lot of time. Scanning for old files to see what space can be saved if they're compressed takes time, too. The Registry has a setting that tells Windows there's no need to scan for compression candidates. I talk about it in Technique 70.

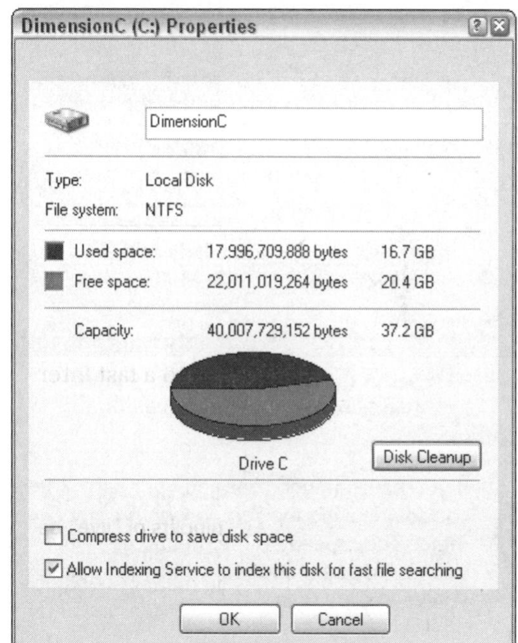

• **Figure 5-10: Properties for my C: drive.**

4. **Check the boxes (see Figure 5-11) next to the types of files you don't need anymore.**

Temporary files are files in `\temp` folders, created by various programs. Unfortunately, intermediate files created by Office that are left in the lurch when Office crashes (`*.tmp` files), don't make it onto this list. You need to look for them and delete them manually.

• **Figure 5-11: Select the categories of files you want Windows to delete.**

If you have enough room on your hard drive, consider leaving the *Temporary Internet Files* intact. They speed up Internet access, when you revisit pages and look at images that you've already seen.

Deleting the files in the Recycle Bin is a one-way trip: After they're gone, you can't retrieve them through normal methods (although you can frequently recover deleted files using a product like R-Undelete, $29 from `www.r-undelete.com`). If there's any chance you might delete something important, click the View Files button and take a good, hard look.

5. **Click OK.**

   Windows deletes the chosen files.

6. **Click the Tools tab.**

   Do *not* click Error-Checking/Check Now. That option sets up a disk scan for the next time you start Windows.

7. **Click Defragment Now.**

   You see the Disk Defragmenter dialog box shown in Figure 5-12.

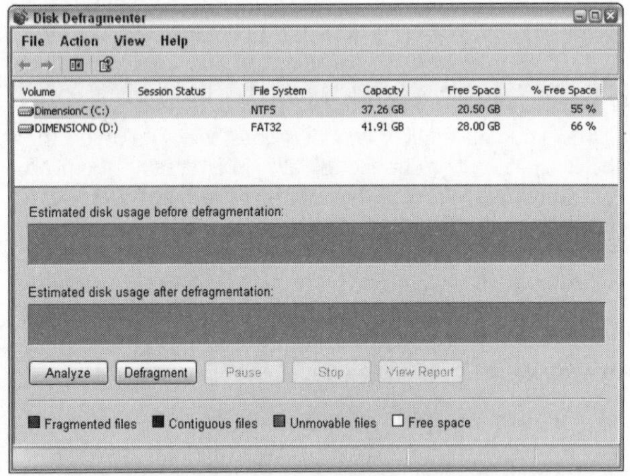

• **Figure 5-12: Maximize the Defragmenter so you can see more details.**

8. **Click Analyze.**

   Chances are very good that Windows comes back with a message that says you don't need to defrag. Heed its advice.

Special-purpose tweaks

Windows XP has three more built-in tweaks that may save time in certain circumstances. Do you meet any of the following criteria?

- You commonly use giant files (maybe you edit several photographs simultaneously or run queries against census data). If you use big files, you might want to tell Windows to save more space for the *system cache* — the place that holds files — and use less space for running programs.

- You keep big, critical programs running in the background (such as a huge Excel recalculation or massive print jobs) while doing noncritical stuff in the foreground (such as Web surfing for fun and profit). If you have important programs running in the background, you can tell Windows to give more time and priority to *background services* — the programs that run without your direct interaction.
- You have two fast hard drives, and you're running out of memory (see "Eliminating the #1 Bottleneck: Memory Drain" earlier in this technique). In that case, you may want to change the *virtual memory* settings — virtual memory being Windows way of using hard drive space when the main memory doesn't have enough room.

To make changes to any of these settings, you have to change some Performance and Maintenance settings in the Control Panel. Follow these steps:

1. **Choose Start⇨Control Panel⇨Performance and Maintenance⇨System⇨Advanced.**
2. **In the Performance box, choose Settings and then click the Advanced tab.**

   Windows presents you with the Performance Options dialog box shown in Figure 5-13.
3. **If you commonly run programs in the background that are more important than what you're doing on the screen, select Background Services.**

   That gives a higher priority to programs that are running by themselves.
4. **If you commonly work with big files — particularly more than one big file at a time — select System Cache.**

   The System Cache is room set aside in memory to hold files that you're working on.

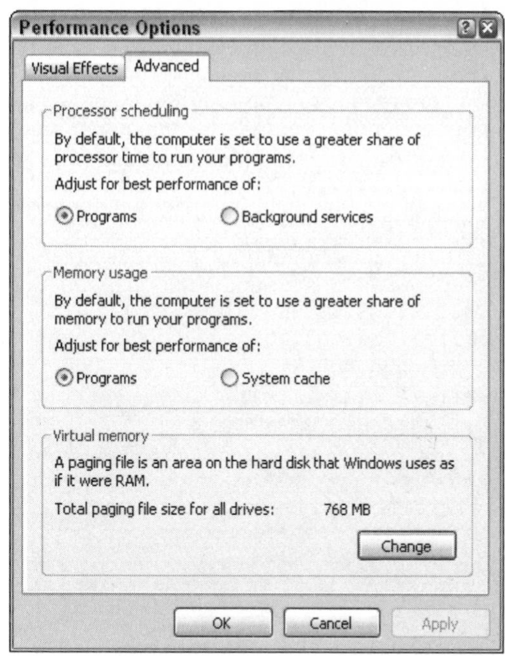

• **Figure 5-13: If you use Windows in unusual ways, these settings can save you a lot of time.**

5. **If you have two (or more) reasonably fast hard drives, and they have a gigabyte or two left on them, click Change in the lower-right corner.**

   The Virtual Memory dialog box appears (see Figure 5-14 and the sidebar, "Understanding virtual memory"). You probably have a sizable amount set aside on your C: drive.
6. **At the top of the dialog box, select each of your other fast hard drives, in turn, and set up Custom initial sizes and maximum sizes on each drive.**

   Make the sizes similar to the sizes set for your C: drive. See the sidebar, "Understanding virtual memory."
7. **Click Set after you enter the numbers for each.**

As long as you have space free on your hard drives, it doesn't hurt to have extra paging files set up, in case you start running low on memory.

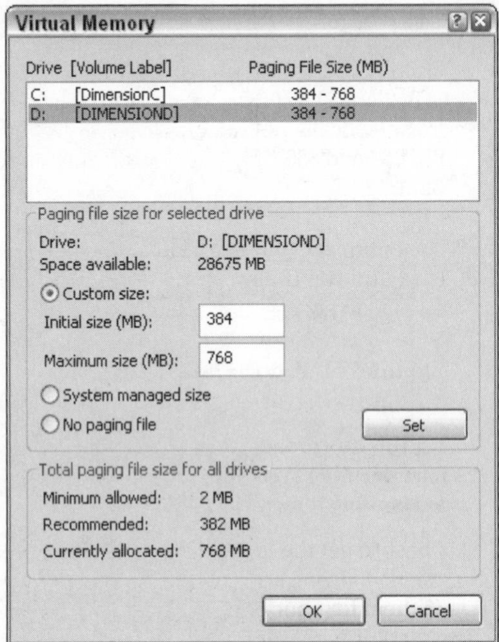

• **Figure 5-14: Establish paging files on all your fast hard drives.**

Understanding virtual memory

When Windows XP runs out of memory — the 128MB or 256MB or even 512MB that you have in your PC — XP needs to shuffle things around quickly. That shuffling is called *paging*, and it's accomplished by copying blocks of memory out to your hard disk.

Think of it this way. Many different programs are running on your computer at the same time. Each needs memory in order to accomplish its tasks. When programs want more memory, they ask Windows to hand some over. When programs are finished with a chunk of memory, they hand it back to Windows. Your memory rapidly turns into a patchwork quilt of chunks, with Windows taking care of parceling out chunks of memory when they're requested and returning them to the available pool when they're no longer needed.

Everything goes along swimmingly until Windows runs out of chunks of memory. Suddenly a program wants more memory, but Windows has already handed out every single chunk. Windows solves the problem by taking a snapshot of a chunk of memory and tossing that snapshot to the hard drive. It then gives the chunk of memory to the program that requested it.

At some point, the program that originally had the chunk of memory wants it back. No problem. Windows runs out to the disk, retrieves the snapshot, sticks it in memory, and hands that chunk over to the old program. (I won't mention the fact that bringing the snapshot into memory may, itself, force Windows to take yet another snapshot and send it out to disk. And so on. But you get the picture.)

The snapshots of chunks of memory out on your disk are called *virtual memory*. Virtual memory sits in *paging files*.

Here's where speed comes in. Windows works like crazy getting programs and their data into the computer. It also works like crazy keeping the virtual memory going. If your virtual memory sits on the same disk as your programs and data, Windows has to hop all over the disk to keep all the programs going. On the other hand, if your paging file sits on a hard disk that doesn't contain your programs, that helps solve the memory problem, simply because Windows can run faster if it's juggling two different disks at the same time. The net result is that you should allow Windows to use all your fast hard drives for virtual memory (er, paging files), providing the drives have room available.

Fine-tuning Intel systems

The only tuning software I've found that really saves time is Intel's Application Accelerator. It's a free utility that automatically tweaks the ATA settings on your disk controller, but it works only on specific Intel systems.

You can tweak many hard drives these days to boost their performance. The problem lies in where the tweak has to occur. The so-called ATA settings (*ATA* being a method for attaching a hard drive to a computer) can make a big difference in drive performance, but these settings aren't easy to tweak, because they're deep inside the hardware. And the tweaks themselves are quite dependent on the hardware that your hard drive plugs into — the disk controller — which is different on each system.

To see whether the utility works on your system, you need to identify the chip set that your PC uses, and verify that your chip appears on a list of chip sets that work with IAA. Here's how to see if IAA will work on your computer:

1. **Go to the Intel main site,** `www.intel.com`.
2. **In the Search box, type** chipid.exe **and click Search.**

   Intel's Web site finds the Chipset ID Utility, called chipid.exe.
3. **Go to the download page and then click the link provided to download and run the chipid.exe program.**

   You may have to click Run twice to get through the security warnings. Chipid.exe gives you a full report on your chip set, as in Figure 5-15. Print the Chipset information. (Typically the easiest way to do so: Press Ctrl+Print Screen to place a copy of the Chipset dialog box on the clipboard; start Word or Paint; choose Edit⇨Paste to put a copy of the dialog box in the document; then print the document.)

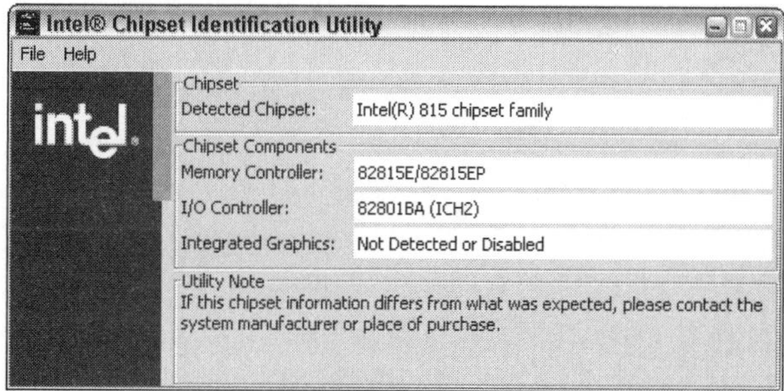

• Figure 5-15: Intel's Chipset ID Utility reliably tells you which chip set controls your computer. In this case, it's an Intel 815, which works with IAA.

4. **Check your chip set number against Intel's list at** `www.intel.com/support/chipsets/iaa/sb/cs-009312.htm`. **If your chip is on the list, IAA works for you.**

   As this book went to press, the following chip sets were supported: Intel 810, 810E/E2/L, 815, 815E/EP/G/EG/P, 820, 820E, 840, 845, 845E/G/GE/GL/GV/PE, 850, 850E, and 860. These chip sets were specifically not supported: 440, 875P, 865G/P/PE, 852 and 855 GM/GME, 855MP, 848P, and 815EM.

If you have a chip set that works with IAA, you need to download and run the program in order to make the tweaks. To do so:

1. **Go to Intel's IAA download page at** `www.intel.com/support/chipsets/iaa/sb/cs-009294.htm`.
2. **Click the download link on that page, choose your operating system, and download the program, saving it on your computer.**

   It's best to get the latest version. Intel keeps old versions hanging around (and, confusingly, presents them for your consideration) primarily for compatibility reasons.
3. **When the download finishes, click Run to run the installer. You may have to click Run a second time to pass the security gauntlet.**

   You need to restart your computer when the installer is done. IAA installs replacement drivers that appear to work better than the ones that ship with Windows. When you restart your computer, those new drivers kick in.
4. **Run IAA's report by choosing Start⇨All Programs⇨Intel Application Accelerator⇨Intel Application Accelerator.**

   The report includes a great deal of hard-to-find information about your hard drive (see Figure 5-16). If changes were made to your system, the report reflects the new, improved settings.

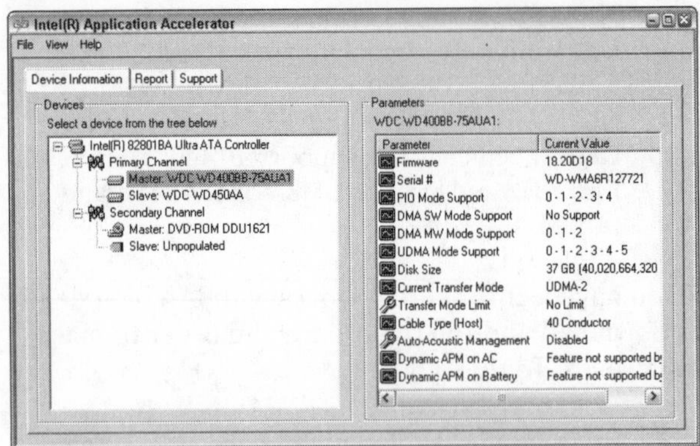

• **Figure 5-16: Intel Application Accelerator speeds up your hard drive(s) by replacing Windows' generic drivers with ones tuned for specific Intel chip sets.**

Technique 6: Shut Down, Restart, and Switch Users Quickly

Save Time By

- Using a special shortcut to shut down Windows quickly
- Restarting your machine in a flash
- Switching users faster than you thought possible

Windows XP contains a bunch of built-in safeguards that, at times, intentionally reduce its operation to a snail's pace. Nowhere is this intentional hobbling more apparent than in the Shut Down, Restart, and Switch Users functions (see Figure 6-1). If you want to turn off your machine, for example, you have to choose Start⇨Turn Off Computer⇨Turn Off and then wait (and wait some more) while Windows slowly fades into the sunset.

Few people realize that Windows XP has a program that allows you to shut off your machine in about half the time of the usual approach. That same program also shaves significant amounts of time whenever you restart your machine. And a second program lets you switch users very, very fast.

That's what this technique is all about.

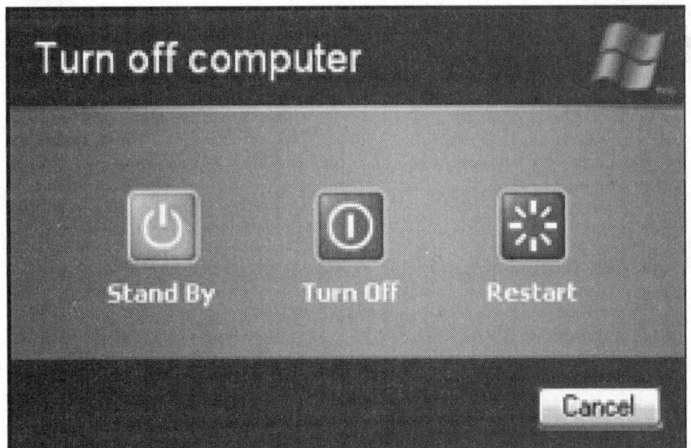

• **Figure 6-1: Time's a-wastin'.**

Creating a Fast Shut Down Icon

Buried deep inside Windows XP lurks a little-known program called `shutdown` that shuts down your system in a very fast — but orderly — way.

Here's how to put an icon on your desktop that shuts down your machine quickly:

1. **Right-click any empty location on your desktop.**
2. **Choose New➪Shortcut.**

   The Create Shortcut Wizard appears (see Figure 6-2).
3. **In the Type the Location of the Item box, type**

   `shutdown -s -t 0`

   It's important that you put spaces before each hyphen, that you have no spaces after each hyphen, and that you use a zero at the end.

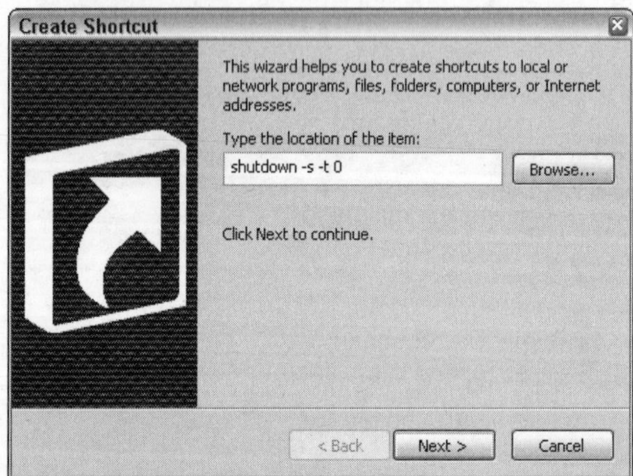

• **Figure 6-2: This shortcut points directly to the Windows program called `shutdown`.**

4. **Click Next.**
5. **In the Type a Name for This Shortcut box, use a name that will remind you that this button is for a *very* quick shut down.**

   Personally, I use the phrase "VERY quick shutdown". No bonus points for originality, but it gets the job done.
6. **Click Finish.**

   You have a new shortcut on your desktop.
7. **Right-click the shortcut and choose Properties. Click the Change Icon button.**
8. **Pick an appropriate icon for the shortcut and double-click it.**

   My favorite appears in the lower-right corner of Figure 6-3.
9. **Click OK, and your new, quick shut down shortcut appears on the desktop.**

• **Figure 6-3: Choose an icon that won't be confused with more prosaic icons on your desktop.**

To test the new, fast shut down icon, make sure no programs are running, and double-click it. On a typical machine, you see the log-off screen in about three seconds, and after another two or three seconds, you get the `It is now safe to turn off your computer` message.

This isn't a leisurely process. Windows gives you a short period of time to save changes in your Office documents, and other applications quit in an orderly way. But after the shut down has begun, there's only one way to stop it. And that's the topic for the next section.

Creating an Icon to Abort a Fast Shut Down

The fast shut down button I show you how to create in "Creating a Fast Shut Down Icon" works quickly and irrevocably. Double-click the icon, and the `shutdown` program takes over — there's no way to stop Windows from shutting down — unless, of course, you set up yet another icon to abort the shut down.

I recommend that you do precisely that. It could come in handy some day.

To create an abort shut down icon on your desktop, follow the steps in the preceding section, but in Step 3, use the command

```
shutdown -a
```

If you start a shut down and change your mind, and you can double-click that new icon before Windows really pulls the plug, Windows XP quits the shut down entirely and returns to normal.

Creating an Icon to Restart Your Computer Quickly

You can use a slight variation on the same technique to put a fast restart icon on your desktop, too.

Follow the steps in the preceding section, "Creating a Fast Shut Down Icon," but in Step 3, use the command

```
shutdown -r -t 0
```

Using Shut Down and Restart Options

You can set up both the Shut Down and Restart icons mentioned earlier in this technique with options that you may find useful.

The number after the `-t` in the `shortcut` command specifies the number of seconds Windows waits before it makes its mad dash to the exits. If you want a bit of additional time, you can change that number. For example, if you use `-s -t 15` Windows counts down for 15 seconds before pulling the plug.

If you have Windows wait a while before it shuts down or restarts, you can add your own message to the countdown dialog box that appears, ticking off the seconds.

The message in the dialog box is controlled by text that you use after the `-c` switch in the shortcut command.

For example, this command:

```
shutdown -r -t 10 -c "To abort the shut
   down, double-click the 'Cancel' icon on
   the Desktop"
```

generates the System Shutdown warning box you see in Figure 6-4. The `-t 10` setting tells Windows to wait ten seconds before shutting down.

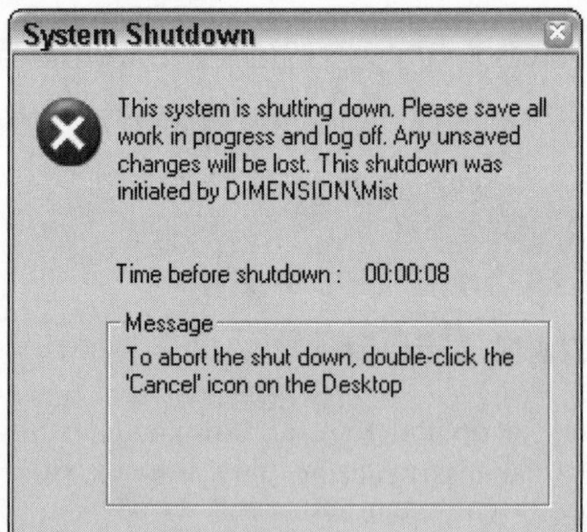

• Figure 6-4: System Shutdown dialog box counts down the seconds.

Creating an Icon to Switch Users

If you have Windows XP set up to allow Fast User Switching (see Technique 8), you can put an icon on your desktop that enables you to switch users very quickly.

If you don't have Fast User Switching enabled — a common situation in large companies where each user is required to log on with his or her own password — this same technique creates an icon that locks the workstation. That means your system goes back to the logon screen, and someone who's authorized to use your computer has to sign on before the system is unlocked.

Here's how to set up an icon that switches users quickly. It's very similar to the shortcuts used earlier in this technique:

1. **Right-click an empty part of the desktop.**
2. **Choose New⇨Shortcut.**
3. **At the top of the Create Shortcut Wizard, type** `rundll32 user32.dll LockWorkStation`

   You must capitalize `LockWorkStation` in precisely that way (see Figure 6-5).
4. **Click Next and give the shortcut a name, such as Switch Users.**
5. **Click Finish.**

   You end up with a shortcut that quickly jumps back to the Windows XP logon screen.

   This is such a handy, fast (and perfectly safe!) icon that I recommend you click it and drag it to your Quick Launch toolbar. If you ever need to switch users, it works in a flash.

• Figure 6-5: To switch users quickly, use `LockWorkStation`**.**

Technique 7

Saving Time (And Your Eyes) On-Screen

Save Time By

- Making characters on your screen easier to see
- Choosing the best combination of screen resolution and zoom factor
- Adjusting ClearType the right way — the first time
- Using multiple monitors in XP Professional

If you're like me, you may have wondered just how much time you have lost because you can't see what's on your %$#@! screen. Even in the best of circumstances, carelessly clicking in the wrong place, deleting the wrong lines, or entering data in the wrong cells is much easier to do than any of us would like to admit.

If your eyes ain't what they used to be, this technique can save you a great deal of time, money, and (literally!) headaches. I talk about a few commonsense timesavers, such as using ClearType, changing screen resolution, zooming in and out to change the appearance of content on-screen, and using multiple monitors.

Applying Basic, Vision-Saving Tactics

All the whiz-bang technology in the world won't save you time unless you set up and use your monitor properly:

- **Keep the monitor clean.** Any high-quality spray glass cleaner works. Just be sure you spray the paper towel, and not the screen. If you spray the screen directly, some of the soap can get down into the innards of the monitor. See Technique 59 for more cleaning tips.
- **Watch out for glare.** If you can't move your monitor out of direct, bright light, get a glare filter. Yes, fluorescent lights can cause a lot of glare, and some people are very susceptible to flicker, particularly when it's reflected on-screen.
- **Line up the monitor so that you're face-to-face (or face-to-monitor, as it were).** Opinions vary, but if your monitor sits right in front of you, the top of the monitor should be a few inches above your eyes, with the face of the monitor parallel to your face.
- **Adjust the darn thing.** Spend a bit of time going through the techniques and apply the options that you're most comfortable using. Whether you're unaware of all the settings or have just been putting off changing them, the most basic adjustments can save you considerable muss and fuss in the long run. Even those "Auto adjusting" LCDs need tweaking.

- **Get a bigger/better monitor.** Although you can't really quantify the amount of time you save by being able to see two documents (or spreadsheets or Web pages) at the same time, there's no question that a larger, better quality screen can improve your efficiency.

Understanding How Characters Appear On-Screen

You and I can whip out a Montblanc and draw swirls and curlicues to our heart's content, but computers have to work with dots. The number of dots, or *pixels* (the word means picture elements), on a screen limits Windows' ability to display characters legibly.

When Windows wants to draw a V on the screen, for example, it looks like Figure 7-1.

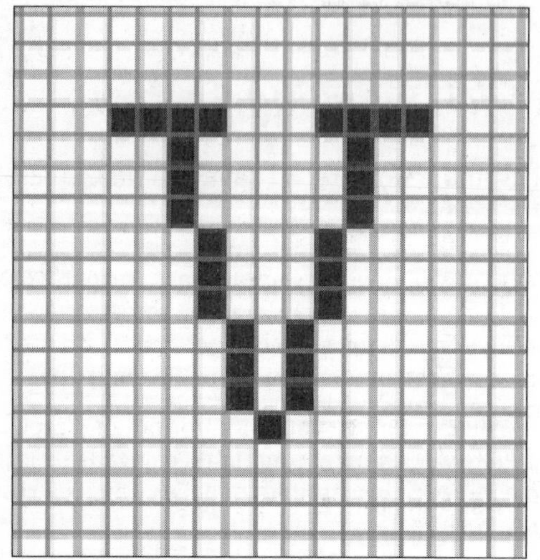

• **Figure 7-1: The letter *V* in a 14-point Garamond font on an 800 x 600 screen.**

Jaggies are the stair-step patterns you see when Windows has to draw a line by filling in the dots on-screen.

That's the best Windows can do as long as it can only turn single dots on or off — it must make each pixel either white or black.

Life isn't so simple, nor so black and white. In fact, each pixel on a color monitor actually consists of three subpixels, one in red, green, and blue — in that order, from left to right. Your brain blurs the subpixels together, to make one dot appear for every group of three subpixels.

Judicious manipulation of the red, green, and blue stripes can significantly decrease the jaggies, as shown in Figure 7-2.

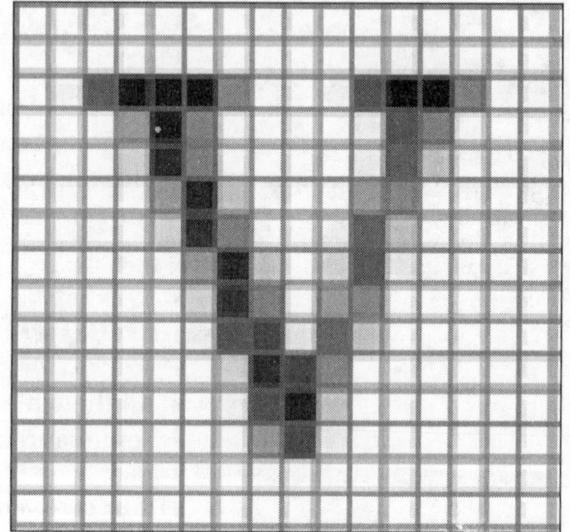

• **Figure 7-2: Manipulating each subpixel individually greatly increases the clarity of a character.**

Many attempts have been made, over the years, to use those three subpixel stripes to improve the legibility of text on a screen. Microsoft calls its approach ClearType.

ClearType is built into Windows XP. However, it isn't turned on automatically. If you try it on an old-fashioned CRT monitor, you'll see why. I talk about ClearType later in this technique.

Flat-panel screens and LCD (liquid crystal display) monitors use three-colored stripes, while traditional monitors use subpixels that look more like dots. That difference is the primary reason that ClearType looks much better on flat-panel displays than it does on traditional monitors.

For a detailed description of subpixel character rendering on color screens, take a look at Steve Gibson's excellent explanation at `grc.com/cleartype.htm`.

Screen Resolution and Zoom on CRTs

If you have a CRT monitor (I'm tempted to say an "old-fashioned TV tube" — you know what I mean), you can also reduce the jaggies by increasing the number of dots on-screen. But this solution works only up to a point. Eventually, the quality of the screen and your ability to squint get in the way. If you haven't adjusted your CRT monitor's screen resolution lately, try it.

LCD displays are generally intended to work optimally for a specific screen resolution (usually 1024 x 768 for 15-inch monitors and 1280 x 1024 for 17-inch). Stick to the intended resolution if you have an LCD monitor. The hardware's designed to work best that way. If you have an LCD display (a flat-panel monitor or laptop), skip this entire section and move to the discussion in "Fine-Tuning ClearType."

Screen resolution refers to the number of pixels Windows places on a screen. For example, the 640 x 480 resolution (which few people use anymore) has 640 pixels across the screen and 480 from top to bottom.

The smaller the numbers used to describe resolution, the bigger the items appear on-screen. However, the larger the stuff that appears on-screen, the less of the big picture you see.

Many people use their current resolution because Windows came that way, out of the box. If you have a 17-inch CRT monitor or larger — or even a good quality 15-inch monitor — try the 1024 x 768 resolution, if you aren't using it already. Most good CRT monitors readily support 1280 x 960 or higher.

The more pixels you can fit on-screen, the more information you can see at one time. Because of all its boxes, Excel is a good application to illustrate this point:

- At 800 x 600, Excel shows you about 300 cells (see Figure 7-3).
- At 1024 x 768, Excel displays around 525 cells (see Figure 7-4). The text is a little smaller, but not exceedingly so, and you get about 75 percent more usable area.

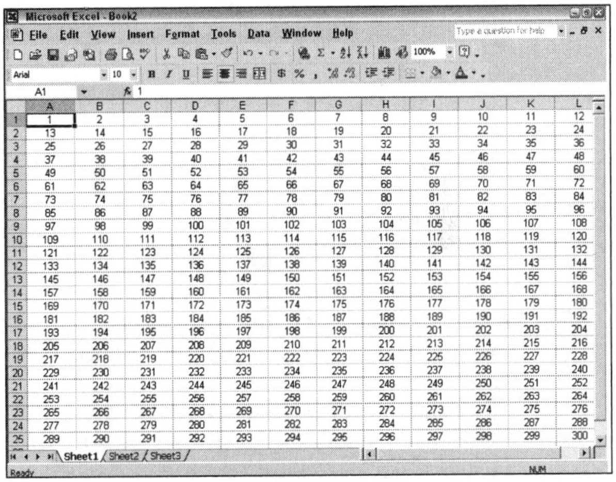

• Figure 7-3: A standard Excel spreadsheet at 800 x 600 resolution.

Table 7-1 compares screen resolution and the number of usable cells in the standard default Excel spreadsheet. It should give you a good feel for the density of information on higher-resolution screens.

Table 7-1: Screen Resolution and Excel Cells

Resolution	Rows	Columns	Cells	Versus 800 x 600
800 x 600	12	25	300	
1024 x 768	15	35	525	+ 75 percent
1280 x 960	19	45	874	+ 190 percent
1600 x 1200	24	60	1440	+ 380 percent

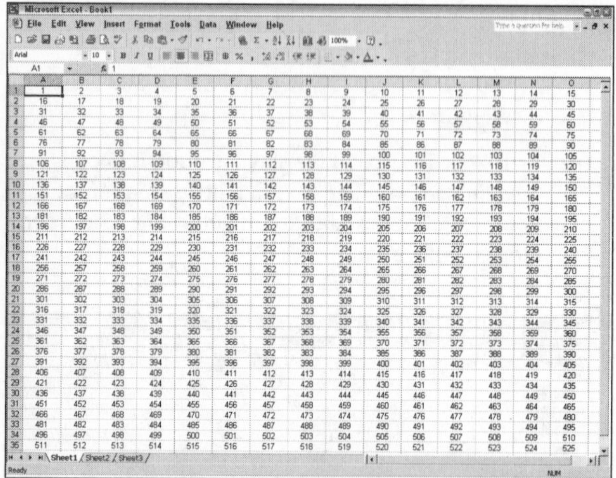

• **Figure 7-4: Boost the resolution to 1024 x 768, and you get 75 percent more cells.**

While you're thinking about changing your screen resolution, you must also take into account the zoom factor. Most major applications these days (including all the Microsoft Office applications) allow you to magnify content within the document, effectively applying a zoom effect to the working part of the application. So you can start at a higher resolution to get more usable area, but then zoom in when you want to see bigger type.

Adjusting resolution settings

The screen resolution and zoom interact in ways that most mortals find confounding — at least, I do.

Here's the technique I use to find the best compromise between screen resolution and zoom:

1. **Start Word and Excel (or your two most frequently used applications). In each application, open files that you've used recently.**

   The intent is to work with the kinds of files you use every day — live, working data.

2. **Right-click any empty spot on the Windows desktop and choose Properties⇨Settings.**

   Windows brings up the Display Properties dialog box, shown in Figure 7-5.

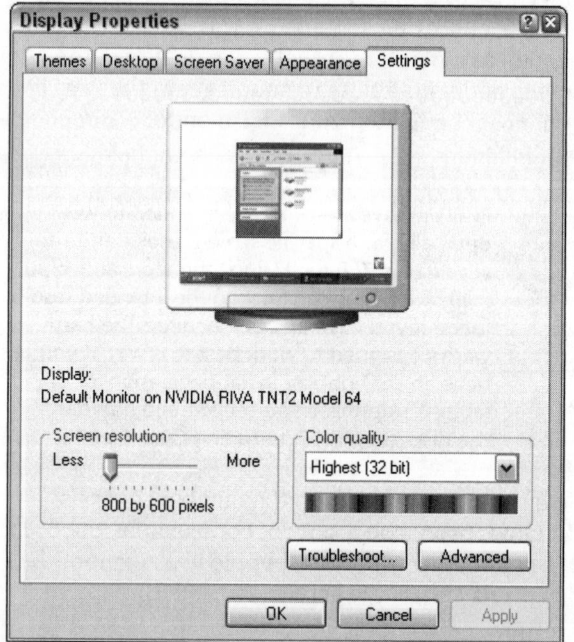

• **Figure 7-5: Adjust the screen resolution here.**

3. **Choose a screen resolution that's one increment larger than the one you're using now. Click OK.**

   The screen flickers for a bit.

4. **If Windows asks you whether you want to keep the new setting, click Yes.**

   If you find yourself trying to decide between 1280 x 960 and 1280 x 1024, keep in mind that the aspect ratio (that is, the ratio of the width to the height of the screen) at 1280 x 960 is the same as the aspect ratio at 1024 x 768. If you want to maintain the same proportions at higher resolution, choose 1280 x 960.

A bug in Windows XP may prevent you from choosing higher screen resolutions or refresh rates, even if your monitor is capable of supporting them. See `support.microsoft.com/default.aspx?scid=kb;en-us;309569` for details.

If this is the first time you've tried a specific screen resolution, take a moment to make sure the refresh rate is set at 72 Hz or higher (see "Handling refresh rate matters" later in this technique).

You may need to adjust the controls on your monitor to make sure that the picture is centered and as large as it can be. Most monitors have buttons or wheels on the front to make the changes easy — but every monitor is different, so play with it and/or read the manual.

5. **Open one of your applications and look at your live data.**

   Work with the application maximized (full screen) by clicking the Maximize button in the upper-right corner, next to the X.

6. **If the application has a zoom setting (see Figure 7-6), adjust it until you feel comfortable with the size of your live text.**

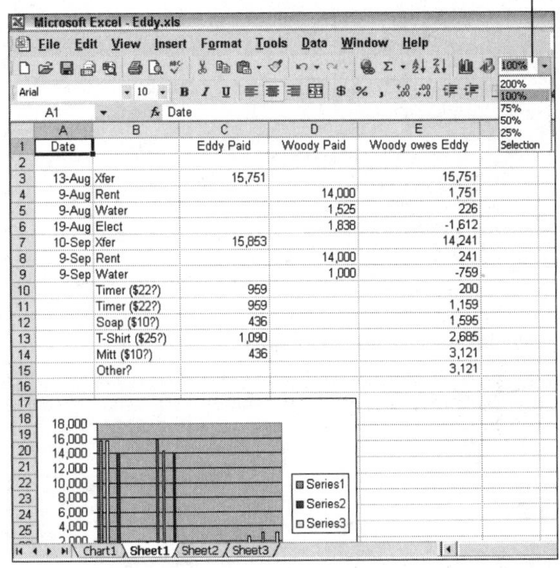

	A	B	C	D	E
1	Date		Eddy Paid	Woody Paid	Woody owes Eddy
2					
3	13-Aug	Xfer	15,751		15,751
4	9-Aug	Rent		14,000	1,751
5	9-Aug	Water		1,525	226
6	19-Aug	Elect		1,838	-1,612
7	10-Sep	Xfer	15,853		14,241
8	9-Sep	Rent		14,000	241
9	9-Sep	Water		1,000	-759
10		Timer ($22?)	959		200
11		Timer ($22?)	959		1,159
12		Soap ($10?)	436		1,595
13		T-Shirt ($25?)	1,090		2,685
14		Mitt ($10?)	436		3,121
15		Other?			3,121

• **Figure 7-6: The zoom setting box in Microsoft Excel.**

All Microsoft Office applications have drop-down zoom boxes on the Standard toolbar.

In most applications (including every application in the Office suite), you're not limited to the choices shown in the drop-down box. Simply type a number into the zoom box and press Enter.

7. **If your application allows it, adjust the size of the icons (see Figure 7-7).**

   All the Office applications allow you to choose between regular and large icons by choosing Tools➪Customize➪Options and checking or unchecking the Large Icon box.

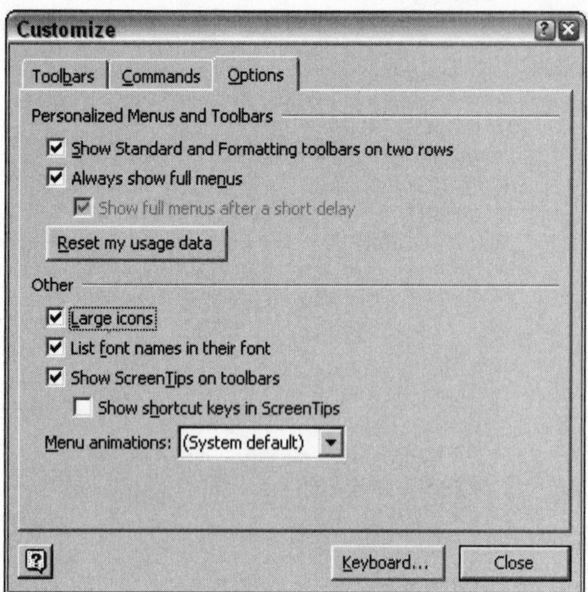

• **Figure 7-7: Microsoft Word supports large icons — particularly handy at resolutions greater than 1024 x 768.**

8. **Try to do some real work with your adjusted screen.**

   Make sure you can select text accurately and the icons are big enough. You should be able to find and click the icons quickly and reliably.

Also make sure that the icons are small enough so they all fit on-screen. Nothing saps time and interrupts your work more than hunting for important icons.

9. **Go back to Step 2 and try a higher resolution. Repeat until you get the highest resolution that's comfortable.**

   Each time you change resolution, you'll hate what you see on-screen. Be sure you adjust the zoom factor and twiddle with the icon size before you give up.

10. **When you're happy with the resolution and zoom on a single application, try working with two of them side-by-side.**

To do that quickly, click one application in the Windows taskbar; then hold down Ctrl and click the other. Right-click either entry in the taskbar and choose Tile Horizontally (or Tile Vertically). From that point, you can easily rearrange the sizes of each.

   You'll probably want to adjust the zoom setting and/or reset the icons on both applications.

11. **When you're sure that you've found the settings you like, close both applications.**

   That ensures the applications retain their zoom and icon size settings.

Most people with CRT screens find that following this one procedure boosts their productivity enormously. A finely tuned screen is a work of art!

If you start working with different applications, go back through the procedure again. Working primarily with Outlook and Word, for example, is quite different from working with Word and Excel. Don't hesitate to fine-tune your screen to match your work.

After you have the screen resolution and zoom factor down, see whether ClearType makes your text any easier to see. (You can find details in "Fine-Tuning ClearType" later in this technique.)

Handling refresh rate matters

Windows' *refresh rate* reflects how frequently the screen gets redrawn: A 60 Hz refresh rate means the screen gets rescanned 60 times per second. For office work on a standard CRT monitor, you want a refresh rate of at least 72 Hz (anything less and the screen flickers like a firefly in heat), and some people work best at refresh rates of 80 Hz or higher.

Flat panel (LCD) monitors are quite different from CRT monitors. With a flat panel, flicker isn't a problem — but slow refresh for fast-moving objects (think of, oh, an Illuminati pointing an intimidating weapon in your direction) can drive ya nuts. Most LCD monitors work best at 60 Hz — although you may want to tinker a bit.

Driving an older monitor at too high a refresh rate may harm the monitor, but you're far more likely to simply see nothing: If you've made a bad choice, Windows simply reverts to the previous setting.

Windows XP may or may not honor the refresh rate setting in the Monitor Settings box, but here's what you can do to find out how your refresh settings stack up:

1. **Right-click anywhere on the desktop.**
2. **Choose Properties⇨Settings, and then choose Advanced⇨Monitor.**

   Windows XP tells you the nominal refresh rate that it's using. See Figure 7-8.

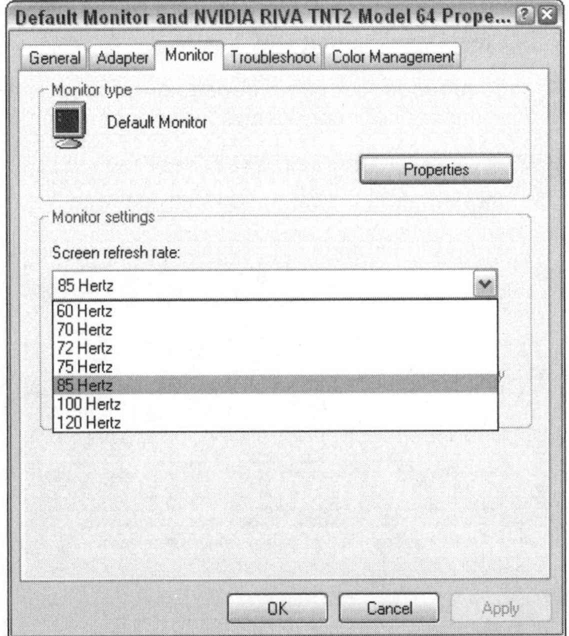

• **Figure 7-8: You can adjust refresh settings manually, but Windows XP may not use them.**

In spite of what has been said and written, it's clear to my eyes (pun intended) that Windows XP uses a refresh rate far in excess of 60 Hz when running business software on CRT displays, even when the Advanced Monitor settings dialog box (refer to Figure 7-8) says it's only running at 60 Hz. Many video card manufacturers have their own software that lets you override Windows settings. The card's software is generally accessible from a Custom tab on the Advanced Monitor settings dialog box.

On the off chance that Windows XP or one of your applications actually looks at the refresh rate setting, I suggest you check it right now and make sure it's set to 72 Hz or higher. You also need to reset the refresh rate manually every time you try a new screen resolution.

High-resolution tricks

The higher your screen resolution, the more likely you bump into limitations that Windows' designers used to make Windows work better on tiny screens. Specifically,

- **Adjust the mouse pointer speed.** Mouse travel at higher resolutions seems sluggish at best. To speed up the mouse, choose Start⇨Control Panel⇨Printers and Other Hardware⇨Mouse⇨Pointer Options and pull the Pointer Speed slider to the right. While you're there, try unchecking the Enhance Pointer Precision box and see whether your ability to click icons and buttons improves.
- **Make desktop and Windows Explorer icons bigger.** Those tiny icons on the desktop are fine-tuned for displaying at 1024 x 768 or smaller. To make them big, right-click the desktop, choose Properties⇨Appearance, and click the Effects box. In the Effects dialog box, check the Use Large Icons box. Click OK and then click Apply. (The big icons don't show up until you click Apply.)

Although it's theoretically possible to fine-tune the size of desktop icons using the Advanced Appearance dialog box, I recommend that you don't. Icons are pre-built at large and small sizes. They don't scale well.

- **Change desktop and window title fonts.** You can change the size of the text underneath desktop icons as well as the size of the title bar in most Windows applications in one fell swoop. Right-click the desktop, choose Properties⇨Appearance, and click the Advanced box. In the Advanced Appearance dialog box's Item box, choose Icon (see Figure 7-9). Then in the Font box, increase the size of the font. I suggest you start with Tahoma 12 point, but your eyes may vary.
- **Save your high-resolution settings.** Some day you may want to retrieve all these settings quickly, so take a moment to give your changes a name. Right-click the desktop, choose Properties⇨Themes, and click the Save As box. Then give your high-resolution desktop a new name and click OK.

• **Figure 7-9: The Icon font also controls the font used in the title bar for many applications — up at the top of Word, for example.**

Fine-Tuning ClearType

If you follow the instructions in Windows Help to enable and adjust ClearType, I can almost guarantee that you'll hate it. The tools Microsoft shipped with Windows XP are a bit coarse, by any standard.

For years, the only tool Microsoft provided for setting ClearType levels was a clunky Web page called ClearType Tuner (`www.microsoft.com/typography/ClearTypeInfo.mspx`). Recently, Microsoft released a PowerToy specifically devoted to ClearType adjustments (see the ClearType Tuner PowerToy at `www.microsoft.com/windowsxp/downloads/powertoys/xppowertoys.mspx`). I still prefer ClearTweak, which I describe in this section.

If you want to give ClearType a decent workout, download Mike Dixon's freeware program, ClearTweak, and give it a shot. Here's how:

1. **Go to `www.ioisland.com`, download ClearTweak, and install it.**

   ClearTweak starts by showing you a text sample using your current settings (see Figure 7-10).

• **Figure 7-10: The sample generated by ClearTweak precisely matches what you'll see on-screen.**

2. **Select the No Font Smoothing or Standard Font Smoothing radio button and see whether the text quality improves.**

   Chances are good that you'll prefer Font Smoothing at higher resolutions. This button changes the Smooth Edges for Screen Fonts setting, found in the Performance Options dialog box, which I discuss in Technique 5.

This kind of font smoothing is traditionally known as *anti-aliasing*. It works by adding various shades of gray pixels (or lower-intensity colored pixels, if the character isn't black) to the edges and corners of characters. This approach is different than ClearType's subpixel smoothing. Details at `www.microsoft.com/typography/links/link9.htm`.

3. **Next try the ClearType Font Smoothing button (see Figure 7-11).**

   You might want to change to a font you work with all the time, such as Times New Roman 11 point (which is Word's default font).

• **Figure 7-11: Try ClearTweak with a font that you use all the time.**

4. **Try sliding the Contrast setting down to 1000, and then all the way up to 2200.**

   Contrast settings between 1000 and 2200 correspond to the full range of ClearType subpixel shenanigans Windows XP has to offer. (The default setting is 1400.)

If your monitor has an "automatic adjust" button, make sure you push it a few times while playing with the Contrast setting. You may find that ClearTweak does a better job than your monitor, or you may find that your monitor's auto adjustment effectively wipes out all of ClearType's advantages. In that case, you have to decide for yourself if choosing the auto adjustment, ClearType with manual monitor settings, or some combination of the two is faster and easier on your eyes.

5. **Click the button that corresponds to the rendering you prefer. If you decide to choose ClearType, set the slider to the contrast level you want. When you're done, click Close.**

   Windows updates with the settings you chose.

   ClearType is worth a try, particularly on flat screens, and you might want to leave it turned on for a day or two to see if you really prefer it.

   Personally, I don't.

Setting Up Multiple Monitors

If you have room on your desk for two monitors and you aren't prone to getting a stiff neck, multiple monitors (either side-by-side or, less frequently, one stacked on top of the other) can save you an enormous amount of time. Windows XP has built-in support for multiple monitors. (So did Windows 98, but I digress.)

When you use more than one monitor, your Windows desktop changes in the following ways:

- Windows divvies up the desktop among the monitors.
- Your mouse roams freely across the monitors.

- Programs that are designed to work with multiple monitors (including all the Microsoft Office applications) can be resized and can float to occupy one, two, or more monitors at a time.

Adding a second monitor isn't exactly easy to do, and requires some hardware skills and knowledge. Because this book isn't geared toward hardware upgrades, I can only give you an overview of the steps that you need to follow. Before you go any further, review these steps.

Here's how to set up multiple monitors on your PC. Be sure that you have the correct version of Windows XP (that is, the Professional version), and follow these steps:

1. **Make sure that you have a multiple-port video adapter, or two or more PCI or AGP video adapters on your machine.**

   A list of adapters that Windows XP supports out of the box is at `support.microsoft.com/default.aspx?scid=kb;en-us;Q296538`. (As of this writing, Microsoft hasn't updated that list in ages, so don't be overly put off if your specific adapter doesn't appear there.)

2. **Turn off the computer, install any cards, plug in the monitors, turn the computer back on, and stand back.**

   The usual startup screen appears on one monitor only. That's your *primary monitor*. Windows is generally smart enough to detect everything automatically.

3. **Right-click an empty part of the desktop and choose Properties⇨Settings.**

   You see numbered boxes (see Figure 7-12) that correspond to the screens you have installed.

4. **Click the 1 box and then click the Identify button.**

   A large number 1 appears on the monitor that Windows has identified as 1.

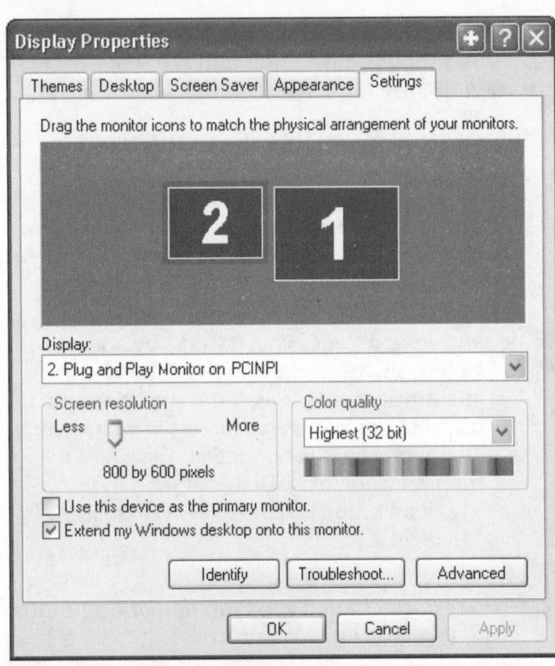

• **Figure 7-12: Numbered boxes identify your screens.**

5. **Click and drag the boxes, rearranging them into the sequence that corresponds to the way you want the mouse to move.**

   For example, if you have three monitors side-by-side, drag the leftmost monitor (identified by its number) all the way to the left. Drag the rightmost monitor all the way to the right.

6. **Click the monitor that you want to be the primary monitor, and check the Use This Device as the Primary Monitor box.**

When Windows boots, it uses the primary monitor for its startup screen. Many Windows applications get confused when they're run on multiple monitors, and they have to run on the primary monitor.

7. **One by one, click the other monitors, and check the Extend My Windows Desktop onto This Monitor box. Click OK.**

Test the configuration by opening a multiple-monitor-friendly application (any of the Office apps work). Try clicking and dragging from one monitor to the next. If you have any problems, return to the Settings dialog box in Step 3.

When you have the settings ironed out (and in many cases that's a Herculean task), the most common problem is *banding* — a light or dark band on one or both of the monitors, possibly traveling slowly up or down the screen. The banding is caused by radio frequency interference (RFI) between the monitors. I've seen reports where changing the refresh rate (see "Handling refresh rate matters," earlier in this technique) on one of the monitors eliminated the banding. You may have better luck using commercial RFI shields — pieces of radio-scrambling material available at electronics shops.

Stopping a Thief with Your Welcome Screen

Save Time By

- Branding your PC with a screen that appears before the welcome screen
- Modifying the welcome screen to deter would-be thieves

Have you ever accidentally picked up a portable that belongs to someone else? Have you ever lost a portable? Talk about a time sink.

One computer insurance company claims that 5 percent of all new portables get stolen *within the first year*. While I'd be the first to admit that insurance companies count stolen portables about as well as coyotes count stolen chickens, sooner or later you're bound to get stung.

You can't stop a determined thief, but you can take steps to "brand" your portable PC. That way, someone who innocently picks it up knows how to return it, and you give would-be bandits a reason to skip over your PC and pick someone else's.

This technique shows you two different fast, easy, cheap ways to do just that. Use one, or use 'em both. Either way, if you have a laptop, save yourself a lot of time-consuming headache down the road and get yer computer branded.

Choosing a Branding Approach

Windows XP owners have two methods at their disposal for branding their PCs, or putting notices on their machines that say something like, "I belong to Woody, and there's a reward for my safe return!"

One branding approach puts an on-screen message (see Figure 8-1) before the Windows welcome screen appears. I call this a *pre-logon screen*, and the capability is built into Windows itself. I explain how this is done in "Building a Pre-Logon Screen" later in this technique.

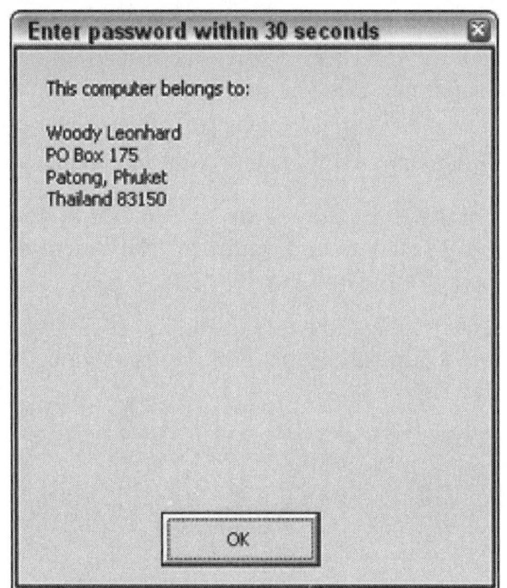

• Figure 8-1: A would-be thief who sees this screen might pass your machine by, and steal something less ornery.

The admonition in Figure 8-1 about entering a password within 30 seconds is pure hokum. Click OK, and Windows proceeds to the welcome screen. But if a would-be thief watches as you bring your system up, they might find that screen a bit . . . unnerving.

A surprisingly small number of people know about this pre-logon screen. You can be sure it'll take a thief by surprise.

A second branding approach modifies the welcome screen itself (see Figure 8-2). That approach uses a free utility you can download from the Web. I explain this approach in "Modifying the Windows Welcome Screen," also later in this technique.

You may use either approach, or both, on any Windows XP machine.

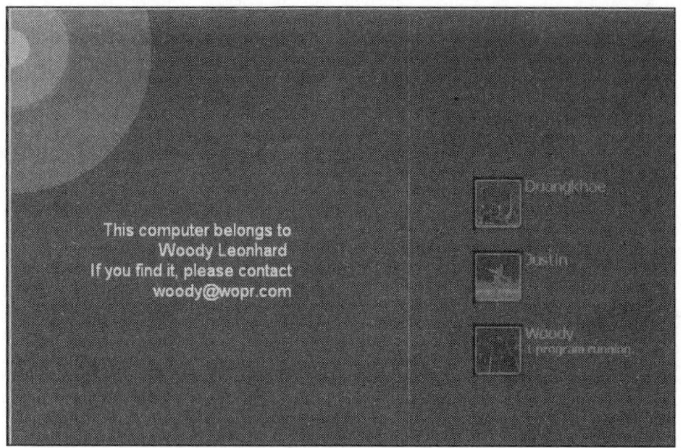

• Figure 8-2: The familiar welcome screen can be changed to brand your machine.

Neither of these approaches locks people out of your PC. If you want to keep unsophisticated users out of your machine, follow the advice in Technique 47, assign yourself a logon password, and don't share any of your folders.

If you want to keep sophisticated crackers away, you need to use Windows XP's Encrypting File System, but it's a bear. It's hard to understand and use, and if you don't do things just right, there's a chance you can lock out everyone, including yourself. If you forget your password, you're outta luck — there's no way to recover it, unless you remembered to create a password reset disk (see Technique 65). And the feature only works with XP Professional. See `support.microsoft.com/?kbid=307877` for details.

Building a Pre-Logon Screen

Here's the quick way to build a pre-logon branding screen like the one you see in Figure 8-1. You have to change the Windows Registry, so some degree of caution is in order.

The Windows Registry isn't as daunting as you might think. Although it's quite true that you can permanently damage your system by randomly deleting entries in the Registry, you really have to make a spectacular mistake in order to bring your system crashing down. Just stick to the instructions I include here and avoid the temptation to poke around in places you really shouldn't go. If you need more detailed instructions, look at Technique 68.

Your pre-logon screen might include

- Your name, e-mail address, and possibly your telephone or fax number
- Your company name, building, and possibly a floor number
- Any other information you can think of that might help a good guy return the PC to you

You definitely should not include

- Your physical address
- Sensitive data, including credit card numbers, Social Security number, your boss's name, and so on

Bringing the pre-logon screen to life

To make Windows show a pre-logon screen

1. **Choose Start⇨Run.**
2. **Type** regedit **and press Enter.**

   The Registry Editor appears. On the left side of the screen, you see a bunch of arcane names that only make sense to programmers (see Figure 8-3).

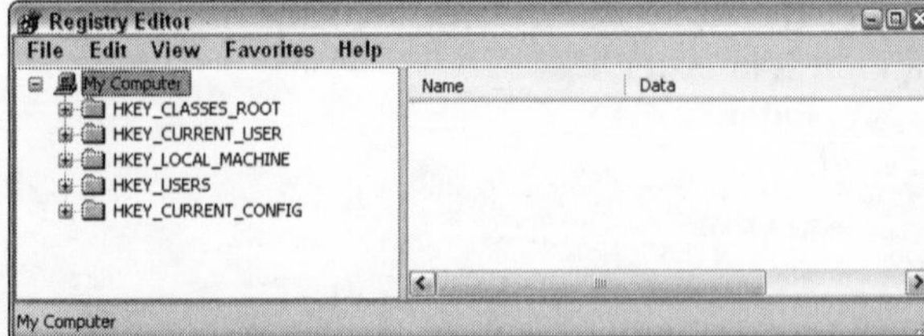

• **Figure 8-3: The Registry Editor lets you change anything in the Registry. Use it with care.**

3. **Double-click HKEY_LOCAL_MACHINE, then SOFTWARE, then Microsoft, and so on, all the way down the tree until you get to**

   ```
   HKEY_LOCAL_MACHINE\SOFTWARE\Microsoft\
      Windows NT\Current Version\WinLogon
   ```

4. **On the right side of the screen, scroll down until you see the LegalNoticeCaption and LegalNoticeText entries.**

   The title that appears at the top of the Windows pre-logon screen is stored in LegalNoticeCaption. See Figure 8-4.

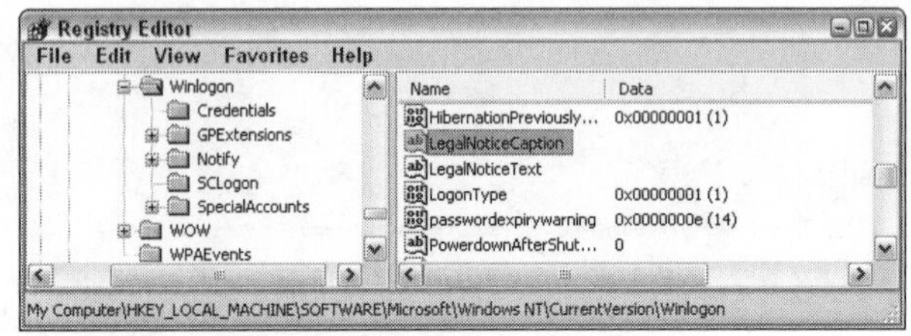

• **Figure 8-4: Windows Registry entries that control the pre-logon screen.**

5. **Double-click LegalNoticeCaption.**

   An Edit String dialog box appears for the LegalNoticeCaption value.

   LegalNoticeCaption is Windows' bizarre jargon for "the text that appears as the title up at the top of the dialog box in Figure 8-1."

6. **At the bottom of the Edit String dialog box (see Figure 8-5), type the title you want to see at the top of your pre-logon screen. Click OK.**

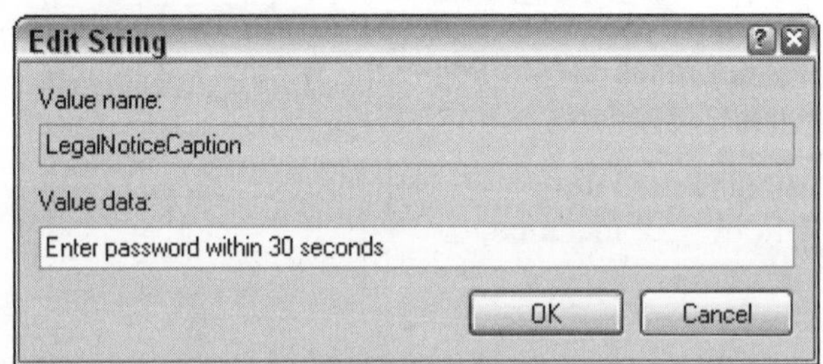

• **Figure 8-5: Whatever you type here appears at the top of the pre-logon screen.**

7. **Double-click LegalNoticeText.**

   An Edit String dialog box appears for the LegalNoticeText value.

8. **At the bottom of the Edit String dialog box (see Figure 8-6), type the text you want to see in the main body of the pre-logon screen. Click OK.**

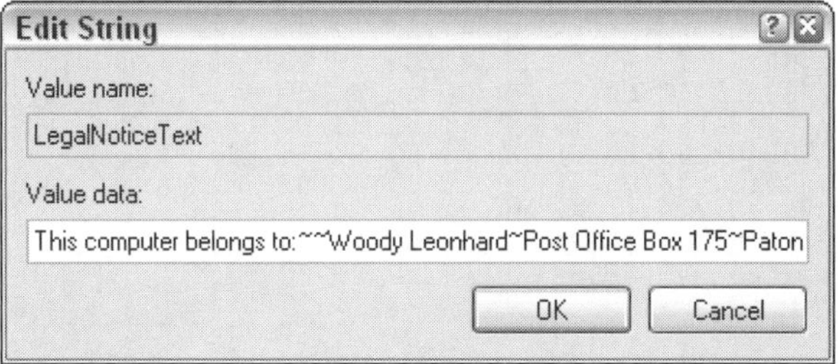

• **Figure 8-6: Whatever you type here appears in the main part of the pre-logon screen.**

I use a trick here to simplify adding line breaks to the pre-logon screen. I put a tilde (~) in LegalNoticeText wherever I'm going to want a line break. See the next section for details, but you can save yourself some time later if, wherever you ultimately want to add line breaks, you use tildes.

9. **Your new Registry entries should look like those in Figure 8-7. When you're happy with them, choose File⇨Exit to get out of the Registry Editor.**

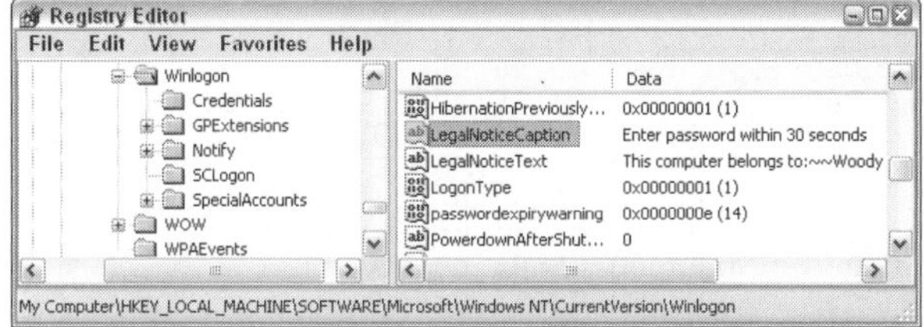

• **Figure 8-7: Final settings for the Winlogon Registry key.**

   The next time you log off (Start⇨Log Off⇨Log Off) or restart your computer, you see the pre-logon screen.

If you ever want to get rid of the pre-logon screen, get back into the Registry Editor by following Steps 1 through 3 in the preceding steps. Then double-click LegalNoticeText and delete everything in the Value Data box. Click OK, and then choose File⇨Exit to leave the Registry Editor. After that, you don't see any more pre-logon screens.

Adding line breaks to your pre-logon screen

Up for a little bit of a challenge? Want to feel like a programmer?

Naw, I didn't think so. Maybe you just have the sensibilities of a poet, arranging text to fill up space, *just so*.

There's a tricky way to make Windows break lines in its pre-logon screen, so that the screen appears the way it's shown in Figure 8-1, with separate lines for my name, address, and the like.

This technique really isn't for the faint of heart. But if you screw up, the worst you do is make the text look funny.

Here's how to get line breaks:

1. **Follow the steps in the preceding section, taking particular care in Step 8 to insert tildes (~) in LegalNoticeText wherever you want line breaks to appear in the body of the pre-logon screen. Wherever you want a paragraph break, use two tildes.**

Nothing is magical about the tilde. I just chose it because it's easy to see.

2. **Bring back the Registry Editor by choosing Start⇨Run, typing** regedit, **and then pressing Enter.**

3. **Navigate to LegalNoticeText (HKEY_LOCAL_MACHINE⇨SOFTWARE⇨Microsoft⇨Windows NT⇨Current Version⇨WinLogon).**

   LegalNoticeCaption and LegalNoticeText appear in the pane on the right.

4. **In the Registry Editor, click LegalNoticeText and then choose Edit➪Modify Binary Data.**

   The Edit Binary Value dialog box appears, as in Figure 8-8. The tildes on the right correspond to the 7E 00 entries on the left — 7E 00 being the hexadecimal computer-code equivalent of a tilde. (Take my word for it.) Two tildes back-to-back form a paragraph break.

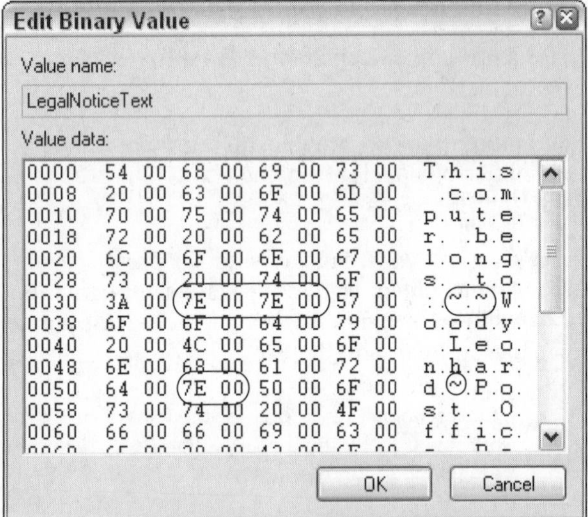

• **Figure 8-8: The tildes appear on the right as text, and on the left as hex numbers.**

5. **On the left side of the Edit Binary Value dialog box, click immediately in front of the 7 in 7E 00, and press the Delete key on the keyboard twice.**

That gets rid of the 7E 00. Notice that I said twice. Not four times. Just twice.

6. **Make sure that your cursor is right where you left it and type** 0d000a00 **(that is, a zero, followed by the letter *d*, then three zeros, a letter *a*, and two more zeros).**

   The original 7E 00 is replaced by 0D 00 0A 00 (see Figure 8-9). That little bit of hex magic just so happens to be Windows' secret code for "end of line."

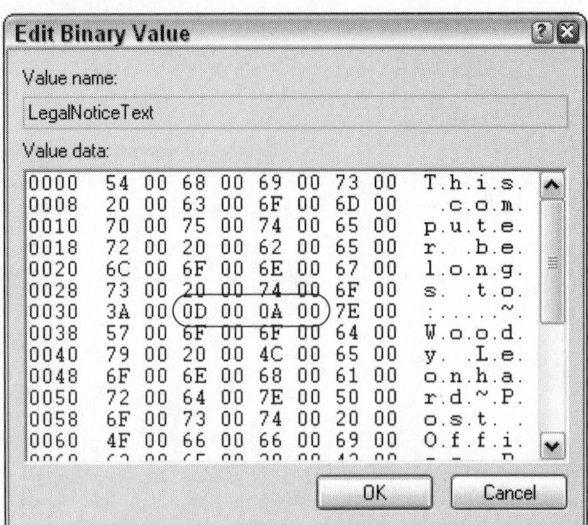

• **Figure 8-9: Replace 7E 00 with 0D 00 0A 00.**

You can type upper or lowercase letters; Regedit doesn't mind.

7. **Repeat Steps 5 and 6 for every tilde in the Edit Binary Data dialog box. If you mess up, click Cancel. When you get it right (see Figure 8-10), click OK.**

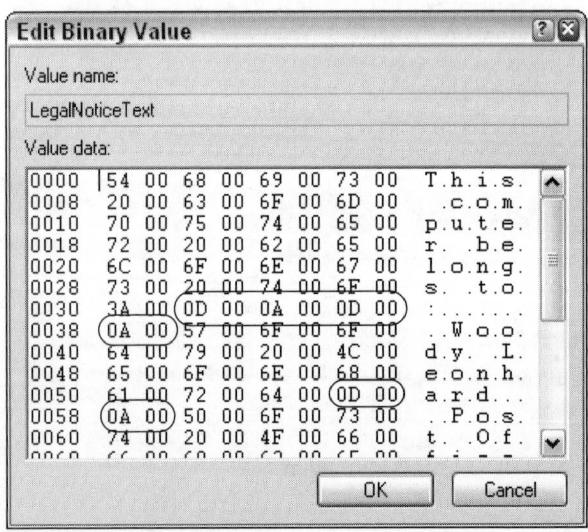

• **Figure 8-10: I replaced all the 7E 00 tildes with 0D 00 0A 00.**

Modifying the Windows Welcome Screen

The Windows XP welcome screen appears every time you start your machine, every time you log off, and every time you switch users. That makes it a good location for a subtle reminder that, in fact, you own the machine, and anybody who gets it better give it back to you!

Modifying the welcome screen isn't what I would call heavy-duty security. If somebody erases the hard drive and reinstalls Windows, your custom welcome screen won't survive.

On the other hand, this technique isn't exactly a featherweight, either. Removing that screen with anything short of a full reformat is very difficult, so the screen could act as a deterrent to a lazy or technically illiterate thief. And it definitely helps if someone innocently picks up your PC.

To brand your welcome screen, you need a free program called LogonStudio from Stardock. You can get it at `www.stardock.com/products/logonstudio`.

After you download and install LogonStudio, the program starts with the welcome screen that Windows XP users have come to know and love (see Figure 8-11). Starting with that foundation, you can then overwrite the prose on the left and/or in the lower-right corner and insert whatever text tickles your fancy.

LogonStudio isn't a polished product. Far from it. At the time this book went to press, I couldn't get the program to save my work before I exited, so losing all your work accidentally is easy to do. Follow these instructions carefully.

To use LogonStudio

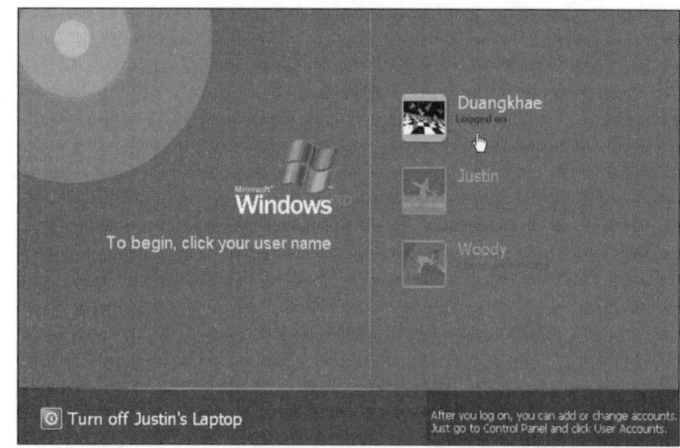

• **Figure 8-11: LogonStudio lets you change any part of the Windows XP welcome screen.**

1. **Choose Start⇨All Programs⇨WinCustomize⇨LogonStudio.**
2. **On the main screen (see Figure 8-12), click the New button toward the bottom of the screen's middle pane.**

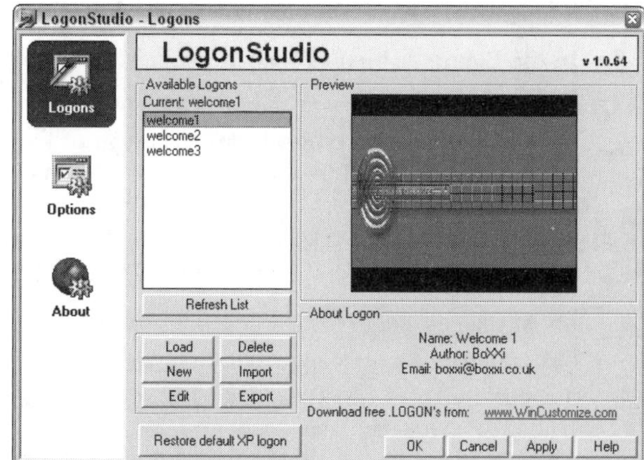

• **Figure 8-12: LogonStudio's main screen.**

The Create New Logon dialog box appears (see Figure 8-13).

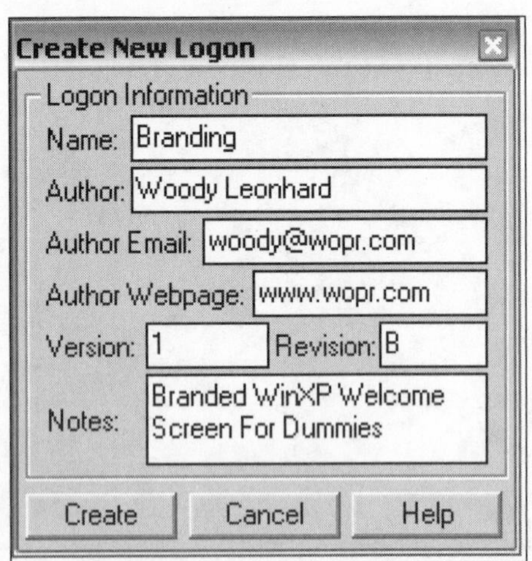

• **Figure 8-13: Identifying information for your custom Windows XP welcome screen.**

3. **Fill in the details on your new welcome screen. When you're satisfied, click Create. Don't click your user name like the screen tells you to; go to Step 4 instead.**

   LogonStudio's Editor shows you a mock-up of the Windows XP welcome screen (see Figure 8-14).

4. **In the Elements box, choose Messages➪Login Notice.**

5. **In the Caption box, type whatever you want to appear on the left side of the welcome screen.**

Use `\n` for a paragraph break.

   My Messages\Login Notice Caption box says:

```
This computer belongs to\nWoody
   Leonhard\nIf you find it, please
   contact\nwoody@wopr.com
```

   That produces the text you see on the left in Figure 8-2.

6. **If you want something to appear at the bottom of the welcome screen, choose Messages➪Notice in the Elements box (refer to Figure 8-14) and type the text in the Caption box.**

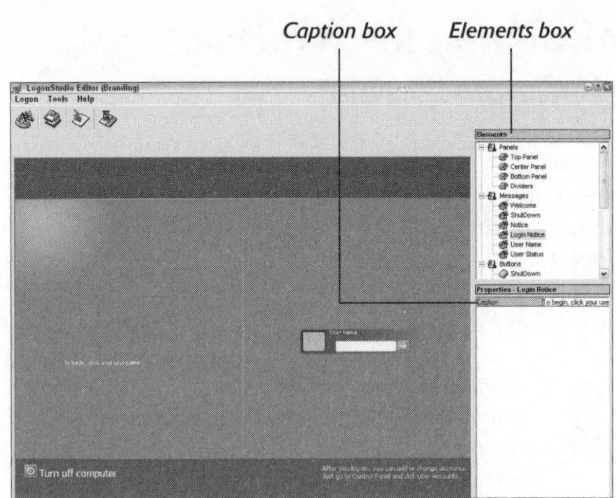

• **Figure 8-14: The beginning of your custom branding screen.**

7. **This is the vitally important step: Before you leave LogonStudio, click the Save and Apply icon in the upper-left corner — the one that looks like two diskettes stacked on top of each other.**

If you don't manually save your changes before you leave LogonStudio (by clicking the X in the upper-right corner), you lose all your work – and waste a lot of time!

   (Yes, *someone* learned this lesson the hard way. Sigh.)

8. **The next time you log off, switch users, or restart your machine, Windows XP uses your custom welcome screen.**

LogonStudio does much more than simply allow you to brand your welcome screen. You can use it to change the color of the screen. In fact, it enables you to change the colors of individual panels on the screen. You can change the logo, if that old "flying flag" Windows XP logo no longer tickles your fancy. Fonts, locations, borders — any aspect of the welcome screen rates as fair game.

Bringing back the welcome screen

Some Windows XP PCs — particularly those attached to BCNs (Big Corporate Networks) — don't use the Windows XP welcome screen. In its place, they have an old-fashioned logon screen that requires you to type in your user name and password.

Although the old-fashioned logon screen is arguably more secure than the welcome screen, disabling the welcome screen also robs you of one important Windows XP feature: the ability to switch among users quickly, dubbed *Fast User Switching*. If a welcome screen doesn't appear when you boot up your PC and you want one to (and you aren't connected to a network where the Network Administration Police will knock down your door), you can bring back the welcome screen simply enough:

1. Choose Start⇨Control Panel⇨User Accounts.
2. Click the Change the Way Users Log On or Off option.
3. Check the Use the Welcome Screen box.

   Optionally, check the Use Fast User Switching box.
4. Click Apply Options.

   The welcome screen jumps back to life.

Technique 9

Rapid Power Passwords

Save Time By

- Establishing passwords only when necessary
- Using fast, easy-to-remember, hard-to-crack passwords
- Setting password requirements judiciously

I waste more time with passwords. Sometimes they're important, but other times, they're just not. Sure, I want my online bank account to have a strong password, and I occasionally want to password-protect a Word document or Excel spreadsheet. I also stick a password on the shared PC in the living room, so my son and I don't accidentally clobber each other's settings.

But most of the time, for me, passwords are overkill. Why should I put passwords on my production machine, when I'm the only one who uses it? Why make my life more difficult by putting passwords on PCs that have shared printers, or shared disks? It doesn't make sense. If I had a sensitive payroll file sitting around somewhere, I'd put a password on the file — not on the computer that the file sits on.

In this technique, I show you what you really need to know about Windows XP passwords. I explain when they're useful and when they aren't. I also cover what they do — and don't — protect. You may be surprised.

The time comes when everybody needs a strong password or two, so this technique lets you in on a secret that I use to quickly create solid, hard-to-crack passwords *that you can remember.*

If you're looking for tips on creating a password reset disk, turn to Technique 65. A password reset disk allows you to log on to a PC, even if you've forgotten your password. If you decide to put a password on your Windows XP account, you need a password reset disk.

Understanding Password Limitations

If you're a fanatic about saving time and you aren't connected to a Big Corporate Network (in Microsoft parlance, a *domain*), chances are good you've already set up Windows XP — or Windows set itself up — so you don't need a password to log on to your PC.

Chances are also good that a nagging voice is inside your head that says, "Passwords are good, you should enable them, and some day you're gonna regret being so cavalier." The voice probably sounds like the same one that tells you to eat your vegetables.

Tell the voice to put a sock in it. Here's what you need to know about passwords in Windows XP:

- Anybody who can get to your computer can retrieve all the data on the PC (even if you use the snarly Encrypting File System, which can be cracked; see the upcoming Warning). The simplest way to do so is with a screwdriver. It takes about a minute to remove a hard drive.

As I mention in other techniques, if you want to keep unsophisticated users out of your machine, follow the advice in Technique 47, assign yourself a logon password, and don't share any of your folders. If you want to keep sophisticated crackers away, you need to use Windows XP's Encrypting File System, which is a bear. It's hard to understand and hard to use, and if you don't do things just right, there's a chance you can lock out everyone, including yourself. If you forget your password, you're outta luck — there's no way to recover it. And the feature only works with XP Professional. See `support.microsoft.com/default.aspx?scid=kb;en-us;307877` for details.

- Anyone with Computer Administrator status can change every user's password. In XP Home, unless you modify things, *everyone* is an administrator. So anybody can change all the passwords on the machine, at any time, no sweat.

Unless you take steps to change things (or you're attached to a Big Corporate Network), Windows XP accounts aren't for security. They don't do anything to make your computer more secure. They exist primarily to help keep well-intentioned users from bumping into each other.

- Nobody can log on to a Windows XP computer — either over the Internet or over your network — using an account with a blank password (or no password).

In Windows XP Home (or XP Professional when the PC isn't tethered to a Big Corporate Network), requiring a password to log on provides a convenient way to keep multiple users from bumping into each other, but that's about it. If you limit the PC to one Computer Administrator account (see Technique 47), put a password on that account, and jealously guard it, XP can provide a substantial amount of security. Still, anybody who's determined or knowledgeable can crack a protected system.

Requiring a Password to Log On

When Windows XP installs itself, all the user accounts it gleans from previous versions of Windows and all the accounts you create during the installation process are turned into Computer Administrator accounts (see Technique 47), and by default, Administrator accounts don't have passwords.

That means anybody walking up to the Windows welcome screen can click your name and start using the computer, and Windows has no way to know that the interloper isn't you.

In Technique 5, I show you how to bypass the Windows welcome screen and automatically log on to Windows. That can be a real time-saver if your machine is physically secure. But if you aren't sure who can get at your PC, it's an invitation to real problems. Best to avoid automatic logon and secure your PC with a password, if anyone can get close to your machine.

If you want to force anyone who uses your logon ID to supply a password, follow these steps:

1. **Choose Start⇨Control Panel⇨User Accounts; then click your account.**

   You see the What Do You Want to Change About Your Account dialog box.

2. **Click Create a Password.**

   Windows shows you the Create a Password for Your Account dialog box (see Figure 9-1).

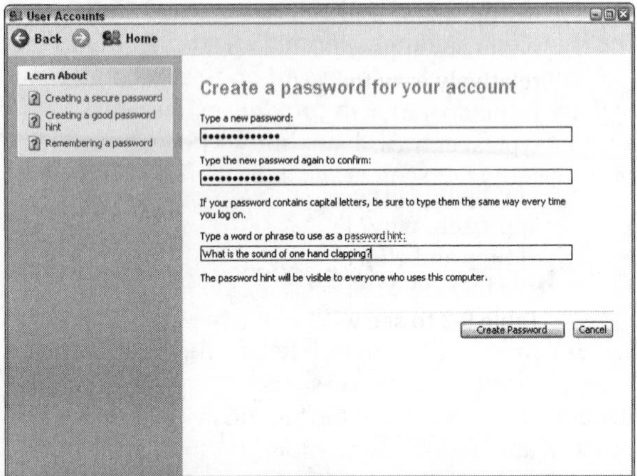

• **Figure 9-1: When you create your first password for an account, the dialog box looks like this.**

3. **Make sure the Caps Lock key is off.**

Turning off the Caps Lock key is a crucial step, and skipping it can cause you no end of time-consuming problems.

4. **Type your new password in the top box and then type it again in the second box.**

   For tips on creating passwords that work, see "Choosing a Quick, Strong Password" later in this technique. For tips on passwords that simply don't work, see the sidebar, "Don't go there: Passwords that won't pass muster," also in this technique.

5. **If you must have a password hint, type it in the bottom box.**

Be aware that anybody who can see your screen can see the hint.

6. **Click Create Password.**

   Windows responds with a helpful offer to make your files and folders private.

7. **Click the Yes, Make Private button or the No button, depending on your circumstances.**

   See Technique 48 for a thorough discussion of the implications of making your files and folders private. It isn't as simple as the dialog box would make you think.

The next time you start Windows or switch users, anyone who wants to use your logon ID has to provide a password (see Figure 9-2). Other people can click the question mark next to the password box; Windows divulges the password hint you've provided without a whimper of a protest.

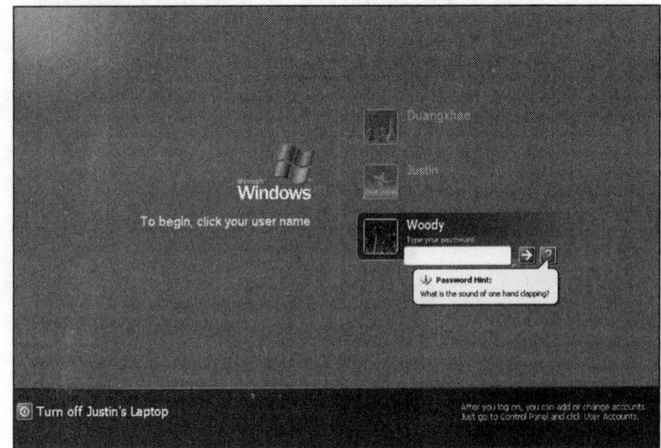

• **Figure 9-2: The password hint appears when you click the question mark button.**

Looking at Passwords from a Cracker's Point of View

A good password is not only hard for a cracker to compromise, but also easy for you to remember. Much has been written about the former. Few have worried about the time-consuming aspects of the latter.

To understand what makes a good password, you need to understand how most crackers go about breaking them. Crackers start with the easiest methods for getting into your system:

- **The D'Oh approach:** You scribble your password on a sticky note and attach it to your console or throw it in your desk drawer. The cracker doesn't have to do too much work on that one. You hit your forehead and say, "D'Oh!" when you figure out what happened.

  Or maybe the cracker concocts some way to con you out of your password. "Hello, Mr. Woody. This is tech support. Our database just crashed. What is your password?" ("D'Oh.")

- **The Hang Your Head in Shame approach:** Passwords that fall into this category include those that use the word *password*, your first name, or any of the other easily guessed passwords I list in the sidebar, "Don't go there: Passwords that won't pass muster" in this technique. You have no excuse.

- **The Dictionary approach:** Crackers can find dozens of ordinary dictionaries from cracking sites on the Web. These specialized "common password" dictionaries include a large majority of all the passwords in common use — names, words, dates, abbreviations, and more. If your password appears in the dictionary, it can be relatively easy to crack your system. (*Relatively* is the operative term.) See Table 9-1 for a few typical entries.

- **The Brute Force approach:** Crackers hate this approach. Why? It can take an enormous amount of time and effort to crack a password when you have to work from scratch. Take a look at Table 9-2 to see why.

Table 9-1: The Most Common (and Most Easily Cracked) Passwords

0	000000	00000000	007	1
110	111	111111	11111111	12
121212	123	123123	1234	12345
123456	1234567	12345678	123456789	1234qwer
123abc	123asd	123qwe	2002	2003
2600	54321	654321	88888888	a
aaa	abc	abc123	abcd	Admin
admin	admin123	administrator	alpha	asdf
computer	database	enable	foobar	god
godblessyou	home	ihavenopass	Internet	Login
login	love	mypass	mypass123	mypc
mypc123	oracle	owner	pass	passwd
Password	password	pat	patrick	pc
pw	pw123	pwd	qwer	root
secret	server	sex	super	sybase
temp	temp123	test	test123	win
xp	xxx	yxcv	zxcv	

Table 9-2: How Long it Takes to Crack a Good Password

Length of Password	Number of Distinct Passwords	Time to Crack
5 characters	6,600,000,000	15 hours
6 characters	600,000,000,000	60 days
7 characters	55,000,000,000,000	15 years
8 characters	5,000,000,000,000,000	1,500 years

Table 9-2 assumes that the cracker is using 46 keys on the keyboard and making 1,000 attempts to crack the password per second. It also assumes that the cracker will hit pay dirt halfway through the process.

Don't go there: Passwords that won't pass muster

Do not use any of the following as passwords. All of them are child's play for any cracker, hacker, or tech-savvy second-grader:

- Password.
- Your name, your nickname, your spouse or significant other's name, your child's name, your parents' name, your pet's name, your boss's name. . . shall I continue?
- Your birthday, your spouse's birthday, your kids' birthdays, D-Day, the date of a major holiday or event, and so on.
- The name of a month, a day of the week, or a color.
- Your telephone number, Social Security number, or e-mail address.
- Anything resembling the most common (and most easily cracked) password list in Table 9-1.

And my two cents on password hints: I wish I had a nickel for every Windows XP user who has "Mother's Maiden Name" or "Dog's Name" or "Home Phone Number" as his or her *uncrackable* password hint. Your password is only as secure as the hint, and if the hint points to information that is readily available, well. . . .

Choosing a Quick, Strong Password

If you look at Table 9-2, you can easily see why most experts recommend you use a password that's at least seven characters long.

In addition, using different kinds of characters in your passwords is important. If you limit yourself to 26 lowercase letters, the MTTC (er, Mean Time To Crack) a seven-character password falls from 15 years to less than a day. That's a huge difference.

On the other hand, if you try to memorize a random seven-character string of letters and numbers and punctuation marks, you'll spend more time dealing with forgotten passwords than you will working on your PC. Guaranteed.

Here's my four-step, blazingly fast method for coming up with a secure password that you can remember:

1. **Pick two words or numbers that go together.**

   Moon and June, Tomato and Tomahto, your mother's maiden name and the city where you were born, your birth date and your son's birth date. Doesn't matter, as long as you don't use your own name or your logon ID. Even if each word or number is easy to crack all by itself (as certainly is the case with your mother's maiden name or your birth date), combining two together makes things far more complicated. Pick two that are easy for you to remember.

2. **Pick a number or punctuation mark.**

   All you need is one.

3. **Use the first word, then the number or punctuation mark, then the second word. Here are some examples:**

   - Moon+June
   - Tomato2Tomahto
   - Holmes8Downey
   - Oct20$Apr11

4. **Make sure that your password has at least seven characters, and at least three of the following:**

   - A lowercase letter
   - An uppercase letter
   - A number
   - A punctuation mark.

   If it doesn't, go back to Step 1.

Because of the way Windows XP encrypts passwords, the toughest ones to crack are exactly 7 or 14 characters long.

That's the easiest, fastest way I know to pick an ultra-secure password that you can remember. It has the added advantage of passing muster on all but the most hidebound top-secret Windows systems.

A surprisingly good, small product called RoboForm (www.roboform.com) not only generates hard-to-crack passwords for you, it keeps track of them, and even automatically fills in passwords when requested on Web pages. As a neat additional trick, RoboForm can keep your passwords on a USB flash drive, so you can carry your passwords with you. Free for the basic version, for personal use; $29.99 for the Pro version.

Changing and Deleting Passwords

So you're tired of having a password on your account? As long as you aren't connected to a Big Corporate Network, it's easy to tell Windows you don't want to be forced to use a password anymore. Here's how:

1. **Choose Start⇨Control Panel⇨User Accounts; then click your account.**

   You see the What Do You Want to Change About Your Account dialog box.

At this point, you can click Change My Password and, uh, change your password.

2. **Click Remove My Password.**

   Windows shows you the Are You Sure You Want to Remove Your Password dialog box (see Figure 9-3).

3. **Click Remove Password.**

   Windows XP no longer requires a password when someone clicks your logon ID on the welcome screen.

If your account is listed as a Computer Administrator, you can change other users' passwords, too — or remove password protection on their accounts entirely.

If you have a Computer Administrator account, you don't need to know another person's password in order to change or delete it. This is a giant-sized security hole that many Windows XP users don't know about, but it's a natural byproduct of the way Windows XP gives new users Computer Administrator status by default.

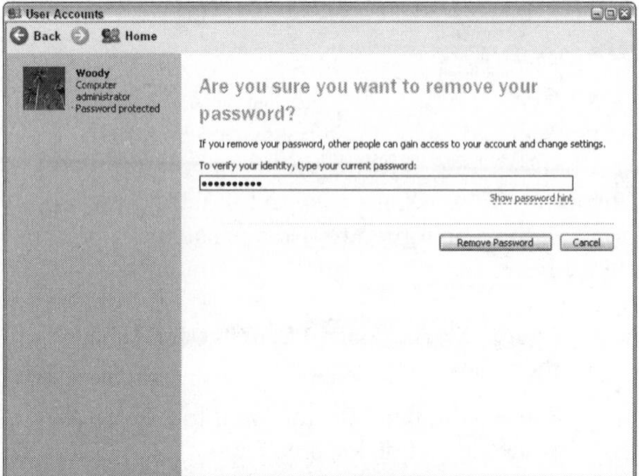

• **Figure 9-3: In order to remove the password, you have to supply the current password.**

Here's how to change another user's password, if you have a Computer Administrator account:

1. **Make sure you can live with the consequences of changing the password.**

   If you change someone's password, he or she automatically

   - Loses all the passwords he or she has stored in Internet Explorer.
   - Loses all the passwords stored for network access, including dial-up accounts.
   - Cannot view encrypted e-mail messages (sent or received).
   - Cannot use current digital certificates that, among other things, are used to sign encrypted e-mail messages.
   - Loses all access to any data protected by the Encrypting File System (see the Warning earlier in this chapter). That EFS data is gone, kaput, and after the password is changed, there's no way you can ever get it back.

2. **Choose Start⇨Control Panel⇨User Accounts; then click the other person's account.**

   You see the What Do You Want to Change About (the other person's) Account dialog box.

3. **Click Change the Password or Remove the Password.**

   The Change (the other person's) Password dialog box appears (see Figure 9-4).

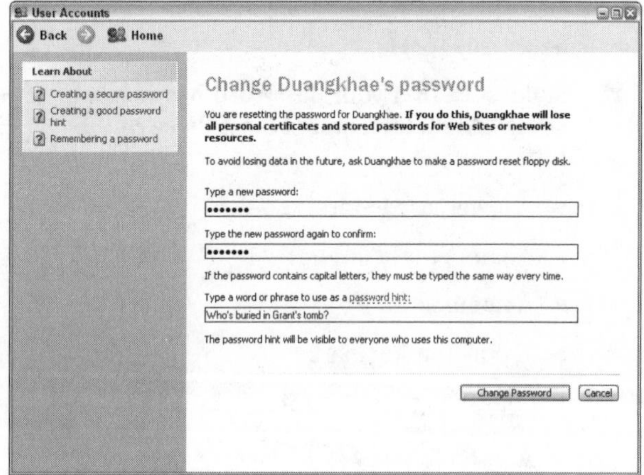

• **Figure 9-4: Changing or deleting another user's password has many serious repercussions.**

4. **If you're absolutely certain that you understand the consequences, fill out the appropriate boxes and click Change Password.**

   I talk about the password reset disk (refer to Figure 9-4) in Technique 65. It allows you to log on to a computer even if you've forgotten your password — and if you're changing another user's password, she should certainly be admonished to create a password reset disk right away.

Keeping Your Password Alive

Windows XP Home doesn't force users to periodically change their passwords. Some XP Professional systems also spare users the bother. Many Windows XP Professional systems, however, require you to change your password periodically.

Providing you've chosen a solid password and you don't let it out, forced password changes rate as a major time-eating annoyance. Fortunately, the problem's very easy to fix if you know how, and you have permission — by no means a given on Big Corporate Networks.

If Windows requires you to change passwords periodically, and your password is about to expire, you get a message such as the one shown in Figure 9-5 as soon as you log on.

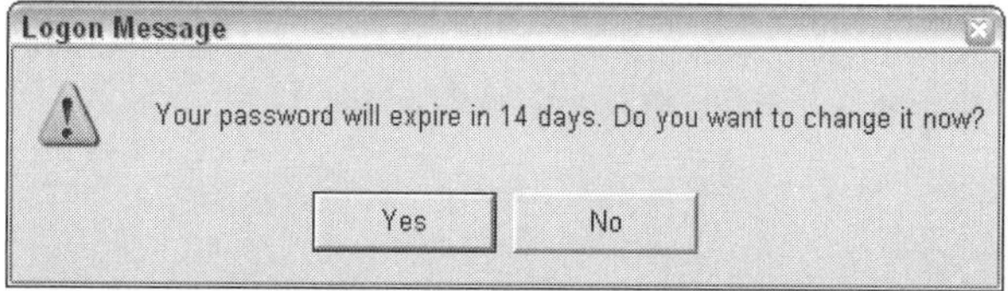

• **Figure 9-5: The password expiration warning.**

Unless some administrator has overridden the XP Professional defaults and made your life miserable, your password is valid for 42 days, and you start getting those warning messages 14 days before the password is due to expire.

If you play along with the game, you may discover that you can re-enter your old password as a "new" password and go your merry way.

If you don't play along and let your password expire, it may take an act of Congress (or at least an act of mercy from your network admin) to get your account going again.

Here's how to tell Windows XP Professional that you want it to let you keep your password forever:

1. **Log on with a Computer Administrator account.**
2. **Choose Start⇨Run and type**

   `control userpasswords2.`
3. **Press Enter, and then click the Advanced tab.**

   Windows brings up the User Accounts dialog shown in Figure 9-6.

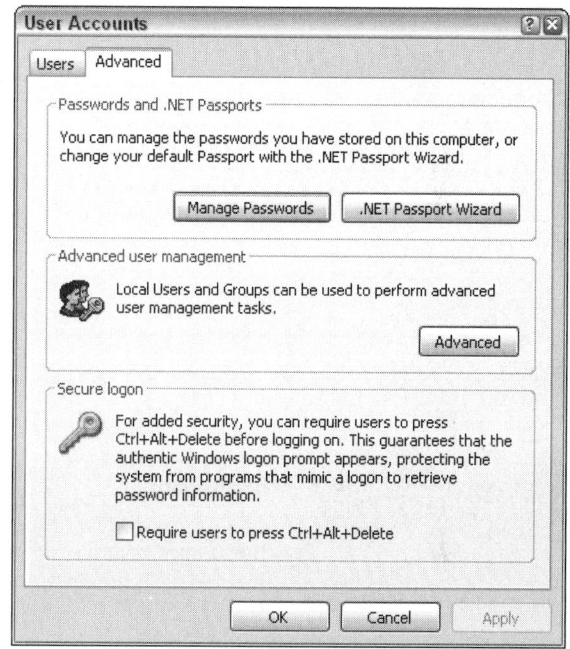

• **Figure 9-6: Override passwords here.**

4. **In the Advanced User Management box, click Advanced.**

   It can't get more advanced than this, eh? Windows shows you the Local Users and Groups dialog box, shown in Figure 9-7.

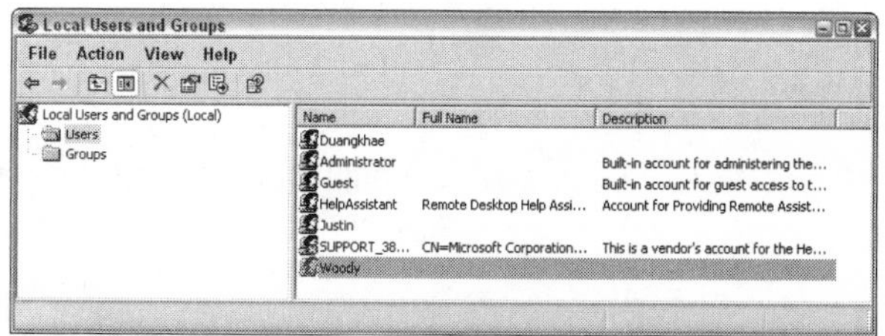

• **Figure 9-7: Manage users and groups on this machine.**

5. **On the left, click Users. On the right, double-click the name of the user whose password should never, uh, pass away.**

   The Properties dialog box for the selected user appears (see Figure 9-8).

6. **Click the Password Never Expires check box; then click OK.**

• **Figure 9-8: Keep the password forever.**

Windows Power Management

Save Time By

- Using Stand By or Hibernation mode to restart quickly
- Getting Windows to turn off the power when you shut down
- Making smart, power-saving choices that also save you time

This technique tells a tale of two standards. It was the best of times. It was the worst of times. Oops. Wrong plot.

Good power management saves energy, saves money, saves the earth, and saves your time. Bad power management forces you to hunt for the off button on your computer every time Windows tells you, "It is now safe to turn off your computer." Windows XP supports some versions of the older power management standard — called APM — as well as the newer standard, dubbed ACPI. (Actually, calling APM a "standard" is a bit of a stretch. Just about every PC manufacturer had its own, unique "standard.")

This technique tells you just what you need to know to standby, hibernate, and power down completely and quickly. It should also make you feel much less guilty about adjusting power-saving options to save you time.

Understanding the Standards

Not that many years ago, power management decisions took place deep inside your PC. When the computer's BIOS (Basic Input/Output System, the program that talks directly to the hardware) detected that you weren't using a portable's hard drive, for example, the BIOS cut off power to the drive to conserve battery life. APM, or Advanced Power Management, refers to this older, hardware-based version of power management. It suffers from many problems, including the inability to tell whether your USB peripherals are busy.

A number of hardware manufacturers got together with Microsoft and created ACPI, or Advanced Configuration and Power Interface (`www.acpi.info`). ACPI puts Windows in the driver's seat, making decisions about what parts of the computer can be powered down.

If you bought a PC new with Windows XP installed, ACPI works with no problems. If you installed Windows XP on an existing computer, you may or may not have ACPI or APM support. Windows XP installs APM only on systems with specific BIOSs that appear on its compatibility list.

If you're having any sort of power problem — your battery drains too fast, the computer stays on too long, your computer doesn't shut off when you shut down Windows — it's worth the effort to go into the computer's BIOS setup program and turn off all the power management settings, leaving Windows in control. Do so even if you think that you have the correct ACPI power management settings. See your PC's documentation or the manufacturer's Web site for details.

Using Stand By and Hibernate

The ACPI standard (`www.blueowltechnologies.com/pmtACPI.asp`) defines six power states, but you're only interested in four of them: On, Off, Stand By, and Hibernate.

In *Stand By* mode, everything except the memory is shut off. You still draw some power, but returning to the On state is very quick. If the battery runs out while you're in Stand By, you lose everything in memory.

Of course, you should always save everything before going into Stand By mode.

In *Hibernate* mode, the contents of memory are written out to the hard drive and then all the power is turned off. Returning to On takes a while because the PC has to spin up the hard drive and then transfer the saved data back into memory. But if the battery goes south, you don't lose any data.

To go into Stand By or Hibernate mode if your computer isn't connected to a Big Corporate Network:

1. **Choose Start➪Turn Off Computer.**

   Most desktop computers show Stand By as the first option in the Shut Down dialog box (see Figure 10-1).

• **Figure 10-1: Most computers have Stand By for the first shut down option.**

2. **Hold down the Shift key.**

   If your computer supports Hibernate mode, the first option changes from Stand By to Hibernate (see Figure 10-2).

• **Figure 10-2: Hold down Shift to change the first option.**

3. **Click Stand By or Hibernate as appropriate, but if you use Stand By, be sure the power doesn't go out!**

If you have a newer portable computer, chances are good it has a Soft Off button. Push the button briefly, and Windows XP goes into Hibernate. Press it for several seconds, and you get a full Shut Down. (Soft Off buttons don't send a PC into Stand By mode.) Consult your PC's documentation or the manufacturer's Web site for details.

If you are connected to a domain (that is, a Big Corporate Network), your shut down screen probably gives Stand By and Hibernate as separate options in the What Do You Want the Computer to Do drop-down box.

Forcing Power Off on Shut Down

Many Windows XP users who upgraded their machines from earlier versions of Windows have bumped into a simple power management problem: They shut down Windows, but the computer stays on — even if the computer used to turn itself off before the upgrade.

Instead, Windows XP puts up a screen that says, `It is now safe to turn off your computer.` Why can't Windows XP turn off the computer? Particularly if lowly Windows 98 did everything just fine.

There's a reason why: Windows XP probably doesn't know that it can use the older APM commands to turn off your PC. To give Windows a clue:

1. **Choose Start⇨Control Panel⇨Performance and Maintenance.**

2. **Click Power Options (at the bottom)⇨APM.**

   Windows XP shows you the Power Options Properties dialog box in Figure 10-3.

If you don't see the APM tab in the Power Options Properties dialog box, Windows didn't detect an APM-compatible BIOS. You're outta luck.

3. **Check the Enable Advanced Power Management Support box and then click OK.**

   If this step works, Windows puts up a balloon in the notification area (down near your clock) that says, `Windows has found a Microsoft APM Legacy Battery.`

4. **Choose Start⇨Turn Off Computer⇨Turn Off. (Or, if you're connected to a Big Corporate Network, choose Shut Down from the drop-down list).**

   If Windows figured out how to talk to your PC's BIOS, it turns off the computer.

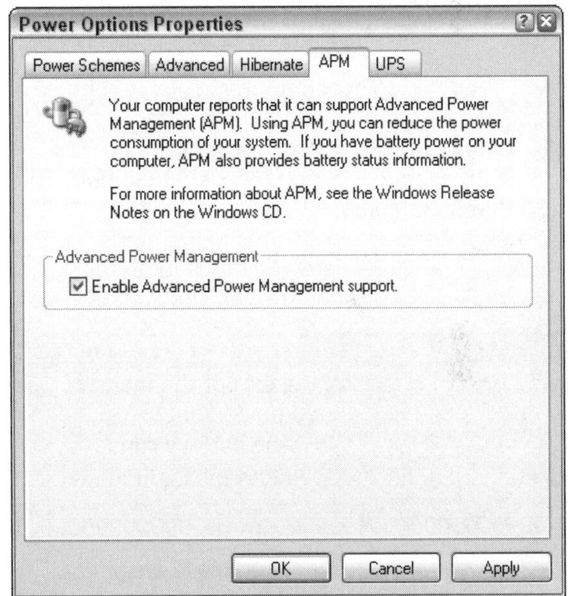

• Figure 10-3: Enable old-fashioned Advanced Power Management here.

Timesaving Settings for Power Users

Sure, you want to configure your computer to save power — but you also want the settings to save you time. Powering down a hard drive after it's been idle for a minute makes no sense, if the drive takes yet another minute to come back up to speed. This section includes my favorite settings to keep power consumption down — but not get in the way while you're working.

How much power does a computer use?

Unless you have an enormous number of peripherals, or you're running your processor full-tilt for extended periods of time, a typical computer these days uses about as much power as a 100 watt light bulb – maybe two. The single largest power drain is a regular, old computer monitor.

That said, if you really want to save power, switch to a flat-panel LCD monitor. That one action alone saves as much as all the other "green" power settings in Windows combined.

Here's how I set up my computers:

1. **Choose Start⇨Control Panel⇨Performance and Maintenance⇨Power Options (at the bottom)⇨Power Schemes.**

   Windows shows you the Power Options Properties dialog box, shown in Figure 10-4.

• **Figure 10-4: Saving power and saving time are often at odds.**

2. **For a desktop machine, I click the down-arrow under Power Schemes and choose Minimal Power Management. If you have a portable, skip to Step 3.**

   This step ensures that the largest single power drain — the monitor — gets turned off after 15 minutes of inactivity. Everything else is set to Never, so that it's all powered and ready to go.

3. **For a portable, I choose the following settings from the drop-down lists:**

   - **Turn Off Monitor:** After 15 minutes
   - **Turn Off Hard Disks:** After 30 minutes
   - **System Standby:** Never
   - **System Hibernates:** Never

On my portables, I always go into Hibernate or Stand By mode manually (using Start⇨Turn Off Computer), and I choose between modes based on how much battery life I have left at the moment.

4. **To set your power buttons like mine, click the Advanced tab (see Figure 10-5) and choose Ask Me What to Do from the drop-down lists in the Power Buttons area.**

   I don't trust the Power Off and Hibernate buttons on my computers, because they're too easy to press when I'm in a hurry. I always have Windows ask me what to do when I press them.

5. **Click the Hibernate tab and check the Enable Hibernation box.**

   The only reason you would want to disable hibernating is if you have a PC that can boot to different operating systems. Hibernating in that situation can be quite disastrous.

6. **Save your custom settings by clicking the Power Schemes tab. Then click the Save As button, type a name, and click OK.**

• **Figure 10-5: Most portable users want to show the power icon in the notification area (first check box).**

Keeping Programs from Starting Automatically

Save Time By

- Tracking down drivers and other programs that won't load
- Finding and deleting those annoying auto-starting programs
- Trapping auto-starting programs before they get into your system

I once visited a friend at a prestigious university, known for its outstanding computer science faculty and courses. He took me over to his office PC and booted it. Windows XP came up with a notice that it had detected a bad driver and wouldn't load it.

I asked him about the notice.

"Oh that?" he said. "My PC has been doing that ever since I installed this CD burner. I just check the Don't Display This Message box, and then click Cancel. When the notification box comes up by the clock that says the driver isn't being installed, I click the X over there."

Every time he boots Windows XP, he clicks three times in three different places, just to get his PC running. And this guy has an IQ that'd fry an egg.

There's something seriously wrong here.

Recognizing You Have a Problem

If your PC runs a program that you don't want every time you start it, you have a problem. I don't care if the interloper is a cutesy greeting of the day, a vicious piece of won't-let-go advertising, or a direct connection to the XXX Internet Search Page: If you got it, and you don't want it, you need to get rid of it. More than that, you need to make sure that similarly scummy programs don't have a chance to infect your PC again.

Far too many people think it's normal for Windows XP to hiccup on startup: Bad drivers are common, especially on older systems. (*Drivers* are small programs that control specific devices, such as printers or video cards.) A bad driver can trigger a warning such as the one in Figure 11-1.

The seemingly commonsense solution to bad drivers is to tell Windows Don't Display This Message Again, click a few times, and hope that the problem goes away the next time you boot. It doesn't.

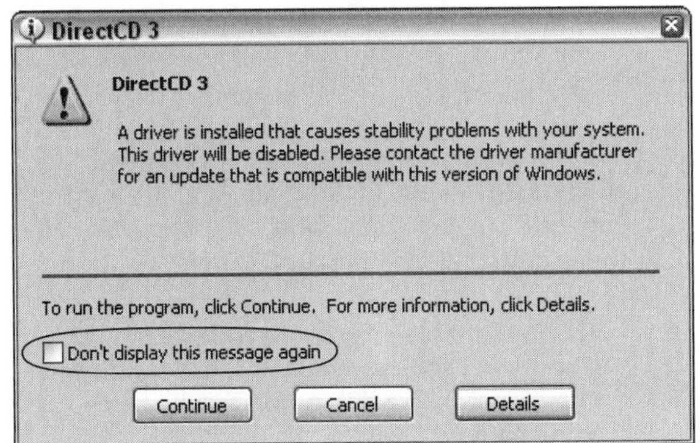

• **Figure 11-1: A telltale sign of an auto-starting program attempting to load a bad driver.**

Each time you install a new application, you have a fair-to-middlin' chance the new application will launch some part of itself every time you start the computer.

The application may also put an icon in the *notification area* (the box on the lower right of the Windows screen, next to the clock), and you may or may not be able to get rid of the program using the application itself or the Control Panel's Add/Remove Programs feature. After six months or a year of operation, your machine could easily be launching two dozen programs every time it starts — and you may want or need only a few of them.

If you bought your PC with Windows preinstalled, every two-bit gewgaw the manufacturer threw in to get you to buy a product (or to collect royalties from a software vendor) is bound to automatically start something as well.

More and more viruses and other pieces of malware auto-start themselves using Windows XP's features. The best way to stop them is with a program called Startup Monitor, which I discuss at the end of this technique.

It has to stop. Literally. Although unneeded programs don't slow down your system perceptibly, having to click three times to bypass a bad driver every time Windows boots is a pain. Mostly, auto-starting programs make it tough to wade through the icons in the notification tray, pose some security risk, and can contribute, in often mysterious ways, to lock-ups, crashes, and all sorts of time-gobbling problems.

In addition to programs and drivers, Windows itself starts a bunch of programs (called *services*) that take care of miscellaneous Windows activities. Although Windows services are generally benign, some services that most folks don't need have security holes in them that cretins love to exploit. Microsoft itself has seen the error of its ways; many of the services that were launched automatically, mindlessly in earlier versions of Windows XP have been cut off at the knees in Service Pack 2.

Finding and Eliminating Auto-Starting Programs

Sometimes, a computer suddenly starts doing something that you didn't tell it to do — such as putting a message on-screen, dialing your modem, running your video camera, or hanging an extra toolbar on Internet Explorer. Or maybe you get a message about a driver that won't load, or one that would make the system unstable. In such cases, the most likely culprit is an auto-starting program. If your computer suddenly starts hanging or crashing, the cause may be an auto-starting program, too.

Many times, you can install auto-starting programs without knowing it. File-sharing programs (such as KaZaa and iMesh) are notorious for installing many auto-starting programs — which many people call *scumware*. You may have accidentally installed an auto-starting program when a perfectly legitimate-looking Web site asked if it could install some sort of custom "download content."

If you have a particularly scummy program starting all by itself for no apparent reason, your first line of defense should be SpyBot-Search & Destroy. I talk about SpyBot extensively in Technique 52.

Ridding yourself of the auto-starting vermin is a three-step process.

1. You have to find the programs that start when Windows starts.
2. You have to figure out whether the programs are good or bad.

   Not all auto-starting programs are bad. The ones listed in Table 11-1 appear on almost all systems.
3. You need to unhook the bad ones so that they don't start by themselves. You might want to delete the programs, too.

Understanding where auto-starting programs live on your computer

When Windows XP starts and you log on, programs from dozens of places run automatically. Here are some of the main hideouts for auto-starting programs:

- **The Registry:** I talk about the inner workings of the Registry in Technique 68. Many auto-starting programs run because they're mentioned in specific places inside the Registry. Programs mentioned in the `\Run`, `\RunOnce`, and `\RunOnceEx` keys (under both `\Windows` and `\WindowsNT`) are run automatically every time Windows starts, as are those in the `\Windows\Load` and `\System\Scripts` keys, plus `\Winlogon\Userinit` and `\ShellServiceObjectDelayLoad`. If you go spelunking in your Registry looking for wayward auto-starting programs, you need to look at all of those keys.

The Registry won't jump up and bite you, but if you go in and change things, make sure you know what you're doing. See Technique 68 for some hard-won advice.

- **Startup folders:** Windows XP automatically runs everything in the system's Startup folder (`C:\Documents and Settings\All Users\Start Menu\Programs\Startup`) and your personal Startup folder every time you log on.
- **Scheduled Tasks:** These get run, too, from the `C:\Windows\Tasks` folder.
- **Group Policy scripts:** If you're attached to a Big Corporate Network, the domain's network administrator can tell Windows to run even more programs when you log on.

Table 11-1: Common Auto-Running Programs

Name	What It Does	What to Do with It
`userinit.exe`	Gets network connections going and starts the Windows shell.	Keep it. This program is vital.
dumprep	Apparently checks the Windows Kernel for problems.	Keep it.
`osa.exe`	Prelaunches parts of Microsoft Office programs so they run faster.	Optional.
`ctfmon.exe`	Speech recognition software for Office XP.	Optional. To remove it, see the sidebar, "Getting Rid of Microsoft Office's speech recognition."
PostBootReminder	No idea.	Keep it.
CDBurn	Apparently a hook for Windows XP's CD-Writing Wizard.	Keep it.
Webcheck	Seems to be for an ancient Internet Explorer feature called Channels.	Keep it.
Systray	Puts icons in the notification area (next to the clock).	Keep it. This program is also vital.

Those of you who grew up with Windows might expect to find auto-running programs listed on the `run=` or `load=` lines of a file called `win.ini`. As far as I can tell, that old method doesn't work in Windows XP.

If Windows XP has a definitive list of all the places auto-running programs can hide, I've never seen it. The official Windows documentation falls far short of the mark.

Detecting and deleting auto-starters

Four widely available free tools can find auto-starting programs. Unfortunately, none of them offers a complete solution.

Here's my school-of-hard-knocks advice for using the best of each to perform a quick and thorough scan:

1. **Run Autoruns, a tool from Bryce Cogswell and Mark Russinovich.**

   Download this free program from Sysinternals at `www.sysinternals.com/files/autoruns.zip`. Unzip it and run the `autoruns.exe` program. You see a report similar to that in Figure 11-2.

2. **Identify any auto-starting programs that you don't immediately recognize.**

   In Figure 11-2, for example, I find a program called `osa.exe` that claims to be a Microsoft Office component — whatever that is.

You can easily print a list of all the programs Autoruns identifies. In Autoruns, choose Entry➪Copy to Clipboard. Start Word (or Wordpad), paste into a clean document, and then print.

For a quick cross-check, you can find a list of almost 100 auto-starting programs and their associated applications at `www.pacs-portal.co.uk/startup_content.php`.

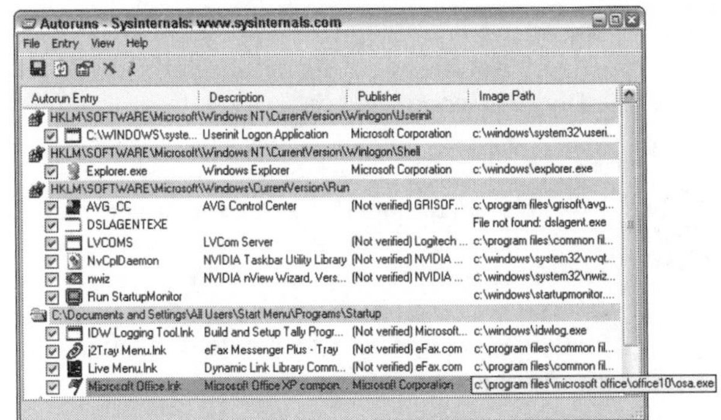

• **Figure 11-2: Autoruns catches all the auto-starting programs (at least, all the ones I know about).**

3. **Select each program you don't recognize, in turn, and then choose Entry➪Properties.**

   Windows shows you the Properties sheet for that particular program (see Figure 11-3).

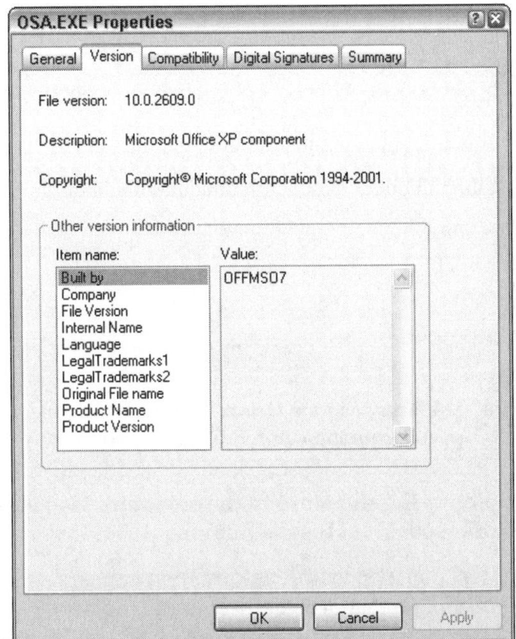

• **Figure 11-3: Internal identifying information about the auto-starting program.**

4. If you still don't recognize a program or if you have any doubts about its authenticity, click the Digital Signatures tab.

If you don't see a Digital Signatures tab, you're looking at an unsigned — and therefore immediately suspicious — program. The signature(s) associated with the program are listed (see Figure 11-4). Even if you see a signature, though, you shouldn't take it at face value; you must look at the details.

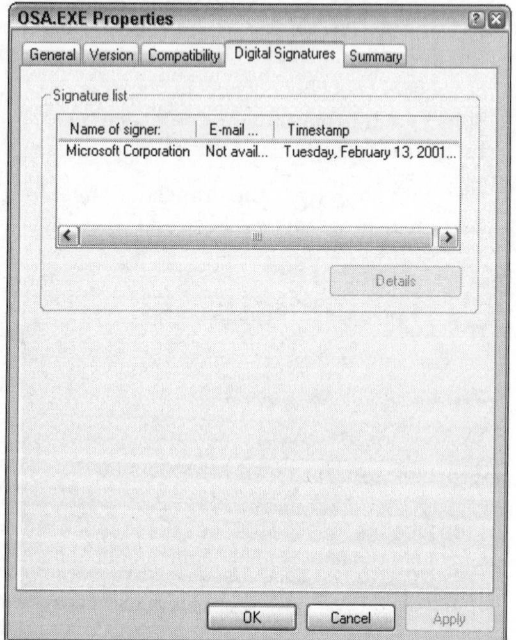

• **Figure 11-4: This program claims to be from Microsoft Corporation, but you need to verify it.**

5. Select the signature in the Signature List, and then click the Details button.

Full digital signature information appears. Although digital signatures aren't foolproof — Microsoft had one "hijacked" in 2002 — Thawte and VeriSign are reliable.

Anybody can generate a self certification. If you see a self certificate — even one purportedly signed by Bill Gates — realize that the certificate has no independent verification and doesn't really signify anything. You must follow Step 5 to make sure that a certificate-granting organization has verified that the signer is who it says it is.

6. Repeat Steps 3 through 5 for each program that you don't recognize.

Keep track of the programs' names and where they reside. Although Autoruns is the most thorough program available for catching auto-starting programs, its tools for stopping them are rudimentary.

Refer to Table 11-1 for a list of very common auto-starting programs that shouldn't concern you — providing the certificates are valid.

If you find an auto-starting program that looks the least bit suspicious, start Internet Explorer, go to Google (`www.google.com`), and look up the name of the program. Check and see what other people are saying. You'd be amazed what some of these programs do.

7. To get rid of auto-starting programs that you don't want, start with the program itself.

This is the cleanest, easiest, fastest way to get rid of auto-starting programs. Many programs give you the option to turn off the auto-starting component. In some cases, it's as simple as right-clicking the program's icon in the notification area (next to the clock), and choosing Disable.

8. If that doesn't work, try the Control Panel's Add/Remove Programs feature.

Providing you can figure out which application spawned the offending auto-starter, you may be better off removing the entire application. Choose Start⇨Control Panel⇨Add or Remove Programs, click the application, and remove it. Restart Windows and rerun Autoruns to see if that did the trick.

9. **If you can't get rid of the auto-starting program via the Control Panel's Add/Remove Programs feature, or you would rather not remove the entire application from your hard drive, see the following section, "Using a third-party auto-starter disabler."**

Using a third-party auto-starter disabler

You may be a bit frustrated that you can't get rid of those dreaded auto-starter files without going into the Control Panel and removing the entire program. Well, that's not entirely true. If you want to disable the auto-starting program alone, without removing the entire application, try one of these applications:

- **Windows' built-in MSConfig utility:** Choose Start➪Run, type **msconfig**, and press Enter. MSConfig misses a lot of auto-starting programs, and it's very intrusive because it inserts itself into the Startup sequence.
- **Startup Cop Pro:** *PC Magazine*'s utility, originally written by Neil Rubenking, is free for *Mag* subscribers, or $5.97 for the unwashed masses. Download it from `www.pcmag.com/utilities`. Recently revamped, the Pro version catches most problematic auto-starting programs. (It remains to be seen if the *PC Mag* folks will keep the program updated — the original version was left to twist in the wind for years.) Startup Cop Pro has a great user interface, a hallmark of the legendary Rubenking.
- **Mike Lin's free Startup Control Panel:** Although Mike's utility misses a few of the auto-starting programs that Autoruns catches, it's a dynamite small program that works well, indeed.

If Autoruns doesn't catch your two-timing program, I urge you to try Mike Lin's Startup Control Panel. Here's how to use it:

1. **Download Startup Control Panel.**

   It comes in two versions; I prefer the standalone program, called `Startup.exe`. Get the file from `www.mlin.net/StartupCPL.shtml`, unzip it, and put `Startup.exe` someplace convenient.

2. **Run Startup Control Panel and look for auto-starting programs that you want to disable.**

   Click the various tabs (see Figure 11-5) to find the program you want to snip. You'll probably notice that most, but not all, of the programs identified by Autoruns appear on the tabs.

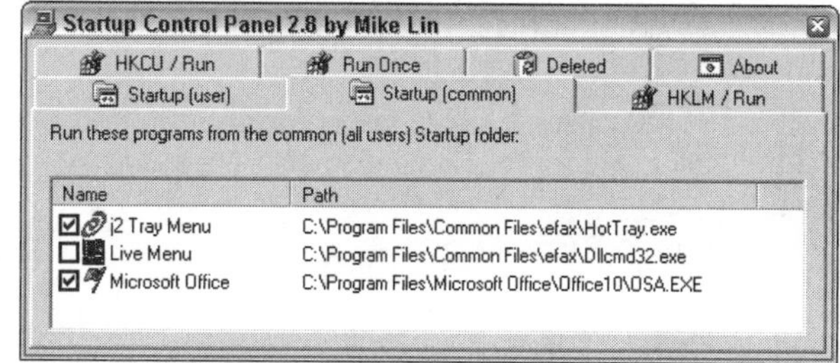

• **Figure 11-5: Locate the programs you want to disable.**

3. **Uncheck the boxes next to the programs that you don't want to run.**

   Your computer runs just fine, even if you uncheck *all* the programs listed in Startup Control Panel.

4. **When you finish, click the X in the upper-right corner of the dialog box and restart Windows.**

   If you have any problems, go back into Startup Control Panel and uncheck the appropriate boxes. Windows always starts, but you may have trouble getting a specific piece of hardware (or even a specific program) to run.

Some of the programs that Autoruns lists don't appear in either Mike Lin's Startup Control Panel or PC Mag's Startup Cop Pro. You can try to use MSConfig to stop those programs. Or you can go directly to the settings in Autoruns by clicking the program in question and then choosing Entry➪Jump To. I recommend the latter approach only to people who feel very comfortable working with the Registry and the Startup folder.

The programs listed by Startup Control Panel and Startup Cop Pro are all expendable: You can turn them off without bringing down Windows. By contrast, some programs listed in Autoruns and in MSConfig are vital: Mess around with them too much, and Windows may not reboot. Be very careful if you use Autoruns or MSConfig to make modifications.

If all else fails, you can follow Microsoft's official approach for eliminating aberrant auto-starting programs at `support.microsoft.com/?kbid=316434`.

Getting rid of Microsoft Office's speech recognition

My vote for one of Office's most frustrating "features": speech recognition. For people with disabilities, it's a godsend. For many business users, it's insufferable. Worse, it's almost impossible to figure out how to turn it off, if you ever have the misfortune to turn it on. The Office help files are all wrong.

When you perform a "Full" installation of Office XP, you get speech recognition whether you like it or not. Microsoft showed some restraint in Office 2003, where speech recognition only comes to haunt you if you specifically ask for it in a "Custom" install.

Unfortunately, disabling speech recognition isn't as easy as unchecking the `ctfmon.exe` box in Startup Control Panel. If you do try to get rid of this annoying auto-starting component of speech recognition, the next time one of the Office applications starts, it puts `ctfmon.exe` back on the auto-starting list. (Remember the old Office paper clip — the one that kept popping up, no matter how hard you tried to get rid of it? The sins of the father are visited on this son, methinks.)

To turn off `ctfmon.exe` for good, choose Start➪Control Panel➪Date, Time, Language and Regional Options➪Regional and Language Options➪Languages, and then choose Details➪Language Bar. Check the Turn Off Advanced Text Services box. Then click OK and/or Yes as many more times as it takes to get out. That has to be the most arcane setting ever.

Alternatively, you can uninstall speech recognition from Office XP itself, but that's an entirely different pain in the neck.

Preventing New Auto-Starters

Now that you've gone to all that trouble of cleaning up your auto-starting programs, stopping new programs from adding their demon offspring to the auto-start lists is easy.

Mike Lin has a nifty free utility called Startup Monitor, which watches and warns you when intransigent applications try to tell Windows to auto-start programs. For example, Figure 11-6 shows you how Startup Monitor trapped Office's attempts to put `ctfmon.exe` back on the auto-starting list (see the sidebar, "Getting rid of Microsoft Office's speech recognition").

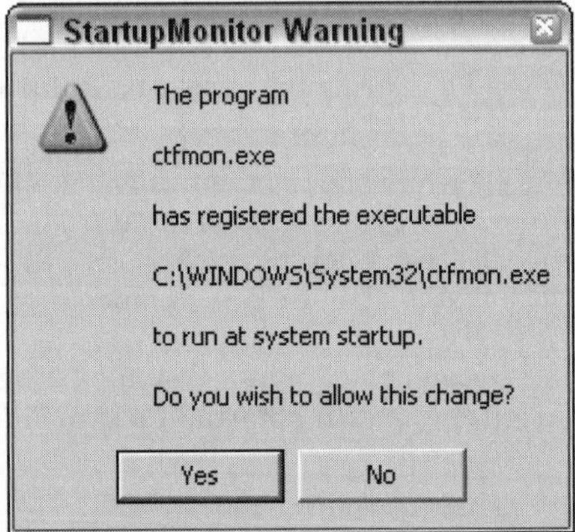

• Figure 11-6: Startup Monitor watches and warns you when an attempt is made to add a program to Windows' auto-starting lists.

To use Startup Monitor, follow these steps:

1. **Download the file at** `www.mlin.net/StartupMonitor.shtml`.

2. **Unzip it and run the** `StartupMonitor.msi` **program.**

That's all it takes. From that point onward, Startup Monitor keeps watch. I bet you'll be surprised by how many auto-starters it catches.

If you use and like Mike's programs, go to his Web site and leave him a tip. A couple of bucks goes a long way for a college student. Yep, Mike's a student at MIT. Bright kid.

Removing and Reinstalling Programs

Save Time By

- Getting rid of pesky vestiges of "removed" programs
- Reinstalling cantankerous programs so they work
- Removing Windows Messenger, Auto Update, and more
- Replacing Microsoft's programs with The Competition

Into every program's life a little rain must fall. For some programs it's a gentle mist. For others, it's a monsoon-borne torrent. There are many good reasons for getting rid of programs that are causing you problems. Even programs that you use all the time — Outlook and Word come to mind — occasionally become unstable and need to be uninstalled and reinstalled.

The rub comes when removing a program and reinstalling it doesn't fix things: Lingering problems — which are usually in the Registry, but sometimes in a "bad" file — can keep reinstalled programs misbehaving just as badly after the makeover as before (see Figure 12-1).

Here are the tips you need to oust the offal — quickly, reliably, the first time.

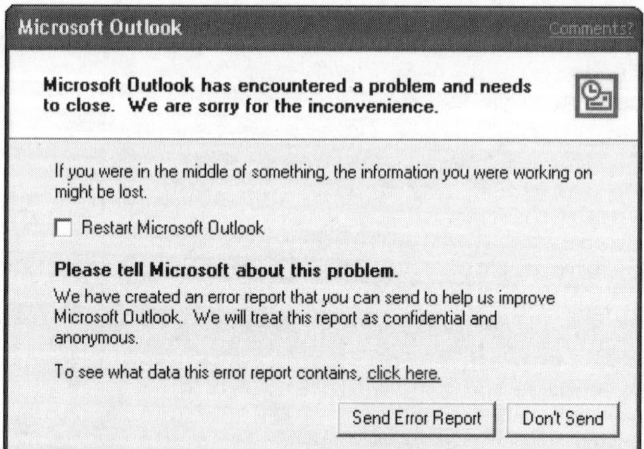

• **Figure 12-1: Outlook has encountered a problem.**

Removing Programs Thoroughly

Sometimes, the only way you can get a program to work again is by removing and then reinstalling it. Sometimes you just want to get rid of the stupid thing — forever.

You can use a few tricks to save yourself a bunch of time. To truly remove a program, follow these steps:

1. **Choose Start⇨Control Panel⇨Add or Remove Programs.**

   Windows shows you the Add or Remove Programs dialog box in Figure 12-2.

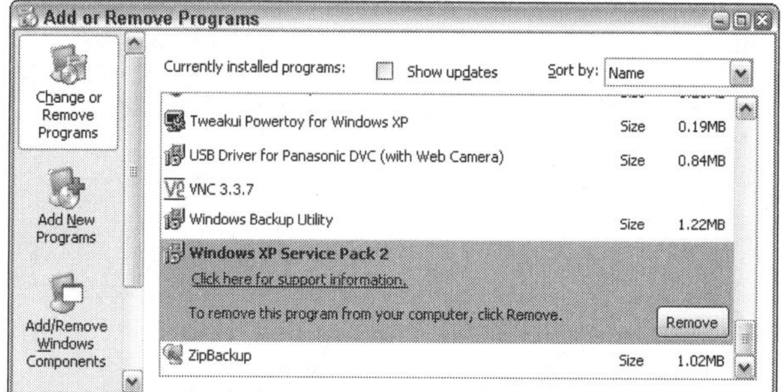

• **Figure 12-2: All well-behaved installers leave an entry here.**

2. **Make sure to click Change or Remove Programs on the left; then click the program you want to remove.**

   If you want to try something less drastic than removing the program, click the Click Here for Support Information link (if it's available). The program responds with a list of help resources, similar to that in Figure 12-3.

Microsoft Office components give you a Repair option in the Support Info dialog box. Sometimes running a repair at this point can fix a problem. If the repair works, it's much less time-consuming (and hair-raising) than a complete Removal/Reinstall. Give it a try.

3. **If you're certain that you want to remove the program, click Remove in the Add or Remove Programs dialog box.**

Different programs label their buttons differently: Some say Remove, others Change/Remove, others Change. No matter what the label, removing the program is always an option.

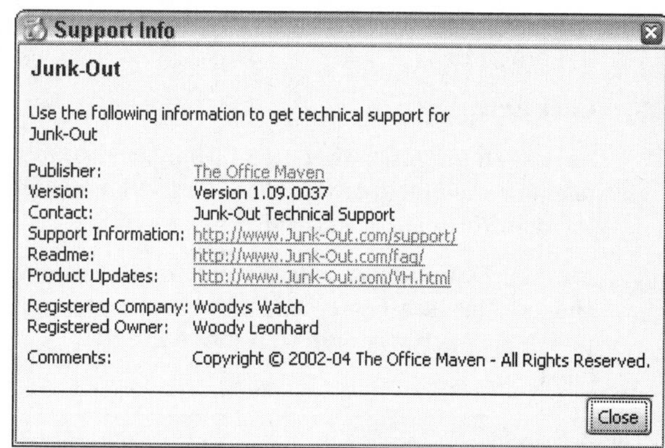

• **Figure 12-3: Typical contact information for support, if you aren't yet ready to remove the program.**

If you're uninstalling a Microsoft program (see Figure 12-4), you get the option to repair it. Try the Repair option before removing the program completely. A repair takes much less time than a removal followed by a reinstall. In the latest versions of Office, the Repair option works reasonably well.

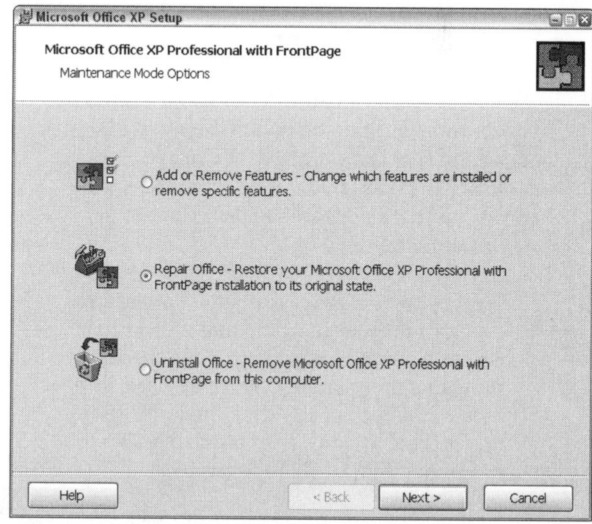

• **Figure 12-4: When given the option in a major Microsoft product, run a repair instead of removing and reinstalling.**

Windows asks if you're sure you want to remove the program.

4. **Click Yes.**

   Almost all programs that aren't from Microsoft use unInstallShield or the Wise Uninstaller, called Unwise. You want to know that in a moment.

5. **Inevitably, Windows asks if you want to remove shared files (see Figure 12-5). Unless you have a pointed, specific reason to remove the file, click No.**

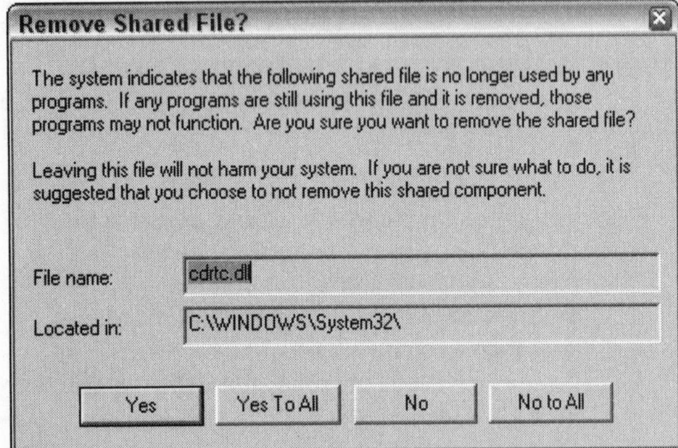

• **Figure 12-5: Always click No when asked if you want to remove shared files.**

Windows keeps a count of how many different programs use specific files. When you install a program that uses that particular file, the counter is raised by one. When you delete a program that uses the file, the counter is lowered by one.

The counter isn't always right. If you leave a program on your machine that's never used, you lose a tiny sliver of hard drive space. If you remove a program that has to be used sometime in the future, you could be in for some, uh, interesting times — a completely different program might crash, for example.

When the uninstaller finishes, look hard to see if there's any indication that something could not be removed. In Figure 12-6, for example, unInstallShield indicates that some "elements" couldn't be removed.

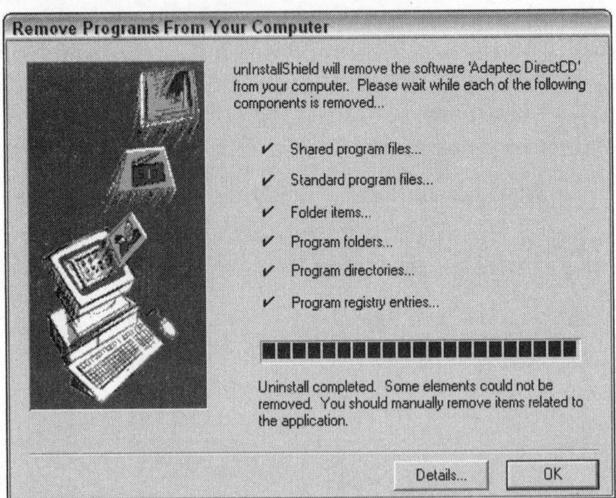

• **Figure 12-6: unInstallShield admits that it couldn't do its job.**

6. **To find out what the uninstaller left behind, click the Details button.**

   The Details dialog box shown in Figure 12-7 appears.

7. **Try to manually remove whatever the uninstaller left behind.**

   In the case of the remaining Registry entry shown in Figure 12-7, bring up the Registry Editor (choose Start➪Run, type **regedit**, and press Enter). On the left side, navigate to the key mentioned and delete it. See Technique 68 for more details on editing the Registry.

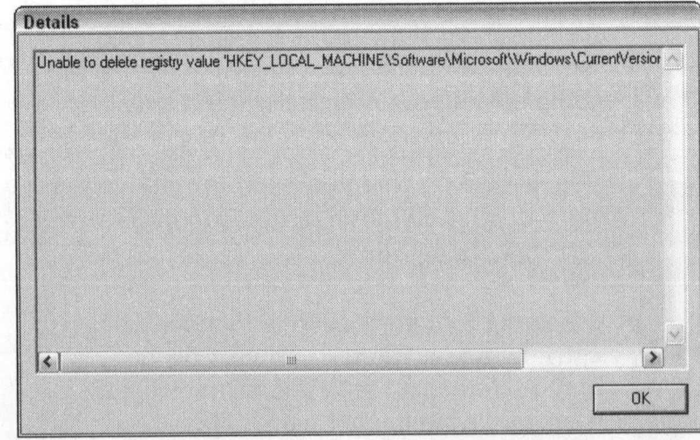

• **Figure 12-7: The Details reveal that a specific Registry key couldn't be removed.**

Updating the Add or Remove Programs List

Sometimes an uninstaller won't remove the entry for the program itself in Add or Remove Programs. For example, you may successfully remove a utility, but the uninstaller leaves the entry for that utility in the Add or Remove Programs list. Here's how to get rid of the entry manually:

1. **Choose Start➪Run. Type** regedit **and press Enter.**

   The Registry Editor appears.

2. **On the left, choose HKEY_LOCAL_MACHINE➪SOFTWARE➪Microsoft➪Windows➪Current Version➪Uninstall.**

   Under the Uninstall folder, on the left, you see a list of all the programs that appear in the Add or Remove Programs list (see Figure 12-8).

   You also see a lot of lengthy {numeric} entries. You can safely ignore those.

   My favorite recalcitrant uninstaller is iMesh's Ads-Support, shown in Figure 12-8. Yes, I am being facetious.

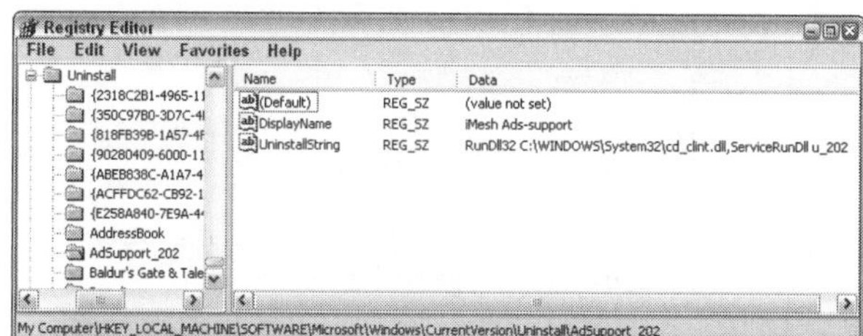

• **Figure 12-8: iMesh Ads-Support won't remove its own entry from Add or Remove Programs.**

3. **Right-click the appropriate key and click Delete.**

4. **Choose File➪Exit to leave Regedit; then choose Start➪Control Panel➪Add or Remove Programs and make sure the entry is gone.**

Cleaning Up before a Reinstall

Sometimes removing a program and reinstalling it isn't sufficient; the program continues to cause problems in the same way it did before you went through this mind-numbing process. In some cases, pieces of the old program get left behind, even if the uninstaller tells you that it got everything.

If you believe that remnants of an old program are hampering your attempts to get it to reinstall correctly, try this:

1. **Use Add or Remove Programs, as described earlier in this technique, to remove the program.**

2. **Even if the uninstaller tells you that it got everything, choose Start➪Run, type** regedit, **and press Enter.**

   I talk about the Registry Editor in detail in Technique 68.

3. **Inside the Registry Editor, search for the name of the program by choosing Edit➪Find (see Figure 12-9).**

   Make sure all three boxes — Keys, Values, and Data — are checked. You might not be able to find the precise program name, but you may be able to find something similar to it, or possibly the manufacturer's name.

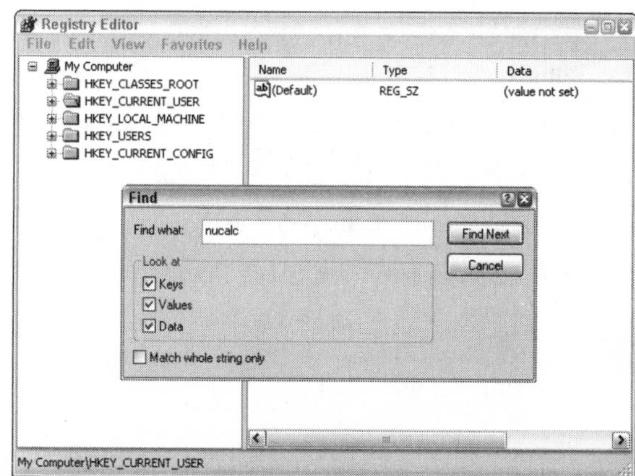

• **Figure 12-9: Searching the Registry for the program nucalc.**

4. Keep searching (use the F3 key or the Find Next button) until you find a major entry for the program.

Usually you can find a major entry for the program itself, as opposed to minor entries for certain kinds of documents or filename extensions.

5. If you find an entry that seems to include lots of settings for the program, right-click it and choose Export (see Figure 12-10).

The Export Registry File dialog box appears.

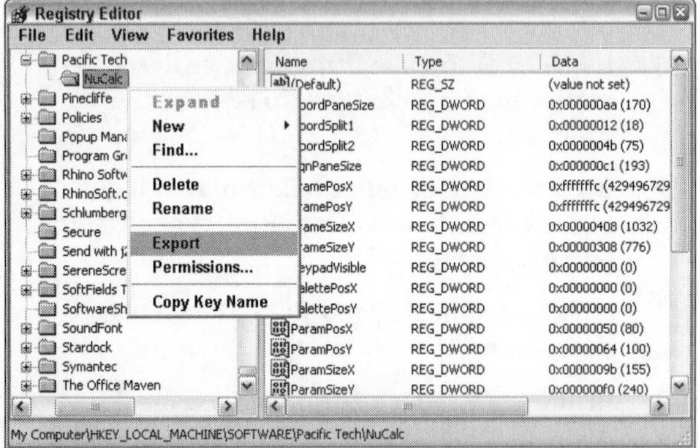

• **Figure 12-10: Export the Registry key.**

6. Use the Export Registry File dialog box to put the contents of this key on your desktop.

Give the exported Registry key a filename that you can remember and click Save.

7. In the Registry Editor, click this key and press Delete.

That removes all the old information about the entry from your computer — and may help knock loose whatever was preventing the reinstallation from working correctly.

8. Reinstall the program that's been giving you problems.

You'll probably insert a CD or double-click a downloaded file.

Chances are very good that going through the additional step of scouring the Registry to remove all the old, potentially bad settings makes the program work right.

9. If the reinstalled version of the program *still* doesn't work, double-click the Registry key on your desktop to put the Registry back the way you found it.

That doesn't fix the problem. But it does mean any changes you made to the Registry are undone.

Adding Windows Components

If you didn't install all the pieces of Windows XP — or if the PC manufacturer didn't before it shipped your PC to you — then you might find references to a program you just don't have. Perhaps you can't find one of the Windows games, or you read about the Windows Calculator or WordPad, and you can't find those on your PC.

If you ever think that parts of Windows haven't been installed, grab your Windows CD and follow these steps:

1. Choose Start⇨Control Panel⇨Add or Remove Programs.

2. On the left, click Add/Remove Windows Components.

Windows brings up the Windows Components Wizard, shown in Figure 12-11.

For a greatly expanded Windows Components Wizard, see the last section in this technique.

3. Select check boxes to add or remove components.

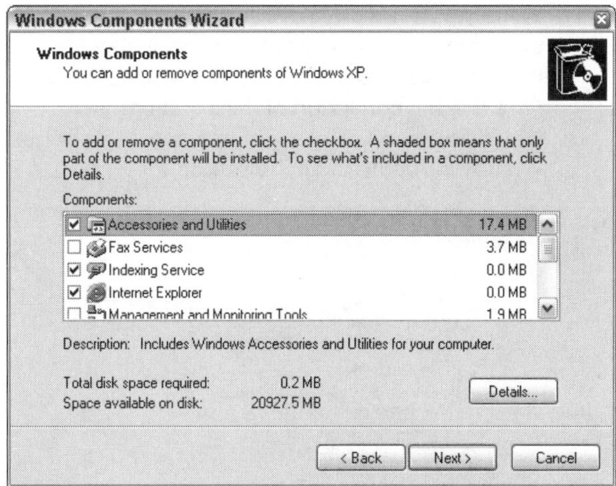

• **Figure 12-11: Windows manages its own version of Add or Remove Programs.**

You might think that unchecking the Internet Explorer box in Figure 12-11 would remove IE. It doesn't. For the full story, see the next section.

If you think you have a bad Windows file, don't bother fiddling with Add or Remove Programs. You need the System File Checker, which I discuss in Technique 63.

Using Non-Microsoft Replacements

As part of Microsoft's antitrust settlement, Windows XP was modified to make it much easier to use non-Microsoft products for browsing the Web, reading e-mail, sending instant messages, and playing media files.

Top choices for alternatives include

- **Mozilla Firefox:** Microsoft hasn't had any real competition in the Web browser arena since IE 4.0 — and it shows. IE 6 is a bloated, buggy embarrassment. It has virtually no new features, compared to IE 5. And the security holes in IE 6 boggle the imagination. Microsoft has let some well-known security holes languish for months. Finally, Firefox offers an alternative to Internet Explorer that doesn't harbor legions of known, unplugged security holes, and boasts dozens of better features to boot. `www.mozilla.org`
- **Trillian:** The MSN Messenger alternative that lets you talk to anybody using almost any instant messaging program. Not as flashy as MSN Messenger, but far more useful. I talk about Trillian in Technique 27. `www.trillian.cc`
- **iTunes:** I'm no fan of Apple, and I've sworn at QuickTime for years. But iTunes (which, admittedly, runs with QuickTime) actually works as a media player, has a decent interface and, most of all, doesn't help Microsoft further entrench its music file formats. Windows Media Player ain't the only game in town — see Technique 33. `www.apple.com/itunes`
- **Opera:** A quick, sometimes quirky browser. `www.opera.com`
- **Eudora:** E-mail from Qualcomm. Getting long at the tooth, but some people still prefer it to Outlook or Outlook Express. Qualcomm's most endearing characteristic (and greatest deterrent to malware writers) is the fact that it *isn't* Outlook or Outlook Express. `www.eudora.com`
- **Real Media:** Whatever Real Media happens to call its media player this week. `www.real.com`

Your PC manufacturer may have set up non-Microsoft programs for you. They aren't necessarily better. Make up your own mind — don't feel compelled to use the manufacturer's choices.

Some people think that Microsoft took Internet Explorer, Outlook Express, Windows (MSN) Messenger, and Windows Media Player, respectively, out of later versions of Windows XP. Nothing could be further from the truth. All those applications are alive and well in Windows XP. In fact, IE and OE are there whether you want them or not.

If your PC manufacturer installed different (non-Microsoft) messaging or media playing software for you and you want Microsoft's applications, downloading and installing the latest versions of the Microsoft applications is as simple as visiting `windowsupdate.microsoft.com`.

If you want to use programs other than Internet Explorer, Outlook (or Outlook Express), MSN Messenger, and/or Media Player, follow these steps:

1. **Install the alternative program, start it, and if it asks, allow it to become your default program for Internet access, e-mail, messaging and/or media.**

   Some programs are smart enough to replace the Microsoft equivalents all by themselves, but you may need to manually boot some of them.

If you've installed a Web browser or e-mail application, click Start and see if it appears at the top of the Start menu. If it doesn't, continue with these steps.

2. **Choose Start⇨Control Panel⇨Add or Remove Programs.**

   The Add or Remove Programs dialog box, shown in Figure 12-12, appears.

3. **On the left, click Set Program Access and Defaults.**

   If the Add or Remove Programs dialog box does not have a Set Program Access and Defaults icon on the left, you have an older version of Windows XP. If you feel so inclined, use `windowsupdate.microsoft.com` to install the latest Service Pack for Windows XP. (A *Service Pack* is a big collection of fixes and patches, which Microsoft releases all at once. I talk about Windows Update in Technique 55.)

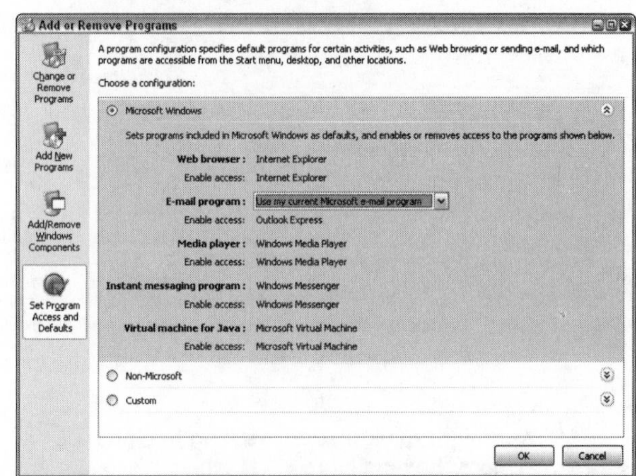

• **Figure 12-12: It's easy to get out of the Microsoft rut for Web browsers, e-mail packages, messaging, and playing media files.**

4. **Click Custom and then click the down-arrow to the right of Custom.**

   Change any defaults you wish.

5. **When you're done, click OK.**

   Your new program(s) appear everywhere that Microsoft's built-in programs used to appear.

Don't worry. The old Microsoft programs are still there — and they should still work just fine. When you make this change, the Microsoft programs simply won't appear as your default Web browser, media player, e-mail program, and the like.

Nixing Windows Messenger (And Other Hidden Programs)

If you read the preceding section, you know that you can easily substitute your own messenger service — say, Trillian, ICQ, AOL Instant Messenger, or Yahoo! Messenger — for Microsoft's Windows/ MSN Messenger.

But what if you don't want *any* instant messenger? After all, they're pretty obnoxious things, always asking you to sign up. You might want to remove Windows Messenger completely from your system if you're tired of it constantly pestering you to get a Passport.

Permit me to stand on a futuristic soapbox. Right now, e-mail and spam are the greatest time-sinks for most knowledge workers. (Raise your hand if you agree.) Five years from now, I predict, instant messaging will be considered the greatest time-waster. At least with e-mail, you can reply at your own rate. (Put your hand down now.) With IM, if you ain't there, you ain't there. Bottom line: I suggest that you learn to rely on Messenger as little as possible. Your productivity will thank you for it.

In previous versions of Windows, the Add or Remove Programs dialog box had all sorts of components. Windows XP doesn't offer as many choices, but all is not lost.

There's a trick for getting Windows XP to allow you to remove Windows Messenger and bring back a few choices in the Add or Remove Programs dialog box:

1. **Choose Start⇨Search.**
2. **In the resulting dialog box, click All Files and Folders.**
3. **Check the following boxes: Search System Folders, Search Hidden Files and Folders, and Search Subfolders.**

   You may have to click the down arrow in More Advanced Options.
4. **Type** sysoc.inf **in the upper-left box and click Search.**

   Windows (finally!) finds the `sysoc.inf` file.
5. **Right-click the file and choose Open With⇨ Notepad.**

   Notepad shows you the `sysoc.inf` file, as shown in Figure 12-13.
6. **For each Windows application that you want to remove, go to the appropriate line in the** `sysoc.inf` **file and delete the word *hide*.**

   See Table 12-1. Don't delete the commas before or after. Just delete the word *hide* (or *HIDE*).

If you want to delete all instances of the word *hide* in one fell swoop, choose Edit⇨Replace, type **hide** in the Find What box, leave the Replace With box blank, and click Replace All.

7. **Choose File⇨Exit and tell Notepad that yes, you want to save changes.**
8. **Choose Start⇨Control Panel⇨Add or Remove Programs, and then click Add/Remove Windows Components.**

   The Windows Components Wizard appears, but now it includes all the programs that were previously hidden with the "hide" entry in `sysoc.inf`. See Figure 12-14.
9. **Remove the programs that you don't want.**

   I explain how to do this in "Removing Programs Thoroughly," earlier in this technique.

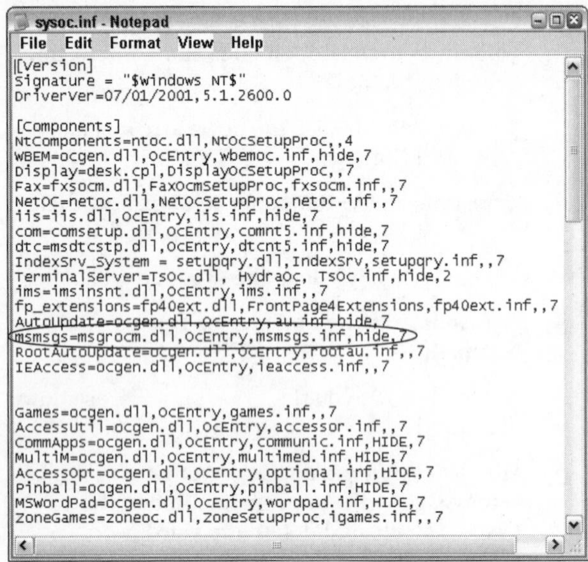

• **Figure 12-13:** `sysoc.inf` **holds the key to completely removing Windows Messenger.**

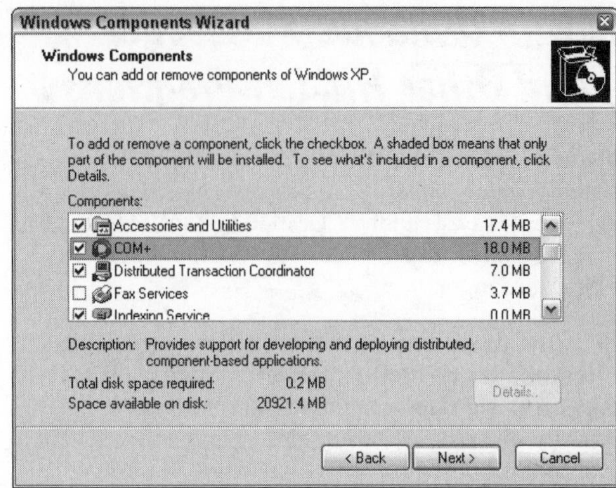

• **Figure 12-14: Modify** `sysoc.inf` **to get back dozens of additional Windows-streamlining choices.**

TABLE 12-1: SYSOC ENTRIES FOR SELECTED HIDDEN WINDOWS COMPONENTS

Entry	Application	Timesaving Advantage of Removing This Application
TerminalServer	Terminal Server (Remote Desktop, Remote Assistance)	Eliminates one more potential security hole, although you won't be able to request Remote Assistance (see Technique 61).
AutoUpdate	Windows Update	See Technique 55.
msmsgs	Windows Messenger	Eliminates annoying, repeated requests to sign up.
CommApps	Chat, Hyperterminal, Phone Dialer	Most people don't need these.
MultiM	Media Player, Volume Control, Sound Recorder	If you never use your PC to play CDs or DVDs or music from other sources, these can go.
AccessOpt	Accessibility Wizard (Control Panel)	Many people never need these utilities, which are geared to people with physical challenges.
Pinball	Pinball	What? Give up Pinball? You must be mad!
MSWordPad	WordPad	For most people with Office, WordPad isn't really necessary. Word and Notepad suffice.

Part III

Convincing Windows to Work Your Way

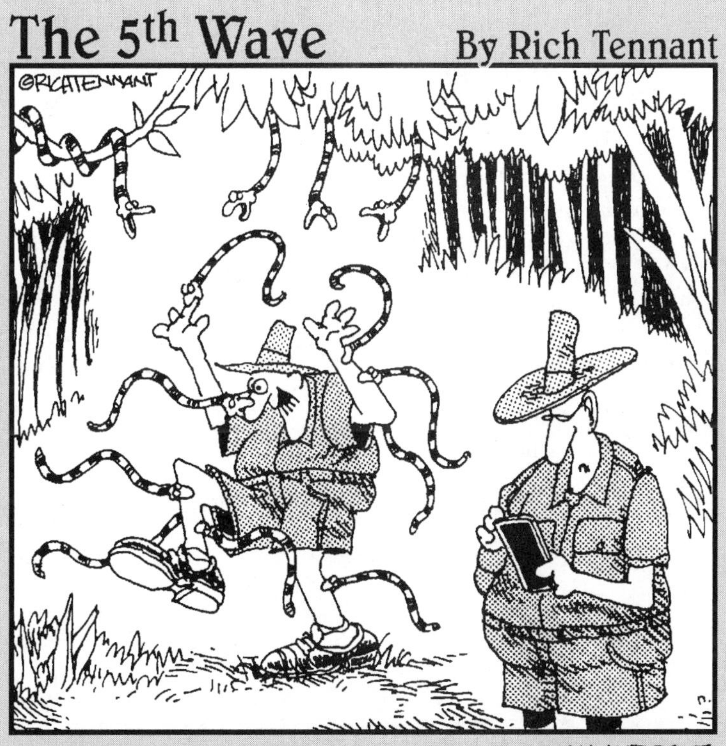

"OK — ANTIDOTE, ANTIDOTE, WHAT WOULD AN ANTIDOTE ICON LOOK LIKE? YOU KNOW, I STILL HAVEN'T GOT THIS DESKTOP THE WAY I WANT IT."

Streamlining the Start Menu

Save Time By

- Supercharging the Start menu
- Sticking the programs *you* choose on the Start menu
- Organizing the All Programs menu (Yes, really)
- Turning the click-click-click Control Panel into a quick cascading menu

The Start menu: It's the one place you go back to, over and over again. Microsoft set up the Start menu so that it works well for the average Windows XP user. Unfortunately, there's no such thing as an average Windows XP user (or, if there is, he or she certainly isn't reading this book!).

Changing the Start menu couldn't be simpler. Changing it to do the work you want, as quickly as you want it, presents an ongoing challenge. A pre-customized Start menu appears in Figure 13-1.

This technique shows you the key tools at your disposal to mold the mother of all Windows menus. It's a great place to organize, consolidate, group, and simplify.

• Figure 13-1: Justin's Start menu, before this technique's makeover.

Navigating the Start Menu

If you look closely at the Start menu in Figure 13-1, you can see that it's divided up into different sections:

- At the top you see the name and icon of the current user. To change your icon — or, yes, even your name! — see Technique 47.
- In the upper-left, just above that really faint line, sit the programs, folders, or shortcuts that you want to get to quickly. These items are *pinned*, which means that, after you put 'em there, they stay put. Windows starts with Internet Explorer and Outlook (or Outlook Express) in the list. I pontificate on pinned programs, pieces, and places in "Pinning and Unpinning," later in this technique.
- Below that, there's the Most Frequently Used list. They really aren't your most frequently used programs. Microsoft builds a bias into determining what's "frequent." Your best bet is to limit what Microsoft can do with this space and make more room for pinned items. See the sidebar "Adapting the adaptive menu," later in this technique.
- Then comes the All Programs submenu. It doesn't list all your programs — you didn't *really* think it was that simple, did you? But you can clean up this submenu to make it more useful. The details are in "Reining In the All Programs Submenu," later in this technique.
- All along the right side is a list of various locations and system programs that you can modify — to some extent — to reflect how *you* use XP. See "Cascading to Save Time," later in this technique.

A hierarchy of needs is at work on the Start menu. You'll save an enormous amount of time, every day, if you make the Start menu work your way. Put the programs you use many times a day on your Quick Launch toolbar (see Technique 16), pin the ones you need frequently in the upper-left corner of your Start menu, rearrange the structure of the All Programs submenu so that you can find infrequently used programs with some ease, and judiciously choose the entries for the right side of the Start menu.

To speed up the Start menu — and the rest of the Windows interface, for that matter — in another way that makes sense, check out the section about no-nonsense tweaking in Technique 5. Turn off the time-consuming animations that you don't want, and the Start menu speeds up.

Pinning and Unpinning

The following sections show you how to pin and unpin items on the left side of the Start menu so that you can put this area to work for you (and not Microsoft).

Unpinning Internet Explorer and Outlook from the Start menu

Most people use Internet Explorer and their e-mail program (Outlook or Outlook Express) so much that the IE and Outlook/OE icons really should be on the Quick Launch toolbar, not pinned to the top of the Start menu. In Technique 16, I show you how to put icons for both IE and Outlook/OE on the Quick Launch toolbar.

Here's how to remove both Internet Explorer and Outlook (or Outlook Express) from the top of the Start menu:

1. **Right-click Start; then choose Properties⇨Start Menu.**

   Windows shows you the Taskbar and Start Menu Properties dialog box, shown in Figure 13-2.

2. **Choose Customize⇨General.**

   The Customize Start Menu dialog box appears (see Figure 13-3).

3. **In the Show on Start Menu area, uncheck the Internet and E-mail boxes.**

• **Figure 13-2: Set Start menu options here.**

• **Figure 13-3: Remove the Internet Explorer and Outlook icons from the Start menu.**

4. **Click OK twice; then click Start to verify that the two pinned items are gone (shown in Figure 13-4).**

5. **Don't forget to put both your Web browser and your e-mail program on the Quick Launch toolbar (see Technique 16).**

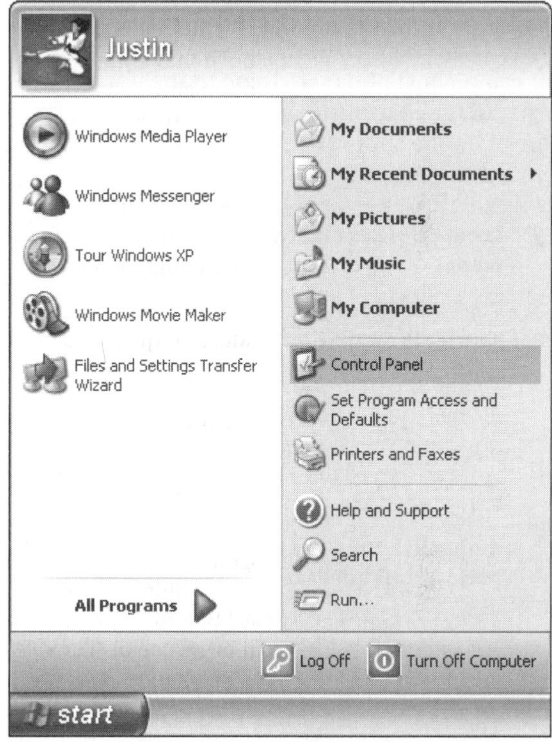

• **Figure 13-4: IE and Outlook are gone from the Start menu, but don't forget to put them on your Quick Launch toolbar.**

Instead of pinning IE to the Start menu, consider pinning two or three specific Web sites. That way when you want to launch IE, you can click its icon on the Quick Launch toolbar, but if you want to go to a specific site — say, a news site you visit daily or to retrieve a stock quotation — you can use the Start menu.

Unpinning IE and Outlook works a little differently than unpinning the stuff that you add. See the next section for details.

Pinning what you like to the Start menu

The programs you use all the time really belong on the Quick Launch toolbar. That makes them easy to find. On the other hand, you don't want to put too many icons on the Quick Launch toolbar — they're tiny and hard to click — so programs (and documents and Web sites and . . .) that you use less frequently should be pinned to the Start menu.

You can pin just about anything to the upper-left corner of the Start menu quickly and easily, if you remember one simple trick: Right-click and drag. Here are the details:

1. **Locate the item that you want to pin to the Start menu.**

   You can put programs, folders, documents, or shortcuts on the Start menu.

   To find the item you're looking for, you can navigate to it using Windows Explorer (Start⇨My Computer, say, or Start⇨My Documents). Or you can use Windows Search (see Technique 21) to find what you want.

2. **Right-click the item, drag it over the Start button, and hover there.**

   It's important that you right-click, because if you left-click you may move the program or document.

   The Start menu appears.

3. **Drop the item where you want it in the pinning area on the Start menu. If you're given a choice, select Create Shortcut Here.**

   You can see the results in Justin's modified Start menu, shown in Figure 13-5.

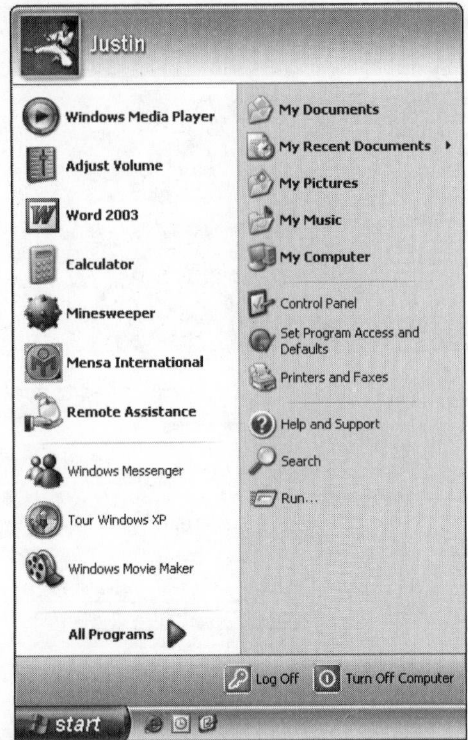

• **Figure 13-5: It takes a few seconds to completely customize the Start menu.**

Another item that's difficult to pin to the Start menu? A Web address.

1. **Start Internet Explorer, and make sure it's *restored* — that is, click the box next to the X in the upper-right corner so that IE doesn't occupy the entire screen.**

2. **Navigate to the site that you want to put on your Start menu.**

3. **Click and drag the IE logo from the address bar to the desktop.**

   I'm talking about the logo that appears to the left of a site's address in the address bar (see Figure 13-6).

   The logo turns into a shortcut on your desktop.

4. **Click the shortcut, drag it to the Start button, hover your mouse pointer over the Start menu, and then drop the shortcut in the pinned area on the Start menu.**

Ever get the feeling that nobody in Redmond ever tried to pin a URL on the donkey . . . er, Start menu?

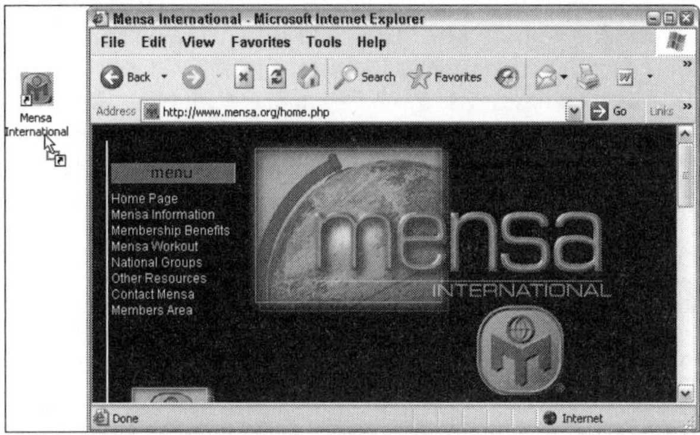

• **Figure 13-6: Click and drag the IE logo to move it to the desktop.**

Take control of your Start menu by filling up the pinned items area. Don't be bashful. Windows controls the Most Frequently Used list below the pinned items — and Windows has its own biases.

Creating more room for pinned items

Windows may bellyache that you've pinned too many items onto the Start menu. (Imagine! Windows doesn't have enough room to put MSN Explorer on your Most Frequently Used list — even if you've never used MSN Explorer. Oh, the horror!)

To make room for all the pinned items you need, take away space from Microsoft . . . er, the Most Frequently Used list. Here's how:

1. **Right-click Start, choose Properties⇨Start Menu, and then choose Customize⇨General.**

   You see the Customize Start Menu dialog box (refer to Figure 13-3).

2. **To make the icons and text on the left side of the Start menu smaller, click the Small Icons radio button.**

If you want to pin several items to the Start menu, the small icons can help you squeeze in more stuff. (See Figure 13-7.)

At first blush, you might think that it's better to pin more items on the Start menu, and to reduce icon size to accommodate. For many people that's not the fastest choice. Larger icons make it easier to scan and "hit" the items you want. More items make it that much slower to read everything. Personally, unlike Justin, I keep only five or so items pinned to the Start menu, so I use big icons. The specific items change almost daily, depending on what projects I'm working on.

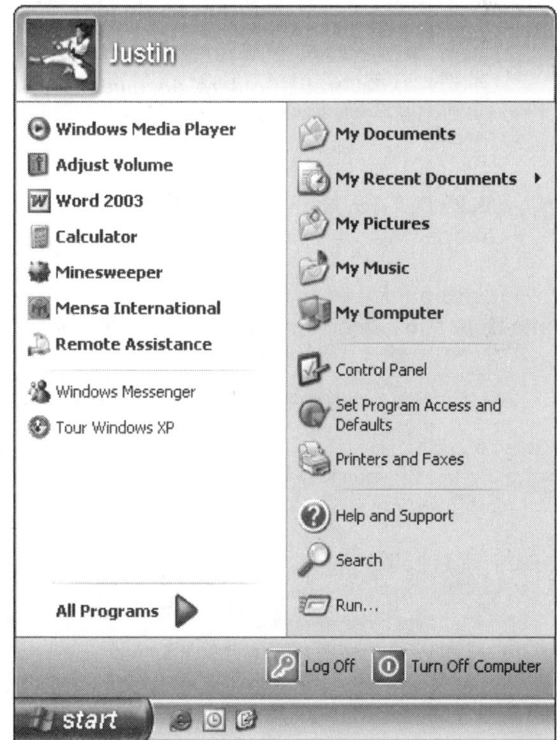

• **Figure 13-7: Justin's Start menu with small icons and the Number of Programs on Start Menu set at 2.**

3. **To reduce the space reserved for Most Frequently Used programs, decrease the Number of Programs on Start Menu setting.**

   In spite of the heading, Number of Programs on Start Menu, this setting does not change the number of programs pinned to the Start menu. It merely adjusts the amount of space saved for the Most Frequently Used programs. See the related sidebar, "Adapting the adaptive menu" for more details.

Usually, you don't want to run this setting down to 0, because a couple of Most Frequently Used programs can come in handy. To make the Start menu fast and easy to use, I recommend that you limit the number of items on the adaptive menu to 4 (at most), and use the reclaimed real estate to pin more items up above it. Details are in the preceding section.

4. **Click OK twice; then click Start to look at your changes.**

To remove a pinned item, right-click it and choose Unpin from Start Menu or Remove from This List.

Adapting the adaptive menu

Microsoft calls the area below the pinned items on the Start menu the Most Frequently Used programs list.

Bunk.

There's a list of programs that never make it onto the list at `support.microsoft.com/?kbid=282066`. That's the official story. Here's the unofficial story: Windows salts the list with programs it wants you to try.

Instead of listing the most frequently used programs, Windows adapts the menu (in sometimes inscrutable ways!), taking into account how many times you use specific programs. In short, it's an *adaptive* menu — and there's precious little you can do to keep it from, uh, adapting. However, you *can* right-click any entry that offends you and click Remove from This List.

There's a Registry key that prevents Windows from showing the Most Frequently Used list entirely. I don't recommend that you use it — the method for reducing the number of items on the Start menu in the preceding section works just as well — but if you're curious, details are at `www.jsifaq.com/SUBL/tip5700/rh5776.htm`.

Reining In the All Programs Submenu

Every time you choose Start⇨All Programs, Windows reaches into four folders and assembles the entire tangled mess you see on-screen. (If you've been using your PC for more than a few months, I bet All Programs looks like the front page of *The New York Times*.) If you want to untangle and organize the mess, unfortunately, you have to understand where the things on the menu come from.

Rearranging the All Programs menu rates as a high-payoff timesaving technique. If you've ever lost five minutes wading through All Programs' endless (and frequently meaningless) menus, you know why.

Where All Programs comes from

Items on the All Programs menu come from combining the contents of four folders:

- `C:\Documents and Settings\All Users\Start Menu`
- `C:\Documents and Settings\All Users\Start Menu\Programs`
- `C:\Documents and Settings\`*`<username>`*`\Start Menu`
- `C:\Documents and Settings\`*`<username>`*`\Start Menu\Programs`

So, for example, if you're logged on as the user Justin, every time you choose Start⇨All Programs, the menu items you see come from the four folders I just listed.

To look at these folders on your system quickly, right-click the Start menu and choose Explore. Windows opens Windows Explorer at your `\`*<username>*`\Start Menu\Programs` folder. If you right-click Start and choose Explore All Users, you're magically transported to `\All Users\Start Menu\Programs`.

In Figure 13-8, you can see the contents of a very simple `\All Users\Start Menu` folder. It's typical of a brand-new system with Microsoft Office 2003 installed. (If you have Office 2000 or XP, your folder is considerably more complicated.)

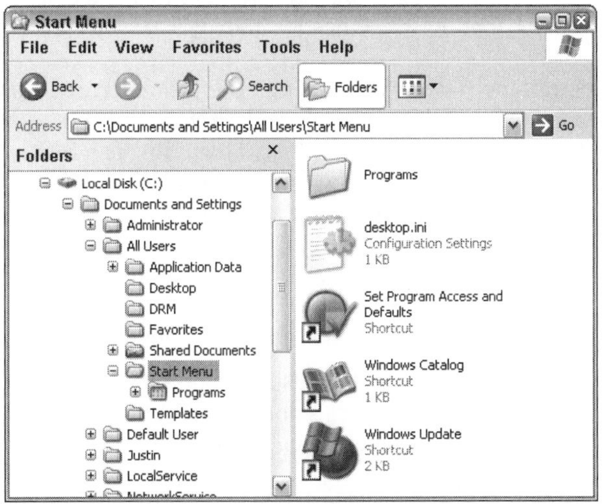

• **Figure 13-8: A very simple** `\All Users\Start Menu` **folder.**

One level down, in `\All Users\Start Menu\Programs`, though (see Figure 13-9), things start getting complicated. Microsoft put its advertisement . . . er, its shortcut, for MSN in the folder. Office 2003 puts a folder in there, too. (That sure beats Office 2000 and XP, which insist on cluttering this folder with lots of files.)

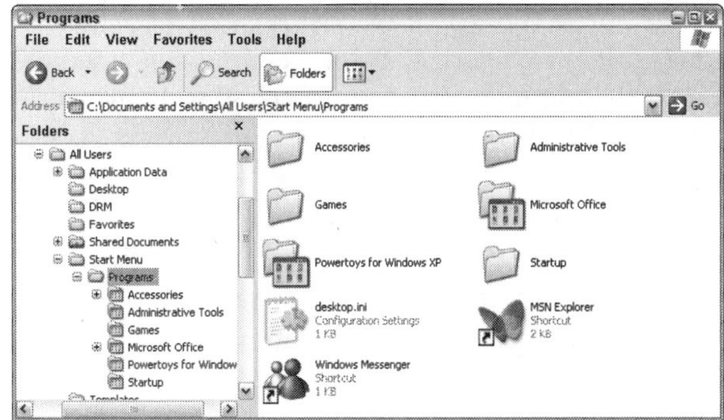

• **Figure 13-9: The** `\All Users\Start Menu\Programs` **folder.**

Justin's Start Menu folder is empty, but `C:\Documents and Settings\Justin\Start Menu\Programs` looks like Figure 13-10 — a typical bare-bones Programs folder in Windows XP.

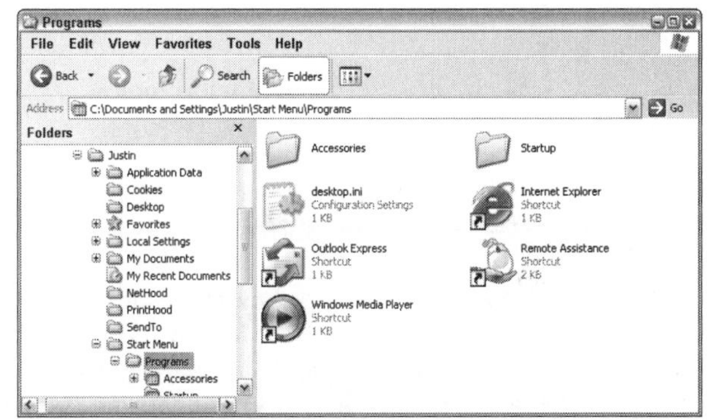

• **Figure 13-10: Justin's Programs folder.**

When Justin chooses Start⇨All Programs, Windows combines those three folders (plus `\Justin\Start Menu`, which is empty) to produce the All Programs menu you see in Figure 13-11. Items from the Start Menu folders go above the horizontal line. Items from the Programs folders go below the line. Folders turn into submenus. And shortcuts turn into individual entries on the menu.

For example, the `\All Users\Start Menu\Programs\Games` folder in Figure 13-9, for example, becomes the Games fly-out menu in Figure 13-11. MSN Explorer from the All Users side turns into the MSN Explorer item on the menu, and `\Justin\Start Menu\Programs\Windows Media Player` turns into the Media Player item on the All Programs menu.

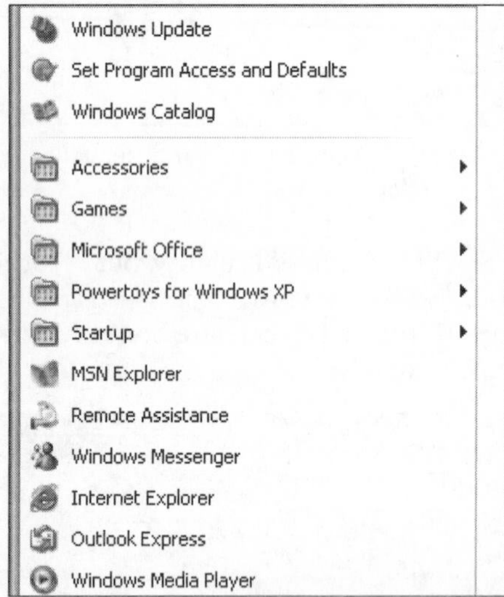

• Figure 13-11: Justin's All Programs menu.

Although it's certainly good for Microsoft's bottom line to put Windows Catalog, MSN, and Media Player in your face every time you choose Start⇨All Programs, there's no reason in the world why you should have to wade through all that garbage when you're trying to get some work done. Follow the steps in the next section to take back the All Programs real estate you paid for.

Rearranging the All Programs submenu

One of the truly significant improvements in Office 2003 was the removal of a whole lotta garbage from the All Programs menu. If you're still running Office 2000 or Office XP, like most Office users, you know what I mean: half a dozen programs scattered all over the All Programs menu, getting in the way every time you want to get some work done.

Lest you think I'm railing exclusively about Microsoft, I'm not. Many hardware manufacturers put really annoying little programs at the highest level of the All Programs menu, too. Most software manufacturers, though, got a clue long ago. They typically put their programs in a fly-out menu that occupies a minimum of space on All Programs. Thankfully, Microsoft Office finally showed us some respect, starting with Office 2003.

You need to be set up as a Computer Administrator in order to change the All Users folder. That's where you're likely to find the most junk that needs trimming.

Permit me to step you through the clean-up process that Justin performed on his All Programs menu. (Justin's a Computer Administrator.) This is a real-life demonstration of the timesaving methods I talk about in this section, and should give you a number of ideas for taking control of your own All Programs menu:

1. **Right-click Start and choose Explore.**

   That put Justin in his Start Menu folder, shown in Figure 13-12. There's nothing in there to gum up the All Programs menu. Whew.

• Figure 13-12: A clean `\<username>\Start Menu` **folder.**

2. Double-click the Programs folder, and make any worthwhile changes here.

Now you're getting to the garbage (Justin's original Programs folder appears in Figure 13-10).

Justin has Internet Explorer on his Quick Launch toolbar, as I recommend in Technique 16. There's no reason to have it on the All Programs menu, too, so he deletes that icon (right-click and choose Delete). He already pinned Windows Media Player at the top of the Start menu, so it doesn't need to go here, either — right-click and delete. No need for Outlook Express: right-click, delete. He uses Remote Assistance, though (one of Windows XP's hidden gems; see Technique 61), so it stays. The final result is shown in Figure 13-13.

• **Figure 13-13: Justin's final** `\Start Menu\Programs` **folder.**

3. Right-click Start and choose Explore All Users. Start trimming away by right-clicking individual shortcuts and choosing Delete.

Explore All Users put Justin in the `\Documents and Settings\All Users\Start Menu` folder, which was shown in Figure 13-8. What a bunch of junk.

Windows Catalog is a joke — it's a link to one of Microsoft's "all ads, all the time" Web sites. The Set Program Access and Defaults icon is a joke, too — and most Softies would agree; it's yet another part of Windows that was designed by antitrust attorneys. Running Windows Update, on the other hand, can be useful at times (see Technique 55), so it stays.

4. Double-click the Programs folder and slash and burn.

Justin started out with the Programs folder you see in Figure 13-9.

MSN Explorer and Windows Messenger get the right-click-and-delete treatment they deserve.

If you have Office 2000 or XP, you'll undoubtedly see four Office application icons in the Programs folder. If you want to move them to a location on your All Programs menu that's a little less obnoxious, right-click the Microsoft Office Tools folder, choose Rename, and rename it MS Office. Then click and drag each of the four Office applications, in turn, into the newly renamed MS Office folder.

When he finishes, Justin's `\Documents and Settings\All Users\Start Menu\Programs` folder looks like Figure 13-14.

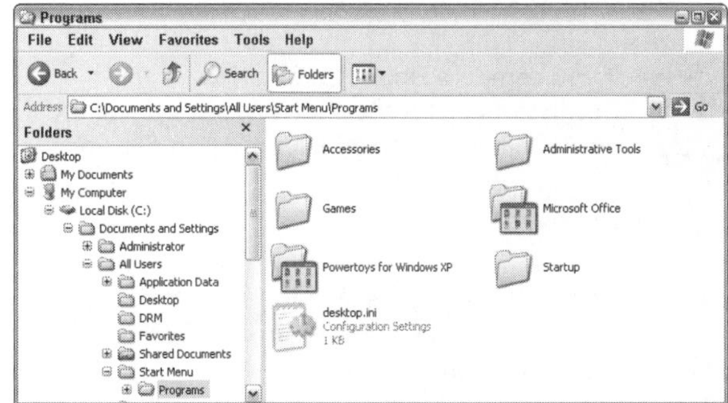

• **Figure 13-14: Final version of the** `\Documents and Settings\All Users\Start Menu\Programs` **folder.**

5. **Choose File⇨Exit to leave Windows Explorer.**

6. **Choose Start⇨All Programs and make sure the menu looks right.**

   Justin's final All Programs menu looks like Figure 13-15. When it comes to saving time, day in and day out, this All Programs menu runs rings around the original, Microsoft-built behemoth in Figure 13-11.

• Figure 13-15: Justin's final All Programs menu.

Cascading to Save Time

Figure 13-16 shows you what the Start menu looks like with all the available options selected.

If you compare Figure 13-16 to Figure 13-5 (Justin's original pinned Start Menu), you'll notice that you can add a lot more to this area.

Here's what each entry does:

- **My Documents:** Starts Windows Explorer based in the My Documents folder. You can also turn this into a fly-out submenu.
- **My Recent Documents:** A list of recently opened documents, occasionally accurate, modified by Windows. Some programs forget to register the documents they open with Windows; those documents never appear on the list. In addition, Windows modifies the list to "hold onto" different kinds of files: If you open two graphics files, for example, then two dozen documents, the graphics files still appear on this list.

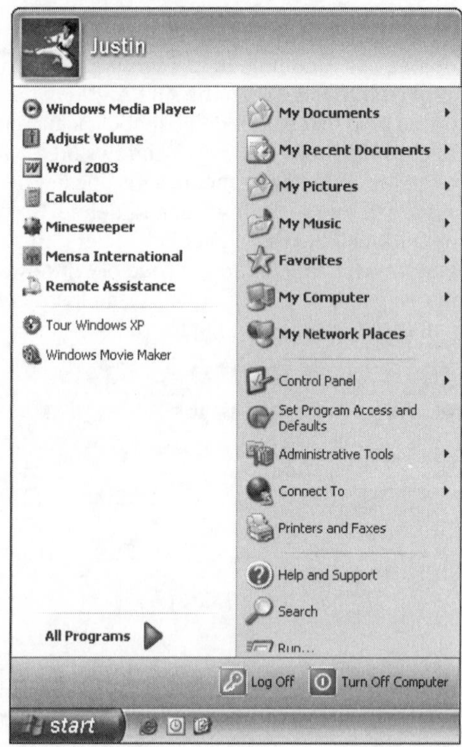

• Figure 13-16: All the options available for display on the right side of the Start menu.

- **My Pictures:** Starts Windows Explorer based in `\My Documents\My Pictures`.
- **My Music:** Starts Windows Explorer based in `\My Documents\My Music`.
- **Favorites:** This fly-out menu shows your Favorites list in Internet Explorer (and occasionally in other applications).
- **My Computer:** Starts Windows Explorer based at My Computer. From there, you can easily get to any of your hard drives, floppies, CDs, or other drives, or get to any user's My Documents folder.

- **My Network Places:** Starts Windows Explorer based at My Network Places, which is the place to look for folders, printers, and other devices shared across your network (if you have one).
- **Control Panel:** Brings up the Windows Control Panel.
- **Set Program Access and Defaults:** Brings up the Add or Remove Programs panel for changing the default Internet browser, the media player, and the e-mail and instant messaging programs. See Technique 12.
- **Administrative Tools:** Gives you quick access to the various management tools that control devices, users, performance, and the like. Also includes the System Event Viewer, which tells you when there's been a problem.
- **Connect To:** Lets you choose among available dial-up connections to ISPs (they're called *connectoids*). Also lets you see all connections, including broadband/DSL/ISDN/cable connections and network cards.
- **Printers and Faxes:** Same as choosing Start⇨Control Panel⇨Printers and Other Hardware⇨Printers and Faxes.
- **Help and Support:** Brings up the Windows Help System (see Technique 62).
- **Search:** Brings up Windows Search (see Technique 21).
- **Run:** Opens the Windows command line, which allows you to type and run terse commands.

Unfortunately, you can't click and drag anything onto the right side of the Start menu. It'd sure be nice if you could put Shared Documents directly underneath My Documents, for example, but you can't. Don't waste your time trying to find the correct magical incantation.

However, you *can* click and drag any item from the right side of the Start menu onto the pinned list on the left. Go figger.

You can turn nine of the items on the right side of the Start menu into fly-out menus: My Computer, My Documents, My Recent Documents, My Music, My Pictures, Favorites, Control Panel, Administrative Tools, and Connect To.

Five of the items appear *only* as fly-out menus: Favorites, Network Connections, My Recent Documents, Administrative Tools, and Connect To. If you don't like fly-out menus, it's best to avoid those.

To choose which items you want to appear on the right side of the Start menu:

1. **Right-click Start and choose Properties.**
2. **On the Start Menu tab, click Customize.**
3. **Click the Advanced tab and change the settings in the Start Menu Items area, shown Figure 13-17.**

   Table 13-1 shows what Justin chose and why.

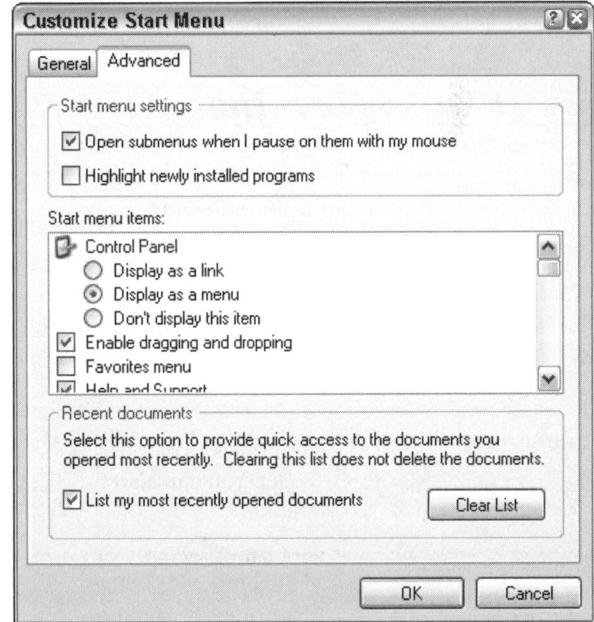

• **Figure 13-17: This one dialog box controls the entire right side of the Start menu.**

4. **At the bottom of the dialog box (for reasons known only to Microsoft), a separate box controls whether My Recent Documents appears on the Start menu. Check it if you wish.**

5. **While you're here, uncheck the Highlight Newly Installed Programs box, at the top.**

   That prevents Windows from popping up dialog boxes and putting yellow stripes on your Start menu every time you install a new program.

6. **Click OK twice.**

Figure 13-18 shows you Justin's final Start menu. He cut out all the marketing garbage, and (finally) made Windows ready to rumble!

• **Figure 13-18: Justin's final Start menu.**

Table 13-1: Justin's Start Menu Picks

Thumbs Up	Thumbs Down	Why
My Documents		Use it all the time. I made it a link because the fly-out menu is too unwieldy.
	My Pictures	Who needs ya, baby? All my camera pics are in Shared Pictures anyway.
	My Music	Same reason I scrapped My Pictures.
	Favorites	If I want a Web page, I'll start Internet Explorer.
My Computer		Having the fly-out menu to show all my drives is useful.
My Network Places		Vital.
Control Panel		I like it as a fly-out, to save time.
Network Connections/ Connect To		Sometimes I need to connect or disconnect a modem or DSL line.
	Printers and Faxes	These rarely need troubleshooting.
Scroll Programs		Makes Windows show All Programs as a scrollable list. Handy if All Programs grows too big.

Thumbs Up	Thumbs Down	Why
	Set Program Access and Defaults	You gotta be kidding, right?
Help and Support		Another one of those marginal things. A good book is better, but Help and Support does in a pinch.
Search		Yeah, but without the Search Companion.
Run		How else do I get into the Registry?
System Administrative Tools		Can be very helpful, especially if you're trying to track down the System Event Log. Most people find it's sufficient to put it on the All Programs menu only.
My Recent Documents		This one is occasionally useful.

Building a Power Desktop

Save Time By

- Getting your desktop right (now)
- Working effectively with multiple programs
- Optimizing your new right-click menu

Does your desktop look like the cat licked it? Yeah, mine, too. See Figure 14-1. The desktop is a horrible place to organize things. But it's a great place to stick stuff temporarily.

Or so I'm told. Hey, do as I say, not as I do, okay?

This technique is more a set of rapid-fire mini-techniques. I step you through a handful of tricks for turning your desktop into the lean, mean face of your machine that it should be. I also explain what to avoid ("Active" anything) and what doesn't really hurt (screen savers). Finally, I show you some truly masterful, timesaving ways to make Windows work your way, building on several rarely seen (and in some cases completely undocumented) settings that you can use, right now.

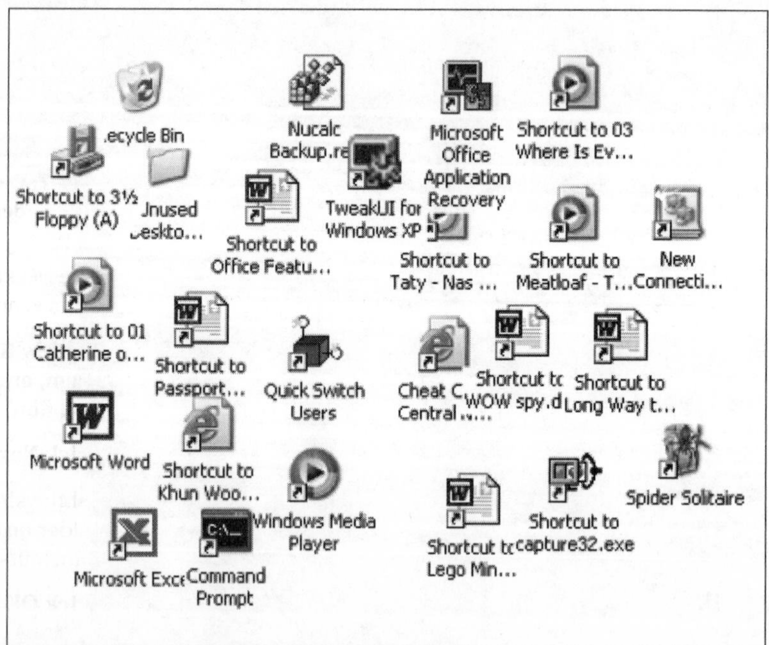

• Figure 14-1: My desktop has seen better days.

Desktop Brevity: The Soul of Wit

Your desktop is just like your kitchen table. It's where you put things for a short period of time; it's where you place files you don't want to forget about. At least, that's the conventional wisdom. When is enough enough? The problem, of course, is that when you place things on the desktop, even temporarily, you can easily forget to put those things where they rightly belong. Then your convenient kitchen table looks a little more like a heaping mess.

Here are my five favorite, fast tips for tuning up a Windows XP desktop.

Cleaning up old icons

Your desktop is a great place to park things for short periods of time, but a lousy place for organizing anything long term. Start by cleaning up the mess that's there right now.

The first time you use the following procedure, I take you through the Desktop Cleanup Wizard. If you've already been through this once (or if you've already used the Desktop Cleanup Wizard and found it, uh, wanting), start at Step 7:

1. **Right-click an empty location on the desktop and choose Properties⇨Desktop.**
2. **Click Customize Desktop.**

   You see the Desktop Items dialog box in Figure 14-2. Don't believe what you read about Desktop Cleanup, by the way. The straight story follows.
3. **Click Clean Desktop Now.**

   The Desktop Cleanup Wizard appears.
4. **Click Next.**

The Desktop Cleanup Wizard scans only for shortcuts. It doesn't even look at other kinds of files or folders (or zipped/compressed folders). Follow this procedure all the way to the end to move all your unused, or rarely used, desktop items.

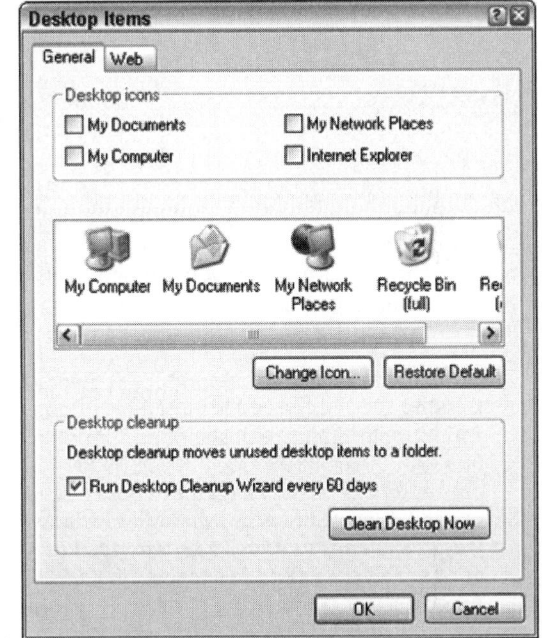

• **Figure 14-2: Desktop Cleanup doesn't move unused desktop items.**

The Desktop Cleanup Wizard presents the results of its scan (see Figure 14-3).

5. **Review the shortcuts with check marks next to them, and feel free to check any shortcuts that you don't expect to use in the near term.**
6. **Click Next, and then click Finish.**

   All the shortcuts you checked are shuffled to a folder on the desktop called Unused Desktop Shortcuts.
7. **Click OK twice to clear out the dialog boxes.**

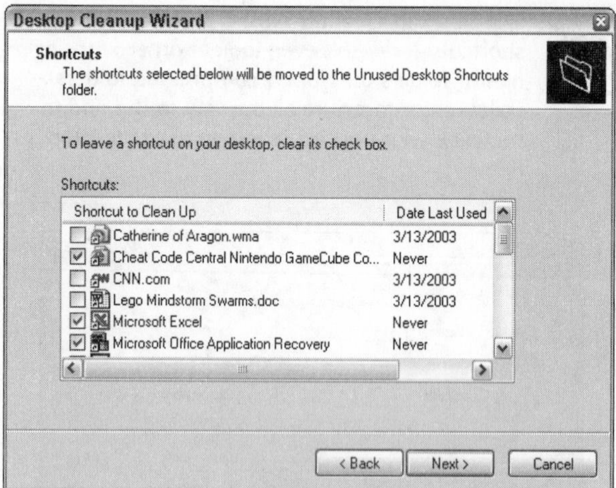

• **Figure 14-3: This is a partial list of your unused desktop items.**

Some of the Date Last Used entries in the Desktop Cleanup Wizard are just plain wrong. For example, I found that shortcuts to MP3 files with the name "Shortcut to . . ." didn't appear on this list, although they had been opened multiple times by Windows Media Player. Shortcuts to Web pages also failed to appear. This is a wizard in a teapot ("full of sound and fury / Signifying nothing") — except it has one good side effect. Keep reading.

Exploring unused desktop shortcuts

In the previous section, "Cleaning up old icons," I show you the cookie-cutter, kiddies approach to cleaning up your desktop. The Desktop Cleanup Wizard misses lots of old, dead files, but it *does* set up a new folder that you can use for genuine time-savings, populating it with a few well-chosen shortcuts. There's a tricky way to look at all the items remaining on your desktop, figure out how long it's been since you used them and, based on that information, manually shuffle the ones you really don't need into the Unused Desktop Shortcuts folder.

To take control of your desktop and sweep away the dead wood, follow these steps:

1. **Right-click the new Unused Desktop Shortcuts folder and choose Explore.**

   Windows Explorer opens with Unused Desktop Shortcuts showing (see Figure 14-4). All the icons you just cleaned up are there.

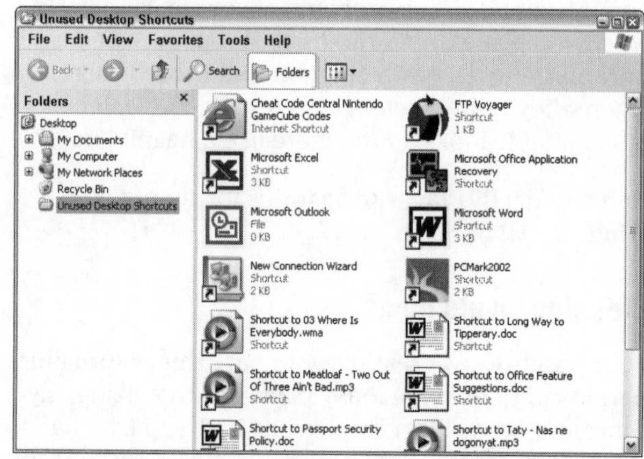

• **Figure 14-4: The recently created Unused Desktop Shortcuts folder.**

2. **Click the Up icon on the main toolbar.**

   You move up to the Desktop folder. This folder holds all the items on your desktop.

3. **To show more information about each folder and file on your Desktop, choose View⇨Details, right-click the Name column header, and choose More.**

   Explorer shows you the Choose Details dialog box in Figure 14-5.

   Unless you change things, Explorer lists four details for each file: Name, Size, Type, and Date Modified.

4. **Check the Date Accessed box and click OK.**

   Explorer lists all of the four original details for each file or folder, plus Date Accessed.

5. **Click the Date Accessed column header.**

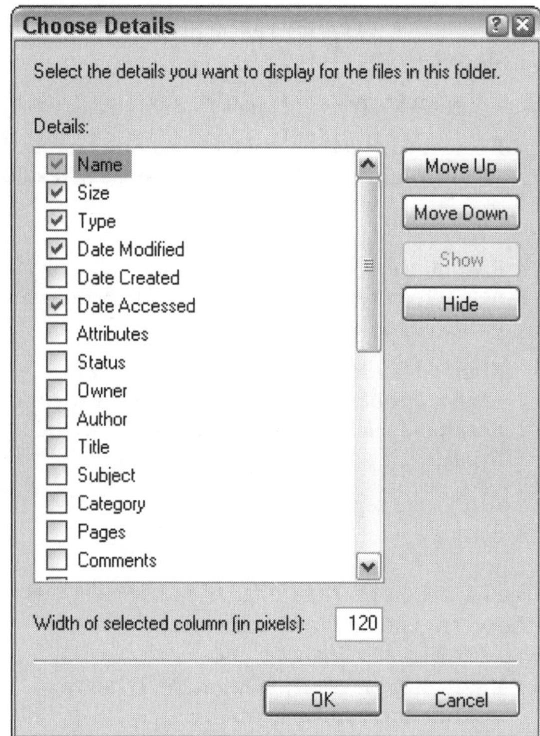

• Figure 14-5: Choose which columns appear in Windows Explorer.

Explorer sorts the list of files on your desktop, based on the date and time you last accessed them (see Figure 14-6). Folders come first, but after that, individual desktop items appear with the oldest one on top.

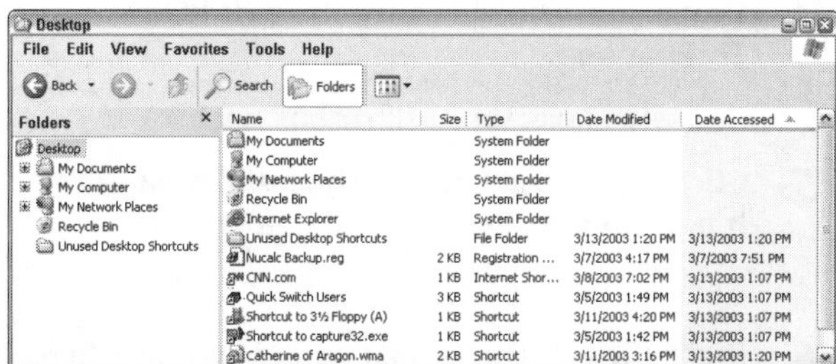

• Figure 14-6: The real list of unused (or little-used) desktop items.

6. **Click desktop items (in the pane on the right) that you don't want to appear on your desktop anymore, and drag them to the Unused Desktop Shortcuts folder.**

   This is the easiest, fastest way to remove unwanted icons from your desktop. If you ever need to get at an icon that used to appear on your desktop, just double-click the Unused Desktop Shortcuts folder, and there it is.

Windows pops up every 60 days to remind you that you can clean your desktop. When you see that notification, flip back to Step 1 of this procedure and really clean your desktop by manually scraping off your unwanted icons.

Aligning icons

Are your icons dangling all over the place? Ever had a problem finding an icon because it was covered up by another one? Windows makes it easy to automatically align your icons — but a couple of tricks can save you even more time.

To quickly line up the icons on your desktop:

1. **Right-click an empty part of the desktop.**
2. **Choose Arrange Icons By, and if Align to Grid is not checked, check it. (See Figure 14-7.)**

   The icons are "snapped" to an invisible grid on the desktop.

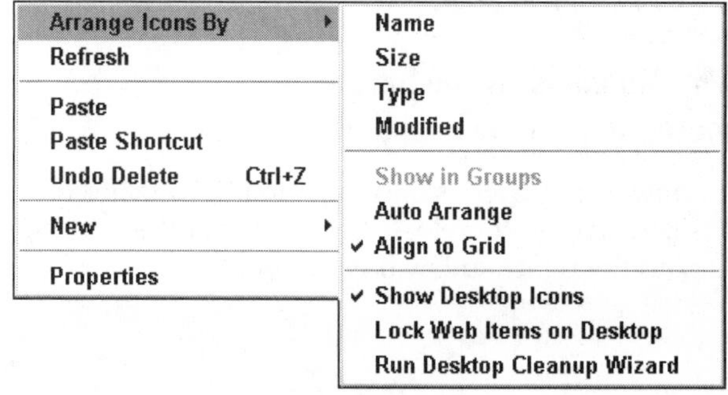

• Figure 14-7: Alignment options.

After the icons are aligned, I always uncheck Align to Grid, because it allows me to put related icons next to each other without worrying whether Windows will jump in and rearrange everything. When my icons get so jumbled I can't work with them any more, I align them to the grid again. But in the interim, I want control over where they sit.

You can select groups of icons (by using Ctrl+click or Shift+click or "lassoing" groups of them) and drag them all together. They stay aligned with each other after the move. These two very quick tricks can come in handy if you want to move a bunch of icons all at once.

Although the procedure is quite time-consuming, if you're dead-set on changing the size of the grid that Windows uses to align icons, you can do so by right-clicking an empty part of the desktop and choosing Properties⇨Appearance⇨Advanced. Then modify the Icon Spacing (Horizontal) and Icon Spacing (Vertical) settings.

Avoid the temptation to use any of the other Arrange Icons By settings. Name, Size, Type, and Modified (refer to Figure 14-7) reorder your icons in often inscrutable ways. Leaving the Auto Arrange option checked forces Windows to drag your icons back into line, no matter where you move them. After you jumble your icons using one of these settings, undoing the change is impossible.

Moving icons so you have more room on the desktop

To quickly force icons into the upper-left corner of the screen (and thereby free up space at the bottom and on the right), follow these steps:

1. **Right-click an empty spot on the desktop and choose Properties.**
2. **Click Settings.**
3. **Reduce your screen resolution. For example, if you're running at 1024 x 768, choose 800 x 600.**
4. **Click Apply.**

   If Windows asks whether you want to keep your new screen resolution, click Yes. The icons move to the upper-left corner of the screen.
5. **Right-click an empty place on the desktop, choose Properties⇨Settings, and return your desktop back to its original resolution. Click Apply.**

   Windows keeps the icons in the upper-left corner.

To free up the entire right edge of the screen, pushing the icons aside, follow these steps:

1. **Right-click an empty spot on the Windows taskbar and choose Properties.**
2. **Uncheck the Lock the Taskbar box and the Auto-Hide the Taskbar box. Click OK.**
3. **Click any unused part of the taskbar and drag it to the right edge.**

   After you have the taskbar in place, you can see that Windows moves all the icons out of the way.
4. **Right-click an empty area on the taskbar, click Properties, and check the Auto-Hide the Taskbar box.**

   Leave the Lock the Taskbar box unchecked.
5. **Click any unused part of the taskbar and drag it back to wherever it originated.**

   None of the icons are disturbed.
6. **Right-click an empty spot on the taskbar, choose Properties, and check the Lock the Taskbar box. If you don't want the taskbar to auto-hide — see Technique 15 — uncheck the Auto-Hide the Taskbar box.**

Adding Other Icons — Maybe

Your Quick Launch toolbar should have shortcuts to programs, documents, and folders that you use several times a day. That's the fastest, easiest place to find 'em.

Programs, documents, and folders that you use daily or almost daily should have shortcuts pinned to your Start menu. That's the second-easiest place to find 'em.

The desktop isn't a good place to put stuff you use all the time. Finding things there is hard after your icon count has run up above ten or so, unless you meticulously reserve sections of the desktop for specific kinds of icons – and you have a big enough screen to organize it all. If you want to save time, reserve the desktop for temporary parking: stuff you've downloaded and will use soon; that file you have to edit and hand off to your coworker tonight; the, uh, funny picture that guy in Chattanooga sent you. Put the items you use all the time on the Quick Launch toolbar or on the Start menu.

Here's how you can put a few common system icons on the desktop:

1. **Right-click an empty location on the desktop and choose Properties➪Desktop.**
2. **Click Customize Desktop.**

   Windows brings up the Desktop Items dialog box (refer to Figure 14-2).
3. **Check the boxes for the icons you want.**

   You can choose from My Computer, My Documents, My Network Places, and Internet Explorer.
4. **Click OK and the icons appear on your desktop.**

The middle area in the Desktop Items dialog box (refer to Figure 14-2) lets you change the picture associated with the various system icons. The picture marked "Recycle Bin (full)" is mislabeled. That's the icon Windows uses when there's *anything* in the Recycle Bin – not when it's full.

Avoiding Active Content

If you want to save time, you need to avoid so-called *Active Content* (sometimes called "Web Content" or "Active Web Content") like the plague. Windows' Active Content feature takes constantly updated information from the Internet — say a stock ticker or a weather map or news headlines — and puts that information on your desktop, as a kind of living background.

You can get to the Active Content dialog box, shown in Figure 14-8, by right-clicking an empty spot on the desktop, and then choosing Properties➪Desktop➪Customize Desktop➪Web.

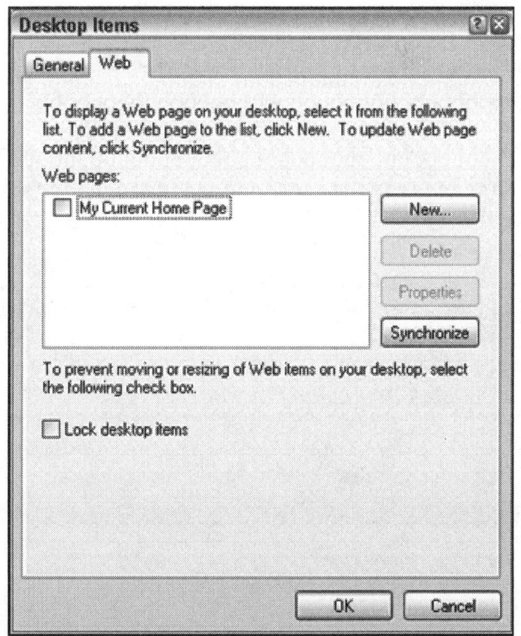

• **Figure 14-8: Avoid Active Web Content on your desktop.**

Microsoft introduced this bandwidth-sucking destabilizing “feature” in Windows 98/Internet Explorer 4. Very little has been done to improve it — the 20-minute-delayed stock ticker that Microsoft offers, for example, hasn’t changed a bit. Savvy users ignore the whole mess, although you’ll find many books, magazines, and Web sites that recommend Active Content.

If you want to watch a constantly updated stock ticker, try `www.javaticker.com` or simply keep a browser window open at your favorite business site, and click the Refresh button when you need it. You have better things to do than stare at a 20-minute-delayed ticker that simultaneously sucks up your computer power and makes Windows significantly less stable!

If you have Active Content on your desktop, right-click an empty spot on the desktop and then choose Properties⇨Desktop⇨Customize Desktop⇨Web to bring up the dialog box shown in Figure 14-8, uncheck any boxes in the Web pages list, and click OK.

A note on screen savers

Bottom line on screen savers: They don’t do any good, but they don’t do any harm, as long as your energy saving settings kick in properly. (Some PCs have a hard time reconciling specific screen savers with your power-shutoff settings. If in doubt, try turning off the screen saver.)

That said, one screen saver may save you some time. Then again, it may waste your time. Hard to say. If you have a (figurative) ton of digital pictures sitting on your PC, you should use them in the Windows XP My Pictures Slideshow screen saver. Windows cycles through all the pictures in a folder of your choosing, showing each picture on the screen. If your resolve is better than mine, you’ll save time by not having to wade through all those folders. Of course, if you see a picture that you remember, and dig into the file to take a longer look — well, sometimes saving time isn’t *everything*, is it?

To crank up the My Pictures Slideshow screen saver, right-click the desktop, and choose Properties⇨Screen Saver. In the Screen Saver box, click My Pictures Slideshow (see the following figure). Choose Settings⇨Browse and point Windows at a folder with lots of pictures.

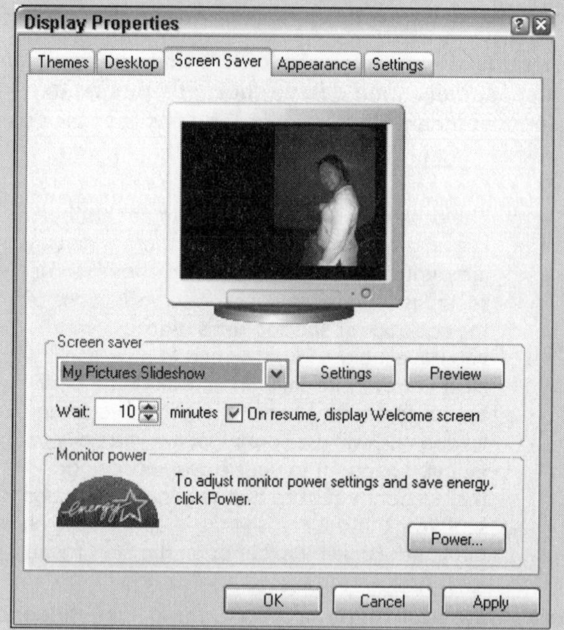

Oh. I get an enormous number of requests at AskWoody.com for the ultra-realistic aquarium screen saver. The original one is at `www.serenescreen.com`, but there are many others. Try a Google search on **free aquarium screen saver**.

Trimming the New Right-Click Menu

When you right-click an empty spot on the Windows desktop and choose New, Windows responds with an enormous list of potential choices — different kinds of documents, files, and on and on. (See Figure 14-9.)

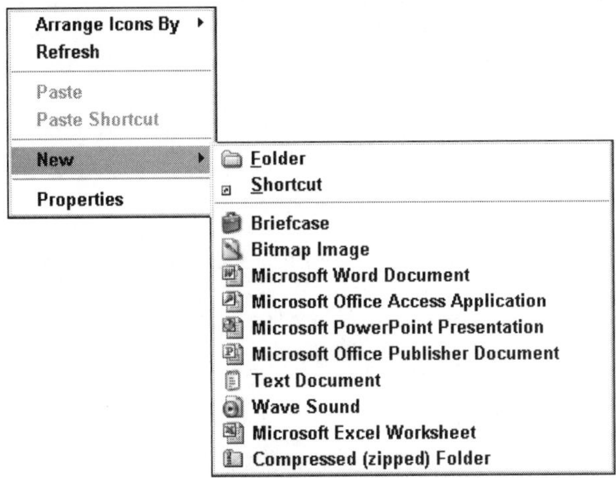

• **Figure 14-9: The New context menu.**

If you use the New right-click menu, paring down the list is worth the effort — simply to minimize the chances of accidentally picking the wrong option.

Pruning the New list is easy:

1. **Download and install TweakUI.**

   I talk about TweakUI in Technique 5.

2. **Choose Start⇨All Programs⇨PowerToys for Windows XP⇨TweakUI for Windows XP.**

3. **On the left, click Templates.**

   TweakUI shows you a list of all the programs on the New right-click menu (see Figure 14-10).

4. **Uncheck the boxes next to the items that you want removed from the New right-click menu.**

Any changes you make affect all users on the PC. Everybody has the same New right-click menu, so if you change it, make sure other users on your machine can live with the results.

Don't click the Delete button. If you do, all the unchecked New menu items are permanently deleted from TweakUI's list — for you, and for everybody else on your PC — and there's no way to bring them back.

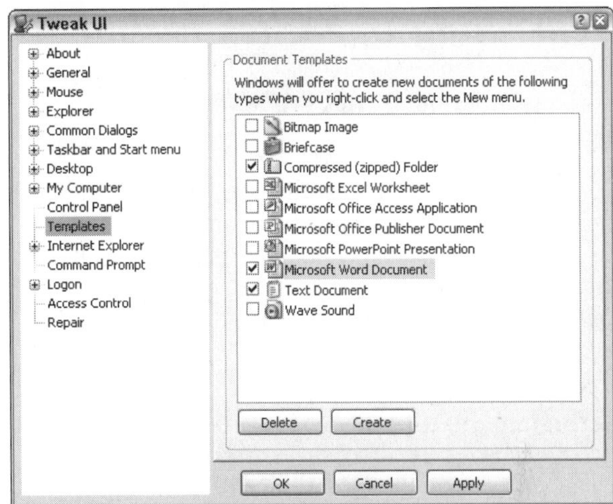

• **Figure 14-10: Each item on the New right-click menu is associated with a template listed here.**

5. **Click OK. Check the results by right-clicking a blank spot on the Windows desktop and choosing New.**

   The newly trimmed — and much more usable — list of available templates appears on the desktop. See Figure 14-11.

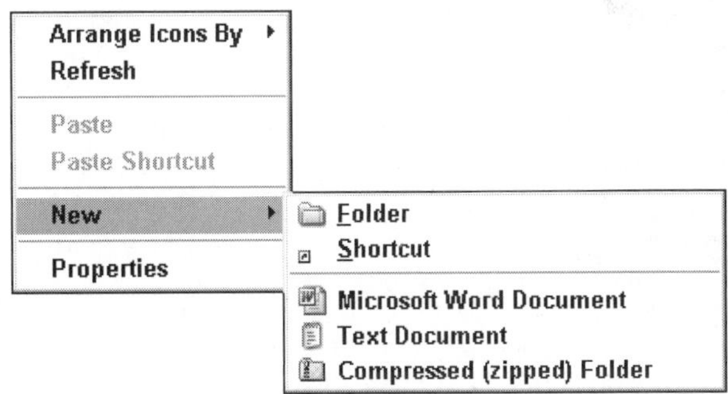

• **Figure 14-11: Save time by scaling back on the New right-click menu.**

Generating One-Click E-Mail

Here's another quick trick I've never seen documented anywhere.

Say you have to e-mail a status report to the same people every day. You can create an icon on the desktop which, when clicked, starts your e-mail editor (Outlook, Outlook Express, or some other client), and creates a new message all filled out and ready to go.

Setting up the e-mail

Here's how to set up basic one-click e-mail:

1. **Right-click any empty spot on the desktop.**
2. **Choose New⇨Shortcut.**

   Windows responds with the Create Shortcut Wizard shown in Figure 14-12.

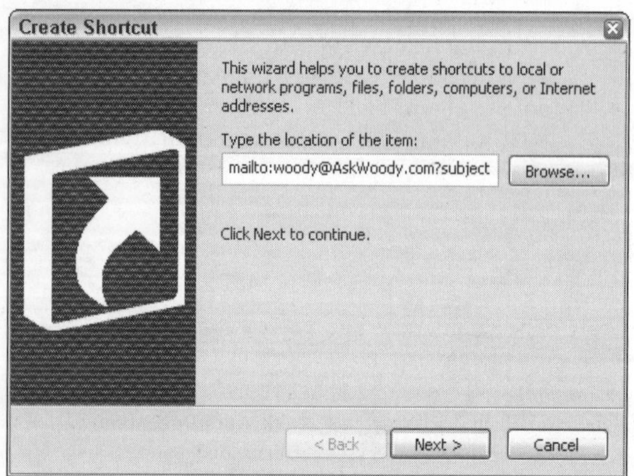

• **Figure 14-12: Send an e-mail message with the Create Shortcut Wizard.**

3. **In the Type the Location of the Item box, you need to type the e-mail recipient's address in a very specific way, using the `mailto:` command. It takes the form**

   ```
   mailto:somebody@somewhere.com?
     subject=SomeSubject
   ```

   For example, I might type

   ```
   mailto:woody@AskWoody.com?
     subject=ThisJustIn
   ```

   The e-mail address immediately following the colon is the recipient of the message. The text to the right of the equal sign is the subject.

The Create Shortcut Wizard isn't smart enough to work with spaces. Avoid putting spaces anywhere in the entire line — specifically, you cannot put spaces in the `subject=` field. Unfortunately, you can't use quotation marks either.

4. **Click Next.**

   You see the Select a Title for the Program dialog box.

5. **In the Type a Name for This Shortcut box, type a label for the shortcut.**

   For example, you might type `AskWoody News`.

6. **Click Finish.**

   The shortcut icon appears on your desktop.

7. **Double-click the new icon.**

   Your e-mail editor kicks in, creating a new e-mail message to the person whose information you entered in Step 3.

   In my example, a new message to `woody@AskWoody.com`, with the subject ThisJustIn, appears (see Figure 14-13).

8. **Complete the e-mail message, as usual, and click Send.**

In addition to individual e-mail addresses, you can create a `mailto:` shortcut that sends a message to all the members of an Outlook Distribution List. To do so, follow the steps, but instead of entering a single e-mail address, use the name of the group. For example, if you have a Distribution List called Department Heads, create a shortcut that says `mailto:DepartmentHeads`.

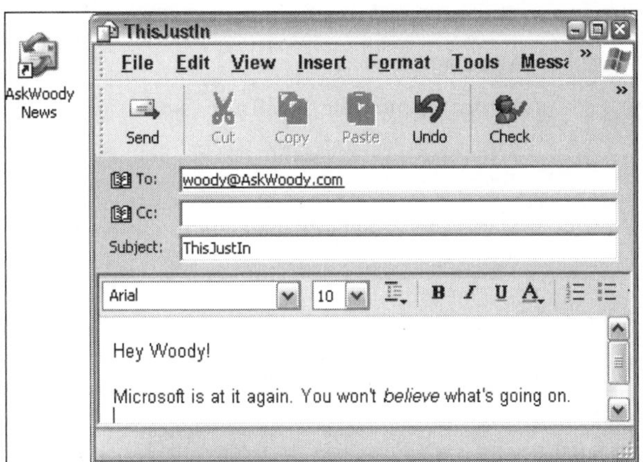

• **Figure 14-13: A very quick way to create new e-mail messages.**

Improving one-click e-mail

But wait! There's more! After you create a shortcut that generates e-mail, you can go back and modify it, making the subject much more legible, sending copies or even blind copies. You can even specify text that's supposed to go in the message.

To look at it another way, it's easy to put a single icon on your desktop that, when double-clicked, creates an e-mail message that looks like, oh:

```
To: myboss@myworkplace.com

Cc: herboss@myworkplace.com

From: woody@AskWoody.com

Subject: Status Report

We're on schedule. No problems to
   report. Looks like we won't have any
   difficulties making the end-of-month
   target. Will keep you posted. Let me
   know if you have any questions.
```

When you double-click that icon, the message appears in Outlook or Outlook Express, properly formatted and ready to go. All you need to do is click Send, and your status report goes out. ***Note:*** Unfortunately, this technique doesn't work with AOL Mail.

To embellish the one-click e-mail icon you constructed in the preceding section, follow these steps:

1. **Right-click a shortcut that was created by following the steps in the preceding section.**
2. **Choose Properties⇨Web Document.**

   Windows brings up the shortcut's Properties dialog box, as shown in Figure 14-14.

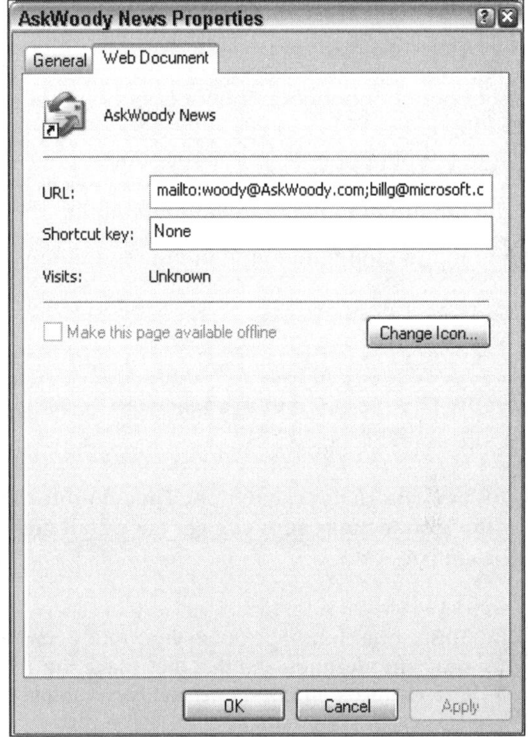

• **Figure 14-14: Entries here are analogous to a template for quick new e-mail messages.**

3. **In the URL box, use any combination of the symbols and fields in Tables 14-1 and 14-2 to create the message you want.**

   For example, I generated the e-mail message in Figure 14-15 from this entry in the URL box:

```
mailto:woody@AskWoody.com;billg@
   microsoft.com?cc=steveb@microsoft.
   com&subject=Can you confirm?&body=
   I just heard from an old friend that
   MS is going to sell off the Windows
   Division. True?
```

Spaces and most punctuation marks pose no problem at all. Also, you're limited to 255 characters in the URL box.

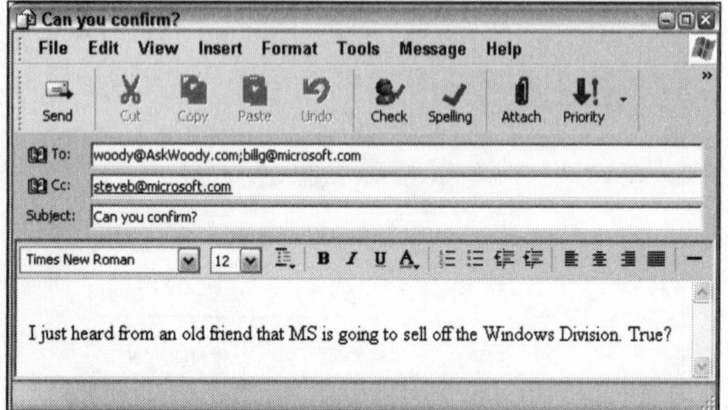

• **Figure 14-15: An e-mail message generated by clicking a simple shortcut.**

4. **When you're done, click OK. Then double-click the icon to make sure you get the e-mail message you want.**

This approach doesn't circumvent your e-mail program's features, and that may make the 255-character limit less onerous. For example, if you have an automatic entry that turns `billg` into `billg@microsoft.com`, you only need to use `billg` in the shortcut's URL box.

After you create this icon on the desktop, you can easily pin it to the Start menu, or move it down to the Quick Launch toolbar by simply clicking it and dragging.

Table 14-1: E-mail Shortcut Symbols

Symbol	Meaning
;	Separates multiple e-mail addresses
?	Separates address(es) in the To: field from other fields, such as cc: or bcc:
&	Marks the end of one field and the beginning of the next

Table 14-2: E-mail Shortcut Fields

Field	Meaning
mailto:	To: address(es) follow
cc=	cc: addresses follow
bcc=	bcc: addresses follow
subject=	Subject field
body=	Text inside the message

Starting Multiple Programs at Once

Sometimes you want to start multiple programs or open multiple documents at the same time. It's easy if you know the trick:

1. **Choose Start⇨All Programs or Start⇨My Documents.**
2. **Navigate to the first program or file that you want to open.**
3. **Hold down the Shift key.**
4. **Start the program or open the document by double-clicking it (just as you normally do).**
5. **Keep holding down the Shift key and click the second program or file.**

   The Start menu stays open indefinitely as long as you hold down the Shift key.

If you find yourself commonly opening the same group of documents using a single program, some programs (including the Office programs) allow you to set up a single shortcut that opens all the documents at once. It doesn't work all the time — as you will see, there are size limitations — but for people who always open the same group of files, this can be an enormous timesaver.

Here's how to set up a single shortcut to have a program open multiple documents at once (for example, to have Excel open three spreadsheets):

1. **Choose Start⇨All Programs and navigate to the program in question (in this case, Excel).**
2. **Right-click the program and drag it onto the desktop. Release the mouse button and choose Copy Here.**

   You have a shortcut to the program on your desktop.
3. **Choose Start⇨My Documents and navigate to the first document that you want to open with the program.**
4. **Right-click the document and choose Send To⇨Desktop (Create Shortcut).**

   A shortcut appears on your desktop that points to the document.
5. **Repeat Step 4 for each document that you wish to open.**

   At this point, you have a shortcut for the program on the desktop and separate shortcuts for each document. In Figure 14-16, I have a shortcut for Excel, plus shortcuts for three spreadsheets.

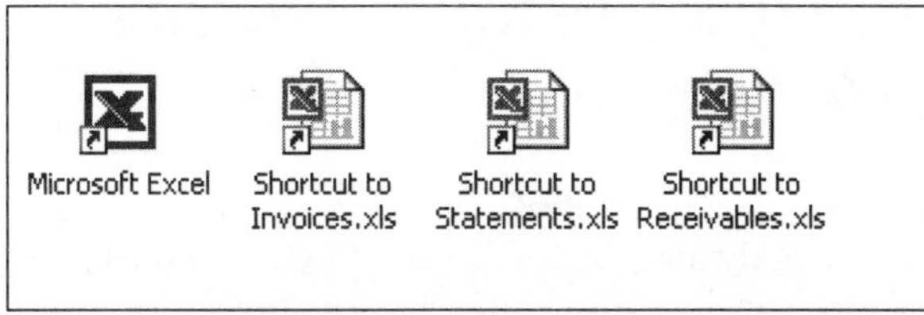

• Figure 14-16: Shortcuts for Excel and three spreadsheets.

6. **Right-click the program's shortcut icon and choose Properties.**

   Windows shows you the Properties dialog box for the program (such as the one in Figure 14-17).

   In this example, the Target box says:

   ```
   C:\Program Files\Microsoft Office\
     Office10\EXCEL.exe
   ```

   That's the most common location for Excel 2002 — the version in Office XP. If you have Office 2003, Excel is probably located at `c:\Program Files\Microsoft Office\Office11\EXCEL.exe`.

For no apparent reason, the Target box is limited to 259 characters.

7. **Press End and then press the spacebar.**

   That puts a space at the end of the Target box and leaves your cursor precisely where it needs to be.

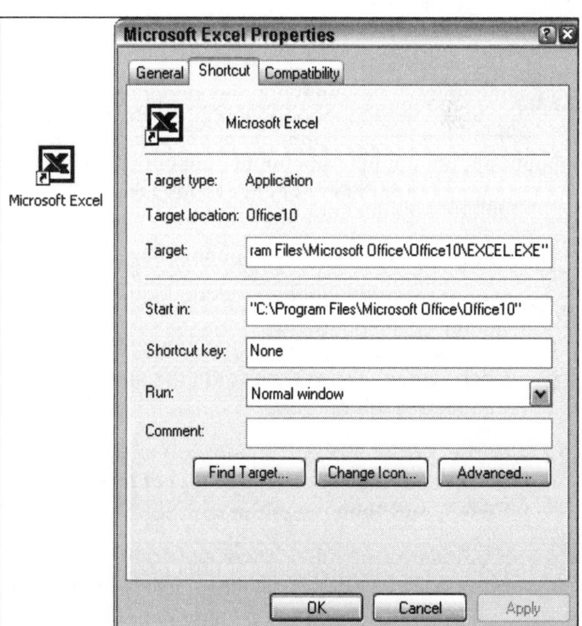

• Figure 14-17: Build on the Target box.

8. **Right-click the shortcut to one of the documents you wish to open and choose Properties.**

   You see the Properties dialog box for the shortcut, as in Figure 14-18. Note that the location of the document is highlighted in the Target box.

• **Figure 14-18: The full name of the document (including its location) is in the Target box.**

9. **Immediately press Ctrl+C.**

   That copies the full name of the document onto the Windows Clipboard.

10. **Click Cancel and return to the program's Properties dialog box.**

11. **In the Target box, with your cursor positioned at the end of the text in the Target box, press Ctrl+V, and then press the spacebar.**

    That pastes the full name of the first document into the Target box. The cursor is in position for you to enter the next document name.

12. **Repeat Steps 8 through 11 for each of the documents you wish to open.**

    When you're done, the Target box looks something like this:

```
C:\Program Files\Microsoft Office\
   Office10\EXCEL.EXE" "C:\Documents and
   Settings\Woody\My Documents\Invoices.
   xls" "C:\Documents and Settings\
   Woody\My Documents\Payables.xls"
```

    and so on, with spaces between each filename.

13. **If you run out of room in the Target box (that is, if a filename gets truncated), change the Start In box to point to the folder that contains one or more of your documents.**

    For example, if you change the program shortcut's Start In box to

```
C:\Documents and Settings\Woody\
   My Documents
```

    Then the filename in the Target box can be simply

```
Invoices.xls
```

    This may take some jiggling, but a little perseverance now results in a shortcut that you can use over and over again.

14. **When you finish with the Target box, click OK. Then double-click the icon and make sure it works.**

Don't forget that you can move this shortcut from the desktop to the Quick Launch toolbar (see Technique 16), or you can pin it to the Start menu (see Technique 13).

Arranging Multiple Windows Side-by-Side

You can arrange multiple windows on your desktop very quickly and easily. You can tile them side-by-side (vertically) or one-on-top (horizontally). Here's how:

1. **Make sure both the windows are open and thus have icons that appear on the Windows taskbar.**
2. **On the taskbar, click one window's icon, hold down the Ctrl key, and click the other window's icon.**
3. **Right-click one of the selected icons and choose Tile Horizontally or Tile Vertically.**

   The selected windows are tiled, as shown in Figure 14-19.

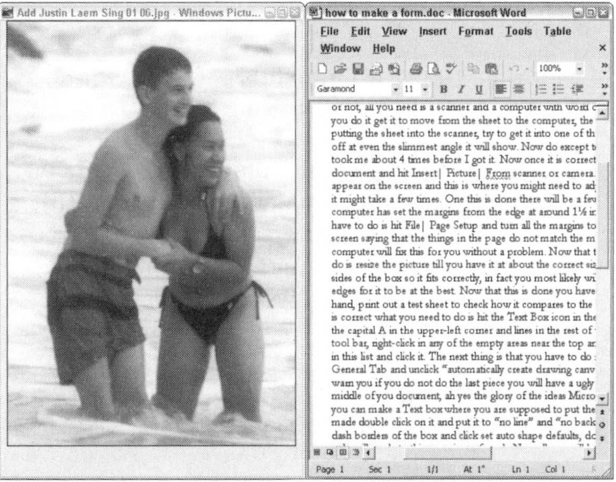

• **Figure 14-19: These windows are tiled vertically.**

Shooting a picture of your desktop

Sooner or later — probably sooner — you'll want to take a picture of your desktop. You might want to do this for a lot of reasons — some more socially acceptable than others:

- **To get all the details of an error message.**
- **To show a friend how to do something, or to show them what went wrong.**
- **To bypass print restrictions.** Some demo versions of programs allow you to open files, but not print them. The easy, fast workaround is to take a screen shot and print the screen. Of course, if you use the program you should buy it — and a printout of a screen shot is a very poor substitute for a genuine printed document. But if you're in a pinch, this works.
- **To circumvent onerous Information Rights Management restrictions.** If you haven't bumped into IRM yet, don't worry, you will. The IRM features built into Office 2003 and supported by Windows 2003 Server allow the author of a document to specify who can open, edit, print, copy, or even forward that document. Some people see IRM as a step forward in allowing companies to control their documents. Other people (present company included) see it as a horrendous way for some people to make other peoples' lives miserable — particularly when somebody screws up granting permissions for a specific document that you need to use. If you're allowed to view a file, but not copy it or give it to someone else, taking a shot of the screen is almost as good.

Quick pictures are a, uh, snap with Windows XP:

1. **Line up the picture that you want to take.**

   Setting up the screen shot is an art unto itself, but it helps if you use a high screen resolution and take great care to make sure the overlapping windows don't obscure anything important.

2. **To take a snapshot of the entire screen, press the PrtScr (or the Print Screen) key on your keyboard.**
3. **Alternatively, to shoot the active window or dialog box — the one that's "on top" — press Alt+PrtScr.**
4. **Start a graphics program, Word, or even Windows Paint.**
5. **Press Ctrl+V or choose Edit⇨Paste to place the screen shot in your document.**

Tip: If you have a friend who wants some help, but has a hard time explaining exactly what he's doing, have him start a Word document. Tell your friend how to use this technique to snap screen shots, and have him paste a sequence of shots into the document as he goes along.

Technique 15: Tricking Out the Taskbar

Save Time By

- Making the Windows taskbar work your way
- Jumping to important Web sites quickly
- Putting any folder on the taskbar
- Creating a custom pop-up menu for the taskbar

When you're trying to save time, the taskbar (shown in Figure 15-1) takes the cake: That little strip at the bottom of your screen is the one place you can get to quickly, easily, from any place in Windows, at any time.

To look at it a different way, the taskbar is, quite literally, where you go before you venture over to the Start menu.

Microsoft realizes the taskbar's supremacy in the timesaving pantheon, and because of that, provides us Windows customers a myriad of settings for tweaking, mashing, and mangling the bar. Unfortunately, many of those settings get in the way of saving time. This technique presents the ones you should consider if you want to make Windows work more effectively for you.

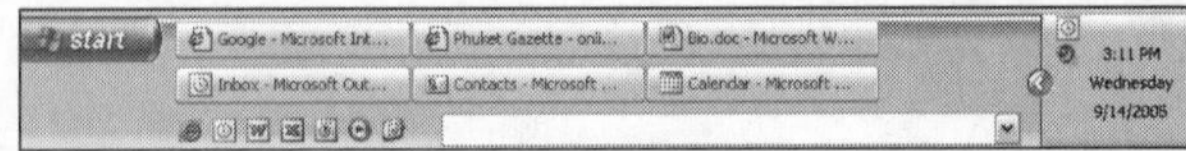

• Figure 15-1: The familiar Windows XP taskbar.

Customizing the Taskbar

One taskbar tweak rates as a no-brainer. If you haven't already changed your taskbar so it's two (or even three!) lines tall, do so now:

1. **Right-click an empty part of the taskbar and uncheck Lock Taskbar.**

   Before you can make changes to the taskbar, you have to unlock it. When it's unlocked, you can see a pattern of dots immediately to the right of the Start button (see Figure 15-2).

2. **Hover the mouse pointer over the taskbar until you see the double-headed arrow.**

3. **Click and drag upward to make the taskbar taller.**

If you're running at a screen resolution of 800 x 600 or 1024 x 768 (see Technique 7), you probably want the taskbar to be at least two lines tall. At higher resolutions, three can help.

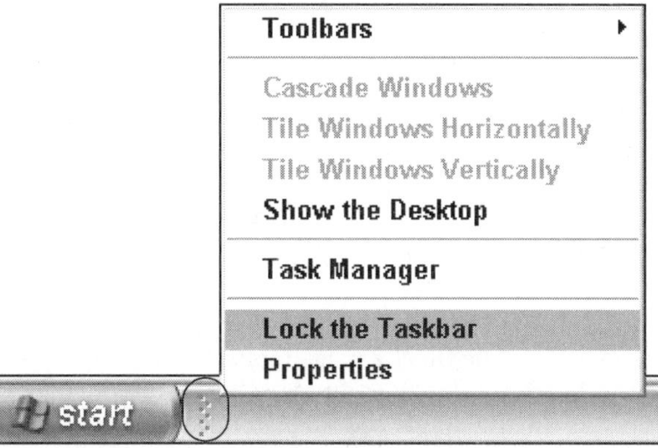

• **Figure 15-2: An unlocked taskbar.**

4. **Right-click the taskbar again and check Lock Taskbar.**

   Your taskbar now looks something like the one in Figure 15-3. Note that the area on the right — called the *notification area* or system tray — now shows the date as well as the time.

• **Figure 15-3: With a taller taskbar, Windows shows you the date, too.**

When the taskbar is unlocked, you can move it to the top, left, or right side of the screen by clicking in an unused area on the taskbar and dragging it. Because it's relatively easy to move — and most people don't want to move it — I recommend that you leave the taskbar locked unless you specifically need to unlock it.

Beyond that one no-brainer — making the taskbar at least two lines tall — I recommend a second bunch of timesaving settings for every Windows XP user. Check out Table 15-1.

Changing taskbar settings in one fell swoop

Are you ready to change your taskbar? Good. It should be changed, and as you can see in Table 15-1, there's no dearth of timesaving options.

Follow these steps:

1. **Right-click an empty place on the taskbar and choose Properties⇨Taskbar.**

   Windows shows you the Taskbar and Start Menu Properties dialog box.

2. **To enable the features you want, check the appropriate boxes (refer to Table 15-1).**

   Personally, I check all of them and recommend that you do, too.

TABLE 15-1: TASKBAR OPTIONS

Name	What It Does	Timesaving Bonus Info
Lock the Taskbar	Keeps you from accidentally doing something stupid, such as dragging the taskbar to the top of the screen. When the taskbar is unlocked, you can see a bunch of dots to the right of the Start button.	I keep the taskbar locked all the time. Justin prefers to keep his unlocked, so (among other things) new icons on the Quick Launch toolbar always show up.
Auto-Hide the Taskbar	Keeps the taskbar out of the way until you roll your mouse to the bottom of the screen (or to the side, if you moved the taskbar). As soon as you're through using the taskbar, it disappears.	I always auto-hide the taskbar to maximize my available screen real estate. Justin, on the other hand, likes to keep his showing, so he can switch programs without "bouncing" the mouse against the bottom of the screen.

(continued)

Table 15-1 *(continued)*

Name	What It Does	Timesaving Bonus Info
Keep the Taskbar on Top of Other Windows	Floats the taskbar up and down like any other window.	If you don't check this box, you may have trouble finding the taskbar. It's hard to imagine why anybody would float the taskbar.
Group Similar Taskbar Buttons	When Windows runs out of room on the taskbar, it looks to see if any one program has more than one button on the taskbar. If so, Windows groups the buttons for a single program together. For example, you may have five Internet Explorer windows grouped together under one taskbar button, and that button says you have five Internet Explorer windows. (Rocket science, eh?)	You do have some control over the way Windows combines buttons. See "Grouping Windows" later in this technique.
Show Quick Launch	Puts the Quick Launch toolbar on the taskbar, to the right of the Start button (see Figure 15-4).	The Quick Launch toolbar is the best location for your most heavily used programs, documents, Web pages, and the like. See Technique 16 for important details.
Show the Clock	Shows the clock, which is synchronized automatically with an ultra-accurate clock (either the National Institute of Standards and Technology clock — widely regarded as the premiere clock in all the world — or Microsoft's mirrored version of that same clock).	Let's be honest — your Windows clock is the most accurate one in your house or office. No, Microsoft doesn't use its clock to spy on you, but if you're concerned, switch over to the NIST clock by choosing Start➪Control Panel➪Date, Time, Language, and Regional Options➪Date and Time➪Internet Time.
Hide Inactive Icons	A program's icon should appear in the notification area only when the program is running.	Click Customize if you want to show a particular program's icon whether or not it's running.

3. **Click OK to put your choices in action.**

Figure 15-4 shows the left part of Justin's taskbar, with the Quick Launch toolbar activated.

• **Figure 15-4: The left part of Justin's taskbar.**

As with so many parts of Windows, there's no one "right" setting or group of settings. Justin and I disagree on two key points: auto-hiding and locking. You say "potato"; I say "potatoe."

Grouping Windows

Each time you start a program or open a document, and sometimes when you open a new Web page, Windows puts a button down on the taskbar. Sooner or later, you have so many programs running simultaneously that the taskbar runs out of room.

When that happens, Windows looks at the Group Similar Taskbar Buttons setting on the Taskbar and Start Menu Properties dialog box (refer to Table 15-1).

If you don't allow Windows to group similar buttons (which is to say, all the buttons associated with one specific program), the buttons keep getting smaller and smaller, until you can't see much at all (as in Figure 15-5).

• **Figure 15-5: With 15 active windows, you can't see much.**

On the other hand, if you do allow Windows to group similar buttons — if you have checked the Group Similar Taskbar Buttons box — Windows tries to figure out which program is being used the least and groups buttons for that program (see Figure 15-6).

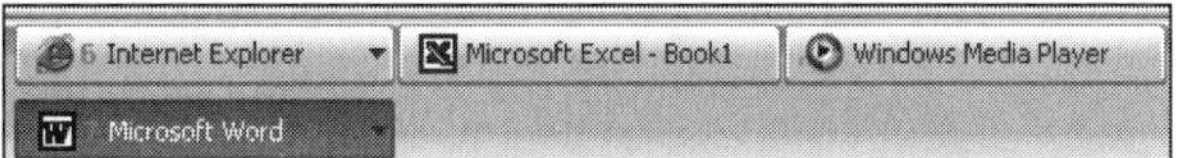

• **Figure 15-6: Least-used programs are grouped first.**

If you start even more programs or open more documents, Windows groups together another set of buttons, and so on.

The timesaving problem: When buttons are grouped, they're harder to find and slower to use. If you commonly have many programs, documents, or Web pages open simultaneously, it can take a lot of time to switch among them.

You have some control over how Windows decides which buttons to group:

1. **Download and install TweakUI.**

   Full details are in Technique 5.

2. **Choose Start⇨All Programs⇨PowerToys for Windows XP⇨TweakUI.**

   The TweakUI About screen appears.

3. **On the left, click Taskbar and Start Menu⇨Grouping, as shown in Figure 15-7.**

4. **Choose a Button Grouping option.**

   If you commonly have many Web pages open, for example, but you don't switch among them as frequently as open Word documents, you might want to choose Group Applications with the Most Windows First.

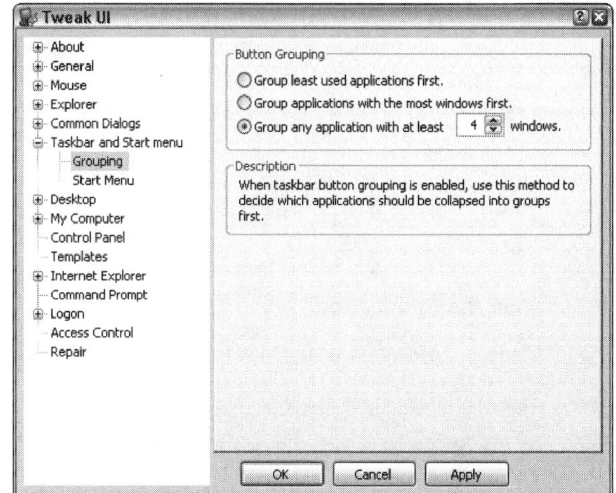

• **Figure 15-7: Use TweakUI to tell Windows how to group taskbar buttons.**

   Alternatively, if you don't mind seeing small buttons but want the button grouping to kick in eventually, you might tell Windows to wait until an application has four or five taskbar buttons before grouping them.

5. **Click OK.**

Some applications have tools for switching among open documents. All the Microsoft Office applications, for example, allow you to switch among open documents by choosing Window on the main menu and then picking the document from a list.

In Office XP and Office 2003, most of the applications (Word, Excel, PowerPoint, and Access) can be told to put only one button on the taskbar. If you tell your Office application to use this option, you then use the application's own internal mechanism for switching among open documents.

The difference can be substantial. For example, Figure 15-8 shows how telling Word to use just one taskbar button can make a big difference in the amount of information you can see about other active applications.

• **Figure 15-8: Word occupies only one taskbar button.**

To tell any Office XP or Office 2003 application (except Outlook) that it should use only one taskbar button, follow these steps:

1. **Start the application.**
2. **Choose Tools⇨Options⇨View.**

   The application shows you an Options dialog box.
3. **In the Show area, uncheck the Windows in Taskbar box.**
4. **Click OK.**

To tell Outlook 2002 or 2003 to use only one taskbar button, right-click the Outlook icon in the notification area (next to the clock) and check the Hide When Minimized line.

Blitzing the Address Bar

People on the move should activate another buried treasure available on the taskbar: a full-fledged rendition of the Internet Explorer/Windows Explorer Address bar.

Before your eyes glaze over, realize that the Address bar lets you type or paste

- **Web addresses** (but you already guessed that).
- **Any command that you would use in the Start⇨Run command box**, including `regedit`, `calc` (to bring up the Windows calculator), `winword` (to start Word), `ping`, `mspaint`, `msconfig`, `tracert`, and many more.
- **The name of a folder.** Press Enter and Windows Explorer appears, starting at that folder.
- **The name of a document** (generally, you have to include the full path). Windows starts the appropriate program and opens the document.
- **Any text.** Windows fires up Internet Explorer and starts a full-scale Web search, using your chosen search engine, such as Google (which I discuss in Technique 24).

Because of a very bad design decision at Microsoft that limits where you can put the Address bar, in order to take full advantage of the Address bar you probably need to expand the taskbar so that it occupies three lines. If your screen resolution is 1024 x 768 or higher and you auto-hide the taskbar, that shouldn't be an insurmountable problem. Auto-hiding becomes more and more important as you add features to the taskbar.

Here's how to put a lean, clean Address bar on your taskbar:

1. **Right-click any open area on the taskbar and choose Toolbars⇨Address.**

   The word *Address* appears on the right, near the notification area (see Figure 15-9).

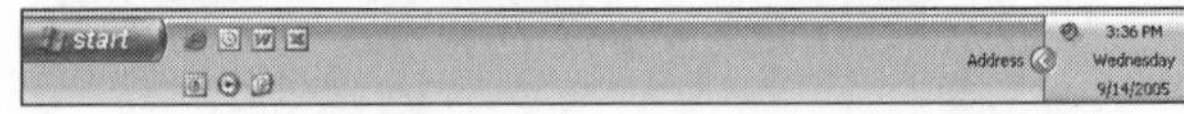

• **Figure 15-9: At first, the Address bar is completely inaccessible.**

2. **Right-click any open area on the taskbar and uncheck Lock the Taskbar.**

   You see the now-familiar dots — the Address bar's resizing handle — to the left of the nascent Address bar (see Figure 15-10).

• **Figure 15-10: Resizing dots on the Address bar.**

3. **Click the dots and drag the Address bar's resizing handle to the left.**

   Drag it far enough to the left so that you can see all three parts of the Address bar — the word *Address*, the box where you enter addresses, and the Go button (see Figure 15-11).

• **Figure 15-11: The three elements of the Address bar — two of which are completely useless.**

4. **Choose Start⇨Control Panel⇨Network and Internet Connections⇨Internet Options⇨ Advanced. Scroll down to near the end of the Browsing section and uncheck the Show Go Button in Address Bar box. Click OK.**

   The Go button does precisely the same thing as pressing Enter. There's no reason to have it on the Address bar. After you uncheck the box, the Address bar looks like the one shown in Figure 15-12.

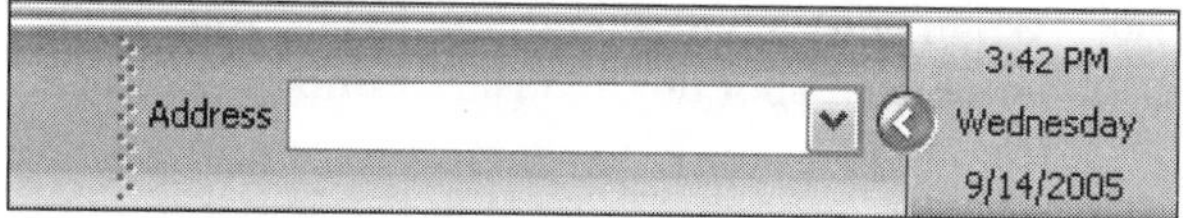

• **Figure 15-12: The Address bar *sans* Go.**

5. **Right-click the word *Address* and uncheck the Show Title box.**

   The word *Address* in the Address bar is completely superfluous as well.

6. **Click and drag an empty part of the Quick Launch toolbar, relocating it to the lower-left corner of the taskbar.**

   I discuss the Quick Launch toolbar in Table 15-1 and discuss it in depth in Technique 16.

Unfortunately, Windows XP doesn't let you put the Quick Launch toolbar and the Address bar just anywhere. It's a very bad design restriction, but there doesn't appear to be any way around it. I've come to the conclusion, after lots of trying, that the best way to arrange things is with the Quick Launch toolbar on the left and the Address bar on the right, on the lowest level of the taskbar. You can try rearranging things differently, but I bet you come to the same conclusion.

7. **Click the dots to the left of the Address bar and drag the bar to the right of the Quick Launch toolbar.**

   You may want to click and drag the top part of the taskbar, turning it into three lines. The net result looks something like the taskbar shown in Figure 15-13.

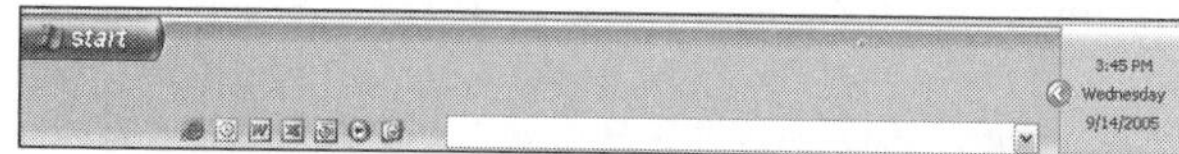

• **Figure 15-13: Nothing can go under the Start button.**

8. **Right-click an unused part of the taskbar and check Lock the Taskbar.**

   Justin's final, three-line taskbar looks like the one shown in Figure 15-14.

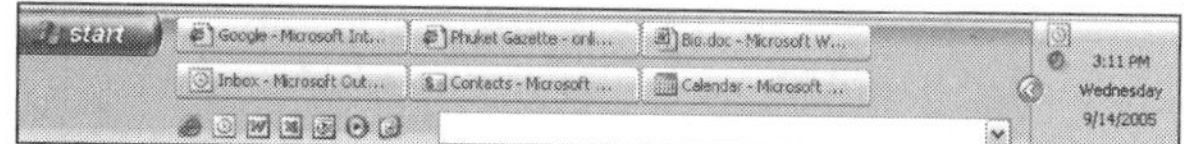

• **Figure 15-14: A very fast, easy, versatile, timesaving taskbar.**

Navigating from the Taskbar

This technique isn't for everyone. It's for those of you who frequently need to navigate around a hornet's nest of folders and don't want to do the navigating from inside a specific program (such as Word or Excel). Instead, you can put a pop-up menu — a *new toolbar*, in Windows parlance — on the taskbar. This toolbar whisks you directly to a folder, and from that point, subfolders turn into submenus. You can navigate through the folder maze to individual files, as shown in Figure 15-15.

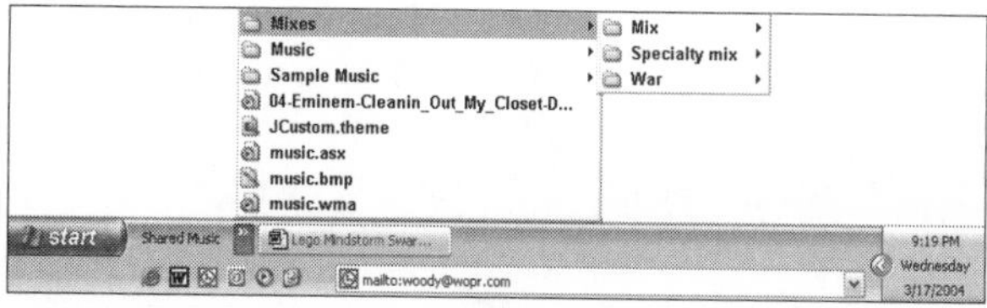

• **Figure 15-15: The Shared Music folder on the taskbar.**

Most people don't need the extra cascading toolbar: You can navigate through your program's usual File Open menu with no problem. For most of us, this fancy custom toolbar just takes up room on the Windows taskbar — where space is in short supply anyway. But if you have a bunch of folders that you navigate frequently, it can really save a lot of time.

To put a new toolbar on the Windows taskbar:

1. **Right-click any unused part of the taskbar and choose Toolbars⇨New Toolbar.**

   You see the New Toolbar dialog box shown in Figure 15-16.

2. **Navigate to the folder you want as the root of the pop-up menu, and click OK.**

   The contents of this folder will appear on your new toolbar. In Figure 15-16, Justin chose to put the Shared Music folder on the taskbar.

3. **Your new toolbar appears on the taskbar. Right-click the taskbar and uncheck Lock the Taskbar.**

4. **Click and drag your new toolbar, relocating it wherever you want.**

   If you play with it a bit, you see that Windows restricts the placement and sizing of the toolbar quite drastically.

• **Figure 15-16: New Toolbars are just folders.**

5. **When you're happy with the result, right-click an unused spot on the taskbar and check Lock the Taskbar.**

   Try using the new toolbar a bit and see if you get used to it.

If you change your mind and want to get rid of the new toolbar, right-click an open place on the taskbar, choose Toolbars, and uncheck the line that mentions the new toolbar.

Technique 16: Launching Your Most-Used Programs Quickly

Save Time By

- Customizing your Quick Launch toolbar
- Identifying Quick Launch programs instantly
- Opening documents and starting new documents in a flash

Are you tired of the Start⇨All Programs⇨Blah⇨Blah⇨Blah hunt-and-click routine? Do you have a small handful of programs you run every day? Man, have I got a toolbar for you!

The Quick Launch toolbar contains small icons that let you open programs quickly. In its initial state, it holds little icons for Internet Explorer, Outlook, Windows Media Player, and a few more programs (the company that manufactured your PC may have jimmied the mix a bit).

Windows XP Professional users have their Quick Launch toolbars turned on automatically. For reasons I can't begin to fathom, XP Home users — who need this speed-demon feature as much as anyone — have to turn it on themselves. In this technique, I show you how to bring the Quick Launch toolbar to life and turn it into your number-one timesaver.

This technique and Technique 15 go hand-in-hand. You can tackle them in either order, as long as you go through them both.

Using the Quick Launch Toolbar

The Windows Quick Launch toolbar sits immediately to the right of the Start button on the Windows taskbar (see Figure 16-1). It's a very convenient place to put your own icons so that launching programs — or even opening frequently used documents — is just a click away.

• Figure 16-1: The programs available directly from my Quick Launch toolbar.

After many years of kicking and futzing with the Windows desktop, I've settled on a simple hierarchy that really streamlines Windows, and in my opinion, the Quick Launch toolbar stands at the top of the timesaving food chain. Table 16-1 shows you how to organize Windows for maximum efficiency.

Table 16-1: Organizing Programs by Frequency of Use

Do This	See Also
Put programs and documents that you use several times a day on the Quick Launch toolbar. Assign shortcut keys to these frequently used programs and documents, as well.	Technique 18
Put programs, folders, and documents that you use at least once a day on the Start menu.	Technique 13
Use the Windows desktop as a temporary parking area and clean it up as frequently as you possibly can.	Technique 14

Following those three guidelines ensures that the programs, documents, and folders you use most are the easiest ones to find.

Making the Quick Launch Toolbar Appear

If you can't see the Quick Launch toolbar next to the Start button on your Windows taskbar, that's because you haven't activated it yet. Here's what you need to do:

1. **Right-click any open spot on the Windows taskbar.**
2. **Choose Toolbars⇨Quick Launch.**

   Windows creates your new Quick Launch toolbar with icons for Internet Explorer, the desktop, and the Windows Media Player. If you have Outlook installed, chances are good that it appears on the Quick Launch toolbar, too.

Adding Programs to the Quick Launch Toolbar

There's no need to settle for Windows' bone-stock Quick Launch toolbar. Any program that you want to get at quickly deserves to be there. Here's how to add your frequently used programs to the toolbar:

1. **Navigate to the program you want to put on the Quick Launch toolbar.**

   Most commonly, you'll want to click Start or Start⇨All Programs and work your way to the program in question.

2. **Right-click the program and drag it to the Quick Launch toolbar.**

   An I-beam appears where the new quick launch icon will go (see Figure 16-2).

• **Figure 16-2: The I-beam tells you where the icon will go.**

3. **When you release the icon, choose Copy Here.**

   The icon appears on the Quick Launch toolbar (see Figure 16-3).

• **Figure 16-3: I added Excel to the Quick Launch toolbar.**

Never choose Move Here. If you do, the entry on the Start menu disappears! If you accidentally move it off the Start menu, not to worry: You can simply click the icon on the Quick Launch toolbar, and drag back up to wherever it's supposed to go on the Start menu.

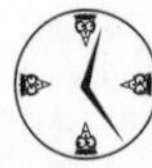

To remove a program from the Quick Launch toolbar, right-click it and choose Delete. That does not delete the program from your computer. It only deletes the icon on the toolbar.

Making Room for More Programs on the Quick Launch Toolbar

It won't take long before you run out of room for Quick Launch icons. Although keeping the number of icons manageable is important so that you can readily remember what each one does, in my experience, feelings of claustrophobia rapidly overcome deficiencies in long-term memory.

To give your icons more elbow room

1. **Right-click any open spot on the Windows toolbar.**
2. **Uncheck the Lock the Taskbar box.**

   A domino pattern of dots appears, marking the edges of the Quick Launch toolbar (see Figure 16-4).

• **Figure 16-4: Drag the dots to resize the Quick Launch toolbar.**

3. **Drag the dots left or right to make the Quick Launch toolbar area bigger or smaller.**

If you can remember what all the icons mean, or you take the time to make the Screen Tips meaningful (see the following section, "Changing Quick Launch Screen Tips"), there's no reason to be stingy with Quick Launch real estate. Personally, I drag the entire Windows toolbar up so it occupies three rows (see Figure 16-5), and leave plenty of extra room for Quick Launch icons.

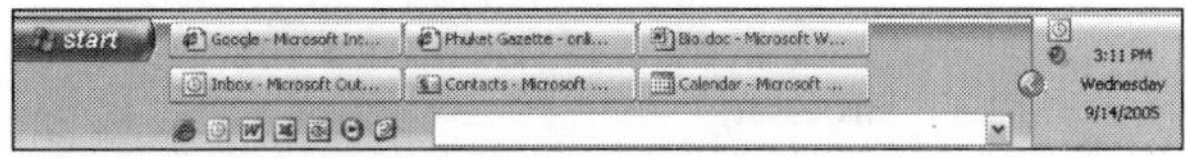

• **Figure 16-5: Leave lots of room for the taskbar and the Quick Launch toolbar.**

4. **When the Quick Launch toolbar is the right size for you and in the location you want, right-click any unused part of the Windows taskbar, and check Lock the Taskbar.**

My son, Justin, leaves the taskbar unlocked all the time, so it's easier and faster to rearrange things. If you find yourself adapting to many different working situations on any given day, this may be the most efficient approach.

Auto-Hiding the Taskbar

I like to see as much of my screen as possible, so I make the Windows taskbar auto-hide itself. To auto-hide the taskbar, follow these steps:

1. **Right-click the taskbar and choose Properties.**
2. **Check the Auto-Hide the Taskbar box.**

   The taskbar no longer takes up precious screen space.

When you move the mouse to the bottom of the screen, the taskbar reappears. Make sure you go through Technique 15 for a bunch of hard-hitting taskbar timesaving tips.

Changing Quick Launch Screen Tips

When you hover your mouse pointer over an icon on the Quick Launch toolbar, a Screen Tip appears directly above the icon. Although Windows uses lots of Screen Tips that are frequently more of a bother than a help, the Quick Launch Screen Tips can be very helpful, particularly if you have more than a few Quick Launch icons.

Unfortunately, many companies (and I won't mention Microsoft by name) put ridiculously long essays in their Screen Tips. The Screen Tip for Word 2003, for example, reads (I kid you not): `Microsoft Word / Create and edit text and graphics in letters,` reports, Web pages, or e-mail messages by using Microsoft Office Word. Nothing like a quick and snappy Screen Tip to increase your efficiency, eh?

Depending on the way you created your Quick Launch icons — or the way they were created for you — you might have such illuminating Screen Tips as `Shortcut to capture32.exe` or `CorelDRAW 10 Launch CorelDRAW 10`, which, no doubt, originated in Corel's Department of Redundancy Department.

To make your own Screen Tip for a Quick Launch icon:

1. **Right-click the icon and choose Properties.**

   Windows creates the Screen Tip on the fly by combining the name at the top of the Properties box with the Comment at the bottom. Figure 16-6, for example, shows you the stock Word 2002 Properties. Windows combines "Microsoft Word" at the top with "Create and edit text..." from the Comment.

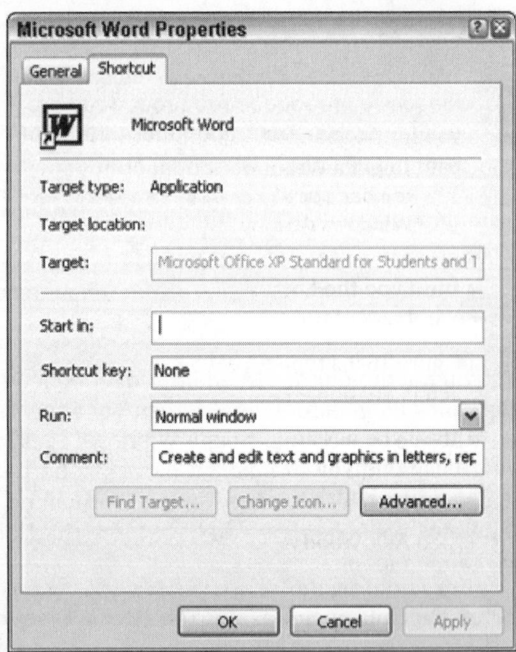

• Figure 16-6: The components of the Quick Launch toolbar's Screen Tips.

2. **Unless you really want to see the verbiage in the Comments box every time you hover over a Quick Launch icon, delete everything in the Comments box.**

3. **Click the General tab at the top of the Properties dialog box.**

   The General tab for the Internet Explorer icon looks like Figure 16-7.

4. **Type whatever you want to appear as the Screen Tip in the top box on the General tab. Click OK.**

   I change Internet Explorer's name to a short, sweet "IE 6".

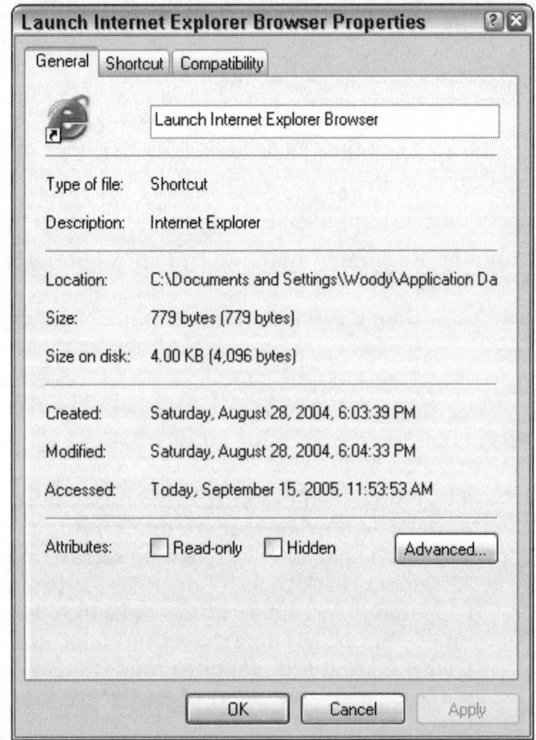

• Figure 16-7: This is where the Quick Launch toolbar picks up the text "Launch Internet Explorer Browser."

You also can change the first entry on the General tab by right-clicking the Quick Launch icon and choosing Rename. Unfortunately, renaming this way doesn't wipe out the comments and may not have the effect you want.

Opening Documents Quickly

Do you have a document that you open every day — or even several times a day? If so, adding the document to the Quick Launch toolbar can save you all sorts of time. Here's how to add a document to the Quick Launch toolbar:

1. **Locate the file you want to put on the Quick Launch toolbar.**

   You can use Windows Explorer, or File➪Open from inside the application.

Surprisingly, this quick tip doesn't work if you try to grab the file from Windows' Start➪My Recent Documents list.

2. **Right-click the file and drag it to the Quick Launch toolbar.**
3. **Place the I-beam where you want the document's icon to appear.**
4. **Release the mouse button and choose Create Shortcut Here.**

   Figure 16-8 shows how I placed a shortcut to a Word document at the end of the Quick Launch toolbar.

I added a Word document to the Quick Launch toolbar.

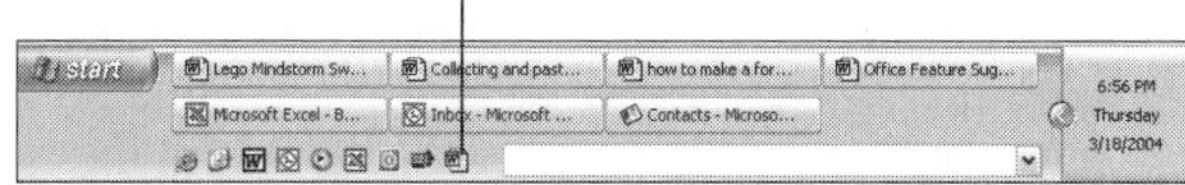

• **Figure 16-8: A Word document on the Quick Launch toolbar.**

Opening Web Pages Quickly

You can create a Quick Launch toolbar icon that opens a specific Web page in many different ways.

Here's my favorite, fast way:

1. **Right-click an empty spot on the desktop and choose New➪Shortcut.**

   Windows responds with the Create Shortcut Wizard (see Figure 16-9).

• **Figure 16-9: To put a Web page on the Quick Launch toolbar, start by making a shortcut on the Windows desktop.**

2. **In the Type the Location of the Item box, type the address of the Web page. Click Next.**

   In Figure 16-9, I typed **www.AskWoody.com**, which is my home page.

3. **In the Type a Name for This Shortcut box, type a name that you want for the shortcut's Screen Tip. Click Finish.**

   I typed **Ask Woody**.

4. **Click and drag the newly created shortcut to the Quick Launch toolbar (see Figure 16-10).**

   After the Quick Launch icon is in place, double-clicking it launches Internet Explorer and brings up that specific Web page.

• **Figure 16-10: The last icon on this Quick Launch toolbar goes directly to AskWoody.com.**

Adding a Blank E-Mail Message to the Quick Launch Toolbar

You can use the same method to create a Quick Launch icon that starts a blank e-mail message addressed to whomever you wish. Follow these steps:

1. **Right-click an empty spot on the desktop and then choose New⇨Shortcut.**

   Windows responds with the Create Shortcut Wizard.

2. **Type** mailto: **and then type the recipient's e-mail address.**

   For example, type **mailto:woody@AskWoody.com**.

3. **Click Finish.**
4. **Click and drag the newly created shortcut to the Quick Launch toolbar.**

   Clicking that icon starts your e-mail program, with a blank e-mail to the address you specified in Step 2, ready for you to complete and send.

Creating New, Template-Based Documents Quickly

If you frequently create new documents (Word documents, Excel spreadsheets, and the like) from the same template — say, a report you prepare every day — here's a technique that you can use. This technique is also helpful if you use a particular form letter on a regular basis that you want to access from the Quick Launch toolbar.

Here's how to make it one-click easy to create a new document, using the Quick Launch toolbar:

1. **Locate the template for the document.**
2. **Right-click the template and drag it to the Quick Launch toolbar.**
3. **Release the mouse button and choose Create Shortcut.**

It's that easy, if you can find the template.

Many Windows applications make it deucedly difficult to locate templates — they're tucked away in hidden folders. Here's the easiest way to find an existing template in Word or Excel:

1. **Start Word or Excel. Click the New button to create a new document in Word, or a new spreadsheet in Excel.**
2. **Click the Save button.**
3. **In the Save as Type box, choose Document Template (for Word) or Template (for Excel).**

   You find yourself in the middle of all the templates (see Figure 16-11).

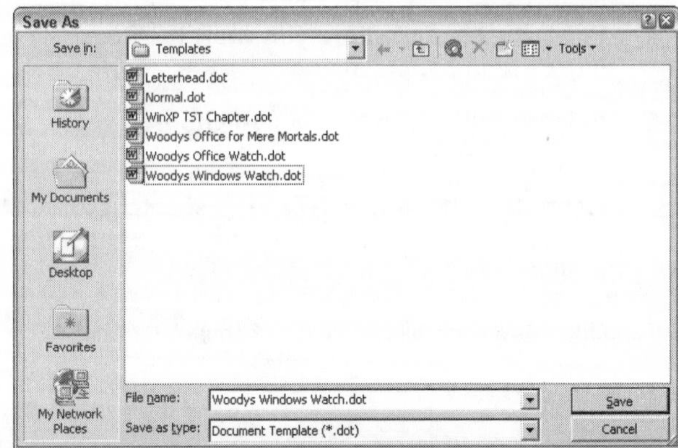

• **Figure 16-11: Use the Save As trick to quickly get to all the hard-to-find templates.**

4. **Click and drag a template anywhere you like. Just click Cancel when you're done.**

Making Programs Run Your Way

Save Time By

- Running the programs you choose whenever Windows starts
- Setting up programs so every user on the computer can run them
- Making programs start your way — right away

Windows XP is nothing without programs. Hey, I'm not saying Windows isn't nice, but your work (and play!) gets done inside programs — word processors, e-mail programs, spreadsheets, *Warcraft XIX: The Prequel* . . . you get the idea.

Windows has all sorts of hooks for making programs run in a specific way — and gotchas to trap the unwary. Windows is the ooze that all the programs have to play in. And if they play well, you can push and nudge Windows to control the programs themselves. You don't have to write a program. You don't need to be a Computer Science grad. All you need is a little gumption and good ol' fashioned ingenuity.

This technique contains three program-controlling tips that you can use right now to save time and take control of your PC. Twiddling program controls is a two-way street: The same methods that allow scumware programs to start automatically on your PC can be used for good, to start the programs *you* want. In Technique 11, I show you how to turn auto-starting programs off. In this technique, I show you how to save time by making the program(s) you use most often start up with Windows.

Running a Program when Windows Starts

Many Windows XP users run some specific program every time they get on their computers. Personally, I run Outlook every time, but Justin likes to get Windows Media Player and the Calculator going. Odd combination, that.

Here's how to tell Windows to run a specific program each time it starts:

1. **Right-click the Start button.**

   You can run the program whenever you log on to your PC, or you can run the program no matter who logs on to the PC.

2. **Choose Explore to run the program when a specific user logs on. Choose Explore All Users to run the program regardless of which user logs on.**

   Windows Explorer opens to the Start Menu folder.

3. **Double-click your way down to Start Menu⇨Programs⇨Startup.**

   Any shortcut that sits in the Startup folder runs whenever this particular user signs on to the PC.

4. **Navigate to the program you want to start automatically.**

   If a shortcut is already on the Quick Launch Toolbar (see Technique 16), you have all you need. Otherwise, go through the Start⇨All Programs route. Say you want to start Windows Media Player every time you log on. In that case, you choose Start⇨All Programs, then hover your mouse (but don't yet click) over Windows Media Player.

5. **Right-click the program and drag it into the Startup folder. Release the mouse button and choose Create Shortcut Here.**

If you click the program and hover the mouse over the Startup folder on the Windows taskbar, the folder opens (sooner or later), making it easier to complete the drag.

The Startup folder looks similar to Figure 17-1.

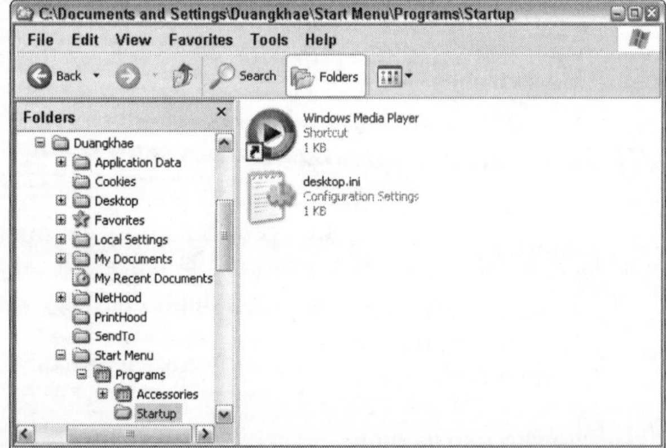

• **Figure 17-1: The shortcut to Windows Media Player sits inside the Startup folder.**

6. **Log off (Start⇨Log Off⇨Log Off), and then log back on again.**

   The program you placed in the Startup folder runs as soon as you log on.

You can place as many programs as you like in the Startup folder.

Allowing Other Users to Run Your Programs

Tell me if you've heard this one before.

Justin installed one of *The Sims* games on the family room PC and he took me through a quick demo. Cool stuff. I was interested in the, ahem, mathematical simulation capabilities, so one day while he was at school, I logged on to the PC in the family room, chose Start⇨All Programs and . . . no *Sims*.

Huh?

Turns out that Justin had installed *The Sims* for one user only — it doesn't show up on the Start⇨All Programs menu for anybody but Justin.

Many older programs install themselves for the current user only. More recent ones frequently give you the option of installing for just one user or for all users. If you have the option, unless you have a very compelling reason to do otherwise, always install for all users.

I could go into Windows Explorer and look for *The Sims*, but that's a pain in the neck. In the end, I put the shortcuts for *The Sims* on everybody's Start⇨All Programs menu. Here's how:

1. **Log on as the user who can get to the program.**

   In this case, Justin logged on as himself.

2. **Right-click Start and choose Open. On the right, double-click the Programs folder.**

   You end up in the `Start Menu\Programs` folder for the user who's logged on.

3. Find the folder that contains the programs you installed.

The folder that contains the *The Sims* is called Maxis (see Figure 17-2). That's the name of the company that makes *The Sims*.

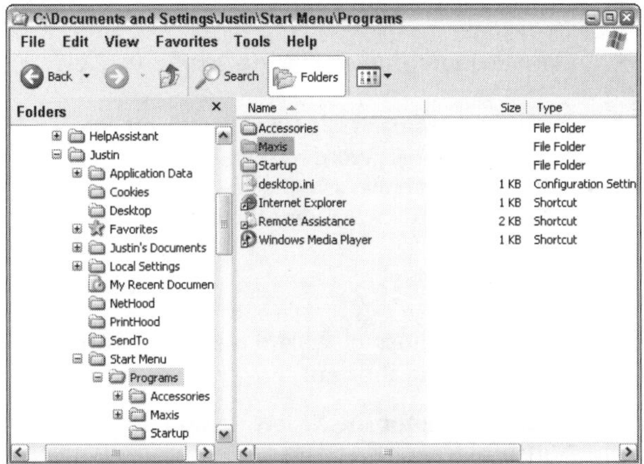

• **Figure 17-2: Find the folder in the** `Start Menu\Programs` **folder that contains the shortcuts you want.**

You may have to click and search a bit to find the folder you need, but make sure you get the main folder — the one that contains all the shortcuts.

4. Right-click the folder and choose Copy.

Do not click Copy This Folder over on the left. Although you can use Copy This Folder to eventually get the folder copied to its proper location, these steps show you a much simpler, faster way.

5. Right-click Start and choose Open All Users. Double-click the Programs folder, and then right-click in a blank spot on the right side of the Explorer window and choose Paste.

The program shortcut folder (in this case, to the folder Maxis) appears in the `All Users\Start Menu\Programs` folder, as shown in Figure 17-3.

By virtue of its location in that folder, Maxis appears on the Start➪All Programs menus for every user.

• **Figure 17-3: Placing the Maxis folder here ensures that it appears on the Start Menu for all users.**

Bringing Back Word's Last Document

Many programs use *command line switches* — little directives that tell the program what to do when it starts. All the Office applications have various command line switches — most of which are widely ignored and rarely used.

One of the most useful Office command line switches tells Word that it should open the last-used document when it starts.

You can use that switch to put an icon on your desktop that, when double-clicked, starts Word with the last-used document open, ready for you to dig in.

Here's how to use a command line switch in order to tell Word to open with the last document you were working on:

1. Right-click any open spot on the desktop, and choose New➪Shortcut.

The Create Shortcut Wizard appears.

2. **Click the Browse button and locate `winword.exe` — the program better known as Word.**

   Unfortunately, finding programs can be a challenge in and of itself. For example, Word's location varies depending on which version of Word you use. Use Table 17-1 as a start.

To find out which version of a specific Office application you're using, start the application (Word, Outlook, Excel, PowerPoint, and so on), and choose Help⇨About and the product name. For Word, you choose Help⇨About Microsoft Word; for Excel, it's Help⇨About Microsoft Excel, and so on. The dialog box tells you which version is running.

3. **When you find `winword.exe`, click it once, and then click OK.**

   The Create Shortcut dialog box looks similar to Figure 17-4.

• **Figure 17-4: The location of `winword.exe` for Office XP/Word 2002.**

4. **Press the End key.**

   You're taken to the end of the long line in the Type the Location of the Item text box, which points to `winword.exe`.

5. **In the text box after `winword.exe`, type a space, type `/mfile1`, and then press Enter.**

   The net result looks like this:

```
"C:\Program Files\Microsoft Office\
  Office10\WINWORD.EXE" /mfile1
```

   Note that one space is before `/mfile1`, after the double-quote, and no space is inside `/mfile1`.

The `/m` command is a Word command line switch that tells Word to run a built-in program (also known as a macro). In this case, the File1 macro simply opens the last-used file.

6. **Click Next.**

   The Create Shortcut Wizard asks you to provide a name for the shortcut.

7. **Type a name for the shortcut and click the Finish button.**

   I call this shortcut Last Doc, but you can call it Gefilte Fish if you like. You end up with a new shortcut on your desktop.

8. **Double-click the new shortcut.**

   Word opens with the last-used document and ready for edits.

If you commonly start Word and want to open the last-used document, put a copy of this new shortcut on your Quick Launch Toolbar, or even on the Start menu. Usually, you want to leave the old Word shortcut in place, so you can quickly decide whether to open Word normally or open the last-used document.

Microsoft finally (finally!) published a complete and accurate list of Word 2000, 2002, and 2003 command line switches at `support.microsoft.com/default.aspx?kbid=210565`. (Pardon me if I sound excited. I've been complaining about the lousy switch documentation for a decade.) I'm still looking for definitive lists for other Office applications.

Table 17-1: Places You Usually Find Winword.exe

Version of Office	Default Location
Office 97/Word 97	C:\Program Files\Microsoft Office\Office\winword.exe
Office 2000/Word 2000	C:\Program Files\Microsoft Office\Office\winword.exe
Office XP/Word 2002	C:\Program Files\Microsoft Office\Office10\WINWORD.EXE
Office 2003/Word 2003	C:\Program Files\Microsoft Office\OFFICE11\WINWORD.EXE

Using Built-In Keyboard Shortcuts

Save Time By

- Picking and choosing the keyboard shortcuts you need most
- Finding the right shortcut quickly

Windows abounds with shortcut key combinations. Did you know that holding down the Alt, Shift, F1, End, and Print Screen keys simultaneously brings up a secret picture of Bill Gates wearing a T-shirt that says, "Hey-Hey! No-No! Open Source Has Gotta Go!"?

Naw. Just joking.

Arguably the most important key combination is Ctrl+Alt+Del — the combination that's used to shut down Windows Me and 98. That three-finger salute (or is it a Vulcan Mind Meld?) brings up the Windows Task Manager, shown in Figure 18-1, from which you can halt programs that are misbehaving. (I talk about other features from the Windows Task Manager in Technique 5.)

This technique makes it easy and fast for you to find the shortcuts that you need. Training your fingers is up to you.

• Figure 18-1: The Windows Task Manager gives you control over all running programs.

Shortcuts Everybody Needs

I have a very short list of shortcut key combinations that every single Windows XP user needs to memorize. They work in practically every Windows program ever made. Table 18-1 shows you the Big Three shortcut keys that go back to the ancient days of personal computing and, man, do they come in handy.

Tattoo these to the inside of your eyelids.

There's a handful of additional keys (see Table 18-2) that are recognized in almost every program — and, usually, in Windows itself.

Table 18-1: Shortcut Keys Every Windows XP User Must Know

Key	What It Does
Ctrl+C	Copies the selected items to the Clipboard
Ctrl+X	Cuts the selected items to the Clipboard
Ctrl+V	Pastes the contents of the Clipboard at the current cursor location

In most applications, you can use Alt+underlined letter (for example, the "F" in File), and the menu behaves as if you clicked it. Fast touch typists find this approach useful because it saves them from moving their fingers to the mouse.

Table 18-2: Shortcut Keys that Work Almost Everywhere

Key	What It Does
Ctrl+A	Select everything.
Ctrl+Z	Undo the last thing you did.
Ctrl+click	Selects items one-by-one: Click something to select it; then hold down the Ctrl key and click something else. Both things are selected. To select more, hold down the Ctrl key again, and select another one. To deselect items that you have selected, hold down the Ctrl key and click the thing you want to get rid of.
Shift+click	Similar to Ctrl+click, except this action selects everything in between. Say you're working on a list of files. Click the first file to select it. Hold down the Shift key and click another file. Every file between the first one and the last one is selected.
Tab	Go to the next item (in, say, a dialog box, or to fill in a form on the Web). Just to confuse things, if you want to move from tab to tab in a tabbed dialog box, use Ctrl+Tab.
Shift+Tab	Go to the previous item.
Alt+F, Alt+X, and then Enter	In most (but not all!) applications, this combination starts an orderly shutdown of the application. If your screen suddenly goes black — perhaps a power outage? — and you need to bail out quickly, hold down the Alt key, press F and release it, wait a second, press X and release it, release the Alt key, wait a few more seconds, and press Enter to save whatever file you've been working on. Press Enter a few more times for good measure, and you're usually okay.
F1	Help.
F5	Refresh (in other words, go back out and check things all over again). In Word, F5 is Find/Replace.

Important Windows Key Combinations

Sometimes Windows goes out to lunch and you need a key combination to get it back. Other times, the shortest distance between two points, er, programs, is a simple key combination. You'll use the keyboard shortcuts in Table 18-3 over and over again.

A Grab-Bag of Application Shortcuts

These key combinations can be incredibly useful for some people — but probably rate as real duds for most of us. Scan Table 18-4 and try the ones that look good in your favorite programs.

Table 18-3: Important Windows Commands

Key	What It Does	Timesaving Bonus Info
Ctrl+Alt+Del	The infamous Three-Finger Salute brings up the Windows Task Manager. When Windows freezes tighter 'n' a drum, this is the way out.	Doing the Ctrl+Alt+Del combination twice no longer results in an automatic reboot of Windows.
Alt+Tab	Once known as the "CoolSwitch," holding down the Alt key and repeatedly pressing Tab cycles through all running programs. Unfortunately, the desktop isn't one of your choices.	This approach can be faster than using the taskbar you don't have many programs running. It's also if convenient if your machine freezes and you want to see if any other programs are available.
Shift	Holding down the Shift key when you insert a CD temporarily overrides Windows' attempts to run, play, copy, or otherwise automatically do something with the inserted CD.	If you need to insert the Windows installation CD to retrieve a file, hold down the Shift key while you slide in the CD, and you don't have to close out of the installer's starting screen.
Shift+Del	Permanently deletes an item — it isn't placed in the Recycle Bin.	Windows asks if you're sure you want to delete the file.
Ctrl+drag	Hold down the Ctrl key while you drag an item, and you make a copy.	I tend to use a right-click drag because it gives more options, and it's just one less key combination I need to memorize.
Windows key *or* Ctrl+Esc	Brings up the Start menu.	Easy way to exit Windows if your mouse freezes.
Windows key+M *or* Windows key+D	Minimizes all open windows so that you can see your desktop immediately.	After you get that key combination down, you can take the desktop icon off the Quick Launch toolbar to give way to another shortcut.

Table 18-4: Miscellaneous Commands for Almost Every Program

Key	What It Does	Timesaving Bonus Info
Esc	Stops whatever is happening.	If you get to the point where you really need it, chances are good Esc won't work. But it's great for closing open dialog boxes and closing drop-down or pop-up menus.
Alt+F4	Closes the current program.	I use Alt+F, X, Enter (refer to Table 18-2) because it seems to work in more programs, but your mileage may vary. In programs where this option works, it saves you a step when compared to Alt+F, X, Enter.
Home	Moves the cursor to the beginning of the current line or list.	Ctrl+Home moves the cursor to the beginning of the document.
End	Moves the cursor to the end of the current line or list.	Ctrl+End moves the cursor to the end of the document.
Ctrl+B	Bold (usually toggles bold on or off — if it was off, this shortcut turns it on, and vice-versa).	If you're typing and your text suddenly turns bold, press Ctrl+B to turn off the bold.
Ctrl+I	Italic (usually a toggle).	Same as the bold eliminator (see earlier entry).
Ctrl+U	Underline (usually a toggle, too).	Same as bold and italic.

Odds 'n' (Sometimes Useful) Ends

Some of the keyboard shortcuts in Table 18-5 don't amount to much more than parlor tricks. But if you need to do something over and over again, memorizing one or two of these is worthwhile.

Finally, Table 18-6 contains a mercifully short list of shortcuts that may help if you spend a lot of time navigating through Windows Explorer (say, when you choose Start➪My Computer or Start➪My Documents). A great collection of Internet Explorer keyboard shortcuts is in Technique 23.

Table 18-5: Windows Shortcuts that Might Come in Handy

Key	What It Does	Timesaving Bonus Info
Windows+E	Opens Windows Explorer, starting at My Computer.	Beats Start➪My Computer when you don't want to dive for the mouse.
Windows+F	Same as Start➪Search.	In earlier versions of Windows, Search used to be called Find — thus, F.
Windows+R	Same as Start➪Run.	Many people find it faster to start Word by pressing Windows+R and then typing **winword**, instead of click-click-clicking.

Table 18-5 *(continued)*

Key	What It Does	Timesaving Bonus Info
Windows+Pause (or Break on some keyboards)	Brings up the System Properties dialog box.	This dialog box is a pain in the neck to get to. The second-fastest way is to click Start, right-click My Computer, and then choose Properties.
Shift+F10	Same as right-clicking.	Shows the context menu at the current cursor location.
Windows+L	If Fast User Switching is enabled (see Technique 8), brings up the welcome screen. If Fast User Switching is not enabled, brings up the logon screen.	This is a good boss key. If the boss is coming, hit Windows+L and your game of Solitaire (or anything else) disappears. To get it back, just log on.

Table 18-6: Windows Explorer Shortcuts

Key	What It Does
F2	Rename the selected folder or file.
F3	Bring up the Search Companion.
Backspace	Move up one folder or level.

Making Your Own Keyboard Shortcuts

Save Time By

- Creating your own hot keys to run programs, open files, create files, or bring up Web pages
- Running a PowerPoint presentation by pressing one hot key
- Starting an e-mail message with a hot key
- Using ActiveWords — the hot key capability that Windows XP should have

All the techniques in this part help you use the Windows desktop efficiently and effectively. There's one additional desktop technique you should add to your timesaving arsenal: the ability to designate your own hot key (Windows calls it a *shortcut key*) to start a program, bring up a Web page, or open a folder or file.

Unfortunately, for reasons known only to the folks in Redmond, the Windows custom hot key capability has many limitations. I tell you about those limitations — and how to work around many of them, of course! — in this technique.

At the end of this technique, I talk about an extraordinary shareware product called ActiveWords, which gives Windows outstanding hot key capabilities.

Putting Custom Hot Keys to Work for You

Windows has had a hot key capability since the heady days of Windows 95. The basic idea is pretty simple: You tell Windows that you want to use a specific key combination to run a particular program or to bring up a Web page, document, or spreadsheet. For example, you might make Ctrl+Alt+G bring up the Google Web site, or have Shift+F9 create a new invoice.

Hot keys are particularly handy in the following scenarios:

- You run the same program many times a day.
- You create a new document based on the same template many times a day.
- You update a document many times a day.
- You perform any of the preceding actions, and diving for the mouse is a pain in the neck.

Hot keys save most people enormous amounts of time. Maybe you run a consulting business, or maybe you're an attorney. Whatever you use Windows XP to do, you can come up with a hot key that saves you time. In fact, you even might want to set up hot keys for your time-management program. If you have a small business, setting up a hot key to create a new invoice or sales slip can shave lots of time off the click-click-click routine.

Knowing What You Can't Do with Hot Keys

Hot keys have some strange limitations, many of which aren't documented anywhere. Here's a short list of the most confounding restrictions:

- **You can only assign a hot key to a shortcut.** There's no way to assign a hot key to a program, document, or folder. But it's easy to assign a hot key to a *shortcut* to a program, document, or folder. Go figger.
- **Generally, you can assign hot keys only to shortcuts that are on the desktop or the Start menu.** For example, you can't add a hot key to a shortcut that's buried in a subfolder of your My Documents folder.
- **You cannot assign a hot key to anything pinned to the Start menu — which is to say, anything in the upper-left corner of the Start menu.** Again, it makes no sense. That's just the way it works.
- **You cannot assign a hot key to some icons on the Quick Launch toolbar.** For example, you can't assign a hot key to the Show the Desktop icon that Windows automatically puts on the Quick Launch toolbar.
- **You *can* assign a shortcut key to an icon on the Quick Launch toolbar or to a shortcut pinned to the Start menu, but it won't work.** Alas, you may think you have a shortcut key assigned, but the shortcut key won't work. I have no idea why.

These restrictions lead to some senseless hoop-jumping when you set up a hot key (see the next section).

After you have the hot key up and working, it keeps on working — to the point of overriding a hot key that previously existed inside the program you're using. For example, if you're using a program that recognizes Shift+F11 as a specific command, but you've told Windows that you want Shift+F11 to run the calculator, every time you press Shift+F11, Windows probably trumps the running program, and the calculator takes over (although I've seen a few situations where the program wins).

Creating and Organizing Hot Keys

From your point of view, you press a hot key, and a program runs (perhaps with a document open or a Web page loaded). Simple.

From the computer's point of view, pressing a hot key isn't so simple. Windows has to watch what you're typing and jump in whenever it detects something that could be a hot key combination — primarily odd combinations of Ctrl and Alt keys or Shift and function keys (such as F1). When Windows sees you press one of those strange key combinations, it goes out and looks for shortcuts that have that particular key combination listed as the shortcut's hot key. If Windows finds a shortcut and that particular hot key is associated with the shortcut, Windows runs the shortcut.

For example, say you set up a shortcut to the Windows Calculator and put that shortcut inside a folder on your desktop. You tell Windows that Ctrl+Alt+C is the hot key for this particular shortcut. Windows watches as you use the keyboard. When you press Ctrl+Alt+C, Windows recognizes that as a possible hot key combination. It then looks in a handful of places for shortcuts with that combination. One of the places Windows looks is inside all the folders on the desktop. So sooner or later, Windows finds that you have a shortcut to the Windows Calculator with Ctrl+Alt+C as its hot key. Ba-da-bing ba-da-boom, Windows runs the Calculator.

Generally, you have to jump through a few different hoops in order to get a hot key working:

- If a suitable shortcut doesn't already exist, you have to create one.
- You need to change the properties of the shortcut to reflect the specific hot key that you've chosen.
- You have to organize your hot keys. Well, you don't *have* to. But if you want to save time, you should.

Theoretically, shortcuts with hot keys can go anywhere on the desktop or inside any folder that sits on the desktop. I've found that it's much easier to organize and find things if I put all the shortcuts with hot keys inside a single folder on the desktop. That way, if I ever wonder what hot keys I'm using, I can look inside the folder and check out the properties for each of the shortcuts. It's also a good way to make sure I don't accidentally delete a shortcut with a hot key.

If you haven't yet created a folder devoted to hot key shortcuts, it's easy:

1. **Right-click an empty part of the Windows desktop and choose New⇨Folder.**
2. **Type** Hot Key Shortcuts **(see Figure 19-1) and press Enter.**

Setting up a proper shortcut — one that can support a hot key — can be very easy or ridiculously difficult. I run you through the gamut in the following sections.

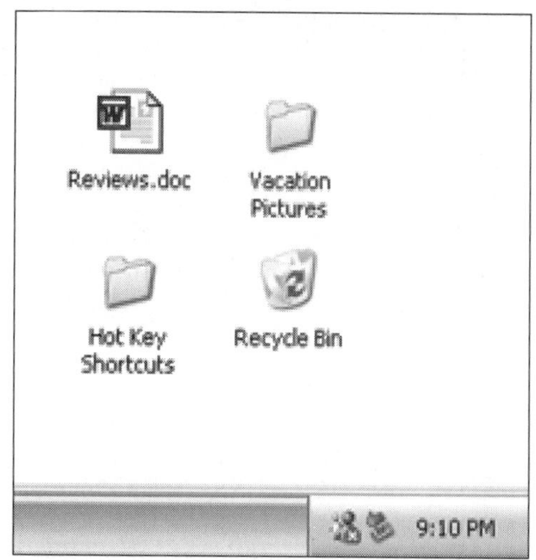

• **Figure 19-1: Create a new folder to hold your hot key shortcuts.**

Starting a program with a hot key

If you want to establish a hot key for any program on the Start⇨All Programs menu, the method is quite simple:

1. **Choose Start⇨All Programs and navigate to the program that you want to launch with a hot key.**

   For example, if you want to set up Ctrl+Alt+C to start the Windows Calculator, choose Start⇨All Programs⇨Accessories⇨Calculator, but don't actually open the Calculator.

2. **Right-click the program and choose Properties⇨Shortcut.**

   Figure 19-2 shows you the Properties dialog box for the shortcut to the Windows Calculator.

3. **Click in the Shortcut Key box.**

   If you press the Backspace key at this point, the Shortcut Key reverts to None. That's how you get rid of a hot key that's already assigned.

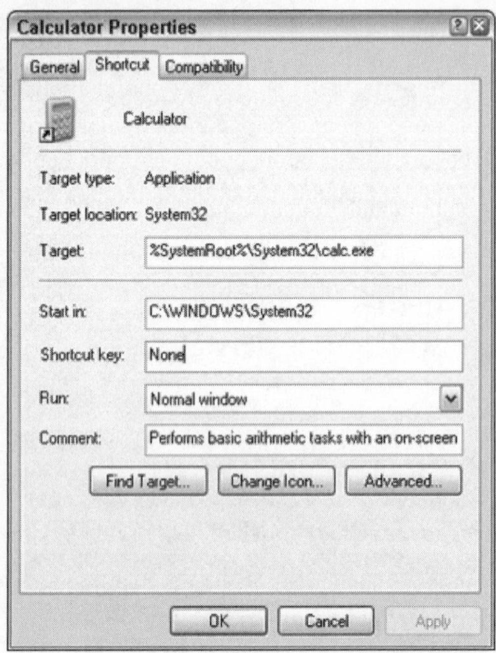

• **Figure 19-2: No hot key has been assigned for this shortcut.**

4. **Press the key or keyboard combination that you want to use as a hot key.**

By default, Windows uses Ctrl+Alt for most keyboard shortcuts. Simply type the letter that you want to associate with Ctrl+Alt, and Windows fills in the rest for you without any extra fuss or muss.

Windows recognizes several odd combinations, and a bunch of very common ones (including all the function keys), but to avoid confusion and conflict with the programs you commonly use, I recommend that you stick to the list in Table 19-1.

If you press a hot key combination that's already being used, Windows brings up the conflicting program. For example, if you already have Ctrl+Alt+P set up to launch Windows Paint, and you try to assign Ctrl+Alt+P to a different program, as soon as you press Ctrl+Alt+P, Paint starts running. There's no way to use Ctrl+Alt+P a second time.

5. **If another program suddenly appears when you type a keyboard shortcut, choose a different key combination for this program, or change the other program's hot key.**

6. **Click OK.**

   Press the hot key combination and make sure it works.

Immediately check to see whether the hot key combination you chose works. Some combinations just don't seem to work on some machines. I have a PC that refuses to recognize Shift+F12, for example. You may encounter similar problems.

TABLE 19-1: RECOMMENDED WINDOWS XP HOT KEYS

Use This	Plus	Example
Ctrl+Alt	Any letter, A thru Z	Ctrl+Alt+A
Ctrl+Alt	Any number, 0 thru 9	Ctrl+Alt+1
Ctrl+Shift	Any letter or number	Ctrl+Shift+1
Alt+Shift	Any letter or number	Alt+Shift+1
Shift	Any function key	Shift+F2
Ctrl	Any function key	Ctrl+F2
Alt	Any function key	Alt+F2

Opening a folder with a hot key

It's relatively easy to set up a hot key that starts Windows Explorer with a specific folder open and ready to go. Say you want to quickly access a subfolder of My Documents. Here's how:

1. **If you don't already have a Hot Key Shortcuts folder set up on your desktop, follow the steps in "Creating and Organizing Hot Keys" to do so.**

Although Windows doesn't absolutely require you to set up a special folder for hot key shortcuts, you end up saving more than a few gray hairs by creating the folder. It's so much easier if you put shortcuts to all files, folders, and programs that contain hot keys in one place. That way, you can quickly locate them and find out the properties of the shortcut in case you forget the hot key.

2. **Double-click the Hot Key Shortcuts folder on your desktop to open it.**

3. **Right-click anywhere inside the Hot Key Shortcuts folder, and choose New⇨Shortcut.**

   The Create Shortcut Wizard appears (see Figure 19-3).

• Figure 19-3: Use the Create Shortcut Wizard to create a shortcut to a folder.

4. **Click Browse and in the Browse for Folders dialog box, find the folder you need. Click OK.**

   In Figure 19-4, I choose the AskWoody folder.

5. **Click Next, type a name for the shortcut, and click Finish.**

   The new shortcut appears in your Hot Key Shortcuts folder.

• Figure 19-4: Pick the folder that needs a hot key.

6. **Right-click the shortcut you just created and choose Properties⇨Shortcut.**

   Windows shows you the Properties dialog box for the shortcut, shown in Figure 19-5.

7. **Click in the Shortcut Key box.**

8. **Press the key or key combination that you want to use as a hot key.**

   I recommend that you pick from the list in Table 19-1. In Figure 19-5, I used Ctrl+Alt+1.

If you press a hot key combination that's already being used, Windows brings up the conflicting program. Simply choose another key combination for this program, or change the other program's hot key.

By default, Windows uses Ctrl+Alt for most keyboard shortcuts. If you type the letter or number that you want to associate with Ctrl+Alt, Windows fills in the rest for you.

9. **Click OK.**

   Press the hot key combination and make sure it works.

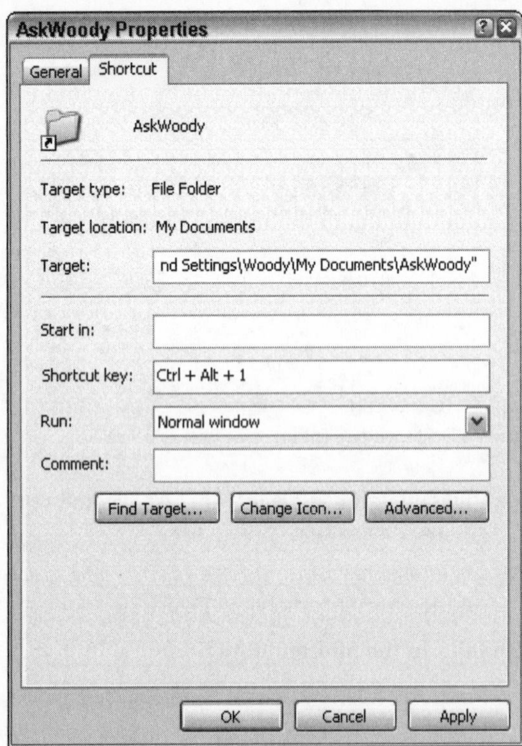

• **Figure 19-5: The properties for the shortcut to the AskWoody folder.**

Surfing to a Web site with a hot key

If you know the precise URL of a Web page, it isn't too difficult to set up a hot key that launches Internet Explorer and runs out to retrieve the page. You're well on your way to saving yourself time.

To open Internet Explorer to a specific Web address with the touch of a few simple keys, follow these steps:

1. **If you don't already have a Hot Key Shortcuts folder set up on your desktop, follow the steps in "Creating and Organizing Hot Keys," earlier in this technique.**
2. **Double-click the Hot Key Shortcuts folder on your desktop to open it.**
3. **Right-click an empty place inside the Hot Key Shortcuts folder, and choose New⇨Shortcut.**

   The Create Shortcut Wizard appears (refer to Figure 19-3).
4. **Type the exact location of the Web page in the Type the Location of the Item box.**

   Windows helps a little bit by offering to fill in Web locations you've used recently. You can select a location by using the mouse, or simply type a location such as **http://www.askwoody.com** (see Figure 19-6).

• **Figure 19-6: It's important that you get the exact address.**

To make sure you get the right address the first time, copy and paste it from Internet Explorer's Address Bar.

5. **Click Next, type a name for the shortcut, and then click Finish.**

   The new shortcut appears in your Hot Key Shortcuts folder.
6. **Right-click the shortcut you just created and choose Properties⇨Web Document.**

   Windows shows you the Properties dialog box for an Internet shortcut.

7. **Click in the Shortcut Key box.**

8. **Press the key or key combination that you want to use as a hot key.**

   I recommend that you pick from the list in Table 19-1. In Figure 19-7, I pressed the letter **A**, which resulted in a hot key of Ctrl+Alt+A.

By default, Windows uses Ctrl+Alt for most keyboard shortcuts. Simply type the letter that you want to associate with Ctrl+Alt, and Windows fills in the rest for you.

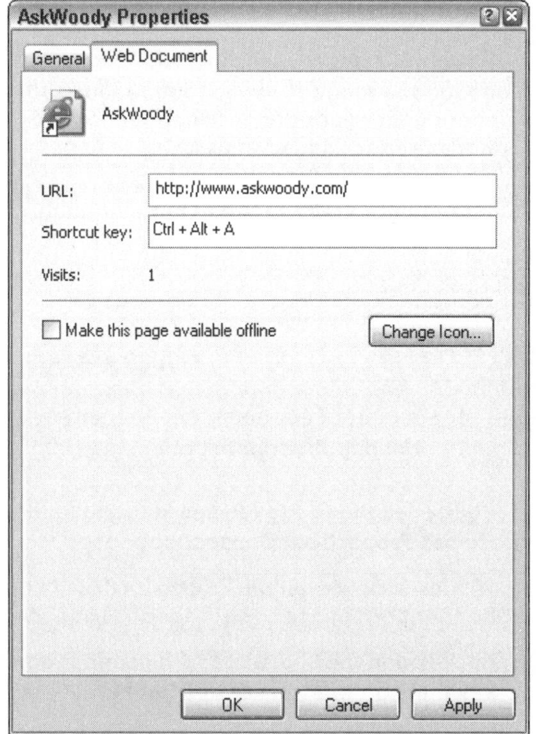

• **Figure 19-7: The www.AskWoody.com shortcut's properties.**

If you press a hot key combination that's already being used, Windows brings up the conflicting program.

9. **Choose a different key combination for this Web site, or change the other shortcut's hot key.**

To change a different shortcut's hot key, right-click the shortcut and choose Properties. Click in the Shortcut Key box, type whatever new hot key you wish, and click OK. Now you know why it's so much easier to have all your shortcuts with hot keys in one place!

10. **Click OK.**

    Press the hot key combination and make sure it works.

Sending e-mail with a hot key

You can set up a hot key that, when pressed, fires up your e-mail program and starts a fresh new message addressed to whomever you wish. You can have one key combination to start an e-mail message to your boss, another combination for a message to your mom, and a third for your stock broker — very slick. And the approach works for most major e-mail programs, including Outlook and Outlook Express. Give it a try and see if it works on your machine.

This trick can be a real godsend to people who send many e-mail messages to the same person in one day. I won't mention your boss by name.

To do it, follow the steps in the preceding section, "Surfing to a Web site with a hot key." When you get to Step 4, try this: Type **mailto:** followed immediately by the e-mail address of the recipient. For example, in Figure 19-8, I typed **mailto:woody@AskWoody.com**.

When you're done, test the hot key. A new e-mail message appears, addressed to the person on the `mailto:` line.

• **Figure 19-8: Using** `mailto:` **to create an e-mail message.**

Opening a file with a hot key

Hot keys for documents work in two ways, both of which can be major timesavers for people who work with the same document over and over again:

- If the document isn't already open, pressing the hot key starts the program associated with the document and then opens the document.
- If the document is already open, pressing the hot key directs Windows to find the document and maximizes the document so that it appears on top of all other open documents.

That's a dynamite, useful combination.

Here's the fastest, easiest way I know to make a Windows application open a specific file when you press the magical hot key:

1. **If you don't already have a Hot Key Shortcuts folder set up on your desktop, follow the steps in "Creating and Organizing Hot Keys," earlier in this technique, to do so.**
2. **Double-click the Hot Key Shortcuts folder on your desktop to open it.**
3. **Start the program that created the file.**

   For example, if you're trying to create a shortcut to an Excel spreadsheet, start Excel.
4. **Inside the program, choose File⇨Open and navigate to the document you want.**
5. **In the Open dialog box, right-click the document, and drag it to the Hot Key Shortcuts folder.**

   If you can't immediately see the Hot Key Shortcuts folder, you may need to drag the document down to the Windows taskbar, hover your mouse over the button for the Hot Key Shortcuts folder, and then drag the document into the Hot Key Shortcuts folder.
6. **Release the mouse button and choose Create Shortcuts Here.**

   Windows creates a shortcut called *Shortcut to* whatever file you've chosen. For example, the shortcut in Figure 19-9 is called Shortcut to Woodys Fruit Company Sales Log.

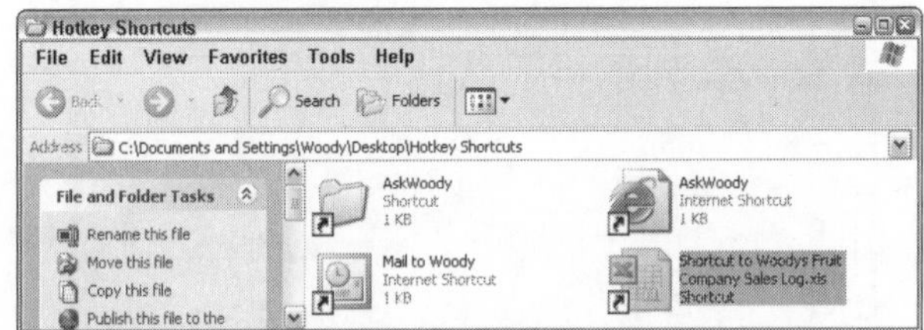

• **Figure 19-9: A shortcut created by dragging a file into the Hot Key Shortcuts folder.**

7. **Right-click the newly created shortcut and choose Properties⇨Shortcut.**

   Windows shows you the Properties dialog box for the shortcut, such as the one in Figure 19-10.
8. **Click inside the Shortcut Key box and press the key that you want to use as a hot key.**

   I recommend that you pick from the list in Table 19-1. In Figure 19-10, I used Ctrl+Alt+F.

   If you press a hot key combination that's already being used, Windows brings up the conflicting program. In that case, you have to choose a different key combination for this program, or change the other program's hot key.

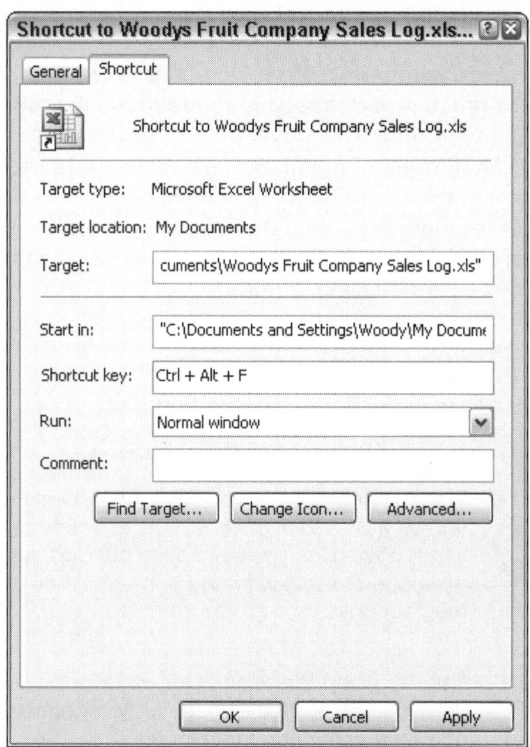

• **Figure 19-10: This keyboard shortcut opens the spreadsheet document.**

By default, Windows uses Ctrl+Alt for most keyboard shortcuts. If you type the letter that you want to associate with Ctrl+Alt, Windows fills in the rest.

9. **Click OK.**

   Press the hot key combination and make sure it works.

Creating new documents with a hot key

In Technique 16, I tell you how to create an icon that generates a new document based on an existing template every time you click it and put the icon on the Quick Launch toolbar.

With a couple of slight twists, the same approach works with hot keys. This technique can come in really handy if you have to create 10 invoices every day, or file two-dozen status reports. (Hey, some days that's how I feel.)

Here's how to set things up so that pressing a hot key combination creates a new Microsoft Office document based on an existing template. This general approach works for Word, Excel, PowerPoint, and many other applications:

1. **Start the application and create a new, blank document.**

   In all Office applications (and most other applications), you can click a New button on the main toolbar.

2. **Click the Save button.**

   The application's Save As dialog box appears.

3. **In the Save As Type box (see Figure 19-11), click any option that includes the term template. For example:**

   - In Word, click Document Template.
   - In Excel, click Template.
   - In PowerPoint, click Design Template.

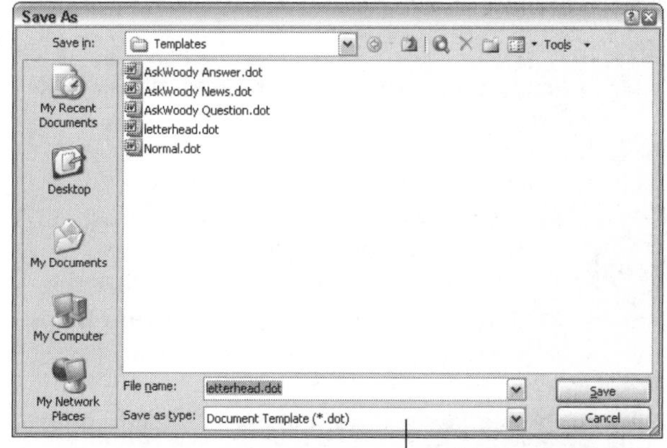

• **Figure 19-11: The fast way to put yourself in the middle of all the templates.**

4. **Right-click the template you want, and drag it to the Hot Key Shortcuts folder.**

   You may need to drag the template over the Windows taskbar, hover the mouse over the button for the Hot Key Shortcuts folder, and then drag the template into the Hot Key Shortcuts folder.

5. **Release the mouse button and click Create Shortcuts Here.**

   Windows creates a shortcut called *Shortcut to* your selected template (see Figure 19-12).

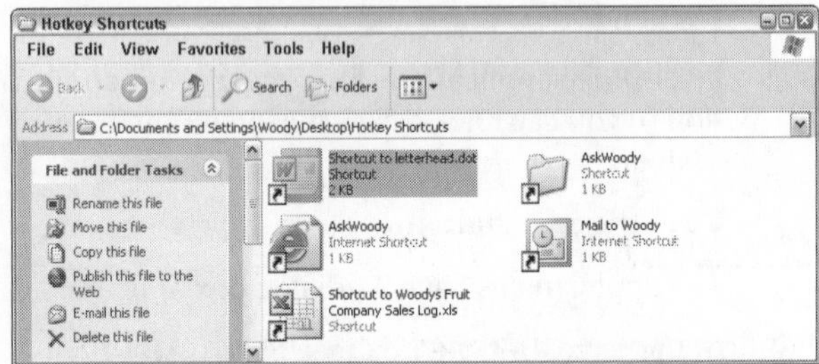

• Figure 19-12: A shortcut created by right-clicking and dragging the Letterhead template from Word into the Hot Key Shortcuts folder.

6. **Right-click the newly created shortcut and choose Properties⇨Shortcut.**

   Windows shows you the Properties dialog box for the shortcut.

7. **Click in the Shortcut Key box and press the key or key combination that you want to use as a hot key.**

By default, Windows uses Ctrl+Alt for most keyboard shortcuts. Simply type the letter that you want to associate with Ctrl+Alt, and Windows fills in the rest for you without any extra fuss or muss.

8. **If the hot key you want to use is already in use, choose another.**

9. **Click OK.**

   Press the hot key combination and make sure it works.

Running presentations with a hot key

There are many tricks for making hot keys work effectively. As an example, in this section, I show you how to set up Windows XP so that pressing Ctrl+Alt+P runs a specific PowerPoint presentation. That could come in handy if you use a portable computer for making presentations, and you don't want to go to the hassle of hooking up the mouse just to start the presentation.

Say you have a PowerPoint show called `GreatShow.pps` in a folder called `\My Documents\Presentations`. Here's how to tell Windows that you want to run the presentation every time you press Ctrl+Alt+P.

This tip works great if you have the presentation on a USB flash drive, as long as you know which drive letter corresponds to the card. Just make the shortcut point to the presentation on the flash drive.

If you're going to use a hot key to launch a PowerPoint presentation, take a few extra minutes to save the presentation as a show: Go into PowerPoint, open the presentation (which has a `.ppt` extension), choose File⇨Save As, and choose PowerPoint Show (*.pps) in the Save As File Type box. With the presentation saved as a show, you can't accidentally modify it while you're standing at the podium talking!

To set up the hot key, start by putting a shortcut to the presentation in the Hot Key Shortcut folder. To do so, follow these steps:

1. **If you don't already have a Hot Key Shortcuts folder set up on your desktop, follow the steps in "Creating and Organizing Hot Keys," earlier in this technique, to do so.**

2. **Double-click the Hot Key Shortcuts folder on your desktop to open it.**

3. **Right-click an empty place inside the Hotkey Shortcuts folder and choose New⇨Shortcut.**

   The Create Shortcut Wizard appears (refer to Figure 19-3).

4. **Click Browse, and in the Browse for Folders dialog box, click the + sign to get to your presentation; then click OK.**

   For example, I followed the path `\My Documents\Presentations\GreatShow.pps` (see Figure 19-13).

5. **Click Next, type a name for the shortcut, and click Finish.**

   The new shortcut appears in your Hot Key Shortcuts folder.

6. **Right-click the shortcut you just created and choose Properties⇨Shortcut.**

   Windows shows you the Properties dialog box for the shortcut.

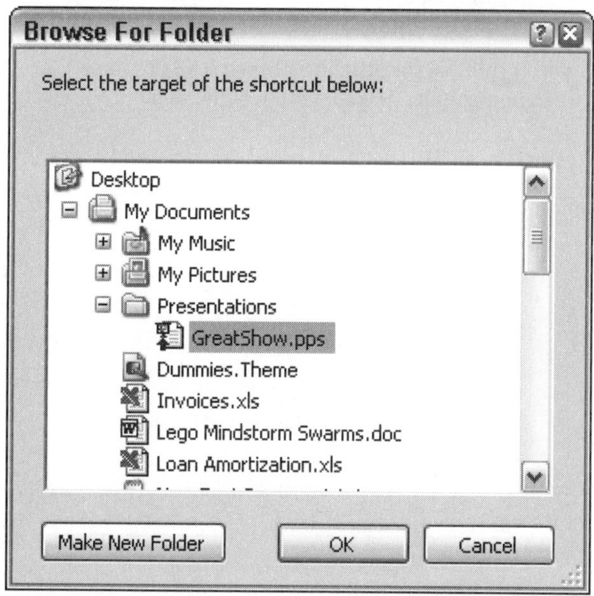

• **Figure 19-13: Pick the PowerPoint presentation.**

7. **Click in the Shortcut Key box.**

8. **Press the key combination that you want to use as a hot key.**

   I pressed P, which set Ctrl+Alt+P as the hot key combination.

By default, Windows uses Ctrl+Alt for most keyboard shortcuts. Simply type the letter that you want to associate with Ctrl+Alt, and Windows fills in the rest for you.

9. **If you press a hot key combination that's already being used, Windows brings up the conflicting program.**

   In that case, you have to choose a different key combination for this program, or change the other program's hot key.

10. **Click OK.**

    Press the hot key combination and make sure it works. In this example, you can press Ctrl+Alt+P, and the `GreatShow.pps` show springs into life.

Undoing Hot Keys

Windows hot keys work great — most of the time. Occasionally (as I mention several times in this technique), their behavior is odd, more than odd, or downright bizarre.

Sometimes, you can find solutions to these anomalies. Case in point: A friend of mine reassigned a key combination that she uses for formatting in Word. Instead of formatting text, she changed Ctrl+Shift+F10 so it started the Pinball game. After playing Pinball a few times, she decided she wanted Ctrl+Shift+F10 back for her work in Word. Cool. She reassigned the hot key to format text again and . . . Ctrl+Shift+F10 still brought up Pinball.

She tried everything she could think of to dislodge the Ctrl+Shift+F10 key combination, and nothing worked — until she restarted Windows. Then, miraculously, everything went back to normal: Ctrl+Shift+F10 did its formatting thing in Word. Pinball didn't enter the picture.

If you have trouble getting a hot key assignment "unstuck," try restarting Windows. It shouldn't be necessary. But sometimes it is.

At other times, however, finding a workaround isn't so simple. I personally have a hot key combination that creates a new spreadsheet based on an Excel template. The hot key combination works just fine — except when I'm in Excel. I have no idea why, but Excel "swallows" the hot keys. I haven't found any solution.

Hot keys are powerful, useful timesavers — when they work right. They don't always work right.

Using ActiveWords for Expanded Hot Keys

If you have read the majority of this technique (and Technique 18, as well), you have some idea of the enormous timesaving power available through Windows' native hot keys. Now I introduce you to a product that takes hot keys into a new dimension.

It's called ActiveWords, and the concept couldn't be simpler. Instead of limiting your hot keys to odd key combinations, ActiveWords lets you type just about anything and then press F8, and whatever command you associate with the active word takes effect.

For example, you can set up ActiveWords so that typing **myadd** followed by F8 "types" your name and address wherever the cursor happens to be.

More than that, you can have it bring up programs: Typing **calc** and then pressing F8 might bring up the Windows Calculator; typing **xl** and pressing F8 could start Excel.

Ah, but there's more:

- Typing **cnn** and pressing F8 can start Internet Explorer and bring up the CNN Web site.
- Typing **mb** and pressing F8 might start an e-mail message to `billg@microsoft.com`.
- Typing **inv** and pressing F8 could start Excel using your invoice template to create a new invoice.
- Typing **lthd** and pressing F8 might bring up Word with a new letter, based on your letterhead.
- Typing **Mxyzptlk** and pressing F8 could call Superman . . . well, you get the idea.

ActiveWords SE, `www.activewords.com`, is $19.95 for personal use, and you get a 60-day free trial.

Exploring Effectively

Save Time By

- Coaxing Windows into showing all your files — the first time
- Finding things quickly and reliably in Windows Explorer
- Navigating the Open and Save As dialog boxes quickly

Windows XP's Explorer provides the lens by which you see all the files and folders on your computer. It was designed to look good and feel comfortable for first-time users: When you choose Start⇨My Documents for the first time, Microsoft wants you to be able to look around and get warm and fuzzy vibes all over.

But if you want to save time, you need to take off the training wheels.

Underneath Explorer's docile exterior beats the heart of a powerful, adroit assistant. You need to push it here and poke it there, but if you spend a few minutes to apply the suggestions in this technique, you can emerge with a world-class file handler that saves you time, day after day.

Even if you never use Explorer, and you don't have time to go through this entire technique, please read the first section, which describes how (and why!) to make Windows show you filename extensions. It's the single most important tip in the whole book.

If you want to apply the changes I describe in this technique, be sure to follow the tips in the technique in order; you may get unexpected results if you apply the tips at the end before you apply the tips at the beginning. Take a few minutes right now to work through these timesaving customizations. Start with the first procedure in this technique and make Windows show you filename extensions. Then continue from there.

Making Windows Show Filename Extensions

Yes, this is the most important tip in the entire book. If you let Explorer hide filename extensions, you vastly increase your chances of being zapped by a virus or a worm. Microsoft executives — people who should know better — have been bitten by Explorer's intransigence. Don't let it bite you.

Every computer program since the dawn of time (okay, so maybe I'm exaggerating a *little* bit) puts a handful of letters on the end of each file's name, to identify which program goes with the file. For example, Microsoft Word files are branded with `.doc`; WordPerfect files usually get `.wpd`; Excel has `.xls`; Adobe Acrobat uses `.pdf`; Windows Remote Assistance uses `.msrcincident`. (No, I don't make this stuff up.)

If you save a file in WordPerfect and call it `ByeByeBallmer`, WordPerfect automatically converts the name to `ByeByeBallmer.wpd`.

The stuff that goes on the end of the filename is called a *filename extension*. Although the extension is commonly three letters long, in fact there are no hard-and-fast rules.

Certain generic types of files are inexorably bound to their extensions: `.jpg` files are JPEGs, `.gif` files are GIFs, `.pcx` files are PCXs, and I bet you can guess what `.mp3` files are called.

Somebody sitting in a dark cave in Redmond decided that filename extensions were too confusing for the average user. As a result, Windows Explorer hides filename extensions from you. They're still there, and they can definitely bite you in the posterior if you aren't careful. Renaming files can be enormously complicated if you can't see the extension (try re-naming `some.doc` to `some.txt` and you'll see what I mean).

Most importantly, nearly all the recent major viruses and worms that come in attached to e-mail messages take advantage of this blind spot to propagate: Fizzer, Klez, BugBear, Nimda, Goner, Irok, Happy99, ExploreZip, the Anna Kournikova virus, Frethem, Freelink, Myparty, Badtrans, Magistr, Navidad, Bubbleboy. ILOVEYOU, too.

When you hear of a *blended threat* virus, you can bet that a big part of the "blend" falls squarely on the shoulders of the people who decided to have Windows Explorer hide filename extensions.

Here's how it works:

- You get an e-mail message with an attached file. The file looks innocent enough. Maybe it's called, oh, `resume.txt`.
- You know that text files can't hide viruses, so you double-click `resume.txt` to see what's inside.
- A minute or two later the text file isn't open, and you wonder why your hard drive is whirring like crazy. What happened? You forgot to tell Windows Explorer to show you filename extensions. The file that you thought was called `resume.txt` is, in fact, `resume.txt.exe` — a program. But by the time you realize that you've launched a virus instead of opening a text file, it's too late: The virus is stuck in your system, and it's madly shipping out copies of itself to everyone in your address book.

That isn't a hypothetical doomsday scenario. It's how one variant of Klez actually works. An entire industry of e-mail attachment-borne viruses and worms has grown up around this one truly awful design decision: Windows doesn't show filename extensions unless you tell it to.

If you ever receive an infected file, and you're tempted to open it without knowing exactly what it is, this one quick procedure pays for the cost of this book, all by itself:

1. **Double-click any folder to open it, or choose Start⇨My Computer.**

   Windows Explorer appears.

2. **Choose Tools⇨Folder Options⇨View.**

   You see the Folder Options dialog box.

3. **Uncheck the Hide File Extensions for Known File Types check box.**

   Remarkably, unchecking this check box doesn't just force Windows to show you filename extensions inside Explorer itself. The setting actually ripples all the way through Windows and every application.

4. **Click the Apply button.**
5. **Click OK and then choose File➪Close.**

If you want to continue with the settings in this technique, leave the Folder Options dialog box open.

Customizing Explorer for Speed

I don't know why, but every time I get into Windows Explorer — by choosing Start➪My Computer or Start➪My Documents, or via some more devious means, such as right-clicking the Start menu — I'm always in a hurry. Many of the standard settings in Explorer drive me nuts: Scrolling through dozens of identical pictures of folders, for example, makes me see red.

If you ever want to jump quickly to the end of a whole bunch of files or folders, press Ctrl+End. To go back to the top, press Ctrl+Home.

You can make a handful of changes to Explorer that greatly simplify and speed up the way you work. Most of the changes are simply cosmetic, but when you strip away some of Windows' happy face, it's a whole lot easier to get to the meat.

In the next few sections, I take you through the customizations that I find most beneficial — *most* time-saving, if you will.

Unfortunately, you must apply all the changes in the order presented here. Changing one setting sometimes clobbers others.

There's a sneaky way to make sure folders and files you use all the time "rise to the top" in folder lists. Put an underscore at the front of the folder's or file's name. For example, if you always want to see your company's Human Resources folder at the top of every list, call it _Human Resources. You can use any symbol or punctuation mark, in fact.

You can use a dozen different ways to name folders (and files) so they stay in order. Using numbers at the beginning of the folder's name works well: 00 Admin, 01 Copy Edit, 02 Tech Edit, and so on. So does 2003 09 Invoices, 2003 09 Statements, 2003 10 Invoices, 2003 10 Statements, and such.

Seeing all your files and folders

Windows has this nasty habit of hiding files from you. As long as you're beyond the abject beginner phase — and you know enough to refrain from deleting files with names like `cmd.exe` or `shell32.dll` — there's no reason in the world why you can't see all the files on your computer.

If you try to get into your system folders, Windows has the audacity to show you this message:

```
These files are hidden. This folder con-
  tains files that keep your system work-
  ing properly. You should not modify its
  contents.
```

I figure that message has stopped, oh, maybe 10 people from looking at their system folders.

To make Windows show you all your files and folders without giving you a hassle about system folders

1. **If the Folder Options dialog box is not currently visible, choose Start➪My Computer, and in the My Computer window, choose Tools➪ Folder Options➪View.**

   You see the Folder Options dialog box.

2. **Check the Display the Contents of System Folders check box.**

   That bypasses the toothless warning screen.

3. **Click the Show Hidden Files and Folders radio button.**

   These are files and folders with the so-called "hidden attribute" set.

4. **Uncheck the Hide Protected Operating System Files (Recommended) check box.**

   Windows tosses up a warning saying that you shouldn't mess around with system files, and asking whether you're sure you want to make them visible.

5. **Click Yes, dear.**

   Your Folder Options dialog box now looks like the one shown in Figure 20-1.

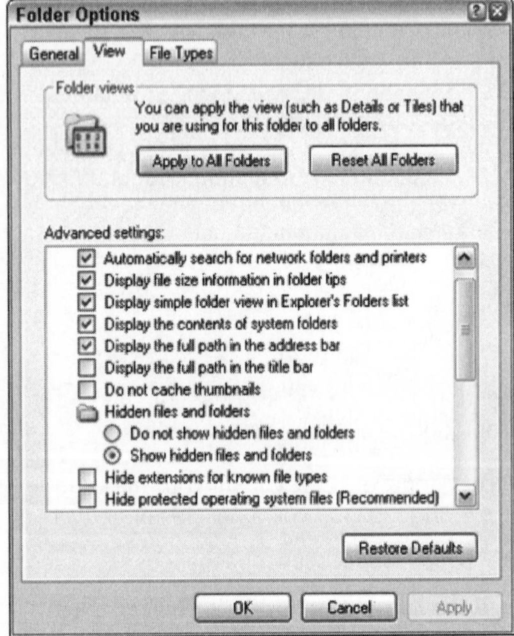

• **Figure 20-1: Make Windows show you all your files and folders.**

6. **Click Apply in the lower-right corner.**
7. **If you want to continue with the settings in this technique, leave the Folder Options dialog box open. Otherwise, click OK, and then choose File⇨Close to get out of Windows Explorer.**

Seeing pathnames in Explorer's title bar

Windows Explorer lets you traverse folders within folders within folders, buried so deep you may never get out. But it doesn't give you one, simple place to look that tells you precisely where you are.

Usually, the Explorer title bar tells you basically nothing. But if you make one small change in the Folder Options dialog box, though, Explorer's title bar suddenly tells you precisely where you are and how to get there — the folder's path (see Figure 20-2).

• **Figure 20-2: Now the title bar tells you where that Outlook folder is located.**

To make Explorer use its title bar to show you the full path to the current folder

1. **If the Folder Options dialog box is not currently visible, choose Start⇨My Computer, and in the My Computer window, choose Tools⇨Folder Options⇨View.**

   You see the Folder Options dialog box; refer to Figure 20-1.

2. **Check the Display the Full Path in the Title Bar check box.**

   That makes Explorer display all the information shown in Figure 20-2.

   Your Folder Options dialog box looks like the one in Figure 20-3 — which is my preferred set of Explorer Folder Options settings.

3. **Click OK, and then choose File⇨Close.**

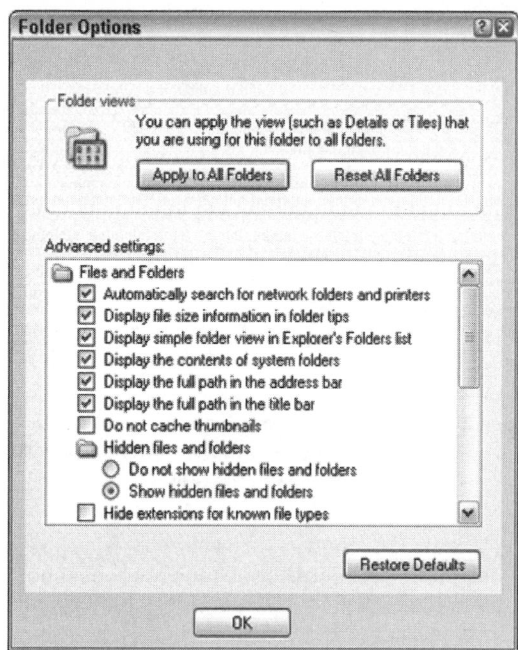

• **Figure 20-3: Make Explorer show you the full path in the title bar.**

Choosing the Right View

Explorer offers you many options for viewing your folders and files, and you can change the view in each individual folder. To switch among views, open the folder you want to change, click View, and choose from one of these:

- **Filmstrip:** This option, shown in Figure 20-4, shows you thumbnails of all your pictures across the bottom, and lets you click through your pictures to see an enlargement of the selected picture. This view is the fastest, easiest way to work with pictures.

Filmstrip view is only available inside folders that are associated with a Pictures or Photo Album template. See the "Setting Folders' Behavior" section, later in this technique.

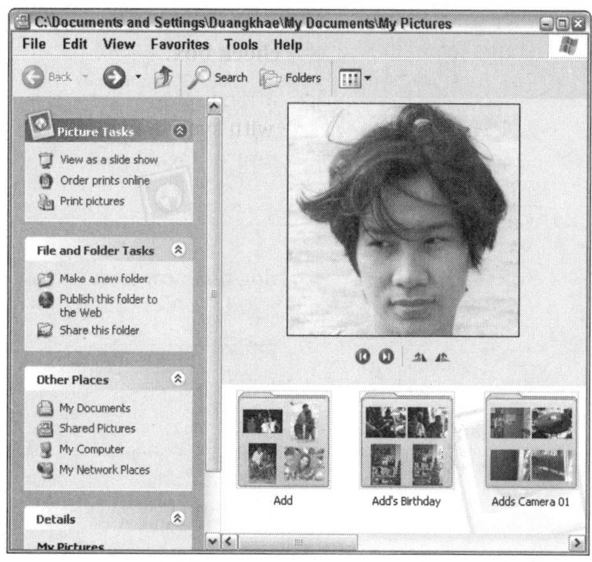

• **Figure 20-4: Filmstrip view lets you rotate pictures with a click.**

- **Thumbnails:** The only reason to use this view (shown in Figure 20-5) is if you really need to work with a lot of pictures, all at the same time. Even then, Filmstrip view or Details view may help you work more efficiently.

• **Figure 20-5: I rarely use Thumbnails view.**

- **Tiles:** This option (shown in Figure 20-6) uses large icons to represent different kinds of files, folders, and devices. The icons are generic (all picture files, for example, have the same icon), and for each file, you have enough room for three lines of description.

• **Figure 20-6: Tiles view takes up a lot of screen real estate, but it has some detail.**

- **Icons:** This option (shown in Figure 20-7), puts small icons next to each file or folder name. Looks pretty, but makes finding things difficult.

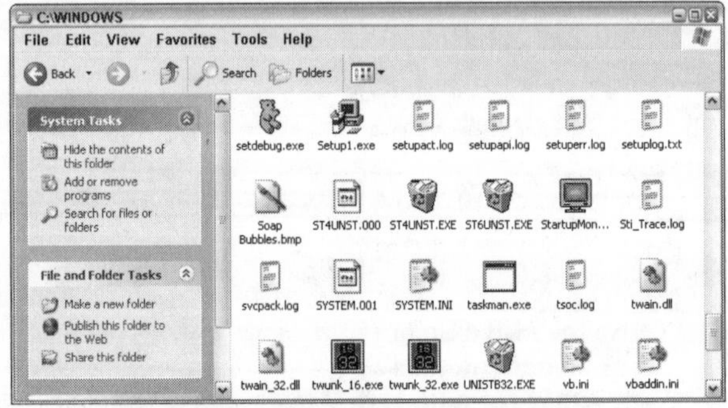

• **Figure 20-7: Icons view puts a pretty face on everything — but where's the beef?**

- **List:** This view (shown in Figure 20-8) puts a workmanlike list of names on-screen, but the horizontal scroll bar (which only lets you scan from left to right) and the lack of any information about the files makes this a limited view.

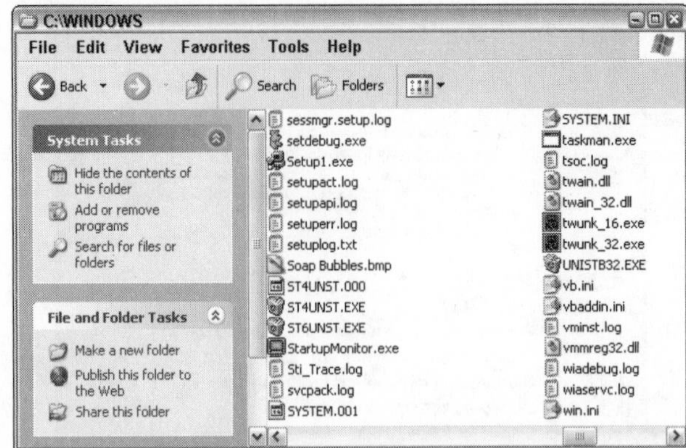

• **Figure 20-8: List view shows a lot of filenames, but nothing else — and the horizontal scroll bar drives many people nuts.**

- **Details:** This option (see Figure 20-9 in the next section) ranks as the view of choice in almost all situations. It shows you important information about your files and folders, and you can customize the information in no time at all (see the next section, "Working with Details view").

I find that most people work best with Details view in almost all their folders — the only significant exceptions being My Computer (which looks gorgeous in Tiles view) and various media folders. In the following section, I explain how to set up Explorer to use a modified version of Details view in precisely this way.

If you're tired of Windows Explorer's glamorous face and you're ready to get down to work, here's a sparse overview of what you gotta do:

1. Modify Details view in one folder to show you the specific details that you can use.
2. When you're happy with the details that appear, apply that set of details to all your folders.
3. Go back and change the settings of specific folders — primarily media folders — to use other views.

In the rest of this section, I show you what to do in more detail.

Working with Details view

Here's how to customize the Details view so it shows you the details you want to see:

1. **Choose Start⇨My Documents.**

   For most people, the My Documents folder is a good place to try out different details.

2. **Choose View⇨Details.**

   Windows Explorer switches to Details view (see Figure 20-9).

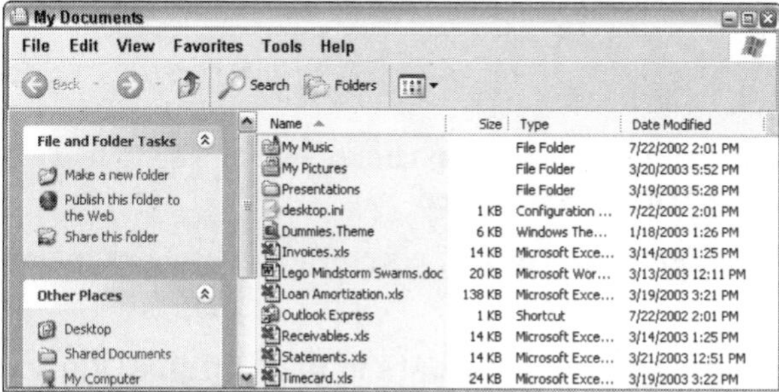

• **Figure 20-9: The standard Details view.**

3. **Right-click one of the column headings (such as Name) and click More.**

   The Choose Details dialog box appears (shown in Figure 20-10).

4. **Check the boxes next to the details you want to see.**

Think of these details as values you can sort by: name, size, or date. When you want to get the right file, fast, the first time, the details lead the way.

You rarely look for a file based on the Type column, simply because the column contains such bizarre names. If I'm looking for a Word `.doc` file, my natural inclination is to scan for `.doc` or, at worst, W. To me, it's completely counter-intuitive to look under M — for "Microsoft Word Document" — right next to the `.xls` Excel spreadsheets and `.ppt` PowerPoint presentations. Still, I include the File Type column in the details that I use, and suggest you do, too. Once in a blue moon, it helps. When all else fails, look at the icon on the left.

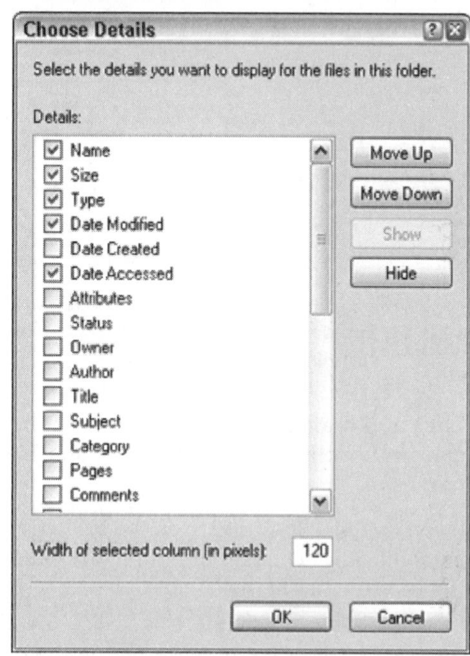

• **Figure 20-10: Pick which columns you want to see in Details view.**

In Figure 20-10, you can see the details that I use: Name, Size, Type, Date Modified, and Date Accessed.

5. **Use the Move Up and Move Down buttons to arrange the details in the order that helps you find files (or folders or programs) the fastest.**

   The order I prefer is Name, Size, Date Accessed, Date Modified, and then Type.

See the box at the bottom that says Width of Selected Column (in Pixels)? Don't bother with it. I show you a much better way in the next few steps.

6. **Click OK.**

   Windows Explorer comes back with your chosen details, in the sequence you specified (see Figure 20-11).

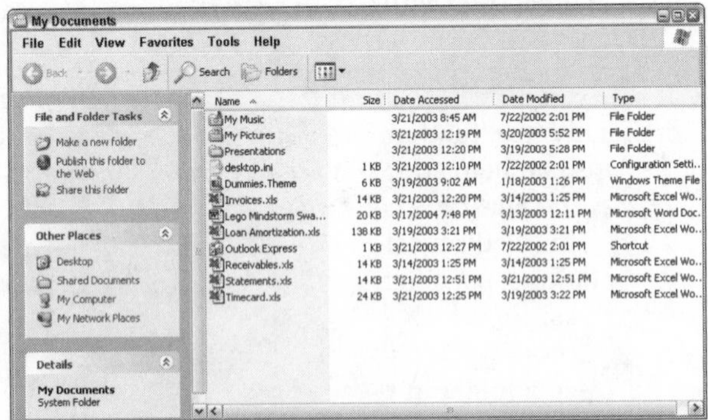

• **Figure 20-11: Explorer is set up for quick, powerful scanning.**

7. **Click and drag the vertical bars separating the column headings to make the columns wider or narrower.**

   If you double-click directly on the bar, Explorer automatically adjusts the width to accommodate the widest entry in the column.

Alternatively, you can hold down the Ctrl and Alt keys, and press the + sign on the number pad, and every column adjusts to accommodate the widest entry.

If you've never used Details view columns to sort a list of files, you should try it now. If you click the Date Modified column heading, for example, Explorer sorts the entire list, with folders on top and files on the bottom, by the date the file (or folder) was last modified, oldest date first. Click Date Modified again, and Explorer reverses the sort order, with newest date first. When you're done, click Name to set the sort order back to normal.

When you're satisfied with the list of details, tell Explorer to use these specific details in all its folders:

1. **Choose Start⇨My Computer, and in the My Computer window, choose Tools⇨Folder Options⇨View.**

   You see the Folder Options dialog box (refer to Figure 20-1).

2. **Click the Apply to All Folders button.**

   Explorer warns you about the consequences of your actions. Don't worry — I don't know what this dialog box means, either.

3. **Click OK.**

4. **Click OK and then choose File⇨Close to leave Windows Explorer.**

   Your changes take effect when you open Explorer again.

Returning crucial folders to their original views

If you have followed the steps in the previous section and set all your folders in Details view, you may want to follow another one of my strong recommendations: Spend a minute or two and turn a very few folders back to their original views. That way you see your pictures in Filmstrip view, for example.

To return some folders to their native views, follow these steps:

1. **Choose Start⇨My Computer⇨View⇨Tiles.**

   My Computer simply looks and works better in Tiles view.

2. **Choose Start⇨My Pictures.**

   Your My Pictures folder appears in Details view.

3. **Choose View⇨Filmstrip (or Thumbnails, if you prefer Thumbnails view).**

   Done.

Converting one folder to Filmstrip (refer to Figure 20-4) or Thumbnails view this way is easy. If you have only one folder with pictures in it, you're done. But if you have a lot of folders with pictures, there's also a reasonably fast, not-the-least-bit-obvious, way to convert all of them to Filmstrip view. Follow these steps:

1. **Open My Documents and click the Folders button on the toolbar.**

   You see a folder tree on the left, and the current folder is selected.

2. **Press the Down arrow key on your keyboard to move to the next folder.**

   Explorer shows you the folder in Details view (see Figure 20-12).

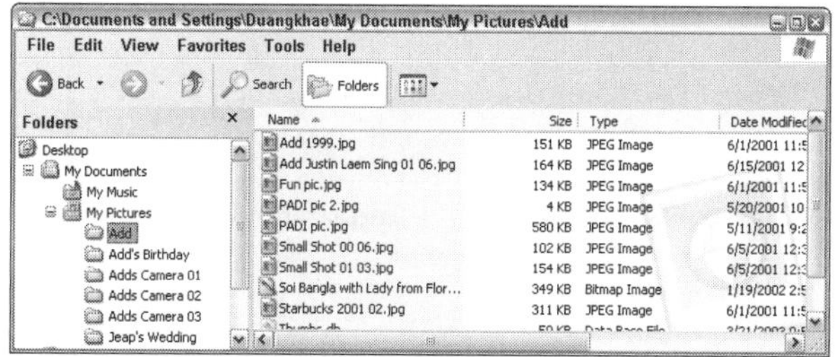

• **Figure 20-12: A picture folder in Details view.**

3. **Choose View➪Filmstrip (or Thumbnails, if you prefer).**

   The current folder is converted to Filmstrip (or Thumbnails) view (refer to Figure 20-4).

4. **Repeat Steps 2 and 3 to quickly move through all the folders and convert them to Filmstrip (or Thumbnails) view.**

   If you have folders inside of folders, press the Right arrow key on the keyboard to make them visible and then continue with the Down arrow.

You can use this same quick approach to convert groups of music files to Tiles view or to apply other specific views to groups of folders.

If the Filmstrip view isn't available in a particular folder's View list, see the section, "Setting Folders' Behavior," later in this technique.

Sorting files by group

Windows Explorer includes a rudimentary capability for grouping files together. If you group by name, for example, Explorer puts a big letter A above the files whose names start with A, then B, and so on.

Yawn.

I've found one situation, though, where showing files in groups can help speed up my scanning — and it involves the File Type column, which I begrudgingly included in the discussion of Details view earlier in this technique, specifically so that this timesaving trick works:

1. **Open a folder in Details view.**

   This trick works particularly well if you're looking at a folder with several different kinds of files.

2. **Click the File Type column.**

   The list of files gets sorted by File Type.

3. **Choose View➪Arrange Icons By➪Show In Groups.**

   Explorer breaks up the list visually, based on File Type (see Figure 20-13). Although the specific File Type itself may be a bit obscure, the fact that you can look at groups of files of similar type frequently makes it easier to pinpoint the file you want.

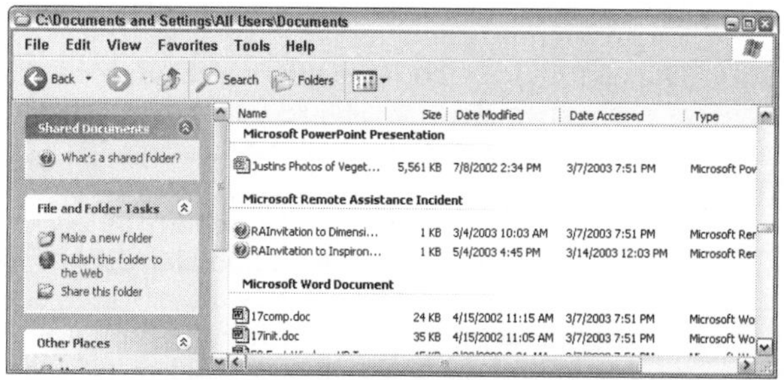

• **Figure 20-13: Viewing by File Type can make it easier to rummage around long lists of files.**

Setting Folders' Behavior

Windows Explorer uses a fixed set of folder templates to control what you see. For example, the folder templates control

- The actions available in the folder's task pane (such as View as a Slide Show, Order Prints Online, or Play All Videos).
- The views available (specifically Filmstrip view).
- How many pictures can be superimposed on the folder in Thumbnails or Filmstrip view (one or four).
- The background graphic (a small, lightly colored picture in the lower-right corner) that appears when you open the folder.

In addition, when you change the template, Explorer automatically changes the View setting inside the folder.

You can waste a lot of time futzing with these settings, but every time-conscious Windows user needs to know two things:

- If you can't get a folder's contents to appear in Filmstrip view (say you click View, and Filmstrip isn't available), you need to change the folder's template to Pictures or Photo Album.
- You can put your own picture on a folder to help you move through folders quickly and visually. The picture you choose appears in Thumbnails and Filmstrip view.

To change a folder's behavior

1. **Use Windows Explorer to open the folder.**
2. **Right-click any blank area inside the folder and choose Customize This Folder.**

   The folder's Customize dialog box appears (see Figure 20-14).

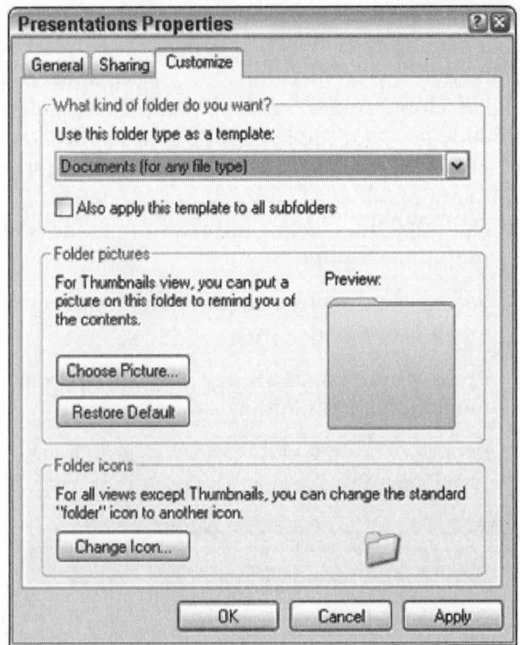

• Figure 20-14: Customize the appearance of the folder and its behavior.

Not all folders have Customize This Folder as a right-click option. Sometimes you can customize the appearance of the folder by right-clicking and choosing Properties⇨Customize. Sometimes, for reasons known only to Microsoft, you can't even do that — no Customize tab is in the folder's Properties dialog box.

3. **Choose a template from the Use This Folder Type as a Template box.**

   In particular, if you want to see the contents of the folder as a Filmstrip, you must choose either Pictures or Photo Album.

4. **If you want to put a picture on the folder, click Choose Picture and find the picture you want.**

   The picture appears when you view the folder itself in Thumbnails or Filmstrip view.

5. **Click OK.**

The view inside the folder is now changed.

There is only one difference between the Pictures and Photo Album templates: When you click OK with the Pictures template, Explorer goes into Thumbnails view. When you click OK with the Photo Album template, you go into Filmstrip view.

Copying Files Quickly

If you copy files into the same location over and over again, you can save time by putting the destination on the right-click Send To menu. That way, you select the file(s) or folder(s) you want to copy, right-click, choose Send To, and the destination you want appears. In Figure 20-15, I use this approach to copy the `Reviews.doc` file to the Shared Backup folder, which is a subfolder in my Shared Documents folder.

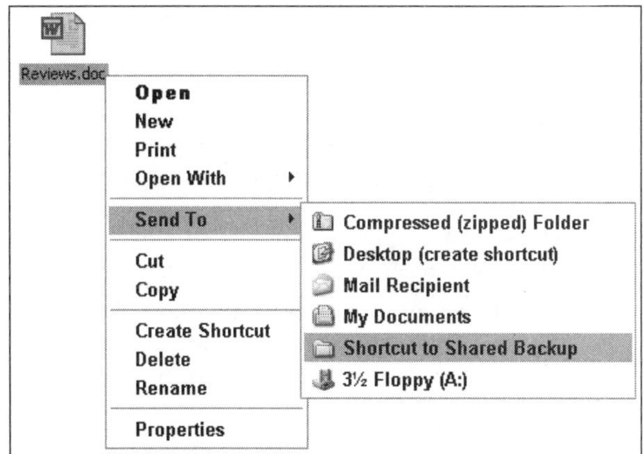

• Figure 20-15: Copying files and folders is a right-click away.

Here's how to put your commonly used folder on the Send To menu:

1. **In Windows Explorer, locate the folder you want to copy things into.**

In this example, I go to the `Shared Documents\Shared Backup` folder.

2. **Right-click the folder and choose Copy.**

3. **Right-click the Start button and choose Explore.**

This quick trick gets you to the Send To folder.

4. **Immediately above the Start Menu folder, on the left, click Send To.**

That puts you inside your Send To folder (see Figure 20-16).

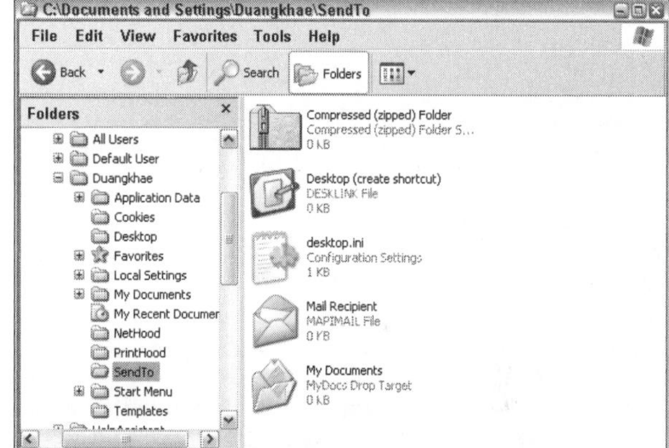

• Figure 20-16: The fast way to your Send To folder.

5. **Right-click a blank spot in the Send To folder and click Paste Shortcut.**

See Figure 20-17.

6. **Choose File⇨Close to leave Windows Explorer. You should also File⇨Close out of the originating folder.**

When you right-click a file or folder, your chosen destination appears in the Send To listing (refer to Figure 20-15).

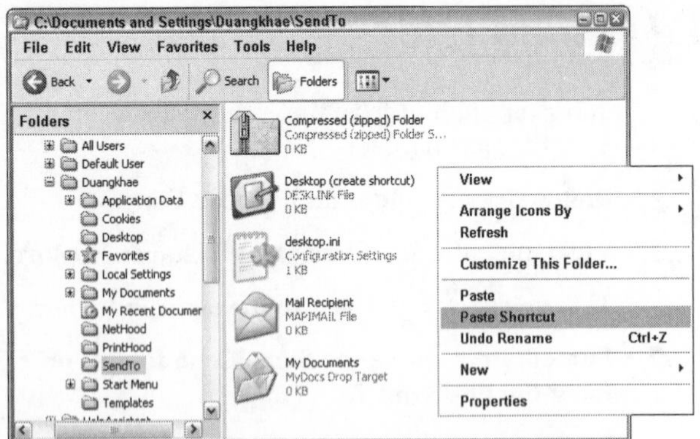

• Figure 20-17: Paste a shortcut to your intended destination inside the Send To folder.

Zipping

Zipped (or "compressed") folders contain files that have been squished down in size. That may sound a bit odd, but the technology has been around for many years. A very large percentage of all the files available on the Internet, for example, are zipped. Zipping involves scanning a file to determine what chunks are duplicated, and then replacing the duplicated entries with much smaller pointers. For example, you could scan "How much wood would a woodchuck chuck if a woodchuck could chuck wood?" and perform the substitution <1>=" wood"<2>="chuck". The resulting phrase, "How much<1> would a<1><2><2>if a<1><2>could <2><1>?" is considerably smaller than the original. Wood.

In practice, file compression methods are much more complex, but you can probably understand why a typical text file can be compressed to half of its original size.

Windows XP makes it easy to zip a file and stick it in a special kind of folder called a zipped (or compressed) folder. Simply select the file or files that you want to zip, right-click and choose Send To⇨Compressed (zipped) folder. Although Windows goes to great lengths to hide the fact from you, the compressed folder is actually a file with a `.zip` filename extension. If you send the folder to a friend, attaching it to an e-mail message, your friend receives a `.zip` file.

Changing Filename Associations

From time to time, really obnoxious programs take over your filename associations. One day, you double-click `.gif` files, and they open in the Windows Picture and Fax Viewer, as they should. The next day, they open with Billy Bob's Giffy Deluxe Pro.

What happened?

Chances are good that you have recently installed a new program and, whether you gave your permission or not, that program took over the `.gif` filename extension.

You can easily see which program is associated with a specific filename extension and change the association, too, should Billy Bob's Giffy Deluxe Pro take over:

1. **Open Windows Explorer.**

   For example, choose Start⇨My Computer.

2. **Choose Tools⇨Folder Options⇨File Types.**

   Explorer displays the Folder Options dialog box, shown in Figure 20-18.

3. **Click the filename extension that's been shanghaied, and then click Change.**

   Explorer brings you the Open With dialog box, shown in Figure 20-19.

4. **Pick the program you want to associate with this filename extension, and then click OK.**

If the program you want isn't listed, click the Browse button and find it.

• **Figure 20-18: Associating filename extensions with specific programs.**

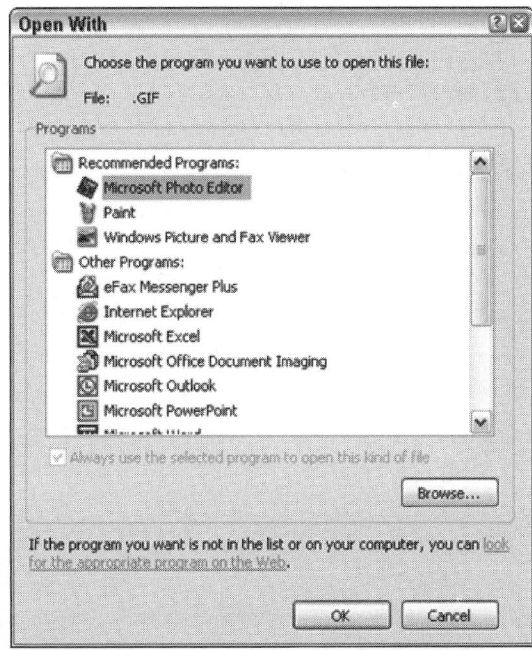

• **Figure 20-19: Choose the program you prefer here.**

Renaming Files En Masse

Do you have a bunch of files with such scintillating names as `DSCN1886.JPG`, `DSCN1887.JPG`, and so on?

You could rename these files individually, but chances are that you have better things to do, like watching grass grow. Windows Explorer has a limited ability to rename groups of files like that:

1. **Select the files you wish to rename.**

   You can use Ctrl+click to select individual (noncontiguous) files, or click at the beginning of a bunch, hold down the Shift key, and click the last of the bunch (see Figure 20-20).

2. **Right-click the first of the bunch, choose Rename, and type in a name that identifies the whole bunch.**

   In Figure 20-20, I right-clicked the `DSCN1886.JPG` file, choose Rename, and typed **Adds Party.jpg**.

• **Figure 20-20: Select a group of files.**

3. **Press Enter.**

   Explorer renames the first file `Adds Party.jpg`, as expected. It calls the second one `Adds Party (1).jpg`, then `Adds Party (2).jpg`, and so on. See Figure 20-21.

   No, there's no way to change this very rigid naming convention. But any identification at all is better than `DSCN1886.JPG`, eh?

You can undo the naming, one file at a time, by pressing Ctrl+Z.

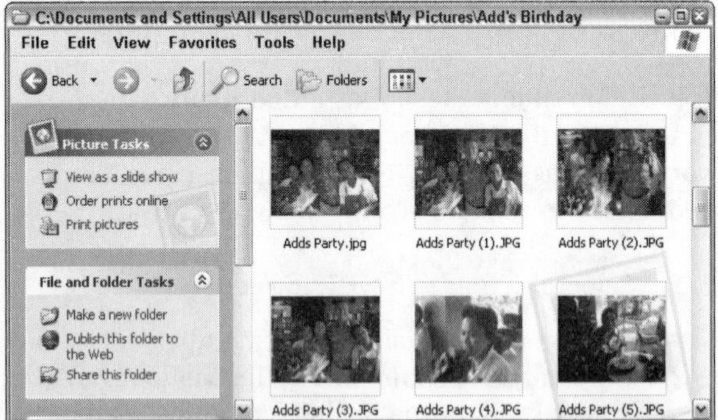

• **Figure 20-21: Giving multiple files user-friendly names.**

Customizing the Open and Save As Dialog Boxes

Several Windows applications, including Windows Media Player, Notepad, WordPad, and Paint, use the standard Windows dialog boxes for Open and Save As.

(None of the Microsoft Office applications use the standard dialog boxes, nor do any of the major applications from other companies.)

If you use Notepad, WordPad, or Paint extensively, you may be able to save yourself some time by customizing the Places bar on the left side of the dialog boxes. The idea is you replace Microsoft's places with places that *you* frequently use.

To customize the Places bar on the left side of these dialog boxes, follow these steps:

1. **Download and install TweakUI.**

   Full details are in Technique 5.

2. **Choose Start➪All Programs➪PowerToys for Windows XP➪TweakUI.**

   The TweakUI About screen appears.

3. **On the left, click Common Dialogs.**

   See Figure 20-22.

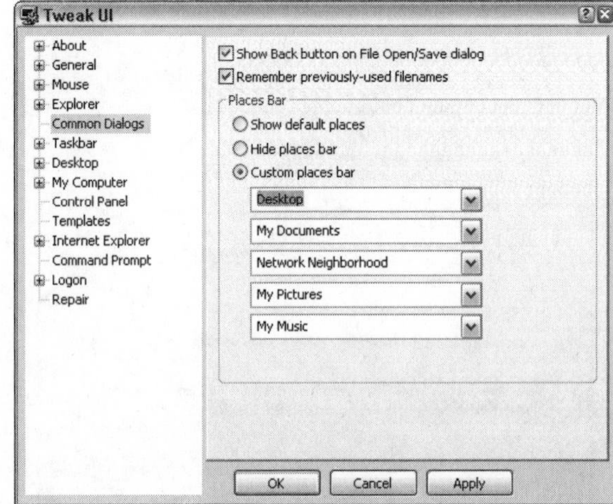

• **Figure 20-22: Use TweakUI to modify the Places bar on the left side of common dialog boxes.**

4. **On the right, choose the locations you want to appear in the customized Places bar.**

5. **Click OK.**

   The Places bar now looks something like Figure 20-23.

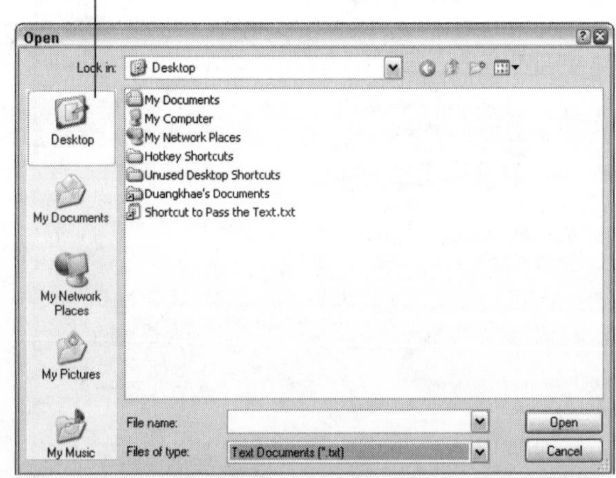

• **Figure 20-23: The Open dialog box with a customized Places bar.**

Finding the Files You Want Fast

Save Time By

- Cutting through the cute interface
- Searching intelligently
- Recycling searches
- Saving time with Copernic

Rover, the Search Companion, may look cute, but he'll eat into your time. No, I don't have anything against dogs, even ones who tell me they want to "play fetch" when I really want to find a file quickly. To tell the truth, Rover isn't the problem. The problem lies with the way Windows XP puts layers of time-eating feel-good interference over the top of its search engine.

Microsoft has made search products for years: MSN Search on the Internet, Rover's search on the desktop, Word and Excel search in the Office arena, and the Windows Indexing Service, the mother of all PC search engines. One minor problem. With the possible exception of Word/Excel search in Office 2003, not one of Microsoft's search tools comes close to its competitors. The Windows Indexing Service, in particular, has been riddled with bugs for many years.

As this book went to press, rumors appeared almost daily about Microsoft's much-anticipated entry into the search engine market. Everything I've seen reinforces the fact that the new search capability — both on the desktop, and on the Internet — will be a "version 1.0" product, in the pejorative sense of the term. If the Redmondians remain true to form, that means we have at least one, and possibly two, full revisions ahead before Microsoft irons out the kinks. In the interim, the nostrums in this technique can serve you well.

If you want to search the Internet, this technique isn't the place to look. Even though Windows Search claims to run on the Internet — and it does, to a point — don't waste time with the Microsoft-bound version. Go for the real thing, Google, which I talk about in Technique 24.

Before you start thinking about searching for files, you need to be able to see the full filename. Make sure you follow the steps in Technique 20 and make Windows show you filename extensions.

Speeding Up Searches

You might think the best way to speed up your searches involves some arcane setting, or checking the box that the Search Companion frequently displays asking if you want to make future searches faster.

Wrong.

The best way to speed up searches is to make searching for files and folders the right way, for the right thing, easier for you to do the first time.

Starting with advanced searches

If you've used Windows Search and come away confused, there's a reason why. The options you have to wade through can be obfuscating and misleading.

Working directly with the search engine is far better. Microsoft calls it Advanced Search. I call it getting rid of the glitz.

To do so, follow these steps:

1. **Choose Start⇨Search.**

   Windows Explorer brings up the Search Companion.

2. **Click Change Preferences.**

   The Search Companion asks How Do You Want to Use Search Companion? (See Figure 21-1.)

3. **Click Change Files and Folders Search Behavior.**

   You see the settings in Figure 21-2.

4. **Check the Advanced — Includes Options to Manually Enter Search Criteria. Recommended for Advanced Users Only button.**

5. **Click OK.**

   At this point, you're ready to start using Windows Search.

• **Figure 21-1: Taking off the training wheels.**

• **Figure 21-2: Search settings.**

Nixing the mutt

Rover is Windows' anointed Search Companion (whom you can see in most of the figures in this technique).

You might think that having Rover around slows down your searches. He (she? it?) won't. The animation itself doesn't slow down your computer. But the distraction might cause you to waste time. Take Rover, change him, or leave him, with impunity. The Rover overhead is sorely overstated. Say that ten times fast.

To change Rover to another Companion (or get rid of him completely), follow these steps:

1. **Choose Start⇨Search.**

   If you made the change to Advanced Search, which I describe in the preceding section, you see the search criterion in Figure 21-3.

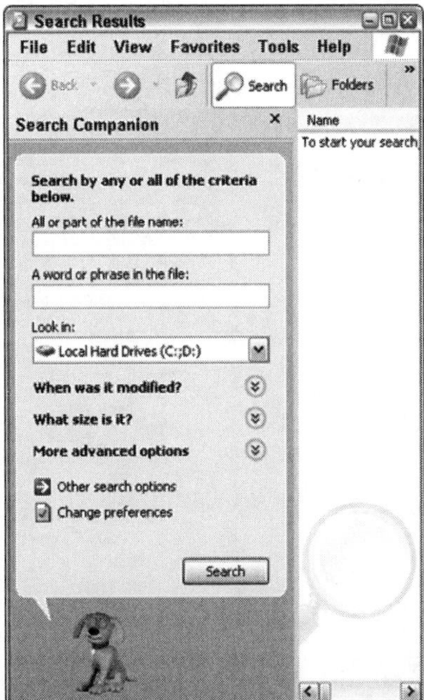

• **Figure 21-3: Advanced Search — without the training wheels.**

2. **Click Change Preferences.**
3. **If you want to replace Rover, click With a Different Character. If you want to get rid of Rover and don't want another character to replace him, click Without an Animated Screen Character.**

   If you decide to replace Rover, step through the Rogue's Gallery by pressing the Back and Next buttons.

4. **Click OK.**

Engaging Your Brain Before the Search

All the search engines in the world can't help until you have your act together. You can save a lot of time and frustration by following these suggestions:

- **Visualize exactly what you want.** Don't search for *lightning* if you're looking for *lightning bug.*
- **Work with the best tools.** If you're looking for a Word document, Excel spreadsheet, or Outlook message, use the search tools inside Word (which are quite extensive), Excel, or Outlook (which can be frustratingly limited). They're honed specifically for the task. Windows Search, out of the box, doesn't even look inside Outlook or Outlook Express's collections of e-mail messages.
- **Narrow down the search ahead of time.** If you're looking for a file that you last opened a few days ago, why have Search look at all files?
- **Stay flexible.** If you keep typing the same search string, you keep getting back the same answers — guaranteed. Any idea how many different ways you can spell "Shakespeare" — correctly?
- **Use every trick in the book.** *This* book, of course.

Running a Simple Advanced Search

Here's how to run an advanced search for a file, if you know part of the filename. I assume that you made the change mentioned in the first steps in this technique, so you're using Windows advanced search:

1. **Choose Start⇨Search.**

   The advanced Search pane appears (refer to Figure 21-3).

2. **Click the More Advanced Options down arrow.**

   You see the options in Figure 21-4.

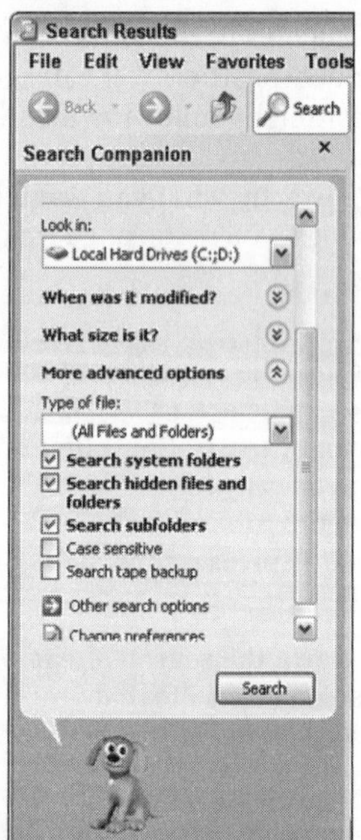

• **Figure 21-4: An important option.**

3. **Check the Search Hidden Files and Folders box.**

If you leave this box unchecked (Windows doesn't check it for you), you may miss a file that you thought you'd get. For example, Office stores the templates that you create in hidden folders.

4. **In the All or Part of the File Name box, type as much of the name as you can remember.**

   Use the examples in Table 21-1 as a guide.

5. **Click Search.**

   Windows returns the results of its search in the right side of the window.

6. **To open one of the chosen files, double-click it. To move Explorer to the folder that holds the file, right-click and choose Open Containing Folder (see Figure 21-5).**

7. **When you're done, choose File⇨Exit to leave Explorer.**

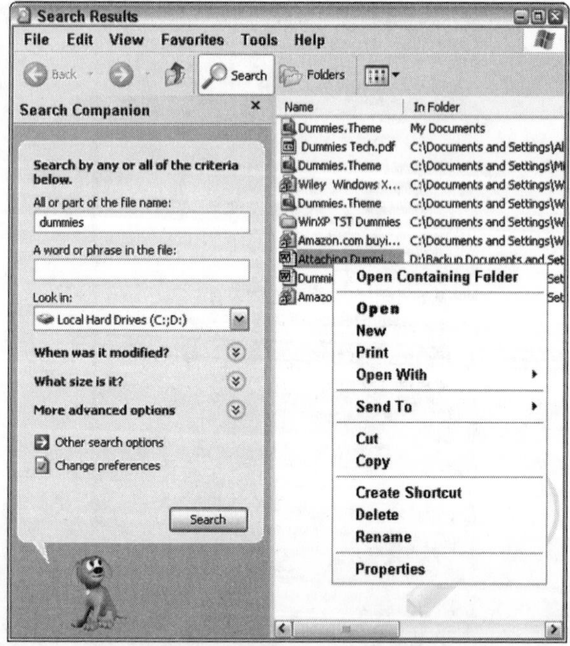

• **Figure 21-5: Right-click to move to the found file's folder.**

Table 21-1: Filename Matches and Misses

When You Type	Search Finds	But Search Does Not Find
`dummies`	`more dummies.doc`	`dummie.doc`
`timesaving`	`timesaving techniques.ppt`	`time saving.ppt`
`fax`	`faxes.xls`	`fa.xls`

Searching for Contents and Metadata

Windows can look for text inside files. It can also look for *metadata* — the pieces of text associated with a file, and which are used to describe its contents. For example, many music files have the name of the artist attached to them. Most Office documents include the name of their authors as metadata.

If you're looking for a file based on its contents or its metadata, use the application associated with that kind of file to search for the file. This method is almost always faster, easier, and more efficient.

Here are some example searches and the best ways to do them:

- **If you want to search for an Office document, use Word or Excel.** In Office XP and Office 2003, you can use Word, Excel, or Outlook to search for Outlook e-mail messages — and many people find that using Word is the easiest and fastest of the three.
- **To search for a file in your Media Library, use Media Player (choose Media Library⇨Search).** If you have media files that aren't yet in the Media Library, add them first (Tools⇨Search for Media Files).
- **To search for HTML (formatted Internet) files or even `.txt` text files (if you have Office XP or Office 2003), use Word.** Putting together searches the Word way is much easier — although, surprisingly, you can't store and reuse searches. If you want to use searches of that sort, see "Saving and reusing searches," later in this technique.

With that as a warning, you might want to use Windows Search to look for simple strings, particularly if you're not sure what kind of file you're looking for — maybe you want to look in Word documents and Help files, too. Here's how:

1. **Choose Start⇨Search.**

   The Advanced Search pane appears (refer to Figure 21-3).

2. **Type the text you want to find in the A Word or Phrase in the File text box.**

   If you type more than one word, Search interprets what you type as a phrase. In my example, the precise phrase *file name extensions* must appear in the file.

3. **If you can remember when you created, changed, or last opened the file, click the When Was It Modified down arrow.**

   In fact, Windows lets you search on three different dates, as you can see in Figure 21-6. You can choose

   - **The date on which the file was modified**
   - **The date the file was created**
   - **The date the file was last opened**

4. **If you remember about how big the file is, click the What Size Is It down arrow.**

   Pick the size by using the Specify Size radio button.

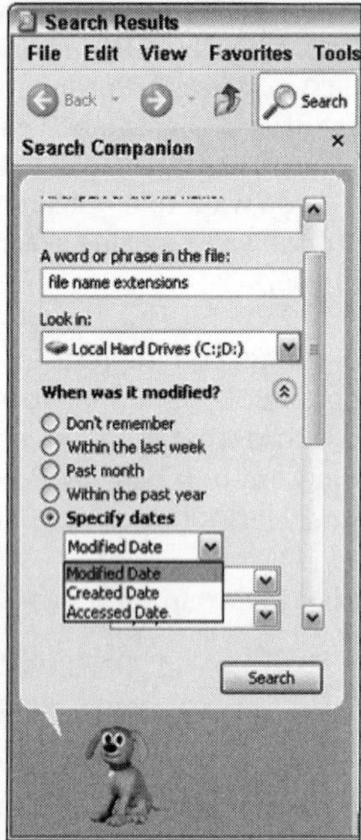

• **Figure 21-6: Narrow down the search by date.**

5. The More Advanced Options arrow holds several options (see Figure 21-7).

If you want to choose a file type using the verbose Windows substitutes for standard, simple, filename extensions (for example, if you want to choose "Microsoft Word Document"), you can do so here.

Except in very unusual circumstances, the first three boxes under More Advanced Options should always be checked. The Case Sensitive box applies only to text. (Filenames and folder names are never case sensitive.) Search Tape Backup applies only if you are using Windows XP's backup.

6. Click Search.

The results appear in the pane on the right.

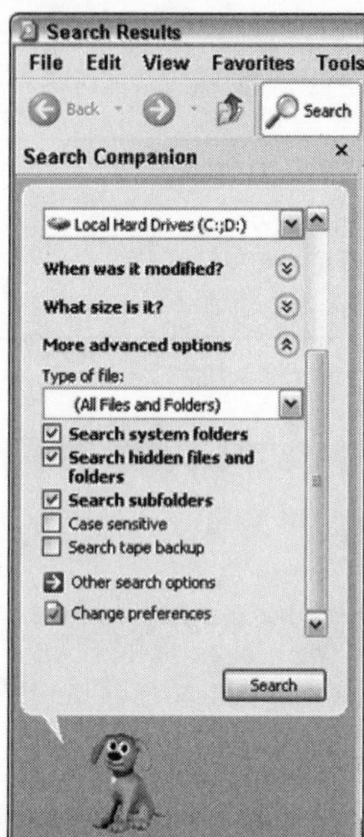

• **Figure 21-7: Usually you just want to leave the top three boxes checked.**

The date, size, and other more advanced options in Steps 3, 4 and 5 are *sticky*: They don't return to their former state. You must go back and change them immediately after running a search, or they stay in effect for your next search.

7. If you made any changes in Steps 3, 4, or 5, go back and clear them before proceeding.

If you ever run a search and it doesn't make sense, check those sticky settings!

Employing Wildcards

Windows Search recognizes two wildcards inside filenames:

- ? can stand for any single letter
- * can stand for zero or more letters

Wildcards work only in the All or Part of the File Name box. They do not work in the A Word or Phrase in the File box (the one for text).

To see how wildcards work, see Table 21-2.

Table 21-2: Filename Wildcard Matches and Misses

When You Type	Search Finds	But Search Does Not Find
`du?mies.doc`	`dummies.doc`	`dumies.doc`
`time*saving`	`timesaving techniques.ppt, time saving.ppt`	`timesave.ppt`
`fa*x`	`faxes.xls, fa.xls`	`fx.xls`

When you type something in the All or Part of the File Name box, Windows effectively puts a * at the beginning and end of what you type. Thus, if you type **timesaving**, Windows acts as if you typed ***timesaving***.

If you want to override that behavior, use quotes around your search term. For example, typing "**timesaving.doc**" with the quotes returns only files named **timesaving.doc**.

Saving and Reusing Searches

Windows (unlike recent versions of Word, Excel, and Outlook) lets you save a search so you can reuse it:

1. **Choose Start⇨Search and formulate the search.**

   In Figure 21-8, I typed the search term **dummies*.doc** to search for files.

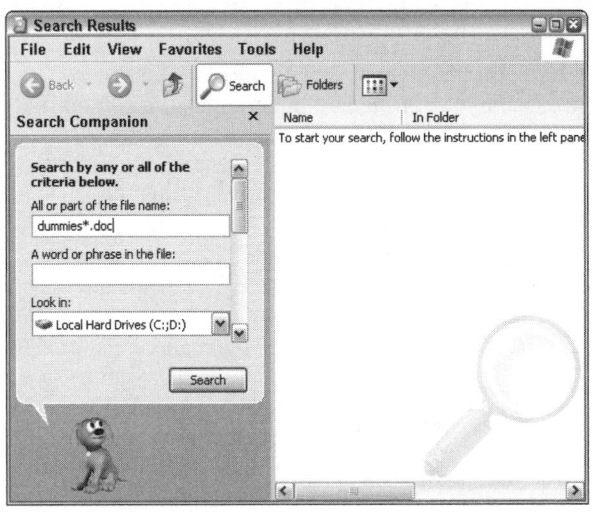

• **Figure 21-8: Perform the search.**

2. **Click Search.**

   For reasons known only to the programmers at Microsoft, you have to start the search before you can save it.

3. **Click Stop.**

   You can stop the search immediately. No need to let it run all the way.

4. **Choose File⇨Save Search.**

   Windows shows you the Save Search dialog box.

5. **Navigate to a location where you can find the search again — most likely on the desktop, and click Save.**

To reuse a search, just double-click it.

Finding Files That Got Lost

Wish I had a nickel for every time people ask me why Windows stole their files. The story always goes like this: "Woody, I used to have a whole bunch of important files in My Documents\Someplace, and now they're gone! What did Windows *do* with them?"

Oy.

When you discover that your files are lost, save yourself a lot of time and headaches and remember that there are only four possibilities:

- You moved them somewhere (Probability: 90 percent).
- You deleted them, and they're still available (Probability: 9 percent).
- You permanently deleted them and it will be difficult, but probably not impossible, to get them back (Probability: less than 1 percent).
- Little green men broke into your office in the middle of the night and ate them (Probability: varies).

First, don't panic

If you suddenly discover that some of your files are "lost," here's the fastest, most reliable way to get them back:

1. **Don't panic.**

   Douglas Adams' sage advice pertains.

2. **Don't create any new files or delete any existing ones.**

Do not choose this *particular* moment to defragment your hard drive. Even when you "permanently" delete a file, all the data remains on your disk until it is overwritten.

3. **Open Windows Explorer and look at the folders near the one that used to contain the "lost" files.**

   Chances are very good you accidentally moved the files while you were in Explorer. Accidentally dragging a bunch of files to a nearby folder is easy. If you go back to the scene of the crime, you may be able to retrace what went wrong.

4. **Run Search to find one of the lost files.**

Don't bother trying to find all the lost files at the same time. Just look for one of them. With a little luck, you can remember one lost file's name, or part of a name.

5. **If you find one of the lost files, right-click the filename and choose Open Containing Folder (refer to Figure 21-5).**

6. **If the files (or file) are in a regular, everyday folder, select them, click Move in the task pane on the left, and move them back where they belong.**

7. **If you find the lost files in the Recycle Bin, select them and click Restore This Item in the task pane on the left.**

Second, get determined

If you can't find the files with a simple search, it's time to haul out the big guns. Or at least the bigger guns:

1. **Go to your desktop and double-click the Recycle Bin icon.**

   Windows brings up the contents of the Recycle Bin, as shown in Figure 21-9. Any files that you deleted are probably in the Recycle Bin.

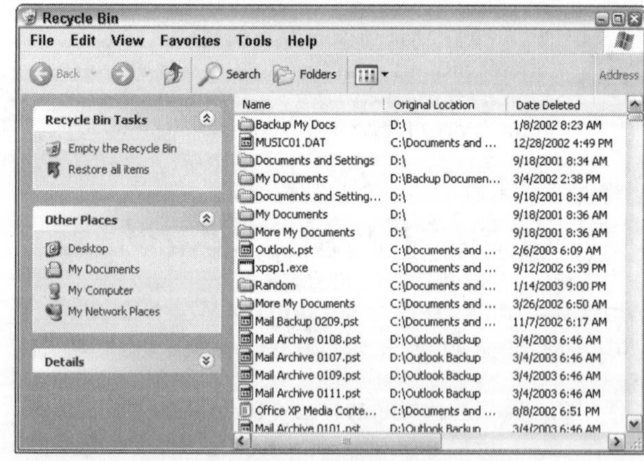

• **Figure 21-9: Look through the Recycle Bin.**

2. **Scan the Recycle Bin for your lost file.**

   You've already tried searching, but maybe you didn't spell the name exactly right — the Achilles heel of searches. A little bit of eyeballing might turn up the culprit. Usually it's fastest to look at the most recently deleted items first. To do so, click the Date Deleted column heading.

3. **If you find the lost files, select them, and in the task pane, click Restore This Item (or These Items).**

4. **If that still doesn't work, shut your machine down, and go buy a file recovery program.**

   Even if you've "permanently" deleted a file, its remnants remain and can frequently be put back together. Norton Utilities has long been the product of choice for undeleting files, but there are dozens of competitors, all of which basically do the same thing. It's important that you follow the instructions *precisely* in order to maximize your chances of getting your file back.

5. **If you still can't find the file, and there aren't any suspicious green men lurking about, and you are willing to spend many hundreds of dollars getting your data back, look for a data recovery company.**

   These folks can scan every bit on your hard drive and bring seemingly lost files back from the dead. Here's the best way to find a data recovery company, short of a recommendation from a satisfied customer: Go to Google (www.google.com) and search on the phrase **data recovery services**.

Advanced Searching with Copernic

Windows XP has the capability to scan and set up an index for certain types of files on your PC. A computer index, just like the index in this book, contains a list of words, and the words are linked to their locations. In particular, the Windows XP Indexing Service identifies and indexes the words in all kinds of Office documents — including Outlook and Outlook Express e-mail messages, text files, and HTML files.

I tried for years to get Windows Indexing Service to work as advertised. I had absolutely no luck at all, until I bumped into the pioneering research done by Richard Gamberg (www.xpsearch.info/xps1.htm). He managed to overcome many of the bugs and inanities in Indexing Service. If you're ever forced to work with Windows' own indexing program, start at Richard's site. Strap on your hip waders first.

Fortunately, a company called Copernic has come up with a free indexing and search engine that runs rings around anything Microsoft ever made. If you search for files on your computer (and who doesn't?) you owe it to yourself to download and install Copernic Desktop Search.

Here's how to get Copernic Desktop Search going:

1. **Crank up Internet Explorer and go to** www.copernic.com. **Download Copernic Desktop Search.**

2. **Double-click** copernicdesktopsearch.exe **to run the installer.**

   You may have to click through a couple of security warnings.

3. **Follow the steps in the wizard to install the program and then run it.**

   If given permission, the program indexes all your files. That can be a gargantuan task, but Copernic is smart enough to run in the background if you have more important work to do.

4. **In the Copernic Desktop Search main window (see Figure 21-10), choose what type of search you want to conduct — on the Web, within your e-mails (Outlook and Outlook Express only), in files of all types, music files, pictures, contacts,**

and so on. Type your search string in the Search For box and click the right arrow to search.

The speed of the search is breathtaking, particularly if you're accustomed to Windows search's sluggish pace.

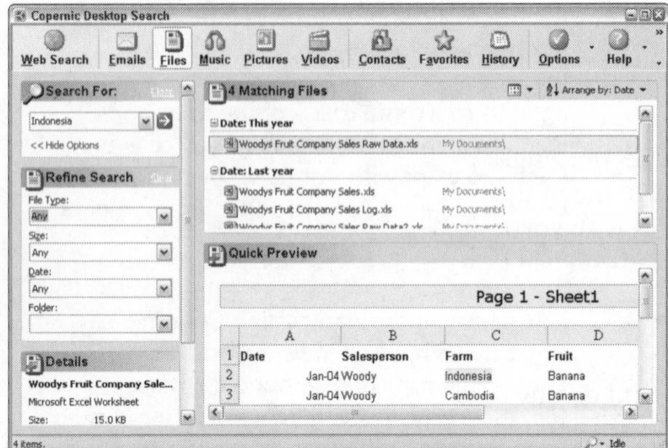

• **Figure 21-10: Copernic Desktop Search runs at lightning speed.**

5. **To put a search box on your Windows taskbar, right-click any open spot on the taskbar and choose Toolbars⇨Copernic Desktop Search.**

   Copernic puts a Search For box on your Windows taskbar, complete with a hovering control pane that lets you choose what kind of search you want to run (see Figure 21-11).

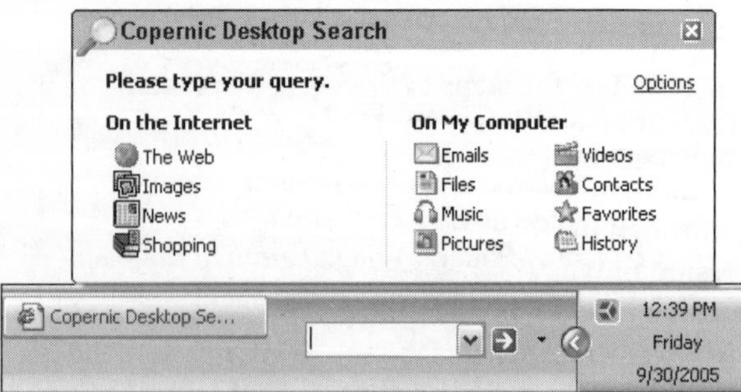

• **Figure 21-11: Copernic's search box on the Windows taskbar.**

To see how a Web search works from the taskbar, type **ask woody** in the Search For box, hover your mouse until the Copernic work pane opens, and then click The Web. Copernic searches AllTheWeb.com for the string you typed (see Figure 21-12).

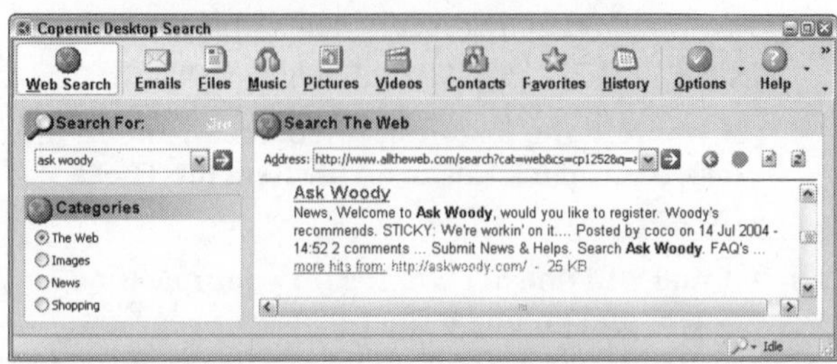

• **Figure 21-12: Copernic uses AllTheWeb.com for Web searches.**

As of this writing, Copernic Desktop Search did not have the ability to change the default Web search engine. But it lets you conduct full Boolean searches (AND, NOT, OR, and the like), and the preview pane lets you look at files before opening them.

Most of all, it's fast and unobtrusive. Your PC won't slow down while indexing is under way, and the typed search queries yield results that change as you type them. Quite astonishing, and well worth the few minutes it takes to download and install.

Listing Files Quickly

Save Time By

- Listing all the files in a folder with one click
- Sorting files by filename extension
- Printing a list of files automatically

How many times have you wanted to get your hands on a list of all the files in a folder? Amazingly, there's no way to do it in Windows. Never has been. It's one of the gaping holes left in Windows Explorer — right up there with sorting files by filename extension, which is another important thing you can't do, for love nor money.

This technique presents three variations on the "list filenames" (or "print directory") theme. When you're done with the technique, you'll be able to right-click any folder and do any of the following:

- **Create a list of all the files in a folder:** The list you create is poured into a file, which is automatically opened in Notepad. From there, you can search, look at, print, or copy the information into Excel, Word, or any other program, to do with what you will.
- **List files by extension:** The list is the same as in the previous bullet, only it's sorted by the `.doc`, `.xls`, and `.exe` filename extensions that control so much of your files' destinies. The trick I explain in this technique is the only way I know (short of writing a very hairy macro) to get a list of all files in a folder sorted by the filename extension.
- **Print file listing:** The list you create is sent to the printer. The list is then automatically deleted, all with one click.

I also let you in on a couple of additional undocumented tricks. Cool stuff.

Barry Simon and I originally came up with many of these tricks in *The Mother of All Windows 95 Books*, ten years ago. At the time, we had no end of problems wading through the File Types and Edit Flags bugs in Windows 95. The first version of Windows XP not only included essentially all the old bugs, but also has added several new ones. Progress. I'm happy to report, though, that Microsoft finally fixed the most glaring bug in Windows XP Service Pack 1 — and it's still fixed in Service Pack 2.

Getting Started by Fixing a Windows Bug

There's an old, old bug in Windows that may or may not affect your PC. Microsoft finally fixed the bug (after nearly a decade of letting it sit there) in Windows XP Service Pack 2. If you have Windows XP Service Pack 2 installed, skip to the next section, "Showing Directory Listings." If you don't have SP2, or if you aren't quite sure, here's how to set things right.

This is important stuff. If you use any variation of the technique presented here, and you don't have a patched PC, the bug makes Windows do very weird stuff. It all has to do with the menu that you see when you right-click a folder, and the reasons are . . . complicated. Suffice it to say that a simple change to the Registry can make everything all right.

If you're worried about changing the Registry, don't be. Just avoid dashing around the Registry, changing or deleting entries willy-nilly. As long as you follow the steps here, you'll be just fine.

To see if you have the default Directory action bug in Windows XP, and to fix it if you do:

1. **Choose Start⇨Run. Type** regedit **and press Enter.**

   The Registry Editor appears (see Figure 22-1). You see typical Registry gobbledygook, full of sound and fury, signifying nothing (unless you happen to mess around with the wrong entry).

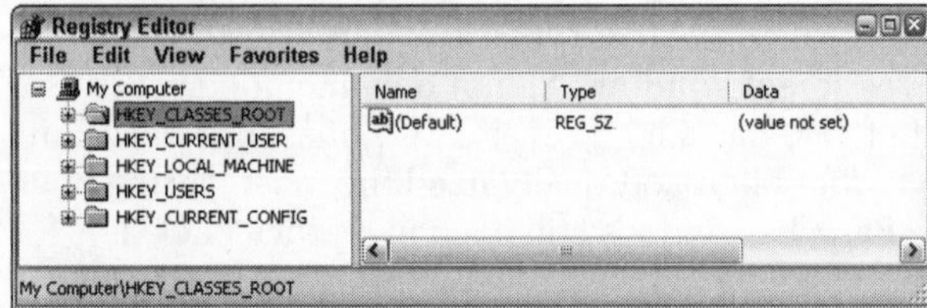

• **Figure 22-1: The Registry Editor lets you change anything in the Registry. Use it with care.**

2. **On the left, choose HKEY_CLASSES_ROOT⇨Directory⇨Shell.**

   Although it takes a bit of scrolling, the Registry Editor moves down to the location shown in Figure 22-2.

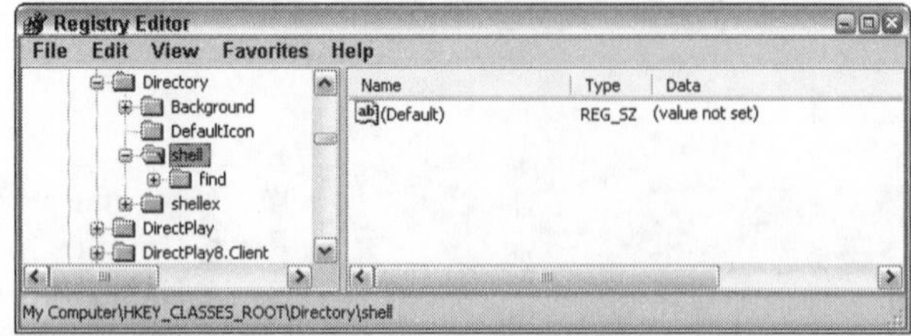

• **Figure 22-2: Move to the correct entry.**

3. **If you see the word** `none` **under the Data column on the right side of the screen, all is well with the world. You've been patched already. Choose File⇨Exit to leave the Registry Editor, and then go to the next section in this technique, "Showing Directory Listings".**

4. **On the other hand, if you see** `(value not set)` **under the Data column on the right side of the screen (as is the case in Figure 22-2), you have the bug, and you need to fix it. Click (Default) once and then choose Edit⇨Modify.**

   You see the Edit String dialog box, shown in Figure 22-3.

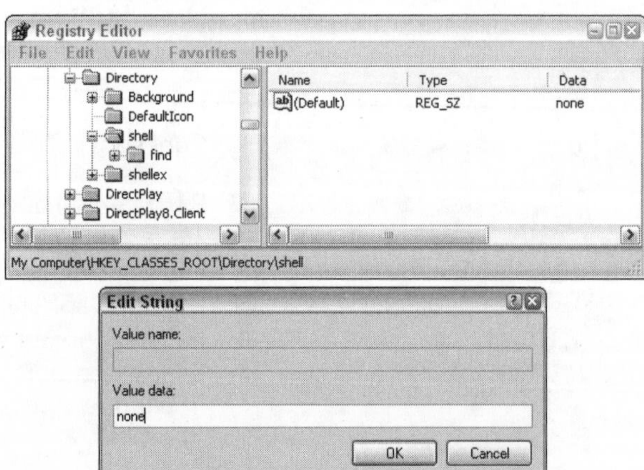

• **Figure 22-3: Type in the value of the (Default) string.**

5. **In the Value Data box, type**

```
none
```

6. **Click OK and then choose File➪Exit to exit the Registry Editor.**

   Windows XP is now ready for you to make modifications to the right-click menu for all folders.

Of course, it's best to install Service Pack 2. If you don't, for whatever reason, it doesn't hurt to change the (Default) string to `none` even if you decide that you don't want to use the methods in this technique. By following the preceding steps, you're correcting a known bug in Windows — an obscure one that comes into play if you change the right-click menus for your folders. I've been kvetching about this bug in print for ten years. Looks like the Softies finally fixed it.

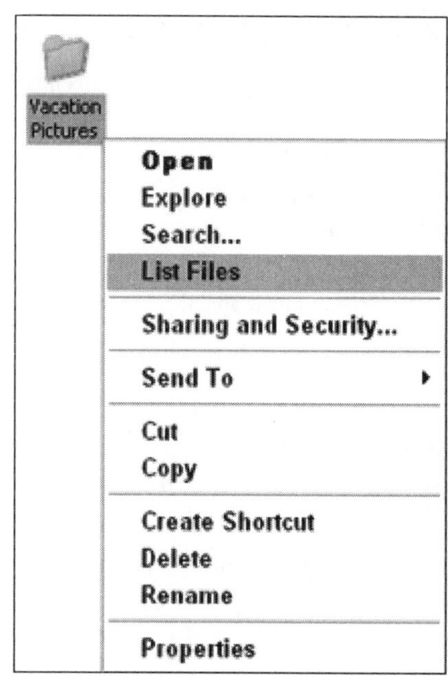

• **Figure 22-4: The new List Files entry on the right-click menu for all folders.**

Showing Directory Listings

Follow the steps in this section to create a new entry for the right-click menu on every folder. When you're done, if you right-click a folder, you see that the context menu includes a List Files entry, as shown in Figure 22-4.

Click List Files, and Notepad appears with a sorted list of all the files and their sizes, as shown in Figure 22-5. Okay, so it's not pretty, but it's better than anything that Windows currently allows you to do.

Here's what you see in the list:

- **The size of the file:** The number of bytes.
- **The name of the file:** The fourth file in the list in Figure 22-5 is called `Add in Bay`.
- **The filename extension:** In the case of Figure 22-5, the files are all images with the `.jpg` extension.

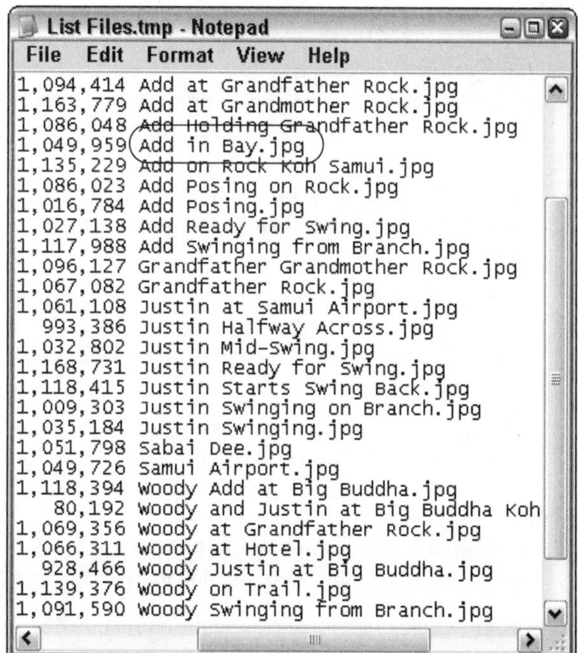

• **Figure 22-5: A list of files ready for you to search, print, or copy into another program.**

Writing a program to show directory listings

To write the two-line program that creates the list:

1. **Choose Start⇨My Computer.**
2. **Double-click the C: drive and then double-click Program Files.**

   If Windows puts up a scary warning about hidden files (see Figure 22-6), just click Show the Contents of This Folder, Turkey. While you're at it, make a mental note to follow the steps in Technique 20 to whip Explorer into shape so that you don't see this warning again.
3. **Right-click an empty spot inside the Program Files folder and choose New⇨Text Document.**

   Windows creates a new document for you called `New Text Document.txt`.

These files are hidden.

This folder contains files that keep your system working properly. You should not modify its contents.

Show the contents of this folder

• **Figure 22-6: Just don't delete anything while you're here, okay?**

4. **Immediately overwrite the name that Windows created by typing** List Files.bat **and pressing Enter.**

   If you forget and do something else before typing the file's new name, just right-click `New Text Document.txt`, choose Rename, and type **List Files.bat**.

   Windows tosses out a message warning you about changing filename extensions.
5. **Click Yes.**

   You now have an empty text file called `List Files.bat` in your Program Files folder.
6. **Right-click** `List Files.bat` **and choose Edit.**

   Notepad opens with `List Files.bat` loaded and ready for mangling. Er, editing.
7. **Type this two-line program into Notepad.**

```
dir %1 /o:gn /n /-p > "%temp%\List
   Files.tmp"
start notepad "%temp%\List Files.tmp"
```

Make sure that you don't press Enter at any point, except immediately before the word `start`. See Figure 22-7 for an exact rendition. An explanation of all the strange commands is in the sidebar.

8. **Choose File⇨Exit to leave Notepad. Be sure you save the changes.**

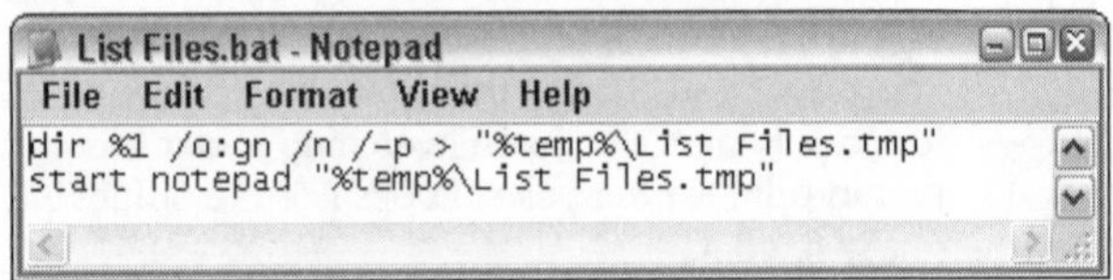
List Files.bat - Notepad
File Edit Format View Help
dir %1 /o:gn /n /-p > "%temp%\List Files.tmp"
start notepad "%temp%\List Files.tmp"

• **Figure 22-7: The two-line program that runs List Files.**

Understanding what all those funny characters mean

Here's a handy babelfish for all that programming tomfoolery. Strip away the funny stuff, and you get this gem:

```
dir %1 > "%temp%\List Files.tmp"
```

That command tells Windows to put a list of everything in the current ("%1") directory into a file called `List Files.tmp`, which is located in the temporary folder. Then

```
start notepad "%temp%\List Files.tmp"
```

simply starts Notepad and feeds it `List Files.tmp` from the temporary folder.

Everything else is embellishment. The switch

```
/o:gn
```

tells Windows to put the folders first, and to sort by filename. (No, I have no idea why "put folders first" is `g`. Programmers are trained not to ask such insightful questions.) The switch

```
/n
```

(continued)

tells Windows to put the filename on the right. (n stands for "new". Don't ask.) Finally,

```
/-p
```

tells Windows to override another switch, which can force the whole command to hang when the file gets too large. I told you not to ask.

Feel like a programmer now? Great. Choose Start⇨All Programs⇨Accessories⇨Command Prompt and type **dir /?** the first chance you get. That shows you all the options you have available for the `dir` command. I use several of them in this technique.

Adding the program to the right-click menu

If you followed the steps in the previous section, you now have a program that shows you a list of all the files in a folder. That's all well and good, but if you want to access the program quickly (and, therefore, save time), the next step is to hook the program into the right-click menu for folders. Follow these steps:

1. **Choose Start⇨Control Panel⇨Appearance and Themes⇨Folder Options⇨File Types.**

   Windows grinds away for a few seconds and then shows you the File Types list in Figure 22-8.

2. **Click File Folder, and then at the bottom of the dialog box, click Advanced.**

   You see the Edit File Type dialog box shown in Figure 22-9.

3. **Click New.**

   The New Action dialog box appears, as shown in Figure 22-10.

4. **In the Action box, type** List Files. **Then click the Browse button and navigate to** `C:\Program Files\List Files.bat`**. Click** `List Files.bat` **and then click OK twice.**

   In the Edit File Type dialog box, you now see List Files in the Actions box, as shown in Figure 22-11.

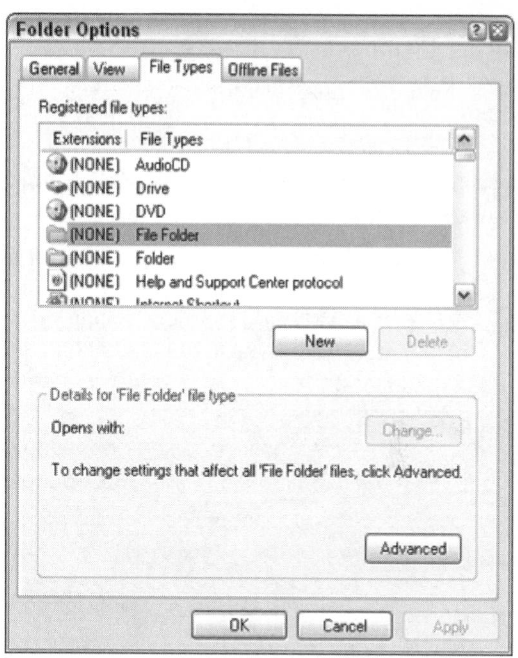

• **Figure 22-8: Where the right-click menus are buried.**

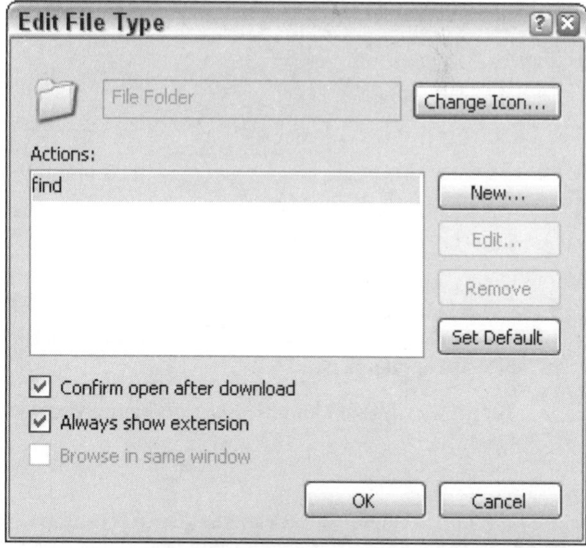

• **Figure 22-9: Right-click actions that are specific to file folders appear here.**

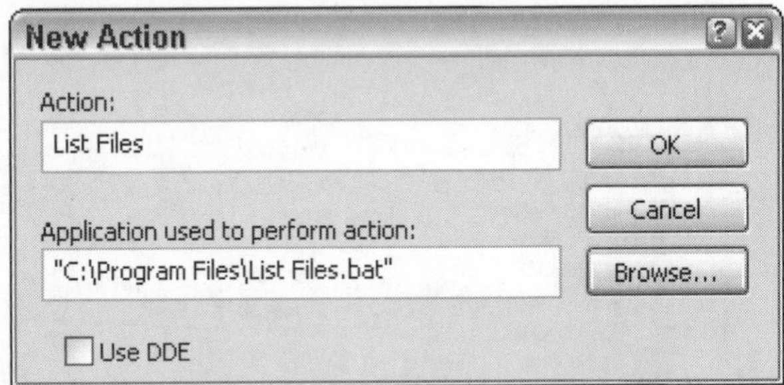

• **Figure 22-10: Creating a new List Files action for the right-click menu.**

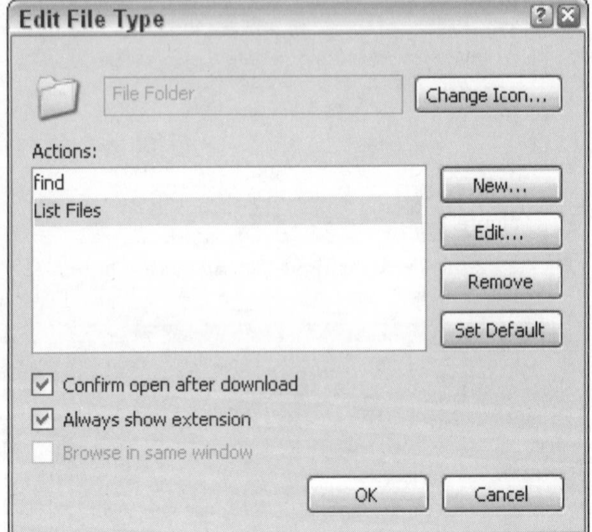

• **Figure 22-11: The new List Files action, ready to go.**

5. **Click OK one last time, close the Control Panel Appearance and Themes window, and the List Files program is ready.**

   Test it by right-clicking a folder and choosing List Files.

If you accidentally click the Set Default button in the Edit File Type dialog box (refer to Figure 22-11) and turn Find into the default action for folders, you'll soon discover that double-clicking any file folder launches Windows Search. Blech. Unfortunately, getting back to normal is a little difficult. Starting in the Edit File Type dialog box (the result of preceding Step 2), click New and create a new action called Open by following steps similar to the preceding steps. In this case, type Open in the Action box, click Browse and navigate to `C:\windows\explorer.exe`, and click `explorer.exe` to make it appear in the Application Used to Perform Action box. Click OK to get back to the Edit File Type dialog box, click Open in the Actions list, and then click Set Default. That straightens things out.

Listing Files by Filename Extension

I'm still fuming that Windows Explorer doesn't let me sort files by filename extension — the three-or-more letters at the end of a filename — and I've been complaining about it, in print, since the days of Windows 3.1.

Until Microsoft gets a clue, at least you can generate a list of files by filename extension. It isn't anywhere near as effective as, say, clicking a column heading in Explorer. But if you can find the file you're looking for in the generated list, it's reasonably easy to go back to Explorer and find it.

Writing a program to list files by filename extension

Here's how to build the program that does the trick:

1. **Choose Start➪My Computer.**
2. **Double-click the C: drive and then double-click Program Files.**

   If you see a warning (refer to Figure 22-6), click Show the Contents of This Folder and make sure you go to Technique 20 to get Explorer out of your face.
3. **Right-click an empty spot inside the Program Files folder and choose New➪Text Document.**

   Windows creates a new document for you called `New Text Document.txt`.

4. **Immediately overwrite the name that Windows created by typing** List Files by Extension.bat **and pressing Enter.**

5. **Windows warns you about changing filename extensions. Click Yes.**

   You now have an empty text file called `List Files by Extension.bat` in your Program Files folder.

6. **Right-click** `List Files by Extension.bat` **and choose Edit.**

   Notepad opens `List Files by Extension.bat`.

7. **Type this two-line program into Notepad.**

```
dir %1 /o:ge /x /-p > "%temp%\List
   Files.tmp"
start notepad "%temp%\List Files.tmp"
```

Make sure that you don't press Enter at any point, except immediately before the word `start`. See Figure 22-12.

• **Figure 22-12: The two-line program that runs List Files by Extension.**

8. **Choose File⇨Exit to leave Notepad, and save your changes.**

Making the program show up in your right-click menu

Now that you have the program ready and waiting, you need to hook this program into the right-click menu for folders. The procedure you use is essentially the same as the one in the preceding section, where you hooked the directory listings program (List Files) into the right-click menu.

To put the program on the right-click menu for folders:

1. **In the Program Files folder, choose Tools⇨Folder Options⇨File Types.**

   Windows shows you the File Types list (refer to Figure 22-8). This is the same list that you can see by going through the Control Panel.

2. **Click File Folder and then, at the bottom, click Advanced.**

3. **Click New.**

4. **In the Action box, type** List Files by Extension. **Then click the Browse button and navigate to** `C:\Program Files\List Files by Extension.bat`. **Click** `List Files by Extension.bat` **and then click OK twice.**

   The Edit File Type dialog box now shows List Files by Extension in the Actions area (see Figure 22-13).

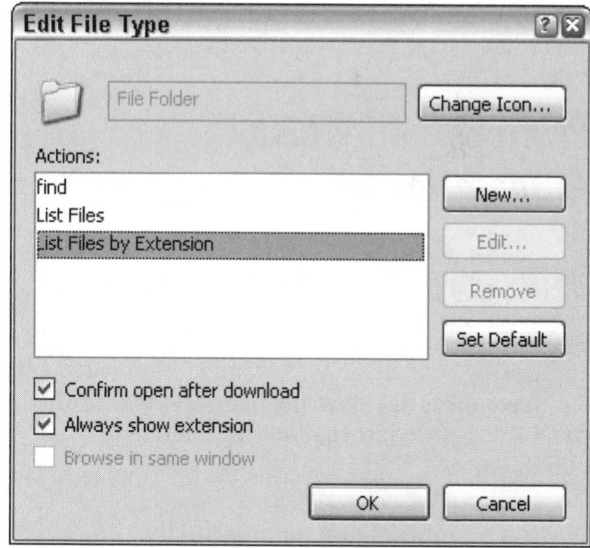

• **Figure 22-13: The new List Files by Extension action.**

5. **Click OK, and the List Files by Extension program is ready.**

   Test it by right-clicking a folder and choosing List Files by Extension (see Figure 22-14).

I set up this program to show you old-fashioned short (so-called "8 plus 3") filenames in a column just before the real filenames. I did that to make it easier to scan for filename extensions — a big timesaver. If you'd rather drop the short filenames, perhaps to minimize confusion with people who don't understand short filenames, remove the /x switch in the first line of the program.

```
List Files.tmp - Notepad
File  Edit  Format  View  Help
    3,528 DOCUME~1 RTF Document Collaboration Spyware Demo.rt
   11,951 AUTOMA~1 RTF Automatic Spy.rtf
    5,668 MYFAVO~1 THE My Favorite Theme.theme
  274,288 SHOTFR~1 TIF Shot from Inspiron 00.tif
  148,960 SHOTFR~4 TIF Shot from Inspiron 03.tif
   48,936 GAZETT~1 TIF Gazette01.tif
  148,960 SHAAC5~1 TIF Shot from Inspiron 04.tif
  145,902 SHOTFR~2 TIF Shot from Inspiron 01.tif
  469,318              wxpaio04.tif
  272,885              wxpaio01.tif
  148,960 SHOTFR~3 TIF Shot from Inspiron 02.tif
  142,072              Gigi.TTF
    6,981              leonjm4a.txt
    2,495 USHOLI~1 TXT US Holidays 2003-6.txt
    8,900 JEFFSK~1 TXT Jeffs Kids Passport Experience.txt
    2,569 HOLIDA~1 TXT Holidays 2003-6.txt
      747              Guninski.txt
   10,371 PASSTH~1 TXT Pass the Text.txt
    1,972 WINXPU~1 TXT WinXP Undelete.txt
   20,480 INVENT~1 XLS Inventory.xls
```

• **Figure 22-14: List Files by Extension at work.**

Printing a File List Automatically

You can print lists of files that are presented by the programs I show you how to create earlier in this technique. Simply create a list and then choose File⇨Print in Notepad.

But this book is about saving time. Sometimes all you want to do is just right-click a folder and print the contents.

Writing a program that automatically prints a file list

Here's how to create the program you need to print the list:

1. **Choose Start⇨My Computer.**
2. **Double-click the C: drive and then double-click Program Files.**

   If Windows presents you with a warning (refer to Figure 22-6), click Show the Contents of This Folder. (I tell you how to get rid of the message completely in Technique 20.)
3. **Right-click an empty spot inside the Program Files folder and choose New⇨Text Document.**

   There's a new document called `New Text Document.txt`.
4. **Immediately type** Print File List.bat **and press Enter.**
5. **Windows warns you about changing filename extensions. Click Yes.**

   You have an empty text file called `Print File List.bat` in your Program Files folder.
6. **Right-click** `Print File List.bat` **and choose Edit.**

   Notepad opens `Print File List.bat`.
7. **Type this three-line program into Notepad.**

```
dir %1 /o:gn /n /-p > "%temp%\List
   Files.tmp"
start /w notepad /p "%temp%\List
   Files.tmp"
del "%temp%\List Files.tmp"
```

For a complete list of switches for the `start` command, choose Start⇨All Programs⇨Accessories⇨Command Prompt and type **start /?**. (Equivalently, choose Start⇨Run, type **cmd**, and press Enter.) The `/w` switch, for example, tells the program to wait until Notepad finishes before deleting the file. Notepad is so slow that, if you don't tell the program to wait, the file is deleted before Notepad has a chance to run!

You press Enter only twice, immediately before the word `start` and again before the word `del`. See Figure 22-15.

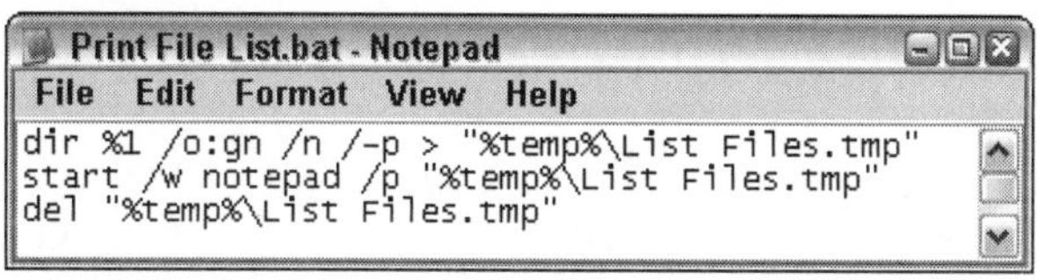

• Figure 22-15: The three-line program that prints a list of files.

This program prints to the "default" Windows printer — the one that Notepad prints to when you click the Print icon. Unfortunately, there's no easy way to switch printers.

8. **Choose File⇨Exit to leave Notepad and save changes.**

Adding the program to your right-click menu

After you have the Print File List program under your belt, make it really useful by hooking it into the right-click menu.

To put the program on the right-click menu for folders

1. **Choose Start⇨Control Panel⇨Appearance and Themes⇨Folder Options⇨File Types.**

   Windows shows you the File Types list (refer to Figure 22-8).

2. **Click File Folder and then at the bottom click Advanced.**
3. **Click New.**
4. **In the Action box, type** Print File List. **Then click the Browse button and navigate to** `C:\Program Files\Print File List.bat`. **Select** `Print File List.bat` **and then click OK.**

   In the New Action dialog box, Print File List now appears in the Action box and "`C:\Program Files\Print File List.bat`" now appears in the Application Used to Perform Action box (see Figure 22-16).

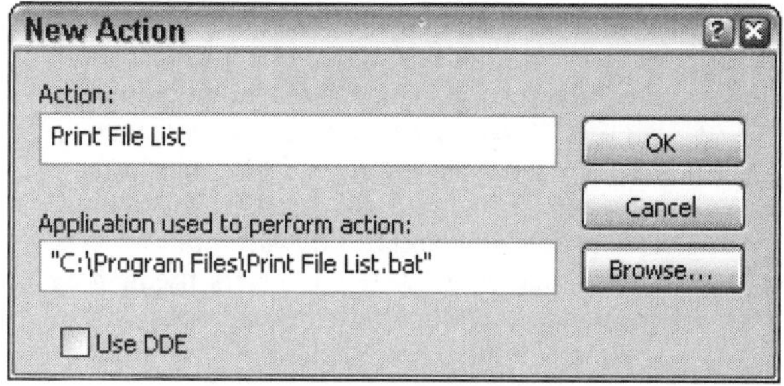

• Figure 22-16: The new Print File List action.

5. **Click OK.**

   If you've created commands for all the actions in this technique, the Edit File Type dialog box looks like the one shown in Figure 22-17, with four actions in the Actions box (which include the default find action).

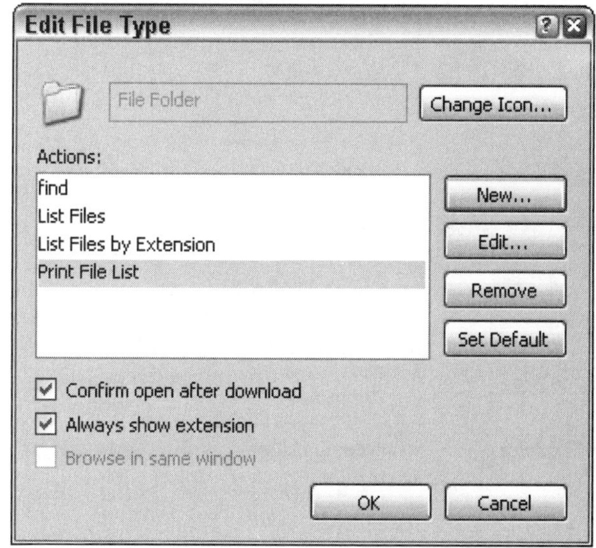

• Figure 22-17: All three of this technique's actions.

6. **Click OK, and the Print File List program is ready.**

   Test it by right-clicking a folder and then choosing Print File List (see Figure 22-18).

You can mix and match any of the switches discussed in this technique. Many valid, useful, timesaving combinations are a great help in specific situations. For example, you may want to print "8+3" filenames, or create a listing in Notepad, print it, but not delete it. The best way to see what you can do (short of taking a course on old-fashioned DOS commands) is by consulting the list of switches, as I described in the preceding section "Writing a program that automatically prints a file list."

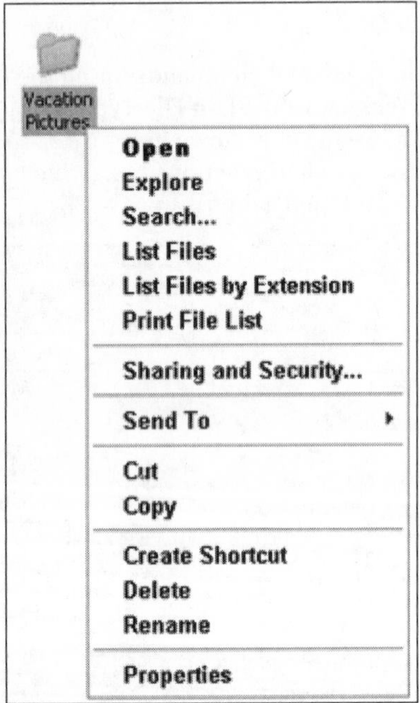

• **Figure 22-18: The three commands on the right-click menu.**

Getting Rid of Listing Entries

If you ever change your mind and decide to get rid of these right-click context menu entries (or any other entries that Windows blocks in the File Types dialog box, for that matter), here's how:

1. **Choose Start➪Run. Type** regedit **and press Enter.**

   The Registry Editor appears (refer to Figure 22-1).

2. **On the left, choose HKEY_CLASSES_ROOT➪Directory➪Shell.**

   Each action that you added through the File Types dialog box appears under Shell (see Figure 22-19). Windows changes spaces to underscores, but you can figure out which one is which.

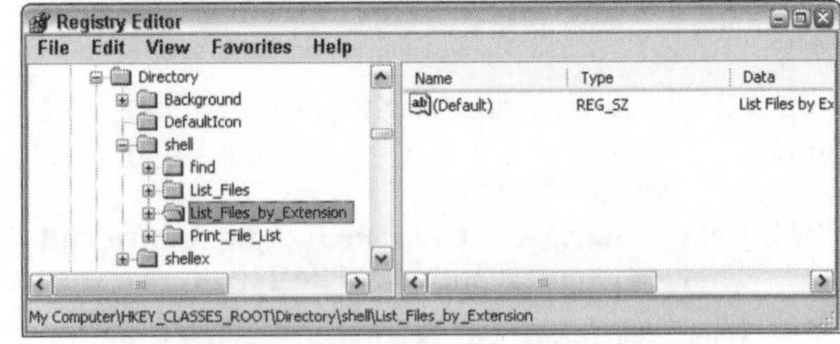

• **Figure 22-19: The actions you added appear here.**

3. **Right-click any unwanted entries and choose Delete.**

   That deletes the key, which in turn removes the action from the right-click menu. It doesn't get rid of the program, but these programs are tiny and probably not worthy of eradication anyway.

4. **Choose File➪Exit to get out of the Registry Editor.**

Part IV

Making the Most of Internet and E-Mail

"I heard you say you needed a new Web dowser, Andy, and I thought old gramps could help out, but dang if I can find one that'll work!"

Technique 23: Customizing Internet Explorer

Save Time By

- Making IE work quickly and to your specifications
- Using timesaving methods to bypass IE inanities
- Taking control of your Favorites list and other key parts of IE
- Configuring security zones so you don't get stung
- Uninstalling and reinstalling IE

The best way to speed up Internet Explorer (IE) is to get a faster Internet connection. The second best way is to adapt IE to your way of working. Or vice versa.

Internet Explorer abounds with settings that not only make it work faster, they make it work more like the way you work. Which is to say, rationally. Many of IE's default settings are rigged to line the pockets of a certain company in Redmond. Others are simply . . . bizarre.

Microsoft isn't the only one to blame. Some scummy Web sites take over your Back button. Others trick you into changing your home page. Still more find ways to get you to fill up your Favorites. And of course you can't ignore the pop-ups, which are still being used by big-name places such as CNN.com and even <*shudder!*> Microsoft.com.

You don't have to put up with it. IE has plenty of tools to help you fight back. This technique shows you how.

Internet Explorer ain't the only game in town. When Microsoft "won" the browser wars years ago, the Softies started resting on their ill-gotten laurels. As a result, IE has languished, the victim of developer neglect. Mozilla Firefox, as of this writing anyway, holds great potential and merits your consideration as a feature-rich, less buggy, more secure alternative. See `www.mozilla.org/products/firefox` **for details, and Technique 12 for installation instructions.**

Speeding Up IE

If you look around on the Web you'll find dozens — hundreds — of shopworn tips on how to speed up Internet Explorer. One minor problem: Most of the methods don't work, and those that do work have unintended consequences.

In this section, I step you through IE speed-up techniques that actually save time. They all entail a change in the way IE works, and you may not like their side effects. That's why I give you instructions on how to *undo* each specific tweak, so you can return IE to its original state.

I don't know about you, but I find the adaptive menus in IE's Favorites list distracting and a waste of time. Adaptive menus move items around depending on how often you use them. One day, your link to the Teletubbies site is in one place, and the next day it's been moved, without your knowledge or consent. In my opinion, adaptive menus are evidence that programmers think they're smarter than you and me. To get rid of adaptive menus in your Favorites list (that is, to keep menu items where you put them), start Internet Explorer, choose Tools⇨Internet Options⇨Advanced. Then uncheck the Enable Personalized Favorites Menu box.

Using a blank home page

Microsoft stacks the deck on new Windows XP installations; if you install Windows XP on a clean machine, for example, Internet Explorer always starts by running out to `www.msn.com`, Microsoft's MSN main page, retrieving the page, and displaying it on your screen. If you bought your computer with Windows XP preinstalled, your home page may have been set to the MSN site, or to some other equally advertising-laden corner of the Internet.

Content owners pay for the privilege of having IE directing itself to their home pages every time you open the browser. The number of hits increases exponentially, as does the small chance that you'll actually buy something.

Getting stuck with a big, slow home page rates as a first-class time sink, which you should change immediately. If you want IE to come up with no page at all — a *blank page* — every time it's started, here's how:

1. **Start Internet Explorer.**
2. **Choose Tools⇨Internet Options⇨General.**

   You see the Internet Options dialog box shown in Figure 23-1.

• **Figure 23-1: Every time IE starts, it shows you the home page listed in the Address box on the General tab.**

3. **Click the Use Blank button and then click OK.**

   From this point on, every time you start IE, it starts as quickly as possible — with no time lag while IE goes out and grabs a page you probably don't want anyway.

If you have an overwhelming need to always see a specific Web page every time you open Internet Explorer (or if you want to override the blank page you set up in the preceding steps), simply navigate to the page you want to become your new home page and choose Tools⇨Internet Options⇨General, and then click the Use Current button (instead of Use Blank).

If you look around on the Web, you'll find some reference to adding a `-nohome` switch to the command that starts Internet Explorer. It's an old trick that supposedly starts IE without a home page, and it's both cumbersome and buggy. Avoid `-nohome`.

Some unscrupulous Web pages may hijack your home page by tricking you into clicking something that takes over this setting. If you start IE one day and a strange Web page appears, follow the preceding steps to get your home page back (or, better, make it blank).

Showing placeholder pictures

Most of the time, pictures add a lot to Web pages (just take a look at Figure 23-2 if you don't believe me). In fact, you'll frequently have a hard time figuring out what a Web page is supposed to be showing you if you can't see the images.

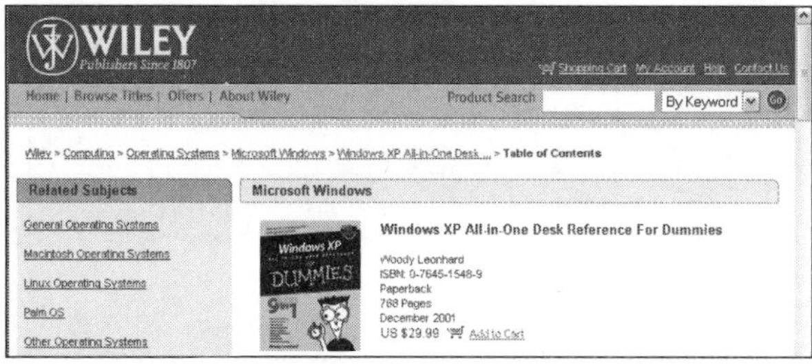

• **Figure 23-2: Pictures make the text-heavy Internet more colorful.**

Other times, though, you need only the text, thank you very much. In times like these, you can save tons of time by telling Internet Explorer to forget about the pictures, and simply show boxes where the pictures should go (see Figure 23-3).

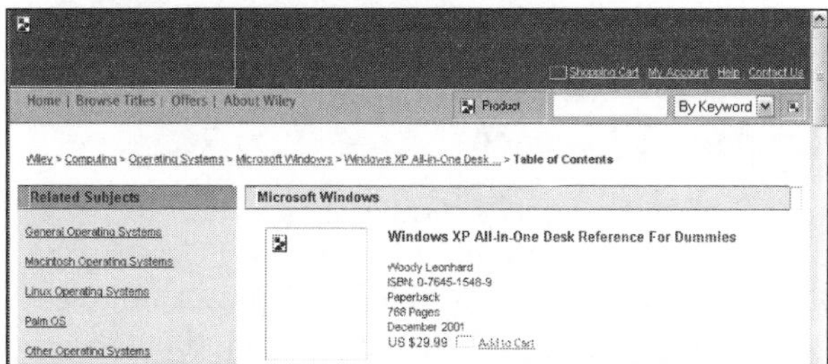

• **Figure 23-3: The same page as the one in Figure 23-2, without the pictures.**

Savvy Web site designers put pieces of text underneath their pictures, so if you visit a well-designed site, you can get the gist of what's going on without seeing the pictures themselves.

Here's how to tell IE that you don't want to see pictures:

1. **Start Internet Explorer.**
2. **Choose Tools⇨Internet Options⇨Advanced.**

   The Internet Options dialog box in Figure 23-4 appears.
3. **Under Multimedia, uncheck the Show Pictures box.**
4. **Click OK.**

   The setting takes effect on the next page you view.

To show pictures again, you have to follow the preceding procedure and check the Show Pictures box.

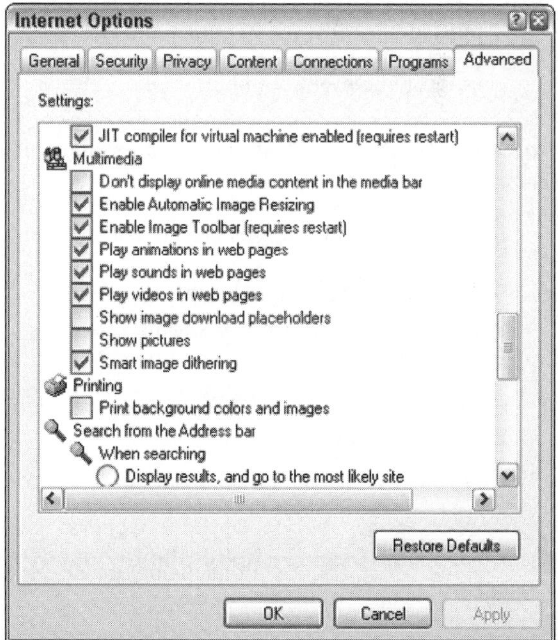

• **Figure 23-4: Make IE show picture placeholders instead of pictures.**

Stopping script debugging

How many times have you run across a message like the one shown in Figure 23-5?

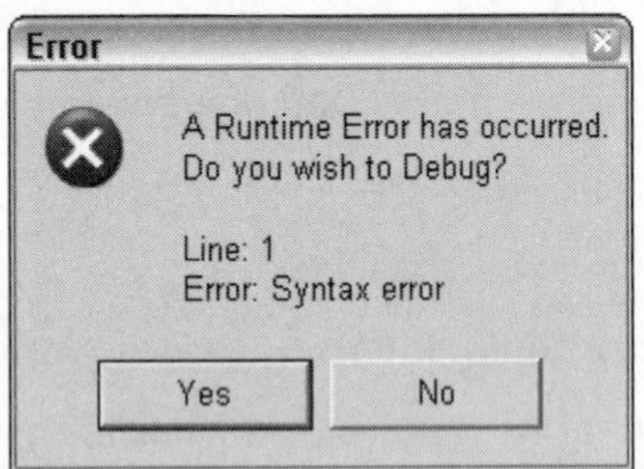

• **Figure 23-5: Why on earth would you want to debug a Web page?**

This is one of the most annoying so-called *features* in Internet Explorer. If a bug is in a Web page — that is, if the person who created the Web page made a mistake — why would *you* want to fix it?

If you're worried that you somehow screwed up IE, and that triggered more of these Debug messages – relax. You didn't do anything. The messages occur when IE can't figure out how to read a Web page. The person who wrote the Web page screwed up. Not you.

Fortunately, turning the blasted error messages off, permanently, is easy:

1. **Start Internet Explorer.**
2. **Choose Tools➪Internet Options➪Advanced.**

   The Internet Options dialog box in Figure 23-6 appears.
3. **Check the Disable Script Debugging box, in the Browsing section.**

   It's probably checked already, but make sure it stays that way.
4. **Uncheck the Display a Notification About Every Script Error box.**

   Different versions of Windows XP have different default settings. If the box is checked, whether by default of Windows or, uh, de fault of de owner, you see the `Do You Wish to Debug?` messages when IE gets confused. Because you can do precious little, unless you're an expert at HTML programming, uncheck the box and tell IE to put a sock in it.
5. **Click OK.**

   You're never asked to debug a script again.

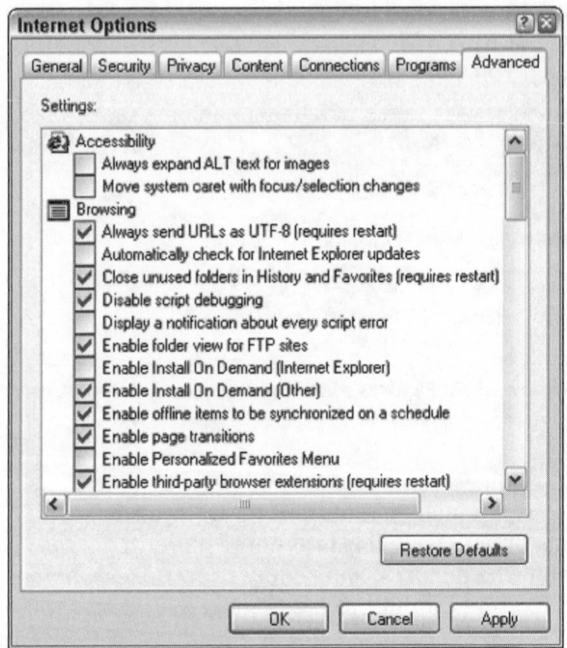

• **Figure 23-6: Turn off debugging.**

Bumping up the cache

Internet Explorer *caches* Web pages — that is, it saves Web pages and pictures on your PC as it goes along and, whenever possible, pulls pages and pictures from your PC instead of retrieving them from the Web again.

In spite of what you may have read in those breathless pieces of spam (Did YOU know that YOUR computer has COPIES of EVERY PICTURE you've SEEN on the INTERNET?), caching is a good thing. It speeds up your Web surfing enormously, especially if you tend to come back to the same page — or view related pages with the same graphics — over and over again. Those "Temporary Internet Files," as Windows calls them, really come in handy.

With the IE cache, as with any cache, the question boils down to how much room on your hard drive you're willing to give up in exchange for shaving a few seconds off the time it takes for the computer to do its thing.

IE offers four cache level settings, described in Table 23-1. Unless you have an overwhelming reason to change it, use Automatically, the default setting. I use it, although when I'm surfing, I frequently push Ctrl+F5 (a handy IE shortcut) to make sure that IE goes all the way out to the Web site to get the latest page.

Here's how to jiggle the settings in the way that gives you the most speed:

1. **Start Internet Explorer.**
2. **Choose Tools⇨Internet Options⇨General.**

   You see the Internet Options dialog box.
3. **In the Temporary Internet Files area, click Settings.**

   You see the Settings dialog box, shown in Figure 23-7.

• **Figure 23-7: Adjust the size of the cache here.**

TABLE 23-1: INTERNET EXPLORER CACHE LEVEL SETTINGS

Level	What the Level Means
Every Visit to the Page	When you view a page, IE checks whether a copy of the page is cached. If a copy is in the cache, IE then looks to see if the page available on the Web has the same characteristics (Microsoft doesn't say *what* characteristics) as the one in the cache. If they match, IE doesn't download the page, and the cached version comes up lickety-split.
Every Time You Start Internet Explorer	When you view a page, IE checks to see whether a copy was put in the cache on the current day, during the current IE session. (One "session" lasts from the time you start IE until you close the last open browser window.) If the current day and session doesn't have a cached page, IE retrieves a copy from the Web.
Automatically	IE starts by using the preceding method — but it keeps track of the pages you visit and how frequently they change. Using some magic formula (which, again, Microsoft doesn't divulge), IE figures out which pages you view change a lot, and which change very little. Ultimately, IE decides whether or not to look for a new copy on the Web.
Never	You only get what's in the cache. The first time you go to a Web page, it's put in the cache, but after that, you have to hit the Refresh icon or press F5 to update it.

I increase the size of the cache until it hurts. As long as you have a lot of hard drive space available, increasing the Web cache size to 2MB or more is a good idea.

4. **In the Temporary Internet Files Folder, increase the Amount of Disk Space to Use (cache size) and click OK twice.**

   Your changes take effect immediately.

Downloading pages overnight

You can tell IE that you want it to save a Web page — stick it in the cache — and even schedule the caching to take place overnight, while you're asleep (assuming your PC is connected to the Internet). Any page that doesn't change very often is a good candidate for caching. If you retrieve those sluggish pages while you're dreaming, you save a whole bunch of time when you're sitting at the monitor.

Of course, some pages aren't suitable for caching at all: news sites, for one, or any other Web site that changes frequently.

You can always save a Web page: There's no need to set up an automatic download if all you need to do is save the current page. To save a Web page in Internet Explorer, choose FileÍSave As. If you set the Save As Type drop-down box to save a Web Archive, Single File (`*.mht`), you get the entire Web page, including graphics, in one single file.

You can tell Internet Explorer to download a bunch of pages early in the morning and then look at them when you get to the office. The cached pages download much quicker than pages you retrieve right from the Internet. To make sure IE uses the page that's saved in the cache, choose File⇨Work Offline. To go back to working directly on the Internet, choose File⇨Work Online.

The simplest, fastest way to cache a Web page is to tell IE you want to cache it when you add the page to your Favorites list:

1. **Start Internet Explorer.**
2. **Navigate to the Web page you want to cache and choose Favorites⇨Add to Favorites.**

   IE shows you the Add Favorite dialog box shown in Figure 23-8.

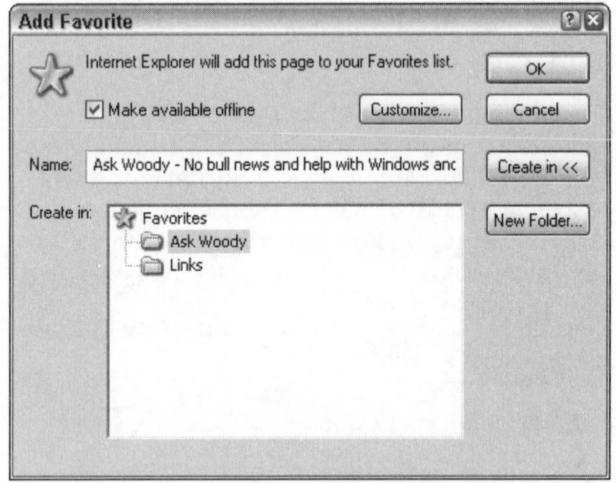

• **Figure 23-8: Caching a Web page is fast and easy when you add it to your Favorites list.**

3. **Check the Make Available Offline box and click the Customize button.**

   The Offline Favorite Wizard springs to life.

4. **Click Next.**

   The Offline Favorite Wizard asks you about caching linked pages, too.

5. **If you regularly want to link from the cached page to other pages, set the depth.**

The deepest I ever go is 2. Even so, if the page I'm caching has 10 links, and each of the pages *it* links to has 10 links, I'm asking Internet Explorer to download 100 pages just to cache this one. Imagine what that number would be like if I set the depth for 10.

6. **Click Next.**

   The wizard asks if you want to perform the caching manually (which usually doesn't make a whole lot of sense), or whether you want it to take place automatically.

7. **Select the I Would Like to Create a New Schedule radio button and click Next.**

   The wizard gives you an opportunity to set the schedule (see Figure 23-9). This caching takes place independently of Windows Scheduler (which I discuss at length in Technique 56).

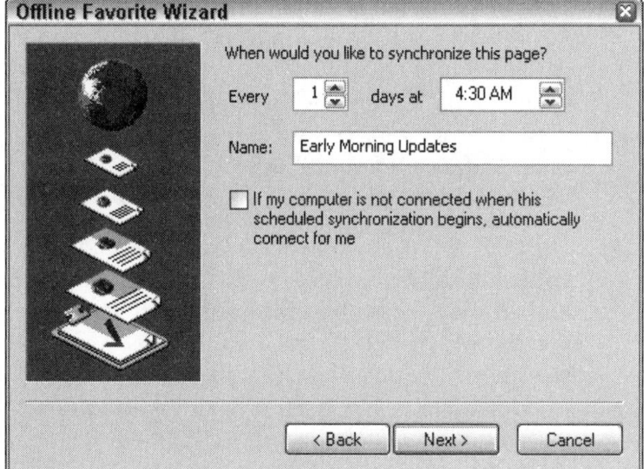

• **Figure 23-9: Set the schedule.**

If you have Check Disk or a defrag run scheduled for the early morning hours, consider running your Web caching either before or after.

8. **Choose the schedule you want and click Next.**

9. **Provide a password, if necessary, and click Finish.**

If the page you want to cache is already in your Favorites, the procedure is similar:

1. **Start Internet Explorer.**

2. **Choose Favorites⇨Organize Favorites.**

   IE shows you the Organize Favorites dialog box.

3. **On the right, select the page you want to download automatically and check the Make Available Offline box.**

   IE puts a Properties button on the Organize Favorites dialog box (see Figure 23-10).

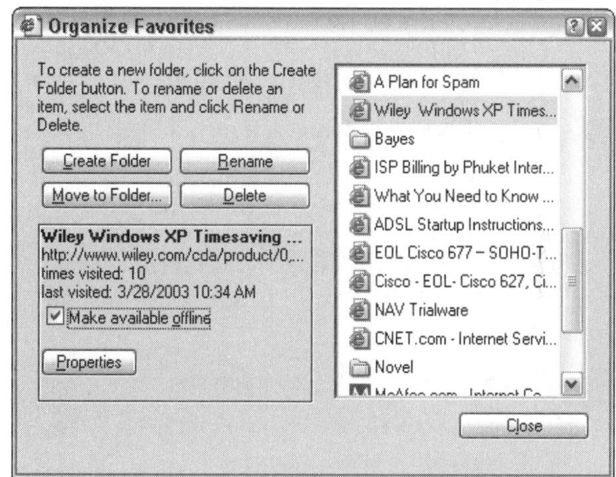

• **Figure 23-10: The Properties button only appears after you check Make Available Offline.**

4. **Click Properties.**

   IE responds by showing you a shortcut dialog box specifically for Internet shortcuts.

5. **Click the Schedule tab.**

   On the Schedule tab, tell IE when to download the page. It's similar to the Offline Favorite Wizard's schedule settings.

   You can choose one of the existing download times or create a new one. If you have a Disk Cleanup or Defragmenter session going on with Windows Scheduler (which is an entirely different part of Windows), make sure the download(s) you request don't coincide with times that your computer is preoccupied.

6. **Make your scheduling choices and then click the Download tab.**

   Here (see Figure 23-11) you choose whether pages referenced by the current page are to be downloaded and, if so, how far down the chain IE should go. As I explain earlier in this technique, I never go more than 2 links deep — and try not to go that far.

On the Download tab, you can also have IE send you an e-mail when a page has changed. Unfortunately, the notification doesn't tell you much (there's no Sender e-mail address and no body text in the message) and your Junk Mail filter (if you have one) may well kick it out as junk.

7. **Make download changes, if any, and click OK.**

From this point on, the page downloads into the cache according to the schedule you set.

• **Figure 23-11: Download details.**

Finding Uncommon Methods for Common Tasks

There's a core set of IE skills — and features that you should use all the time — if you want to speed up your browsing enormously. Unless you have an abysmally slow Internet connection, the following sections are required reading.

Using important IE keyboard shortcuts

Here are three timesaving key combinations that every IE user should know:

- **Ctrl+Enter:** If you type the middle part of an address in the Address bar — say, `wiley` — and then press Ctrl+Enter, IE immediately puts an `http://www.` on the front, and a `.com` on the back. Type **wiley** and press Ctrl+Enter, and IE immediately knows to look for `http://www.wiley.com`.
- **Ctrt+F5:** If you think that the Web page is "stuck" — it isn't being updated properly, perhaps because it's been put in the cache on your PC — pressing Ctrl+F5 forces IE to go out and get the latest copy of the current page. In theory, IE even blasts past copies that are cached with your Internet service provider (which can be a real headache if your ISP is slow to update cached pages).
- **Shift+click:** When you click a link, sometimes you want to leave the old page in place while you look at the new page — for example, if you're going through Google and want to look at several search-results pages at the same time. To force IE to open a Web page in a new window, hold down Shift while you click the link.

Put a sticker on your monitor with those three key combinations until they become ingrained in your fingers' little gray cells.

The rest of the shortcuts (see Table 23-2) are gravy. They can save you some time if you fear rodents, or if you repeat some specific action many times in a day. But I wouldn't lose a lot of sleep over them.

Unhijacking the Back button

Have you ever surfed to a Web page and noticed that the Back button suddenly doesn't work? You can click Back over and over again, and you never get off the page. I think Dante reserved the sixth ring of hell for Web sites that hijack the Back button. Or at least he should've.

Table 23-2: Worthwhile Internet Explorer Keyboard Shortcuts

Press This Key (or Keys)	And IE Does This
F5	Refresh the current page (same as clicking the Refresh button), but if you really want to refresh the current page and bypass your Internet service provider's cache, press Ctrl+F5.
F11	Full Screen Mode — eliminate all but the Standard Button bar. Return to normal by pressing F11 again.
Ctrl+mouse wheel	Increase or decrease the size of the font on the current page. This doesn't work on all Web pages.
Ctrl+D	Add the current page to the bottom of your Favorites list, which is probably the last place you want to put it.
Esc	Stop loading the current page.
Home	Go to the top of the page.
End	Go to the bottom of the page.
Page Down or spacebar	Scroll down one screen. If your cursor is in a text box, pressing the spacebar doesn't work.
Page Up or Shift+↑	Scroll up one screen.
Alt+← or Backspace	Same as clicking the Back button.
Alt+→	Same as clicking the Forward button.

Unfortunately, you can't do anything to prevent the hijacking. But you can do something to bypass it.

If you right-click the Back button, a list of the sites you have visited recently appears. Even if the Web page commandeers your Back button, it can't wipe out your history. Right-click Back and move back to someplace safe.

Creating custom shortcuts from the Address bar

When most people first start using IE, they think they have to type in the full URL, or Web address, and they worry that upper- and lowercase letters matter. So they type something like:

```
http://www.Wiley.com
```

Pretty soon, most people learn that you don't need the `http://`, and that lowercase and uppercase are all the same on the new frontier. So this works fine:

```
www.wiley.com
```

If you read the section, "Using important IE keyboard shortcuts," earlier in this technique, you have probably hit the first stage of enlightenment: You know that typing

```
wiley
```

and pressing Ctrl+Enter takes you to the same place.

Are you ready for the next step?

TweakUI has a capability called Search String, which lets you set up your own shortcuts for the IE Address bar. For example, if you regularly visit AskWoody.com, you can set up IE so that the keyword `aw` takes you to `www.askwoody.com`. But that's not all.

Some Web sites are set up to move you directly to a page based on some parameter that you can provide. For example, if you have a Microsoft Knowledge Base article number, you can go straight to the article by typing `support.microsoft.com/?kbid=` **and then the number. You can use this capability with**

keywords to open a page in a few nimble keystrokes, bypassing whatever click-scroll-type-paste routine you might otherwise have to use.

For example, I'm constantly going to the Microsoft Knowledge Base (KB), looking for specific articles.

Using the TweakUI search shortcut, I can simply type **kb** and the article number in the Internet Explorer Address bar, as shown in Figure 23-12, and press Enter. IE goes directly to the article I want.

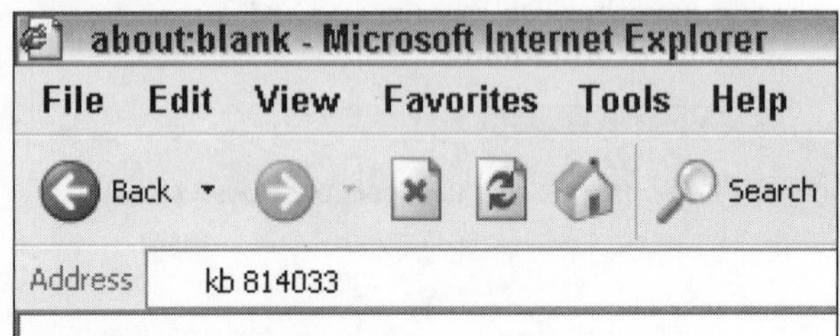

• **Figure 23-12: With this trick, I just type kb and the article number I'm looking for.**

Full details on what TweakUI does, finding it (for free online), and downloading it are in Technique 5. When you have the program set up, you can use it to get to specific pages on indexed sites like this very, very quickly. Here's how to set up TweakUI to do your bidding:

1. **Download and install TweakUI.**
2. **Choose Start➪All Programs➪PowerToys for Windows XP➪TweakUI.**

   The TweakUI About screen appears.
3. **On the left, choose Internet Explorer➪Search.**

   The Search Prefixes screen appears on the right (see Figure 23-13).
4. **Click Create.**

   TweakUI brings up a Search Prefix dialog box (see Figure 23-14).
5. **In the Prefix box, type whatever shorthand you want to use for the Web site.**

   In this case, I want to be able to type **kb** and have it go to the MS Knowledge Base.

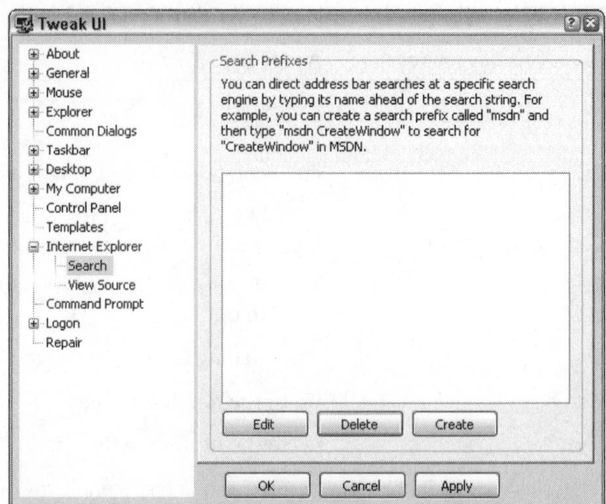

• **Figure 23-13: TweakUI calls these *search prefixes,* but they aren't limited to searches.**

6. **In the URL box, type the Web address of the site you want, using** %s **wherever your typed string should go.**

   In this case, `support.microsoft.com/?kbid=%s` takes the string that I type after `kb` (the Knowledge Base article number), slaps the entire address together, and makes IE go out and find the site (and article) I'm looking for.
7. **Click OK and then click the Close (X) button to exit TweakUI.**

   You need to shut down any open IE windows and start IE again. Test the shortcut by typing a sample string (in my case, I typed **kb 814033** to verify that Internet Explorer goes straight to Microsoft Knowledge Base article 814033).

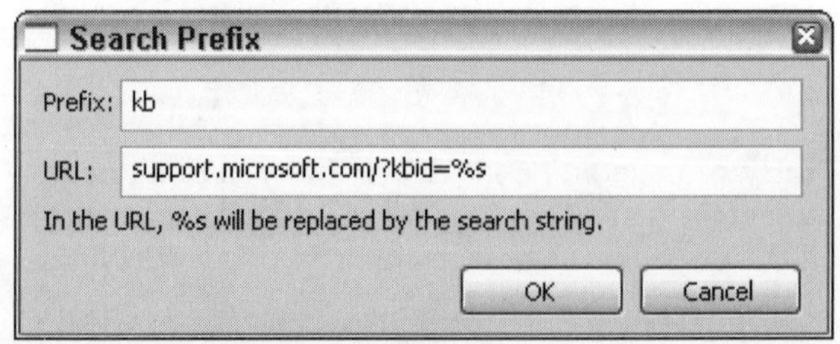

• **Figure 23-14: Set up the prefix.**

Controlling Favorites — Directly

Many people save time with a well-organized bunch of Favorites, each placed in the correct folder. Keeping Favorites organized is every bit as important as organizing the My Documents folder structure — more so, if you spend a lot of time with IE.

Some folks have good intentions, but never get around to organizing their Favorites very well. See Figure 23-15 for a horrible real-world example from my, uh, my er, my messy alter ego. Honest, I've been meaning to clean it up. The dog ate it.

A big part of the problem in organizing favorites is the hokey user interface Internet Explorer uses to "help" people keep it clean.

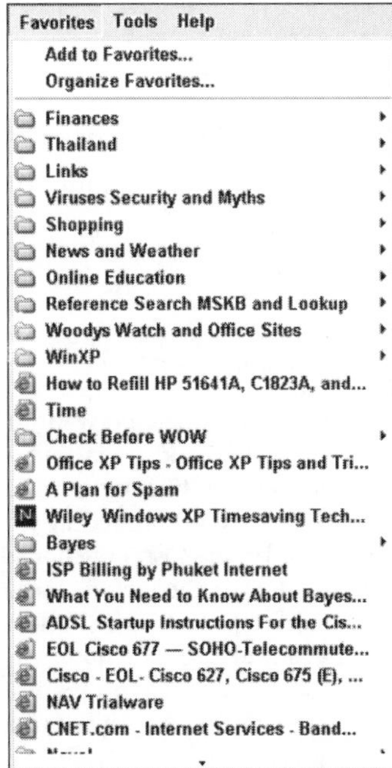

• **Figure 23-15: Don't let me fool you. This was my Favorites list before I cleaned it up.**

Believe it or not, the IE Favorites list is actually based on a folder — more precisely, a bunch of folders — that IE uses to reconstruct the list on the fly. You'll find it much easier, faster, and more accurate to abandon the IE user interface and work directly with the Favorites folder. Here's how:

1. **Start Internet Explorer.**
2. **Hold down the Shift key and then choose Favorites⇨Organize Favorites.**

   If you hold down the Shift key, you go straight to the location on your hard drive where IE keeps its Favorites list. Windows Explorer opens in your Favorites folder (see Figure 23-16).

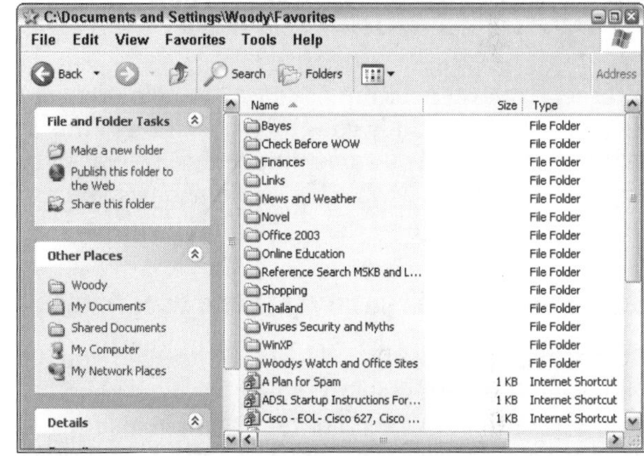

• **Figure 23-16: The folder structure that gives rise to the spaghetti in Figure 23-15.**

3. **Make changes to speed up your navigating through the Favorites maze.**

   You can create new folders, rename them, and move them around. You can also create shortcuts to documents or other folders, anywhere on your hard drive — or even on a shared folder.

4. **When you're happy with the organization, choose File⇨Exit to leave Windows Explorer.**
5. **Back in Internet Explorer, click Favorites to confirm that you like your changes.**

   There's a key final step. Reorganizing folders and shortcuts sets up the structure of the Favorites list, but the order of the items on the list is stored deep inside IE.

6. **To list your favorites in the order you want them to appear, open your Favorites menu in IE, and click and drag any folder or items to new locations.**

   When you drag any line in the Favorites list, you see a dark bar where the item will go. Simply right-click, drag, and release to move folders and individual shortcuts.

7. **Close any open IE windows.**

   All your changes are now saved.

Keeping IE under Control

Internet Explorer goes out of its way to help you, and in some cases, it simply goes too far: Although the features may save you some time, they also leave you exposed in various ways. This section shows you how to turn off some of those "helpful" features.

Removing "saved" passwords and user names

Back when you first started using IE, it asked you if you wanted the program to remember your passwords, so you didn't need to type them in again. Chances are pretty good you let IE have its way. IE is possibly storing your passwords even now.

I have a few objections to allowing IE to save my passwords:

- **I don't like to have my passwords sitting around in a file somewhere, even if they're protected and encrypted.** I don't trust IE to absolutely, positively keep my passwords safe from every clever virus or worm that's running around. Call me paranoid.
- **I've learned the hard way that if I don't type my passwords on a semi-regular basis, I forget what they are.** Memory's the second thing to go, right?
- **I don't like the idea that anyone casually walking by my PC, who can log on to Windows with my ID, can then log on to any site and pretend to be me.** That's particularly distressing if any of my credit card information has ever been entered on any form — and my bank accounts? Fuhgeddaboutit.

The minute you let anyone sit down at your PC, he or she can break anything on it. It should send shivers down your spine that anybody who can guess your Windows password immediately has access to any Web site, and he or she can do anything you can do (in your name), including shopping with your credit card or sending wire transfers from your bank account.

Besides, typing in a user name and password takes only a few seconds. That's time well spent, in my opinion.

Don't let IE hold onto your passwords. Period. To keep IE from storing away your passwords, follow these steps:

1. **Start Internet Explorer.**
2. **Choose Tools⇨Internet Options⇨Content.**

   IE shows you the Internet Options dialog box shown in Figure 23-17.

3. **Click AutoComplete.**

   IE brings up the AutoComplete Settings dialog box shown in Figure 23-18.

In general, to save time, you want to have IE remember the Web addresses that you type. I don't like the idea of IE storing my credit card number to be used automatically when filling out forms on the Web, so I uncheck the Forms box. That's a tough choice for timesavers because it also tells IE that it shouldn't store your name, address, phone number, and so on, to use on forms — but them's the breaks. I figure I'm potentially saving myself more than simple time by playing it safe. But you may disagree.

Use Table 23-3 to figure out how to handle the last two check boxes.

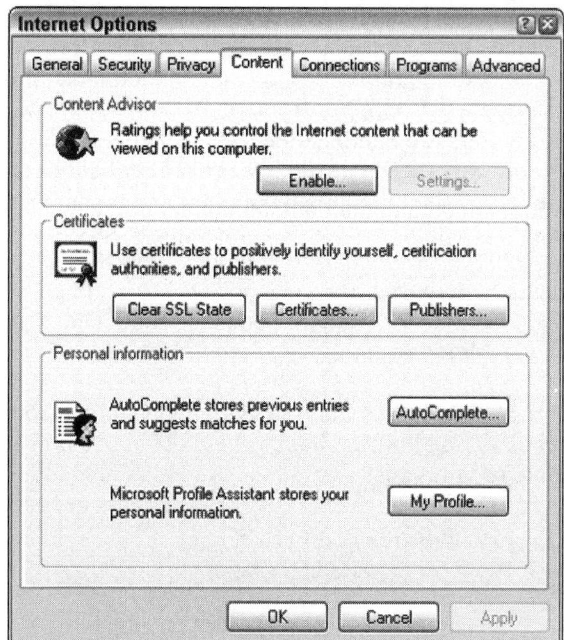

• **Figure 23-17: The Content tab holds a hodgepodge of settings.**

4. **In the Use AutoComplete For area, choose the settings that work best for you.**
5. **If you want to clear out any of IE's current AutoComplete data, click the appropriate button.**

   If you click Clear Passwords, IE deletes all the passwords that it has stored. If you click Clear Forms, all the data IE has — including all user names and passwords, in addition to addresses, telephone numbers and the like — gets the heave-ho.

6. **Click OK twice.**

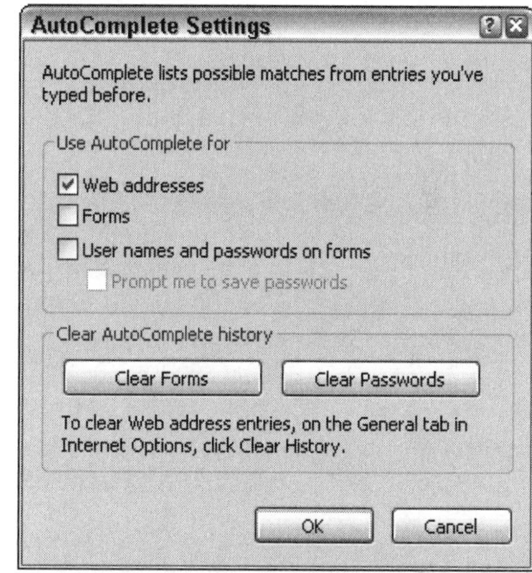

• **Figure 23-18: Deciding on the last two boxes can be tricky.**

TABLE 23-3: CONSEQUENCES OF INTERNET EXPLORER AUTOCOMPLETE OPTIONS

User Names and Passwords on Forms	Prompt Me to Save Passwords	IE Does This
Checked	Checked	IE stores all the user names you enter on forms, but it only stores passwords if you explicitly give permission when you type the password. If you can remember to tell IE that it's okay to remember relatively unimportant passwords (say, the password to log on to a news site, or a vendor's support site), but can always remember to tell IE to not remember important passwords (for example, on a banking site), this is a good, timesaving combination.
Checked	Not Checked	This is the most dangerous combination. IE remembers all the user names and passwords that you enter and offers them when anyone using your Windows ID reaches the logon Web page.
Not Checked	N/A	IE doesn't store any user names or passwords. The most secure — but most time-consuming — option. This is the one I use.

If you want to delete some AutoComplete entries (such as your credit card numbers) but want to use others (such as your name and address), there's a way. The next time you fill out a form on the Web and you see some data you don't want IE to remember, double-click the box that's coming up with your sensitive data, and then click the unwanted entry once and press Delete. That gets rid of it.

Untrusting trusted publishers

How many times have you seen a dialog box like the one in Figure 23-19?

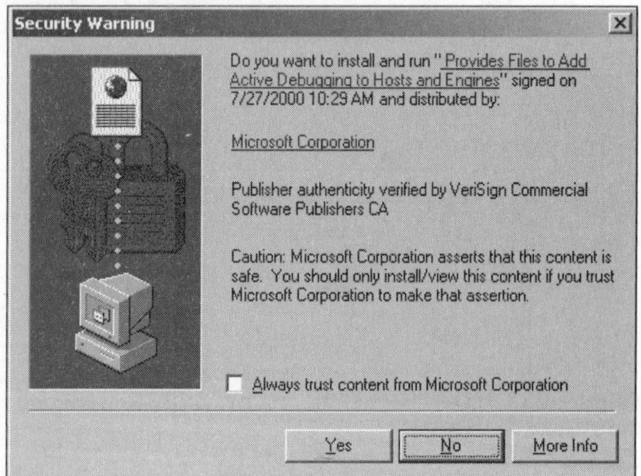

• **Figure 23-19: A typical digital signature warning dialog box from Microsoft — or is it?**

Chances are good that you checked the Always Trust Content from Microsoft Corporation box and never thought twice about it.

Or did you?

On January 29 and 30, 2001, VeriSign — the company that issues those certificates — handed out two completely bogus certificates to an, uh, enterprising fellow who managed to convince the VeriSign folks that he represented Microsoft. Of course, he didn't.

The situation isn't quite as dire as you might think because checking the Always Trust Content from Microsoft Corporation box doesn't, in fact, mean that IE always trusts content from Microsoft Corporation. The reasons are complicated, but they have to do with the way these certificates are authenticated on individual PCs (see `www.microsoft.com/technet/security/bulletin/MS01-017.mspx` for details).

Nonetheless, I strongly urge you to not trust content from *any* corporation — much less Microsoft.

If you have checked that Always Trust Content from Microsoft Corporation box in the past, here's how to atone for your sins:

1. **Start Internet Explorer.**
2. **Choose Tools⇨Internet Options⇨Content.**

   IE displays the Internet Options dialog box.
3. **Click Certificates.**
4. **Using the arrows to the right of the tabs, move to the Trusted Publishers tab (see Figure 23-20).**

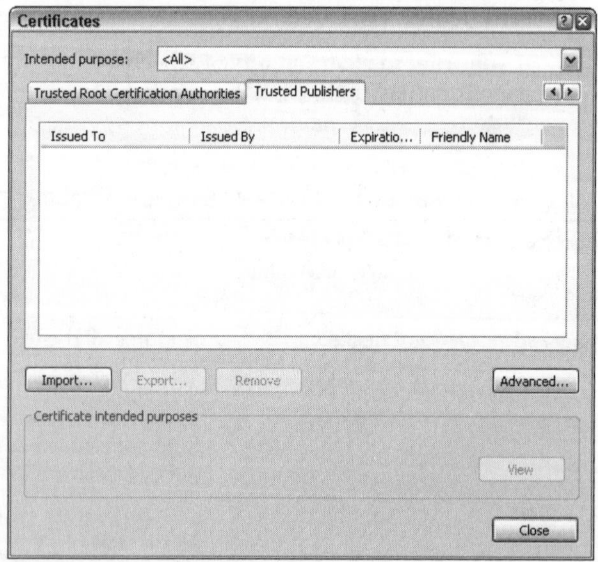

• **Figure 23-20: Any company that you've told IE to trust is listed here.**

5. **If the Trusted Publishers list contains any entries, select each entry, one by one, and then click Remove.**

   In the future, don't trust anyone, okay?

Checking for add-ons and parasites

A *parasite* is a program that's been installed, usually without your knowledge, usually through Internet Explorer, that doesn't benefit you in any way. An add-on is a program that's been installed, usually without your knowledge, that may or may not be of any benefit.

See the difference?

Typically, you get parasites when you download and install a free software package. Sometimes, you install the parasite as a byproduct of installing a program that you really want, after clicking Yes to a warning like the one in Figure 23-19. Frequently, the good program's installer has a tiny notice buried in the End User License Agreement (EULA) that says you grant your permission for the parasite to be installed.

If you had an extra lifetime or two, you could go over the EULAs with a fine-toothed comb. It's far better simply to check your PC for parasites from time to time. You can use a good (but not infallible) checker at www.doxdesk.com/parasite. It's free. Use it.

With Service Pack 2, Internet Explorer now gives you the ability to manage the programs that have insinuated themselves into IE. If you think you have a rogue program that's taken over IE — perhaps the home page keeps resetting itself to a porn search site, or you keep getting redirected to a "helpful" shopping site — check and make sure that IE is only using add-ons that you approve:

1. **Start Internet Explorer, and choose Tools⇨Manage Add-Ons.**

   You can choose to see a list of the currently loaded add-ons, or all the add-ons that IE has run recently (Figure 23-21).

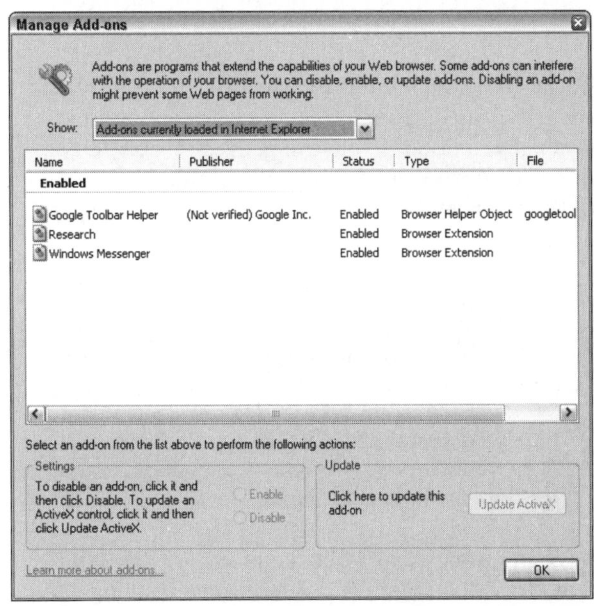

Figure 23-21: Internet Explorer can show you a list of all the add-ons that have been run.

2. **If you come across any suspicious add-ons on the list, try running a Google search (if you can!) to see if any other IE users are experiencing problems with the add-on.**

   The names of problematic add-ons can be quite innocuous. If you don't know what a particular add-on does, a quick trip to Google can provide some illumination.

3. **To disable an add-on, click it, and in the Settings area at the bottom, click Disable.**

4. **When you're done, click OK.**

   IE returns to browsing.

Once in a blue moon you may disable an add-on that does something useful. If that happens, IE simply won't run the program — typically, it does nothing when you click a button and expect something to happen.

Configuring security zones

Internet Explorer's security zones offer a fast way for you to control what specific Web pages can do to your PC.

Every Web site belongs to a security zone. Each security zone has its own set of rules and limitations. If you don't do anything, every Web site goes into the Internet zone. And if you don't do anything to the Internet zone, sites in the Internet zone can't do much.

Make sense?

You can spend the rest of your weekends this year tweaking security zone settings, but you won't accomplish much. If a site wants to get you, it must find a way to bypass the security zones anyway — in other words, find a new bug in Internet Explorer.

Once in a very great while, you may need to tell IE that it can "trust" specific sites. Some banking sites, for example, work only if you move the site into the Trusted Sites zone. Here's a fast, accurate way to put a site in the Trusted Sites zone:

1. **Start Internet Explorer.**
2. **Bring up a page on the site you want to trust.**
3. **Select the site's address in the Address bar, and press Ctrl+C to copy the address that you want to trust.**
4. **In the lower-right corner of the IE screen, double-click the Internet icon.**

   IE brings up the Internet Security Properties dialog box (see Figure 23-22). You can also open the dialog box by choosing Tools➪Internet Options➪Security.
5. **Click Trusted Sites and then click the Sites button.**

   IE shows you the Trusted Sites dialog box in Figure 23-23.

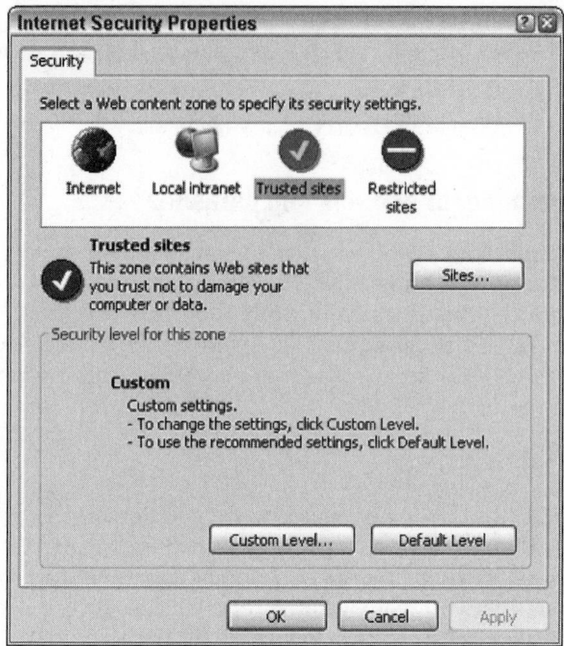

• Figure 23-22: Control the security of each zone and assign sites to zones in this dialog box.

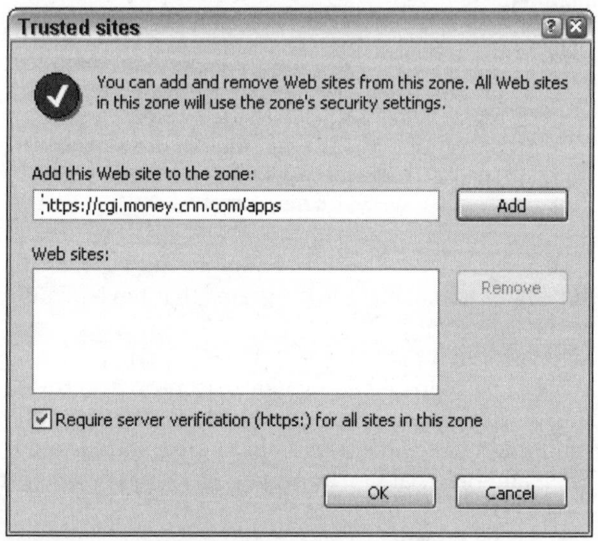

• Figure 23-23: Add specific pages or entire sites to the Trusted Sites zone.

6. **Click in the Add This Web Site to the Zone box. Press Ctrl+V to paste the current Web page's address into the box. Then click Add.**

   The page or site that you add becomes part of the Trusted Sites zone. In Figure 23-23, adding `https://cgi.money.cnn.com/apps` to the Trusted Sites zone means that any page under `https://cgi.money.cnn.com/apps` — including, say, `https://cgi.money.cnn.com/apps/abc.html` — is also in the Trusted Sites zone.

7. **Click OK twice, and the change takes effect immediately.**

Riding herd on pop-ups

When was the first time you saw a pop-up (or pop-under) ad? I bet it was in 2001. That's when pop-ups started appearing in earnest. You were surfing on one of the main sites at the time — maybe nytimes.com, drkoop.com, or weather.com. (Nowadays it doesn't matter whether a site is big or small — many of them have succumbed.) You closed all the Internet Explorer windows you had opened, and there it was: a little, lonesome window with an ad for an amazing new "tiny wireless camera" called the X10, beckoning you to click through to the X10 Web site. And click you did.

In May 2001, the X10 Web site was the fifth most-visited site on the Internet. The X10 people laughed all the way to the bank. Several banks. And the Web has never been the same.

The generic term *pop-up ad* covers:

- **True pop-ups:** These ads appear as separate, smaller Internet Explorer windows on top of the Web page you're trying to see.
- **Pop-unders:** These ads appear underneath the page you're trying to see. Pop-under ads are more common than pop-ups. They don't get in your face. You don't even bump into a pop-under ad until you minimize or exit out of the main page. There's usually a bit of ambiguity about how a pop-under gets there: Any page you've visited could've, uh, deposited it.
- **Pop-overs:** These ads usually appear when you try to exit a page. They're incredibly obnoxious — you're trying to leave a site, and a pop-over pulls you back in. The best way to get out of a pop-over is to press Ctrl+Alt+Del, click the Internet Explorer task(s) that's running the pop-over, and click End Task.

If you've installed Windows XP Service Pack 2, your copy of Internet Explorer acquired a pop-up blocker. Not a great pop-up blocker, mind you: It's definitely a "version 1.0" product, with plenty of surprises. For example, IE's pop-up blocker doesn't block some pop-ups but it sure does block a lot of windows that aren't pop-ups, including many on microsoft.com!

Worse, the pop-up blocker can cause Internet Explorer to crash. An early bug in the pop-up blocker crashed IE when you surfed to Microsoft's own Windows Update site. See `support.microsoft.com/?kbid=883820`.

When IE encounters a pop-up ad, it's supposed to put a line underneath the address line alerting you to the fact, and it's supposed to block the pop-up (see Figure 23-24). It's not supposed to crash, but you probably guessed that.

• Figure 23-24: The yellow Information Bar lets you override IE and make it show you the blocked pop-up.

Overriding the double download inanity

Far too frequently, IE blocks actions that you specifically request. For example, if I go to TechSmith.com and try to download SnagIt, their award-winning screen capture utility, IE doesn't let me. I navigate to the download page, click the Download button, and IE's Information Bar jumps in to block the download (see Figure 23-25).

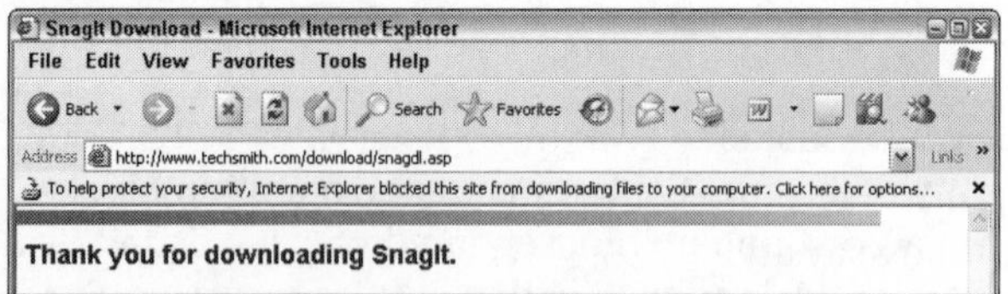

• **Figure 23-25: IE's Information Bar stops the action and gets in the way far too often.**

Of course, IE jumping in at this point is absolutely ridiculous. You've already specifically told the computer that you want to download a file. And even after you tell IE to download it, you need to jump through two (or more) dialog boxes before you can actually run it. What a waste of time!

To force IE to download files automatically, bypassing the Information Bar warning and its concomitant click shuck-and-jive:

1. **Start Internet Explorer. Choose Tools⇨Internet Options⇨Security.**

   IE shows you the security settings for the Internet Zone, which is the "zone" that almost all Web pages fall into.

2. **Click Custom Level.**

   That allows you to alter the default security settings for most Web pages.

3. **Scroll down to Downloads. Under Automatic Prompting for File Downloads, click the Enable button.**

4. **Click OK twice to go back to IE. (After clicking the first OK, you may get a dialog box asking if you're sure about the new setting.)**

   The Information Bar never complains about downloading a file again. Note that you still get the Security Warning in Figure 23-26, every time you download a file.

• **Figure 23-26: Even with the Information Bar disabled for downloads, you still get a Security Warning like this one.**

Saving Time with Google

Save Time By

- Installing and using the Google Toolbar
- Making your Web searches work right — the first time
- Playing Google like a violin

Even though everybody says that Google is the best search engine, not everybody knows just how great Google is. Some of the engine's most timesaving parts are also its best-kept secrets. That's a shame, really, because folks who spend time searching the Web for information can save a lot of effort if they know how to use Google effectively. And folks who *don't* spend time searching the Web for things should.

This technique has the potential to save you more time than all the other techniques in this book put together — especially if you spend a lot of time doing online research. If you can learn to search for answers quickly and thoroughly — and cut through the garbage on the Web just as quickly and thoroughly — you can't help but save time in everything you do.

Microsoft's alternative, MSN Search, doesn't ring my chimes. Your results may vary – and you should certainly give MSN Search a run around the block – but my experiences with MSN Search leave a lot to be desired. As a real-world example, I tried running a search for "Windows XP SP2 Cannot Start Firewall" through both search engines. Both engines returned the standard Knowledge Base article on top (which didn't solve my problem). The next three results in Google were germane; the next three in MSN Search didn't come close. See Figure 24-1 for details.

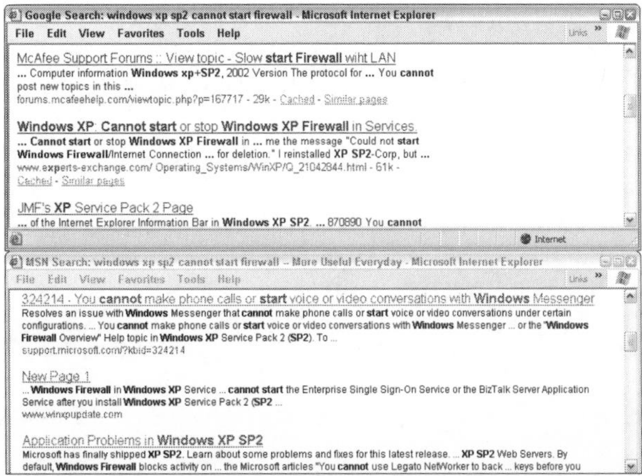

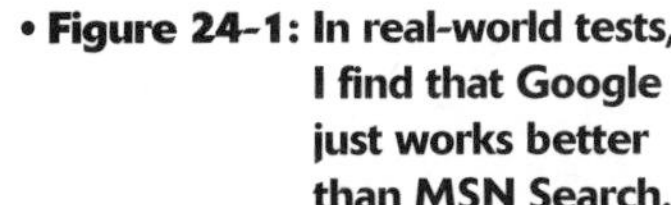

• Figure 24-1: In real-world tests, I find that Google just works better than MSN Search.

Using the Google Toolbar

The folks at Google created the Google Toolbar, shown in Figure 24-2, so you would use their Web search engine more often: The toolbar's surprising flexibility makes searching for almost anything easy as can be. Because you probably want to use Google for Internet searches anyway, putting the toolbar in your copy of Internet Explorer makes a whole lot of sense.

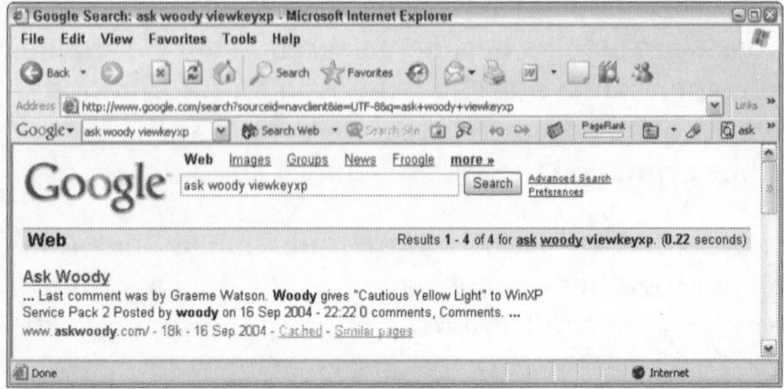

• **Figure 24-2: The Google Toolbar.**

If you spend any time at all searching the Web, the Google Toolbar rates as a timesaver of the first degree. It's also free.

The Google Toolbar is not without controversy. If you tell the Toolbar that you want it to rank the importance of pages — that is, if you use the so-called "Advanced" Toolbar, you also consent to sending information about your surfing behavior to Google's database. The two work together: the more people who look at a page, the higher its rating. In order to keep track of how many people go to a page, the database has to keep track of what you do (although Google says it doesn't collect any personally identifiable information). So if you want to participate in this part of Google's PageRank system, you have to allow Google to track what you're doing. For more about the PageRank controversy, more is at `www.google-watch.org/pagerank.html`.

You can use the Toolbar without sending any information to Google. But to take full advantage of PageRank, you have to let some go. Fortunately, Google makes the choices clear, obvious, and unambiguous.

Installing the Toolbar

You can install the Google Toolbar in your sleep:

1. **Start Internet Explorer and go to** `toolbar.google.com`**.**
2. **At the bottom of the page, pick your language and click Download Google Toolbar. After the file downloads, run it (you may have to click Run and/or OK to get past the security warnings). Read the Terms of Use and then click Agree.**

   The Google company has a very up-front warning about its "spying" on your Web behavior (see Figure 24-3). The key question is whether you want the Google Toolbar to silently send information about your Web surfing behavior to the giant Google database in the sky. It's not an easy choice, but I've decided to go ahead and let Google watch over my shoulder, in exchange for more advanced capabilities. You need to choose whatever makes you comfortable.

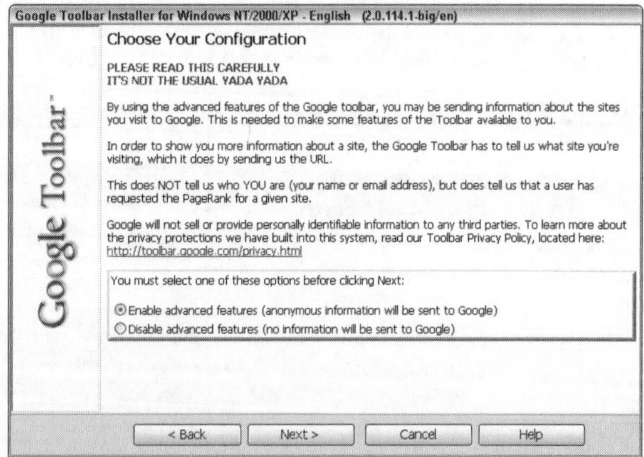

• **Figure 24-3: Whether to have PageRank or not, that is the question.**

You have every reason to be queasy about allowing a program — one that looks like a toolbar — onto your machine, knowing that it does send out information about you and that the precise nature of that information could be modified in the future, if you're ever asked for permission to update the Toolbar. Or, to put it in a somewhat different light, I trust Google. I don't trust Microsoft. How about you?

3. **If you're willing to let the Toolbar send detailed information about your surfing behavior (but not about you, personally) to the Google database, click the Enable Advanced Features option. Otherwise, click the Disable Advanced Features option. Then click Next.**

4. **Pick a default Google site, verify that you want to make Google your default search engine, and then click Next.**

If you make Google your default search engine, the next time you use IE's Search pane, you won't be accosted by that %$#@! canine, Rover, and his intelligence-inhibited actions. Instead, you get a simple, clean search pane with a place to type your search criteria, and no cutesy agents.

When the Google Toolbar is installed, you see it (as shown in Figure 24-4).

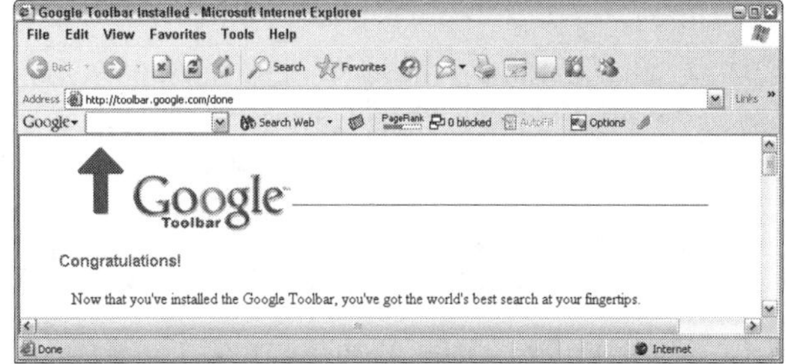

• **Figure 24-4: The Google Toolbar installer makes very certain that you see your new Toolbar.**

5. **Test the Google Toolbar by typing your name in the Search box and pressing Enter.**

Bet you didn't know that your name was so popular.

If you ever want to turn off the Google Toolbar, right-click any empty spot on any toolbar and uncheck the Google option.

Getting around the Toolbar

The Google Toolbar packs a lot of wallop into a small space. Here are the high points:

- **Google Menu:** The drop-down Google Menu (see Figure 24-5) lets you jump directly to various Google pages, so you can use Google's more sophisticated search features quickly. The page you're most likely to jump to is the Advanced Search page.

  The Google Menu also allows you to customize the Google Toolbar. I tell you more about that in the next section.

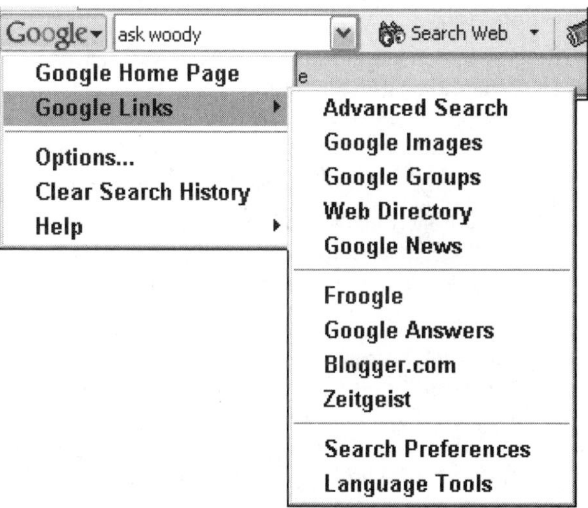

• **Figure 24-5: Jump straight to various Google pages.**

- **Search Terms box:** You'll spend most of your time working in the Search Terms box (see Figure 24-6). Type the words that you want to find in this box, and then press Enter or click the Search Web button. Google searches the Web for what you ask.
- **Search Site:** If you're working on a Web site that doesn't have its own search engine, the Search

Site button can help. A lot. You have to set up the toolbar specifically to show you the Search Site button (I show you how in the next section). After you do, type the terms you want to find in the Search Terms box and then click Search Site. Google performs the search, restricting itself to the current Web site.

Frequently, a Google search of a site is more useful — and faster — than using the site's own built-in search engine.

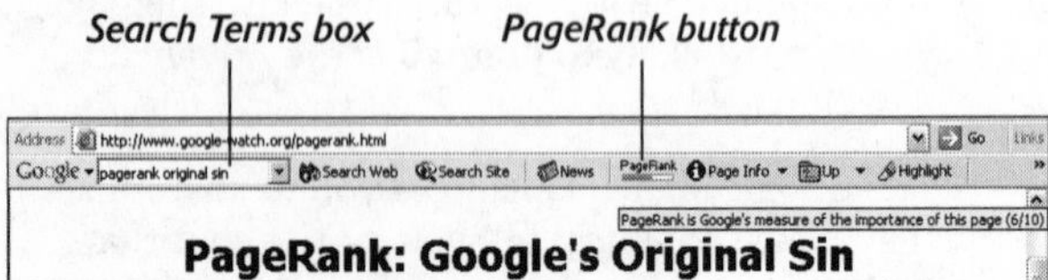

• **Figure 24-6: The Search Terms box.**

- **News:** You might think, given the way Search Web and Search Site behave, that typing something in the Search Terms box and clicking the News button would bring up the Google News service, with a search on those terms.

  You'd be wrong. When you click the News button, Google goes to its News page and ignores whatever is in the Search Terms box.

- **PageRank:** When you hover your mouse over the PageRank button — assuming you opted for the Advanced Google Toolbar — you see Google's assigned PageRank, on a scale from 0 to 10 (see Figure 24-6). A PageRank of 6 or higher generally means you're looking at a reliable page that many other sites refer to.

- **Page Info:** Click the Page Info button, and Google shows you a copy of the page as it was originally scanned, a list of similar pages, a list of pages that link to this page, or a machine-generated (and, generally not very good) translation of the page into the language you're using.

- **Up:** The Up button lets you move up from the current Web site. If you're looking at `www.AskWoody.com/books/WindowsXP` and you click the Up button, IE moves to `www.AskWoody.com/books`. You have to install the Up button manually — see the next section.

- **Highlight:** If you click the Highlight button, Internet Explorer highlights the words in the Search Terms box that appear in the Web page, each with a different color.

Getting the most out of the Toolbar

No two people search the same way. (There's something metaphysical about that statement.) Ultimately, you need to find the best Google Toolbar configuration for you. Check out Tables 24-1 and 24-2 for my recommendations on which options you should check (meaning, "Yes, Google, I want to use this option") and what you can skip (meaning, "Nope, Google, I can live without this option").

The recommendations in Tables 24-1 and 24-2 are designed to place the most powerful buttons where you can get to them immediately. If you are running at a screen resolution higher than 1024 x 768 and can fit more buttons on your Toolbar, go for it.

To make changes to the Google Toolbar options, follow these steps:

1. **Download and install the Google Toolbar, using the procedure at the beginning of this technique.**
2. **Click the Options button on the Toolbar, if you can see it, or choose Google⇨Options.**

   Google shows you the main Toolbar Options page, shown in Figure 24-7. Check and uncheck buttons according to your preferences, based on the guidelines in Table 24-1.
3. **Click the More tab and make your selections according to Table 24-2.**
4. **At the bottom of the page, click OK.**

   Your new Google Toolbar is available immediately.

Table 24-1: Timesaving Google Toolbar Settings

Setting Name	How to Set It	Additional Info
Open a New Window	Unchecked	There's no need to tell Google to open search results in a new window, because you can automatically do that by holding down the Shift key when you click Search Web or Search Site, or press Enter to start a search.
Drop-Down Search History	Checked	Use the Toolbar's Search History features. If you want to erase the history, choose Google➪Clear Search History.
Highlight Button	Checked	Makes it easy to find the terms you searched for — and equally easy to turn off highlighting if the stripes get too distracting.
Word-Find Buttons	Checked	Google Toolbar creates one button for each word you type. Instead of using Edit➪Find to find the search terms on a page, you can simply click the button associated with the word. Very useful — if you have room for all the buttons.
Enable Browse By Name	Checked	Type a name in IE's address bar, push Enter, get a search. Or, if Google's pretty sure, you go straight to the site.
PageRank display	Checked	A number from 0 to 10 that reflects how many sites refer to the page and how many people look at it. This number drives the Google search engine, so a quick check of any Web page's PageRank can give you some indication of its importance. You can see the PageRank only if you volunteer to let Google keep track of your Web surfing. I use it, but you may be spooked by the privacy implications, for good reason. See the discussion in the section, "Using the Google Toolbar," earlier in this technique.
Page Info Menu	Unchecked	Lets you quickly find a cached snapshot of the current page, similar pages, a list of pages that link to the current page, and a very rudimentary language translation.
Popup Blocker	Unchecked	IE has its own pop-up blocker that works reasonably well. Two is overkill, and potentially confusing.
AutoFill	Unchecked	I'm always leery of storing my personal information and having a browser regurgitate it automatically.
Blog This!	Unchecked	Connects to Google's Blogger, which is cool if you're into that kind of thing. A blog (= weB LOG) is a journal posted on the Web. Updating a blog is quite easy, and many people use blogs as personal journals.
News	Checked	See "Viewing the news" later in this technique.
Options	Unchecked	If you want to change the options, choose Google➪Options.

Table 24-2: A Few More Timesaving Google Toolbar Settings

Setting Name	How to Set It	Additional Info
Up	Checked	Moves one level up from the current Web site: Press this button when you're at `www.microsoft.com/search`, and you move up to `www.microsoft.com`.
Next & Previous	Checked	Much like the Back and Forward buttons in IE itself, moves back and forth among the latest Google searches.

(continued)

Table 24-2 *(continued)*

Setting Name	How to Set It	Additional Info
Search Site	Checked	Performs a Google search within the current site.
Search Images	Up to you	If you frequently search for pictures — stock art, clip art, almost any kind of graphic image — you definitely want to check the Search Images box. Like the other Search buttons, all you have to do is type search criteria in the Search Terms box and click Search Images, and you're presented with a flood of options.
Search Groups	Checked	Google's ability to search USENET newsgroups is one of its most powerful features. I talk about it later in this technique.

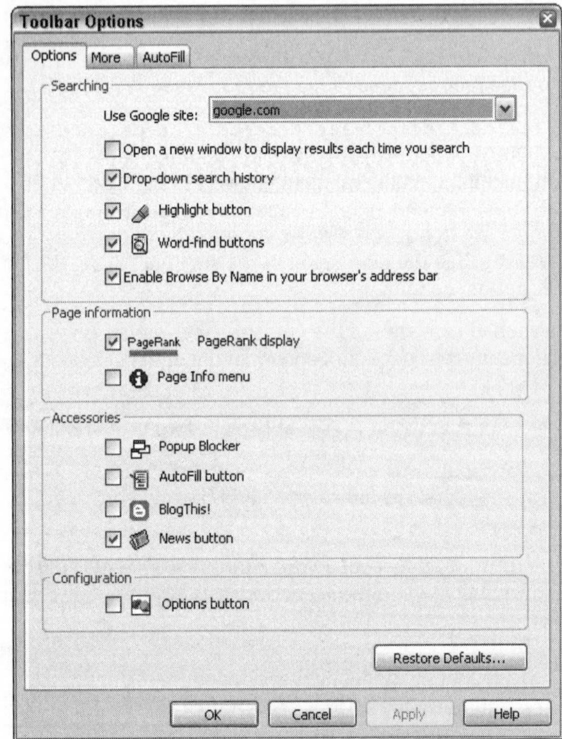

• **Figure 24-7: Google lists an entire page of Toolbar options — and there's More.**

Using Google Effectively

After you install the Google Toolbar, the entire power of the search engine lies just a click or two away. It's well worth learning the inner workings of the beast.

Saving time with search terms

Obviously, you should choose your search terms precisely. Pick words that will appear on any page that matches what you're looking for: Don't use *Compaq* when you want *Compaq S710*. That's true of any search engine.

Beyond the obvious, the Google search engine has certain peculiarities that you can exploit (these peculiarities hold true whether you're using the Google Toolbar, or you venture directly to `www.google.com`):

- **The first words you use get more weight than the latter words.** If you look for **phuket diving** you get a different list than the one for **diving phuket**. The former list emphasizes Web sites about Phuket that include a mention of diving; the latter include diving pages that mention Phuket.
- **Google shows you only those pages that include all the search terms.** The simplest way to narrow down a search that returns too many results is to add more specific words to the end of your search term. For example, if **phuket diving** returns too many pages, try **phuket diving beginners**. In programmer's parlance, the terms are "anded" together.

Google doesn't pretend to be a natural language search engine, such as Ask Jeeves. You can't type a question and expect an answer. Google ignores a handful of short words (such as *who, how, where, to*, and *is*) as well as single-digit numbers. The results page tells you whether it ignored certain words.

- **You can use OR to tell Google that you want the search to include two or more terms — but you have to capitalize OR.** For example, **phuket OR samui OR similans diving** returns diving pages that focus on Phuket, Samui, or the Similans.
- **If you want to limit the search to a specific phrase, use quotes.** For example, **diving phuket "day trip"** is more limiting than **diving phuket day trip**, because with the former, the precise phrase *day trip* has to appear on the page.
- **Exclude pages from the results by putting a hyphen in front of the words you don't want.** For example, if you want to find pages about diving in Phuket, but you don't want to associate with lowly snorkelers, try **diving phuket -snorkeling**.

You can combine search tricks. If you're looking for overnight diving, try **diving phuket -"day trip"** to get the best results.

- **Google doesn't support wild card searches.** You can't search for **div*** and expect to find both diver and diving.
- **Just like the points in *Who's Line Is It Anyway?*, capitalization doesn't matter.** Search for **diving phuket** or **diving Phuket** — either search returns the same results.

Using Advanced Search

The Google Toolbar can directly handle almost all the searches people normally perform.

The one kind of search that's difficult to perform from `www.google.com` but easy to do from the Toolbar is the Search Site, which requires a mere click of a button on the Toolbar.

If you need to narrow down your searches — in other words, if you want Google to do the sifting, instead of doing it yourself — you should become acquainted with Google's Advanced Search capabilities. Here's a whirlwind tour:

1. **On the Google Toolbar, choose Google⇨Google Links⇨Advanced Search.**

   You can also navigate to `www.google.com/advanced_search`. Both approaches put you on the Google Advanced Search Page (see Figure 24-8).

2. **Fill in the top part of the page with your search terms.**

   Anything you can do in the top part of this page can also be done with the shorthand tricks mentioned in the preceding section. If you find yourself using the top part of the page frequently, save yourself some time and brush up on the tricks (such as OR, -, "") that I mention in "Saving time with search terms" earlier in this technique.

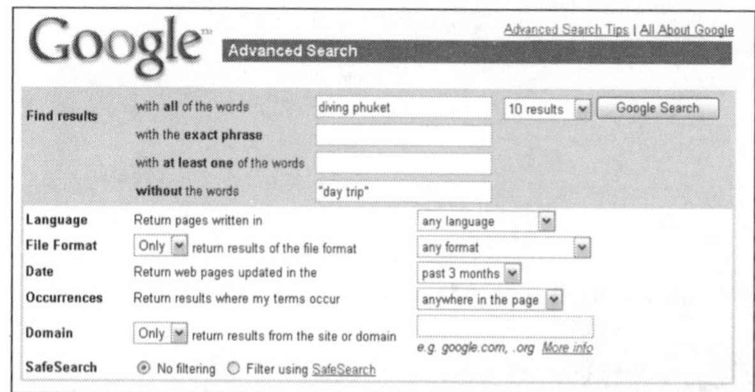

• **Figure 24-8: Google's Advanced Search Page makes it easier to combine search criteria.**

3. **In the bottom part of the Advanced Search Page, further refine your search by matching on**

   ▶ The identified source language of the page (not always accurate).

   ▶ A specific filename extension (such as `.pdf` or `.doc`).

This setting is generally used for finding downloadable files — not Web pages.

   ▶ When the page was last updated (although this information, too, is not always accurate).

   ▶ Whether the search terms appear in the URL, the title, or links to the Web page.

   ▶ The domain name, such as AskWoody.com.

You can also tell Google whether it should use its offensive-page filter, called SafeSearch, on this specific search.

4. **Press Enter.**

   The results of your advanced search appear in a standard Google search results window (see Figure 24-9).

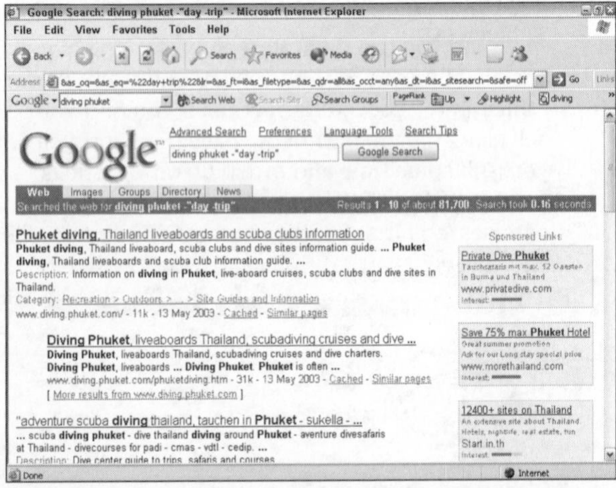

• **Figure 24-9: The results of the search in Figure 24-8.**

Viewing the news

The Google News site contains automatically generated headlines culled from more than 4,500 continuously monitored Web news sites. What you see in Google News is a completely automated distillation of the current contents of key news sites on the Web.

That's good and bad. It's good because you get to see a cross-section of how the news is being reported in many different places. It's bad because the automatic distiller ain't perfect.

To see the news on the Google Toolbar, click the News button if you can see it; otherwise, choose Google➪Google Links➪Google News or navigate to `news.google.com`.

You can search the Google News site using search terms in the same way you use terms on Google's main search site. The results reflect recent news reports on the Web — and nothing else.

Scanning newsgroups

One of Google's most important (but largely unknown and underutilized) gems is the ongoing archive of USENET newsgroup postings. For many, many years, the USENET newsgroups on the Internet served as a vital person-to-person link, with hundreds of millions of absolutely uncensored messages on every conceivable topic.

Google, being Google, has indexed the messages, built a credible viewer that shows you who replied to what message and when, and even assembled a very serviceable front-end so that you can post your own messages on the groups.

To search for a message in the massive Google newsgroups archive

1. **On the Google Toolbar, choose Google➪Google Links➪Google Groups.**

   Google shows you the Google Groups search page (see Figure 24-10).

• **Figure 24-10: Search about a billion posted messages in the Mother of All Message Databases.**

2. **Type your search terms in the box and press Enter.**

   Google returns a list of all the messages that meet your criteria (see Figure 24-11).

If you have the Search Groups button on your Google Toolbar, simply type the search terms in the Toolbar and click Search Groups.

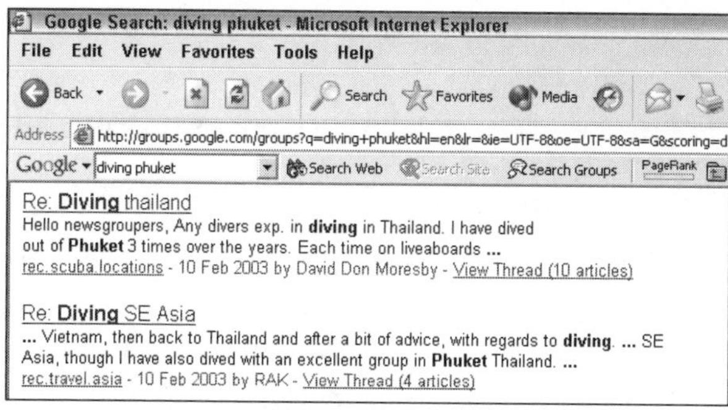

• **Figure 24-11: An enormous wealth of sometimes-accurate information awaits in the newsgroups.**

The results are normally presented to you in order of Google's calculated relevance. You may find it more enlightening to click the Sort By Date line at the top of the results list.

3. **You almost always want to see the entire *thread* (the message itself, with all the messages that came before it and after it), so click the View Thread link next to a search result.**

   Google shows you the thread (the list of messages, who posted them, and an indication of who they responded to) on the left. Messages appear on the right. (See Figure 24-12.)

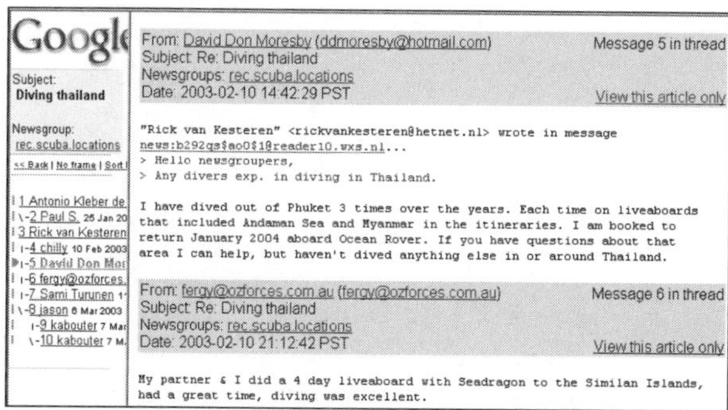

• **Figure 24-12: Google Groups show fully threaded messages.**

4. **To reply to a message, locate and click a Post a Response to This Message link.**

   You may need to sign up for a Google account, which takes only a few seconds. As soon as you're signed up, you see a Posting form.

5. **Type your message in the space provided and click Post.**

   Your message appears on the group in short order.

   That's how hard it is to talk to anyone, on any subject, anywhere in the world.

Using the Directory the timesaving way

Another largely unknown fact: Google has a directory that organizes Web sites by their contents. The Directory lets you look for answers based on general categories, as opposed to typing specific search terms.

Many people drill down through the topics and subtopics, but there's a much better way to kick-start the Google Directory. It isn't infallible, but it's one whole heck of a lot faster than trying to wade through five or six or seven layers down in some manual search tree:

1. **On the Google Toolbar, type a few relevant words in the Search Terms box and press Enter.**

   Google comes back with a typical search results page.

2. **At the top of the page, click the Directory list that most closely narrows in on the topic that interests you.**

   In this case (shown in Figure 24-13), the second Directory list looks far more promising than the first.

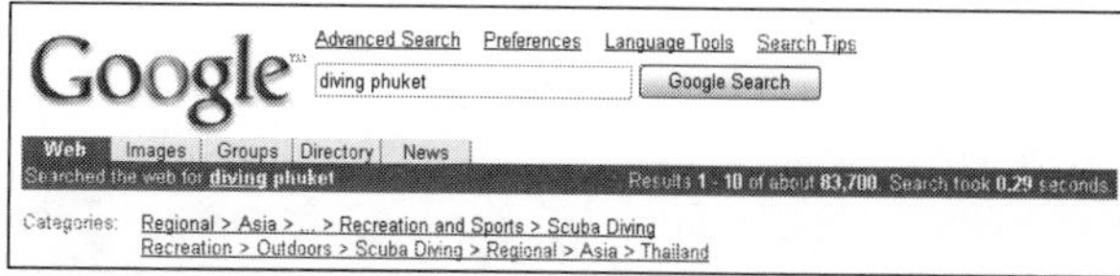

• **Figure 24-13: The top of the results page for *diving phuket*.**

3. **Move around the Directory to zero in on your goal.**

   When you're inside the Directory at a good starting point, it's comparatively easy to move up and down (see Figure 24-14).

4. **If you can't find what you want, go back to Step 1 and try different search terms.**

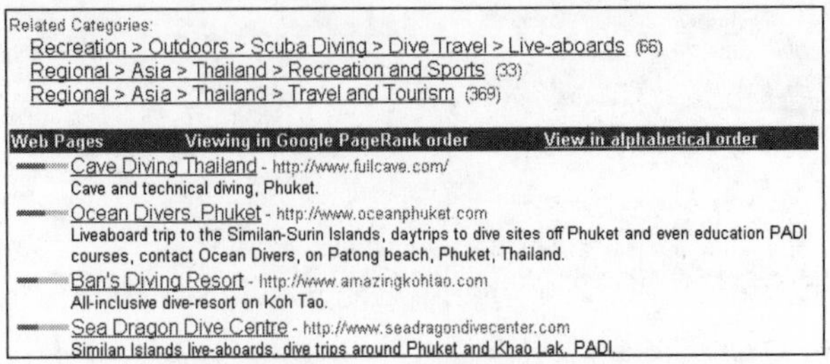

Related Categories:
Recreation > Outdoors > Scuba Diving > Dive Travel > Live-aboards (66)
Regional > Asia > Thailand > Recreation and Sports (33)
Regional > Asia > Thailand > Travel and Tourism (369)

Web Pages | Viewing in Google PageRank order | View in alphabetical order

Cave Diving Thailand - http://www.fullcave.com/
Cave and technical diving, Phuket.
Ocean Divers, Phuket - http://www.oceanphuket.com
Liveaboard trip to the Similan-Surin Islands, daytrips to dive sites off Phuket and even education PADI courses, contact Ocean Divers, on Patong beach, Phuket, Thailand.
Ban's Diving Resort - http://www.amazingkohtao.com
All-inclusive dive-resort on Koh Tao.
Sea Dragon Dive Centre - http://www.seadragondivecenter.com
Similan Islands live-aboards, dive trips around Phuket and Khao Lak, PADI.

• **Figure 24-14: The Directory allows you to hop from topic to topic, or company to company.**

Technique 25: Locating and Sharing Files on the Internet

Save Time By

- Finding the files you want quickly
- Getting good files — the first time
- Understanding what you can and can't share

Yes, most of the people who use file-sharing programs, such as Shareaza, Morpheus, SoulSeek, BitTorrent, Ares, iMesh, and KaZaA, send and receive copyrighted material or, ahem, pictures of dubious artistic intent.

No, not all the files exchanged are illegal, immoral, or fattening.

Napster started it all, but its congenital defect — a centralized design — left it vulnerable to legal action, and Napster went down in flames. Roxio bought the Napster name and promptly turned it into a me-too music download site. But the spirit of file sharing lives on with dozens of Napster progeny offering programs to fill the void. Few concepts in the computer industry have spread as quickly as file sharing. There's something here, and it's about much more than breaking copyright laws.

This technique shows you how file sharing works in the post-Napster era. If you're curious about the legalities and intricacies of *P2P* (person-to-person) file sharing, you need to understand the technology behind it. I also show you how to use my favorite free file-sharing program, Shareaza, without getting burned or beaten — and how to stay inside the law while you do it.

Infected files get shared, too. Many worms these days propagate through file-sharing programs. If you share files, it's imperative that you scan each and every incoming file before opening it — and that your antivirus program have the latest updates.

Deciding What Files Are Worth Sharing

So what can you share?

Just about anything, really. Obviously, illegal copies of music and video files abound on the file-sharing scene, as do photographs of questionable taste, pirate copies of software, hackers' kits, and other "underground" files. For lack of a better term.

You can also share music *honeypots* — large fake files (some distributed by folks in the music industry) designed to clog your Internet connection and hard drive with useless files that look like genuine songs and albums. Several viruses/worms now travel via P2P file-sharing programs, planting themselves in infected computers' shared folders. It's a jungle out there.

On the plus side, though, an ever-growing amount of legitimate material is being distributed by file sharing: freely distributed songs and video clips, high-quality travel photographs, written material of highly variable quality, even screen savers and utility programs. File sharing is an easy way for people to distribute almost anything without going to the hassle and expense of posting it on the Internet.

If you're disappointed by the majority of the files on offer today, check back in six months or a year. I bet you'll be pleasantly surprised.

Understanding How File Sharing Works

On the surface, P2P file sharing is pretty simple: You have files you're willing to share with anybody who wants them; someone out there has files that you want. It all boils down to a question of figuring out where the files are and how to get to them.

The term *sharing* gets bandied about quite a bit, and it has several different meanings:

- If you're connected to a network — either a Big Corporate Network, or a small one in your home or office — you share folders (and printers and who-knows-what-all). That kind of sharing only works across your local network: The users and computers on the network talk to each other, and can get at specific folders (and printers, and so on) on other computers on the same network.
- Many people think of posting a file on the Internet as sharing. It is: The file sits in one location, and other people can download it onto their computers. The same concept applies when you share pictures by posting them on a family Web site.
- File sharing, in the sense that I use the term in this technique, is fundamentally different from those other two types of sharing. When you use a file-sharing program, such as Shareaza or BitTorrent or KaZaA, you tell the program that you're willing to share all the files sitting in a specific folder on your hard drive. The programs reach out over the Internet and connect to other PCs running similar programs. You aren't sharing over a local network, because you're sharing with anyone running a similar program on the Internet — anywhere. You aren't sharing in the sense that you've posted a file on the Internet, because there's no single Web address for the file. Instead, with a file-sharing program, you're participating in a network that runs inside the Internet, hooking together like-minded programs wherever they may be located.

File sharing takes place over a network that exists inside the Internet itself: File-sharing programs connect to each other via these P2P networks that run on the Internet. The best-known and most frequently used networks are Gnutella (the original), Gnutella2 (a favorite for many Shareaza users), Edonkey 2000, and BitTorrent.

Following Napster's rise and fall

It's hard to mention file sharing without saying Napster in the same breath. Napster was the original file-sharing mega-company. It pioneered the use of the Internet to share files. The Napster technology proved revolutionary and enormously popular. Ultimately, Napster died because of a single weak point. Not a technical weak point, mind you. A legal weak point.

If you want to understand file sharing today, you have to understand what brought Napster to its knees.

Back in the larcenous not-so-good ol' days, when you logged on to Napster, your PC told the Napster central computer which files you had to offer. The

Napster computer added you to a list that detailed which files were available and who had them.

When you asked Napster for a list of all documents, say, containing the words *Toyota Repair Manual,* the Napster computer gave you a list of all the computers that were logged on that offered a file called Toyota Repair Manual. You scanned the list, picked the file you wanted, and clicked a button. Then your computer connected directly to the other computer and retrieved the manual.

Two key points here. First, Napster maintained a central database. Second, once you found the file you wanted using that central database, your PC connected directly to the PC that had the file; there was no link through the Napster central computer.

Napster's key claim to legitimacy was that the file you wanted — the Toyota Repair Manual — never existed on the Napster computer. Thus, if this particular Toyota Repair Manual was restricted because of copyright laws, Napster claimed (legitimately but disingenuously) that it wasn't transmitting copyrighted material.

It only took a little while for several powerful groups to convince a judge that Napster was enabling copyright violations on a massive scale — to the tune of 60,000,000 connections per month. Kerplunk. Napster shut down, went into bankruptcy, and was ultimately bought out by Roxio.

Napster lives on as the name of a music download site — a revolting development, to my way of thinking. It's sort of like taking a great Rolling Stones anthem and turning it into the marketing jingle for a greedy software company. Come to think of it . . .

Distributing the Napster concept from one peer to another

With Napster out of the way and about 100,000,000 people around the world seeking a replacement for their free-music fix, it didn't take long for other approaches to fill the void.

Although pirated music made Napster famous — and completely swamped many universities' internal networks — the technology holds huge potential for all sorts of peer-to-peer file distribution: Anybody who wants to share a file but doesn't want to post it on the Internet can use file sharing quickly and easily. Graphic artists use file sharing as an electronic gallery. Budding musicians, uh, strut their Buds. Writers do what they always do — act as Samuel Johnson's blockheads. The file-sharing artists' contingent is growing.

Other companies realized the Napster potential, and took up the challenge — spurred no doubt by the huge numbers of Napster faithful, but also mindful of legitimate (and potentially lucrative) applications of the technology.

The most popular file-sharing programs today — Shareaza, LimeWire, BearShare, Morpheus, SoulSeek, BitTorrent, Ares, iMesh, KaZaA, and more — all use *peer-to-peer* systems that don't depend on one single, central computer or group of computers. They avoid Napster's Achilles heel by eliminating the big central database.

Here's how they work, using iMesh as an example:

1. When you download and install iMesh, it has a built-in list of many other computers that participate in iMesh's network.
2. When you start iMesh, it reaches out to computers on that list, to see if any of them are running iMesh.
3. When you ask for a file, your request is passed on to the other computers connected to your PC that are running iMesh.
4. To spread the workload around, iMesh periodically updates its list of participating computers.
5. When an iMesh computer receives a request for a file, the computer looks to see if the file is on the current machine and passes the request along to all the other iMesh computers that are connected to it.

For example, say your PC, which is running iMesh, is connected to eight other PCs running iMesh, and each of those are connected to eight more running iMesh, and so on. If your request goes out five deep, your request can be passed to more than 32,000 computers in a very short period of time.

6. To keep from completely over-running the system, a limit is placed on how deep a search can go.

   If each PC is connected to eight more, and your request could go 10 levels deep, you'd be asking a billion computers whether they have your file. Not a good idea.

The important legal point in all these systems is that there's no central database — all the search information is built, more or less, on the fly. All the communication is between the users; there's no central server. Without a managing server, there's no way to shut down the network. For example, if a court in Kansas decides that iMesh is violating some sort of court order, there's no way the Kansas police can shut down the service without shutting down the Internet itself. That was Napster's Achilles heel.

Whether P2P software companies will be able to pass muster in court remains to be seen. But the peer-to-peer technology is definitely here to stay.

Using a file-sharing program doesn't absolve you from copyright restrictions. If you're sharing files illegally on the Internet, you may feel the long arm of the law some day. Students at several universities have been threatened with suspension or expulsion over their file-sharing activities — in some cases, because record companies have threatened to pull the plug on the universities. Others have incurred the ire of their Internet service providers, apparently in response to pressure from media companies. And of course we've all heard about the schoolkids and grandmothers who were sued by the RIAA. . . .

Setting the limits

Other folks can see only the files you've put in one of the program's shared folders. And you can see only those files that others have put in their shared folders. Outsiders cannot see the rest of your computer.

Or can they?

File-sharing programs have been hacked — bad guys have been able to find holes in the programs that let them sneak onto your computer and wreak havoc. The holes are generally plugged quickly. But you need to stay on your toes.

File-sharing programs are notorious for bundling pop-up ads, obnoxious add-ons, and various kinds of scumware. It's important that you only use file-sharing software that's 100 percent scum-free. To get an unbiased analysis of the scumminess of popular file-sharing programs, drop by `www.zeropaid.com`.

If you share an MP3 that somebody ripped from an audio CD, are you doing anything illegal? Short answer: Probably.

Downloading and Installing Shareaza

It's hard to pick a single "best" file-sharing program — although it's relatively easy to spot the scummy dogs. Justin and I used iMesh for quite a while. Then we discovered Shareaza. It's a fast, reasonably capable sharing program that talks with all of the other major file-sharing programs, because it hooks into the most popular file-sharing networks — Gnutella, Gnutella2, Edonkey, and BitTorrent.

Best of all, Shareaza (as of this writing anyway) is absolutely, totally, 100 percent scum-free.

Here's how to get Shareaza going on your PC:

1. **Go to** `www.shareaza.com` **and click the Download button.**

   Shareaza is an open source program, which means the source code for the program itself is available to anyone (see Figure 25-1).

• Figure 25-1: Shareaza shares files across all the major file-sharing networks.

2. **Ask for a direct download, and save the program on your PC.**

   You may need to click to bypass Internet Explorer's download blocking, and you may need to click again to get past a security warning.

3. **Double-click the downloaded file and run the installer to get Shareaza going.**

4. **Follow the instructions on-screen to pick a language, and use the Quick Start Wizard to get registered on the network.**

   Shareaza correctly detects if you're using Windows XP Service Pack 2 (see Figure 25-2). SP2 limits the number of Internet connections that you can have going at a time to ten. Because Shareaza can keep lots and lots of connections going simultaneously, SP2 puts a significant crimp in Shareaza's performance.

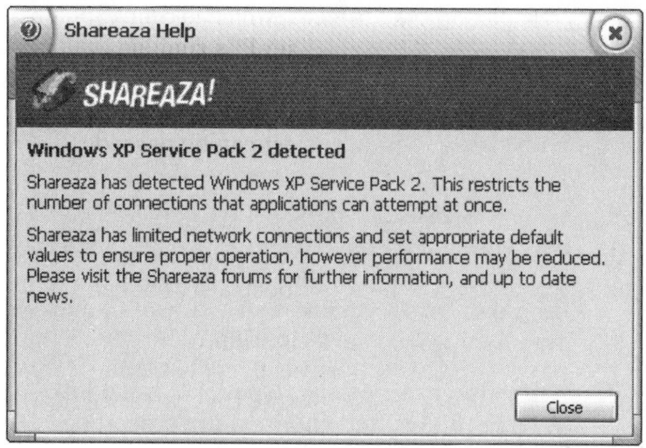

• Figure 25-2: Shareaza works with SP2 — albeit more slowly.

5. **Shareaza asks you to designate which folders you can share across the P2P network. I strongly suggest that you remove the automatically generated folders by selecting each one, in turn, and clicking Remove. If you feel the need to share a folder, go into your Shared Documents folder (Start⇨My Documents⇨Shared Documents), and create a new folder specifically for Shareaza (right-click any empty space and choose New⇨Folder). Then, back in the Shareaza installer, click Add and choose the folder you just created (see Figure 25-3).**

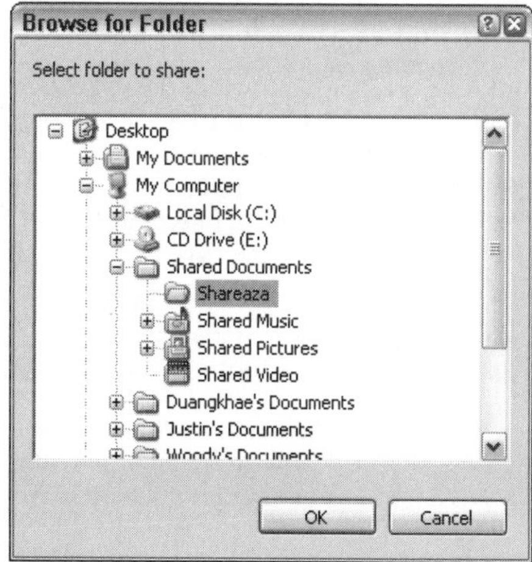

• Figure 25-3: Create a new folder for Shareaza.

By placing the Shareaza shared folder in your Shared Documents folder, anybody using your computer, or anybody on your home network, can get at the Shareaza files, with a minimum of fuss.

6. **When the installer finishes, Windows Firewall tells you that it has blocked Shareaza (see Figure 25-4). If you trust the Shareaza people to keep their program updated so it can't be taken over by a worm, click Unblock.**

7. **With Shareaza running, type a keyword into the search box, and choose a file type. (See Figure 25-5.) Click Start Search.**

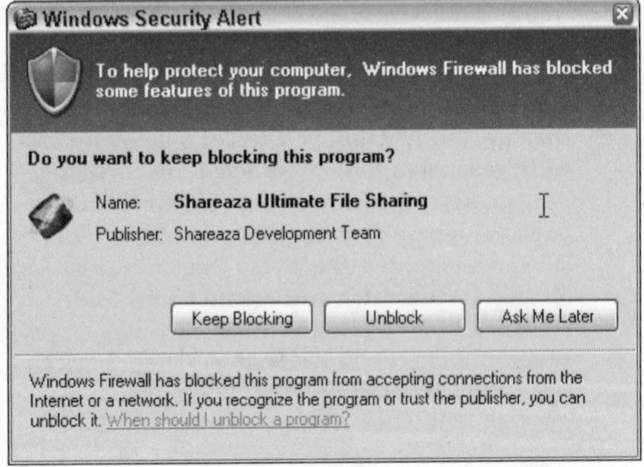

• Figure 25-4: The moment of truth. Do you trust Shareaza to keep its program safe from worms that may be trying to break into your computer?

Shareaza goes out to all available P2P networks and retrieves a list of files that match your search criteria.

If Shareaza doesn't appear to be responding, you probably need to poke a hole through Windows Firewall to let it out. See Technique 50 for details.

• Figure 25-5: You can tell that Shareaza is connected to a P2P network by looking at the Connection box at the lower left, or on the status bar.

Sometimes, it takes a while for Shareaza to search way down in the P2P networks. If you see a note that says `The network has not returned any matches yet / Click here to search again` rest assured that your search is still underway. Patience is a virtue and all that. Shareaza recommends you wait at least five minutes before canceling a search, to see if anything turns up.

8. **If you see a file that looks interesting, hover your cursor over it and Shareaza shows you the file's details (see Figure 25-6).**

Keep in mind that the details go along with the file, and anybody with an inclination to do so can modify the data; thus, don't be surprised if the file ultimately bears no resemblance to its description.

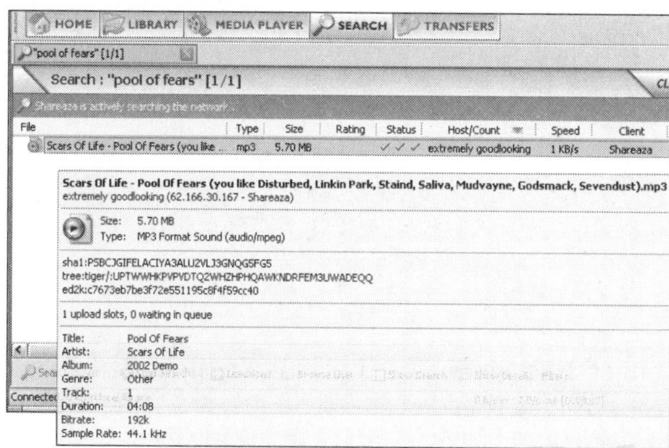

• Figure 25-6: Some bands make their music freely available for sharing. Scars of Life recently signed with a major record label, aided by the publicity they received from free downloads like this one.

9. **If you want to download a file, double-click it.**

   Shareaza switches to the Transfers window (see Figure 25-7), and then starts the download, depositing the file in the folder that you specified in Step 5.

You can preview and/or play many different kinds of shared files using the tools built into Shareaza. Check out the Media Player.

Always, always, always run an antivirus scan on every file that you download before you open it!

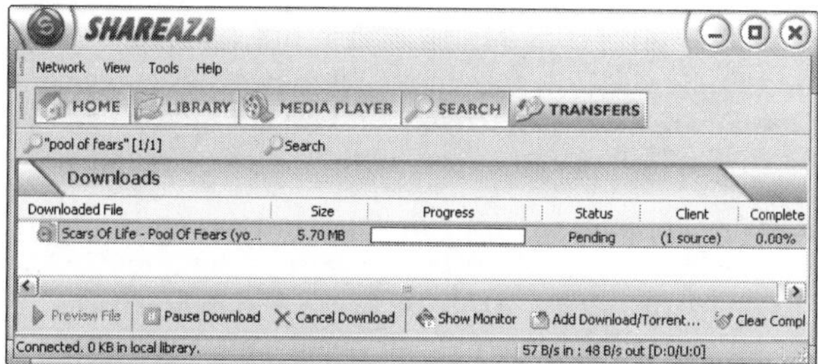

• Figure 25-7: Downloading a file is as simple as double-clicking it.

Finding the Good Stuff

From Justin's big bag of P2P tips

- **Search often.** P2P networks have no "memory," so the collection of available files is entirely dependent on who's online at any given moment — if you can't find what you want right now, it may well be available in six or twelve hours. The largest number of people are online around noon to midnight New York time.
- **Don't limit yourself to songs or movies.** Plenty of good, legal stuff is online — but you'll never find it if you don't look for it. I like to search on a movie's name (say, *Matrix*), but look for documents, not videos. I've found a lot of interesting reviews, analyses, rants, all sorts of stuff. Copies of movies online can be really, really bad — poor video quality, bad sound tracks, skips, a lot of junk. I'd much rather see a good movie on the big screen. But the stuff *about* movies can be very interesting. And it's legal.
- **Look for original art posted by the artist.** Many truly fantastic artists and graphic designers share their creations via file sharing. Look for dragons, alchemy, magic, scientific drawings, travel, or anything to do with religions or beliefs, real or imaginary. There's original music, works of fiction, even fiction posing as fact (after all, this *is* the Internet).
- **Don't bother downloading music or video files that are too small to be true.** Chances are good they're of poor quality or messed up some other way.
- **Don't bother downloading WMA or AAC files.** Chances are good they have Digital Rights Management restrictions. The person who posts WMA or AAC files may get them to play on his machine, but they won't play on any other.
- **If you want to download a big file, get Shareaza going just before you go to bed.** It's smart enough to reestablish a dropped connection and retrieve the whole file before you wake up.

Keeping Messenger in Line

Save Time By

- Using Messenger on your terms
- Blocking people you'd rather avoid (while letting key people talk to you)
- Using low-tech, but easy and free, telephone connections

Windows Messenger. MSN Messenger. I hate it. Er, them. Talk about a time sink. All my friends feel free to just start chatting with me every five minutes. It's worse than having a compulsion to answer your phone every time it rings. You know, before caller ID?

Blech.

Ever wondered about the difference between Windows Messenger and MSN Messenger? There *is* a difference. They're both free. One's more obnoxious than the other. I show you the differences in this technique.

There are some tricks to using Messenger — Windows or MSN flavors — that give you at least a little bit of peace and quiet. And when you really *do* want to chat, you can keep the experience from swallowing every waking hour.

This technique shows you the secrets.

Saving or Shooting the Messenger?

Before you dig into this technique, permit me to save you some time:

- If you're absolutely convinced that you don't want to run instant messaging — and believe me, I sympathize — skip this technique completely. Technique 12 tells you how to remove Windows Messenger. (Well, you don't actually *remove* Messenger, but you cut off enough of its offensive parts so you don't need to deal with it. Close enough.)
- If you don't have a very good reason for running Windows and/or MSN Messenger, take a look at Trillian, which I discuss in Technique 27. Trillian may not have all the latest whiz-bang features (Oh My! Icons that blow kisses *and* hearts!), but it works very well, and it talks to anybody using MSN Messenger, AOL Instant Messaging, or Yahoo! Messenger.

As of this writing, if you run Windows or MSN Messenger, you can only converse with other people who are running Windows or MSN Messenger. (Or Trillian.) Some people have good reason to stick with Windows or MSN Messenger — some companies, for example, take advantage of specific Windows Messenger features. But the vast unwashed masses, present company included, prefer a polyglot instant messenger such as Trillian, even if Trillian doesn't have a "feature" that makes the screen shake. Oy.

- If you decide to stick with Windows or MSN Messenger, use the advice in this technique to minimize your exposure to spam, messenger-based attacks, and simple intrusions on your privacy. You'll be glad you did.

In spite of the names, Windows Messenger and MSN Messenger are two entirely separate programs. Every Windows XP system includes Windows Messenger. You have to download and install MSN Messenger separately. Microsoft doesn't make any money from Windows Messenger, so it doesn't get many updates, new features, and the like — but it's also more stable than its offspring. MSN Messenger sports those fancy blowing kisses and shaking windows, but it's also considerably more obnoxious than the original program, pushing you constantly to sign up, sign on, and slap out your credit card.

You should think about whether you want the extra features — and extra intrusion — offered by MSN Messenger. If so, you need to download and install MSN Messenger separately.

There's no problem at all running both Windows Messenger and MSN Messenger on the same machine. True to form, MSN Messenger installs itself as the default messaging service and tries to get you to log on all the time, whereas Windows Messenger merely sits and waits. You can even run both Windows Messenger and MSN Messenger at the same time, providing you have two different .NET Passport accounts. That's easy. The rest of this technique takes you through the paces.

To download and install MSN Messenger:

1. **Start Internet Explorer and navigate to** `messenger.msn.com`**.**

   MSN shows you the home page for MSN Messenger.

2. **Click the Download Now! link.**

   MSN Messenger wants you to sign up for a Passport (see Figure 26-1). (Note: Passport is the same thing as .NET Passport, MSN Passport, Microsoft Passport, and Windows Passport. It's the giant Microsoft database, and you must be assimilated into The Passport Borg if you want to use Messenger. See the next section for tricky details.)

3. **Whether you have a Passport or not, whether you're a Registered MSN User or not, click the Have a Hotmail or MSN E-mail Address/Get MSN Messenger/GO button.**

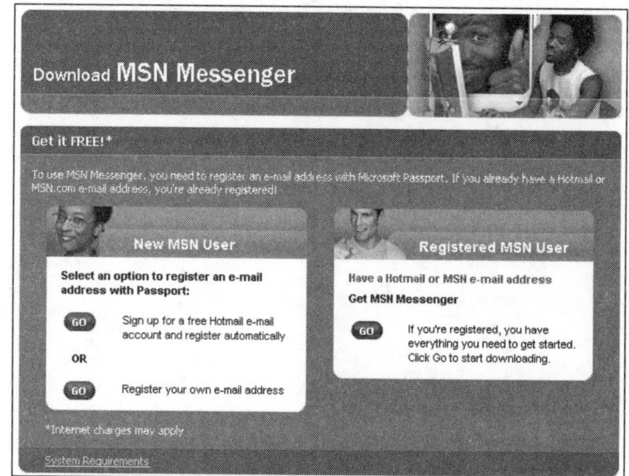

• **Figure 26-1: Ignore the instructions. Click the Go button on the right.**

The installer starts. If you have Service Pack 2 installed, Internet Explorer's pop-up blocker kicks in. (The irony of it, eh? IE blocks Microsoft's own site!) If you get blocked, click the line at the top of the screen and choose Install ActiveX Control.

4. **If IE shows you another security warning, click Install.**

   Can't have too much security, I s'pose.

5. **Follow the steps in the (thankfully short) Setup Wizard to get MSN Messenger installed.**

   You have to agree to a six-page-long Terms of Use agreement.

6. **When the installer asks if you want to install the MSN Toolbar, if you want to make MSN Search your default search engine, or if you want to make MSN Home your default Internet Explorer home page, click I Don't Want to be Assimilated Today, Thank You Very Much. Oops. Sorry. Politely uncheck the boxes, think Resistance is *not* Futile, and click Next.**

   The installer winds down, and MSN Messenger appears.

7. **MSN Messenger asks you to Sign In (see Figure 26-2). *Don't do it*. Follow the instructions in the next section to make sure you log on the right way, the first time.**

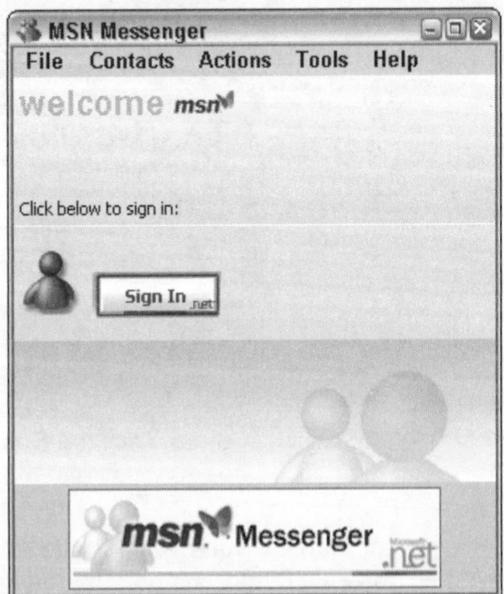

• **Figure 26-2:** Don't sign in just yet. You have to get some ducks in order.

Getting the Skinny on User IDs

If you plan well, you can minimize Messenger's intrusiveness — and save yourself tons of time down the road. The trick lies in acquiring multiple free user IDs, passing out those IDs to the right people, and logging on with the correct ID at the right time.

The best moment to put the plan into action is right now, before you log on to Messenger (either Windows Messenger or MSN Messenger) for the first time.

To save time, I recommend using more than one user ID for all your messaging needs. For example, I have three IDs that I use exclusively for Messenger, Hotmail, and Passport. Here's a list of user ID-related things you can do to keep meaningless messaging to a minimum:

- **Choose a user ID for fun time:** Ideally, this ID is one that you don't mind sharing with the rest of the world. For example, I don't mind sharing with you, dear reader, that my fun-time ID is `WoodysWatch@hotmail.com`. I use it on alternate Wednesday mornings between 3:00 and 3:15, which are my allotted fun-time hours. Everybody knows about that ID. Now you do, too.
- **Choose a user ID for travel time:** Don't broadcast this ID. For example, try something like `WoodyOnTheRoad@hotmail.com` to minimize the amount of e-mail traffic coming in. Only a few people have the ID that I *really* use for this purpose. I encourage them to use it when they want to send e-mail to me, or chat with me, when I'm on the road.
- **Choose a user ID for first-tier friends:** From `SomeOtherID@hotmail.com` to `NoneofYourBeeswax@hotmail.com`, this user ID is the one you hand out only to immediate family, close friends, and any essential work colleagues. That's the ID you use when you want to get some work done. No, you can't have it.

You might've noticed that I don't use my regular e-mail address, `woody@AskWoody.com`, for Windows Messenger. I have many reasons why, but the fundamental sticking point is that I refuse to let my real IDs be assimilated by The Borg . . . er, I refuse to put my real IDs in the Passport database.

Making Messenger forget your password

Have you already told Windows Messenger to sign you in automatically? Now that you understand how to use multiple accounts with Messenger, do you regret that choice?

Yeah. I know what you mean. Been there. Done that. Got the scars — or the arrows in the back.

If you have a Messenger ID that's set to sign in automatically, you can switch it back to manual: Choose Start➪Control Panel➪User Accounts➪User Accounts. Double-click your account and, in the upper-left corner, click Manage My Network Passwords. Click the account that you want to wipe out, and press Delete.

Setting Up Your Messenger Account

It's none of Microsoft's business what IDs you use. If you need a Passport to run Messenger — or to participate in Office 2003 collaboration, or open a locked Office document, or use any other piece of Microsoft software that you've already bought and paid for — I say use one of Bill's *free* IDs, thank you very much.

Here's how:

1. **Figure out if you need one, two, or three (or more) IDs.**

   Most people can do quite well with two — one they hand out in general, and one that's only given to a close circle of friends.

2. **Follow the steps in Technique 2 to sign up for a Passport and Hotmail account, for each of the IDs.**

You have to log on to Hotmail at least once shortly after you create the IDs, and then once a month thereafter, to keep the IDs alive.

3. **Start Messenger.**

   You can do that by choosing Start➪All Programs➪Windows Messenger or MSN Messenger, or by double-clicking the bubble boy icon in the notification area (near the clock). If you just finished the steps in the preceding section, Windows Messenger is already on-screen.

4. **Click the Sign In line.**

   Windows Messenger takes you to a Passport sign-in screen (see Figure 26-3). For no apparent reason, the dialog box says .NET Messenger Service.

5. **Fill in the Passport sign-in box with your "give it to anybody" Messenger ID, and your password, but *do not* check the Sign Me In Automatically box. Click OK.**

• **Figure 26-3: Sign in to Passport, but don't save the password.**

You don't want Messenger to sign you in automatically, because you want to make it easy to use different IDs, depending on how busy you are.

The MSN (or Windows) Messenger main window appears (see Figure 26-4).

6. **Immediately click the down arrow to the left of your Messenger ID and choose Personal Settings.**

   Messenger shows you an Options dialog box.

7. **In the My .NET Service Display Name box, type the name that you want people to see when you're talking to them in Messenger.**

   This name appears at the top of the screen, next to your ID.

8. **Click the General tab.**

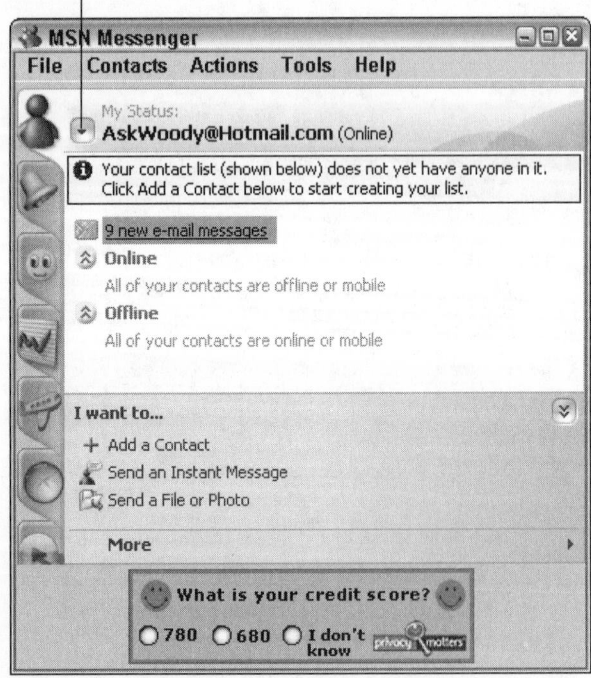

• **Figure 26-4: Messenger's main window.**

9. **Adjust the preferences according to your predilections.**

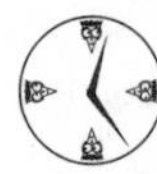

MSN Messenger has a potful of useful settings — and a whole bunch of settings that can eat into your time. Figure 26-5 shows you my suggestions for saving time and keeping your sanity — but still using Messenger when you absolutely have to.

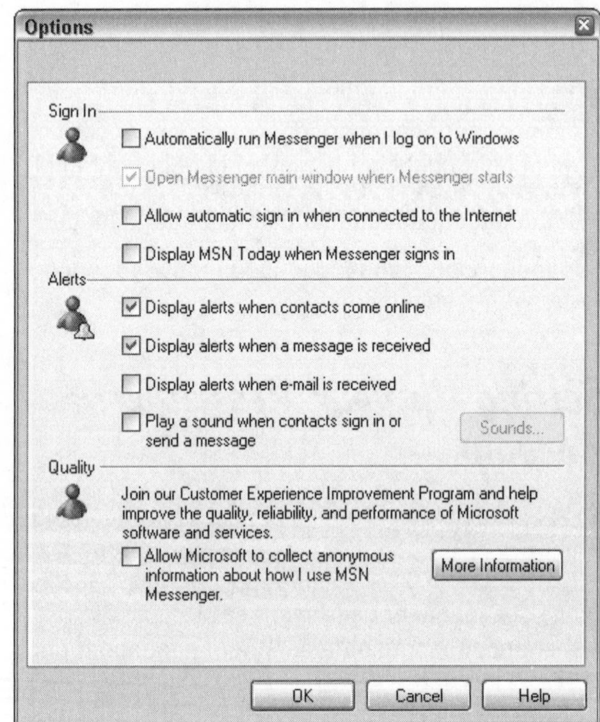

• **Figure 26-5: My General tab.**

10. **Click the Privacy tab (see Figure 26-6).**

    The Privacy tab — think of it as a cloaking device — lets you decide who can see you and who can't.

11. **If you're using your "give it to anybody" Messenger ID, leave All Other Users in the left column. If you're working on any other Messenger ID, select All Other Users and click the Block button.**

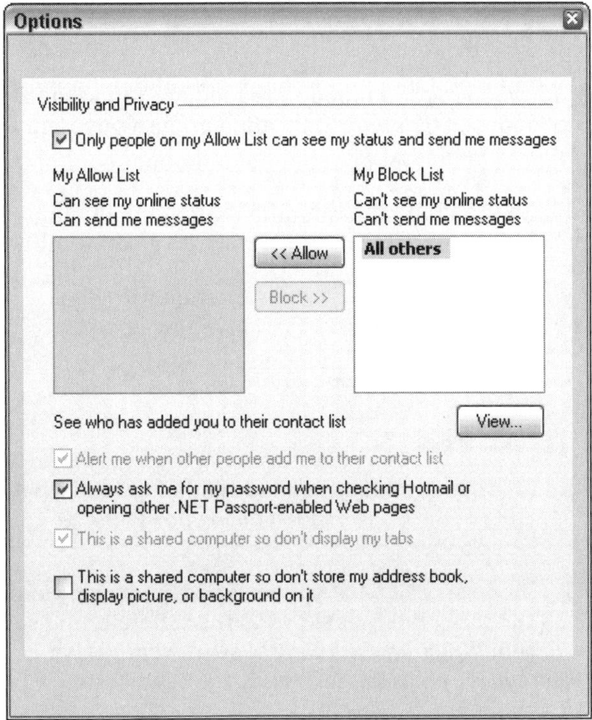

• **Figure 26-6: Do you want to let anybody who has your ID see that you're available?**

If you follow this advice, anyone who has your "give it to anybody" Messenger ID can see when you're online. That's good. But if you block All Other Users for your other Messenger IDs, you can pick and choose specifically who can see you when you're logged on with one of your less promiscuous IDs.

12. Click OK.

You return to the main Messenger dialog box, but this time your name appears at the top.

At this point, if you have the IDs of your friends who are Messenger-enabled, you're ready to start adding Contacts.

Contacts are people you can contact readily: Messenger knows about them, notifies you when they're signed in to Messenger, and lets you start a conversation with them by simply clicking their names.

The Contacts list is not restrictive; anybody on the Contacts list who has your Messenger ID can start a conversation with you when you're online (unless you specifically block them — refer to Step 11).

Messenger Contacts aren't the same as Outlook or Outlook Express Contacts. They're completely separate entities.

13. Choose Contacts⇨Add a Contact.

The Add a Contact Wizard appears. See Figure 26-7.

• **Figure 26-7: The Add a Contact Wizard.**

14. Make sure the Create a New Contact By Entering Their E-Mail Address or Sign-In Name radio button is selected, and click Next.

The second pane of the wizard appears (see Figure 26-8).

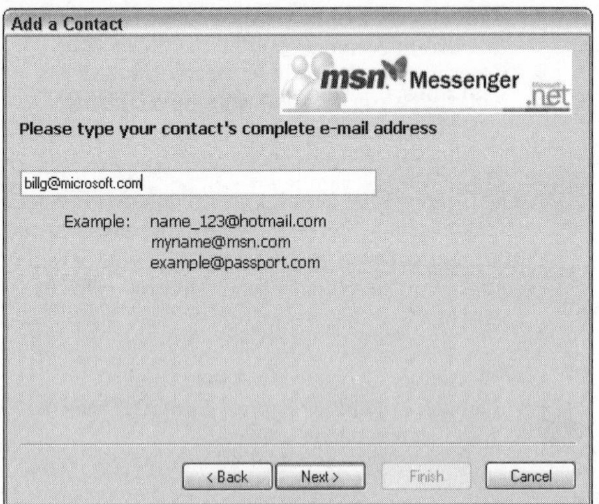

• **Figure 26-8: Get the e-mail address exactly right.**

15. **Type the e-mail address of your contact and click Next.**

    Messenger tells you that the contact has been successfully added. Two important notes:

    - Don't let the "Success!" gibberish fool you. Messenger didn't go out and verify the address. If you typed it incorrectly, you'll never connect with your contact.
    - If you click the Send E-mail button, you send a piece of insufferable, automatically generated e-mail to the person you added to your Contacts list. Don't contribute to the spam problem. Drop your contact a hand-typed message.

16. **Click Next to enter another contact or click Finish to quit.**

As soon as you've set up your "give it to anybody" Messenger ID, choose File⇨Sign Out, and then repeat Steps 4 through 16 for each of your IDs.

Making Contact

If you add a contact and he is signed in to Messenger, you immediately see a notification in the lower-right corner of your screen.

To initiate a conversation with the person, double-click his or her name in the Messenger main window.

If your contact initiates a conversation with you, Messenger starts a Conversation dialog box.

To pick up on the conversation

1. **Just type.**

   Whatever you type appears in the box at the bottom of the Conversation dialog box (see Figure 26-9).

2. **You can edit what you've typed by clicking and pressing the usual keys: arrows, Delete, and so on. When you're ready to send what you've typed, press Enter or click the Send button.**

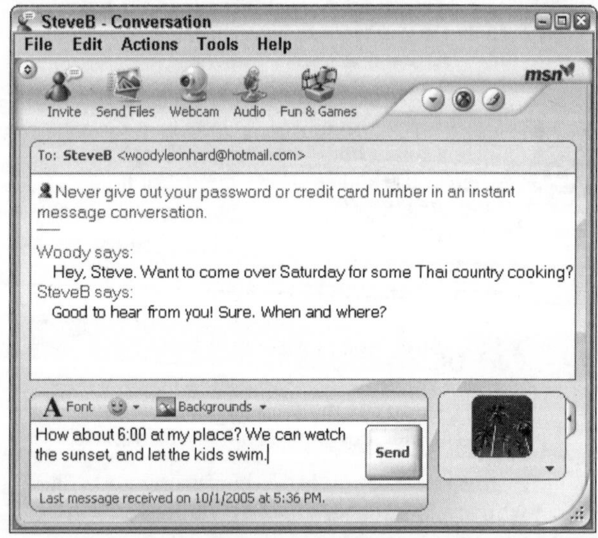

• **Figure 26-9: Anything you type appears at the bottom of the dialog box.**

You also can cut, copy, and paste text, down in the box at the bottom of the dialog box.

3. **To put a cute smiley face in your message, type :) or :D. Better, try (A) for an angel, (6) for a devil, (b) for a mug of beer, or :[for a very cool bat. If you must, click the Emoticons button and choose from a bunch of icons (shown in Figure 26-10).**

• Figure 26-10: A simple click to emoticons.

4. **When you're done with the conversation, choose File⇨Close or click the Close (X) button to leave the Conversation dialog box.**

   Messenger returns you to the Messenger main window.

5. **If you don't want to allow anyone to contact you, click the down arrow next to your name and choose Appear Offline.**

Using the Fancier Features

After you establish a conversation, you may have some success clicking one of the buttons at the top of the Messenger main screen. Here's what each button does:

- **Invite:** Click here to invite other contacts to join the current conversation.
- **Send Files:** Click Send Files and choose a file to send via Messenger. Your correspondent is asked whether she wants to receive it and, if so, she's warned of the (significant) dangers of receiving a file via Messenger (see Figure 26-11).

• Figure 26-11: Heed the warning. You may *think* you know who's sending you the file, but you never know for sure.

- **Webcam:** Both you and your correspondent have to be using Windows XP. Click Start Camera. You see a notification that a request has been sent. If your correspondent accepts the notification, and you both have cameras, you can see her and she can see you. Go to `www.silverhairs.co.uk/help14.htm` for real-world advice.
- **Audio:** Click this icon to talk over the Internet (using a technology called *VoIP* — Voice Over IP). You and the person you're talking to must both have Windows XP, and you should both have microphones and working speakers, headsets, or telephones plugged into your PCs. Click Start Talking. A notification goes out. If your contact accepts it, you can start talking over the Internet. If you have a reasonably fast Internet connection, the results can be quite good.
- **Fun & Games:** This feature patches you straight into the MSN Instant Game center, where you're invited to spend, spend, spend.

Technique 27

Polyglot IMing with Trillian

Save Time By

- Using one instant messenger for all your needs
- Connecting to everyone, no matter which IM program they use

If you gotta have Windows Messenger or MSN Messenger, you gotta have 'em. But if you have just a little bit of say-so in your instant messaging pursuits, you owe it to yourself to try Trillian.

Trillian Basic is free for the downloading — and it sports no ads, no spyware, no scum. And it won't pester you to death with ads for Microsoft products. Trillian Pro sets you back $25. The Pro version includes major upgrades and full technical support by e-mail for a year.

Weighing Trillian Against the Competition

Trillian boasts four major advantages over Windows or MSN Messenger:

- It communicates with anyone who uses Windows Messenger, MSN Messenger, AOL Instant Messenger, or Yahoo Messenger. It also works with ICQ and IRC (bonus points if you have ever heard of those pioneering instant messaging programs). You set things up once, you use one set of contacts, you learn one way of doing things, and Trillian does all the heavy lifting.
- Trillian doesn't constantly bug you about signing on, or signing up, for anything. The Trillian folks aren't trying to accumulate the world's largest user database.
- It doesn't slam non-stop obnoxious advertising in your face. The makers of Trillian don't have other products to sell you.
- And, most of all, it ain't Microsoft.

That said, Trillian has a downside. If the big instant messaging companies — Microsoft, AOL, or Yahoo! — don't play fair, they can knock out Trillian for a while. Yahoo!, in particular, makes sudden changes in its system that cut Trillian off from Yahoo! Messenger users — a half-dozen times in 2003, and again in June, 2004. The same thing happened for Messenger users when Microsoft made changes to it in October, 2003.

It's dirty-business-as-usual for the instant messaging market. Microsoft started MSN Messenger in 1999, back when AOL Instant Messenger (AIM) ruled the roost. The first version of upstart MSN Messenger interacted with AIM. Then AOL changed AIM in a way that cut off MSN Messenger from the AIM network. Microsoft fought back, patched MSN Messenger — and then AOL made another change. That went on for many months. Ultimately, Microsoft gave up, citing "security issues."

Installing Trillian

Downloading Trillian is like falling off a log:

1. **Crank up Internet Explorer and go to** `www.ceruleanstudios.com`**.**
2. **Download Trillian Basic.**

   Trillian Basic is the free version.
3. **Double-click the downloaded file to run the installer.**

   Installation goes very quickly.
4. **Go back to** `www.ceruleanstudios.com` **and download and install any patches to Trillian Basic.**

   As this book went to press, Trillian Basic has one important security patch. Look around the download page and if you see any patches, be sure to install them.

Using Trillian

Getting Trillian to run also couldn't be simpler:

1. **Double-click the Trillian icon on your desktop and start the Trillian Configuration Wizard.**

   The wizard is quite straightforward. Of course, I unchecked the Allow Trillian to Send Anonymous Usage Statistics box.
2. **Type your AOL, MSN, and Yahoo! information. (Make sure you follow the advice in Technique 26 to create anonymous IDs for MSN Messenger.)**

   When Trillian finishes its setup, you see the sleek Trillian main window shown in Figure 27-1.

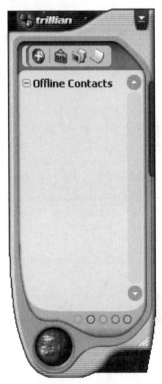

• **Figure 27-1:** Trillian fresh out of the box.

3. **Click the "+" icon to add a new contact.**

   Trillian brings up the Buddy Wizard, shown in Figure 27-2.
4. **In the Medium drop-down list, choose which IM network the new contact uses, and click Next.**

   In Figure 27-2, I chose to add a "Buddy" who's using Windows or MSN Messenger.
5. **Type the Buddy's e-mail address in the location indicated, and click Add Buddy!**

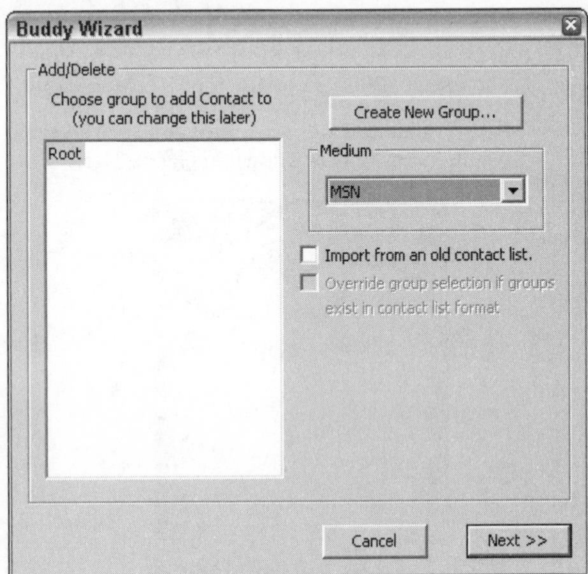

• **Figure 27-2: Trillian uses the terms "Contact" and "Buddy" interchangeably.**

6. **Continue adding Buddies until you finish and then click Done.**

   Trillian takes you back to the main window.

7. **Click the "talk" circle in the lower-left corner and choose Connection⇨Connection Manager.**

   Trillian brings up the Connection Manager dialog box shown in Figure 27-3.

8. **Type in your Passport (MSN Messenger) ID and password, and then click Connect.**

   Trillian springs to life.

Those little circles on the lower right keep track of which IM network(s) are live. Right-click a circle and choose Toggle Status Window to see what's really going on with your connections.

9. **Double-click a Buddy to initiate a conversation.**

Trillian works much like any other IM program: Type your message, press Enter, and your Buddy sees it. Your Buddy responds similarly (see Figure 27-4).

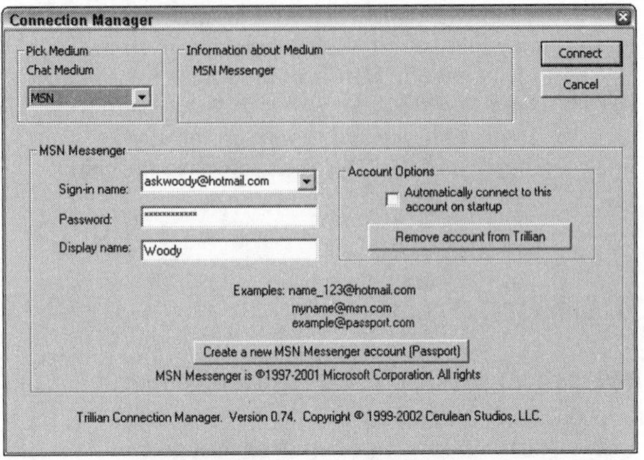

• **Figure 27-3: Establish the connection to Windows/MSN Messenger's network here.**

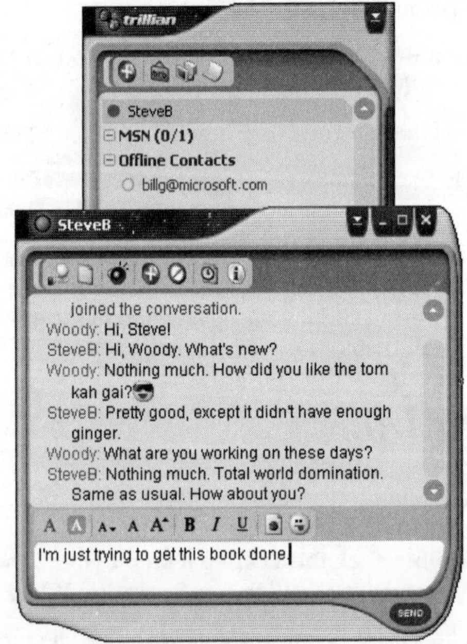

• **Figure 27-4: Trillian conversations work the same way as in other IM programs.**

Trillian has built-in multiple Buddy messaging. Click the icon at the upper left of the conversation window — the one that looks like a hand with a crystal ball on top — to initiate a multiway conversation.

Try Trillian for a while. Bet you'll like it. Don't forget the long list of additional features available if you decide to upgrade to the full Trillian Pro: separate Buddy lists for each IM network; groups of Buddies; autocorrect spell checking; tabbed chat windows; more and better skins. A most impressive product.

Streamlining Outlook Express

Save Time By

- Setting up Outlook Express for multiple users (the right way)
- Overriding and fixing annoying Outlook Express features
- Backing up and restoring messages

I want to make sure we're all on the same page here. This technique covers Outlook Express (OE for short). Basically, it includes all the timesaving tricks you really need to know that Microsoft and many other books don't tell you.

Outlook Express is not Outlook. Outlook Express is an e-mail program (in computer lingo an *e-mail client*) that comes with Windows XP. If you have Windows XP, you have Outlook Express.

Outlook, on the other hand, comes with Microsoft Office. If you have Outlook, you paid for it. (Outlook's also commonly installed on Big Corporate Networks — the kind that use Exchange Server and other worse-than-senseless things.)

Except for their names, Outlook and Outlook Express have almost nothing in common.

Arranging Your OE Desktop

Outlook Express, out of the box, does a pretty good job of hiding the more, uh, flamboyant optional parts of OE (see Figure 28-1). More on those in a moment.

Follow these steps to make OE's interface lean and (relatively) clean:

1. **Choose View⇨Layout.**

   You see the Window Layout Properties dialog box, as shown in Figure 28-2.

2. **Follow the suggestions in Table 28-1 to choose the visual elements that don't slow you down.**

3. **Click OK.**

   Your changes take effect immediately (see Figure 28-3).

Table 28-1: Recommended Quick OE Desktop Settings

Setting	Value	Why
Contacts	Up to you	This way, you can easily start a message by double-clicking a contact; if you have more than a few dozen contacts, this option is probably best left unchecked.
Folders bar	Unchecked	Takes up a lot of space (see Sent Items in Figure 28-1) and doesn't do anything.
Folder list	Checked	The easiest, fastest way to get around OE.
Outlook	Unchecked	Mindless glitter — see the bar at the far left of Figure 28-1. One of the few things OE borrowed bar from Outlook, and not worth the space or distraction.
Status bar	Checked	The strip along the bottom. Occasionally says something useful.
Toolbar	Checked	Icons at the top. You need it. Easy to change: Right-click and then click Customize.
Views bar	Unchecked	Drop-down list at the top (Show All Messages in Figure 28-1). Great if you use custom views, but most people don't.

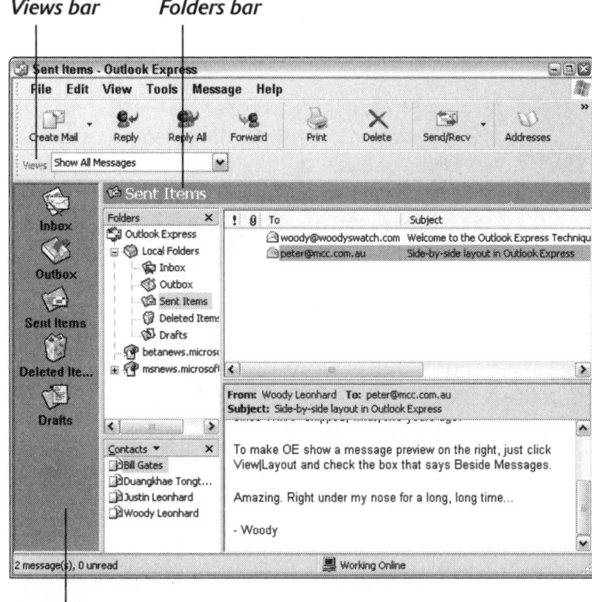

• **Figure 28-1: Three bars you probably don't need — the Views bar, Folders bar, and Outlook bar.**

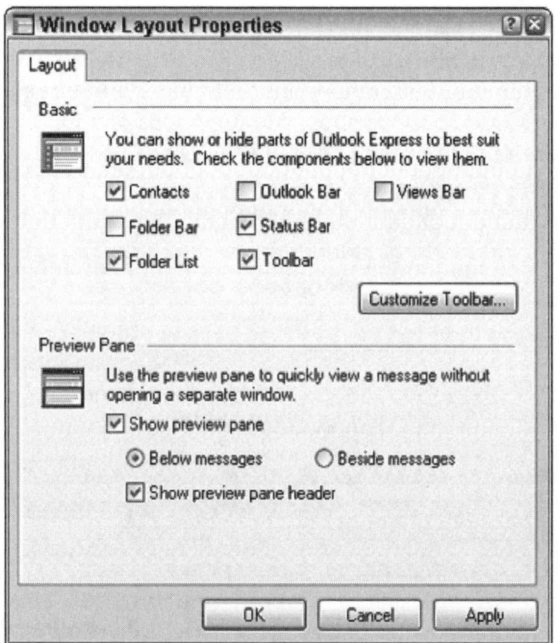

• **Figure 28-2: Control your OE desktop.**

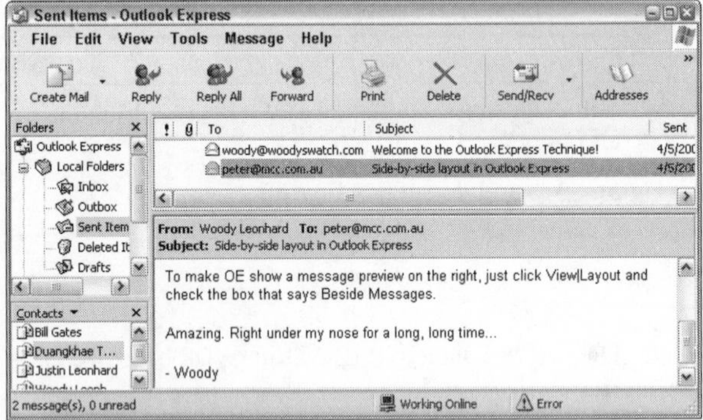

• **Figure 28-3: OE with the options recommended in Table 28-1.**

Disabling Windows Messenger Automatic Sign-In

In some cases, when you start Outlook Express, it automatically kicks in MSN or Windows Messenger (assuming Messenger wasn't running already). OE does that so it can show you the status of your Messenger contacts, as shown in Figure 28-4.

• **Figure 28-4: Icons next to your Messenger contacts indicate whether they're online or not.**

If OE starts Messenger automatically, as soon as Messenger kicks in, everybody who has you on his or her Messenger Contacts list sees that you've signed in. Many people feel that's an intrusive, time-sapping side effect of starting Outlook Express. It's also an incredibly stupid security exposure, hanging a "kick me" sign on your computer for no good reason at all. If you agree, it's easy to turn off:

1. **Choose Tools⇨Options⇨General.**

   OE shows you the Options dialog box.

2. **Uncheck the Automatically Log On to Windows Messenger box.**

   Messenger calls it sign in, not log on, but what's a foolish inconsistency among friends?

3. **Click OK.**

   The next time you start Outlook Express, it doesn't attempt to start Windows Messenger.

Making OE Wait to Send and Receive

As soon as Outlook Express starts, it looks for mail. If you haven't changed the out-of-the-box settings, OE continues to check for mail every 30 minutes, whether you want to or not.

By default, Outlook Express is set up to send messages the moment you finish composing and click the Send button. Wish I had a nickel for every time I've sent out a message and immediately wished I could take it back. E-mail messages, like computer geeks, get better with age. At least, that's what I tell my girlfriend.

I think it's much better to force OE to wait until you click the Send/Receive button before either receiving or sending any mail. Here's how:

1. **Choose Tools⇨Options⇨General.**

   You see the Options dialog box.

2. **Uncheck the Send and Receive Messages at Startup box and uncheck the Check for New Messages Every . . . Minutes box.**

3. **Click the Send tab.**

   OE shows you the Send settings in Figure 28-5.

4. **Uncheck the Send Messages Immediately box.**

5. **If you use a dial-up Internet connection, click the Connection tab.**

   OE displays the Connections settings.

6. **Check the Hang Up after Sending and Receiving box.**

   Your changes take effect immediately.

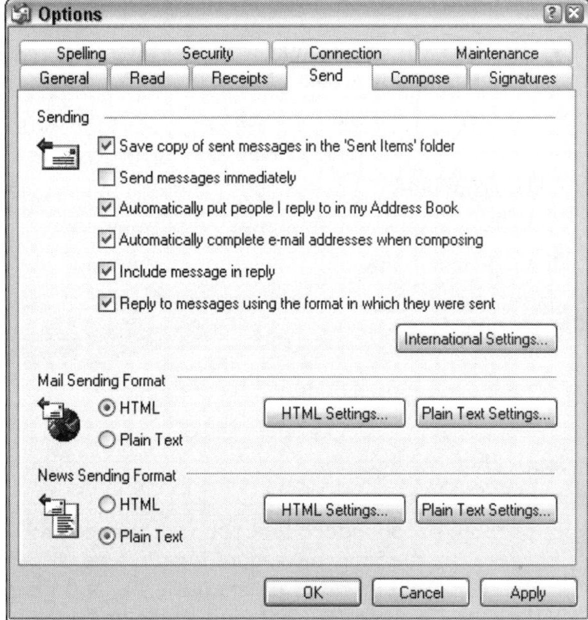

• **Figure 28-5: Disable automatic sending.**

Dealing with Read Receipts

When people send you a message, they can request a *read receipt*. As soon as you open or preview a message with a read receipt requested, you get the dialog box shown in Figure 28-6. These receipts are yet another time-consuming pain in the neck.

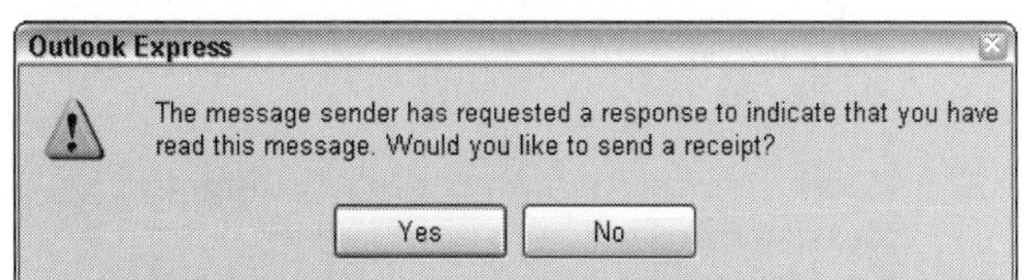

• **Figure 28-6: The sender wants to know if you got the message.**

If you click Yes, Outlook Express automatically generates a message back to the sender that looks like the one in Figure 28-7.

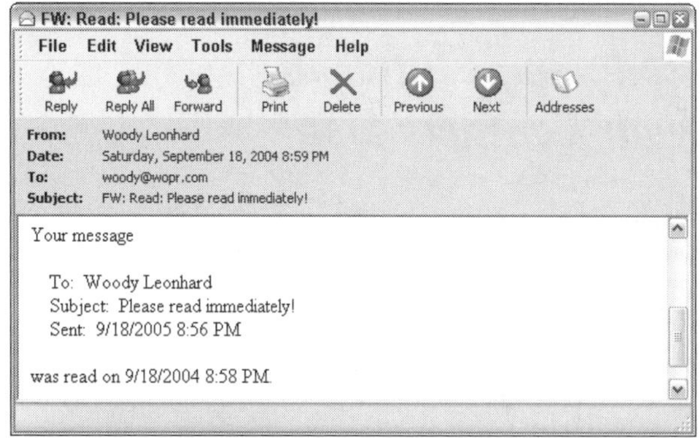

• **Figure 28-7: The computer-generated read receipt response.**

Generally, read receipts do nothing but waste your (and the sender's) time. If you receive a message with a read receipt, are you any more likely to respond to it? No way. If you receive a read receipt, do you know that your intended recipient actually saw the message? Well, no — at least, not unless you're absolutely certain you got the right e-mail address, and that nobody else reads the recipient's mail.

You can deal with read receipts in two easy ways. One is to always send a receipt; the other is to never send a receipt. My personal predilection is to never send a receipt because I don't want to encourage people to use the blasted things!

If you ask OE to always send a receipt or never send a receipt, at least you can bypass that time-consuming dialog box. To make a permanent yes-or-no decision:

1. **Choose Tools⇨Options⇨Receipts.**

   OE shows you the Receipts tab.

2. **Click the Never Send a Read Receipt radio button (or, if you must, click Always Send a Read Receipt).**

3. **Click OK.**

A pox upon you and your kin if you check the box that says Request a Read Receipt for All Sent Messages.

Reducing Clutter in Your Contacts List

Outlook Express can be overly paternalistic. Case in point: Whenever you send a message to someone (even if it's a reply to a message that was sent to you), the person you send the message to is automatically added to your Contacts list.

More than that, if you add someone to your Windows Messenger Contacts list, and you open OE with Windows Messenger running, Outlook Express scarfs up the name and puts *it* in the Contacts list, too.

That might be well and good if OE had a way to identify and eliminate duplicates, or tell if you really wanted to keep a specific reply-to e-mail address. But it doesn't.

To tell OE that you don't want it to add names to your Contacts list automatically:

1. **Choose Tools⇨Options⇨Send.**
2. **Uncheck the Automatically Put People I Reply to in My Address Book box.**
3. **Click OK.**

You probably want to go through your Address Book and get rid of the duplicates. Choose Tools⇨Address Book, and be braced for some hard work.

Any time you want to add someone who has sent you a message to your Contacts list, simply right-click the person's name at the top of the message (or in any list of messages, such as the Inbox or the Deleted Items list) and click Add to Address Book.

Using Signatures the Smart Way

Most people sign their e-mail messages, typically with their name and e-mail address, and perhaps a line (or two or ten) of additional . . . stuff.

Here's the easiest way to create a signature for your messages:

1. **If you want a plain text signature, start Notepad (Start⇨All Programs⇨Accessories⇨Notepad).**

   If you want a formatted signature, start any program (such as Word) that's capable of creating an HTML file.

   I have a plain text signature, so in Figure 28-8, I open Notepad.

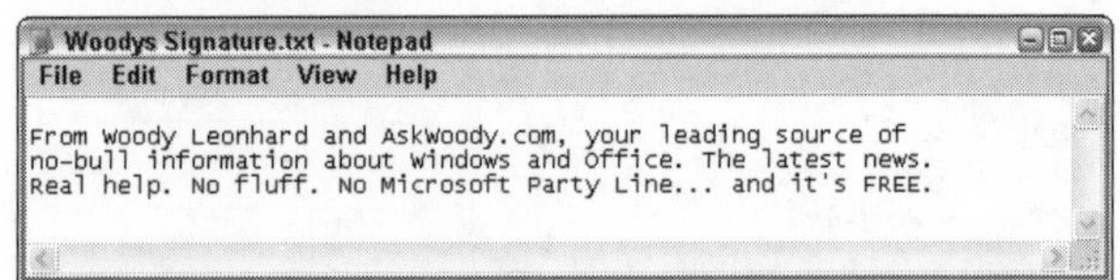

• **Figure 28-8: My signature.**

2. **Create the signature that you want to use and save the file in a convenient location, as either a `.txt` (text) or `.html` (formatted) file, and then exit the application (Notepad or Word, for example).**

   In this example, I save the file as `Woodys signature.txt`.

3. **In Outlook Express, choose Tools⇨Options⇨Signatures.**

   OE shows you the Options dialog box with the Signatures tab displayed.

4. **Click the New button (at the top), click the File button (down below), and then click Browse. After you find the signature file you created in Step 2, click Open.**
5. **Check the Add Signatures to All Outgoing Messages box.**

   The Options dialog box looks like the one shown in Figure 28-9.

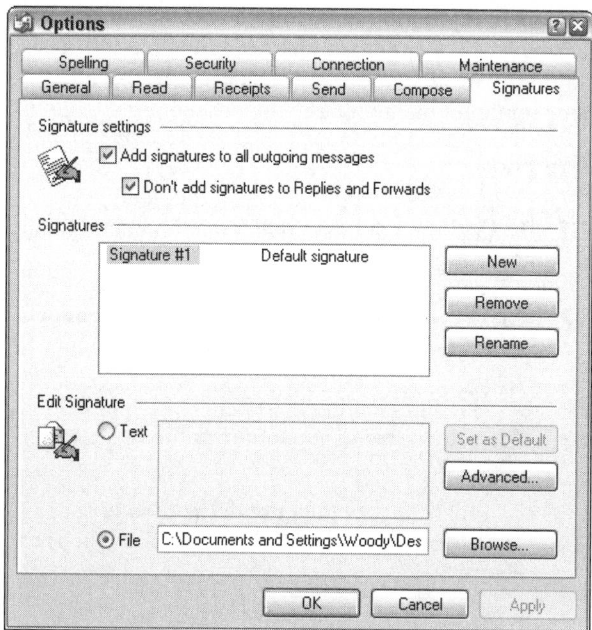

• **Figure 28-9: Tell OE to use your signature for new messages.**

6. **Click OK.**
7. **Test your signature by clicking the Create Mail icon in OE.**

   Your signature appears at the bottom of the new message (see Figure 28-10).

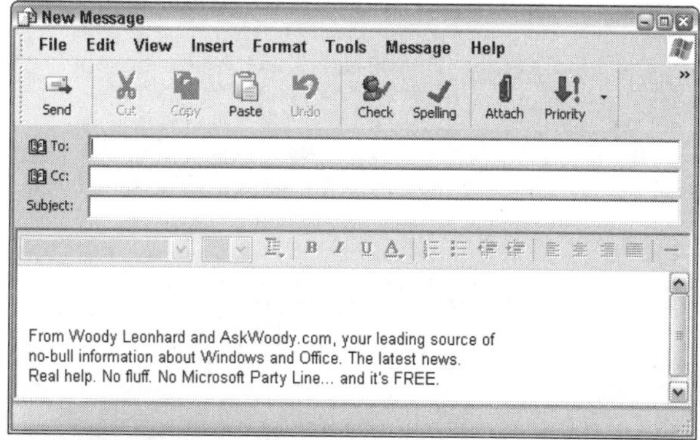

• **Figure 28-10: New messages have your signature at the bottom.**

Using a Business Card

There are many complicated ways to create and send electronic business cards (sometimes called vCards), but this way has to be the easiest:

1. **In Outlook Express, choose File⇨New⇨Contact.**
2. **Fill out a Contact entry for yourself.**

   You can see an example in Figure 28-11.

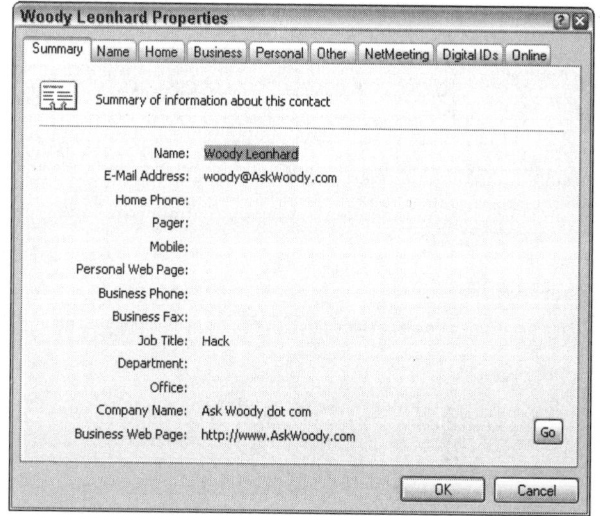

• **Figure 28-11: My contact information.**

3. **Click OK.**

   You now have an entry for yourself in your Contacts list.
4. **In Outlook Express, click the Addresses icon.**

   The Contacts list (Outlook Express calls it an Address Book) appears.
5. **Click your entry, and then choose File⇨Export⇨Business Card (vCard).**

   You see the Export dialog box.
6. **Pick a good location for the vCard, and then click Save.**
7. **Choose File⇨Close or click the Close button to exit the Address Book.**

8. **When you want to attach a vCard to a message, start the message, navigate to the vCard location, click the vCard, and drag it to the message.**

It's very easy to do this if the vCard is on the desktop; you merely click the vCard and drag it over the Windows taskbar button for your message. Hover for a second — the message opens, and you can drop the vCard into the message. The result looks like Figure 28-12.

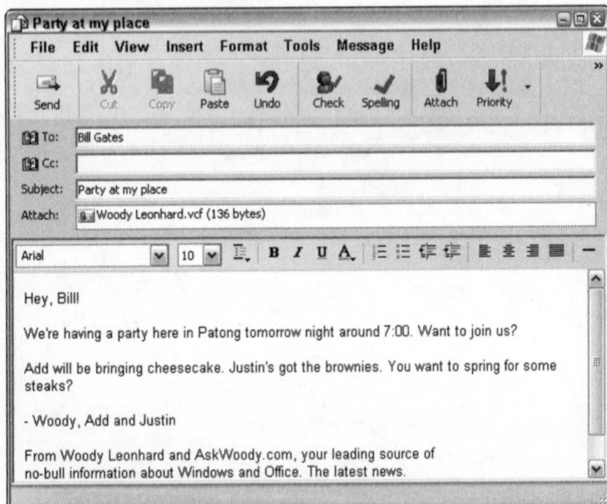

• **Figure 28-12: Drag and drop a vCard onto messages that need them.**

Most people can use two or more vCards — one for business situations, the other (perhaps with directions to the house) for social situations. There's no limit to the number of vCards you can create, although if you have more than a couple, you should put them in their own folder so you can find them easily.

Organizing Contacts in Folders

Outlook Express does have a point of diminishing returns. When you have hundreds of contacts or start wrestling with thousands of e-mail messages, you should look for an alternative, such as Outlook (in Microsoft Office) or Eudora (`www.eudora.com`).

That said, if you're going to stick with Outlook Express for the foreseeable future, using folders inside the Contacts list/Address Book to organize your contacts makes sense.

Here's how:

1. **In Outlook Express, click the Addresses icon.**

   OE shows you the Main Identity's Address Book.

2. **On the left, right-click Main Identity's Contacts, and then choose New⇨Folder.**

   OE responds with a Properties dialog box.

3. **Type the name of the folder in the box and click OK.**

   OE creates a new folder with that name, under Main Identity's Contacts, as you can see in Figure 28-13.

   From this point, you can easily click and drag contacts into whichever folder you feel is appropriate.

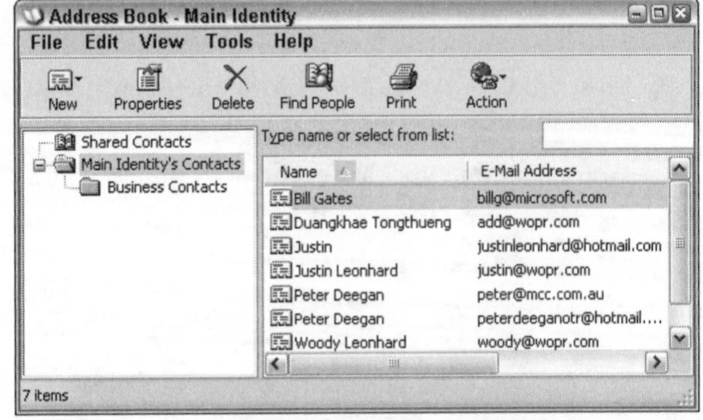

• **Figure 28-13: New folder for Business Contacts.**

Setting Up Outlook Express for More Than One User

If more than one person uses your PC (and Outlook Express), this section's for you.

Outlook Express has a feature called Identities that lets multiple people use OE: When you log on to your Identity, OE shows you your messages, your contacts, and loads up your settings.

Don't use Identities.

Instead of having everything lumped together in one big file and switching among users in OE, why not opt for the much simpler, cleaner, and safer approach of using multiple copies of Outlook Express? More specifically, everyone who uses Outlook Express should have his or her own personal data store.

So what's the brilliant part about allowing each user to run an individual copy of Outlook Express? You don't have to lift a finger. It happens *automatically.* Automatically? Automatically.

Just set up a user account for each person (see Technique 47), have each user sign onto Windows using his or her user name, and start Outlook Express — and that's all you have to do. Windows sorts out all the details.

That's the easy part. Eliminating your old Identities and moving old data to the new Windows user accounts is considerably more complex.

Bringing old Identities into the fold

If you have Identities set up in Outlook Express, you may want to bring all the messages back into the main account. Consolidating messages helps you get rid of the vestiges of Identities — and anything that lets you minimize your exposure to Identities is A Good Thing. It's also an important first step in setting up new user accounts (see the next section for details). To consolidate messages, follow these steps:

1. **Start Outlook Express.**

   If necessary, choose File⇨Switch Identity to change to the Main Identity — the one that holds all the messages.

2. **Choose File⇨Import⇨Messages.**

   OE shows you the Outlook Express Import dialog box, shown in Figure 28-14.

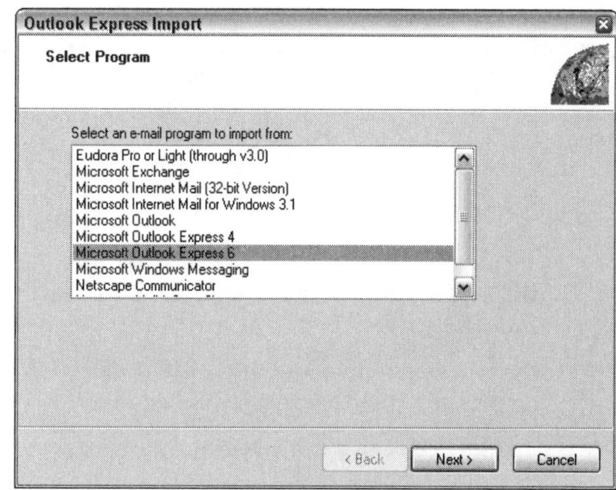

• **Figure 28-14: Consolidate Identities by importing them.**

3. **Click Microsoft Outlook Express 6 and click Next.**

   You see the Import from OE6 dialog box.

4. **Click the Identity that you want to fold into the Main Identity, and then click OK.**

   You see the Outlook Express Import dialog box.

5. **Click Next.**

   OE lets you choose which folders you want to roll into the Main Identity's folders.

6. **Click All Folders, click Next, and then click Finish.**

   When you get back to Outlook Express, you discover that the other Identity's messages are rolled into the main folders.

If you want to pull in the addresses from a different Identity, follow the same steps, but choose File⇨Import⇨Address Book in Step 2.

After you consolidate all the information from an Identity back into the main data store, you can delete the Identity by choosing File➪Identities➪Manage Identities.

Importing existing messages for a new user

If you want to import existing messages into a new user's copy of Outlook Express (more correctly, into the new user's Outlook Express data store), follow these steps:

1. **Log on to Windows as the original user (the one who's been using OE all along), and then start Outlook Express.**
2. **If you have multiple Identities, use the steps in the preceding section to consolidate them.**

   That way you can get at all of the messages.
3. **Choose Tools➪Options➪Maintenance and click the Store Folder button. Copy down the folder name that you see there.**

   It's a horrendously long thing, something like `C:\Documents and Settings\Woody\Local Settings\Application Data\Identities\{7A28F6CB-C130-4134-ACF4-5FE6209BB56B}\Microsoft\Outlook Express`. It's probably simplest to open Notepad and copy the name of the folder from the Store Folder window.
4. **Shut down Outlook Express. Make sure Outlook Express is not running under any Windows user.**
5. **Log on as the user who's going to be taking the copy.**
6. **Start Outlook Express.**
7. **Choose File➪Import➪Messages.**

   You see the Import dialog box.
8. **Click Microsoft Outlook Express 6 and click Next.**

   You see the Import from OE6 dialog box.
9. **Click Import Mail from an OE6 Store Directory, and then click OK.**
10. **Click Browse and navigate to the horrendously long folder name you wrote down (or copied into Notepad) in Step 3, and then click OK.**

    You go back to the dialog box from Step 9, but this time the folder is listed.
11. **Click Next.**

    OE lets you choose the folders.
12. **Click All Folders, click Next, and then click Finish.**

    The new user's Outlook Express gets filled with the old messages. You can do the same with the Address Book by choosing File➪Import➪Address Book in Step 7.

Dealing with E-Mail Attachment Security

Outlook Express 6 Service Pack 2 *blocks* — that is, it refuses to show you — any file attached to an inbound e-mail message with a name that ends with certain "dangerous" filename extensions (see Technique 20, with specific information at `support.microsoft.com/?kbid=291369`).

Of course, the concept of a "dangerous" filename extension is laughable. Up until September 2004, the `.jpg` filename extension was considered "safe." Then somebody discovered that it was possible to stick a killer program inside a JPEG picture file, and a filename extension that was once considered innocuous became, overnight, one of the world's Ten Most Wanted. Conversely, Microsoft doesn't block `.doc` Word documents or `.xls` Excel spreadsheets, even though both are notorious for harboring infections of many different types. Danger is in the eye of the beholder, eh?

If you can exercise a tiny amount of caution when handling files attached to e-mail messages, and if you have an antivirus program that's worth its salt, there's no reason to have OE block your inbound files. Here's how to override the setting:

1. **Start Outlook Express.**
2. **Choose Tools➪Options➪Security.**

   You see the Security tab.
3. **Uncheck the Do Not Allow Attachments to Be Saved or Opened That Could Potentially Be a Virus box.**
4. **Click OK.**

Of course, you should never, ever, ever open or run a file attached to an e-mail message unless you know the person who sent it to you, and you know that they actually *did* send it to you. If you have any doubt, send them a message and confirm that they sent you the file before you open it. If you get confirmation, save the file, and run your favorite antivirus package on it *before* you open it.

Forcing OE to remember your password

Some people hit a bug in Outlook Express that keeps OE from remembering your e-mail account's password. It's a frustrating problem because each time you try to send or receive mail, you have to type in your password.

This snarly problem has a very complex solution. You can find details at `support.microsoft.com/?kbid=264672`.

Removing the "You Have Messages" Notice

The Windows welcome screen says you have "18 unread messages" but you have at least 20 times that many. What gives?

Microsoft isn't very clear about where the number comes from or what it means. If you want to permanently prevent Windows XP's welcome screen from telling you that "You have mail!" follow these steps:

1. **Download and install TweakUI.**

   I explain the specifics in Technique 5.
2. **Choose Start➪All Programs➪PowerToys for Windows XP➪TweakUI for Windows XP.**
3. **On the left, choose Logon➪Unread Mail.**
4. **Uncheck the Show Unread Mail on Welcome Screen box and click OK.**

Zapping Junk Mail

Save Time By

- Avoiding spammers' traps
- Staying off e-mail lists
- Getting rid of junk mail — accurately

I downloaded 455 e-mail messages this morning. 418 of them were spam. Sound familiar?

Don't get me wrong. I really *do* want to buy an *amazing* printer cartridge that never runs out of antigravity ink, refinance my house with the lowest rates in *499 years,* increase my bust size by 17 inches in just *two weeks,* and help Mr. Mungwabe get his $10,368,475,890 out of Nidibia. I'm a New Age kind of guy. But I'd rather not be reminded about my shortcomings every day. And I don't have an extra $100,000.49 to guarantee Mr. Mungwabe's wire transfer.

E-mail is a unique timesaving medium — quite possibly the most effective timesaving communication device since the advent of the telephone. But it has its own set of potential pitfalls. And the continuing onslaught of spam threatens to kill the golden goose. This technique consists of a crash course in spam — if you understand the beast, you're better prepared to fight it — and some school-of-hard-knocks advice about e-mail.

Understanding Spam

Spam — unwanted commercial e-mail messages that tout everything from IQ-building enzymes to calisthenics with barnyard animals — makes me furious. I bet you have a few choice words about it, too.

E-mail set the advertising world on its ear by lowering the bar for direct marketing: Instead of spending thousands or tens of thousands of dollars for a mass mailing campaign via snail mail, an advertiser can send millions of messages for less than $100. You don't have to find very many suckers to make back your investment. And there's one born every minute.

Everybody gets spam. Few take the time to understand how and why spammers construct messages the way they do. Figure 29-1 shows a particularly well-crafted piece of spam:

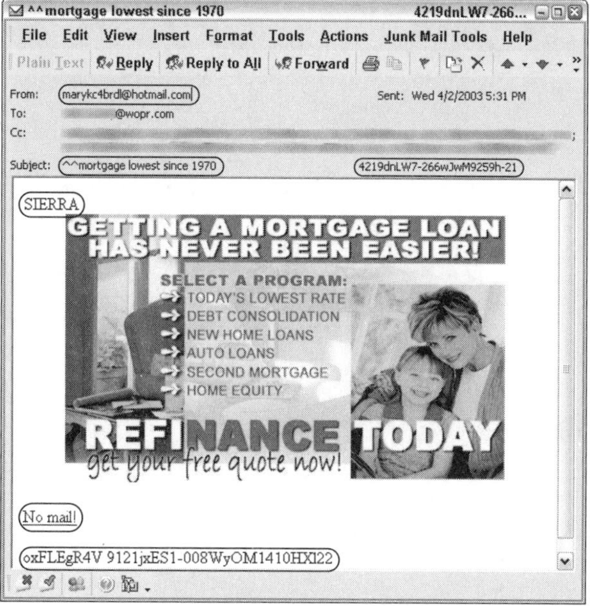

• **Figure 29-1: Anatomy of a spam message.**

- **It came from a Hotmail account.** Microsoft is trying hard (and spending millions) to keep spammers from using Hotmail, but spammers obviously get through the system.
- **The subject doesn't have any trigger words.** Many spam filters look in the Subject line for *trigger* words (key words) such as *mortgage*. This spammer circumvented that kind of filtering by using `^^mortgage`. As an added, uh, bonus, if you sort your messages by subject, `^^mortgage` floats to the top.
- **A unique identifier is in the subject line.** In this case, you can bet that the spammer's database has my e-mail address linked to `4219dnLW7-266wJwM9259h-21`. If I reply to the message or use the subject line in any way, the spammer knows that I got the message. Compare this to Web Beacons, described in the next section.
- **The message starts with a perfectly good word (**`SIERRA`**).** That's used to trip up Bayesian spam filters, which may give high points to messages that contain offbeat words that aren't related to marketing. See the "Filtering out junk e-mail" section in this technique.
- **The ad itself is a picture — no text.** If you have a spam filter that looks at text, there's nothing to look at! Moreover, you can bet that the sender was using a Web Beacon (see the upcoming "Avoiding Spammeisters and Phishers").
- **The No Mail link leads to a Web page that asks you to type in your e-mail address.** No doubt the spammer is trying to trick you into providing yet another valid e-mail address to add to the collection. See the "Unsubscribing — *Not!*" section in this technique.
- **Another unique identifier is at the bottom.** Again, the spammer is trying to bypass filters that look at words in the message.
- **No identifiable company information is in the message.** Can you tell which company sent the message? There's no company name, no Web address, nuthin'. Slick.

If you ever wondered why it's hard to make spam-zappers that catch the bad mail, but let through the good, this example should give you a few ideas.

The CAN-SPAM Act was supposed to put a crimp on this kind of spam, but I've seen more of it now than before the Act went into effect. Some estimates say the number of spam messages more than doubled in the year following enactment of CAN-SPAM. I'd say that's a conservative estimate. Something like three-quarters of all the e-mail on the Internet at this moment qualifies as unsolicited, unwanted junk. Several proposals for limiting spam — and putting technical teeth into the mix — have failed, ultimately because the folks floating the proposals know that spammers can get around them in a matter of days. Hours. Frankly, I'm not optimistic about the future of e-mail.

Phishing Phor Phun and Prophit

Phishing — sending out e-mail messages that try to convince you to divulge personal information — has become breathtakingly clever. Phishers generally rely on spam databases to send out millions of messages. The messages frequently look like real notices from banks (see Figure 29-2), credit card companies, online auction houses, and the like. Most phishing messages tell you that you have to log on to a Web site because your account has a problem.

• **Figure 29-2: A phishing message that looks much like an official notice from Wells Fargo Bank.**

Typically, a phisher tries to trick you into logging onto a Web site that they control. While you may think that you're clicking a link in the message to, say, the Wells Fargo Web site, the real link buried behind the text actually goes to some Web site that was set up just hours before you received the message. You're asked to provide an account number and password, and sometimes other forms of identification. The phisher watches what's being typed into the fake Web site, absconds with your financial information, and then uses it to pull money out of your bank account, con you into something stupid, or do any of the myriad things that identity thieves do.

How do these guys (and they're almost always guys) make any money at it? The numbers. Say someone sends out a million phishing messages purporting to be from Wells Fargo. Maybe 5 percent of those people have Wells Fargo accounts. Maybe 10 percent of the people with accounts are gullible enough to provide their logon information. Do the math. A million messages nets five thousand suckers gleefully typing their logon ids and passwords into an ersatz Web site.

Smart phishers move quickly. That's how they stay ahead of the law. A well-organized phisher can milk hundreds of thousands of dollars in less than 12 hours, and all of it can be done online: setting up the bogus Web site; sending out the phishing messages to a spam e-mail list; waiting for naïve folks to respond; then using the acquired information to drain the victims' accounts. Frequently, the only trail left behind for law enforcement is at the end, where the money from the victim has to make its way to the perpetrator. It's massive fraud, conducted on Internet time.

Avoiding Spammeisters and Phishers

The first step every Windows user needs to take: minimize your chances of being added to a spam list.

Where do spammeisters get your e-mail address? More often than not, they buy it on a CD with millions of addresses, as shown in Figure 29-3. E-mail address compilation CDs cost next to nothing, and if 98 percent of the addresses on the CD are out of date, the remaining 2 percent still represents a huge number of marks. Er, potential customers.

The spammeisters who go out and harvest original new addresses can be quite devious. The worst ones work in cahoots with virus/worm writers, who put spam address-spewing routines into their programs. If you get infected with one of those critters, every e-mail address on your computer gets harvested and sent to the bad guy's address trap. He sells those millions of harvested addresses for a princely sum.

Many times, spam list creators just guess: If `woody@AskWoody.com` is a good address, maybe `woody@AskWoody2.com` is also good — or `woody@microsoft.com`, for that matter. (No, I haven't joined the Dark Side.)

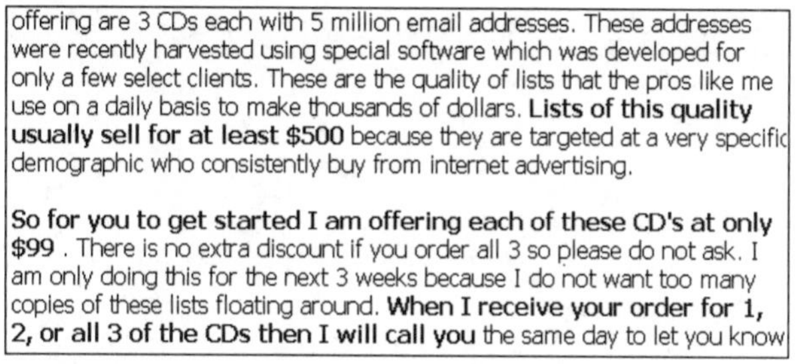

offering are 3 CDs each with 5 million email addresses. These addresses were recently harvested using special software which was developed for only a few select clients. These are the quality of lists that the pros like me use on a daily basis to make thousands of dollars. **Lists of this quality usually sell for at least $500** because they are targeted at a very specific demographic who consistently buy from internet advertising.

So for you to get started I am offering each of these CD's at only $99 . There is no extra discount if you order all 3 so please do not ask. I am only doing this for the next 3 weeks because I do not want too many copies of these lists floating around. **When I receive your order for 1, 2, or all 3 of the CDs then I will call you** the same day to let you know

• **Figure 29-3: Five million addresses for $99. A real ad.**

Lurking in Web Beacons

One of the most common, old-fashioned methods for verifying e-mail addresses employs a method called *Web Beacons*. (You may have heard of them referred to as Web Bugs.) Web Beacons work by using a link to a picture inside a message (instead of a copy of the picture itself) that looks something like this:

```
<img src="http://track3.dealstwoyou.com/
   _o.jpegg>
```

When Outlook Express or Eudora or Hotmail (or whatever e-mail reader you use) sees a code like that, it knows that it needs to reach out to `track3.dealstwoyou.com` and pick up the picture called `_o.jpegg`. Using a link makes the message much smaller, but it takes longer for you to view the message because you have to wait while your e-mail program picks up the picture.

Unfortunately, unscrupulous companies can use linked pictures to determine if a specific e-mail message has been viewed and thus verify your e-mail address. To see how it works, look at the message in Figure 29-4.

The message in Figure 29-4 looks like a typical piece of scum spam, but what you can't see can hurt you. If I right-click the message and choose View➪Source, the HTML working behind the scenes appears and divulges the full story:

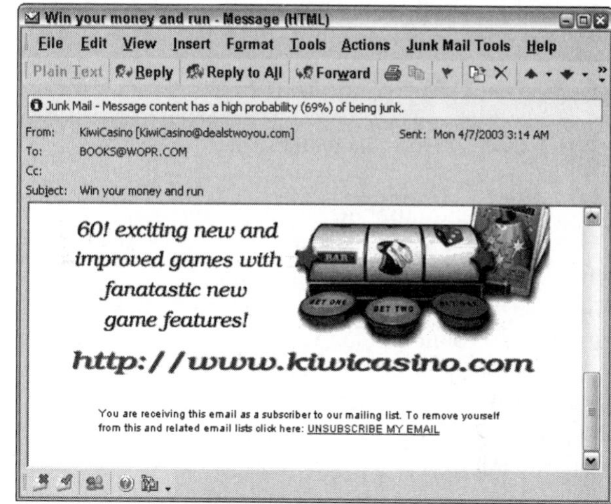

• **Figure 29-4: A typical obnoxious piece of spam.**

- I find the link shown in Figure 29-5 at the bottom of the HTML code. This means that, when you open — or even preview — a message like the one shown in Figure 29-4, your e-mail client (whether it's Outlook, Outlook Express, Eudora, or some other program) reaches its cyber arm out to the `track3.dealstwoyou.com` Internet address and retrieves the file called `_o.jpegg`. In the process of picking up the file, it leaves behind the recipient's e-mail address, `books@wopr.com`.
- As an added flourish, the picture in Figure 29-5 has an on-screen height of 0 and a width of 0. That means your e-mail program retrieves the picture, but doesn't put the picture on the screen: No room is reserved for it. (`Height = 0, Width = 0`. Get it?) Your information goes to `dealstwoyou.com`, you get a picture back, but Outlook (or Eudora or . . .) doesn't even display the picture. That makes this `<img>` tag a so-called Invisible Web Beacon. Slick.

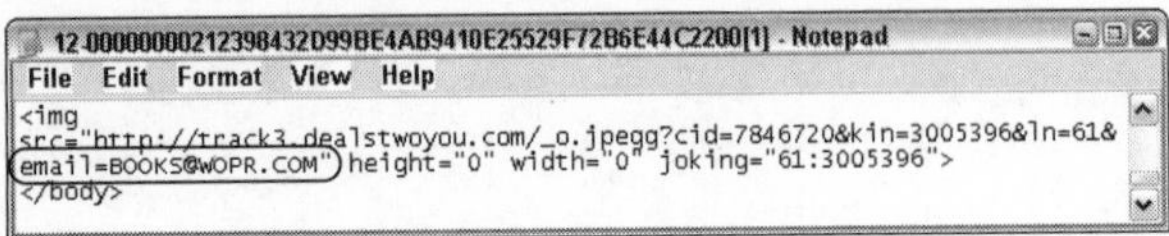

• **Figure 29-5: An invisible Web Beacon.**

Surmising what happened is easy. The people at `dealstwoyou.com` got a list of e-mail addresses somewhere. They sent out messages like the one in Figure 29-4 to everyone on the list, each message customized to include one name from the address list in the body of the Web Beacon. Then they gather e-mail addresses on their Web server, as unsuspecting people open (or even preview) their scummy mail. Ka-ching!

Oh. Did I mention? The list of unscrupulous companies that have used Web Beacons includes a few you probably know: Barnes & Noble, cooking.com, and eToys, among many others, including Microsoft, back in the days before anyone knew what Web Beacons were.

You can do a few things to keep Web Beacons at bay, although these tactics have unfortunate side effects:

- Outlook 2003 and Outlook Express in Windows XP Service Pack 2 have settings (which many people turn off) that disrupt the Beacons by telling Outlook not to open pictures inside e-mail messages. In Outlook, choose Tools➪Options➪Security. In the Junk E-mail Prevention section, click the Settings button (see Figure 29-6). In Outlook Express, choose Tools➪Options➪Security and select the Block Images and Other External Content in HTML E-mail box.

  Unfortunately, many messages are completely incomprehensible without their pictures, so many Outlook users choose to show images. It's Hobbes' Choice: a lose-lose situation.

- You can go through your e-mail with your Internet connection turned off, and that keeps the Beacon from "phoning home."

That's about all you can do.

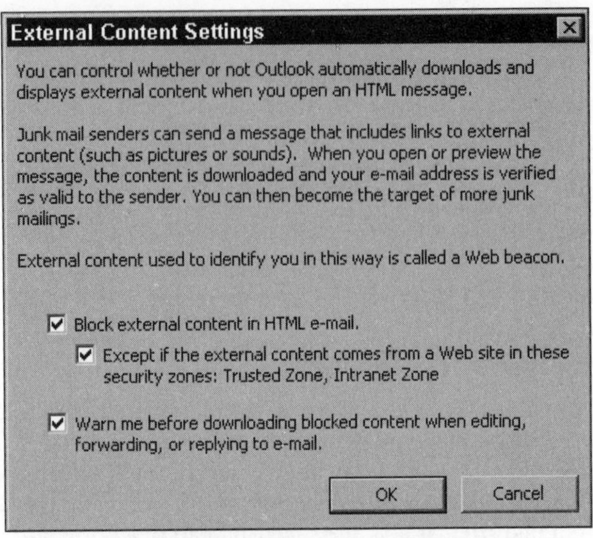

• **Figure 29-6: Blocking Web Beacons in Office 2003 (Office 2000 and XP don't block Beacons, and don't have an analogous setting).**

Crawling and trawling

Giant Web spiders scan millions of Web pages every day, seeking valid e-mail addresses. If your e-mail address is on the Web anywhere — even if it's hidden from view, behind some kind of link on your personal home page, for example — one of the Web crawlers can pick it up.

The crawlers go through all the newsgroups, too, every night. If you post on a newsgroup, make sure you use a return address that can't be automatically lifted. If you want people to be able to send you e-mail, try a combination that's legible to humans, but a real stumper for spiders: `woody@AskWoody.DeleteThisBeforeSending.com` for example.

Some unscrupulous online greeting card companies make most (if not all!) of their profits by skimming From and To e-mail addresses from people sending cards. If you send an online greeting card, stick to one of the big, better-known companies and check their privacy policy before you send.

Unsubscribing — *Not!*

Most vexing: If you follow the instructions to unsubscribe or stop receiving mailings from some spam houses, the company can use the information you provide to confirm that it has your up-to-date, working e-mail address! It's one of the abiding ironies of the CAN-SPAM Act: Every unsolicited e-mail message is supposed to have an opt-out link, so opt-out links are "normal" and expected, so more people click the links, verifying the legitimacy of their addresses.

For example, if I click the No Mail! link in the piece of spam shown in Figure 29-1, I go to the Web page shown in Figure 29-7.

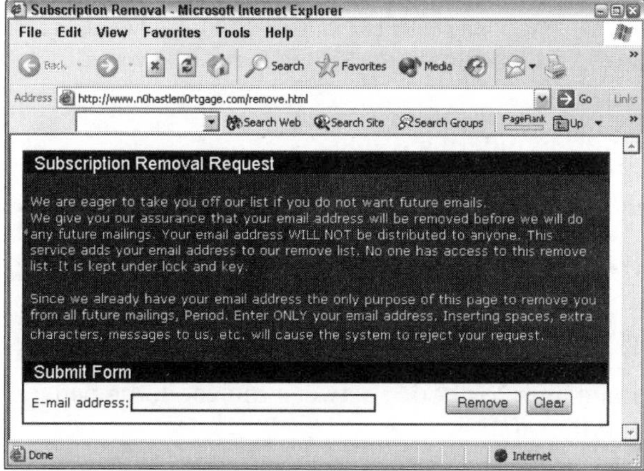

• Figure 29-7: Another scam to harvest more names?

The page in Figure 29-7 is notable because it doesn't include any mention of the e-mail address that received the spam. You have to type in your address. (Remember, the Web Beacon has already confirmed that your address is a good one.) And if you accidentally provide an address that the spammer doesn't have already, there's no telling how the address will be used.

The moral of the story: Don't try to unsubscribe, unless you're looking at a bona-fide message from a big-name company and you know that you personally asked for a subscription in the first place. If you find yourself face-to-face with a form that asks for your e-mail address, think twice before you give it away. Can't win, can't get ahead, can't even get out of the game.

Fighting Back

Spam isn't a black-and-white problem. There are plenty of shades of gray, and zealots (like me) need to temper their anti-spam rabidity with some common sense. That said, spam is probably your number-one computer time sink — if it isn't yet, it will be soon, unless you get sucked in by instant messaging.

So what can you do about spam?

Taking spam action

I wish everyone would use these simple rules about spam:

- **Rule #1: Don't ever, ever, ever respond to spam.** If someone sends you an unsolicited offer to make you look 20 years younger, or add inches here, or take off inches there, don't reply. Don't click the Take Me Off Your List button. Don't click any links. If you respond to one piece of spam in any way, I guarantee you end up on a gold list somewhere and pay for your transgression over and over again. Moreover, if you respond, you only encourage these cretins to keep pestering all of us. Give them the silent treatment. The only exception: established, credible companies. If you click the link to get off the Eddie Bauer direct mail list, rest assured that you're taken off. Just be super certain it's the real Eddie Bauer you're dealing with and not some spammer posing as Eddie Bauer.
- **Rule #2: Tell your friends about Rule #1.**
- **Rule #3: Spammeisters are the scum of the earth.** Treat them accordingly. I know highly experienced and intelligent people who see a piece of spam about something that interests them, and they figure that once — just this once — they'll click through and look at the details. Don't do it.

- **Rule #4: Get mad. And get even.** Legislation against spammers deserves all the support we can muster, as long as the legislation doesn't make matters worse. Sue a few of them, just for practice. Throw the vermin in jail. It may not reduce the volume of spam, but it'll sure make *me* feel better. Lots of resources are on the Web, particularly at `spam.abuse.net`, and the Coalition Against Unsolicited Commercial Email (CAUCE) at `www.cauce.org`.

Biting the phishers

As spammers' evil twins, phishers deserve all the disdain their scummy brothers receive and more. I hate to belabor the obvious, but

- **Rule #1: Don't fill out any form you receive in a message.** I don't care if the message claims that all your credit cards are about to be shredded, the Federal Reserve needs to know about your bank account, *and* the government of Ubistanibia will fall if you don't provide your podiatrist's aunt's maiden name. Send any message asking for any personal information straight to the bit bucket.
- **Rule #2: If you click a link in an e-mail message, assume that you're not in Kansas anymore.** You may think that clicking a proffered link will take you to `citibank.com` or `paypal.com`, but they won't. Guaranteed. Companies that legitimately require your response won't send you mail with a link. If you need to fix your Citibank card, go to Internet Explorer, and type **www.citibank.com**. Or pick up the phone and call the bank.
- **Rule #3: Check your accounts often.** Check any account that has online access every few days. If you see something that doesn't look right, contact your account holder (but *never* by clicking an e-mail link) and yell, real loud, right away.
- **Rule #4: Book 'em, Dan-O.** Phishing takes place in real-time. If you get a suspicious-looking e-mail message that asks you to click through and provide personal information, forward a copy of it to the Anti-Phishing Working Group (`reportphishing@antiphishing.com`) and the U.S. Federal Trade Commission (`spam@uce.gov`). Don't delete the message. Keep it in a safe place, because investigators may want to examine it.

The experts also suggest that you forward a copy of the phishing message to the company that's being clobbered. I once did that, forwarding a copy of a very clever phishing message to PayPal, `spoof@paypal.com`. What a joke! The folks there thought I was trying to report a compromised account. It took more than a week to get it all straightened out — a complete waste of time for all involved. (What's the old saying? "No good deed goes unpunished"?) You may have better luck than I, but I wouldn't bother trying to alert the company involved.

Filtering out junk e-mail

Defining *spam* or *junk e-mail* is very hard. Certainly, the terms include unsolicited e-mail that tries to sell you something, but not all unsolicited e-mail is junk.

And if you and I have a hard time just talking about it, imagine how hard it must be to get an automated spam filter to choose between the good, the bad, and the offal.

Older spam filters just didn't work. They relied on a combination of the following:

- **White lists:** Lists of addresses that are accepted. Any mail from an address on the white list makes it through the junk filter.
- **Black lists:** Lists of addresses (or, more frequently, entire domains) that are rejected. Mail from an address on the black list gets bumped.
- **Bad word lists:** Lists of a thousand (or a hundred thousand) bad words. If any of those bad words are in a message, the message gets filtered out.

No doubt you can come up with a bunch of good reasons why none of those approaches alone work. Black lists and white lists can be helpful, and when you shop around for a spam filter, you should certainly make sure that it supports both. But a good spam filter has to do much more.

Many companies sell spam filtering software and/or services, frequently in conjunction with antivirus or firewall products. I've had very mixed results with them.

Microsoft itself includes a spam filter with Outlook 2003, but many people report problems. For example, in August 2004, Microsoft abruptly yanked the third update to the Outlook 2003 spam dictionary with no warning or explanation, and re-released it several weeks later. Heaven only knows what happened. How can you trust a spam filter like that?

The big spam filters — most particularly Microsoft's filter — suffer from a simple congenital defect: They don't adapt to each individual's specific patterns of spam. They're based on fixed dictionaries that don't vary for each user. A very simplistic example: Outlook 2003's spam filter assigns a negative rating to the phrase "bust enlargement": If the phrase "bust enlargement" appears in a message, chances are good that Outlook 2003 tosses it in the Junk E-mail box. That's bad news if you work in the bust enlargement industry, eh?

More than that, the big companies present a big target. If a spammer (or phisher) can create one message that gets through Outlook 2003's spam filter, they know it can go through every Outlook 2003 spam filter on the planet. That's why using smaller spam fighting programs makes sense.

A new class of spam filters, called *Bayesian filters,* seems to hold the greatest promise. Bayesian filters break down messages into their component parts, and then use sophisticated weighting techniques to determine which messages to allow through, and which are suspect. Most importantly, Bayesian filters, by their very nature, learn which messages are good and bad — and they learn from the master: you.

Microsoft claims that its Outlook junk mail filters (and the filter used by MSN Hotmail) are all Bayesian. That's quite literally true: The "bad word" dictionary is constructed on Bayesian principals, updated by hundreds of millions of pieces of spam. But the Outlook filter doesn't adapt. The only way to change the dictionary is to wait for Microsoft to release (or re-release) a new version.

When you tell a Bayesian junk filter that you have a good message, it adjusts the weight of the words in the message toward the good side. If you flag a message as bad, the filter becomes more wary of words in the bad message.

The results to date have been very encouraging. One researcher has determined that scanning for the color of a formatted message — specifically, rejecting messages with bright red fonts — is a more reliable technique for detecting spam than scanning for specific four-letter words!

Personally, I use a Bayesian junk mail filter called Junk-Out, and I can't imagine living online without it. Last month, Junk-Out automatically filtered out more than 12,500 pieces of incoming spam on my main account. I had two messages identified as spam that weren't — so I still go over the Junk Mail folder periodically. I had a couple dozen pieces of spam that weren't caught, so I "trained" Junk-Out to recognize them as spam; all it takes is one click. All in all, that's an astounding percentage — much better than Outlook 2003.

Junk-Out works only with Microsoft Outlook. It's available in a shareware version, at `www.junk-out.com`.

If you forward messages that look like this:

```
For each person you send this email
to, you will be given $5. For every
person they give it to, you will be
given an additional $3. For every
person they send it to you will
receive $1. Microsoft will tally all
the emails produced under your name
over a two week period and then email
you with more instructions...
```

you're part of the problem. If it sounds too good to be true, it is. Check out `vil.mcafee.com/hoax.asp` **or** `securityresponse.symantec.com/avcenter/hoax.html` **for more information.**

Protecting Your Kids

Save Time By

- Knowing the advantages and limitations of parental control software
- Comparing potential solutions
- Using the approach that's appropriate for you and your kids

Hey, I'm a parent, too. A lot of garbage is on the Internet. No question. Sooner or later, whether your kids look for it or not, they are going to get exposed to some of it. No question.

The big questions are how to minimize their chances of being exposed accidentally — and how to make sure that they move on, quickly, to something a bit more wholesome.

A few tools can help; but in the end, it's a question of how you interact with your kids. The phrase *parental control* rightfully applies to parents — not software.

Evaluating Parental Control Software

Parents seeking a software assistant in their efforts to control kids' access to less-than-stellar material on the Internet need to consider a wide range of potential exposures:

- Web sites with offensive content
- Scummy e-mail messages
- Dubious Internet newsgroups
- Bad chat and instant messaging partners
- Questionable files — not just pictures, but music, documents, and programs, too

The very best parental control software can tackle a subset of those exposures by using

- **Web site white lists:** These feature a list of Web-permitted sites, which you may be able to modify on your PC.
- **Web site black lists:** These feature a list of forbidden sites, again possibly modifiable on your own PC.

- **Web site content scanners:** These typically look for "bad" words on Web pages and ban access to pages with the bad words. These are roughly analogous to the old spam filters (see Technique 29), which bounced messages based on "bad" keywords. These scanners don't work very well.
- **E-mail filters:** These also typically work the old-fashioned way, scanning for "bad" words. Bayesian technology hasn't yet made inroads in the parental control arena. (Find out more about Bayesian technology in Technique 29.)
- **Typing blockers:** These watch what your child types, refusing to pass through strings (including, presumably, a child's address or telephone number) that you specify.

Some parental control software also includes the capability to

- Log every keystroke
- Take periodic snapshots of the screen
- Set time limits — a maximum amount of time a kid is allowed on the PC
- Preset *age appropriate* limits to make it easy to relax the controls for older children
- Work in stealth mode, so transgressions (for example, accessing blacklisted Web sites) are simply logged, not blocked
- Block online games and file-sharing programs, such as iMesh
- E-mail a periodic report with a full log for each child

The best known and highest rated parental control software manufacturers are

- **Net Nanny** (`www.netnanny.com`)**:** This manufacturer consistently ranks high in the reviews, although users fault it for hanging their systems, slowing down browsing, and being hard to administer. No instant message filtering for MSN Messenger or AOL Instant Messenger.
- **CYBERsitter** (`www.cybersitter.com`)**:** This manufacturer also ranks consistently high in the reviews. It adds instant messaging filters, but many parents feel that the controls are too complex. The latest version of CYBERsitter, while drawing good reviews, blocks an enormous number of completely innocuous sites.
- **iProtectYou** (`www.softforyou.com`)**:** Like CYBERsitter, iProtectYou blocks access to many sites that kids should be able to see. It has a few bells and whistles — recognizing different logon names for different kids, and easy tools for setting maximum access time or download sizes — but it has bugs, too.

Here's the truth, right between the eyes: None of the parental control packages can come close to you sitting down with your child and working with her on the Internet. At best, the parental control software locks kids out of the worst sites – but it also locks them out of some perfectly legitimate pages. At worst, the software locks your kids and you out of places you want to go.

All the parental control packages are easily cracked with programs readily available on the Web. (If you don't know about them, your kids do.) Many programs put icons in the notification area, near the clock, so savvy kids know that the spy is watching. Many take the hint from the notification icons and figure out how to kill the programs. It isn't that hard.

The black lists will never include all the "bad" sites. The white lists can be bypassed. Scanning sites for "bad" words pits laughably simplistic tools against a truly complex problem. (How can a filter decide when something is obscene — or even objectionable — when humans rarely agree?) Limitations on typing can be circumvented with tricks so straightforward that many children discover them in minutes. E-mail controls, when present, only cover a tiny fraction of all the "bad" spam kids get. Many adults turn off the parental control software when they want to use the PC and forget to turn it back on. And on and on.

Parental control software might be a part of the solution. But, at best, it's only a small part.

In case you're wondering, Windows XP's Internet Content Advisor blocking doesn't work worth beans. (In Internet Explorer, choose Tools⇨Internet Options⇨Content⇨Enable. It's a clumsy approach that relies on a self-rating system that very few Web sites use.

Going Beyond Parental Control Software

AOL and MSN offer kid-centric Web services, with full parental controls. EarthLink and other major Internet service providers are also starting to roll out similar packages. The problem: Their services suffer from precisely the same defects as parental control software. They're driven by white lists and/or bad word dictionaries, which keep kids away from enormous troves of information.

Ask yourself this. If you were coming up with a white list for one of the Internet providers, would you allow kids to read about the restoration of Michelangelo's *David?* Would you permit them to see the statue? What about the Sistine Chapel? Or any of a thousand different paintings at, say, The Louvre? At what age would you allow a kid to read *Huckleberry Finn*?

For young children, white list limitations aren't as onerous as they can be for older kids and teenagers. You might want to consider using a Web site and browser that are unabashedly limited to "kids only" content. The Children's Internet (`www.childrensinternet.com`), shown in Figure 30-1 offers a fun, safe environment where kids can start learning to use the Web.

There's great merit in this approach. But teenagers won't stand for it.

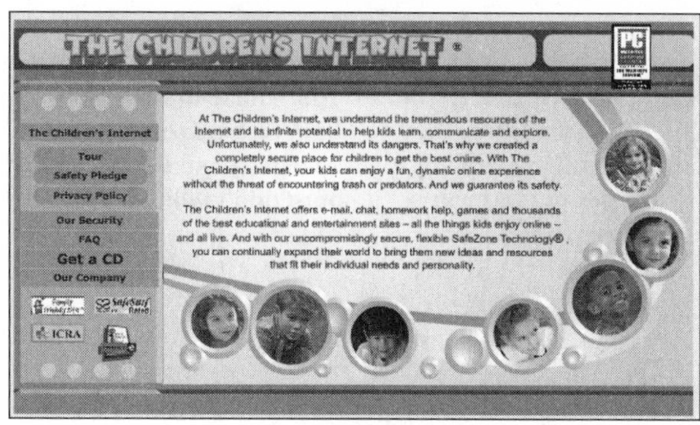

• **Figure 30-1: Many young kids find The Children's Internet delightful – but not very deep.**

Both Linksys (`www.linksys.com/press/press.asp?prid=147`) and ZyXEL (`www.zyxel.com`) offer parental control components as part of their routers. They're based on white lists maintained by independent companies (Netopia for Linksys and Cerberian for ZyXEL).

What I've seen of both offerings leaves me cold. Both Linksys and ZyXEL act as if these features are simply there to add one more item to the reviewers' checklists. Neither appears to support the software, or even publicize its existence.

If you find yourself looking for a *stealthy logger* — a program that surreptitiously logs everything happening on a PC, replete with frequent screen shots — take a look at IamBigBrother (`www.Software4Parents.com`). But more importantly . . . take a look in the mirror. Do you *really* want to invade your kid's privacy to that extent?

Settling on a Workable Plan

As far as I'm concerned, keeping your kids safe all boils down to these basic guidelines:

- **Spend all the time you possibly can with your kids while they're on the computer.** Who knows? They may teach you something.

- **Make sure that your kids understand what you expect — not only in terms of where they can and cannot go on the Internet, but also what information they're allowed to give out while chatting or sending e-mail.** Creepy people hang out in chat rooms. If your child is old enough to type his address, he's old enough to understand when he shouldn't type his address.

Larry Magid, at *The Mercury News* (of San Jose, California) has an excellent article called "Help children know the risks of chat rooms" at `www.larrysworld.com/articles/sjm_chatrooms.htm`.

- **If you can, put the computer where people commonly walk by.** It's an added deterrent.
- **If you use parental control software to block access to Web sites, anticipate the likelihood that your kids will wonder why they're being locked out — and spend an inordinate amount of time trying to circumvent the rules.** They're kids. That's their job.

Before you use *stealth software* (that is, software that hides itself so your kids can't see it) to log your kids' activity on the Internet, consider the consequences. No matter what you do, sooner or later they'll find out.

Part V

Optimizing Your Musical Entertainment

"You should check that box so they can't profile your listening and viewing habits. I didn't do it and I'm still getting spam about hearing loss, anger management and psychological counseling."

Using Windows Media Player

Save Time By

- Getting Windows Media Player 10's settings right
- Customizing and controlling the beast
- Putting the volume control where you can reach it quickly

Microsoft has come a long way from Windows Media Player 8 (WMP 8), which shipped with the original version of Windows XP. For one thing, the old version automatically kept track of what you played and sent Microsoft these great little notices, complete with a "branding" number that identified your PC. In the new version, Microsoft tries to convince you that allowing Mama Microsoft to keep track of your playing and viewing habits is to, uh, enhance your personal experience. Yeah, that's the ticket.

To Microsoft's credit, the new version, Windows Media Player 10, gives you plenty of opportunity to protect your privacy, if you know which check boxes to uncheck. This technique gets you up and running WMP 10 quickly and with a minimum of hassle — now and in the future.

Windows Media Player ain't the only game in town. If you grow weary of WMP's in-yer-face advertising and obnoxious Microsoft-file-format bias, you have plenty of good alternatives. Two stand out: iTunes and Musicmatch. Apple's iTunes (`www.apple.com/itunes`), based on the QuickTime platform (a buggy program I've been railing about for years), has the interface I like best. iTunes makes it easy to print CD case inserts. It even allows you to convert songs from Microsoft's WMA format to Apple's AAC format. Yahoo's Musicmatch (`www.musicmatch.com`) has long led the pack among those who want a simple, no-hassles approach to their music. Musicmatch's greatest saving grace is that it's format-agnostic: Yahoo doesn't care if you use Microsoft's WMA or Apple's AAC. Party on, dude.

Installing WMP 10

If you don't know which version of Windows Media Player you have on your Windows XP PC, start WMP (choose Start⇨All Programs⇨Windows Media Player); then choose Help⇨About Windows Media Player. If the dialog box says you have version 8 (as in Figure 31-1), you need version 10 — quick. Even version 9 needs a makeover.

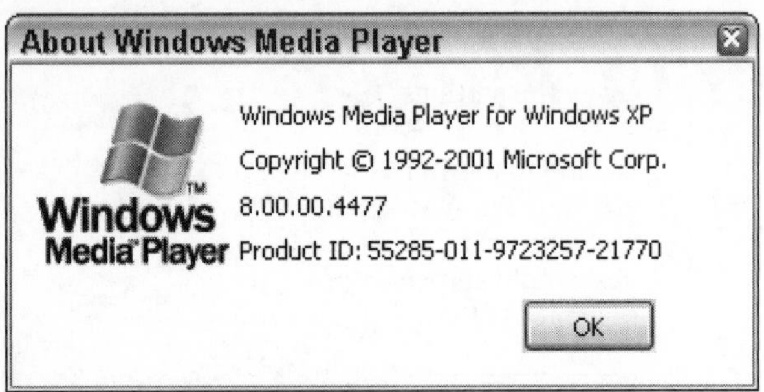

• Figure 31-1: You definitely don't want version 8, identified by the "8.00.00. . ." version number.

To install WMP 10, follow these steps:

1. **Start Internet Explorer and go to** `www.microsoft.com/windows/windowsmedia/download/default.asp`**.**
2. **Under the Windows Media Player 10, click the Download Now button.**
3. **Follow the instructions to save the file** `MP10Setup.exe` **someplace convenient.**
4. **When the download is done, double-click** `MP10Setup.exe`**.**

   WMP greets you with its End User License Agreement. Take heart. The EULA is a little bit longer than this technique, and it's packed with legalese so dense that no two attorneys — especially no two Microsoft attorneys — would ever agree on what it says.
5. **Read the EULA carefully, and then click I Accept.**

   Everyone does. Cough, cough.

   A welcome screen appears.
6. **Click Next.**

   WMP presents you with its privacy questionnaire, as shown in Figure 31-2.
7. **Unless you have very specific reasons for leaving your personal information in Microsoft's databases, uncheck all the check boxes and click Next.**

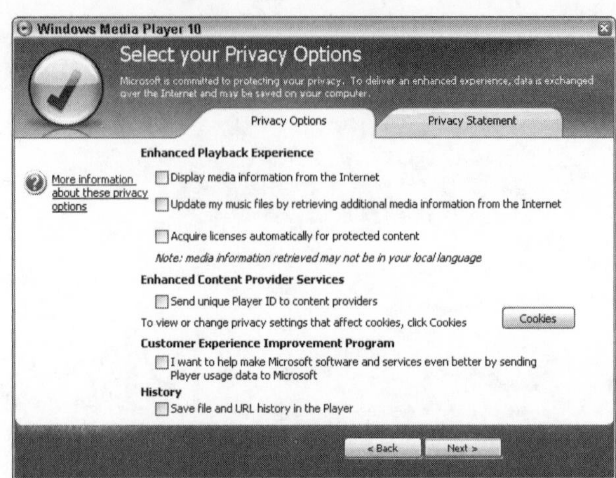

• Figure 31-2: Answer these key questions for Microsoft.

If you wade deep enough through the privacy statements, you find that WMP no longer sends the player i.d. to Microsoft to keep track of what you view and listen to, but MS *does* track your Internet IP address. If you have an "always on" Internet connection — DSL, cable, satellite, whatever — the IP address is almost as specific as the player i.d. WindowsMedia.com, the engine that drives most of WMP behind the scenes, collects even more information, plants third-party advertising cookies, and uses Web Beacons (see Technique 29). If it weren't Microsoft, I'd call that scummy business. Do yourself a favor. Don't give Microsoft even more of your personal information.

WMP warns you that it's going to take over control of all the filename extensions shown in Figure 31-3 — that WMP 10 becomes the default player every time you click a file with one of those filename extensions. Chances are good that you want it to. (To find out more about filename extensions, see Technique 20.)

8. **Unless you need to keep WMP from taking on certain kinds of files, keep all the check boxes checked and click Finish.**

   Windows launches WMP.

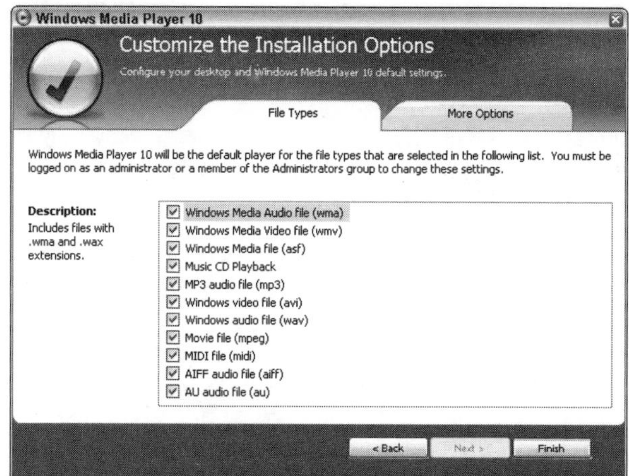

• **Figure 31-3: WMP wants to take over these filename extensions.**

9. When WMP kicks out a little dialog box that shows you how to put a mini-player in your Windows taskbar, check the Don't Show This Message Again check box, and then click OK.

If you want to put the mini-player in the taskbar, right-click an empty place on the taskbar, choose Toolbars, and check Windows Media Player. To give the mini-player the heave-ho, go back and uncheck it.

Chances are pretty good that you're going to get tired of the mini-player — it takes up a lot of precious space on the taskbar, and you can't stack other taskbar buttons below it.

Tweaking WMP

With its newly designed interface (which, ahem, borrows extensively from iTunes and Musicmatch), you'll probably find that you can figure out WMP faster than you can master, oh, a new VCR or DVD recorder.

Until you have your feet on the ground and feel confident you can make your own choices, Justin and I suggest that you immediately go in to WMP and make a few significant changes:

1. Choose Tools⇨Options⇨Player⇨Rip Music.

You see the settings in Figure 31-4.

Getting to the Tools menu may be difficult. If you can't see WMP's File/View/Play/Tools/Help menu bar, click the down-arrow near the upper-right corner — the one to the left of the Minimize button.

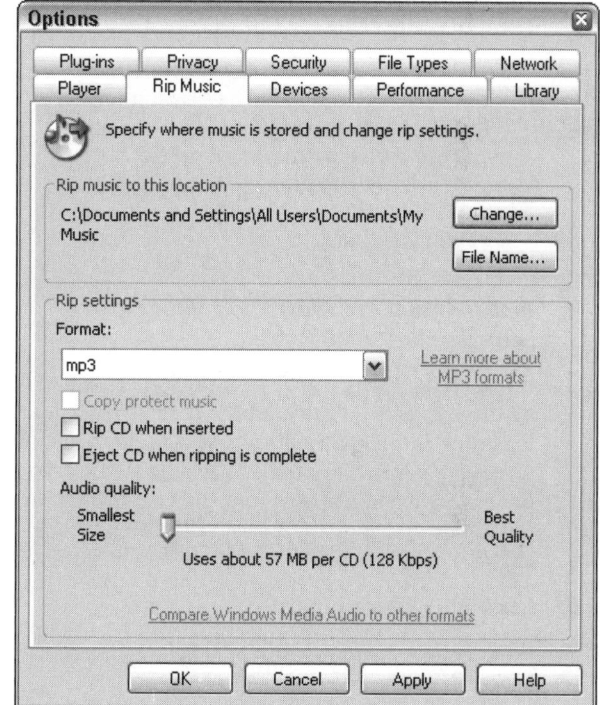

• **Figure 31-4: Key settings for WMP.**

2. If you plan to share your music files with other people on your computer or other people on your network, click the Change button, navigate to the `Shared Documents\Shared Music` **folder, and click OK.**

WMP uses the location you choose to store "ripped" music tracks, when you copy music from an audio CD onto your computer (see Technique 32).

Microsoft's ever-widening digital rights management licensing schemes may trip you up on sharing across a network (you may not be able to play a WMA music file on any machine other than the one on which the file was "ripped"), but in general, the Shared Music folder is the best place to put music files.

Choosing your Shared Music folder as the default location for ripped tracks has the salubrious side-affect of unchecking the Copy Protect Music box.

If this box is checked, every time you rip an audio track and turn it into a Microsoft-format WMA file, WMP marks the file so it can only be played on the machine that ripped it. If you've ever tried to play a WMA file that was created on a different PC and it wouldn't work, now you know why.

3. **In the Format drop-down box, under Rip Settings, choose MP3.**

   If you really, really want to support Microsoft in its drive to control the future of rock 'n' roll (or at least, the format of the files that contain music of all types), you can leave the box set to WMA. If you have any question at all about the best format for the songs you copy from audio CDs, please look at the discussion of file formats in Technique 32.

4. **Click the Privacy tab.**

   WMP brings up its privacy settings, as shown in Figure 31-5.

It's hard to fathom how Microsoft can call individual ID tracking a Customer Experience Improvement Program — especially after the court cases — but here it is, in the flesh. People wonder why I'm so cynical. . . .

5. **Uncheck every check box on the Privacy tab, except the Set Clock on Devices Automatically check box. Then click OK.**

   Yeah, I wimped out on the clock. Can't figure how setting the clock can put money in Microsoft's coffers, but I imagine they'll figure out something. Anyway, now you're ready to use WMP.

• **Figure 31-5: Uncheck every one of these check boxes.**

Running WMP

If you've never used Windows Media Player before, start by going through the steps in the preceding section. Then try playing a CD:

1. **Pop a music CD into your CD drive.**

2. **If Windows XP tosses up a dialog box asking what you want to do, select Play Audio CD Using Windows Media Player and click OK.**

   WMP springs to life, as shown in Figure 31-6. If you've told WMP to protect your privacy and not retrieve information from Microsoft's site on the Internet, chances are good WMP doesn't identify the title of the album, the artist, or the names of the tracks.

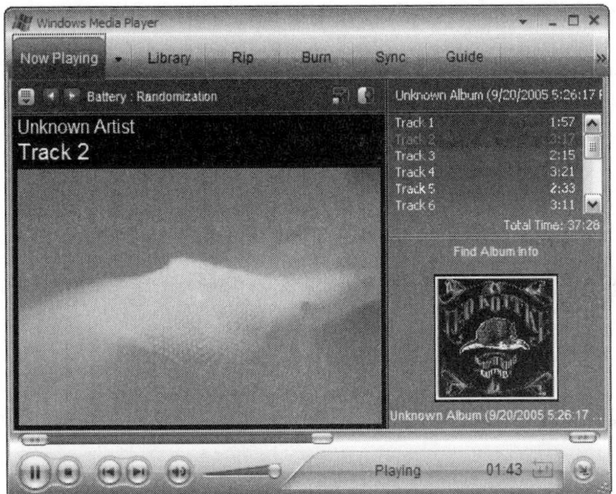

• **Figure 31-6: A view of WMP, playing Leo Kottke's *6- and 12-String Guitar,* without album info.**

At this point, you need to make a choice. You can live with the Unknown Album gibberish. Or, as shown in Figure 31-7, you can have WMP dig into the Microsoft archives and display the details about the album — but at a price. See the "Displaying album info" sidebar.

3. **WMP contains a number of audio settings — *enhancements* in WMP parlance — including control over SRS WOW effects. To leaf through what's on offer, choose View⇨Enhancements⇨ Graphic Equalizer.**

To get to the View menu, you may need to click the down arrow to the left of the Minimize icon, in the upper-right corner of WMP.

Cycle through the Equalizer, the SRS WOW adjuster, video settings, cross-fading (blending the end of one song into the beginning of the next) and auto volume leveling (so each song plays at approximately the same base volume) by clicking the forward and backward arrows. When you're tired of it, click the X in the upper-right corner of the graphic equalizer box.

• **Figure 31-7: *6- and 12-String Guitar* with all the data filled in.**

4. **If you're looking for those far-out *visualizations* — the abstract patterns that move in concert with the music, more or less — choose View⇨Visualizations, and then pick the visualization you want to see.**

   All together now: "Groooooovy."

5. **To get WMP down to its skin, choose View⇨ Skin Mode.**

   The original skin mode looks like something out of *Star Trek.* Nowadays it looks more like a 2D iPod. If you want to put WMP back in Full Mode, click the Return to Full Mode button at the bottom of the skin.

6. **To change skins, go back to Full Mode, and choose View⇨Skin Chooser. Then choose whatever skin suits your fancy.**

Displaying album info

Of course, seeing the album info is great, but before you do, know that you leave behind a record of your request, including your Internet IP address. If you have an "always on" Windows connection, that IP address identifies you (or at least your network) uniquely. Microsoft unabashedly accumulates that information to hone its marketing offers to your preferences. Microsoft claims it won't release the data. Now you know.

To retrieve album information, follow these steps:

1. **Choose Tools⇨Options⇨Privacy.**

   To find the Tools menu, you may need to click the down arrow to the left of the Minimize icon, in the upper-right corner of WMP.

2. **Select the Display Media Information from the Internet check box.**
3. **Click OK.**

   This unlocks WMP and gives it permission to contact windowsmedia.com and retrieve album information. (The information probably comes from AMG, but it may come from your preferred online store.)

4. **Click the Find Album Info line.**

   WMP goes out to the Internet, retrieves the information for the album (sometimes it can't find any!), and returns it to you.

5. **If the information looks correct, click Finish in the lower right. Otherwise, click Search, wait for WMP to retrieve more data from the Internet, and make changes.**

   WMP comes back with the Unknown information filled in (refer to Figure 31-7). But wait. You aren't done yet.

6. **Be sure you replug the hole by choosing Tools⇨Options⇨Privacy, unchecking the Retrieve Media Information for CDs and DVDs from the Internet check box, and clicking OK.**

Controlling WMP from the keyboard

While you can use the on-screen controls for playing and pausing, many people find it easier to use the keyboard controls — especially if the mini-player is on the Windows taskbar. Check out Table 31-1.

One particularly good key to remember: F8 immediately turns off the sound — but only if WMP is the active window.

Table 31-1: Windows Media Player Shortcut Keys

This Key	Does This
F8	Turns off the sound
F9	Decreases the volume
F10	Increases the volume
Ctrl+P	Play/Pause
Ctrl+S	Stop
Ctrl+B	Back one track
Ctrl+F	Forward one track

No-Nonsense Music Gathering

Save Time By

- Adding music on your PC to the Media Library — fast
- Ripping (pulling tracks from audio CDs) the right way, the first time
- Managing playlists so you hear what you want, right now

Hey, if you're a teenager, getting into things is part of your job description. Windows Media Player is full of nooks and crannies and interesting and fun places where you can poke and prod (and learn a lot about computers!) for hours on end.

On the other hand, if you just want to get the %$#@! thing to work, all those little fun places get in the way. This technique shows you how to get songs and video clips into Windows Media Player, and how to organize them so that you can push a button or two and listen to something you really want to listen to. Now.

The next technique talks about buying music on the Internet — downloading it directly to your PC, and possibly from there to your MP3 Player, er, Multimedia Player, uh, Portable Device, well, you know what I mean. It's a field fraught with its own landmines.

Adding Music to the Media Library

Whether you want it or not, whether you tried to or not, your PC already overflows with audio files: grunts and squawks, bleeps and moans, with a few worthwhile songs here or there. If you have a home or small office network, and your son has been ripping CDs since he fell off the turnip truck, you may have a few more tunes sitting around.

Your first step in gathering music? Catalog what you already have. In WMP-speak that's called "adding items to the Media Library."

Making WMP search for music on your hard drive

The first time you use WMP, and any time you copy, delete, or move large numbers of music (or video) files to or from your PC, it's a good idea to tell WMP to scan everything and add your music and video files to the Media Library. It takes a while to scan all your drives, but when you're done, you can get at all your music and videos through WMP itself, instead of having to manually search for songs or videos on your hard drive. To have WMP search your computer for music and videos, follow these steps:

1. **Start WMP by choosing Start⇨All Programs⇨Windows Media Player.**

   Windows Media Player appears.

2. **If you want to retrieve album covers, artist names, and song titles for all the music on your computer, choose Tools⇨Options⇨Privacy and check the Update My Music Files by Retrieving Media Info from the Internet check box, and then click OK. (You may need to click the down arrow to the left of the Minimize icon in the upper-right corner of WMP in order to get at the Tools menu.)**

Be aware that checking this check box gives Microsoft a detailed list of all the music on your computer, along with your Internet IP address, to boot. Check out Technique 31 for more information.

3. **At the top, click Library.**

4. **If this is the first time you've gone to the Library, WMP presents you with the dialog box shown in Figure 32-1. Click Yes.**

• Figure 32-1: A request to put music and videos into your personal Media Library.

5. **If this is not your first time in the Media Library, choose Tools⇨Search for Media Files. (Again, you may have to click the down arrow in the upper-right corner of WMP to get to the Tools menu.)**

   In either event, WMP presents you with the Add to Library by Searching Computer dialog box, as shown in Figure 32-2.

6. **In the Search On text box, choose all the drives you want to scan. (You can also select shared drives by clicking the Browse button.)**

   If you didn't check the Update My Music Files check box in Step 2, there's no need to be concerned about the While Adding Music Files to the Library section shown in Figure 32-2.

The scanner does not look inside compressed folders or Zip files.

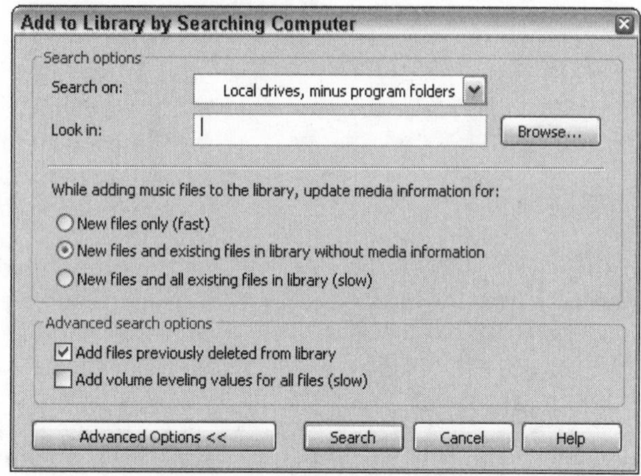

• Figure 32-2: Scan your computer and add music and video files to the Library.

7. **Click the Search button and go have a latte.**

   If you have a lot of files, this takes a while.

8. **When the Cancel button turns into Close, click that Close button.**

   You may want to return to Step 6 and scan other drives, folders, or shared folders.

9. **If you said it was okay for WMP to contact Microsoft in Step 2, you probably want to turn off the phone-home switch: Choose Tools⇨Options⇨Privacy, and uncheck the Update My Music Files by Retrieving Missing Info from the Internet check box, and then click OK.**

Adding new songs to the Library

You should have some music — possibly quite a lot — in your Library.

Sooner or later, you're bound to acquire more songs, and you'll definitely want to put them in the Library, so they are easy to find. Here's how to add more songs to the Library:

1. **Use WMP to rip a track (which is to say, copy a song from an audio CD to your computer).**

   This process is a little confusing because ripping involves three steps:

   - The song gets converted from the format on an audio CD into a form that the computer can understand (typically WMA or MP3).
   - The converted track is placed on your hard drive.
   - Your Library list gets updated to show that you have a new track available.

   While you may think of that as "ripping with WMP," in fact the process involves both copying the track to your hard drive and updating the Media Library database.

2. **Tell WMP to add songs to the Library when you play them by choosing Tools➪Options➪Player and checking the Add Music Files to Library When Played check box.**

   In general, you want to have WMP add a track to its database when you play a track that's on your PC. In general, you *don't* want to add a track to the Media Library when it's on a CD.

3. **Choose File➪Add to Media Library➪Add Folder/File or Playlist/URL.**

   It's possible to link to songs on the Internet this way, although you probably want to download the song.

4. **Have WMP monitor specific folders by choosing File➪Add to Media Library➪By Monitoring Folders.**

   Initially, WMP monitors the folder that you choose to contain newly ripped songs, as well as your My Music and My Videos folders. You can monitor other folders as well by changing the settings, as shown in Figure 32-3.

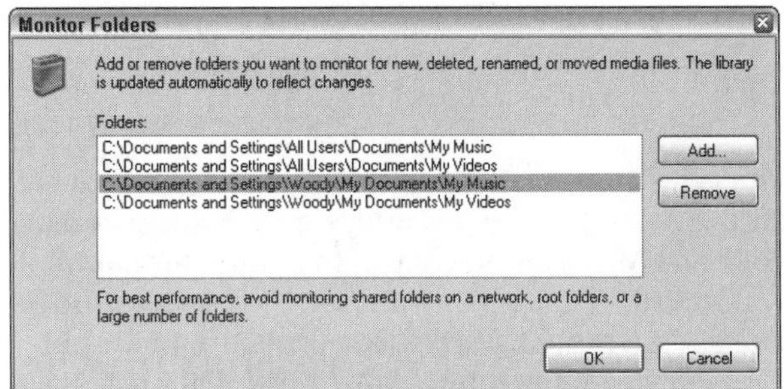

• **Figure 32-3: WMP starts with the folder you selected to store ripped songs (Tools➪Options➪Copy Music) and your My Music folder.**

Ripping CDs You Own

When the topic turns to ripping CDs — the process of pulling songs off audio CDs and putting them on your computer — the first question that inevitably arises is one of ethics.

Ripping ethics

I'm not talking about the ethics of ripping a song and giving the file to another person. There's no question about the ethics of illegally pirating music. You can make copies of music on CDs that you bought for your own private use. People try to hem and haw and weasel their way around the legalities, but their justifications are self-serving. The bottom line's pretty simple. In the U.S., you can make copies of any music that you bought in order to

- Keep a backup for your own private use
- Change the format (for example, so you can download it to a small music player) for your own private use
- Rearrange the order in which the music is played (commonly via a *playlist*) for your own private use
- Make compilations of your favorite songs for your own private use

You also can loan the original CD to a friend, and your friend can listen to it. But your friend can't make a copy of the CD.

That's it. The ethics and legalities of pirating are quite straightforward. The *real* ethics question is whether you trust Microsoft to control the future format of your music. If enough people use Microsoft's proprietary WMA format, Microsoft will have a great deal of influence on the future direction of digital music.

Choosing a file format and sampling rate

Before the time of Windows XP, the vast majority of computer-legible music existed in so-called MP3 format. MP3 is an open standard from the Motion Picture Exchange Group for turning sound into bits. But then the Big Boys arrived on the scene, and they smelled . . . money. Microsoft and Apple both figure that plenty of dough is to be made if the major record labels and movie studios can be convinced to release digital versions of their songs and movies using file formats that belong to the software companies.

Microsoft, Apple, and Real (the company behind Real Audio) have their own music formats, called WMA, AAC and Real, respectively. As of this writing, Real's pretty much dead, and MP3, WMA, and AAC are locked in a celebrity death match duel (trial?) for the hearts and minds of Windows users. If Microsoft or Apple wins, the victor will likely rule the creation and distribution of music and video files well into the next decade. If lowly MP3 wins, Big Software loses — and the major record labels and video companies will find other ways to distribute their wares electronically.

Yes, I know that AAC isn't a proprietary format — it doesn't belong to Apple — *per se*. Apple grafted a copy protection, er, digital rights management scheme called FairPlay onto AAC, and the Apple AAC + FairPlay combination is proprietary. When you download music from the iTunes store, you get AAC (for the music) + FairPlay (to keep you from giving the song to your 100,000 closest friends).

WMA was built, from the ground up, to protect the people who sell music. AAC started out as an open standard, but FairPlay turns the screws. MP3, on the other hand, sprang from the halcyon days when nobody cared very much about digital rights management. You can't copy protect an MP3 file.

The choice of file format isn't entirely a political decision. There are technical considerations, too: After all, the name of the game is high quality music. Each of the music formats has, in effect, a low quality recording level, a couple of high quality levels, and several levels in between. The recording level is called a *sampling rate*. Rates are measured in Kbps, or thousands of bits per second.

As you might expect, all these technical factors have an effect on how many songs you can squeeze into a portable music player (what many call an "MP3 player"), and on how good the music sounds when you play it. See Table 32-1 for a heads-up comparison.

That said, there's one area where WMA and AAC have MP3 beat all to pieces: surround sound. If you have a 5.1 surround sound system built into your computer, don't bother with MP3. And be careful not to stub your toe on that $1,000 subwoofer, okay?

If you have an outstanding audio setup and you love classical music, use 192 Kbps or higher, rather than 128 Kbps. If you want quality above compatibility, be sure to look at the Vorbis OGG format (`www.vorbis.com`). You can't play it on anything, but it sure sounds sweet! Okay, okay. I exaggerated a little bit.

Windows Media Player 10, right out of the box, includes a very good MP3 *codec* — a piece of software that lets you convert audio CDs into MP3 computer files. WMP versions 8 and 9 didn't have an MP3 codec — you had to buy one from a third party.

TABLE 32-1: WOODY'S TAKE ON THE FORMAT CONUNDRUM

Format	Sampling Rate	Hassle Factor	Music Quality	Songs on a 128MB Player	Comments
MP3	64 Kbps	Low	Blech	60–70	Good enough for playing on blah computer speakers.
MP3	128 Kbps	Low	Very Good	30	Woody's Choice Award Winner — if you want to keep Microsoft and Apple from taking over the music distribution business.
AAC	64 Kbps	Medium	So-so	70-80	Not as good as WMA at 64 Kbps.
AAC	128 Kbps	Medium	Best of the bunch	30-35	Apple's AAC-to-WMA converter helps, particularly because so few AAC players exist (other than the iPod and variants, of course).
WMA	64 Kbps	High	So-so	70–80	Why not go up to 128 Kbps?
WMA	128 Kbps	High	Excellent	30–35	A decent choice if you only plan to play music on your PC, or you have a small music player that can handle WMA. But realize that you're helping Microsoft take over electronic music file formats.

The ballad of the MP3 codec

Back when Microsoft first released Windows XP and WMP 8, a hue and cry arose from many corners, saying that Microsoft failed to ship an MP3 codec because it didn't want people to use MP3. Not so, insisted the Softies: Most people didn't rip CDs, so they didn't need an MP3 codec. And, oh, the licensing fees! Adding MP3 support would be enormously expensive. Why should everyone pay extra for something only a few people want?

Yeah, right. MS wanted to get the WMA format on firm footing, and they weren't about to put MP3 support in Media Player.

Fast-forward three years, and MS includes a free MP3 codec in every copy of WMP 10. No wailing about licensing fees. No charge at all. You know why Microsoft did it? Because their competitors had free MP3 codecs, and every WMP review mentioned that fact. Microsoft was forced to keep up with the Joneses. Sometimes competition works, eh?

Ripping A to Z

Ripping a CD is easy. The whole process takes 15 minutes or so for a typical album, and you can do it while you're working on something else.

Here's how:

1. **Start Windows Media Player.**
2. **Choose Tools⇨Options⇨Rip Music.**

   WMP shows you the Copy Music Options, as shown in Figure 32-4.
3. **Set your copy options.**

   In Figure 32-4, I ripped to MP3 format with a sampling rate of 192 Kbps. I also chose not to eject the CD after the ripping stops. Many times an automatic eject amounts to an easy way for WMP to signal me when it's through — otherwise I have to keep checking to see when it's done. But if the CD gets ejected automatically, the music that's playing stops. So if I'm ripping music in a leisurely fashion, listening as I rip as it were, I simply let the music play.
4. **If you're working with a CD that's old and scratched, click the Devices tab, choose your CD drive, click the Properties button, and check the Use Error Correction check box, as shown in Figure 32-5.**

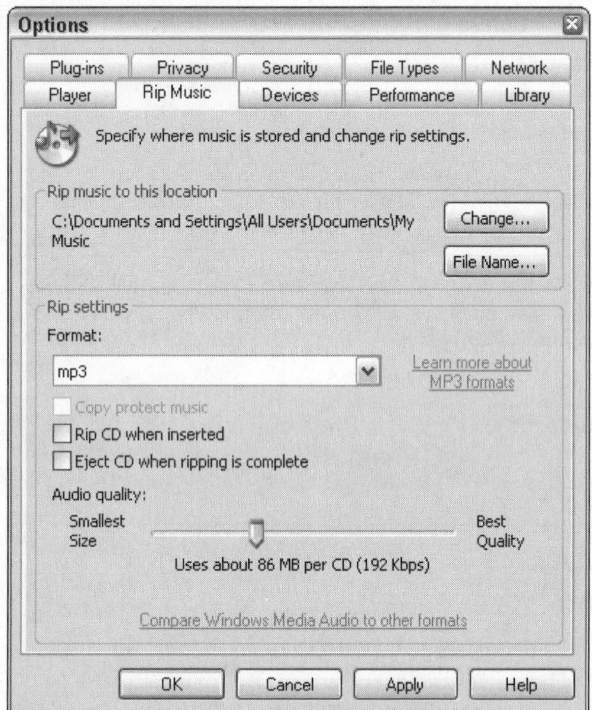

• **Figure 32-4: Your first stop for ripping CDs.**

WMP's error correction rescans dicey tracks. Occasionally, it can reconstruct a bad track, or portions of a bad track. *Playback* in this dialog box is a very poor choice of terms that really means, "when WMP plays a CD." Similarly, *rip* means "when WMP writes a CD."

5. **Click OK until you're back at the main WMP screen.**

6. **Clean the CD you want to rip, and then insert it into the drive.**

   WMP may start playing the CD. That's OK.

7. **Click the Rip button at the top of Windows Media Player.**

8. **If any of the album information is wrong — song title, artist, genre, and so on — you can retrieve that information automatically from Microsoft's Web site, or you can right-click any information that's incorrect and type in whatever you feel is right.**

   To retrieve the information, follow Step 2 in the "Making WMP search for music on your hard drive" section to unblock access to Microsoft's Web site, and then click the Find Album Info button. Finish by following Step 9 in the same section to keep Microsoft from logging your music.

The time to correct information is now, before it gets onto your hard drive. If you get the information right as you're ripping, you don't have to search for the files to change them — and you don't get stuck with mislabeled music. Getting the data right when the song first hits your PC is always best.

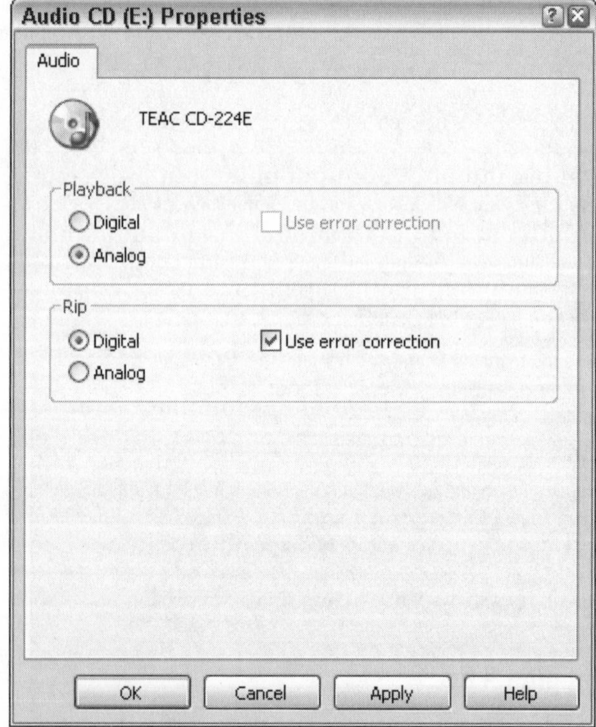

• **Figure 32-5: If your CD is less than pristine, tell WMP to rescan the rough parts.**

9. **If you *don't* want to copy a specific song, uncheck the check box next to it.**

10. **Click the Rip Music button.**

The first time you rip with WMP, Windows Media Player responds with one of the most irritating dialog boxes in all of Windows-dom — a dialog box (see Figure 32-6) that tries to get you to change back to WMA format — even after you've gone to the hassle of finding WMP's buried MP3 setting and turning it on.

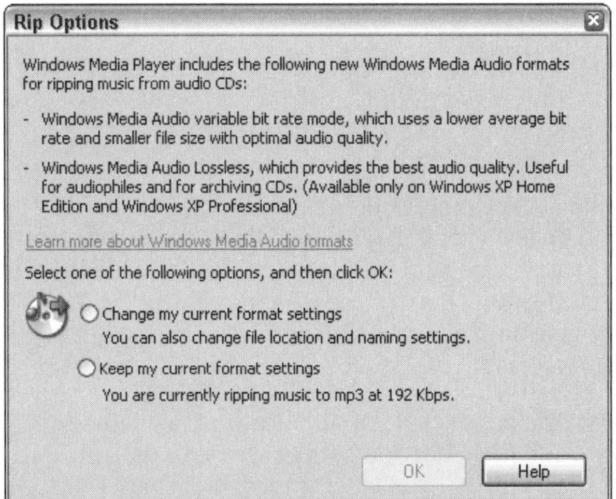

• Figure 32-6: Microsoft's hard sell for WMA. You know the definition of the word *chutzpah?*

Just for the record, WMA Variable Bit Rate mode might reduce file sizes by 20 percent – under ideal circumstances – and WMA Lossless is virtually indistinguishable from MP3 or WMA at 192 Kbps.

11. **Unless you really want to use Microsoft's own WMA format, click the Keep My Current Format Settings option and click OK.**

WMP starts *ripping* — copying the audio tracks from the CD onto your hard drive — in the format you chose, as shown in Figure 32-7.

• Figure 32-7: Rip in progress.

WMP copies faster than it plays the songs. If you have WMP eject the CD after it's done (see Step 3), there's no need to play the CD while you're copying it, or check back to see when WMP is done.

12. **When the CD pops out of the drive, it's done.**

To rip another CD, go back to Step 6.

Technique 33

Buying Music on the Web

Save Time By

- Choosing the right Internet music store for your needs
- Cutting through the marketing hype
- Using the songs you pay for, anywhere (most of the time)

At first blush, you'd think that online music stores have it made. They don't carry any inventory. They don't worry about returns. Most of the transactions are completely automatic. It looks like the kind of low-overhead operation that brings dollar signs to the eyes of any entrepreneur.

Reality, in its inimitable way, begs to differ.

Apple's iTunes Music Store, for example, only retains a small percentage of the money you spend on each song. Reportedly, the recording label gets more than half the sales price, and the copyright holder kicks in with another large chunk. Michael Robertson, who founded `mp3.com`, told a UK news outfit that selling online music is so unprofitable that it's "a race where the winner gets shot in the head."

As of this writing, every Tom and Dick Smothers was jumping into the business. (Well, not Tom and Dick, but you get the idea.) It's unlikely that many will survive.

This technique steps you through the minefield, so you know what questions to ask.

What's Going On Here?

Microsoft leapt into the online music business with the unveiling of MSN Music (`music.msn.com`) in October, 2004. If you have a rusty old calculator sitting around, do the math. No matter how you slice it, even if Microsoft sells 10,000,000 songs a month, there's no way the company can turn a decent profit on the music. No way. Probably won't break even. Ever.

Microsoft may be a lot of things, but it ain't dumb. Why the foray into a line of business that, in analysts' wildest dreams, couldn't possibly contribute more than 0.01 percent to the company's bottom line?

In my opinion, Microsoft saw that it was losing the audio/video file format wars to Apple's astoundingly successful iPod/iTunes effort. The Softies want to make the WMA and WMV file formats industry standards, and it decided that an online music store would help stem the Apple tide. A decade from now, Microsoft wants to collect a royalty on every song and every movie sold. It can't do that unless you and I and all the other Windows consumers shift to Microsoft's WMA and WMV format. That's why Microsoft is willing to spend tens — probably hundreds — of millions of dollars to sink Apple's AAC/FairPlay file format (see Technique 32), and herd us all over to the WMA/WMV fold.

Real — the company behind Real Audio — used to promote its own file format, but it's pretty much given up. That leaves Microsoft and Apple to duke it out for the hearts and minds and pocketbooks of Windows users everywhere.

Behind it all lurks the specter of copy protection — er, excuse me, Digital Rights Management. Microsoft and Apple both want to hold the keys that lock up audio and video files, preventing you and me from copying them at will. That's why I'm an unabashed fan of the MP3 audio format, which — in spite of its manifest shortcomings — can't be copy protected.

Besides, MP3 music can be played on any portable audio player. Yes, the iPod plays MP3.

Making your own MP3s

So you have a whole bunch of iTunes music files (in AAC/FairPlay format), or WMA files that you bought from one of the many online music stores. And you've suddenly discovered that those files have copy restrictions on them — typically you can copy the files to at most five PCs, or burn them onto audio CDs a limited number of times.

Don't know about you, but that really gets my goat. You paid for the music. You aren't allowed to send out a hundred thousand copies of the songs to your closest friends, of course. But you should be able to play them on your PCs, or download them to your music player as many times as you want, or burn them daily for the next hundred years, I figure.

Guess what? You can. Even if your music has the worst copy protection (uh, DRM) restrictions in the world, you can convert that AAC or WMA file to an unprotected MP3. And it's really pretty easy.

First, burn the tracks onto a typical, everyday audio CD. If you have Windows Media Player 10, I give detailed instructions in Technique 35. If you use iTunes, follow the instructions on the Burn tab.

Second, stick the CD back in your PC and rip the songs to MP3 format. Instructions for doing so with WMP 10 are in Technique 32. If you have iTunes, follow the Rip tab.

It's really that easy. There is some loss in quality unless you have very high quality audio files to begin with (in which case you should rip with an MP3 rate that's slightly lower than the original recording rate). But the resulting files aren't copy protected, aren't protect*able*. And they play on any machine, anywhere.

Sorting through the Stores

When you go looking for an online music store, here's what you should consider:

- **The price.**
- **Can you find the kinds of music you want to buy quickly and easily?** Hey, any site has the latest release from Eminem. Not many cover Buckwheat Zydeco. And finding new bands like Buckwheat can be a daunting task.
- **Can you download the music without a hassle?** You can access Apple's iTunes Music Store only through the iTunes media player (which is a very good media player; see Technique 31).
- **What's the format and quality of the songs on offer?** If you have a tremendous computer audio setup, it may be worthwhile looking for WMA Variable Bit Rate. But for most of us whose audio budgets don't approach the national debt, any of the major download sites does fine.
- **Oh. Did I mention? The price.**

To date, the online music stores differ very little, except for the price — and with the inevitable price wars coming, there's no reason in the world to get locked into a single service. For most people the difference between a WMA VBR recording of U2's latest album and a 192 Kbps AAC doesn't amount to a hill of beans. Play the field. Go for price.

So It "Plays for Sure"?

Microsoft's "Plays for Sure" marketing campaign focuses on the fact that you can play Microsoft-proprietary WMA and WMV files on many different audio and video machines.

I start seeing red when I read that an online music store sells music that can't be played on an iPod. What a crock. Granted, you have to go through one extra step (see the sidebar, "Make your own MP3s," earlier in this technique). But every music format can be transformed to a simple MP3 file, unless you've been locked out by a draconian Digital Rights Management deadbolt. And after you turn the song into an MP3, it's free to be played anywhere, any time, even on an iPod.

The intent, of course is to contrast "Plays for Sure" WMA and WMV files (which, it must be said, *can't* be played on an iPod unless they're converted) with copy protected AAC files, which can only be played directly on a small handful of devices (including the iPod).

The "Plays for Sure" campaign strikes me as disinformation of the first degree. Just for starters, any DRM protected file that "Plays for Sure" *won't play on anything* if you go beyond the DRM restrictions. Thus, the fourth or sixth or tenth time you make a copy of a "Plays for Sure" file, that copied file is dead in the water, and nothing you can do brings it back.

In the final analysis, the only songs that "Play for Sure" are plain, old-fashioned MP3 files. Don't let Microsoft's marketing palaver sway you. As long as they're copy protected, files that "Play for Sure" don't.

Tuning In the Radio

Save Time By

- Finding the stations you want — fast!
- Avoiding WMP's incessant attempts to sell you access to radio stations

Windows Media Player's least-used feature has to be the radio tuner. Maybe it's because radio — real radio, the kind with big towers for transmitters and funny guys walking around with visions of vacuum tubes in their eyes — has become so competitive that most cities, sooner or later, draw stations that cater to almost all tastes. Perhaps it's because the quality of radio transmission in the real world is pretty darn good, all in all — and it's free. By contrast, WMP can provide high-quality radio, but you need a big data pipe to support it.

If you have a dial-up Internet connection, don't waste your time on WMP's radio unless you live on a desert island and have no other form of entertainment. At 56K, music sounds muddy (if it comes through at all), and WMP's streaming technology devolves into . . . slogging technology.

If you enjoy listening to offbeat kinds of music, though, and you have a high-speed Internet connection that doesn't charge by the byte or hour, you should give WMP's radio tuner a try. This technique shows you how.

Hey, techno trance ain't that bad. Trust me.

Tuning In a Station

You might figure that the easiest way to find the Windows Media Player radio player is to click the Radio button, up at the top of the screen, right?

Uh, no. Wrong. If you click the Radio button, WMP sends you to MSN Radio, a Web site located at `radio.msn.com`. If you crank up Internet Explorer, you see precisely the same Web page.

Far as I'm concerned, MSN Radio (as of this writing anyway) rates as one of the great ripoffs on the Internet. In general you have two options: You can play a tinny radio station for free, or you can pay by the month for Radio Plus, an MSN feature of dubious value. Worse, Microsoft lists almost a thousand radio stations "like" well-known stations in the U.S. and Canada, such as a station "like" Los Angeles station KHHT Hot 92, and another "like" Country 93.9 — blatantly ripping off the playlists of the commercial stations. They're unlike the real-live stations in that the MSN versions require an MSN Passport, only run self-serving commercials, pester you to pay to download the music being played . . . I could go on.

If you want to use the *real* Windows Media Player radio — the version that's been in WMP for years, the one that has high quality, free radio that isn't run exclusively by Redmond — you have to know where to find it:

1. **Start Windows Media Player 10.**
2. **At the top, click Guide.**

   WMP sends you to the WindowsMedia.com Web page.

3. **Down on the Web page, on the right, click the Radio Tuner line.**

   Don't click the Radio tab. That puts you in the middle of MSN's truly obnoxious radio rip-off section.

   WMP brings up the list of radio stations I discuss in the rest of this technique.

   The radio tuner is actually a Web page, `www.windowsmedia.com/radiotuner/MyRadio.asp`. Microsoft can — and does — change it from day to day, so the Radio Tuner you see may be different from the one shown in Figure 34-1.

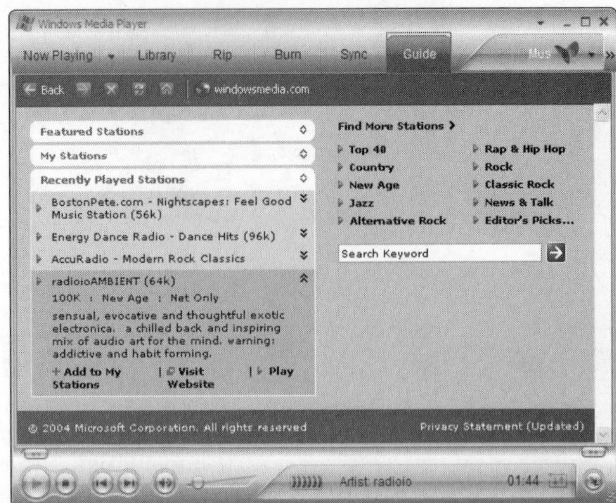

• **Figure 34-1: The tuner helps you find stations in dozens of genres.**

4. **If you see a station you like, click it.**

   More details appear — most importantly the download speed. If you have a dial-up connection, you get much better results if you confine yourself to 56K or slower transmissions.

5. **To listen to the station, click Play or Visit Website to Play.**

   WMP takes it upon itself to launch Internet Explorer and bring up the station's Web page. You can do nothing about it.

Don't be too surprised if you try to play a radio station and IE's pop-up blocker kicks in, advising that a pop-up has been blocked. That noxious pop-up IE has so dutifully quashed is probably the radio station you selected, trying to get out. If you get a pop-up warning (see Figure 34-2), click it and choose Temporarily Allow Pop-ups.

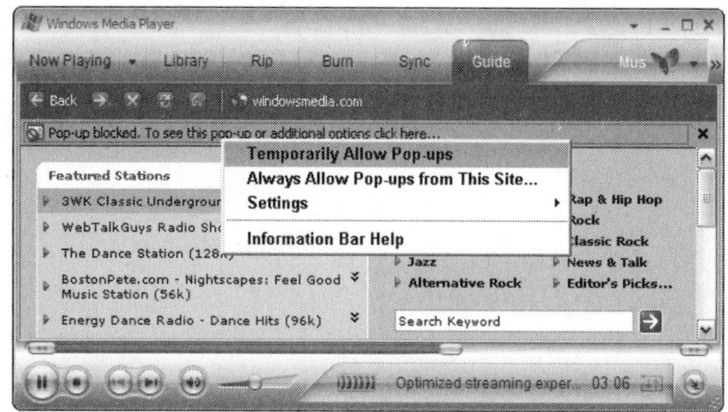

• **Figure 34-2: IE's pop-up blocker frequently gets in the way of playing a radio station.**

6. **If you want to look at WMP's list of stations by musical genre, click the type you like (refer to Figure 34-1) or click Find More Stations.**

You may be asked to fill out a form before you can listen to a radio station. If that happens, pass the station by — thousands and thousands of stations don't require you to give up personal information in order to listen.

If you think you're protected from spam-sucking sleaze sites by using Microsoft-approved radio stations, think again. In fact, WindowsMedia.com, the 100 percent Microsoft owned and operated Web site that drives all this, may be the worst (or, equivalently, most successful) offender of all.

Protecting your privacy is a time-consuming activity. If you want to stay off spammers' lists, you must be diligent. For more info about fighting the illicit marketing onslaught, see Technique 29.

7. **To earmark a station that you like for future listening, click Add to My Stations (refer to Figure 34-1).**

Any station you add to My Stations is readily available on the main Radio Tuner page.

35 Technique

Creating Your Own Music CDs

Save Time By

- Understanding what you can — and can't — do with a CD writer
- Burning CD-R and CD-RWs the right way, the first time
- Troubleshooting common problems

If you have a CD writer, and you've never burned a CD — that is, written data to a CD — you're in for a treat. Windows Media Player truly makes burning audio CDs simpler than ever. In fact, the toughest part of the job is deciding what kind of CD to burn. There are a few tricks, and a couple of potential traps — Microsoft's licensing of its copy-protected WMA files can drive you nuts. But I bet you'll be surprised at how fast and easy burning a CD can be.

Talk about saving time! If you fumble around in your car swapping CDs at 70 miles per hour (or even gently gliding from CD to CD on that big 6-disc changer), you're a great candidate for burning your own mixes, getting more songs on a single CD, eliminating the lousy tracks from an otherwise-good album, or otherwise pulling together the music you want to hear without all the junk in between. It's cheap. It's easy. And now, with WMP, it's fast.

This technique shows you all you need to know.

Choosing the Type of CD to Burn

If you look on store shelves, you see 74-minute CD-RWs, 80-minute CD-Rs, 90-minute CD-Rs — and heaven-knows-what-all from this manufacturer and that. How do you know what works in your CD burner?

Heh heh heh. That's a trick question. Chances are mighty good that your burner — if you bought it in the past couple of years anyway — can handle all those types of CDs. With aplomb.

Almost all CD (and DVD) burners can run the full gamut of CD-R and CD-RWs:

- **CD-R (CD-Recordable):** Record with these discs multiple times — in multiple sessions — but each time, the new stuff appends to the end of the disc. You can't erase and reuse the space occupied by the old stuff.
- **CD-RW (CD-Record/Write):** Record with these discs multiple times, but each time you record a CD-RW, all the old stuff is erased.

DVD-R, DVD-RW, DVD+R and DVD+RW get a touch more complex, but the folks who make DVD burners decided quite some time ago that they should handle all the formats, and do so without bothering you with any details. It's a rare DVD burner these days that can't handle everything.

Mostly, it isn't a question of what your *burner* can handle. The question you need to ask is: What works in your CD *player*?

There's the rub. You can record on almost any kind of CD with fairly recent CD writers, and audio DVDs are like falling off a log. But can your CD player play what the burner has burned?

- Older CD players only play songs in the first recording session on a CD-R.
- Later CD players play multiple recording sessions on CD-Rs and/or recordings on CD-RWs.
- Some CD players can play any kind of audio CD-R or CD-RW, and they can also play MP3 files (or even *gasp!* WMA files) directly. The best of them can also handle DVDs with any kind of file.

This I know from brutal first-hand experience: It's hard to tell by reading a CD player's manual exactly what in the world it can play. Your best bet is to sacrifice a few CDs and try different approaches. If an approach fails, don't throw away the CD. Chances are good the next CD player you buy can handle it.

Picking Songs to Go on the CD

To pick songs that you want to burn on a CD:

1. **Start Windows Media Player 10 and click Library.**

   If you don't yet have Windows Media Player 10 installed, see Technique 31. Yes, it's worth installing.

You will save yourself a lot of headaches if you don't try to burn any copy protected Microsoft-proprietary format WMA files on a CD. If you accidentally ripped audio files in copy-protected WMA format, go back and rip them again. See Technique 32 for details.

2. **Find a bunch of songs that you want to burn — say, by bringing up an album or a playlist.**
3. **Select songs by clicking them, by Ctrl+clicking individual songs, or by Shift+clicking a group of songs.**
4. **Right-click the selected songs and choose Add To➪Burn List (see Figure 35-1).**

• **Figure 35-1: Select the songs you want to burn, right-click, and choose Add To➪Burn List.**

   WMP adds all your selected files to the list of files awaiting burning.

5. **Click the Burn button at the top of WMP.**

   WMP shows you which songs await burning (see Figure 35-2).

Keep an eye on the total amount of space the files require, which appears at the bottom of the Burn List. In Figure 35-2, the selected files occupy a total of 78.81MB, which just barely fits on an 80MB CD-R.

• **Figure 35-2: The list of files waiting to be burned.**

6. **If you have any additional songs you want to copy — or if you want to change the order in which they're burned — click Edit Playlist.**

   The Edit Playlist dialog box appears (shown in Figure 35-3).

7. **Click a song on the left and it appears in the Burn List box on the right. Click a song on the right and click the up and down arrow buttons to change the sequence of songs on the CD you're about to create. When you're done, click OK.**

   Don't worry so much about the total time in the Edit Playlist dialog box; you can get the timing worked out when you're back in WMP itself.

8. **Check and uncheck the boxes in front of individual tracks, to fill up as much of the CD or DVD as possible without going over.**

   You are ready to burn the CD or DVD.

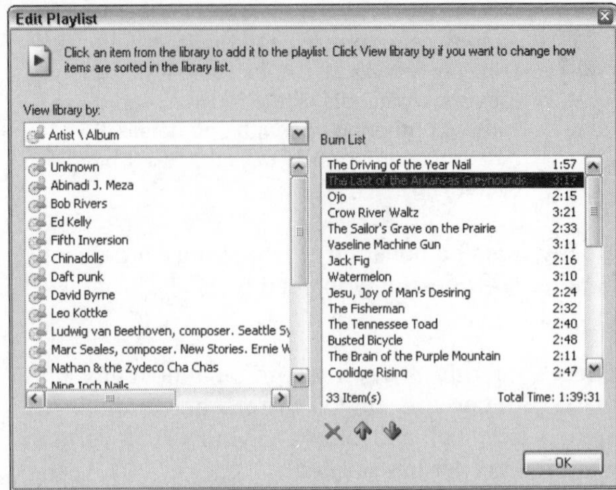

• **Figure 35-3: Change the order of tracks in this dialog box.**

Burning the CD or DVD

After you select the songs for your playlist and determine that all the songs will fit on your CD or DVD, burning an audio CD/DVD is very easy:

1. **Start in Windows Media Player 10 with the songs you want to burn, in the correct order, on the left.**

   Follow the steps in the preceding section if you're not sure how to get the songs set up right.

2. **Put a blank CD in the drive and click Start Burn.**

   Then go grab a good book — or clean your poor, neglected mouse. It takes several minutes to about half an hour to burn a typical CD. Fast burners are popular for a reason, eh?

   WMP 10 starts by converting the songs into a form that works on audio CDs.

WMP 10 puts a two-second gap between each song. You can't change it. If you rip and burn an audio CD that plays songs back-to-back with no gap (I won't mention Nine Inch Nails

by name), you hear an unexpected gap. That isn't an error, or a bad track on the CD. It's just the way WMP does things.

3. **When WMP is done, your computer ejects the CD from the drive.**

4. **Take your new CD to whatever player you intend to play it in, and make sure that it works.**

   As described at the beginning of this technique, compatibility problems with older CD players aren't unusual.

If you want to erase a CD-RW or DVD-RW, click the Burn button at the top of WMP, then click the Erase Disk icon, which is the last icon on the right side. WMP looks at the CD or DVD, figures out if it only contains music files and, if so, erases all the files from the CD-RW or DVD-RW. If your CD or DVD contains other kinds of files (which is to say, any files other than standard audio "CDA" files, MP3, WMA, or WAV files), WMP doesn't erase it.

Dealing with Hard Drive Space Issues

Burning a CD takes a lot of room on your hard drive because WMP has to convert the songs into a format that works on audio CDs. (They're called CDA files, but they aren't "files" in the usual PC sense of the term.) If you don't have an extra 700 to 800MB of free space on your main hard drive, choose Start➪My Computer, right-click your CD-R drive, and choose Properties➪Recording. The CD Drive Properties dialog box appears, as shown in Figure 35-4. Change the drive where Windows can store an "image."

This space is only used temporarily. It has to be on a hard drive, because the CD burning process can't be interrupted. If you have to copy a bunch of files to another computer on your network, or even compress some files to make room for the temporary image area, go ahead. You can always move them back later. Oh. And while the recording session is underway, don't edit that home movie or print 200 vacation pictures, okay? The CD burning routine needs a little room.

Yep, the dialog box refers to "CD-R drives," even if the drive in question is a DVD-RW drive. Not to worry.

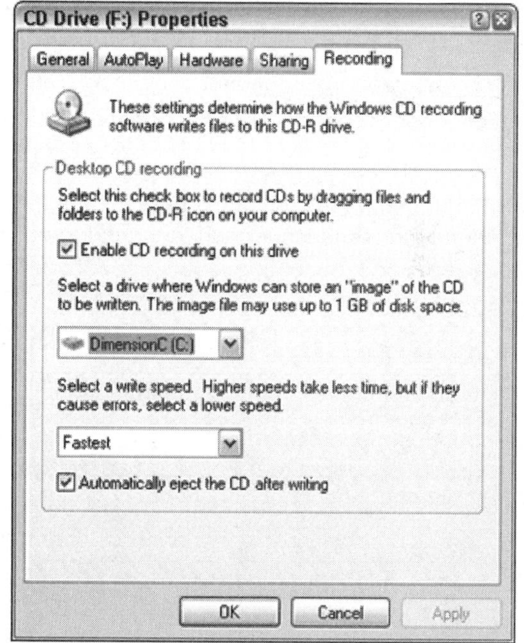

• **Figure 35-4: Specify a temporary storage location here.**

Technique 36: Transferring Music to MP3 Players

Save Time By

- Choosing an MP3 player — what counts, what doesn't
- Copying songs to an MP3 player (or video player) quickly and accurately
- Keeping backup copies of your music

Windows Media Player 10 makes it drop-dead simple to copy MP3 and WMA music from your PC to your MP3 player. (If you have AAC music to go in your iPod, stick with Apple's iTunes, okay?) You have to watch out for a few gotchas, but by and large the entire process goes along with click (and occasional drag) precision. Similarly, copying video onto personal video players rates as drop-dead simple, providing the video player works with Windows Media Player.

CDs are neat, but when it comes to saving time, MP3 players are better. No need to shuffle and scratch those shiny round disks. No need to fumble with all those moving parts. (Tell the truth — when's the last time you tore the top off a CD player?) And, man, the capacity on the new MP3 players boggles my mind. It's like you could keep the songs going for a month and never hear the same one twice (or come pretty close).

As far as the mechanics go, copying files to an MP3 player is every bit as easy — and at least twice as fast — as copying to a CD-R or DVD-R drive (see Technique 35).

This technique tells you how to avoid the gotchas, and how to getcha goin' in no time at all.

Choosing an MP3 Player

People frequently ask me what to look for when they're shopping for an MP3 player. The answer is simple: If you want cool, get an iPod. If you want functional, don't worry about the brand, and go for memory.

A song recorded in MP3 format at 128 Kbps (the setting I recommended in Technique 32) takes about 1MB per minute — so a 256MB MP3 player holds about four hours of music. A 640MB CD-based MP3 player makes it up to 10 hours. A 20GB player holds around 300 hours of music.

Figure out how much memory you need — and whether you have to buy memory cards — and make that the controlling factor when you buy a player.

Everything else falls into the bit bucket. All players do the following:

- Support ID3 (or WMA) tags, so you can see the name of the songs on the player.
- Use USB connections. These connections are good enough, unless you want to transfer a dozen CDs of music every night of your life (in which case, you might want FireWire).

All the players on the market come with their own software that undoubtedly does more than Windows Media Player 10. That said, as long as your music library contains MP3 and/or WMA music files, you'll undoubtedly want to use Windows Media Player 10 to copy music to your MP3 player. Why? Compatibility — you know that WMP works with Windows XP, but you may not be so lucky with the player's software. At any rate, all MP3 players are compatible with Windows Media Player.

Before you actually plunk down your credit card, make sure that you can understand the MP3 player's controls. Some MP3 players have such incredibly inscrutable buttons and on-screen commands that it's hard to believe they were designed to be used by humans.

iPods break all the rules, and I think that's great. I love my iPod, although I use my Nomad, too. If you're going to get an iPod, don't sweat the small stuff. Stick with Apple all the way: The iTunes player and the Apple Music store work great. You may pay a few pennies more, but you get a first-class ride, all the way.

Copying Files to an MP3 Player

The method for copying songs to an MP3 player is virtually identical to the one in Technique 35 for burning CDs.

You save yourself a lot of headaches if you make sure you try to copy only MP3 files — or WMA files without copy protection — to your MP3 player. Some WMA files won't copy at all to any MP3 player. Others require a digital license, which is only granted ten times (you can copy the file ten times, but the eleventh time, you can't copy it). If you download a WMA song from a record company's Web site — or if you buy a WMA version of a song — the record company determines how, when, or whether you can put the WMA file on your MP3 player. MP3 files have no such limitations. In fact, there aren't any hooks inside MP3 files to allow anything of the sort. With MP3, what you see is what you get.

To get songs from the Media Library onto your MP3 player:

1. **Start Windows Media Player 10.**

   If you don't yet have Windows Media Player 10 installed, see Technique 31.

2. **Connect your MP3 player and turn it on.**

   You receive notification from Windows XP, asking what you want to do, as shown in Figure 36-1.

I specifically do not recommend that you go through the manufacturer's steps to insert a driver CD and install the MP3 player before trying the simple trick in Step 2, to see if Windows XP can set up everything all on its own. Usually it does. If you don't receive the notification in Figure 36-1, restart your machine. Start WMP and click the Synch button at the top to see if WMP identified your player. If it isn't there, you have some fun times ahead. Start by following the MP3 manufacturer's instructions for installing any Windows XP drivers.

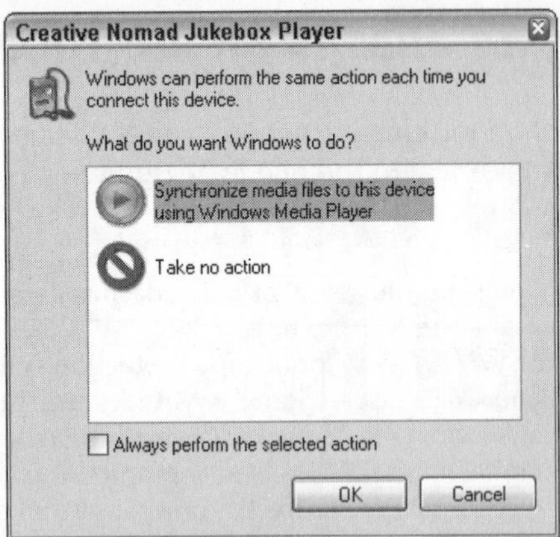

• **Figure 36-1: If Windows XP recognizes your MP3 player, you get this notification.**

3. **Click Synchronize Media Files (you may also want to check the Always Perform the Selected Action box, if you never expect to install your MP3 player manufacturer's software), and then click OK.**

   Windows Media Player appears, with the Sync button selected and your MP3 player identified in the upper right, as shown in Figure 36-2.

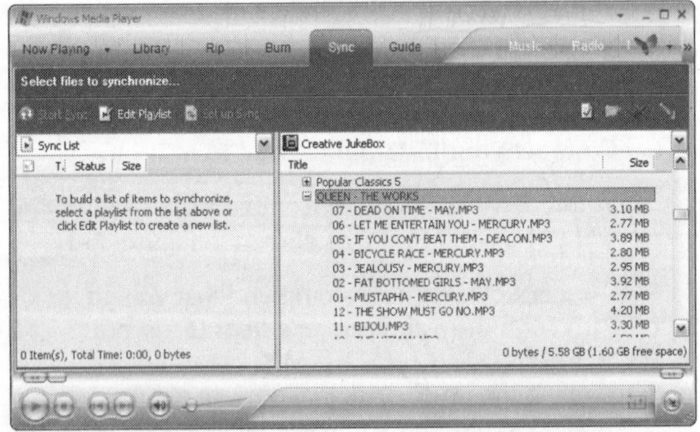

• **Figure 36-2: All the songs on the MP3 player appear on the right side.**

4. **Click the Library button at the top.**

5. **Find a bunch of songs that you want to copy to the MP3 player — perhaps by bringing up an album or a playlist.**

6. **Select songs by clicking them, by Ctrl+clicking individual songs, or by Shift+clicking a group of songs.**

7. **Right-click the selected songs and choose Add To⇨Sync List (see Figure 36-3).**

8. **If you have any additional songs you want to copy, click Edit⇨Playlist and use the method described in Technique 35.**

9. **Check and uncheck the tracks you do or don't want to copy to the MP3 player. When you have the songs set, click Start Sync (in the upper-left corner).**

   WMP copies the songs you've selected onto your MP3 player.

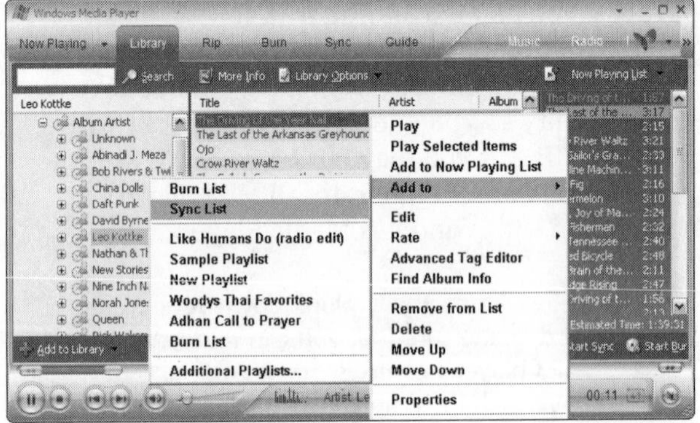

• **Figure 36-3: Right-click tracks and add them to your Sync List.**

Keeping Backups

The MP3 and WMA songs on your computer are files, just like any other files. You can (and should!) back them up. In particular, don't rely on your MP3 player for backup storage — WMP generally doesn't let you copy songs from your MP3 player back onto your PC.

Include MP3 and WMA files in your regular backups (see Technique 60).

Part VI

Having Fun and Saving Time with Visual Media

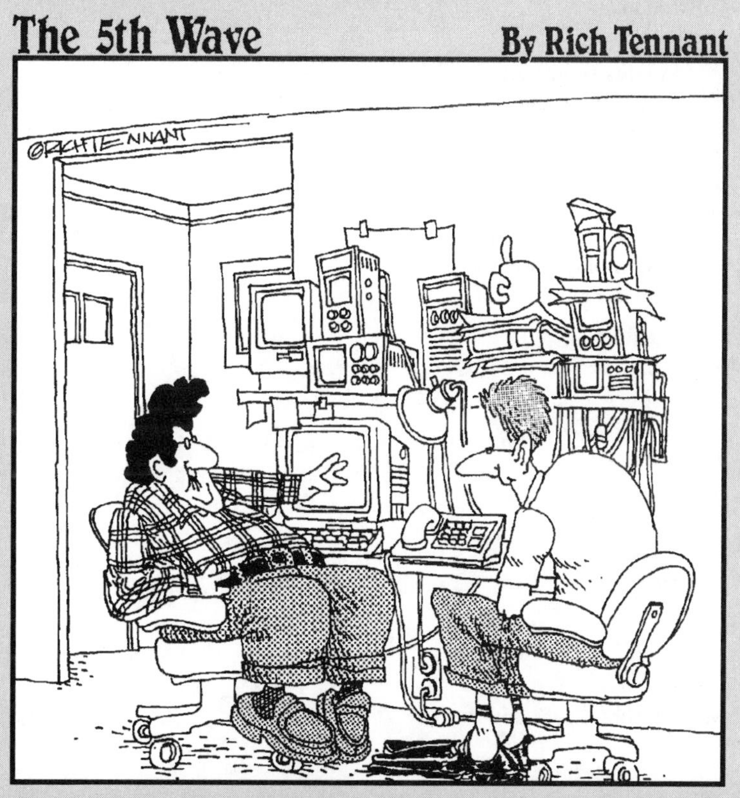

"Now, when someone rings my doorbell, the current goes to a scanner that digitizes the audio impulses and sends the image to the PC where it's converted to a Pict file. The image is then animated, compressed, and sent via high-speed modem to an automated phone service that sends an e-mail message back to tell me someone was at my door 40 minutes ago."

Technique 37 Taking Snapshots with a Webcam

Save Time By

- Taking shots quickly and accurately
- Setting up a camera so you don't look like you just finished vacuuming
- Using time delay for multiple shots — automatically

If you have a Webcam, it probably took you about 30 seconds to figure out that (1) it makes you look like a bag lady — with the bags under your eyes; (2) it produces live, moving images that don't look the least bit like live, moving images; and (3) nobody really feels like looking at your ugly mug on a Webcam unless you're under eight or over eighty.

That said, Webcams are remarkably good at taking still photos — if you set them up right.

A Webcam will never replace a scanner. If you have a flat object and need to reproduce it faithfully, a scanner's your only choice. But the minute you deal with an object that's only slightly more than two-dimensional, a good Webcam and a creative setup can make all the difference.

In general, Webcams install like a dream, they work the first time, and they're so easy to use it's like falling off a log. If you don't need super-high-resolution pictures, and you don't mind having the camera tethered to your computer, they're great. You save money; you save time. This technique shows you how.

If you want good, high quality pics, you should buy a digital camera, of course. (I talk about digital cameras in Technique 40.) But if you only need a quick shot, and your computer's nearby, a cheap Webcam works well indeed — at a fraction of the cost, with very little hassle. I bet you didn't know that snapshots with a Webcam were this easy!

Taking the Shot

If your camera has its own proprietary software, you can probably take snapshots by choosing Start➪*the camera manufacturer's name*➪*the name of the viewing program*.

On the other hand, if you're lucky enough to have a camera that leaves the Windows XP native Camera Wizard in charge, you're in for a real treat. All you have to do is plug the camera into the computer (typically through a USB port) and you're ready to go. Here's what you can do:

1. **Choose Start⇨Control Panel⇨Printers and Other Hardware.**

   Control Panel shows you the Printers and Other Hardware applet.

2. **Click Scanners and Cameras (in the lower-right corner of the screen).**

   Windows Explorer opens to the Scanners and Cameras folder.

3. **Double-click the name of your Webcam.**

   The Scanner and Camera Wizard starts.

4. **Click Next.**

   The preview panel on the left shows you the image taken directly from the camera.

5. **Use the ideas in the next section ("Setting Up the Shot — F/11 and Be There") to set up your shot. When you're ready to take a picture, click the Take Picture icon directly below the camera preview.**

   Your snapshot appears on the right, as shown in Figure 37-1.

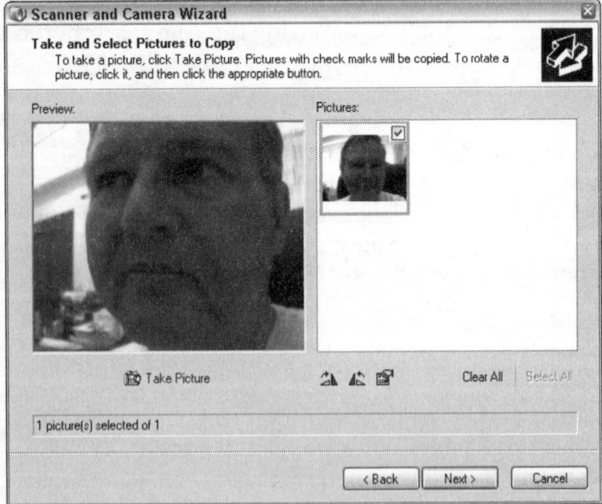

• **Figure 37-1: See what I mean about looking like a bag lady?**

6. **Keep clicking. Rotate the camera 90 degrees or even 180 degrees and click.**

   The pictures gradually fill the panel on the right.

7. **Rotate any pictures at will by first clicking the picture, and then clicking one of the Rotation icons.**

8. **Select the pictures you want to save and click Next.**

   The wizard shows you the Picture Name and Destination pane, as shown in Figure 37-2.

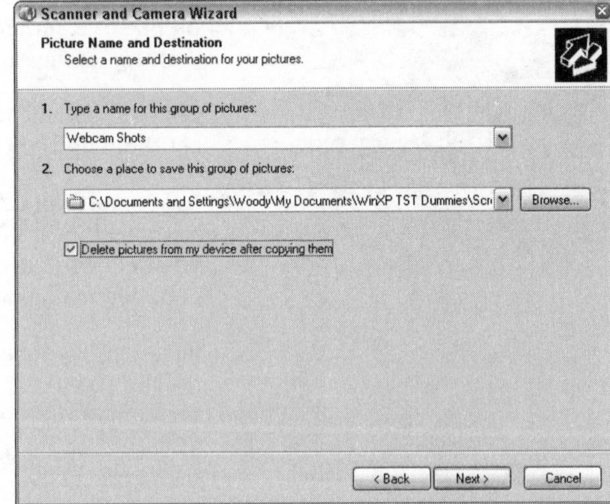

• **Figure 37-2: Pick a destination by clicking the Browse button.**

9. **Type a picture name prefix.**

   For example, if you use the name `Webcam Shots`, the pictures are called `Webcam Shots 001.jpg`, `Webcam Shots 002.jpg`, and so on.

10. **Choose where to save your pics in the second drop-down list. If you want to remove the shots from temporary storage on your PC, check the Delete Pictures from My Device after Copying Them check box. Click Next.**

    The wizard renames and moves the pictures to the location you specified (see Figure 37-3).

11. To leave the wizard, click Next, and then click Finish.

Even at 320 x 340 resolution — typical for a Webcam, although better cams have higher resolution these days — the pictures are at least discernible.

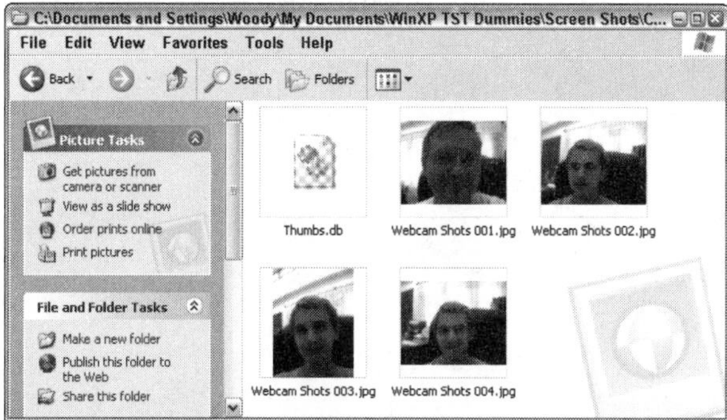

• **Figure 37-3: Note how the picture names are drawn from the entry in Figure 37-2.**

Setting Up the Shot — F/11 and Be There

The single most important part of setting up a Webcam shot?

Lighting

- Put most of the light on the subject that you're shooting — usually that's a face.
- Use small amounts of light on the background. Don't black it out entirely unless you want your Webcam shot to look like a velvet painting of Elvis.
- Never light from underneath. Back in the 1930s, lights under the face were called "monster lighting" because they gave Frankenstein and Dracula that certain . . . something.

Here are some other considerations:

- **Camera location:** You can't really win: Either the camera is too far up, too far down, or too far to the left or right — unless the camera's right in the middle of your screen (which isn't a bad idea, actually, if you're doing snapshots).
- **Subjects:** Have your subjects look straight into the camera. Otherwise, they appear to be untrustworthy. True fact.
- **Focus:** Some cameras have a focus ring. A few have wide-angle and/or *telephoto* capabilities. For the best shot, use the longest telephoto setting you can get away with and still stay in focus.

Using Time Delay

Microsoft has a very cool, free tool called Timershot that lets you take Webcam shots at time intervals that you pick. Timershot doesn't work with all cameras, but it's worth a, uh, shot.

To get it, follow these steps:

1. Start Internet Explorer and go to `www.microsoft.com/windowsxp/pro/downloads/powertoys.asp`.

The PowerToys screen appears.

2. At the bottom of the screen, under Webcam Timershot, download the file called `Timershot.exe`.

Although the file is called `Timershot.exe` on the Web site, when you download it, you see that it's really called `TimershotPowertoySetup.exe`.

3. After downloading this file, double-click `TimershotPowertoySetup.exe`.

You see a very simple, straightforward wizard.

4. Follow the wizard's steps to install Timershot.

5. **To run Timershot, choose Start⇨All Programs⇨Powertoys for Windows XP⇨Timershot; then click the small > chevron in the lower-right corner.**

   Timershot shows you an extensive list of options.

6. **Adjust the frequency, filename, location, and the like; then click Apply Settings and click Close Window.**

   As long as your camera is on, Timershot takes pictures according to your specifications. After you click Close Window, Timershot minimizes itself to the notification area, next to the clock. If you didn't know where to look for its icon, you probably wouldn't know that it was there.

7. **To turn off Timershot, right-click its icon in the notification area and choose Exit.**

Recording Video with a Webcam

Save Time By

- Using your tiny, cheap Webcam to make movies
- Making video from your tiny, cheap Webcam look a little less tiny and cheap
- Recovering quickly from Windows Movie Maker 2.0 freezes

No, that $25 Webcam won't turn you into the next George Lucas. But, yes, it's surprising how much mileage you can get out of a cheap (uh, inexpensive) Webcam. All you really need is a lens, a video chip, and a wire that connects the camera to your computer. If you have a Webcam and you're running Windows XP, you have everything you need to make decent — albeit grainy and possibly jerky — video. Add a cheap microphone, if your Webcam doesn't have one already, and you're sitting on almost everything that an entry-level digital camcorder can offer . . . for about one-tenth the price.

Windows Movie Maker 1.0 — the version that shipped with the original version of Windows XP — was so woefully underpowered and flaky that I found it embarrassing. The latest version, Windows Movie Maker 2.0, lives up to the reputation of a Version 2.0 Microsoft product: It has some really useful features (I'm tempted to use the term *brilliant*), but it has a few limitations, too. Among other things, it freezes all the time. Arrrgh.

If you haven't yet tried to work with digital video on your Windows XP machine, Windows Movie Maker 2.0's limitations can be forgiven. After all, you don't need to spend any money or time searching for a starter package. If you have a Webcam, everything you need is right here, right now.

This technique shows you how to get Windows Movie Maker 2.0 going with just your Webcam.

Installing Windows Movie Maker 2

Windows Movie Maker 2.1 comes bundled with Windows XP Service Pack 2, so you probably have WMM 2.1 or later already. Given the fact that WMM version 1 was only slightly less stable than a ten-foot-high stack of playing cards in a Florida hurricane, it's worth taking a minute to make sure you have version 2. Here's how:

1. **Choose Start⇨All Programs⇨Accessories⇨ Windows Movie Maker.**

   You see the Windows Movie Maker main screen.

2. **Choose Help⇨About.**

   You see the About Windows Movie Maker dialog box, as shown in Figure 38-1. Look at the bottom line of the pedigree list. If it doesn't say Windows Movie Maker Version 2.1 or higher, you need to upgrade.

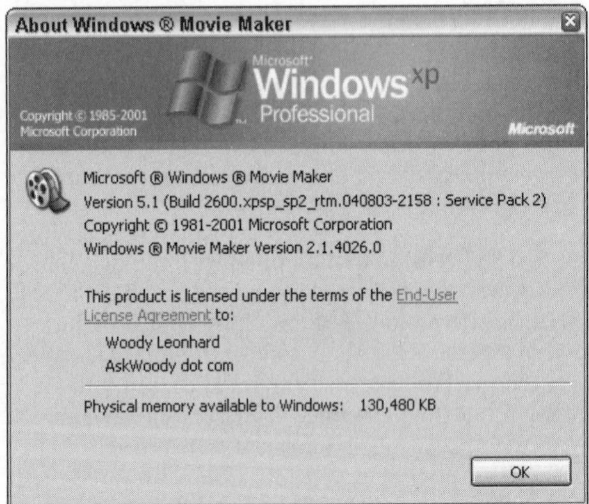

• **Figure 38-1: WMM Version 2.1 comes in Windows XP Service Pack 2.**

As we went to press, WMM 2.1 was the latest version of WMM, and it was only available as part of Windows XP Service Pack 2. Microsoft plugged a bunch of security holes in WMM version 2.1, and the only way to make sure they all got plugged involved changing Windows itself, so WMM 2.1 requires SP2. See Technique 1 for details on installing SP2.

To see if there's a later version of Windows Movie Maker, follow these steps:

1. **Start Internet Explorer.**
2. **Go to the WMM home page at** `www.microsoft.com/windowsxp/using/moviemaker/default.mspx`.
3. **Look around for any reference to a version of WMM that's newer than the one you have. If one's available, you should be able to download it from this page.**

Setting Up and Recording a Video

To record a video using a simple, everyday Webcam

1. **Turn on your video camera and make sure that it's working.**

   If you went through the steps in Technique 37 and have the Scanner and Camera Wizard working, you're in good shape.

2. **Choose Start⇨All Programs⇨Windows Movie Maker.**

   Windows Movie Maker appears on-screen, as shown in Figure 38-2.

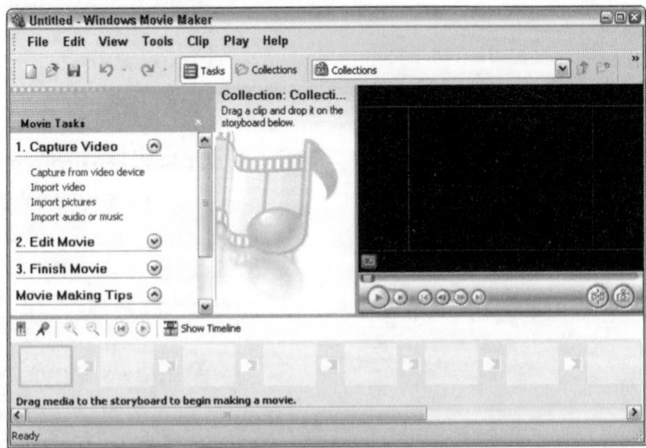

• **Figure 38-2: Movie Maker's smarts are in the upper-left pane.**

3. **Click the Capture from Video Device line.**

WMM brings up the Video Capture Wizard, as shown in Figure 38-3.

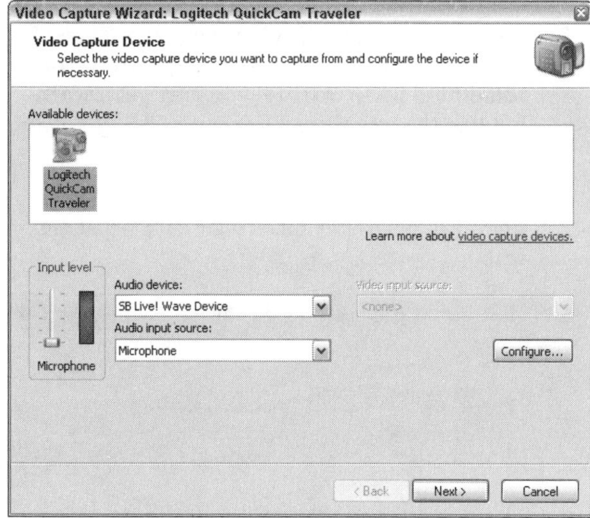

• Figure 38-3: Connecting to your Webcam.

4. **Make sure that your Webcam is highlighted. If you have a microphone and want to capture sound along with the picture, click Configure. Otherwise, click Next.**

The Video Capture Wizard wants a name and location for the video clip(s) you're creating.

The terminology in Windows Movie Maker differs from other computer lingo. When you record a (presumably short) piece of video, it's called a *clip*. You put together clips to form a *project*.

5. **Give the clip(s) a name, and then click Next.**

WMM wants to know what format to use when it's taking the picture(s).

6. **Chances are very good that you want to stick with whatever WMM suggests. Click Next.**

WMM is ready to start recording clips.

7. **To start recording a clip, click the Start Capture button in the Video Capture Wizard. When you're done recording a clip — maybe you want to reposition the camera or bring other people into the scene — click the Stop Capture button. When you're ready to record another clip, click Start Capture again.**

If you record more than one clip, they're all put in the same file, one after the other.

8. **When you're done shooting all the clips that you want to put in one file, click Finish in the Video Capture Wizard.**

WMM stores the clips in their own file and automatically imports the clips into WMM itself, as shown in Figure 38-4.

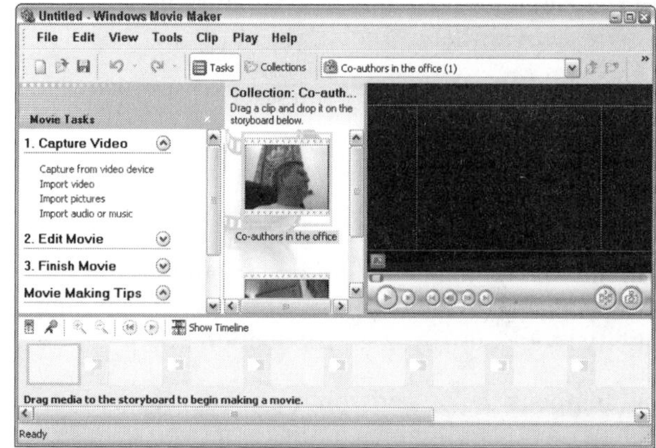

• Figure 38-4: WMM stores the clip and automatically imports it into WMM.

This point is where WMM frequently freezes on me. See the last section in this technique, "Recovering from a WMM 2 Freeze," for instructions on how to kill a frozen instance of WMM and then bring it back.

9. **If you want to start assembling a movie, first choose File⇨Save Project and give your movie a name. Then drag the clip from the Collection in the middle down to the storyboard at the bottom of the screen.**

You see the beginning of a movie, similar to the one shown in Figure 38-5.

• **Figure 38-5: Click and drag a clip to add it to the project, er, movie.**

At this point you're ready to start editing your movie. I cover that in Technique 39.

Recovering from a WMM 2 Freeze

I'm not one to complain too loudly, but Windows Movie Maker (in all its versions) has an astounding ability to lock up my main production PC.

If it happens to you and you're not accustomed to killing off hung programs, here's what you need to do:

1. **Don't worry. You won't break your computer.**

   You won't lose any data (probably).

2. **Press the Ctrl and Alt keys at the same time, hold them down, and press Delete. Then release all three.**

   The Windows XP Task Manager appears.

3. **Click the Windows Movie Maker line. Then click End Task. If WMM was in the middle of something when it froze, you may get a warning like the one shown in Figure 38-6. If you do, click End Now.**

   You can't do anything about lost data. If WMM freezes, it invariably takes your changes along with it.

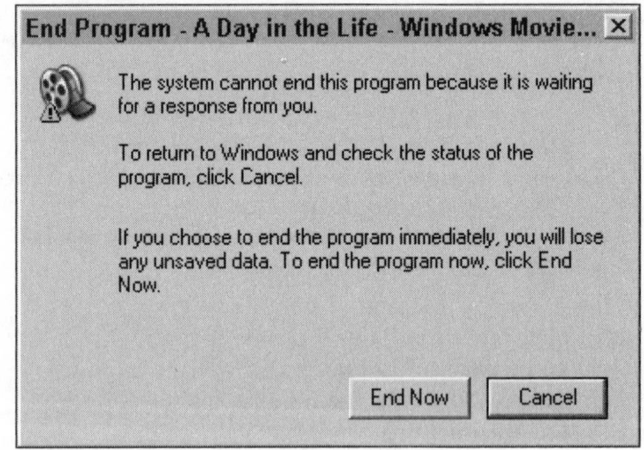

• **Figure 38-6: The system isn't waiting for a response from you. It's just permanently out to lunch.**

4. **Start WMM again by choosing Start⇨All Programs⇨Windows Movie Maker.**

   Maybe someday WMM will be more stable. If it helps, WMM 2 was immeasurably better than WMM 1, and version 2.1 seems better still. Maybe by Version 3, as is the tradition, Microsoft will get it right.

Editing Your Home Movies

Save Time By

- Putting your clips together quickly and accurately
- Using fades and other transitions wisely
- Publishing your finished movie to a hard drive, CD, or on the Web

Windows Movie Maker 2, shown in Figure 39-1, is great despite its ability to cause system lockups.

Movie Maker 2's bag of tricks runneth over, with more than 40 titles ready for you to stick in your movies, 60 transitions, and 30 other effects. In addition, the Auto Movie generator can make serviceable movies from a handful of clips with just a click.

Windows Movie Maker makes great demands on your hardware, particularly if you create long movies (er, "projects"), and/or if you try to edit a movie and stick it back on your digital camera. For big movies, you need big iron. Symptoms of iron deficiency include unexplained freezes and hangs, video getting out of synch with the audio, color splotches or black bands, and video-induced narcolepsy. (Okay, I made that last one up. That's more a side effect of editing ten hours of raw vacation videos down to nine and a half hours of sheer boredom.) To handle big movies, you need to have a fast hard drive with lots of free space — and it helps if the drive has been defragmented recently. See Technique 5 for the skinny on defragmenting.

• Figure 39-1: Windows Movie Maker 2.1.

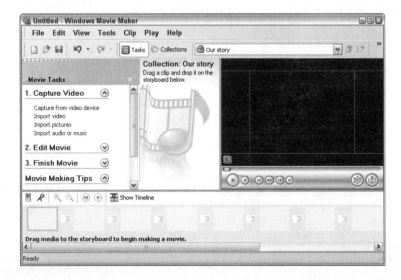

Understanding the Limitations of WMM

You can feed Windows Movie Maker video clips and still pictures in many, many different formats, but it won't take MPEG-2 files, no way, no how. Thus, you can't use Windows Media Center Edition 2004's `.dvr-ms` files, and you can't use files from the Sony MicroMV digital video cameras. Yes, you read that right: You can't use files created by Media Center 2004 as input to Windows Movie Maker.

On the plus side, WMM 2.1 works directly and simply with your digital video (DV) camera, old-fashioned analog video camera, or even a retro VCR. If you have a DV camera, plan on connecting it directly to your computer's USB 2 or FireWire (IEEE 1394) port. (If you don't have a FireWire port, get a FireWire adapter card.) Analog devices, including older video cameras, VCRs, and "video out" connections on just about anything (including cable boxes, satellite boxes, TiVo, television tuners, video game machines, what-have-you) can be connected to an analog capture card, using either S-VHS or standard composite (yellow, red, white) plug-in connectors. WMM works with them all.

It also works great with a plain Webcam, as I explain in Technique 38.

After you're done with your editorial effort, though, you have only a few choices for the final movie you produce:

- **You can turn the new movie into a WMV file.** WMV files can be viewed by Windows Media Player 9, 10, or later — but not with any earlier version of Windows Media Player. That means movies you create with WMM can't be played on Windows 98 PCs (because WMP 9 doesn't run on Windows 98). It also means you have to upgrade to WMP 10 on any other PCs before you can view movies created with Windows Movie Maker. WMV is a proprietary format, owned by Microsoft, lock, stock, and barrel.
- **You can burn the movie on a CD in Microsoft's proprietary HighMAT format.** You can only view that CD on a video machine capable of understanding HighMAT.
- **You can send the movie to digital videotape if you have a DV camera attached to the PC with a FireWire cable.** (You also can produce a DV-AVI format file, which you can subsequently copy onto a DV camera.)
- **You can publish the new movie on the Web if you're willing to pay one of Microsoft's partners for the privilege.** At the time I write this, Microsoft has only two providers available — Neptune Mediashare (`moviemaker.neptune.com`) and POPCast (`moviemaker.popcast.com`). It ain't a growth industry.

Before you create a movie with Windows Movie Maker 2, it would behoove you to consider how and where you're going to view the movie. If you had dreams of burning a DVD with your son's birthday videos, and sending the DVD to your parents so they can watch it on their TV, you have to shell out extra bucks for a product like Sonic MyDVD (`www.mydvd.com`).

Importing and Combining Clips

Start to build a movie from a bunch of clips (see Technique 38 for a great way to make clips with your Webcam) and then follow these steps to put the clips together:

1. **Choose Start⇨All Programs⇨Windows Movie Maker.**

   The main Movie Maker screen appears (refer to Figure 39-1).

2. **Click Import Video.**

   You get the Import File dialog box, as shown in Figure 39-2.

• Figure 39-2: Choose from available clips.

3. Choose one or more video files. (You can use Ctrl+click or Shift+click to pick more than one.) Click Import.

You can have WMM automatically break any file you choose into multiple clips and give each clip a unique number. If so instructed, WMM scans each video file and looks for logical breaks in the action. Each break point starts a new clip. The method for automatically breaking a file into clips isn't perfect, but you can always stitch broken-up clips back together again. (In fact, if you do nothing, you'll never notice a difference because the clips play back-to-back with no interruption.)

Although you may see only one clip in the middle of the screen (as shown in Figure 39-3), WMM really does open all the files you chose.

4. Click the clip that you want to appear at the beginning of the movie and drag it down to the first spot on the storyboard near the bottom of the screen.

You're starting to assemble the movie by using a *storyboard* — a sequence of beginning still pictures in each clip that can help you organize the movie (as shown in Figure 39-4).

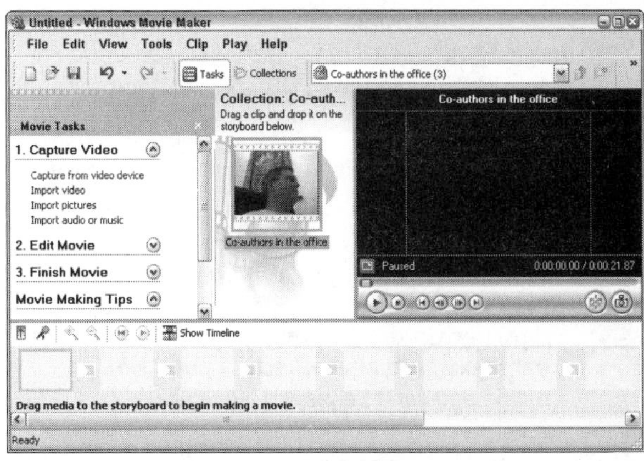

• Figure 39-3: WMM with one clip open.

• Figure 39-4: The storyboard starts to take shape across the bottom of the screen.

5. To see all of the clips that you have open, click the Collections icon on the main toolbar.

Clicking the Collections icon turns the Task pane into the Collections pane. That's where you can see the open clips.

6. Click and drag each clip into place. You can click a file in the Collections pane and drag clips to the storyboard as you see them (as shown in Figure 39-5). You also can click and drag to rearrange clips on the storyboard.

7. See how the clips play next to each other by clicking the Play button.

If need be, rearrange the clips by clicking and dragging them into place until you feel comfortable with the sequence.

8. **This is a good point to save your work. Click the Save icon, give your project a name, and click Save again.**

A project isn't a movie. A *project* is the glue that holds a movie together — pointers to clips, instructions for putting them together, transitions, and other effects — but it isn't a movie and can't be played like a movie.

Click to switch from the storyboard to the timeline.

• **Figure 39-5: Build the clip collection in the correct order.**

Trimming Clips

After you block out the clips, as I describe in the preceding section, I suggest that you trim away the parts at the beginning and end of each clip. You don't have to follow this advice, but you'll discover that the beginning and ending of clips (invariably) don't work out.

When you *trim* a clip, you're just telling Windows Movie Maker to skip over part of the beginning or end of the clip. Nothing in the clip is actually removed — the clip isn't altered in any way.

Trimmin's easy. Just follow these steps:

1. **Open a project.**

   If you're continuing from the preceding section, you already have a project underway.

2. **At the bottom of the project window, click the Show Timeline icon.**

   WMM replaces the storyboard at the bottom with a timeline — a representation of what the movie will show with the timing noted above the clips in the storyboard (as shown in Figure 39-6).

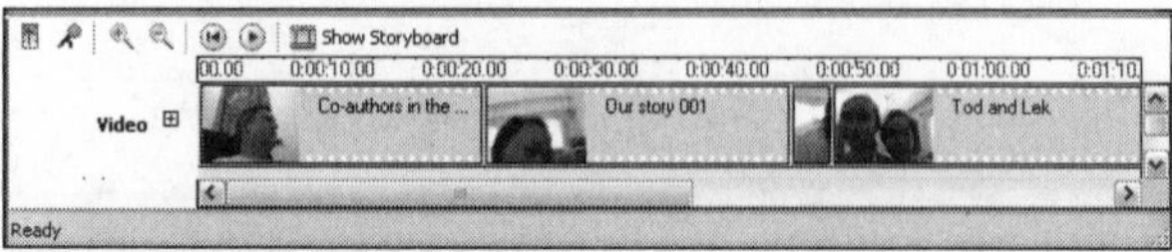

• **Figure 39-6: The movie's timeline.**

3. **Click between clips (or at the beginning of the first clip or the end of the last clip), and your cursor turns into a two-headed arrow (as shown in Figure 39-7).**

• **Figure 39-7: The two-headed arrow used to trim clips.**

4. **Click and drag the double-headed arrow to tell WMM that you don't want to include the beginning or end of the clip in the final movie.**

   It takes a little practice to do this part right. If you drag around long enough, you'll get a feel for what's happening.

5. **Check what you've done by clicking once inside a clip and then clicking the Play button to see what's left after the clip is trimmed.**

6. **This is a good time to save, so click the Save icon on the main toolbar.**

Using Transitions and Effects

With the clips blocked out and trimmed, your next job is to set up transitions between the clips that help tell the story. Mechanically, WMM makes that very easy. Aesthetically, well, that's a fade of a different color.

Here's how I apply transitions and effects:

1. **Start Windows Movie Maker and open the project.**

   If you're continuing from the preceding section, you're in the right place (as shown in Figure 39-8).

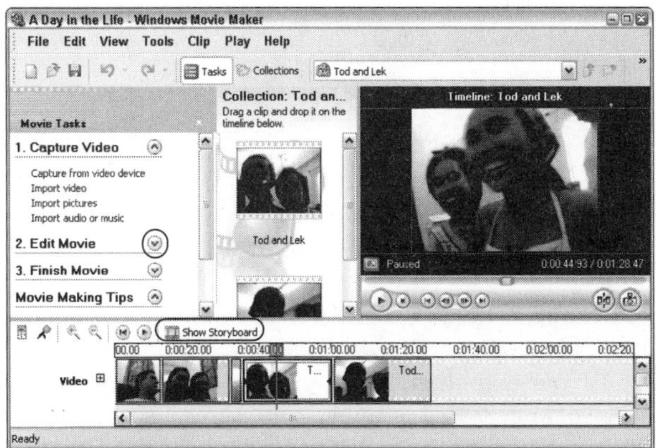

• **Figure 39-8: A Day in the Life.**

2. **At the bottom of the project's window, click Show Storyboard. On the right, click the down arrow next to the Edit Movie task.**

   The Edit Movie steps appear (as shown in Figure 39-9).

3. **If you want a video effect, click the View Video Effects task and drag the desired effect onto the clip that you want to distort.**

   It's unlikely that you'll want to add such an effect, but if you do, you can make the clip look pixilated, brown-toned, or cracked and old, or you can add slow-motion effects.

   The effects are varied and fun, but I bet you get tired of them quickly.

• **Figure 39-9: It's easier to work with transitions if you can see the storyboard.**

Effects are cumulative: If you drag the Sepia effect and the Watercolor effect onto a clip, it shows up watercolored (I call it blotched) and in sepia color. To get rid of one or more effects, right-click the clip and choose Video Effects. Use caution with effects because if you don't like them, you have to waste time removing them one by one.

4. **If you want transitions between the clips, click the View Video Transitions task. Then click and drag the transition you want to the gray box between the clips.**

The two transitions I rate as least jarring are Fade and Wipe — two well-established methods for moving between clips.

5. **Check transitions and effects by clicking a clip and clicking the Play button.**

6. **Now's a good time to save your work. Click the Save button (the one on the main toolbar that looks like a diskette).**

   Note that you're saving the project — not a movie. The project contains pointers to the clips, with instructions for putting the clips together, trimming them, fades, and the like. I talk about saving the entire movie — turning it into a file that can be played — at the end of this technique. For now, save the project.

Adding Titles and Credits

Every movie can benefit from titles. Some justify adding credits. I don't know how many hours I've wasted composing titles in Word (such as, oh, "Kilkenny County" and "County Cork" and "Dublin"), printing those titles out on sheets of paper, filming the printouts, and cutting the titles in with my home movies. Don't laugh. Not many years ago, that used to be state-of-the-art.

Windows Movie Maker 2 makes it easy and quick to show titles.

To get titles working, follow these steps:

1. **If you aren't continuing from the preceding section, start Windows Movie Maker and open a project.**
2. **Click the Edit Movie task, and then click Make Titles or Credits.**

   Windows Movie Maker offers you five places where you can put the title: at the beginning of the movie, before any clip, superimposed on top of the video in any clip, at the end of any clip, or at the end of the movie.
3. **Click Title at the Beginning. WMM has you fill out a template, which translates into a very short title clip (as shown in Figure 39-10). You can change fonts and the way the title fades by clicking at the bottom.**

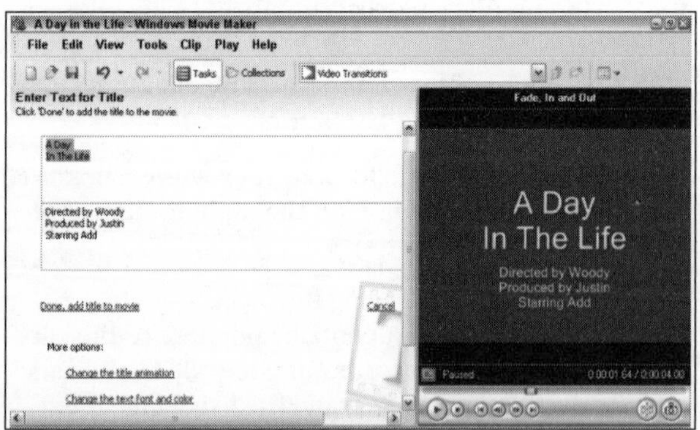

• **Figure 39-10: The intro title is generated automatically from text you type.**

4. **Click the Done, Add Title to Movie link.**

   The title appears as the first clip (in the timeline).
5. **Repeat the same process for anOy other titles you wish to add.**
6. **Click the Save button (the one on the main toolbar that looks like a diskette) to save your project.**

   As noted several times in this technique, the project is not a movie — it's just a bunch of pointers, titles, fades, and so on. To save a real, live movie — one that you can play with Windows Media Player 9 or 10 — see the next section.

Saving the Movie

As mentioned at the beginning of this technique, you have a limited number of options for turning your project into a viewable movie:

- You can make a WMV file (playable with Windows Media Player 9 or 10), which you can save on your computer, send by e-mail, or post on one of Microsoft's partners' for-pay Web sites. You can also post the WMV file on your own Web site, or share it with other people via one of the file-sharing programs, such as Limewire (see Technique 25).
- You can burn a CD in HighMAT format. Windows Media Player has no problem with HighMAT CDs. Very few standalone CD players understand it, though.
- You can record the movie on a DV camera, if the DV camera is attached to your PC, using a file format commonly called DV-AVI.

To create a WMV file, follow these steps:

1. **If you aren't continuing from the preceding section, start Windows Movie Maker and open a project.**
2. **In the Movie Task pane, click the down arrow next to Finish Movie.**

   WMM shows you the output options (as shown in Figure 39-11).
3. **Click Save to My Computer on the left.**

   WMM brings up the Save Movie Wizard.

• **Figure 39-11: The only WMM output options.**

4. **Type in a suitable name, and browse to the location where you want to put your movie. Click Next.**

   The Save Movie Wizard suggests that you save the file in WMV format, but you can click Show More Choices for a wide array of additional options, including a Pocket PC-suitable WMV format, several variants of NTSC (in WMV format, of course), and even DV-AVI in case you want to copy the movie to a Digital Video camera at some point in the future.
5. **Choose the format you like and click Next.**

   WMM converts the specifications in your project and the video in the clips into a real movie.
6. **When WMM is done, click Finish in the wizard's last dialog box and watch your movie.**

Managing Pictures from a Digital Camera

Save Time By

- Using Windows XP's built-in tools to copy, name, and delete pictures
- Reaching inside your camera with Windows Explorer
- Storing Windows files inside your camera

You probably think of your digital camera as an incredibly smart picture-taking machine. If it's built into your mobile phone or PDA, hey, it's gotta be smart. But you may not realize that it includes a reasonably capable computer — one that Windows XP is uniquely capable of manipulating.

Did you know that some cameras let you use their memory almost as easily as an external hard drive on your PC? Talk about a fast way to transfer files when no network is in sight.

Windows XP works with digital cameras so well that you may not want to use your camera manufacturer's software. I don't. When I fill up my camera's memory card with pictures, I whip out a USB cable, plug the camera into the PC, click a couple of times, type in a general description of the pictures (such as "Add's Birthday Party" or "Justin's Diving Trip"), and press Enter. Then Windows does everything else. It's truly breathtaking to see all those pictures move from the camera to the PC, and have Windows handle all the details.

This technique takes you quickly through the ins and outs of digital photography from a Windows XP point of view. And the last section includes a truly memorable way to use your camera as a portable storage device.

Transferring Pictures to Your PC Automatically

You have a digital camera, right? Maybe a camera phone, or a PDA that takes pictures? One with a USB or FireWire attachment? Good. Glad I caught you in time.

Don't install the software that came with your camera. Chances are good that your camera's software only gums up the Windows XP built-in software.

If you've already installed the software, uninstall it. Choose Start⇨Control Panel⇨Add or Remove Programs, pick your camera manufacturer's software from the list, and click Remove.

At the very least, you should give the Windows XP native software a try before you trust your camera manufacturer to write Really Great Software. (Yes, my tongue is planted in my cheek.)

Here's the best way to connect a digital camera to a Windows XP computer, even if it's the first time you've ever hitched your camera up to a computer:

1. **Turn off the camera but leave your PC on.**
2. **Plug the USB (or FireWire) cable into the PC; then plug the cable into the camera.**
3. **Turn on the camera.**

   In most cases, Windows XP asks what you want to do with the pictures (as shown in Figure 40-1).

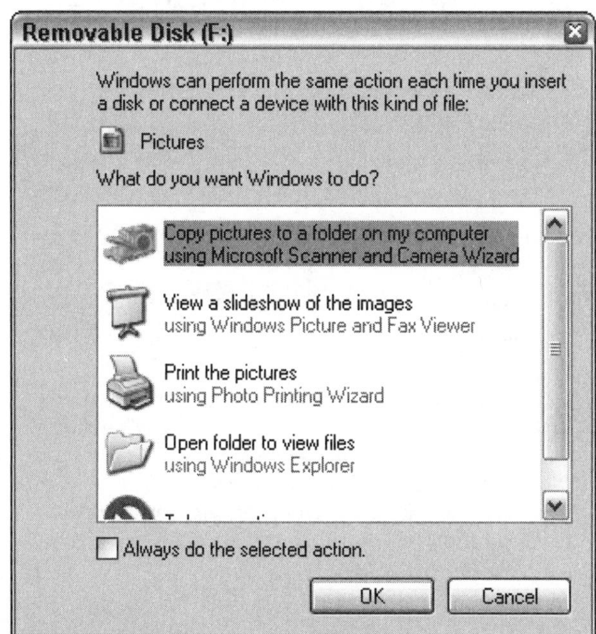

• Figure 40-1: A properly recognized digital camera.

If Windows XP doesn't automatically recognize your camera and the pictures inside it, you can either install the camera manufacturer's software or skip to the next section ("Transferring Pictures with Windows Explorer") and get Windows Explorer to do the work.

Sometimes you really *do* want to install the camera manufacturer's software because it can manipulate settings inside the camera that aren't readily changed from controls on the camera. (I've also had no end of problems trying to get phone cameras to download their pictures without the manufacturer's software.) If you're in that boat — and you really need to change something inside your camera — you don't have much choice. Most camera manufacturers create software that works on almost any computer — at least as far back as Windows 98. It's very difficult to build a program that runs on Windows 98, takes advantage of the features in Windows XP, and stays stable for any length of time.

4. **Click Copy Pictures to a Folder on My Computer Using Microsoft Scanner and Camera Wizard; then click OK.**

   The Scanner and Camera Wizard kicks in.

5. **Click Next.**

   The Scanner and Camera Wizard invites you to choose which pictures to copy (as shown in Figure 40-2).

I always, always select all the pictures and copy them over to the PC because I can see the pictures a whole lot better when they're stored on the PC. These little thumbnails in the wizard don't show you much, and with the photos on my computer, it's one-click easy to delete bad pictures after they're copied anyway. Why take a chance and delete a salvageable picture?

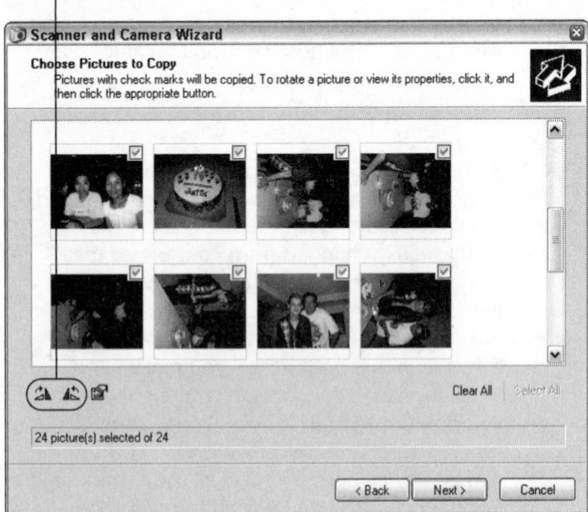

• **Figure 40-2: Always select all the pictures.**

6. **Select any pictures that are rotated (shot with the camera turned); then click the rotation button to bring them topside up.**

   Figure 40-3 shows the portrait pictures from Figure 40-2 rotated right-side-up.

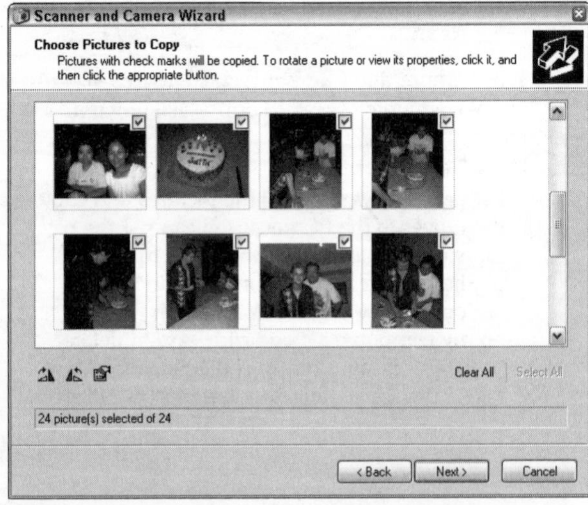

• **Figure 40-3: Rotating pictures is easy and fast.**

7. **Click Next.**

   The Scanner and Camera Wizard asks you to Type a Name for This Group of Pictures and Choose a Place to Save This Group of Pictures.

8. **Type a name for the pictures in the first box.**

   The Scanner and Camera Wizard creates filenames by adding a three-digit number to the end of the name that you type. So if you type `Birthday`, the pictures get the names `Birthday 001.jpg`, `Birthday 002.jpg`, `Birthday 003.jpg`, and so on.

9. **Click Browse and choose a place to put the pictures.**

10. **To save time, check the Delete Pictures from My Device After Copying Them box.**

    That saves you the hassle of going back with Windows Explorer (or the camera's software) and deleting them.

If you accidentally delete pictures on the camera, don't fret. There's a cheap, easy way to bring deleted pictures back. See Technique 41 for details.

11. **Click Next.**

    The Scanner and Camera Wizard takes a while to copy a camera full of pictures, so sit back and watch the screen whiz by.

12. **When the wizard finishes (as shown in Figure 40-4), click Next and then click Finish.**

In Figure 40-4, if you choose to publish the pictures to the Web or order prints, Microsoft just tries to sell you more stuff (specifically, a premium MSN account). Far better to use Google to search for picture-hosting sites on the Web, or ask your friends for their recommendations.

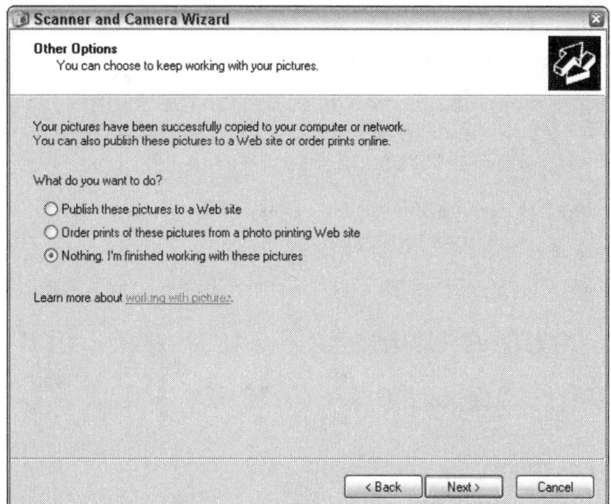

• **Figure 40-4: Pictures are copied to the PC and deleted from the camera.**

Transferring Pictures with Windows Explorer

Sometimes, in spite of all your good intentions, Windows XP just doesn't recognize your camera. When you plug the camera into the PC, you don't get the notification (refer to Figure 40-1).

If you don't get the notification, you should try again. Turn off the camera, unplug the USB or FireWire cable, restart the PC, plug in the cable, and turn the camera back on. Windows might recognize your camera, but if it doesn't, don't fret: You can still use Windows Explorer.

My experience with phone cameras and cameras attached to PDAs has been uniformly lousy. I almost always end up installing the manufacturer's software. Heck, with phone cameras, the manufacturers frequently don't even ship the right software with the phone! Expect to spend some time surfing the manufacturer's Web site to find and install the software you need.

If the Scanner and Camera Wizard doesn't work, you may still have good ol' Windows Explorer to fall back on. Explorer can reach into your camera, retrieve your pictures, copy them to your PC, and, if you so desire, remove the pictures from the camera.

You may want to use Windows Explorer instead of the wizard, even if the wizard *does* work. Here are some reasons why:

- **You like a challenge.** Maybe you figure the wizard's too slow, and you want to go at it by hand. (Ha!)
- **Your camera's batteries are dying.** You don't want to burn through more batteries on your camera, waiting for the pictures to download.
- **Your camera has been separated from its memory card.** For whatever reason, you only have the camera's memory card or memory stick, and you don't want to go fetch the camera.
- **Your ports are all in use.** You don't have an extra USB or FireWire port that you can use to plug in the camera.

Depending on your circumstances, you have many ways to get Windows Explorer to work directly on your camera's memory:

- If the camera's plugged into your PC and the Scanner and Camera Wizard kicks in, click Advanced Users Only on the wizard's first screen. That takes you directly to Windows Explorer, and it shows you the files on the camera.
- Buy a PCMCIA card (PC-card) that accepts your camera's memory card (or stick). If you have a portable with a spare PC-card slot but no spare USB port, either a CompactFlash PC Card Adapter or a Smart Media PC Card Adapter is a good, cheap choice.
- Buy a USB adapter, or even a USB hub, that accepts your camera's memory card (or stick).

This last option is very good if you need more USB ports anyway — for a few shekels more than a plain-vanilla hub, you can get a box that lets you plug your camera's memory card into the hub.

Here's how to use a generic USB hub with a camera's memory card (the PC-card works quite similarly):

1. **Plug the USB hub into your PC.**

   You may need to wait a minute while all the connections are made, drivers are loaded, and so on.

2. **Plug the camera's memory card into the hub.**

3. **Choose Start⇨My Computer; then double-click the removable drive that corresponds to your memory card.**

   You may have to try a few different drives, depending on the hub; but when you finally find the right drive, it looks something like the contents of the G: drive shown in Figure 40-5.

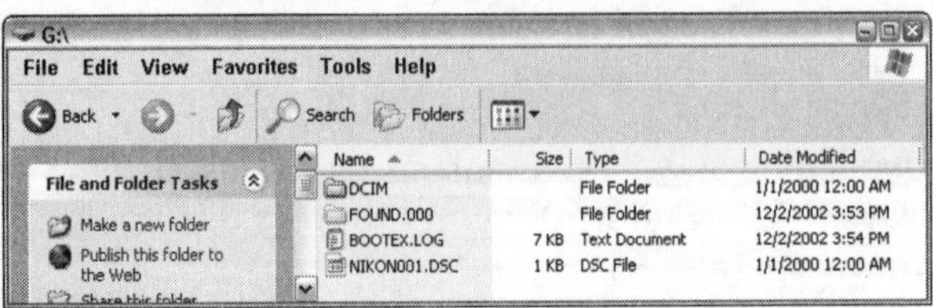

• **Figure 40-5: What a CompactFlash card from a Nikon Coolpix looks like to Windows Explorer.**

4. **Double-click your way down until you find the pictures.**

   On this particular camera, the pictures are stored on drive G: in `\DCIM\100NIKON` (as shown in Figure 40-6).

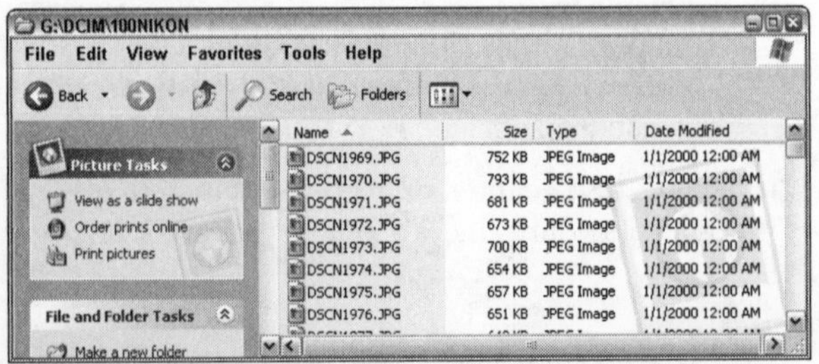

• **Figure 40-6: The picture files are in the DCIM folder.**

5. **From this point, you can treat the picture files on the camera just like any Windows files.**

   For example, you can select all the pictures by pressing Ctrl+A and then copy and paste them to your My Pictures folder.

6. **When you're done, choose File⇨Exit to close Windows Explorer.**

Using a Camera's Memory Card as a Storage Device on Your PC

How many times have you wanted to carry a file around when you travel, but you didn't want to fuss with floppies or a CD, and you didn't have a USB flash drive handy?

Have you ever run out of room on a hard drive and didn't know where to stick a few files while you cleaned out the junk files?

Guess what. If you attach your camera to your PC with its USB (or FireWire) cable, you may be able to use the memory inside the camera in precisely the same way that you use a hard drive or a floppy disk. Most people have a lot of memory inside their cameras. Few realize they can save time and money by using it as portable memory for their computer.

Many digital cameras can handle plain, old, everyday files. They're easy to get to, as long as you have a USB cable and a Windows XP computer. And they work the same way as regular Windows files: Double-click a Word document that's stored inside a digital camera, and Word comes up with the document loaded and ready to go; copy a PowerPoint presentation or an MP3 music file from your desktop to your camera's CompactFlash card and take it with you, inside your camera, when you travel.

With 128MB (and larger) camera memory cards readily available and rapidly growing cheaper, consider using your camera's memory as another kind of external hard drive, particularly if you don't want to spend money for a USB flash drive, or you're traveling, and the camera's coming along with you anyway.

The next time you want to show a PowerPoint presentation to a client, ask if you can plug in your camera. Your audience may forget your presentation by lunchtime, but it'll take a year for anyone to forget your storage medium.

Here's the quick way to get Windows files in and out of your digital camera — assuming that the camera responds to the Scanner and Camera Wizard:

This is most assuredly not something that your camera manufacturer (or even, most likely, Microsoft) wants you to do. Proceed at your own risk. That said, I've never known anyone to have problems, either with Windows or the camera, for saving a Windows file inside a camera.

1. **Turn off the camera, but leave your PC on.**
2. **Plug the USB (or FireWire) cable into the PC; then plug the cable into the camera.**
3. **Turn on the camera.**
4. **When Windows asks what you want to do (refer to Figure 40-1), select Copy Pictures to a Folder on My Computer Using Microsoft Scanner and Camera Wizard. Then click OK.**
5. **In the first screen of the Scanner and Camera Wizard, click Advanced Users Only.**

   The wizard immediately brings up Windows Explorer, with the camera's memory card visible and ready to use (as shown in Figure 40-7).

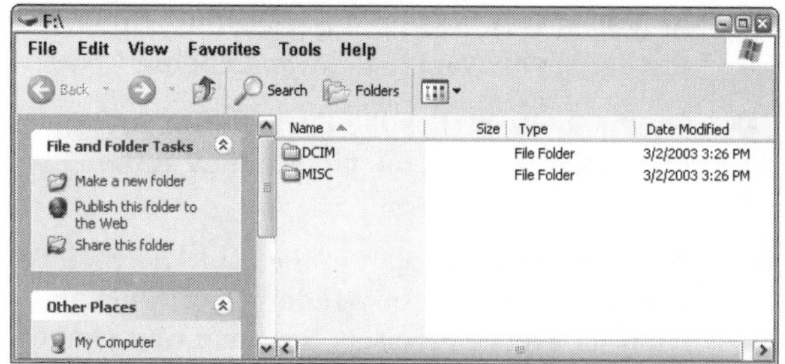

• **Figure 40-7: Windows Explorer is inside the camera.**

6. **Double-click DCIM; then navigate down to where the pictures are stored.**

Although it appears to be possible to put files just about anywhere on the memory card, I prefer to put Windows files among the camera's picture files (as shown in Figure 40-8). Each model of camera stores pictures in a different folder, and it isn't at all clear (to me, anyway) what happens to files that sit in folders other than the one that contains the camera's pictures.

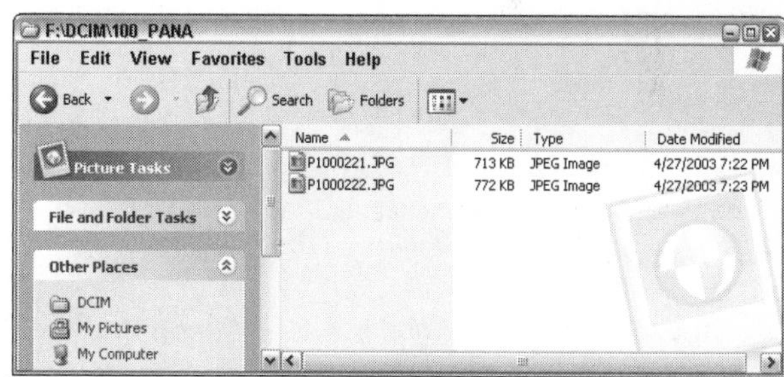

• **Figure 40-8: Dig down into the folder that holds the pictures.**

7. **Click My Computer on the left; then go out and find the file(s) you want to store on the camera.**

   I located a small PowerPoint presentation. Hey, you can pay for a USB flash drive, or you can just use your camera.

8. **In typical Windows Explorer fashion, right-click the file(s) you want to copy and choose Copy.**

9. **On the toolbar, click the Back button and move all the way back to the picture files in the camera.**

10. **Right-click a blank spot in the camera's picture folder (on the right in Windows Explorer) and choose Paste — precisely the same way you paste in Explorer.**

Your copied file appears right next to the picture files (as shown in Figure 40-9).

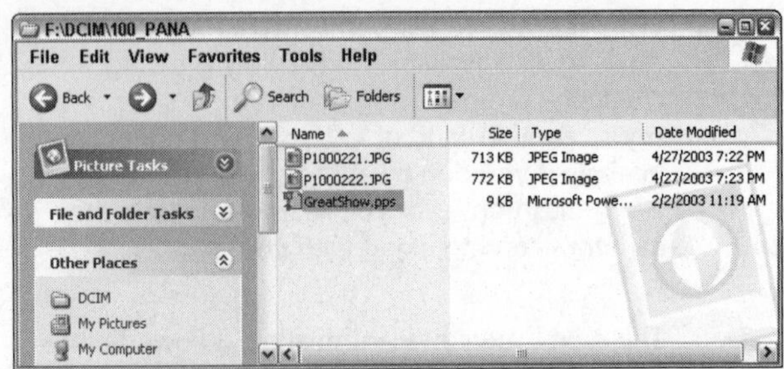

• **Figure 40-9: Right-click and paste the file into the camera's memory card.**

11. **Give it a go: If you copied a document, spreadsheet, presentation, or any kind of graphic file, double-click it.**

Windows behaves in precisely the same way as if the file were inside your computer or on your network.

Doing More with Your Pics

Save Time By

- Using your own pictures for your Windows desktop or screensaver
- Burning pictures — or even an entire slideshow — on a CD
- Retrieving deleted pictures from your digital camera

Have you ever deleted a picture on your digital camera accidentally? Did you know that the easiest way to get that picture back (if it's possible at all) is by running an undelete program on your PC?

Yes, you read that right. You can undelete a picture on your camera *from your PC*. It's easy, it's cheap, and it's so fast you won't believe it.

If you're running out of room on your hard drive and the problem is too many pictures, don't waste your time with compressing and selectively deleting the files you no longer want. Instead, get a CD-R drive if you don't have one already, and simply move a big bunch of pictures to CD. They last longer, and the whole procedure takes just a few minutes.

You may already know that you can view all the pictures in a folder as a slideshow. But you can also do these other things with your pictures:

- Burn a CD with a slideshow.
- Play the CD/slideshow on any Windows computer, not just a computer with Windows XP.
- Use all the pictures in a folder — or even a bunch of folders — for a screen saver. The screen saver randomly picks a picture, shows it on the screen for a while, and then moves on to another randomly chosen picture.

I show you how to do all that and more in this technique.

Putting Your Pic on the Desktop

Do you have a favorite picture that you would like to use as your Windows XP desktop?

Here's the fastest way to do it:

1. **Choose Start⇨My Computer and navigate to the picture you want to put on your desktop.**
2. **Right-click the picture and choose Set As Desktop Background.**

   Your Windows desktop may look great. If so, you're done!

   More likely, the picture you've chosen appears distorted (as shown in Figure 41-1).

• **Figure 41-1: Usually, pictures pressed into service on the desktop are quite distorted.**

3. **If you don't like the appearance of the picture, right-click any open spot on the Windows desktop and choose Properties⇨Desktop.**

   You see the Desktop tab of the Display Properties dialog box.

Usually pictures appear distorted because Windows assumes that you want them stretched to fill the available space on the desktop. In fact, you have three options; you can stretch, center, or tile the image.

4. **From the Position drop-down list, pick one of the position options.**

   If you choose Center, you can specify the color of the desktop that surrounds the picture.

   In Figure 41-2, I chose to have the picture centered and to have the part of the desktop not taken up by the picture to be black.

• **Figure 41-2: Centered picture, black color.**

5. **Click OK.**

You may be tempted to put active content on your desktop — Microsoft's creepy-crawly stock ticker or perhaps a constantly updated Web page. Don't do it. See Technique 14 for details.

Using Your Pictures for a Screen Saver Slideshow

I talk about this nifty (and little-known) Windows XP feature in Technique 14. Here's the whole story on the My Pictures Screensaver.

Windows XP has a built-in screen saver that automatically cycles through all the pictures in a folder. In fact, it can cycle through all the pictures in a folder and all its subfolders. Don't know about you, but on my PC, that can be one whole heckuvalot of pictures!

This feature rates as one of my favorites because old pictures tend to get buried. You shoot them, look at 'em once or twice, and never see 'em again. But if you use this screen saver, everything old is new again — even those really, really bad shots of Aunt Mildred — which, come to think of it, could be a good thing or a bad thing.

To use your pictures for a screen saver slideshow, follow these steps:

1. **Right-click any empty spot on the desktop.**
2. **Choose Properties⇨Screensaver.**

   The Screen Saver tab of the Display Properties dialog box appears.

3. **In the Screen Saver drop-down box, choose My Pictures Slideshow. Then click Settings.**

   The My Pictures Screen Saver Options dialog box appears (as shown in Figure 41-3).

4. **Click Browse and navigate to the folder that contains pictures you want to use for the screen saver.**

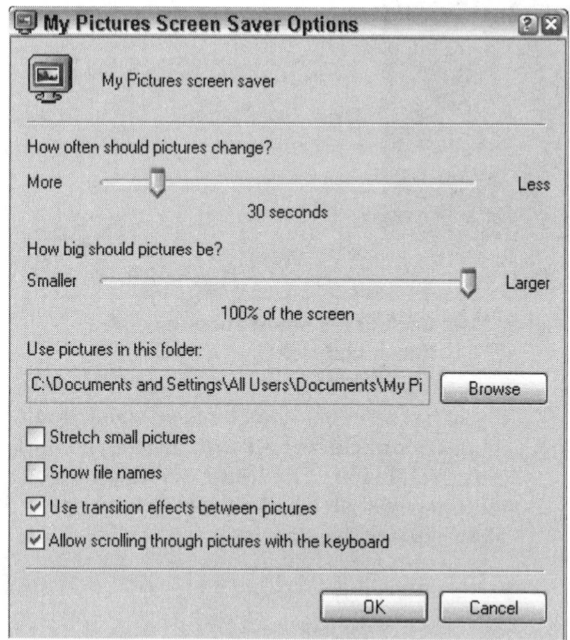

• **Figure 41-3: Control the pictures here.**

Pictures are randomly selected from the chosen folder as well as any subfolders within the chosen folder.

5. **Click OK.**

   The Display Properties box appears again.

6. **Click OK again.**

   Your screen saver is ready for use.

Burning Pictures on a CD

Do you have about a hundred gajillion pictures on your PC eating up hard disk space?

Yeah. I thought so.

If you have a CD-R, CD-RW, DVD-R, DVD+R, DVD-RW, or DVD+RW drive, burning those pictures onto a CD, where they'll last for decades, is very easy. A CD certainly lasts longer than your hard drive, providing you don't gum it up with one of those sticky CD labels (see Fred Langa's experiences at `www.informationweek.com/story/showArticle.jhtml?articleID=15800263&pgno=2`). I talk about backing up files in Technique 60.

Burning pictures couldn't be simpler:

1. **Make sure that your CD-R, CD-RW, DVD-R, or DVD-RW drive is installed and working.**
2. **Start Windows Explorer. (Just choose, say, Start⇨My Pictures or Start⇨My Computer.)**
3. **Navigate to the pictures you want to burn.**

   If you're in a picture or photo album folder (as shown in Figure 41-4), Copy to CD appears in the Picture Tasks list.

You can manually change a folder's type — in particular, you can turn any folder into a picture or photo album folder. For details, see Technique 20.

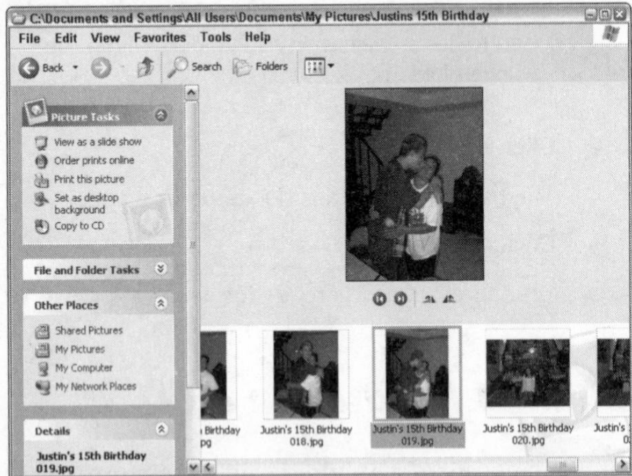

• **Figure 41-4: A photo album folder.**

4. **Select the picture(s) you want to burn; then click Copy to CD in the Picture Tasks list. If Copy to CD doesn't appear in the list, right-click one of the selected files (or folders) and choose Send To➪CD Drive.**

   A small CD icon appears in the notification area, next to the clock.

5. **Keep moving around Windows, gathering pictures that you want to burn.**

   In spite of what the Picture Task list and right-click menu say, Windows actually copies the files you select to a staging area — a place on your hard drive that holds files temporarily, before you burn them to CD.

6. **When you're done gathering files, choose Start➪My Computer➪*your CD burner drive* (whichever drive letter that is).**

   Windows shows you the contents of the CD's staging area, as shown in Figure 41-5.

7. **Put a recordable CD in your CD burner and click Write These Files to CD.**

   The CD Writing Wizard appears.

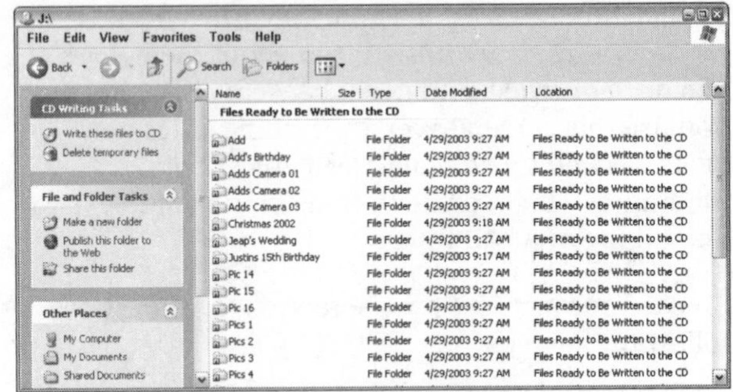

• **Figure 41-5: The CD burner's staging area.**

8. **Type the name you want to be burned on the CD; then click Next.**

   If you've chosen too much data — too many pictures — the wizard alerts you (as shown in Figure 41-6).

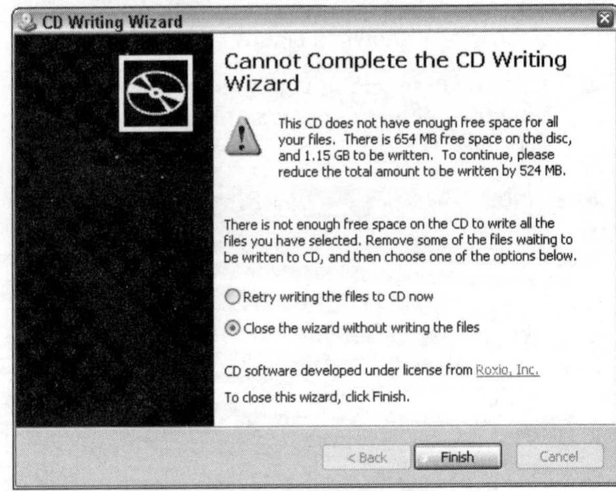

• **Figure 41-6: Can't fit ten pounds of pictures in a five-pound sack.**

9. **If you have too many pictures selected, don't do anything with the wizard. Instead, go back to the staging area and start deleting files or folders (right-click and choose Delete) until you're under the size limit.**

Don't worry — you aren't deleting the pictures. You're just removing them from the staging area.

Unfortunately, neither the wizard nor Windows offers a handy list of folder sizes or suggestions for what to trim. What you can do is right-click a folder, choose Properties, and see the folder's size. For example, the folder shown in Figure 41-7 is 46.2MB, which takes up about half of an 80MB CD.

• **Figure 41-7: The only way to see a folder's size is painstakingly slow.**

10. **When you think that you've deleted enough files or folders, go back to the wizard, click Retry Writing the Files to CD Now (refer to Figure 41-6), and then click Next.**

    If you still have too many pictures selected, you get the warning again. Sooner or later, you have your picture collection trimmed down to the point where it can fit on the CD. At that point, the wizard starts writing files to the CD. Depending on the speed of your burner, it can take 20 minutes or more to burn a full CD.

11. **When the wizard finishes, click Finish.**

    The wizard removes all the files from the staging area.

12. **Immediately try looking at the pictures on the CD.**

    Chances are very good that they're in excellent shape. Oh, and don't forget to label the CD with a Sharpie marker.

Burning a Slideshow on a CD

If you followed the instructions in the preceding section, you have a CD filled with pictures. Plop that CD into any computer that has Windows XP on it and you can use the many Windows XP features to look at the pictures, copy them, and so on. In particular, viewing all the pictures in a folder as a slideshow is easy — just open the folder in Windows Explorer and choose View⇨As Slideshow.

But what about your friends who don't have Windows XP? If you send the CD to people who don't have XP installed, they can open the files, or (on most versions of Windows) view thumbnails of the pics. But they'll have a devil of a time watching the pictures as a slideshow — a feature that older versions of Windows simply don't have.

Fortunately, if you have the foresight, you can burn the CD as a slideshow — one that runs on any version of Windows. This technique is quick, efficient, and surprisingly easy to perform after you figure out what to do.

To burn a slideshow to a CD, follow these steps:

1. **Start Internet Explorer and go to** `www.microsoft.com/windowsxp/pro/downloads/powertoys.asp`.

2. **Download the** `Slideshow.exe` **file.**

   This is more complicated than it should be. The main PowerToys page identifies this particular PowerToy as the CD Slideshow Generator. The program listed for download on that page is called `Slideshow.exe`, but when you download it, you discover that the file is really called `SlideshowPowertoySetup.exe`. Argh.

3. **After `SlideshowPowertoySetup.exe` is downloaded, run it.**

   Windows steps you through a very simple installation wizard.

The CD Slideshow Generator isn't a separate, stand-alone program. Instead, it works by inserting itself as an extra step in the CD Writing Wizard.

4. **Follow Steps 1 through 7 in the preceding section ("Burning Pictures on a CD") to gather the pictures you want to burn on the CD and start the CD Writing Wizard.**

5. **Click Next on the first screen of the CD Writing Wizard.**

   You see a new option to add a picture viewer to the CD.

6. **Click Yes, Add A Picture Viewer; then click Next.**

   The CD Slideshow Generator adds three files to the CD being burned (as shown in Figure 41-8).

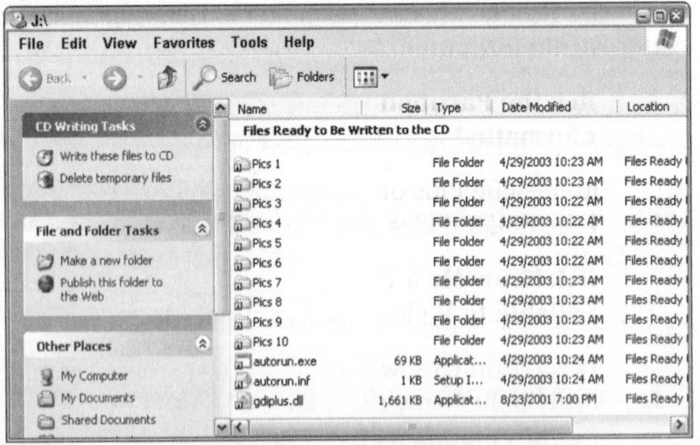

• Figure 41-8: The CD Slideshow consists of three additional files burned to the CD.

7. **Follow Steps 8 through 11 in the preceding section ("Burning Pictures on a CD") to continue burning the CD.**

8. **After you finish creating the CD Slideshow, test the CD by putting it into a machine that's running an earlier version of Windows.**

   A slideshow, such as the one shown in Figure 41-9, appears along with a very simple set of control buttons in the upper-left corner. The slideshow runs all by itself if you don't push any buttons or click anything on-screen. However, you can use the control buttons or arrow keys in the obvious way to move from picture to picture.

• Figure 41-9: This slideshow runs on any version of Windows.

Recovering Deleted Pictures on Your Camera

Tell me whether this has ever happened to you . . .

I just clicked the wrong button on my digital camera and deleted all the pictures I'd stored. I thought I had selected just one file, but my not-so-nimble fingers were working in preprogrammed mode, far faster than my brain. The net result: an entire compact flash memory card wiped out.

Surprisingly, unless your camera manufacturer specifically has a program set up to do it, the fastest, easiest, best way to undelete files on your digital camera is through your PC.

Lots and lots of programs on the market claim to resurrect dearly departed digital image files from your camera. I'm sure most of them work (although I've bumped into several that don't, at least on my cameras).

But I've only hit one company that has the guts to let you download its software and use it to bring back two pictures for free. If you want to undelete more, you have to pay $39.95 for the program. But the two-shot demo version of File Rescue Plus doesn't cost a thing. It's cost effective and saves time, too. Hard to beat.

Here's how to test drive File Rescue Plus:

1. **Start Internet Explorer and go to** `www.softwareshelf.com`.
2. **Pick your location and/or language, and then click File Rescue Plus.**
3. **Fill out the information form, making sure that you choose File Rescue Plus as the Product Download.**
4. **Click Submit.**
5. **Follow the directions to download** `FileRescuePlusDemo.exe`.
6. **After the download has finished, double-click** `FileRescuePlusDemo.exe`.

   Follow the short installation wizard.
7. **Connect the camera that contained the recently deceased picture(s).**
8. **Choose Start⇨All Programs⇨Software Shelf⇨File Rescue Plus to start File Rescue Plus.**

   The program asks about the File Scan mode (as shown in Figure 41-10).

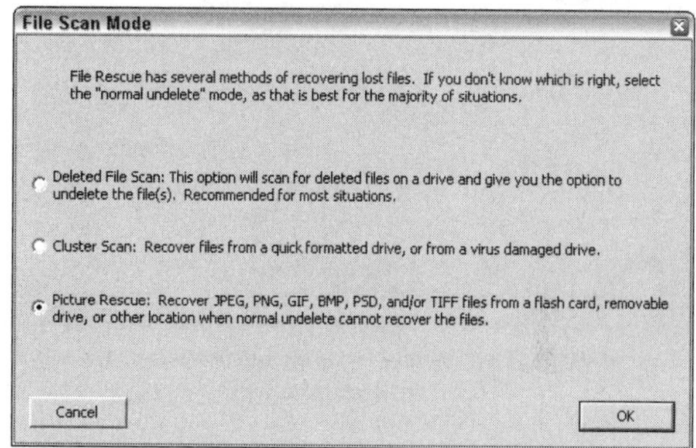

• **Figure 41-10: You want to scan for deleted pictures.**

9. **Click Picture Rescue; then click OK.**

   File Rescue Plus asks you which drive to scan.
10. **If you aren't sure which drive to use, choose Start⇨My Computer and look for your camera.**
11. **Choose the drive that corresponds to your digital camera, and then click OK.**

    Fire Rescue Plus wants to know if the drive has been reformatted. Not likely.
12. **Click the Partition (Drive) Has Not Been Reformatted . . . . Then click OK.**

    Fire Rescue Plus offers to show you thumbnails of the deleted files.
13. **Click Show Me a Thumbnail of the Pictures Available to Be Recovered; then click OK.**

    The first time I saw this happening, I could hardly believe my eyes. Fire Rescue Plus goes into the camera, reconstructs the deleted files, and then presents them to you (as shown in Figure 41-11). This process takes a while, so be patient.

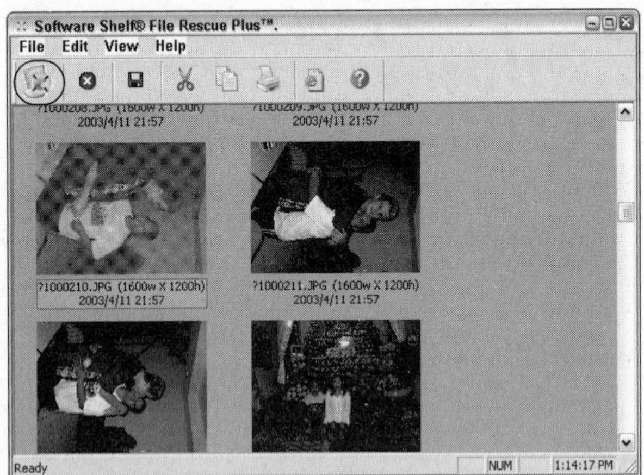

• **Figure 41-11: Fire Rescue Plus reaches into the camera and reconstructs the files.**

14. Click the file (or files) you want to undelete; then click the icon on the main toolbar that looks like a computer monitor with a life preserver in front of it. (I'm tempted to talk about computers as boat anchors, but never mind.)

Fire Rescue Plus asks where you want to put the reconstructed file (as shown in Figure 41-12).

If you put the recovered file back in the camera, you may overwrite a different deleted picture in the process. Only save restored pics back to the camera if you want to keep them on the camera.

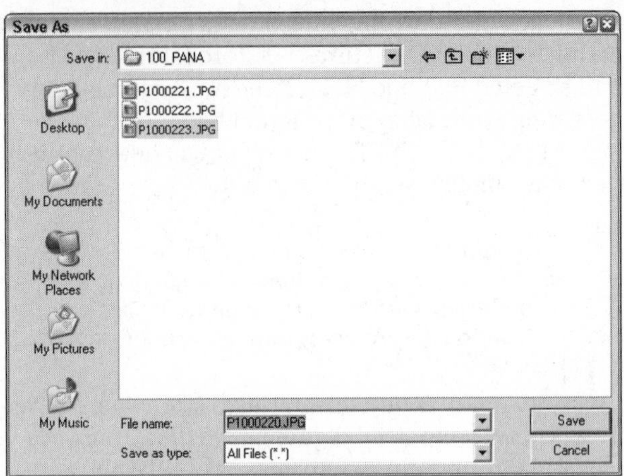

• **Figure 41-12: Save the resurrected file.**

15. Pick a location on your PC, give the file a name, and click Save.

The file is reconstituted and put in the location you choose. You can verify that the picture is alive and well by using Windows Explorer (as shown in Figure 41-13). Chances are good that you can see the picture by using the camera's controls as well.

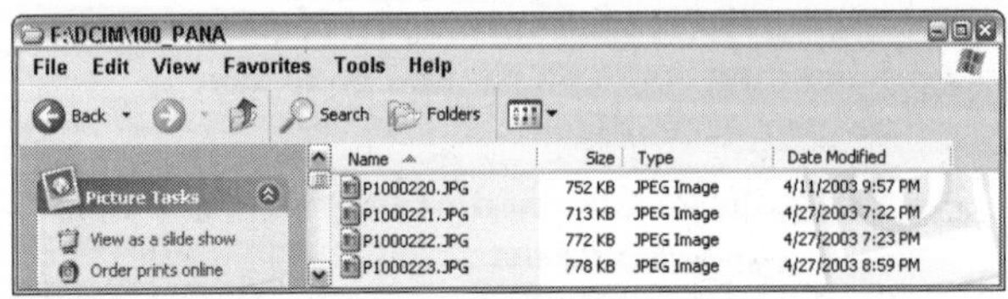

• **Figure 41-13: The picture is alive and well.**

Decreasing Picture Download Times

Save Time By

- Making your picture files smaller so they download faster
- Understanding how picture file size affects viewing quality
- Knowing when you can get away with small files

Do you have one of those umpteen-gazillion pixel cameras? Used to be that 3 megapixels was about as far as a camera could go. Now I'm beginning to wonder if we'll ever see a limit, really.

No doubt you know that more pixels mean better quality pictures (although sooner or later the lens quality sets the upper limit). After all, that's why you shelled out the bucks for a good camera. But the ramifications of all those pixels may not have struck you until you tried to e-mail a picture.

Just one picture can blow someone's e-mail account size limit: Most e-mail accounts have strict limits on the amount of space allotted to each user. Free e-mail accounts rarely accommodate more than a handful of high-quality pictures. Go beyond the limit, and messages get bounced. Gazillions of pixels translates into gazillions of bits. And the bits all take time, time, time to transmit over the Internet.

If you're sending a proof of the next cover of *National Geographic,* hey, use all the pixels you can stand. But if you're just trying to send the grandkids a pic of your new rose garden, all those bits only get in the way. This technique shows you how to find the middle path between humongous file sizes and grainy little snapshots.

Understanding Digital Pic File Sizes

High-resolution digital pictures take an enormous amount of space. But what does it all mean?

A pixel is a dot, give or take a semantic hair or two. If you have a 3.1-megapixel camera, it takes pictures that measure 2048 dots across by 1536 dots high.

Before the camera stores the picture on disk, it uses a compression method — typically JPEG — to reduce the size of the file.

Chances are good that your camera has settings that save pictures in lower resolutions: 1600 x 1200 pixels, 1280 x 960, 1024 x 768, 800 x 600, and 640 x 480 are all possibilities that just happen to correspond to standard Windows screen resolutions. Your camera probably gives these settings truly illuminating names, such as Hi, Med, and Lo.

When you take a shot with a camera that uses 2048 x 1536 dots and you ask for pictures at 1600 x 1200 dots, the compression kicks in, and you end up with a file that's about 750,000 bytes in size, give or take 10,000 or 20,000 bytes. Variations occur because some shots compress more readily than others: Take a picture of the Pillsbury Dough Boy in a blinding winter snow, and you use fewer pixels than shooting, say, Eminem's hair.

Table 42-1 gives you an idea of the size of files you can expect from common picture sizes and how you can expect to use them.

When you reduce the resolution of a picture, you make it a little more fuzzy — but a whole lot smaller, and thus easier to ship over the Internet.

Put another way, if you have a friend with 2MB left on her free e-mail account and you e-mail her just one high-resolution shot from your 3.1-megapixel camera, you take up more than half of her storage allotment. You can't send her two.

But if you convert the high resolution picture to 640 x 480 — which is fine for viewing on a computer screen — the file size goes down to 30 to 40K, and you can send her, oh, 50 pictures without blowing her account out of the water.

In fact, some Internet service providers these days won't allow you to send e-mail attachments larger than 1MB. So you can't even send or receive high quality pics from your 3.1-megapixel camera. None.

TABLE 42-1: CAMERA RESOLUTION AND JPG FILE SIZES

This Resolution	Produces JPEG Files About This Size	So This Many Pictures Fit on a 128MB Memory Card	These Shots Are Suitable For	And Take About This Long to Download on a Good 56K Dial-Up Line
2400 x 1800	1.6MB	80	High-quality enlargements — virtually indistinguishable from (and possibly better than!) 35 mm film	5 minutes
2048 x 1536	1.2MB	100	10 x 12 prints	4 minutes
1600 x 1200	0.8MB	160	8 x 10 prints	2.5 minutes
1280 x 960	0.5MB	250	5 x 7 prints	1.5 minutes
1024 x 768	0.4MB	300	4 x 6 prints (or very high quality shots for documents)	1 minute
800 x 600	0.2MB	500	Wallet-size prints (or good quality Web graphics)	30 seconds
640 x 480	0.1MB	1000	Decent Web graphics (or viewing informal pictures on a computer monitor)	15 seconds

Even if you can send a half-dozen 3.1-megapixel pictures to, say, your lawyer, if he doesn't have a fast line, you tie up his Internet connection for 30 minutes. I don't know how much your lawyer charges for a half hour of staring at Outlook downloading files, but mine wasn't too amused the last time that happened.

Changing the Resolution of Pictures

So you took a bunch of high-resolution pictures, and you used Technique 41 to pull the pictures onto your PC. Or at least that's what I do. I like to have high-resolution pictures hanging around just in case I want to make big prints.

But now the time has come when you need to send some of those pictures over the Internet — birthday pictures to grandma, say, or product pictures to a client.

Here's what you should *not* do: You should *not* send those huge files out over the Internet. Unless you know for a fact that your correspondent can handle big, big e-mailed files, you do her a huge disservice by clogging her inbox with stuff she doesn't need.

If you're sending a photo of your house to a real estate broker so that it can be printed in a four-color glossy brochure, that's one thing. But if you just want to show your sister how the snow's piled up around the house, you're bound by Internet ethics to resize the image before you send it.

Microsoft has a free resizing tool that surprisingly few people know about. Here's how to get it:

1. **Start Internet Explorer and go to** `www.microsoft.com/windowsxp/pro/downloads/powertoys.asp`**.**
2. **Download the file listed as** `ImageResizer.exe`**.**

   The main PowerToys page identifies this particular PowerToy as the Image Resizer. The program listed for download on that page is called `Image Resizer.exe`, but it's really called `ImageResizer PowertoySetup.exe`, as you discover when you download it.

3. **After the file is downloaded, run** `ImageResizer PowertoySetup.exe`**.**

   Windows steps you through a very simple installation wizard, as shown in Figure 42-1.

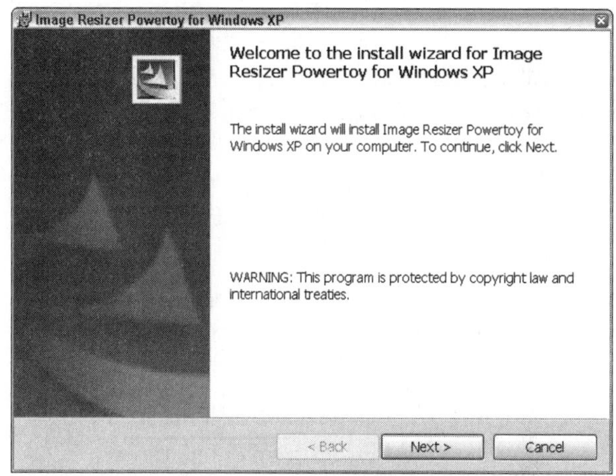

• **Figure 42-1: Another easy installation wizard.**

   The resizer works by attaching itself to the right-click menu for picture files: If you right-click a picture file, or select a group of picture files and right-click them, the resizer appears on the menu. The resizer has no separate program to run.

4. **Use Windows Explorer (say, Start➪My Pictures or Start➪My Computer) to find a picture file that you want to resize.**
5. **Right-click the picture and choose Resize Pictures.**

You also can select a bunch of pictures by using Ctrl+click or Shift+click. Right-click one of them and choose Resize Pictures to resize all the pictures that you selected.

You see a list of resize options, as shown in Figure 42-2.

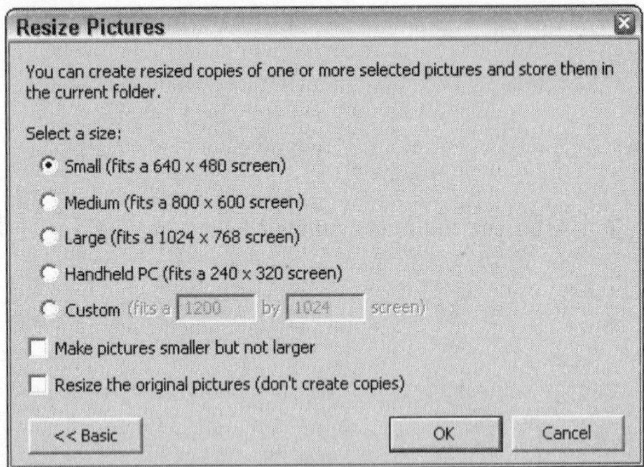

• **Figure 42-2: Choose your resolution.**

6. **Choose the resolution size that you want, keeping in mind the file size approximations in Table 42-1.**

Never check the Resize the Original Pictures (Don't Create Copies) box unless you know for an absolute fact that you have the original file somewhere. If you select this option, the picture gets changed, and the original is overwritten. The net result is that you can't recover the original picture.

7. **Click Next.**

The resizer kicks in and produces a copy of the original picture(s) with the name altered, sticking it in the same folder. For example, if you right-click the `Christmas 2002 023.jpg` picture and choose Small, the reduced-resolution copy is called `Christmas 2002 023 (Small).jpg`, and it's placed in the same folder as the original (as shown in Figure 42-3).

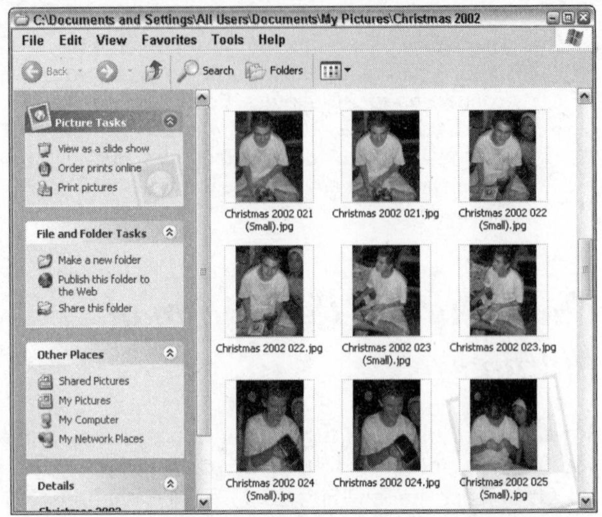

• **Figure 42-3: The copy is marked (Small), (Medium), or (Large).**

The picture in Figure 42-3 was originally at 2048 x 1536 resolution, and that file occupies 1.06MB. The 640 x 480 (Small) version you see only takes up 30.6K — less than 1/30th the size of the original. It could take five minutes or more to download the original on a slow dial-up modem, whereas the (Small) version downloads in seconds.

The resized picture isn't smaller in the sense that it appears smaller in Thumbnails view in Windows Explorer. It's smaller in the sense that the file is smaller.

The resized file is a picture in its own right. You can e-mail it, post it on a Web site, edit it, put it in a document, or use it in any way a picture can be used.

Printing and Posting Pictures

Save Time By

- Printing one picture at a time, quickly and easily
- Printing bunches of pictures on that expensive paper
- Posting your pics to the Web

Some Windows XP features still leave me breathless long after the novelty has worn off. The Photo Printing Wizard certainly deserves mention as one of the Windows XP little-known gems.

You may not have noticed it because you mistakenly thought the Print option just gave you a tired old Print dialog box. In fact, Print has a lot more to it — give it a try and you'll see why.

If you're working with digital pictures in the traditional 4:3 aspect ratio — at resolutions of 2048 x 1536, 1600 x 1200, 1280 x 960, 1024 x 768, 800 x 600, and 640 x 480, or even accurate scans of 35 mm film — the Photo Printing Wizard takes all the guesswork out of printing pictures. It crops and rotates and squeezes the most printable room out of those outrageously expensive fancy papers. It's quite a wizard.

This technique shows you how to get those bits on paper — or on the Web — and save yourself all sorts of time.

Using the Photo Printing Wizard

The Photo Printing Wizard provides a fast, easy way to print pictures stored on your computer. Whether you're looking for professional-quality prints on special photographic paper, or a handful of wallet-size photos on plain paper for your kids' Valentine cards, this wizard delivers the best possible prints, within the limits of your printer and its paper.

The wizard takes the guesswork out of arranging prints on a page, as well. That photo paper is expensive, and the wizard uses every square inch. Table 43-1 shows you how many pictures fit on an 8 ½-by-11-inch page.

Table 43-1: How Many Pictures Fit on a Sheet?

Size of Print	Pictures Per Page
8 x 10	1
5 x 7	2
4 x 6	3
5 x 5	4
Wallet	9
Contact Print	35

If you have one or more pictures ready to print, you're ready for the Photo Printing Wizard. Here's my favorite timesaving way to use the wizard:

1. **Use Windows Explorer (for example, choose Start⇨My Pictures or Start⇨My Computer) to navigate to the picture(s) you want to print.**

   Every picture or photo album folder (as shown in Figure 43-1) has Print Pictures on the Picture Tasks list.

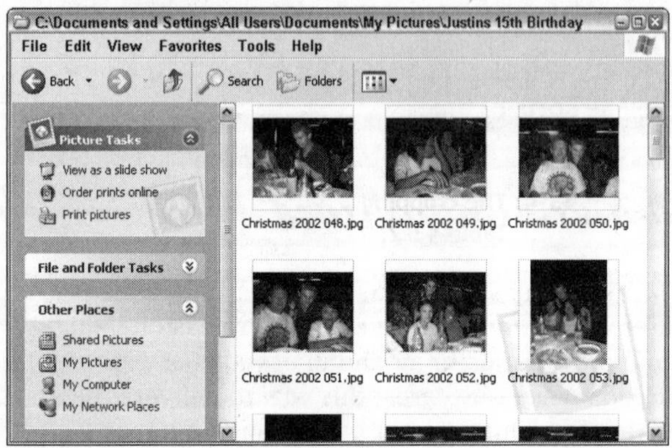

• **Figure 43-1: A photo album folder.**

Every folder has a type. It's easy to get at the Photo Printing Wizard if the pictures you want to print are located inside a folder that Windows identifies as a picture or photo album folder. If you don't see Print Pictures at the top of the task pane of the folder that contains your pictures, the folder hasn't been set up as an official picture or photo album folder. You can set a folder's type by hand — see Technique 20. In this case, you can turn any folder into a picture or photo album folder.

2. **If you want to print only one picture, click that picture once; then click Print Picture. If you want to print more than one picture, select them and click Print Pictures.**

   The Photo Printing Wizard kicks in.

3. **Click Next.**

   The Picture Selection dialog box appears (as shown in Figure 43-2). If you preselected a picture, a check mark appears above it. If you didn't select anything before starting the wizard, all the boxes are checked (also as shown in Figure 43-2).

• **Figure 43-2: Pick the pics to print.**

4. **Choose the pictures that you want to print.**

   Some forethought is worthwhile at this point — although you can always come back. If you're printing on expensive paper and you don't want to waste any, look at the sizing options in Table 43-1 and determine how many pictures you want to print. Then pick that many pictures from the

Picture Selection dialog box. For example, if you're going to print 4 x 6s, you can pick three, six, nine, or twelve pictures to print.

5. **Click Next.**
6. **Choose the printer you want to use from the drop-down box, as shown in Figure 43-3.**

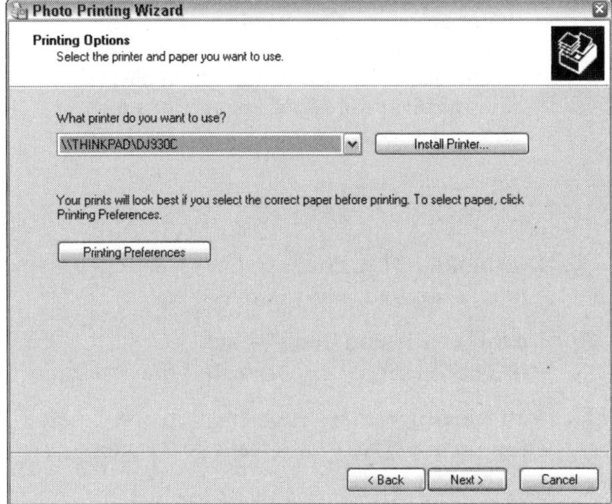

• **Figure 43-3: Pick a printer and paper.**

7. **If you're printing with anything other than plain paper, make sure that you click the Printing Preferences button and tell Windows about it. Click Next.**
8. **In the Layout Selection dialog box (see Figure 43-4), pick a print size and layout for the page, but be aware that many layouts require that the photos be cropped — sides of the pictures will be cut away, so the pictures match the print size you choose.**

   See Table 43-2 for details.
9. **If you want to print each picture more than once, pick the number of times in the Number of Times to Use Each Picture box.**

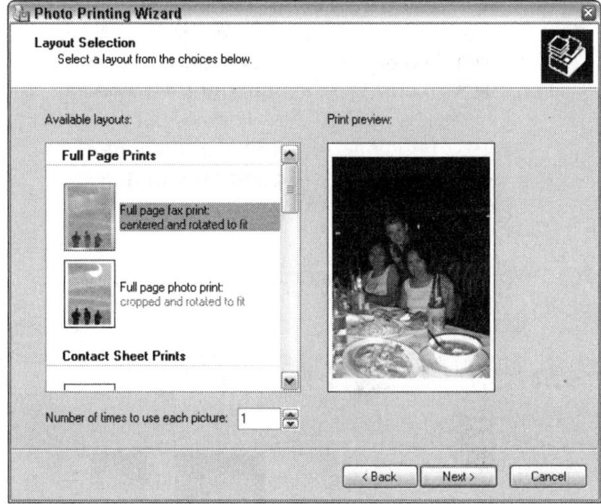

• **Figure 43-4: The cropping details aren't obvious. Consult Table 43-2.**

Table 43-2: What the Layout Options Really Do

This Option	Does This to Pictures with a 4:3 Aspect Ratio
Full page fax	No cropping.
Full page photo	Cropped slightly to print the largest picture possible.
Contact sheet (35 pictures per page)	Pictures are not cropped or rotated, and the filename appears underneath each picture.
8-x-10-inch prints	Cropped significantly on the shorter edges.
5-x-7-inch prints	Cropped significantly on the longer edges.
4-x-6-inch prints	Cropped very significantly on the longer edges. Pictures of people can have part of the head lopped off.
3.5-x-5-inch prints	Cropped significantly on the longer edges.
Wallet prints	Little (if any) cropping; nine on a page.

The limit is 15. I have no idea why, particularly because two pages of wallet prints result in 18 pictures.

10. Click Next.

The pages start printing immediately. This can be rather, uh, abrupt, so make sure that you're ready for it.

If you get an Internal Error message at this point — and I frequently do — the most common cause is a printer that isn't turned on, isn't connected correctly to your PC, or somehow isn't accessible over your network. Make sure that the connection to your printer is working. If necessary, go into the Windows Control Panel's Printer applet (Start⇨Control Panel⇨Printers and Other Hardware) and print a test page.

11. When the printer is done, click Finish.

Posting Pics on the Web

It's surprisingly easy to post your pictures on the Web. Microsoft used to give away free space for posting pics, but now you have to pay for a premium MSN account. Fancy that.

These days, almost any Web hosting service sets you up with more than enough room to post tons of pictures, for a small price. (I've been using `Dundee.net` and `Asianservers.com` for years, but your friends may have better recommendations.) Take your hosting service's tutorial on setting up a Web page. Chances are good you need either FrontPage or some free file transfer utility to get going. After you have a test page in place, you're ready to start uploading pictures.

The best personal pic pages (say that ten times real fast) have an index page, consisting of thumbnails of the pictures available on the site. Many people get a program called Adobe Photo Essentials with their PCs or cameras, and Photo Essentials does yeoman work creating a thumbnail page from a folder of pictures.

My favorite program for transforming a folder of pictures into a bunch of Web pages, including a thumbnail index page, is an odd program from "Alchemist Matt" Monroe who also writes programs that calculate molecular weights, a Rubik's Cube solution monograph, a canonical reference of more than 500 versions of *'Twas the Night Before Christmas*, and. . . well, you get the idea. My kind of guy.

To use Alchemist Matt's program

1. **Download HTML Photo Gallery Catalogeer from** `jjorg.chem.unc.edu/personal/monroe/`.
2. **Unzip the file and double-click** `HTMLPhotoGallery.msi` **to install the program.**
3. **Run the program by choosing Start⇨All Programs⇨HTML Photo Gallery Catalogeer.**

   You see the program's only dialog box in Figure 43-5.

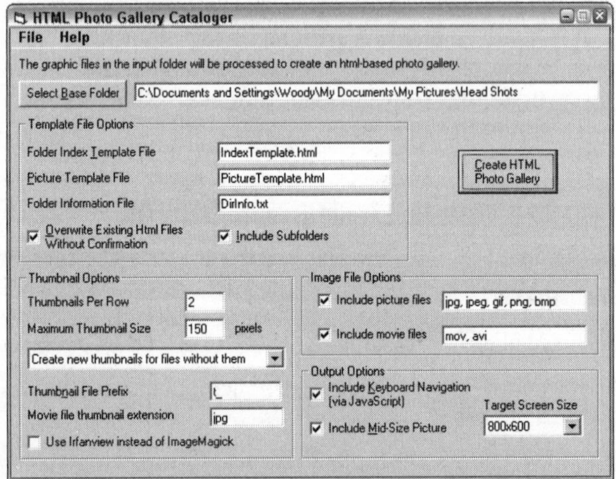

• **Figure 43-5: HTML Photo Gallery Catalogeer creates a page of thumbnails and turns a bunch of pictures into interlocked Web pages.**

4. Pick a folder that contains all the pics you want to post, and click Create HTML Photo Gallery.

Wait a few seconds (or minutes), and you end up with a file called `index.html` that contains thumbnails of all the pictures in the folder, along with a series of HTML files (including navigation buttons) that can be posted on any Web site (see Figure 43-6).

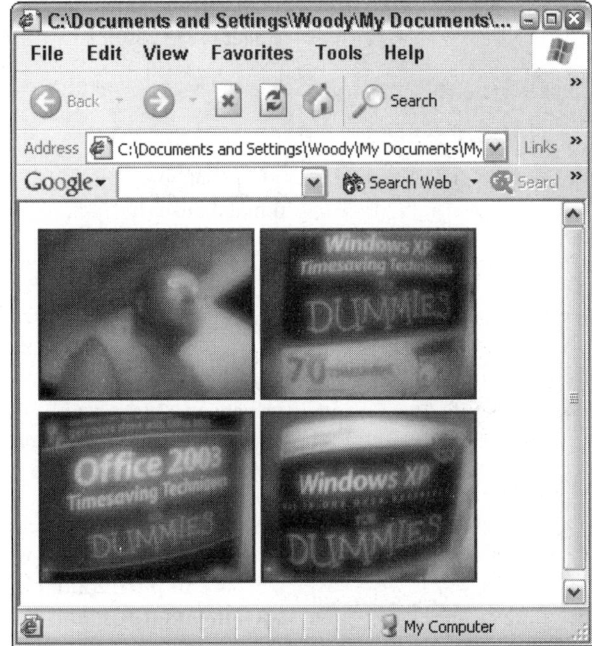

• **Figure 43-6: A folder of pictures turned into an interlocked bunch of Web pages, complete with a page of thumbnails, ready to upload to my Web hosting service. Total time: about 30 seconds flat.**

Using a Scanner Effectively

Save Time By

- Installing your scanner the right way — the first time
- Coaxing your scanner into delivering the highest possible quality scans
- Minimizing the size of the scanned files

Windows XP delivers great scanner support — primarily because Microsoft wanted to build outstanding digital camera support into Windows, and scanners kind of came along for the ride. As long as you have recently purchased a new scanner, the method you use to scan an image is remarkably similar to the one for bringing digital pictures in from a camera.

Although the computer part of getting a scanner to work has become much simpler with the advent of Windows XP, some things never change. In particular, the grunt work — cleaning the scanning bed, dusting the pictures, and on and on — hasn't changed one bit. If you want good scans, you have to work at it. The advantage, of course, is that you only have to do the work once.

This technique shows you the whiz-bang side, but it doesn't neglect the lowly dust speck that can make your scanned documents very hard to read. I show you how to save time when you set up your scanner. I also show you how to get your scans right the first time, so you don't have to go back and retrace your steps.

Getting Your Scanner to Work

Almost all modern scanners come with built-in Windows Image Acquisition support. Even if you aren't sure whether you have a WIA-compliant scanner, as long as it has a USB or FireWire cable, here's the best way to install it:

1. **Plug it in.**

   About nine times out of ten, that's all it takes.

Okay, okay. I skipped over some of the details. In fact, one key detail — unlocking the lamp — is easy to overlook.

Two years ago, I always recommended that Windows XP users throw away the software from their scanner manufacturer, and rely on the software that's built into Windows XP. I don't know why, but in the past two years, scanner manufacturers have improved their software enormously. So it is with great fear and trepidation that I'm changing my long-standing advice: I now recommend that you *read the instructions* that come with your scanner, and install the software per the manufacturer's instructions.

Try these few tricks to get your scanner working:

- Take some time to get the scanner located on top of your desk so you aren't constantly bumping into it. You need to allow room around all the edges, because sooner or later you'll try to scan something that doesn't fit on the bed.
- Before you install the software, log on to the manufacturer's Web site and verify that you have the most recent version.
- Make sure your scanner is turned off before you plug it into the wall, and make sure it's off before you plug the USB cable into your PC.
- After you remove all the tape and gunk from the scanner, make sure you *unlock the lamp*. Almost all scanners ship from the factory with their lamps locked to prevent the lamps from sliding around while they're in transit. When you unpack the scanner, you should see two or three (or ten) pieces of paper that tell you to unlock the lamp, typically by sliding a mechanical switch from one side to the other. It's very easy. But you have to do it.

Guess who forgot to unlock the lamp the last time he installed a scanner.

Understanding DPI

Scanners can produce very coarse scans — which don't take much time and don't occupy much disk space — or they can produce very fine scans — which . . . well, you get the idea. The fineness of the scan is measured in *dots per inch*, or dpi. In theory, you want to match the fineness of your scan to the work at hand: No need to make a very fine scan if you're going to post it on a Web page. In practice, it behooves you to scan at a finer level — at a higher dpi — than your final product requires. Why? Reducing the fineness of a picture is easy (you can use the image resizer I describe in Technique 42, for example). If you want something finer, you have to go back and scan the original again. Windows XP's Scanner and Camera Wizard has settings for 75 dpi (suitable for pictures on the Web), 150 dpi (good quality document setting or for newspapers), and 300 dpi (right for magazine pictures) and up.

Producing Quality Scans

Every scanner manufacturer's software is different, but Windows XP's Scanner and Camera Wizard works with almost every scanner in existence. Getting good scans takes some work. Here's the fastest way I know to use the Scanner and Camera Wizard to produce outstanding scans:

1. **Choose Start⇨Control Panel⇨Printers and Other Hardware⇨Scanners and Cameras (as shown in Figure 44-1). Double-click the name of your scanner.**

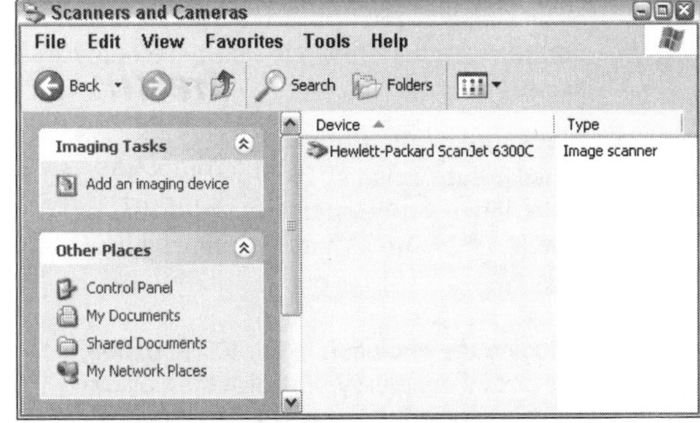

• **Figure 44-1: It takes quite a few clicks to bring up the Scanner and Camera Wizard.**

You see the Scanner and Camera Wizard's opening screen.

2. **Click Next.**

The wizard wants you to choose your color depth preferences (as shown in Figure 44-2).

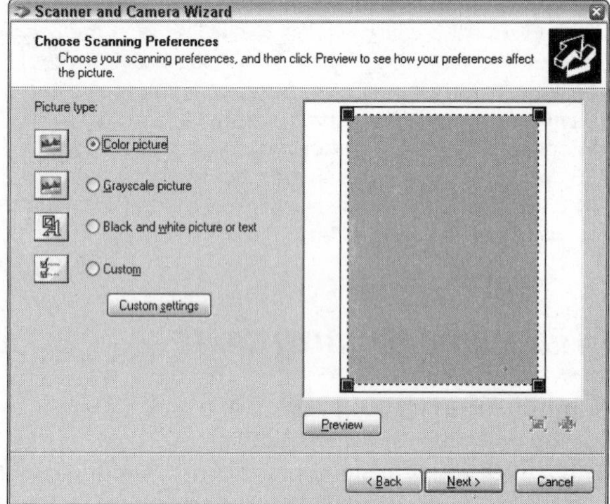

• **Figure 44-2: A limited set of options that work under most circumstances.**

Here's what the preferences mean:

- **Color Picture:** Scans 24-bit color at 150 dots per inch.
- **Grayscale Picture:** Scans 256 shades of gray (8-bit), also at 150 dpi. Use grayscale when you're scanning drawings that have many shades of gray.
- **Black and White Picture or Text:** Scans 1-bit (black/white), also at 150 dpi. Use black and white when you're scanning typed text on a page, or pictures that don't have shades of gray.

Changing the resolution to 75, 100, 150, 200, 300, or 600 dpi is easy: Just click the Custom Settings button. But the only way to change the color depth beyond the three preprogrammed settings is by manipulating the picture after you scan it.

Always scan more than you think that you'll need. In particular, if you're scanning a high-quality black-and-white photo, scan it as a color picture. It's easy to cut back on resolution or color depth after you scan a photo. But if you want more color or a higher resolution, you have to scan again.

3. **Before you put the photo or page in to scan**
   - Clean the scanning surface with an antistatic cloth.
   - Use a photo brush or compressed air to dust off a photo.
   - If the document or photo is smaller than a standard sheet of paper, put a piece of white paper behind it.
   - If the original is bound (as in a book), make sure that all of what you want to scan is flush up against the scanning surface.
4. **Choose the color depth that you want for the scan; then click Preview.**

   Always preview your document before you save it (as shown in Figure 44-3). Too many things can go wrong.

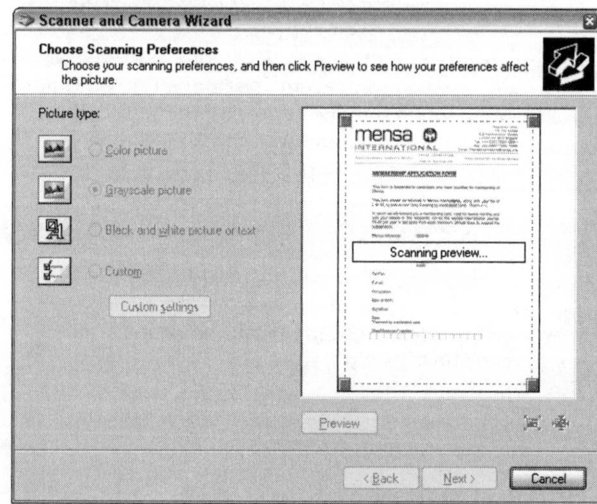

• **Figure 44-3: Always preview the scan.**

5. **Drag the corners around in the preview pane to crop the picture or document; then click the Zoom button to rescan the picture and zoom in on the selected area.**

   The result looks like Figure 44-4.

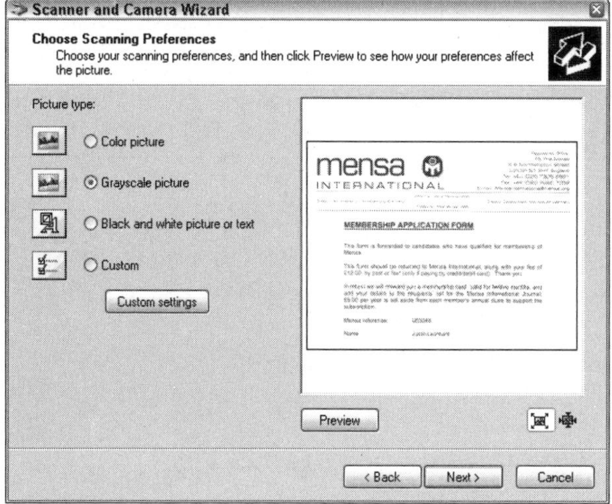

• **Figure 44-4: Zoom in on your final selection.**

6. **When you're happy with the scan, click Next.**

   The wizard then asks what kind of picture file you want and where you want to put the file (as shown in Figure 44-5).

7. **Consult Table 44-1 to pick a good file format; then type in a name, click Browse to select a location, and click Next.**

   The wizard performs a final scan, converts the picture to the specified format, and puts it in the location you chose.

8. **In the final screens of the wizard, click Next and then click Finish.**

9. **Check the final scan by using Windows Explorer to navigate to the picture; double-click it (as shown in Figure 44-6).**

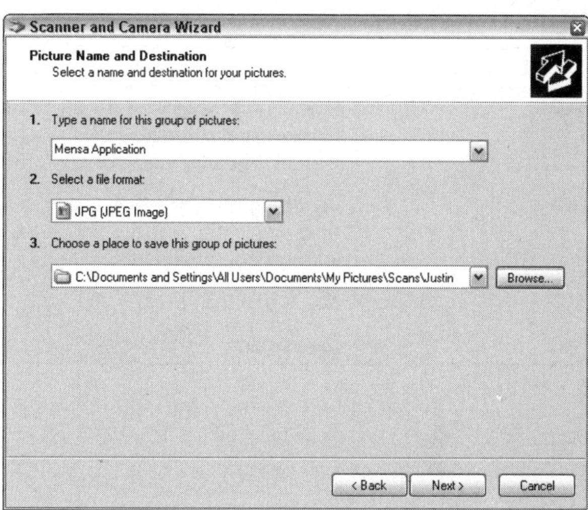

• **Figure 44-5: Tell the wizard what kind of file you want to create.**

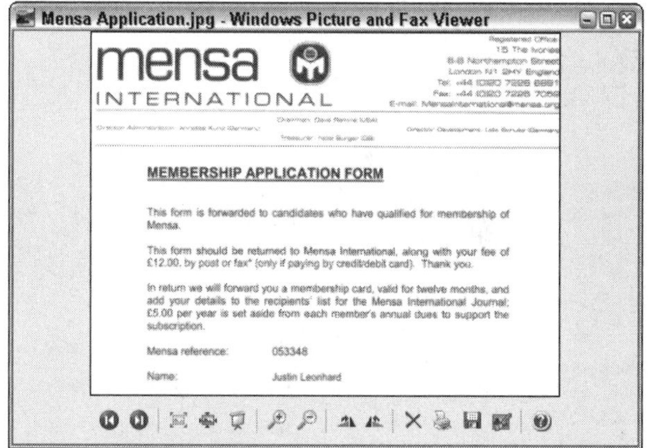

• **Figure 44-6: The final scan.**

If you see horizontal or vertical lines on your scan, Windows didn't do it: Chances are good that your scanner is having a bad day or it's dirty. Less philosophically, plenty of things inside a scanner can go wrong — the lamp, mirrors, the detectors that read pages as they're scanned, and even power supply fluctuations. All those can cause lines. Windows can't.

Table 44-1: Scanner File Formats

Use This Format	For
JPG	Most scans. Microsoft doesn't say how much lossy JPG compression is used — and thus how much of the original image clarity is tossed out — but subjectively, this choice produces decent pictures and high-quality scans of documents. (See Technique 42.)
TIF	Very high quality scans. If you're going to try to print a scanned picture or if you need to scan multiple pages into one file, you need TIF. The files are huge: Apparently the wizard doesn't even apply lossless compression.
BMP	Not worth the effort.
PNG	Rarely used.

Part VII

Ensuring Peak Network Performance

"I guess you could say this is the hub of our network."

Technique 45

Installing a Small Network

Save Time By

- Buying the right equipment — the first time
- Using the Windows XP wizards the right way
- Getting your network up in no time

If you have two or more computers in your office or in your home — or even in your home office — they should be networked. Whether you want to share a printer or a single Internet connection (over a single phone line), or if you just need to transfer a few files every once in a while, a small peer-to-peer network (what Microsoft calls a *domain*) fits the bill. You can throw away your floppies. Stop running up and down the stairs. Whatever weird machinations and incantations you've endured to swap stuff between computers have become a thing of the past. And . . . oh, man, the games!

As long as one of your computers uses Windows XP and the others run Windows 98 or later, setting up a network is fast, cheap, easy — and almost always painless.

Putting the Pieces Together

Most discussions of Windows networking tend to get bogged down in questions of cable types and hub specifications, IP addresses, and DHCP servers. Bah.

Here's the straight timesaving scoop. You have to choose from four different ways to string a network together:

- **If you're networking two PCs, you can use a crossover cable.** This process is cheap and fast, and if you ever need to add more PCs, you just throw the crossover cable away.
- **An increasing number of networks don't use wires.** To go wireless, you need an 802.11b or 802.11g card or USB antenna in each PC (your notebook may have one already) plus an 802.11b or g base station. The base station usually plugs directly into the Internet, or into an existing wired network (in which case it's called a *wireless access point*).

Don't you love these obfuscating buzzwords? 802.11b is a particular way for computers to talk to each other over radio channels. It's very similar to the method used by 2.4 GHz telephones — another obfuscating buzzword. 802.11g is faster, smarter, and better than 802.11b. Given a choice, always go for 802.11g.

- **If the computers you want to connect are sitting on the same desk, consider using a traditional hard-wired Ethernet network.** It's cheap and easy to set up, and you don't have to worry about radio interference. You need a network card in each of the PCs, a cheap box (variously called a *hub, switch,* or *router*) that interconnects the PCs, and enough network cable to hook each PC to the hub.

Ethernet is an ancient technology, predating Windows itself, that still works very well. The terminology can drive you nuts, but 10 Base-T, 100 Base-T, 10/100 Base-T, 1000 Base-T, gigabit, 10/100/1000 Mbps, Category 5, UTP, TPE (Twisted Pair Ethernet), and RJ-45 all refer to Ethernet-related stuff.

- **The best and worst of both worlds come with running two networks — one wired, the other wireless — and connecting the two together.** Nowadays, if you have a fast cable, ADSL, or satellite connection, the easiest and fastest way to work in both worlds involves a *wireless broadband router*. You plug one side of the box into your fast Internet connection, run LAN cables from the router to nearby PCs, and use wireless cards for any other computer on your network. In many cases your Internet service provider can supply the box, and have you going in no time.

Although wireless networks run at a fraction of the speed of hard-wired Ethernet networks (give or take a waffle or two), the speed of a network only comes into play if you're pumping massive amounts of data through it. Someday, when your TV runs directly off the Internet, that'll be important. Right now, it's just marketing hype.

Choosing the right hardware

If you're worried about getting the right hardware, here's a bit of school-of-hard-knocks advice. For hard-wired Ethernet networks, get cheap, get generic. For wireless networks, don't skimp, get everything from the same manufacturer — and make sure that you can return the components if they don't work.

My quick buying guides for network components

- **Wireless base stations/cards:** These are changing so fast, any recommendation I make today will be useless tomorrow, except for one: Don't try to mix and match. Get one package and stick with it. Or throw it away and get another one. Keep on top of the latest developments in wireless technology by visiting `www.practicallynetworked.com`.
- **Network cards (also known as *NICs*, or Network Interface Cards):** Chances are pretty good that any newer PC you own already has one. (Hint: Look for something like a wide telephone jack on the back of your PC.) If you need a card for a desktop PC and you have an extra card slot available, get a generic NIC (less than $20 U.S.) and install it yourself. Installing cards isn't nearly as difficult as it used to be, and most cards now deal with Windows XP quite well. For a portable — or if you're too intimidated to install a card — get a USB Ethernet adapter ($20 U.S.) or PC-card Ethernet adapter ($40 U.S.).
- **Cable:** You can spend a lot, but I'm not convinced that the more expensive ones are any better than the cheaper ones. Look for generic, 8-wire Category 5 cable with telephone-like (RJ-45) connectors on the ends. Buy cables that are long enough to stretch from each PC to the hub.
- **Hubs/Switches/Routers:** A simple $50 eight-port hub is more than most small offices and homes will ever need. If you're going to get a new one, spend a few extra bucks and get one that supports 802.11g wireless access.

Pulling cable through your office or house

Don't. If you have to drill into walls in order to run Ethernet cables, you're far better off going with 802.11g wireless. This job may look easy, but it isn't. If you kink the cable, it may work right for the first day or two. But then it may go all to Hades when you get your first major rainfall or the temperature gets too high or too low.

Typically 802.11g goes through two or three thick concrete walls, and/or up to a couple hundred feet of relatively unobstructed territory. If you need to go farther, all the major wireless manufacturers sell range extenders that relay the signal.

Locating the hardware

In general, it doesn't matter much where you put any of your wired network's components. A wired hub — even if it's a fancy residential gateway — can easily go in a closet. A printer works just as well whether it's attached to the PC in your office or the PC in your living room.

Wireless is a horse of a different color. If you want wireless coverage to extend through several rooms, it helps to put the base station in the middle. Because 802.11b and g use the same 2.4 GHz frequency employed by most cordless phones, keeping the base station away from a cordless phone station is a good idea. Finally, wireless manufacturers recommend that you not place a base station right next to a wall. Reflections can cut down the efficacy of the base station.

The only significant limitation you're bound to encounter is the 100-meter (330-foot) limit on the total length of all the Ethernet cables connecting to a single hub. If that becomes a bother, just go wireless. It's that simple.

Preparing for the Network Setup Wizard

Microsoft's Network Setup Wizard is an amazingly capable piece of software. Many people find that they can set up a network in an hour or less if they use the wizard.

Run the Network Setup Wizard even if you have a wireless network, or a part-wired, part-wireless network.

Before you run the Network Setup Wizard, it's your responsibility to make sure that the hardware is working. For traditional hard-wired Ethernet systems, follow these steps:

1. **Turn off every PC in the network.**
2. **Disconnect the Ethernet cable from the back of every PC.**
3. **One by one, turn on each PC.**

   Make sure that Windows XP boots without rejecting the network card and that the machine itself — along with all its peripherals — is working.

   If Windows needs drivers, it tells you. If Windows tells you that a network card is unplugged, great! That means that everything is working fine.
4. **Again, turn off every PC in the network.**
5. **Connect the Ethernet cables on each PC and double-check to make sure the cables are connected on the hub.**
6. **One by one, turn on each PC.**

   Verify that the light on the hub comes on — that means the PC is talking to the hub — and watch the network card to make sure its light is blinking, too.

If the lights don't come on, go back and check the card and the cable.

7. **Turn off everything — the PCs, the hub, the routers if you have any — everything.**

   You want all the machines off so that you can wake them up, one by one. (Bringing them back one by one can help you minimize — or at least isolate — problems with something called an IP address. See the "Understanding Addresses" section in this technique.)

For wireless networks, you can follow the same basic steps, but you have to consult your manufacturer's manuals to make sure the PCs and base station are talking to each other.

Running the Network Setup Wizard

Everything on the network is turned off, right?

Here's the best way to run the Windows XP Network Setup Wizard, the right way, the first time:

1. **Turn on whatever you have that's connected to the Internet.**

   Whether it's a modem with a power switch, a router, a residential gateway, a hardware firewall, or a miniature paisley homing pigeon, turn it on first. Something called a DHCP server (the box that assigns network addresses; see the "Understanding Addresses" section later in this technique) may need to get itself started.

   If you have an internal modem — one without a power switch — skip this step. It gets turned on when you turn the PC on.

2. **If you have a hub/switch/router and it has a power switch (not all of them do), turn it on. If you have a wireless base station, turn it on, too.**

   Wait another minute.

3. **Turn on all the PCs in the network. Turn on their peripherals, too — especially printers.**

   If you have anything that you don't normally use, leave it off. In particular, if you have a portable with an internal modem that you don't intend to share with the network, don't plug it into the phone jack.

4. **Figure out which Windows XP PC you want to run the wizard on first.**

   If you have a Windows XP PC on the network that controls access to the Internet, that's the one you need to run the wizard on first.

   For example, if you have a PC with a modem that'll be shared by all the PCs on the network, that's the PC you want to go first. If you have a single Windows XP PC that's connected to a router, which, in turn, is connected to the Internet, then that's the one that goes first.

   On the other hand, if all the Windows XP PCs on the network plug into a residential gateway, or if they all communicate with a wireless broadband router, which, in turn, connects to the Internet, it doesn't matter which Windows XP PC you run the wizard on first.

5. **Go to the PC identified in Step 4, and make sure its Internet connection is working.**

   To do so, try running Internet Explorer. Dial up your Internet service provider, if need be.

   If you need to set up a new Internet connection, choose Start➪Control Panel➪Network and Internet Connections➪Network Connections➪Create a New Connection➪Next➪Connect to the Internet➪Next and then follow the instructions from your Internet service provider.

If you can't get connected to the Internet, stop and figure out why. You may have bad connection settings in Internet Explorer (try Start➪Control Panel➪Network and Internet Connections➪Internet Options➪Connections). Your modem may be on the fritz. Your Internet account may be out of money. Your DSL modem may not be set up right. There are a thousand possibilities. But get this one connection working first: There's no reason to continue with this procedure until the Internet connection is working.

6. **Choose Start➪Accessories➪Communications➪ Network Setup Wizard.**

   The Network Setup Wizard splash screen arrives. Finally.

7. **Click Next.**

   A checklist appears. You've already installed the cards, turned on the printers, and connected to the Internet.

8. **Click Next.**

   The wizard has you select a connection method. (See Figure 45-1.)

Network Setup Wizard

Select a connection method.

Select the statement that best describes this computer:

◉ This computer connects directly to the Internet. The other computers on my network connect to the Internet through this computer.
View an example.

○ This computer connects to the Internet through another computer on my network or through a residential gateway.
View an example.

○ Other

Learn more about home or small office network configurations.

< Back | Next > | Cancel

• **Figure 45-1: This connection method defines the way that your network connects to the Internet.**

Click the first button if you want to set up Internet Connection Sharing and you want this computer to be the ICS host. That's the case if the computer connects directly to the Internet — typically through a modem.

Click the second button if you want to connect this computer to the Internet through the network, but you don't want this computer to be the ICS host. That's the case if you've already identified a different Windows XP PC as the ICS host. It's also the case if you have a box (such as a residential gateway, router, DSL router, wireless broadband router, or Internet Address Sharing box) that controls access to the Internet. If you click this button, Windows XP doesn't set up Internet Connection Sharing on this PC, deferring instead to the box that controls Internet access.

Click the third button if (1) each of the PCs on the network connects independently to the Internet (say, each uses its own internal modem); or (2) your network isn't connected to the Internet.

9. **Select your connection method and then click Next.**

   What happens next depends on which connection method you chose:

If you chose the first connection method, the wizard asks you to identify your Internet connection.

This choice can be a little bit tricky because, in many cases, it isn't at all obvious which of your connections go out to the Internet.

If you can't identify your Internet connection offhand, click the Learn More About How to Determine Your Internet Connection link. Windows Help has a few hints that may help — including one trick that involves pulling the cable out of your router. That approach frequently identifies the correct connection quickly!

If you chose the second connection method, the wizard looks for multiple connections.

Typically this happens when you have two Ethernet connections: one for the network, and one for a router, DSL router, wireless router, or Internet Address Sharing box. In that case, the wizard tries to bridge the two connections automatically, effectively connecting one Ethernet network to the other.

In this situation, you don't want Windows XP to set up Internet Connection Sharing. All those duties are taken over by the box that connects to the Internet.

If you chose the third connection method, the wizard narrows down the choices. (See Figure 45-2.)

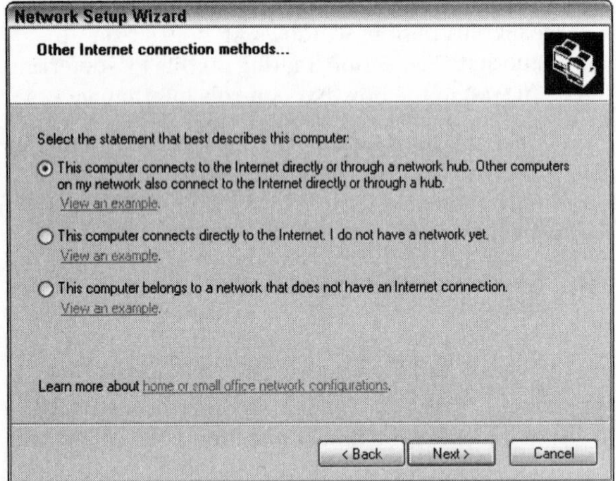

• **Figure 45-2: Pick the configuration that applies.**

If you choose the first method in Figure 45-2 and more than one potential Internet connection is defined on the PC, you're asked to specify which is the correct Internet connection.

10. In all cases, click Next.

The wizard asks for a computer name and description. (See Figure 45-3.) The name is crucial — it's used to identify your computer on your network. The description isn't critical.

You gave your computer a name when you installed Windows XP. If you have wished you could change the computer's name ever since then, do it now. This is the best way and time to change it. If you do change it, make the new name short, simple, and all letters and/or numbers. Avoid spaces or any punctuation marks.

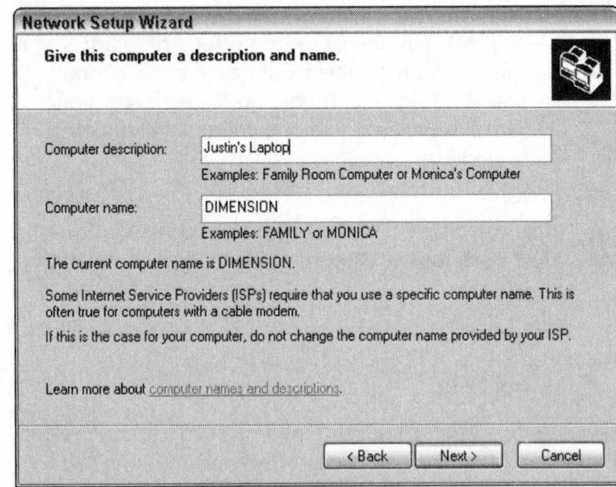

• **Figure 45-3: Give your computer an identity.**

11. Type a new name if you must and then click Next.

The wizard asks for a network name. Unless you have a very good reason to override it, use the default, which may be WORKGROUP or MSHOME.

12. Click Next.

Windows gives you one last chance to change your mind. (See Figure 45-4.)

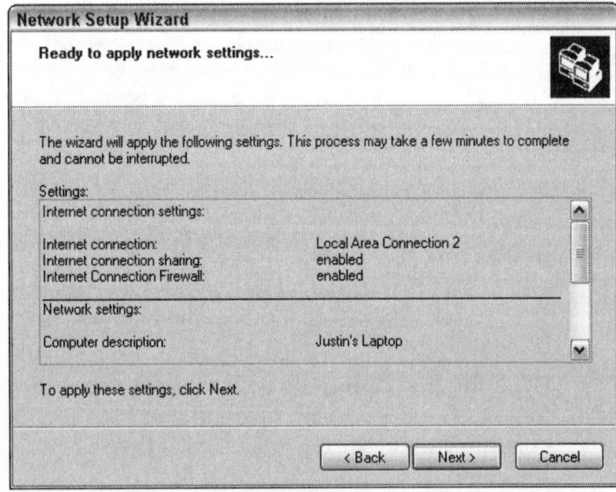

• **Figure 45-4: A quick review of what you've chosen.**

13. Review the settings, and if you need to change something, click the Back button to find the setting. Otherwise, click Next.

The wizard makes all the changes you've specified.

Be patient. Go do something else. This takes a while.

When Windows comes back, it asks how you want to run the Network Setup Wizard. (See Figure 45-5.)

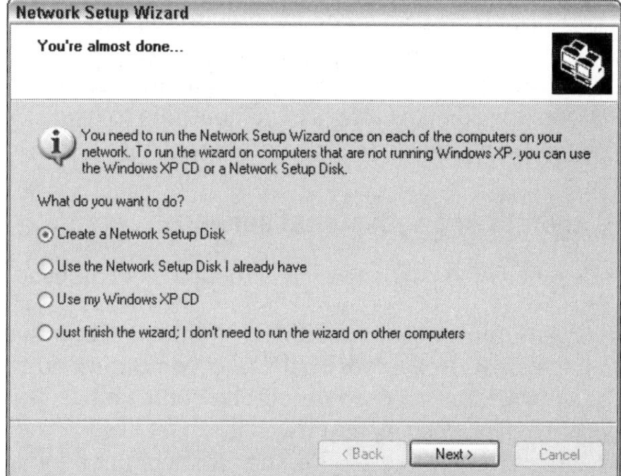

• **Figure 45-5: You always want to create a Network Setup Disk, unless all of your PCs have Windows XP Service Pack 2 or later.**

14. Always, always select Create a Network Setup Disk.

Why? Because Microsoft has released new versions of the Network Setup Wizard after Windows XP hit the stands — and may have released several more updated versions since then. If you use the Network Setup Wizard on the CD, you may have an older (read *more buggy*) version. On the other hand, if you're running Service Pack 2 or later, the version that you can put on a disk right now is the latest Microsoft has.

15. Click Next and go through the steps to create a Network Setup Wizard Disk.

It's easy.

16. When the wizard finishes on this PC, take the disk to each PC in turn. Put it in the disk drive, choose Start⇨Run, type A:\netsetup.exe**, and press Enter.**

You return to Step 6. Make sure that you click the second or third buttons in Step 8 each time. (It won't hurt anything if you make a mistake, but the wizard just won't run.)

Checking the Pieces

After you run the Network Setup Wizard on all the PCs on your network, you need to check to be sure that the computers can see each other.

To do that on a Windows XP computer, follow these steps:

1. Choose Start⇨My Network Places.

Windows Explorer shows you a list of folders that are available on other computers.

2. On the left, under Network Tasks, click View Workgroup Computers.

You see a list of all the computers connected to the network. (See Figure 45-6.)

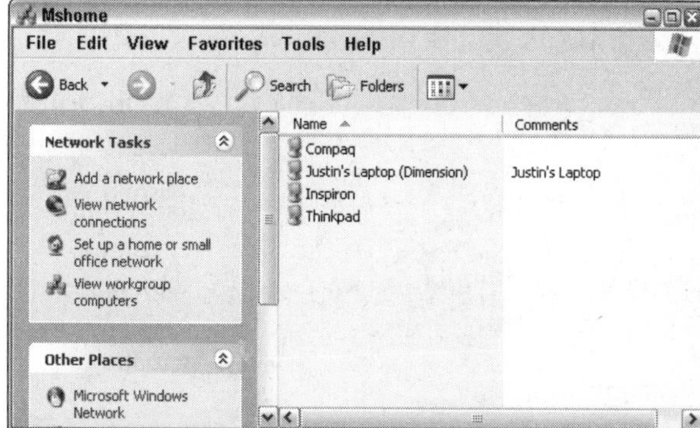

• **Figure 45-6: All the computers connected to the network.**

3. **If you can't see any computers, or only a few, under Other Places, click Microsoft Windows Network and then double-click WORKGROUP or MSHOME (or whatever network name you've chosen).**

4. **If that still doesn't work and you can remember the name of a computer on the network, choose Start⇨Run. Type `\\` and the name of the computer; then press Enter.**

   For example, for the computer called Dimension, choose Start⇨Run, type **\\Dimension** and press Enter. That brings the computer up, dislodging any lingering cobwebs.

Wireless networks are particularly vulnerable to intruders. Most wireless networks, installed precisely according to manufacturers' instructions, have little or no security enabled. That means that a neighbor or passerby may, in certain circumstances, be able to tap into your network. If you have a wireless network, follow the advice in Technique 46.

Understanding Addresses

If your network goes bump in the night, chances are very good that the problem can be traced back to addresses. Every computer on a network has to have an address. That's how computers on a network talk to each other — they use addresses.

IP addresses on the Internet

On the Internet, addresses take a very specific form: Each Internet address (called an *IP address*) is a set of four numbers, each between 0 and 255. For example, this valid IP address `208.215.179.139` just happens to be the address of the *For Dummies* server, `www.dummies.com`. The address for `www.microsoft.com` is `207.46.134.222`.

Perhaps obviously, no two computers can have the same IP address. If two computers had the same address, communication would get horribly messed up — not unlike two different people having the same telephone number or the same street address.

If you dial in to the Internet, every time you dial your Internet service provider, you're assigned an IP address, right there on the spot. Your computer picks up its IP address as part of the logging on process.

If you have a permanent connection to the Internet — typically with a residential gateway, cable modem, DSL router, or the like — you get an IP address, and it's yours to keep as long as you continue to use your current Internet service provider.

IP addresses on your local network

Now comes the part where most people get confused.

Every computer on your office or home network has to have an address, too. That's how computers on the network talk to each other. The confusion arises because these *local* IP addresses look just like Internet IP addresses. `192.168.0.1` is the most common local IP address on a plain-vanilla peer-to-peer small network. Most (but not all!) small networks have one computer with the address `192.168.0.1`. Most (but not all!) computers on a small network have addresses that look like this `192.168.0.x` where *x* is a number between 1 and 254.

Don't let the similarity in numbers fool you. IP addresses on the Internet work on the Internet. IP addresses on your home or office network work on your local network. IP addresses on your neighbor's home or office network work on her local network. Ne'er the twain — er, train — shall meet.

Just as in the case of the Internet, no two computers on your local network can have the same local IP address. That begs the obvious question: Who assigns them?

Assigning local IP addresses

Two ways to assign local IP addresses are available:

- You can type them yourself.
- You can let one — and *only one* — box assign them.

I use the term *box* generically here because several different kinds of assignors automatically assign local IP addresses:

- If you have Windows XP Internet Connection Sharing enabled on a PC, that PC assigns local IP addresses.
- If you have a residential gateway, router, DSL router, cable modem, wireless broadband router, Dynamic Address Translator, or some other Internet box attached to your network, that box may insist on assigning local IP addresses.

Confusingly, more than one box can try to assign addresses. That's when the bits hit the fan.

If you want your local IP addresses assigned automatically, one of the boxes has to be the designated top dog – and the others have to be told to keep their mutts, er, mitts off. If you have more than one box trying to assign local IP addresses on your network at the same time, you will have pandemonium.

See what I mean? It's all about addresses.

Static local IP addresses are ones you dole out by yourself and type by hand. Every time you reboot a PC with a static local IP address, it comes back with the same static local IP address.

Dynamic local IP addresses are assigned by a box called a DHCP Server. Everytime you reboot a PC with a dynamic local IP address, the PC asks the networks' DHCP Server to assign it an address.

Sometimes the only way you can get a network to work is by manually assigning static local IP addresses. Think of it as the last refuge of those whose networks are so messed up the boxes can't be trusted to assign addresses dynamically. Frequently, hardware manufacturers recommend that you dig into each computer and assign its IP address by hand — an approach you should greet with some fear and trepidation, as it indicates you're near the end of the rope. Here's how to switch between static and dynamic local IP address, and change a static addresses manually:

1. **Choose Start⇨Control Panel⇨Network and Internet Connections⇨Network Connections.**

   Windows shows you a list of all the network cards, modems, and any other devices that connect you to the network.

2. **In the list of network connections, right-click the connection to your local network and choose Properties.**

   You may have more than one connection — particularly if you're working on a PC with two network interface cards that bridge your local network to a router that connects to the Internet. Each network connection — which is to say, each network interface card — has its own local IP address. If necessary, in the list of network connections, right-click the connection for your local network and choose Remove from Bridge. Then continue with this step. When you're done, right-click the connection again and choose Add to Bridge.

   Windows responds with the Local Area Connection Properties dialog box, as shown in Figure 45-7.

3. **In the Properties dialog box, click Internet Protocol (TCP/IP); then click Properties.**

   Yes, your local network uses the same TCP/IP protocol as the Internet itself. (A *protocol* is a language that computers use to talk to each other.) Don't be confused. You're dealing with your local network here, not with the Internet.

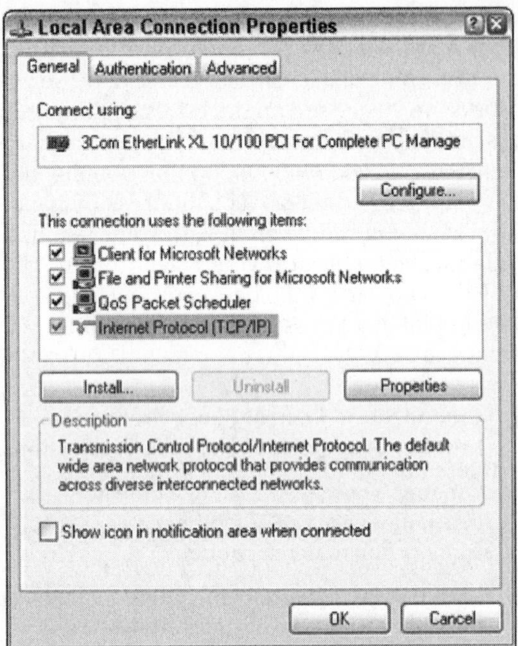

• Figure 45-7: The properties of your local network connection.

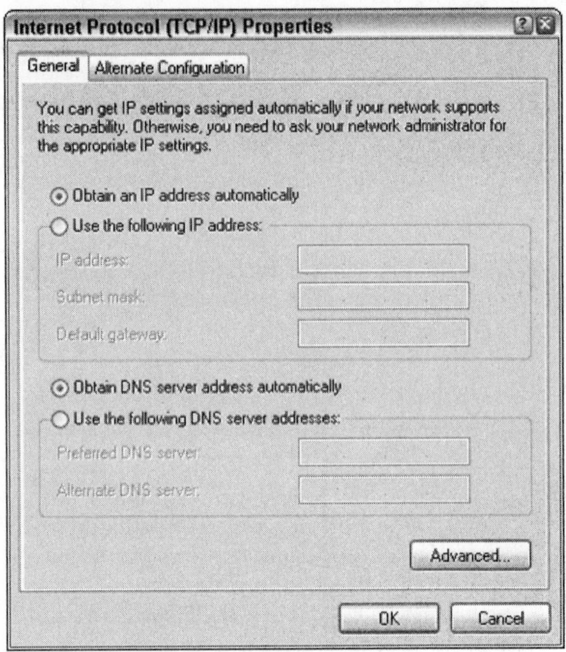

• Figure 45-8: Where your computer gets its *local* IP address.

Windows shows you the Internet Protocol (TCP/IP) Properties dialog box, as shown in Figure 45-8. Again, don't be confused: You're working with the local network, not with the Internet.

4. **If someone has assigned this computer a static local IP address, it appears in the Use the Following IP Address option. If you want to tell the computer to get its local IP address automatically, select the Obtain an IP Address Automatically option.**

5. **Click OK twice (once in the TCP/IP Properties dialog box, and again in the local network connection's dialog box), and the change takes effect immediately.**

More time has been wasted in this dialog box than in all the other networking dialog boxes combined.

Securing Your Wireless Network

Save Time By

- Using the Windows Network Setup Wizard the right way
- Getting your network secure in no time

The most important part of installing a wireless network comes after the network is up. You have to protect it against random intrusions, in spite of all the weird techy terminology. If you don't, your next door neighbor will be able to get onto your network, any time.

My first encounter with wireless networking really drove home the point. A friend of mine came over to the house and helped me put together a wireless network — a Linksys WRT54G wireless broadband router tied into an ADSL line. We had it up and running in no time flat, thanks largely to the Windows XP Network Setup Wizard (which I talk about in Technique 45). My friend started downloading a big file, using his portable and its built-in wireless chip.

One thing led to another, my friend got a phone call, and had to leave. As he was walking near the beach, a hundred meters or so away from the house, he sat down, pulled out his portable and opened it. With absolutely no effort on his part, Windows XP connected to my wireless home network, found its way to the Internet, and continued downloading the file.

Scary, eh?

If you have a wireless network, and you haven't taken the necessary steps to secure it, *anybody* can get onto your network with essentially no effort. He can use your Internet connection and — most alarmingly — go snooping all over your network, just as if he were sitting in your office, plugged into your router.

Securing your wireless network is vitally important.

Running the Wireless Network Setup Wizard

Windows XP Service Pack 2 has a lot of nifty new features, and one of the best is the wizard that helps you plug up your wireless network. You need a USB flash drive, or a USB flash card reader, and a free USB port on every computer attached to the wireless network.

If your wireless broadband router, wireless access point, or other wireless base station has a USB port, and it supports Windows Smart Network Key (another meaningless marketing term), you're in luck: The wizard can configure your entire network in a matter of minutes. If your router doesn't support WSNK, not to worry — entering the requisite codes by hand is pretty easy.

Here's how to get your wireless network secure:

1. **Choose Start⇨All Programs⇨Accessories⇨Communications⇨Wireless Network Setup Wizard.**

   The wizard shows its splash screen. Ignore the bafflegab. I don't think the text on the screen's accurate, but even if it is, it certainly isn't relevant.

2. **Click Next.**

   The wizard asks you to type in a name for your network (see Figure 46-1).

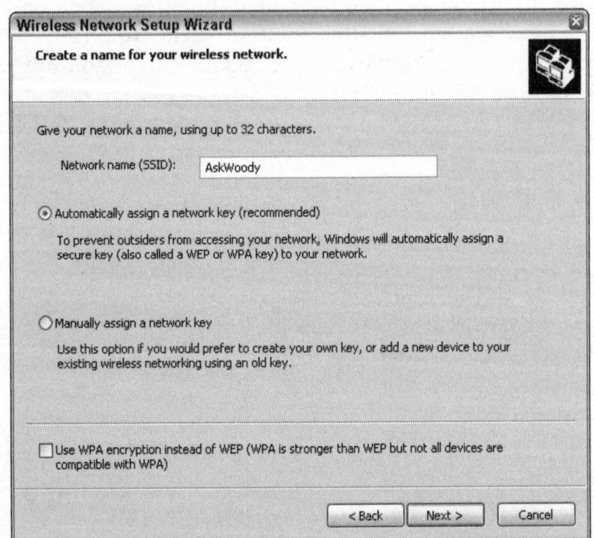

• Figure 46-1: All the security configuration settings are right here, in one easy location.

3. **Type a name for the network.**

   The name of the network is used for the wireless router's SSID (Service Set Identifier — yet another meaningless acronym), which the wireless box typically broadcasts to make it easy to connect. The SSID is the name that appears when you try to connect to a wireless network. Each wireless router has a default SSID: *tsunami*, *wireless*, and *linksys* are all common default SSIDs.

4. **Unless you already have a network key that you absolutely *must* use, select the Automatically Assign a Network Key radio button.**

5. **If your wireless base station and all the wireless cards on your network support WPA (if you have 802.11g, they may or may not; with 802.11b, it's unlikely), check the Use WPA Encryption box.**

   There *is* a performance hit for using either WEP or WPA encryption. Your network will run slower — but your neighbor won't be able to look at your files. Fair trade, eh?

6. **Click Next.**

   Behind the scenes, the wizard generates all the information it needs to set up a secure wireless network.

   The wizard asks if it can use a "key drive" (USB flash drive) to set up the network (see Figure 46-2).

7. **If you have a key drive (USB flash drive) handy, and a free USB port is on every computer on your network, and all of the computers on your network are running Windows XP Service Pack 2 or later, and your wireless router has a USB port *and* it understands WSNK (check the manual), select the Use a USB Flash Drive radio button. If not, select the Set Up a Network Manually radio button. Then click Next.**

   If you click the first button, the wizard takes you through the steps to transfer the settings to all the other computers on the network, as well as the wireless base station. Basically, you schlep the key drive to all the PCs, and they set themselves up.

• **Figure 46-2: Unfortunately, you can only use a key drive if your wireless router has a USB port, and it understands WSNK.**

If your hardware isn't quite up to the Dick Tracy stage yet, the wizard shows you its final instructions, as shown in Figure 46-3.

8. **Click Print Network Settings.**

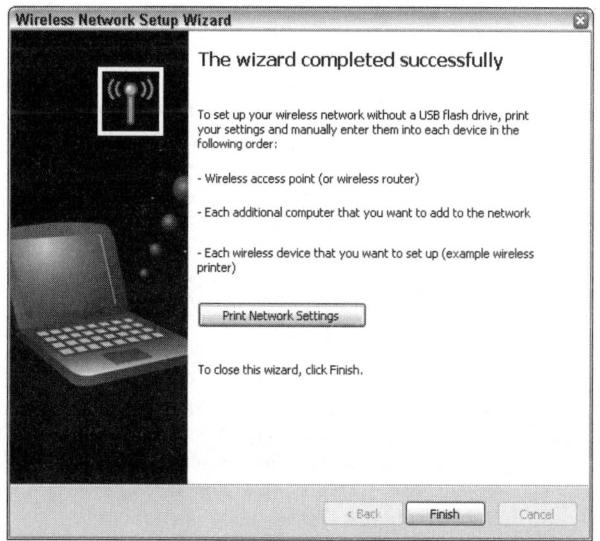

• **Figure 46-3: Print the details and enter them manually.**

The wizard doesn't actually print them. Instead, it opens Notepad and sticks the relevant settings in a new text file (see Figure 46-4).

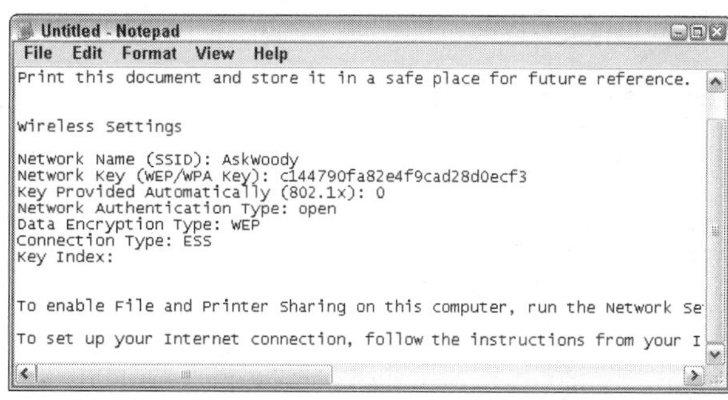

• **Figure 46-4: The settings that have to be entered into each wireless device.**

9. **Print the text file and follow the instructions to transfer the settings to each of your wireless devices manually.**

   It isn't as bad as it looks. See the next section.

Making Manual Changes

So you're stuck with entering wireless network security information by hand. Be of good cheer. The Wireless Network Setup Wizard (see the preceding section) does all the heavy lifting. If you're running Windows XP Service Pack 2 or later, it's pretty easy:

1. **Enter the new settings in your wireless router or access point.**

   Unfortunately, every one is different. You may have to dig into the router's manual. Usually, once you get inside the router, making the changes is easy (see Figure 46-5). The key you need to enter is the one that was generated by the Wireless Network Setup Wizard (refer to Figure 46-4).

2. **Make sure you update/apply/save the changes to the wireless router before leaving.**

   Many routers require you to save the changes manually, so they'll be around if the electricity goes out.

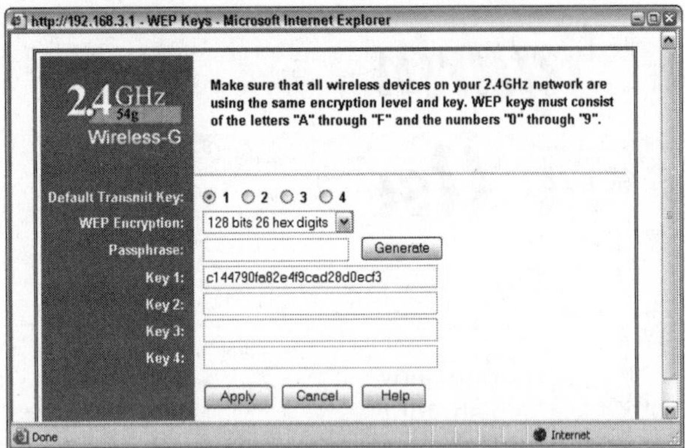

• **Figure 46-5: The Linksys WRT54G's WEP encryption key goes in a specific box. Other routers are similar.**

3. **Choose Start➪All Programs➪Accessories➪Communications➪Wireless Network Setup Wizard.**

   You see that really confusing splash screen again.

4. **Click Next.**

   The wizard asks for a network name (see Figure 46-6).

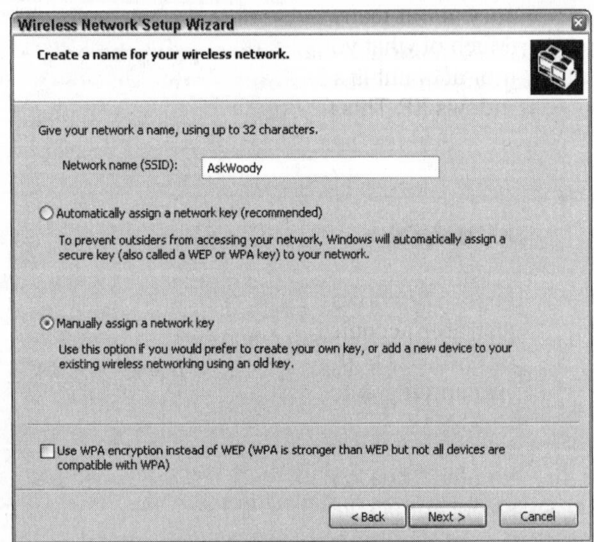

• **Figure 46-6: Tell the wizard that you need to manually assign a network key.**

5. **Type the network name precisely the same way that it appears in the printout from the preceding section. Select the Manually Assign a Network Key radio button and click Next.**

   The wizard asks you to type the key (see Figure 46-7).

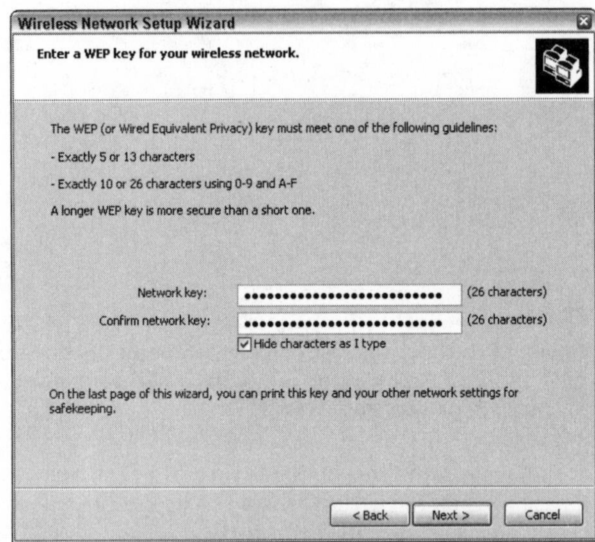

• **Figure 46-7: Enter that abysmally long (but ultra secure!) key.**

6. **Click Next.**

   You end up at Step 7 in the preceding section, from which point you can print your settings or just close down the wizard.

7. **Repeat Steps 3 through 7 on each computer in your wireless network.**

The end result: a very secure wireless network that works like a-ringin' a bell!

If you need help configuring a computer that isn't running Windows XP Service Pack 2 or later — or if you're interested in learning what all those obfuscating three letter acronyms really mean — check out *Wireless Home Networking For Dummies* by Danny Briere, Walter Bruce, and Pat Hurley.

Technique 47: Adding and Configuring a New User

Save Time By

- Setting up new users on your computer quickly and correctly
- Choosing security settings that are right for you
- Understanding the crucial difference between accounts
- Avoiding the bogus information you see in print about the Guest account

If you're connected to a Big Corporate Network (BCN), skip this technique entirely. The network administrator controls all the user capabilities on a Big Corporate Network. The only way you can change anything about users on a BCN is by convincing or cajoling the network administrator into changing things. Bribery may work. Calling him the "Network Admini" is not recommended.

On the other hand, if your computer sits by itself in a corner, or if you have a peer-to-peer *workgroup* network, setting up accounts for each person who uses the computer can be a worthwhile, timesaving endeavor. It won't do much to keep prying eyes from viewing your files, unless you go to great lengths to hide things, but having one account for each user can go a long way toward keeping people from accidentally bumping into each other.

This technique tells you what you need to know about user accounts. It also gives you the straight story about many topics that have been garbled in the press and online: Much of what you may have read about Guest accounts and the Administrator account is accurate for Windows 2000, but completely wrong for Windows XP. This technique sets the record straight.

Grasping User Accounts

If you bought a new computer with Windows XP installed, it probably has two accounts: the Administrator account and the Guest account. You may or may not be able to see either or both. When you first turned on your computer, it may have prompted you to create a new account.

If you installed Windows XP, you set up one or more accounts for the people who will be using the computer. Thus, a minimum of three users are generally available: the Administrator account, the Guest account, and whatever account you set up — probably one with your name on it.

Microsoft has jimmied things a bit, so you may never see the Administrator account or the Guest account. That's probably a good thing. You need both accounts, whether you realize it or not — yes, even if you tell Windows to disable the Guest account because you think it reduces security exposures (it won't, as you see later in this technique).

You have only two good reasons for adding more accounts to your computer:

- Security
- Convenience

Most people add new accounts to their PCs because they think that doing so keeps other users out of their files. That's bogus. Unless you understand the details, adding a user account to keep people out of your files is a waste of time. Boosting security on a plain-Jane Windows XP computer entails much more than setting up a password-protected user account or adding a password to your own account. See "Increasing security with passwords," later in this technique.

On the other hand, having separate accounts for each person who uses a computer can be enormously convenient. It's also a good way to keep neophytes from accidentally clobbering other users. Many a time-consuming tragedy has been averted this way. In some situations, you *can* keep other people out of your files by adding new accounts, but the process is difficult and entails some risk (see Technique 48).

Recognizing account types

Windows XP set up on a Big Corporate Network (a client-server *domain* network) inherits all the account security restrictions imposed by the server. Nothing in this technique applies to PCs running on a BCN. To do anything, you have to contact your network administrator.

In all other circumstances, Windows XP has two built-in types of users:

- **Computer Administrator:** This account has full access to everything on the computer.
- **Limited user account:** People with this type of account can change their own settings, read and write files in their own My Documents folder, and look at files in shared folders. That's it.

Although changing the capabilities of these two types of accounts in some circumstances is possible, at least in Windows XP Professional, you're better off not trying. (You can also add new types of accounts in Win XP Pro.) Making mistakes with difficult, time-consuming repercussions is easy. Stay away from the Windows XP Professional Local Users and Groups console unless you know what you're doing, and you have an overwhelming reason to change how these types of accounts work.

Chances are pretty good your computer has three accounts:

- **One with your name:** This is a Computer Administrator account (not to be confused with *the* Administrator account), with full control over the machine. My original account is called Woody.
- **Administrator:** That's the name of the account. In most cases, you can't see the account called Administrator. That's why it's so confusing. The Administrator account is, as you might imagine, a Computer Administrator account. With apologies to Joseph Heller, Administrator is kind of like having an Army Major called Major Major.

  If you have Windows XP Professional Edition, you gave Administrator a password when you installed Windows — even if you don't remember that password. If you have Windows XP Home Edition, the Administrator account's password is blank.

All this folderol about an account called Administrator probably sounds like a tempest in a teapot, but Administrator can perform some actions that other accounts can't. Many of those actions have to do with resuscitating a nearly dead Windows installation. Under normal circumstances you have no need to use Administrator – indeed, Windows goes to great lengths to hide it from you. But in some dire circumstances (see, for example, Technique 63), you can only use the Administrator account to get your system out of trouble.

- **Guest:** That's also the name of an account. The Guest account is generally invisible unless you specifically make it visible. Guest is a vital account, an account that Windows uses to make many different features work. The Guest account is a limited account, with one additional restriction: You can't put a password on the Guest account.

Computer Administrator accounts are frequently called Administrator accounts, and accounts with Administrator privileges are called Admin accounts, or simply Administrators. Only one account on your PC is actually called Administrator. You can have many accounts that are Computer Administrator accounts.

Of the three initial accounts — the one with your name on it, the Administrator account, and the Guest account — you can usually see only one: yours. The other two are lurking around, though, and as you will see, they are crucial.

By the way, all Computer Administrator accounts are created equal. Just because your account was the first Computer Administrator account doesn't give you any special privileges. (*The* administrator account — that is, the account called "Administrator" — has extra privileges, but they only come into play when you're digging deep inside your computer.) All limited user accounts are equal, too.

Working with account types

Computer Administrator user accounts (including the hidden one called Administrator) can perform the following functions:

- Add or remove other accounts (except Administrator, Guest, and your own account)
- Change passwords and require or remove passwords for any account (except Administrator and Guest)
- Change Windows XP read/write/access permissions for any drive, folder, or file
- Create, open, modify, or delete files anywhere on the PC, except in Encrypting File System protected folders (refer to Technique 8)
- Change Registry settings for all users

An administrator can see the contents of any file on the system unless the file's been encrypted by using, say, the Encrypting File System (refer to Technique 8), an application's password-protection mechanism, or Windows' Information Rights Management technology. All three of those file-locking methods operate independently of Windows XP.

Because Administrator accounts can create files in important places, such as `C:\Program Files`, and administrators can modify the Registry, you usually need an Administrator account to install a program. You also usually need an Administrator account to install new hardware.

By contrast, people with limited user accounts can perform only the following functions:

- Change their own password or require/remove passwords on their own account
- Create, open, modify, or delete files in shared areas, including (usually) the Shared Documents folder
- Create, open, modify, or delete files in My Documents

The powers granted to a limited account usually restrict limited user accounts to running programs but not installing them.

The limited account called Guest can do all those limited account things except require a password for the account.

Increasing security with passwords

Many Windows XP users with stand-alone machines or small (peer-to-peer workgroup) networks think that they can keep other people out of their files by putting a password on their account, and then creating new accounts and requiring passwords on those accounts.

It's a crock.

Windows XP's accounts were built for convenience, not security.

If you want to keep data on one machine from being viewed by users on a different machine, Windows XP, straight out of the box, gives you all the tools you need for coarse, quick, and generally quite usable control. See Technique 48 for details on Simple File Sharing.

If you want to keep multiple users on one machine from seeing or clobbering each other's files, the situation becomes much more complex. You can't simply put passwords on some accounts, or make some accounts limited user accounts. You have to change a bunch of settings — and give up a lot of flexibility. In particular, you have to set up one account that will be in control, and relegate all the other people using the computer to limited user account status. Among other things, that means only one account is capable of installing new programs or hardware. Keeping your data away from the prying eyes of other people who use your computer is a difficult, time-consuming task.

Here's what you have to do:

1. **Use Windows XP Professional Edition.**

   The steps here only apply to Windows XP Professional.

Windows XP Home Edition doesn't have the functionality to completely ensure that multiple users can't access each other's files.

2. **Allow one user to be in control.**

   That one user gets an Administrator account. All other users must have more restricted accounts — typically, that means all the other users must have limited user accounts. If you have more than one Administrator account on a PC, all except one must be deleted. Then you can create new limited user accounts to replace the deleted ones. See the next section for details on setting up new accounts.

Anyone with an Administrator account can change the password of any other user. Unless you spend a substantial amount of time juggling permissions, one user gets an Administrator account, and everybody else becomes a limited user. And that means that only one person can install programs on the PC, add new hardware, and so on.

3. **Password-protect the account of anyone who wishes to protect his or her files from other users of the computer.**

   Refer to Technique 9 for details.

4. **Require any user with a password to create a password reset disk.**

   See Technique 65 for more information.

5. **Put the protected file or folder on a hard drive that uses NTFS.**

   I discuss NTFS in Technique 67.

Old-fashioned FAT32 drives can't be protected.

To see what kind of drive you have, choose Start➪My Computer, right-click the drive, and choose Properties. You see the dialog box shown in Figure 47-1.

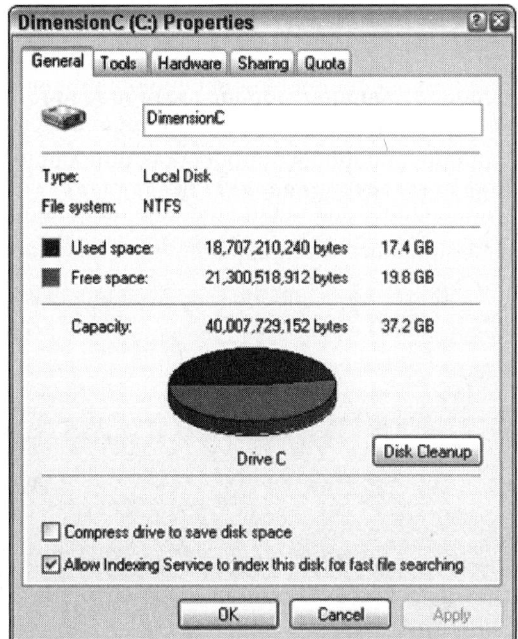

• **Figure 47-1: You can protect only NTFS drives.**

6. **Switch off the Windows XP Simple File System.**

   Simple File System is the default file protection mechanism inside XP. Instead, you want to bring back the old Windows 2000 file sharing system, which I explain how to do in Technique 48.

7. **Explicitly protect the files or folders that you want to keep from prying eyes.**

   See Technique 48 for details.

Those are the steps necessary to make sure that other people using your computer can't see or delete your files. The process is time-consuming and abounds with hidden gotchas. The vast majority of people who believe their PC is set up to protect data from prying eyes or accidental deletion are sadly mistaken. Keeping other people out of your data entails much, much more than requiring passwords or checking an obscure box.

The bottom line: Setting up bulletproof protection from prying eyes and clobbered files takes a lot of time and effort.

Administrator accounts and viruses

Unless you do something to change the situation, every new account created on a Windows XP PC is a full-blown Computer Administrator account. Some people think that you shouldn't use Administrator accounts for everyday work — that most users only need a limited user account.

Many Windows XP experts suggest that you create two accounts for each user:

- An Administrator account that you can use to install hardware and software and make major changes (such as adding a new account)
- A plain, limited account for everyday work

The rationale is straightforward: If you're using an Administrator account and you accidentally run into a virus (or a Trojan horse, worm, or the next big, scary security threat), that bad program automatically inherits your authority. So if you're using an Administrator account, the bad program can wipe out your hard drive or do just about anything it likes.

In actuality, though, the level of protection afforded by running as a limited user isn't all that great. Malicious programs that can crack Outlook's address book, for example, can certainly attack the address books of all accounts on the computer, whether they're Administrator accounts or limited user accounts. And any program that deletes My Documents can get all the My Documents folders on the machine, guaranteed. Anyway, your antivirus software should be looking for malicious programs and protecting your entire machine. That's simply not the job of an Administrator account.

Of course, if you're using a limited account and you bump into a virus, Trojan horse, worm, or some other form of sniveling scumware, the program can't do as much damage. Because malware inherits your authority (and limited user accounts don't have much authority), you may be slightly better off. Slightly. After all, you still have a virus infecting your machine.

Using simple, common-sense protection

If you need intricate file security — where large numbers of individuals or groups of individuals are allowed access to specific folders — you need more than Windows XP. You really need a Big Corporate Network, with servers running Active Directory.

If your file security needs are relatively modest — say, you want to protect your My Documents folder so that only you can see what's inside, and you don't want to allow anyone to delete the files — you can follow the steps in the preceding section and lock down your folder. In order to get that to work, though, everyone else who uses your PC must have a limited user account. They won't be able to install any programs or new hardware.

Windows XP's accounts were built for convenience, not security.

Most individuals, families, and small offices don't need fancy security settings. In most cases, you can keep things simple but secure. I've boiled down a lot of experience into a handful of recommendations:

- **Password-protect files that you don't want others to see.** Use the password protection available in the application that created the file (such as Word, Outlook, or Excel). Most applications allow you to set a password that's required to open a file, and a second password that's necessary to change the file. This doesn't prevent a malicious or misguided person from deleting the file — you always need good backups — but as long as the Recycle Bin isn't emptied frequently, simple password protection works pretty darn well.
- **If a user can't be trusted to use an antivirus program religiously or has a bad habit of downloading and installing scummy programs from the Internet, give that user a limited account.** Better, make Windows show the Guest account on the welcome screen (Start➪Control Panel➪User Accounts➪Guest➪Turn On the Guest Account) and let your neophytes use Guest.
- **Give everybody else a standard (Computer Administrator) account.** But be merciless in your insistence that they use antivirus software.
- **Put files in Shared Documents only if you're willing to see them deleted.**

Creating a New Account

If you have a Computer Administrator account (unless someone has changed it, chances are good your account is a Computer Administrator account), creating a new account couldn't be simpler:

1. **Choose Start➪Control Panel➪User Accounts.**

   Windows shows you the User Accounts dialog box, shown in Figure 47-2.

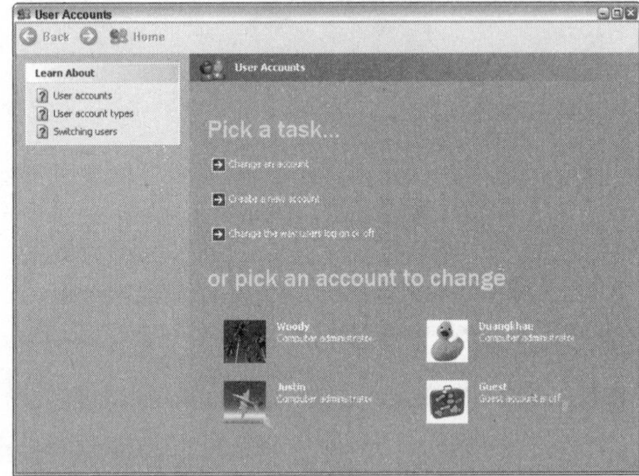

• **Figure 47-2: User Accounts central.**

2. **Click the Create a New Account line.**

   You see the Create a New Account dialog box, shown in Figure 47-3.

   To make your life simpler, use a short, simple name, with no spaces or punctuation marks.

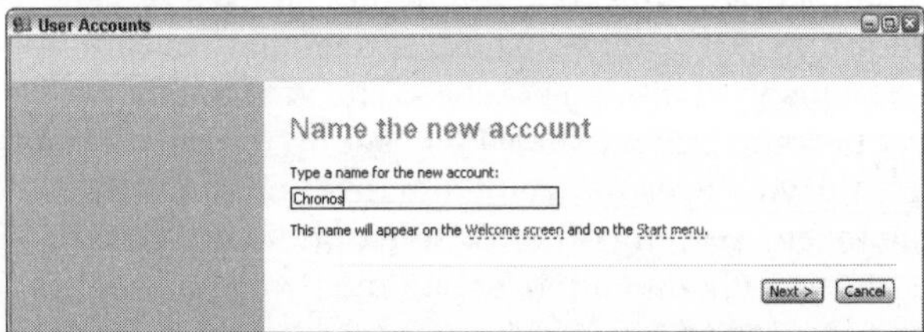

• **Figure 47-3: The name you enter here becomes the name of a folder in the Documents and Settings folder.**

3. Type a name and click Next.

Windows asks you to pick an account type (as shown in Figure 47-4).

If you can trust a person to run antivirus software reliably — and not download any scummy programs from the Internet — she probably is a good candidate for a Computer Administrator account. Besides, if you give her an Administrator account, she can install her own programs, and she won't have to come running to you every time she needs to do something that's "restricted."

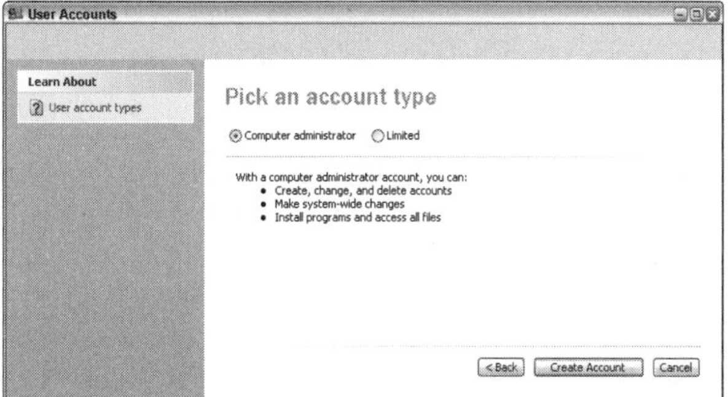

• Figure 47-4: People who don't use antivirus software all the time should probably be assigned a limited user account.

4. Choose between an Administrator account and a limited account and then click Create Account.

The new account becomes available immediately.

Modifying an Account

If you have a limited account, you can change your own name, password, and picture. Computer Administrator accounts, on the other hand, can change every detail of every account. A person with an Administrator account can add new accounts or delete existing accounts — along with all the data associated with an existing account. Administrator accounts can do just about anything.

Yes, you read that right. Say your PC has two Administrator accounts, called Woody and Justin. Woody can go into Justin's account, change Justin's password, then log in as Justin, and do anything that Justin can do. Woody doesn't need to know Justin's current password in order to change it. Conversely, Justin can modify Woody's password, log in as Woody, and do anything Woody can do. Even worse, Woody can delete Justin's account, and all his data — permanently — even if Justin's account has a password, and Woody doesn't know what the password is. See why I say that Windows XP accounts are made for convenience, not security?

If you have an Administrator account and you choose Start➪Control Panel➪User Accounts and then pick an account (see Figure 47-5), you have the following choices:

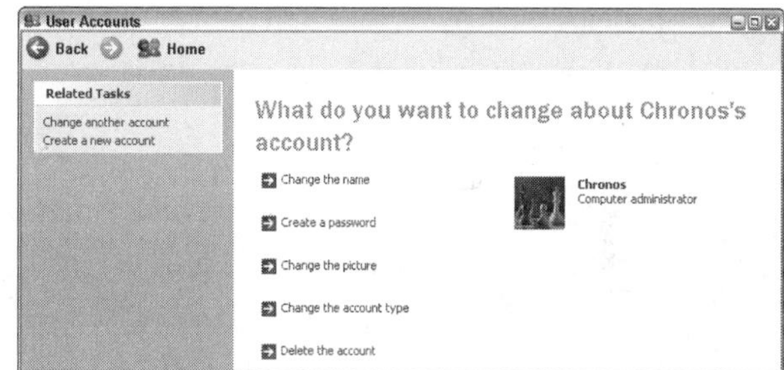

• Figure 47-5: Making changes to Chronos's account.

- **Change the name:** When you set up the account, the name you choose is permanently, indelibly used as the name of the Documents and Settings folder for the user. After the account is set up, changing the name changes only what appears on the welcome screen, at the top of the Start menu, and in this User Accounts dialog box.

The first time you enter a user's name — when you set up the new account — choose something short and sweet, so when you go spelunking through the Documents and Settings folder, you don't have to wade through lots of junk. (You'll probably end up typing the folder name many times, too.) After the account is set up, though, you have no need to be so conservative. Turn the name into anything you like.

- **Create or change a password:** You can force this account to use a password. If you're twiddling with another user's account, setting a password for the user (or changing an existing one) can effectively keep the user off the machine. And you don't even need to know the user's current password in order to make the change. Ouch.
- **Change the picture:** Change the picture that appears on the welcome screen and at the top of the Start menu.

  In the User Accounts dialog box (refer to Figure 47-5), click Change the Picture. Windows responds with the Pick a New Picture dialog box, as shown in Figure 47-6. Click the picture you want, click Change Picture, and then exit the User Accounts dialog box.

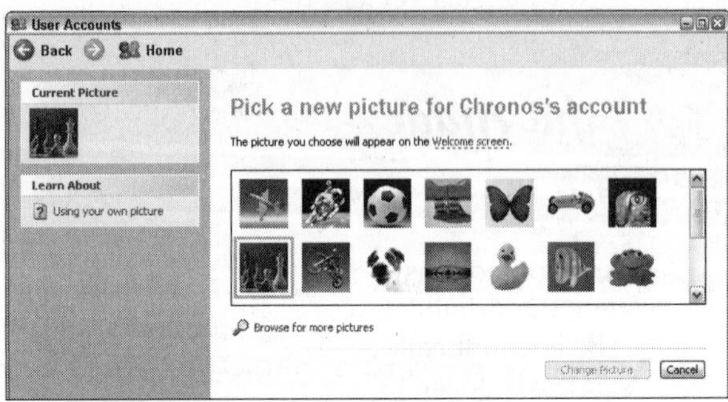

• **Figure 47-6: Pick a pic.**

If you want to stick with Windows' politically correct selection, go ahead and pick a picture from the list. But if you want to have some fun, click Browse For More Pictures. Windows lets you choose a picture from just about anywhere (as shown in Figure 47-7). In fact, Windows squishes any picture down to size for you. Square pictures work best because Windows can squish them down without putting in any white space.

• **Figure 47-7: Pick a picture, and Windows makes a 48-x-48 pixel thumbnail.**

- **Change the account type:** Switch from Computer Administrator to limited and back again.
- **Delete the account:** Delete another user's account. Yes. That's right. Just like that. You aren't given this option if you're working on your own account. The user who's logged on cannot delete his or her own account.

When you delete an account, Windows gives you the option of saving some of the files associated with the account (as shown in Figure 47-8). Save the files! After Windows deletes the files, they're gone for good. They're not in the Recycle Bin. They are really gone.

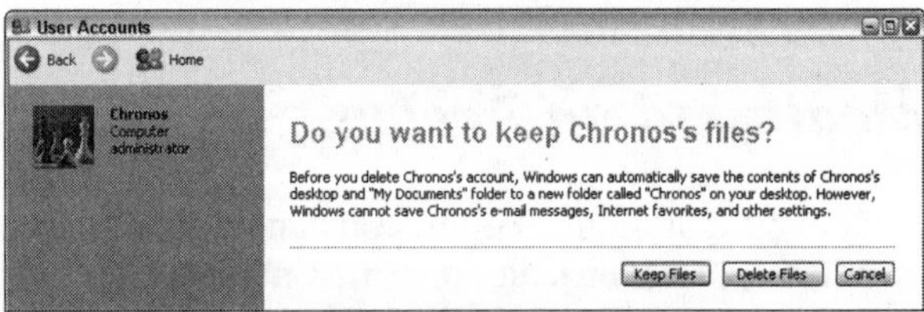

• **Figure 47-8: Deleting a user removes all of that user's folders. Careful!**

Normally, all users except the two hidden users — the account called Administrator and the account called Guest — show up on the Windows welcome screen. In some cases, you may want to remove an account from the welcome screen, thus making it a little bit harder for someone to "accidentally" log on pretending to be you. The easiest way to remove an account from the welcome screen is with TweakUI:

1. **Download and install TweakUI.**

   I talk about TweakUI in Technique 5.

2. **Choose Start⇨All Programs⇨PowerToys for Windows XP⇨TweakUI for Windows XP.**

3. **On the left, double-click Logon.**

   TweakUI shows you a list of all the names on the welcome screen (as shown in Figure 47-9).

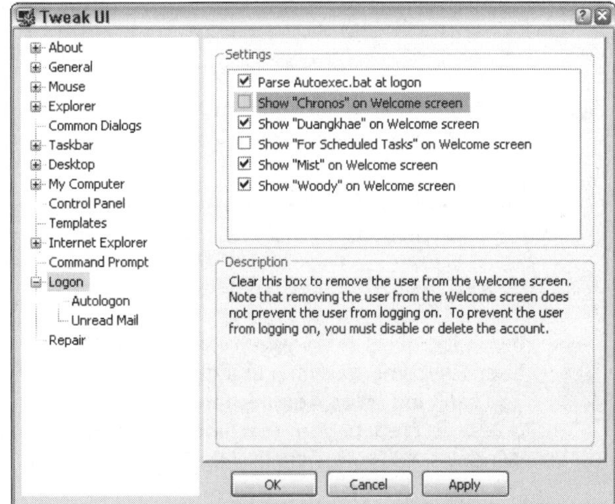

• Figure 47-9: Each name on the welcome screen appears here.

4. **Uncheck the boxes next to the items that you want removed from the welcome screen.**

TweakUI also can set up one ID to log on automatically, bypassing the welcome screen. To do so, double-click Autologon on the left and click the Log on Automatically At System Startup box (as shown in Figure 47-10).

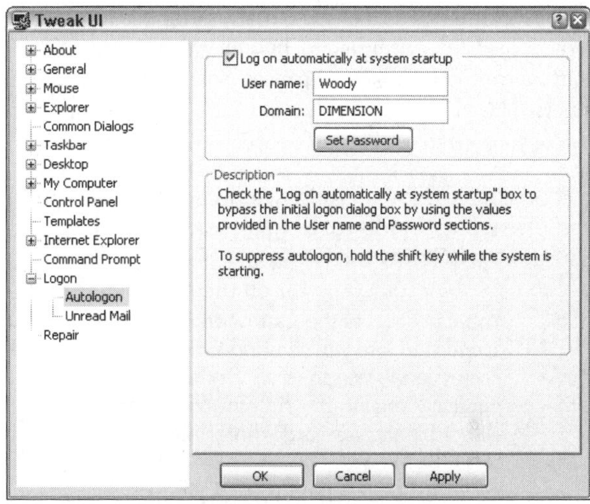

• Figure 47-10: TweakUI can set Windows so it automatically starts one user.

5. **Click OK. Check the results by choosing Start⇨Log Off⇨Switch Users (or use the Fast User Switch icon from Technique 6).**

Using the Hidden Administrator Account

The moment you add just one user account to your system, the Administrator account (which is to say, the account called Administrator) effectively vanishes: It doesn't show up on the welcome screen; there's no Administrator account in the User Accounts dialog box (refer to Figure 47-11); TweakUI won't show it (refer to Figure 47-9); there isn't even an Administrator folder hanging off of the Documents and Settings folder.

Under normal circumstances, you don't want to mess with Administrator: It exists primarily so you can get into Windows in Safe Mode, to run the System Recovery Console (see Technique 63), and to make changes deep inside Windows when an emergency arises. There are occasions when you need to log on with Administrator. For example, if you have only one Computer Administrator account on your PC, that account is password-protected. If you forget the password, your only choice is to log on as Administrator and change the password.

It is possible to log on to the Administrator account if you're using Windows XP Professional. And, of course, if you know the tricks.

You can't access the main Administrator account unless you're using Windows XP Professional. Windows XP Home Edition automatically sets up the Administrator account with a blank password — in effect, no password. But in order to log on as Administrator you must have a password. (Catch-22. Joseph Heller would be proud.) Microsoft intentionally built XP Home Edition this way to keep the unwashed masses from jimmying around their Administrator accounts. If you use XP Home Edition and you absolutely must give your Administrator account a password, choose StartÍRun, type **control userpasswords2**, press Enter, and click the Reset Password button (shown in Figure 47-11).

To log on with the account called Administrator, if you're using Windows XP Professional, follow these steps:

1. **Make sure that every user on the PC is logged off.**

   This is a critical step.

If Fast User Switching is enabled, as shown in Technique 8, everybody has to be logged off the machine before you can log on as Administrator.

2. **At the welcome screen, hold down Ctrl+Alt, and then press the Delete key twice.**

   That brings up a Windows 2000-style logon dialog box.

• **Figure 47-11: The only way to give an XP Home Administrator account a password.**

3. **Type** Administrator **as your user name, enter your password, and click OK.**

   Windows logs you on as Administrator.

If you log on as Administrator and use Fast User Switching to switch to a different user, you can't log on as Administrator again unless you reboot your machine. It's a bug in Windows XP Professional.

If you're using Windows XP Home, there's only one way to log on with the account called Administrator: You must log on in Safe Mode. For details, see Technique 63.

Hobbling the Guest Account

I know, I know. You really want to turn off the account called Guest because you know it doesn't have a password and you're worried that some hacker or bad program is going to get into it.

Relax.

In the old days, a guest account on a networked PC served as a convenient way to let people onto a PC or network temporarily. The guest didn't need to know a password to log on, but the guest couldn't perform as many computing functions, either. That's where the term "guest" came from.

In XP, Windows makes it easy to "turn on" or "turn off" the Guest account. Here's how:

1. **Choose Start⇨Control Panel⇨User Accounts.**

   The Guest account is the last account listed. If Guest appears as one of the accounts on the Windows welcome screen, you see an on-screen message that says `Guest account is on` (see Figure 47-12). If no Guest account is on the welcome screen, Windows says `Guest account is off`.

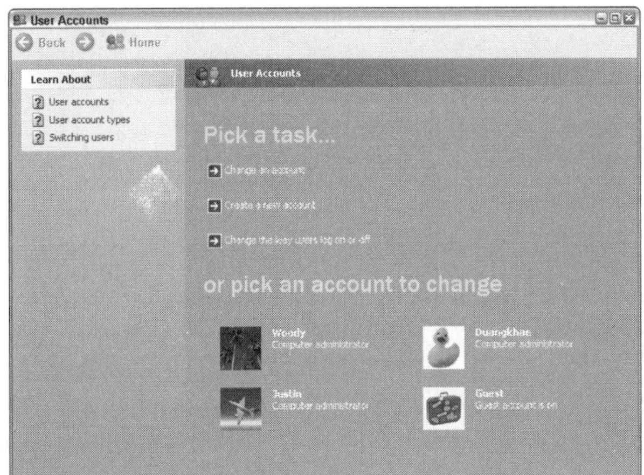

• **Figure 47-12: The Guest account is on — which means that it's visible on the welcome screen.**

2. **Click the Guest account.**

   You see the User Accounts dialog box, as shown in Figure 47-13.

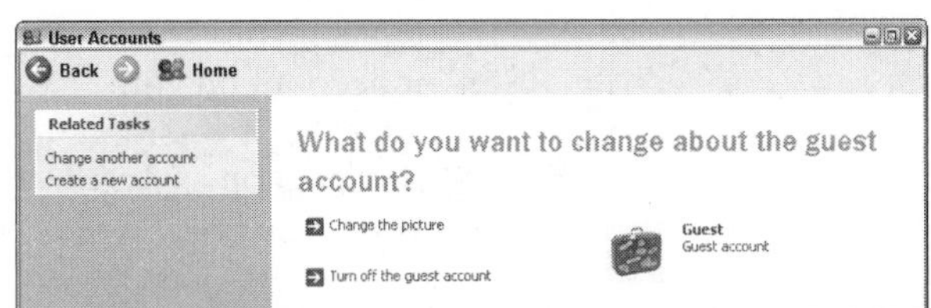

• **Figure 47-13: Not many choices for Guest.**

3. **If you don't want Guest to be visible on the welcome screen, click Turn Off the Guest Account. If you want Guest to be visible, click Turn On the Guest Account.**

4. **Close the User Accounts dialog box.**

You might assume that this procedure turns the account called Guest on or off. It doesn't. Windows XP is fooling you. In Windows XP, Guest plays a pivotal role. Among other things, Windows uses Guest to communicate between computers, run print jobs, and perform a plethora of other behind-the-scenes functions. Windows can't let you turn off the Guest account. If you did, all sorts of things would go bump in the night.

You may find detailed instructions on the Web that show you how to really turn off Guest. It's difficult, but it can be done. Resist the temptation. Leave Guest going.

Guest gets a bad rap

I'm astounded by how much drivel regarding the Guest account has appeared in print, so let me dispel some falsehoods and misconceptions. If you're feeling nervous about the Guest account, the following points should help calm your fears:

- **Nobody and nothing can surreptitiously log on to your computer via the Guest account.** The Guest account hasn't become a convenient entry point for hackers, as one publication put it. If you decide to put the Guest account on your welcome screen, it's like any other limited account. If you don't put it on the welcome screen, nobody can steal it.

- **Guest is the means by which other users connect to your computer.** Say there's a password-protected Administrator account on my machine called Justin. If someone logs on to my machine from the network with Justin's name and password, that person is *not* given Administrator account capabilities — even though Justin is an Administrator account. Anyone who logs on from the network is only given the capabilities of the lowly *Guest* account.

- **The Guest account is absolutely vital.** In addition to providing the means for other people to log on to your computer, Guest operates behind the scenes in Internet Connection Sharing and with file and printer sharing. It's okay to hide the account on the welcome screen, using Windows XP's settings. But don't follow the advice you occasionally see on the Web, dig deep into Windows, and delete the account. You need it.

Technique 48: Sharing Drives and Folders

Save Time By

- Using Simple File Sharing effectively
- Choosing the right level of protection for your drives and folders
- Solving common sharing problems quickly

Most people set up a small office or home network to share an Internet connection, a few files or folders, and a printer or some other piece(s) of hardware.

Although sharing an Internet connection and some hardware is a very straightforward goal — you can either print from all the computers on your network, or something's wrong — file and drive sharing rapidly turns these basic concepts from black-and-white to shades of gray (not to mention fuchsia and indigo).

You can spend a lot of time sweating the intricacies of file sharing; in fact, companies with Big Corporate Networks (BCNs) have entire teams that handle nothing but the inherent turf wars — er, *access permission settings* — that exist in complex information-sharing environments.

If you have a real need for complex sharing rules, you should look into a meatier program, such as Windows 2003 Server's Active Directory, to supplement Windows XP.

On the other hand, if your needs are simple, Windows XP can handle them — quickly, easily, and effectively, if you understand the nuances. That's what this technique is all about: the nuances of sharing folders and drives across a network, or sharing folders among multiple users on a single PC.

Keeping File Sharing Simple

If you use Windows XP Professional on a Big Corporate Network (that is, a client/server network — what Microsoft calls a *domain*), you automatically receive an entire suite of tools for managing who can get at what files or folders or drives on your machine — the *permissions* you grant to let people get at data on your PC. You can choose which individual users or groups of users can see this or change that; you can assign passwords to unlock folders, files, or drives; you can even allow specific users onto your PC or block them entirely, based on the time of the day or the phase of the moon. Okay, I'm exaggerating. A little bit.

You could spend half your working day juggling permissions and sweating endless rivulets of small stuff. If you have a domain, your network administrator gets to deal with most of the arcana. Thank heaven for network admins.

Windows XP Home Edition machines and Windows XP Professional Edition machines that aren't connected to a BCN are automatically set up with Simple File Sharing. *SFS* is a four-sizes-fits-all approach that most people can live with, but some people can't.

In general, SFS is a great fit. In particular, however, SFS won't work for you if you require one or more of the following:

- **The capability for users to have the same access permissions regardless of the computer:** If you want to log on to *any* computer on the network and access your files the same way you could if you were working at your usual machine, SFS won't work for you.
- **The capability to password-protect folders:** You can almost always password-protect individual files by using the application that made the file. You can also password-protect compressed files by using a file compression product, such as WinZip (`www.winzip.com`). But having passwords apply to a whole folder is an entirely different can of worms, and SFS doesn't have a can opener.
- **The capability to grant specific users (or groups of users) on the network unusual capabilities:** If you want to give most users the ability to open all the files in a folder but only give a handful the ability to change them (see Figure 48-1), SFS isn't the tool for you. Windows 2000 lets you fine-tune permissions such as these in great detail. Windows XP Professional even lets you throw out SFS and bring back the (not-so-) good ol' Windows 2000 method of granting permissions. But SFS can't give you this level of control.

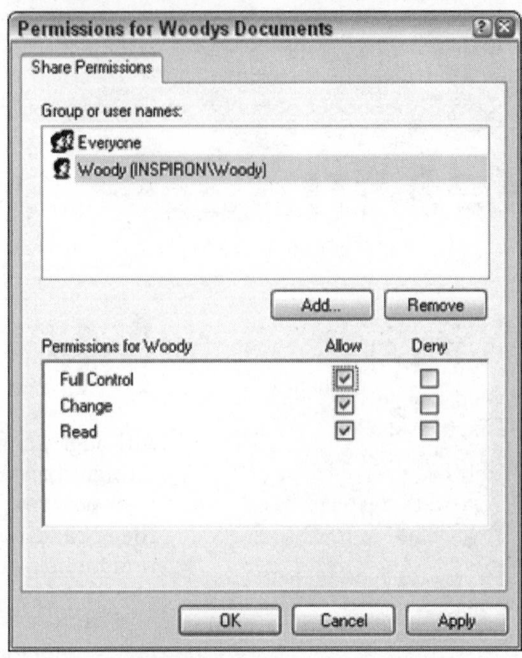

• **Figure 48-1: Windows XP Professional with the old Windows 2000 file sharing enables you to make complicated decisions about who gets access to which folders and files.**

If you need any of those capabilities, there may be hope for you; but you have to meet the following criteria:

- You must be running Windows XP Professional either on a lone machine or as part of a peer-to-peer *workgroup* network.
- Your machine must use the NTFS file system.

If you're not using Windows XP Professional or your hard drive doesn't use the NTFS file system, you're out of luck.

If your machine uses the older FAT32 file system, you can make all these changes — but none of the security settings work. Windows XP doesn't bother mentioning that you have to have NTFS to make any of the old Windows 2000 security settings work.

Although disabling Simple File Sharing on a Windows XP Home computer is theoretically possible, I don't recommend it. The process hasn't been tested well enough – and the last thing you need is to bump into a time-consuming problem running unapproved software. If you need the old-fashioned Windows 2000 security settings, it's best to pay the Redmond Piper and upgrade to Windows XP Professional.

If you're using Windows XP Professional Edition, here's how to disable Simple File Sharing and get at the old Windows 2000 security settings:

1. **Choose Start⇨My Computer.**

   Windows Explorer appears.

2. **Choose Tools⇨Folder Options⇨View.**

   You see the Folder Options dialog box shown in Figure 48-2.

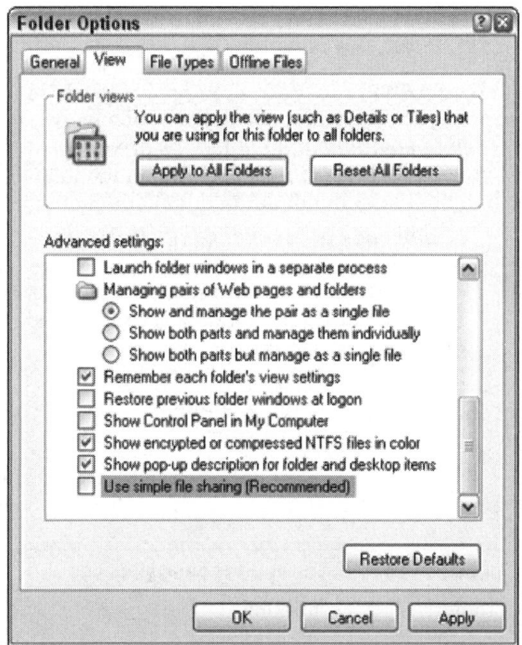

• **Figure 48-2: The Simple File Sharing setting is buried at the bottom of a truly obscure dialog box.**

3. **Uncheck the Use Simple File Sharing (Recommended) check box.**

4. **Click OK.**

   You can set old-fashioned Windows 2000 access permissions (as shown in Figure 48-3) by right-clicking any folder, choosing Sharing and Security, and then choosing items from the Sharing tab and the Security tab. (For more information, see *Windows 2000 Professional Bible* by Michael Desmond, Michael Meadhra, Blair Rampling, and Robert Correll, published by Wiley Publishing, Inc.)

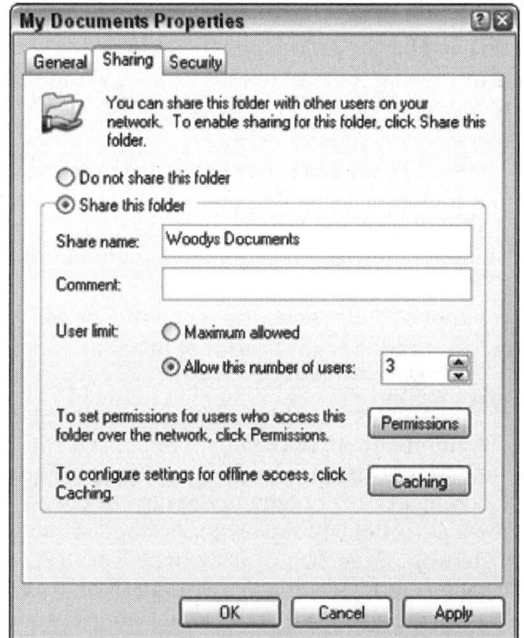

• **Figure 48-3: The Windows 2000 security dialog box, brought to life in Windows XP Professional.**

Using the Four Levels of Protection

Windows 2000 has an enormously rich — and complicated — repertoire of file-sharing settings. For example, you can tell Windows 2000 to allow a predefined group of users to read files in a certain folder, but only allow specific individuals to change files in that folder. You can set passwords for a drive or folder. The number of choices is daunting — and maintaining security settings in such fine detail can be enormously time-consuming.

In fact, unless you specifically need one of the three security features mentioned in the preceding section, you will probably find Simple File Sharing more than adequate – and one whole heck of a lot faster, easier, and simpler to use than the old Windows 2000 security settings.

Simple File Sharing allows you to set four different levels of sharing (or protection) for every folder or drive:

- **Private:** Only you can get at it. Any user can mark his or her My Documents folder as Private, and keep all other users out of it.

You must be using the NTFS file system (not FAT32) on the drive containing the My Documents folder in order to make the My Documents folder Private.

- **Administrators Here Only:** You can tell Windows XP to protect a drive or folder by keeping out any limited user account, and anyone trying to get at the folder from another computer on the network (assuming you have a network). Files in folders marked Administrators Here Only can be read, changed, or deleted by any administrator on that particular PC. All other kinds of accounts are kept out. This is the default setting for all the drives and folders on a PC, except the Shared Documents folder. (Limited user accounts are given full read/write permission for their own My Documents folders, as you expect.)

Unless you specifically change settings, all new accounts on a PC are Administrator accounts (see Technique 47). So if you mark a drive or folder Administrators Here Only, chances are good that people who use your computer can see or clobber anything in that folder. However, if your computer is on a network, other users on the network won't even know that the folder or drive exists – it's hidden from them.

- **Read Only on the Network:** Administrators on this computer can read, change, or delete anything in the folder. Users on other computers can open files in the folder but can't change or delete them, and limited users (including the Guest account) can only read documents without making any changes or deletions, regardless of the computer they use to access the files.
- **Wide Open:** Anybody, anywhere (even people using the Guest account) can read, change or delete anything in the folder or drive. This is the default setting for the Shared Documents folder.

If somebody on another computer deletes a file on your computer, it does not go to the Recycle Bin. You'll have a devil of a time getting it back (see Technique 21). Use the Wide Open option with caution.

Table 48-1 gives you a quick summary of the four levels.

TABLE 48-1: SIMPLE FILE SHARING LEVELS

Level	You Can	Administrators Can	Limited Users Can	Users on Other Computers Can
Private	Read/Write	Do nothing	Do nothing	Do nothing
Administrators Here Only	Read/Write	Read/Write	Do nothing	Do nothing
Read Only on the Network	Read/Write	Read/Write	Read	Read
Wide Open	Read/Write	Read/Write	Read/Write	Read/Write

Microsoft's documentation and dialog boxes hint at a fifth SFS level — a setting called Shared on This Computer, which supposedly allows administrators to read, change, or delete anything in the folder. This setting allegedly grants read-only access to limited users (including Guest) and blocks any access from other computers on the network. Microsoft gives detailed instructions for setting up a folder with this kind of SFS setting, both in a Windows XP dialog box and in Microsoft's Knowledge Base (`support.microsoft.com/?kbid=304040`). Unfortunately, if you follow those instructions, you end up with a folder that is Wide Open.

Files and folders inside a folder inherit the sharing/protection features of the folder that contains them. For example, if you make a folder called Some Folder read-only, then Some Folder\Another Folder (a subfolder of Some Folder) is also read-only unless you explicitly change it.

Making a folder Private

Making My Documents Private requires the NTFS file system. Windows XP encrypts the My Documents folder using the Encrypting File System (see Technique 8). That's how other users are locked out and can't get in.

Using SFS, you can only make your own My Documents folder Private. That's true for all users, all the time, even on a PC that's not connected to a network, and it doesn't matter how many accounts are on the PC. You can't do it to any other folder; nobody else with an Administrator account can do it to you. After you make your My Documents folder Private, you can't make any subfolders "un"private. It's an all-or-nothing deal.

If you make My Documents Private, you'd better put a password on your account. Otherwise, anybody who walks up to the machine can get into the folder.

The minute you put a password on your account, you need to make a password reset disk so that you can retrieve this private data if you ever forget your password. See Technique 65.

To make My Documents Private, follow these steps:

1. **Choose Start⇨My Documents.**

   Explorer takes you into the My Documents folder.

2. **On the Standard toolbar, click the up arrow.**

   Explorer takes you up one level so you can see the My Documents folder.

3. **Right-click the My Documents folder and choose Properties.**

   You see the My Documents Properties dialog box.

4. **Click the Sharing tab.**

   Windows shows you the Sharing settings shown in Figure 48-4.

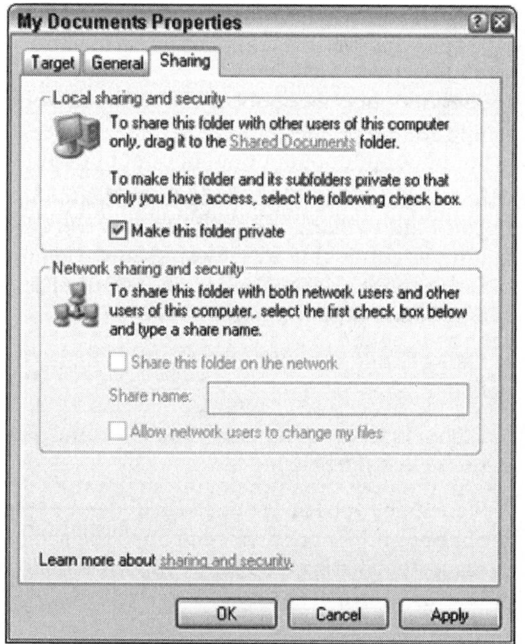
My Documents Properties
Target
General
Sharing
Local sharing and security
To share this folder with other users of this computer only, drag it to the Shared Documents folder.
To make this folder and its subfolders private so that only you have access, select the following check box.
Make this folder private
Network sharing and security
To share this folder with both network users and other users of this computer, select the first check box below and type a share name.
Share this folder on the network
Share name:
Allow network users to change my files
Learn more about sharing and security.
OK
Cancel
Apply

• **Figure 48-4: The check box to make My Documents Private.**

5. **Check the Make This Folder Private box and click OK.**

   Windows encrypts all the data in My Documents. That can take a long time. When it's done, Windows returns to the My Documents Properties dialog box.

6. **Click OK to clear the My Documents Properties dialog box.**

If you have an Administrator account and you add a password to it by using the Control Panel's User Accounts dialog box (see Technique 47), you're asked if you want to make your My Documents folder Private. It's the same setting as the Make This Folder Private setting in Figure 48-4.

Making a folder Administrators Here Only

This is the default setting for My Documents folders — other administrators can read, write, or delete files inside the folder, but limited users (including Guest) can only see inside their own My Documents folders.

If you want to make sure a folder is Administrators Here Only, follow these steps:

1. **In Windows Explorer, navigate to the folder you want to mark as Administrators Here Only. (You might do that by choosing Start⇨My Computer or Start⇨My Documents, or any of a dozen other ways.)**

   Explorer takes you into the My Documents folder.

2. **Right-click the folder and choose Properties; then click the Sharing tab.**

   Sometimes you can right-click a folder and pick Sharing and Security. You end up in the same place, the Sharing tab of the Properties dialog box, as shown in Figure 48-5.

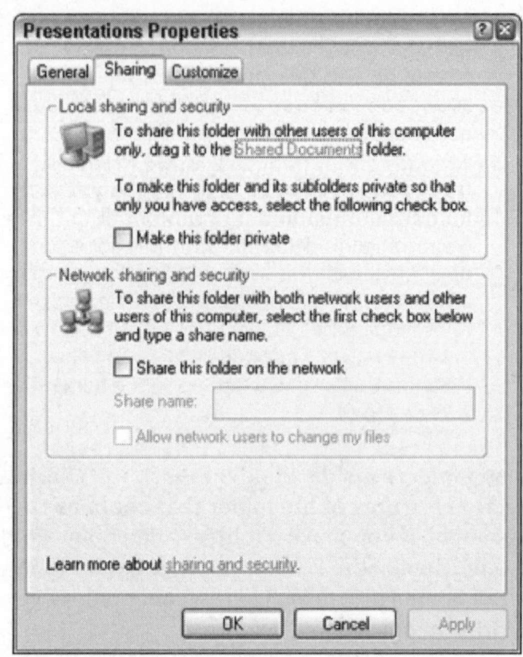
Presentations Properties
General
Sharing
Customize
Local sharing and security
To share this folder with other users of this computer only, drag it to the Shared Documents folder.
To make this folder and its subfolders private so that only you have access, select the following check box.
Make this folder private
Network sharing and security
To share this folder with both network users and other users of this computer, select the first check box below and type a share name.
Share this folder on the network
Share name:
Allow network users to change my files
Learn more about sharing and security.
OK
Cancel
Apply

• **Figure 48-5: Clear the boxes to make a folder Administrators Here Only.**

3. **Uncheck the Make This Folder Private and Share This Folder on the Network check boxes.**

4. **Click OK.**

Making a folder or drive Read Only on the Network

Many Windows XP owners feel more comfortable allowing people on the network to look at their shared files but not change or delete them. If that describes your situation, this setting's for you.

Windows XP discourages you from sharing entire drives. (Among other things, you have to explicitly confirm, in a separate step, that you want to share a drive on the network.) There's a good reason for Windows' caution. If you share the drive that contains Windows (typically your C: drive), other people on the network can get in and see — or possibly even delete — key system files, including files that store passwords and other important settings.

Files in Read Only on the Network folders can be read, changed, or deleted by administrators who are using the PC that contains the folder. Everybody else — limited users on the same PC or even administrators on other PCs — can only open the files.

To make a folder behave this way, follow these steps:

1. **Use Explorer to navigate to the folder.**
2. **Right-click the folder and choose Properties; then click the Sharing tab.**

   Windows shows you the Sharing tab of the folder's Properties dialog box. See Figure 48-6.
3. **Check the Share This Folder on the Network box.**

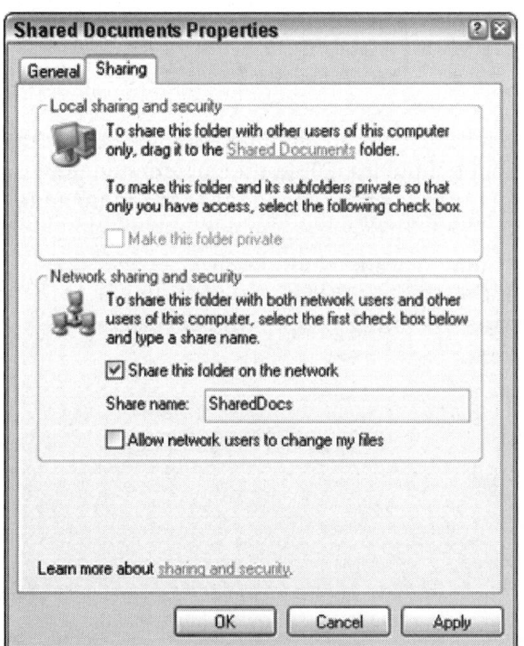
Shared Documents Properties
General
Sharing
Local sharing and security
To share this folder with other users of this computer only, drag it to the Shared Documents folder.
To make this folder and its subfolders private so that only you have access, select the following check box.
Make this folder private
Network sharing and security
To share this folder with both network users and other users of this computer, select the first check box below and type a share name.
Share this folder on the network
Share name: SharedDocs
Allow network users to change my files
Learn more about sharing and security.
OK
Cancel
Apply

• **Figure 48-6: Check to share the folder.**

4. **In the Share Name text box, type a name that other people on the network will recognize as a name for a shared folder.**
5. **Click OK.**

Making a folder or drive Wide Open

Heaven help me, Wide Open is the setting I use for the Shared Documents folder on all my machines. The way I figure it, anybody I'm willing to give network access to has the right to delete any file in my shared folders. All I have to do is be careful what I share and what I keep private.

No, this isn't a very secure setting. Yes, it's very convenient and fast.

To expose a folder to this level of travesty, follow these steps:

1. **Use Explorer to navigate to the folder.**
2. **Right-click the folder and choose Properties; then click the Sharing tab.**

   The Sharing tab of the Properties dialog box appears. (See Figure 48-7.)
3. **Check the Share This Folder on the Network check box.**
4. **In the Share Name text box, give your folder a name that other people will recognize as a name for a shared folder.**
5. **Check the Allow Network Users to Change My Files check box.**
6. **Click OK.**

In general, it's a bad idea to make the root of your C: drive — or whichever drive holds your Windows files — Wide Open. (A *root* of a drive is just the drive letter itself.) If you do share C: (the root of your C: drive), anybody with an IQ above room temperature (Celsius) can go into your `C:\Windows` folder and do all sorts of damage.

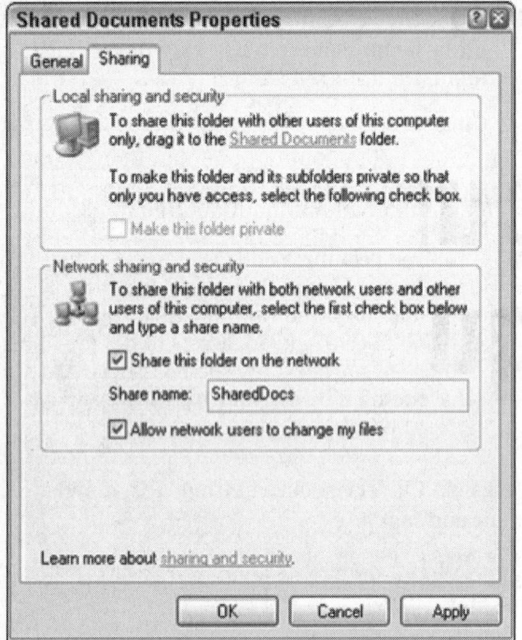
Shared Documents Properties
General
Sharing
Local sharing and security
To share this folder with other users of this computer only, drag it to the Shared Documents folder.
To make this folder and its subfolders private so that only you have access, select the following check box.
Make this folder private
Network sharing and security
To share this folder with both network users and other users of this computer, select the first check box below and type a share name.
Share this folder on the network
Share name: SharedDocs
Allow network users to change my files
Learn more about sharing and security.
OK
Cancel
Apply

• **Figure 48-7: This shared folder is Wide Open.**

If you try to share the root of any drive, Windows responds with a warning message, as shown in Figure 48-8.

On the other hand, it's a very *good* idea to make your CD drive(s) Wide Open. If the CD drive on your machine ever goes on the fritz, you can slap a CD into any other computer on your network and use the other CD drive almost as easily as the one attached to your computer.

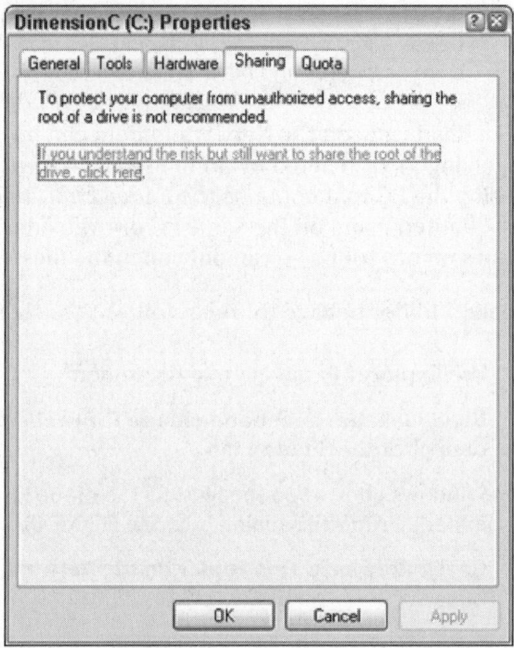
DimensionC (C:) Properties
General
Tools
Hardware
Sharing
Quota
To protect your computer from unauthorized access, sharing the root of a drive is not recommended.
If you understand the risk but still want to share the root of the drive, click here.
OK
Cancel
Apply

• **Figure 48-8: Perfectly good advice for the C: drive. Dreadful advice for a CD drive.**

In general, use your own discretion when sharing the root of any drive. Don't let Windows nag you or scare you into submission. There's nothing inherently wrong with sharing an entire drive. Just understand that everything on the drive is available according to the settings you pick, and be sure that you trust the other people who have access to your network.

Part VIII

Fast Security Techniques

"This is your firewall? This is what you're running? Well, heck – I think this could be your problem!"

Protecting Your PC from Viruses While You Sleep

Save Time By

- Knowing when you're probably infected (and when you aren't)
- Protecting your system quickly and thoroughly
- Not contributing to the problem

You can lose a lot of time — not to mention a lot of sleep — over viruses. Some of the worries are justified. Many are not. I've been working with viruses and antivirus software manufacturers since the first Word macro virus appeared on the scene a decade ago. I was the first person to find a Word 97 macro virus, which was posted on Microsoft's Web site, by a Microsoft employee, attached to a marketing document. And I've been intimately involved in fighting viruses, Trojans, worms, and other nasties up to and including the current "cyberterrorism" phase. Don't tell anybody, but I've even helped Microsoft at times.

You know what I've discovered?

Viruses aren't anywhere near as bad as most people think. Of course, you need to protect yourself by running a good antivirus program, setting up a firewall (you get a decent, but not great, firewall in Windows XP Service Pack 2), and following a few simple rules, which I list in this technique. Network administrators need to stay on their toes to block fast-spreading Internet worms. But for the most part, in spite of what you've read in the papers, well-meaning people trying to fight viruses have done more harm than the viruses themselves have ever caused.

If you want to save time, set up an antivirus program following the rules I give in this technique, get Windows Firewall cranked up (Technique 50) or, better yet, replace it (Technique 51), and then get on with your life.

Understanding Viruses

So much bad information about viruses is floating around the Internet that it's a wonder anybody gets any work done. Before I look at what a virus is, it may be worthwhile to take a look at what a virus isn't. Have you ever received an e-mail message that looks like this?

The objective of this e-mail is to warn all Hotmail users about a new virus that is spreading by MSN Messenger. The name of this virus is `jdbgmgr.exe` *and it is sent automatically by the Messenger and by the address book too.*

The virus is not detected by McAfee or Norton and it stays quiet for 14 days before damaging the system. . . .

IF YOU FIND THE VIRUS IN ALL OF YOUR SYSTEMS SEND THIS MESSAGE TO ALL OF YOUR CONTACTS LOCATED IN YOUR ADDRESS BOOK BEFORE IT CAN CAUSE ANY DAMAGE.

That message has circulated for years in more than a dozen languages. `jdbgmgr` has been blamed for everything from crashing Microsoft Office programs to scrambled hard drives to slow Internet connections to psoriasis. I've heard PC salesmen claim that they couldn't accept a faulty returned PC because it was "infected" with `jdbgmgr`.

`jdbgmgr.exe` isn't a virus. It's a normal part of Windows: You probably have it on your system. The message is a hoax, passed on by (usually) well-intentioned people who simply haven't got a clue.

The point? You can waste a lot of time (and money!) fretting over viruses that don't exist. Spend a few minutes now learning the telltale signs of a virus, and you can laugh at messages like the `jdbgmgr` hoax.

Dissecting a virus

A computer *virus* is a program that replicates. That's all. Viruses generally replicate by attaching themselves to files — programs, documents, spreadsheets — or replacing "genuine" operating system files with bogus ones. They usually make copies of themselves whenever they're run. Even relatively benign viruses can sap your time by bloating your files and making your computer do strange things. Most embarrassingly, viruses can take up enormous amounts of time if you send an infected file to someone else and have to warn the person (or, worse, the organization) after the fact.

You probably think that viruses delete files or make programs go belly-up or wreak havoc in other nefarious ways. Some of them do. Many of them don't. Viruses sound scary, but they really aren't. Most viruses have such ridiculous bugs in them that they don't get very far "in the wild."

Trojans (occasionally called Trojan horses) may or may not be able to reproduce, but they always require that the user do something to get them started. The most common Trojans these days appear as e-mail attachments: You double-click an attachment, expecting to open a picture or a document, and you get bit when some program comes in and clobbers your computer, frequently sending out a gazillion messages, all with infected attachments, without your knowledge or consent.

Worms move from one computer to another over a network. The worst ones replicate very quickly by shooting copies of themselves over the Internet, taking advantage of holes in the operating systems (all too frequently Windows).

Collectively, viruses, Trojans, and worms are known as *malware*. While some malware can carry bad *payloads* — programs that wreak destruction on your system — many of the worst offenders cause the most harm by clogging networks (nearly bringing down the Internet itself, at times), and by turning PCs into *zombies*, which can be operated by remote control.

If your PC is turned into a zombie, the cretin who infected you may be able to retrieve data from (or destroy data on) your computer. Surprisingly, though, most zombie puppetmasters aren't interested in personal data. Some of them make money by mining e-mail addresses from subverted machines, selling the addresses to spammers. Many of them, though, wait until they can get a bunch of subverted machines to work in unison, bombarding a Web site with so many "hits" that the site shuts down. That's the genesis of the so-called *Distributed Denial of Service attack*, a technique that has brought down more than a few controversial sites. Most recently, zombies have been used to send out tons of spam, with the spammers lining the pockets of the puppetmasters. 'Tis a brave new world, eh?

All these definitions are becoming more academic and less relevant, as the trend shifts to *blended-threat* malware. Blended threats incorporate elements of all three traditional kinds of malware — and more. Most of the most successful "viruses" you read about in the press these days are, in fact, blended-threat malware. They've come a long way from old-fashioned viruses.

The first really big virus

The world changed when John McAfee appeared on the *Today Show* in March, 1992, and told Bryant Gumbel that the Michelangelo virus infected more than a million PCs. One week later, the PC world was supposed to end. All the major wire services ran alarming predictions — millions of dollars were forecast to be lost in the wake of the largest computer virus of all time.

The Big Day arrived and . . . nothing. A few thousand systems got clobbered, here and there, but Michelangelo turned into a dud of astonishing proportions. McAfee made millions. The wire services fell silent. We all got huckstered. Does history repeat itself in Internet time?

By and large, malware works in rather predictable ways:

- **By infecting legitimate program files or floppies:** These old-fashioned methods of replicating have all but disappeared because people rarely pass around program files or floppies anymore.
- **By infecting documents:** This type of transmittal works when a user opens an infected document. Other documents on the user's PC become infected. When the user sends copies of those documents to others, the recipients' machines can become infected, too. It's a slow and haphazard approach that's on the wane because antivirus programs have improved enormously and because Microsoft has built antivirus *hooks* into the Office programs. Whenever you open a file in a recent version of Office, your antivirus program scans the file before the program (Word, Excel, whatever) even touches it.
- **By automatically sending copies of infected documents to others:** That's how Melissa (1999) works. If you open a Melissa-infected document in Word, Melissa automatically sends infected documents attached to e-mail messages destined to the first 50 people in your address book. Melissa was so successful that network administrators at hundreds of large installations — including Microsoft and Intel — pulled their networks offline (in some cases, for days). Melissa doesn't have a destructive payload, but it completely brought down e-mail communication in many companies.
- **By sending copies of itself attached to e-mail messages:** ILOVEYOU (2000) arrives attached to an innocuous-looking message that says `kindly check the attached LOVELETTER coming from me`. Anyone using Outlook or Outlook Express who double-clicks the attached file, `LOVE-LETTER-FOR-YOU.TXT.vbs`, unleashes the worm, which immediately sends copies of itself to everyone in the infected user's address book. It also overwrites files. Ford, the Jet Propulsion Lab, the Space Center in Houston, and even the British Parliament were knocked out by ILOVEYOU. Bill Gates once joked that he received infected messages from people who should know better.

The Anna Kournikova virus (early 2001) works much like ILOVEYOU. It arrives as an e-mail attachment called `AnnaKournikova.jpg.vbs`. If you double-click the attachment, copies of the worm are sent to everyone in your address book. One big difference with Anna: It was written with a virus construction kit, readily available on the Web.

- **By sending copies of itself via e-mail and directly infecting other computers on the local network:** Klez (Spring 2002) is a multi-attack opportunist of this ilk. It sends copies of itself attached to e-mail messages addressed to everyone in your address book. For good measure, sometimes Klez retrieves a legitimate file from the infected computer and sends it along with the program itself. (Highly embarrassing!) Klez also *spoofs* the From: address (puts a completely bogus return address on the message) by scanning the address book and sticking randomly selected e-mail addresses in the From: line. At the same time, Klez infects other PCs on the local network by dropping copies of itself in network-accessible folders. The copies have random names, so people using other computers on the network might run Klez accidentally, thinking that they're running some different program. MyDoom (2004) also spreads as an e-mail attachment.

Your best defense is to buy a good antivirus package. Downloading one from the Web takes less than 30 minutes. Setting it up takes another 30 minutes, tops. For an hour's investment, you can save days and days of clean-up.

- **By attacking computers connected directly to the Internet:** The brave new world of attacks involves worms, such as Code Red (Summer 2001) and Slammer (early 2003), that aggressively look for vulnerable PCs that are directly connected to the Internet. Humans are no longer part of the infecting *vector* — these worms are completely self-propelled, scanning randomly generated IP addresses. (Code Red 2 goes one step further by focusing most of its attacks on nearby networks, presumably inside a corporate firewall.) Microsoft's own Hotmail servers were brought down by Code Red, which exploited a known, fixed problem with Microsoft's Internet Information Server. (Yes, Microsoft forgot to patch its Hotmail servers.) Slammer took out SQL Server installations. Many PC users have a SQL Server on their machines, disguised as a product called MSDE. Sobig, Blaster, and Sasser (2003–4) also ran across wide swathes of unpatched Windows systems.

  Code Red took about 12 hours to infect most of its intended victims. During the first minute of its existence, Slammer doubled the number of infected systems every 8.5 seconds. Slammer took about 10 minutes from the moment it was unleashed to infect most of its victims. In fact, the single greatest barrier to Slammer's propagation was the Internet's near-meltdown due to Slammer's fast propagation.

Fast-propagating worms on the Internet are nothing new — the Computer Emergency Response Team (CERT) was initially formed largely in response to Robert Morris' worm, which essentially brought down the Internet in late 1988.

I think it's pretty obvious that the future of viruses, worms, and Trojans lies in these automated direct attacks. Enough do-it-yourself virus-authoring kits are available that the *script kiddies* will keep churning out classic viruses – so it's more important than ever that you use a good antivirus program. But the real killer problems for Windows users will come from previously unidentified or poorly patched security holes in Windows, Windows servers, Internet Information Services, Exchange Server, SQL Server, and the like. Other than setting up a firewall, you can't do much about those. Your network administrator gets stuck holding the ball.

Discerning whether your PC's infected

So how do you know if you're infected?

The short answer is this: Many times, you don't. If you think that your PC is infected, chances are very good that it isn't. Why? Because malware these days doesn't usually cause the kinds of problems people normally associate with infections.

That said, here are a few telltale signs that might mean that your PC is infected:

- **Someone tells you that you sent him an e-mail message with an attachment — and you didn't send it.** In fact, most e-mail malware these days is smart enough to spoof the From: address, so any infected message that appears to come from you probably didn't. Still, some dumb old viruses that aren't capable of hiding your e-mail address are still around. And if you get an infected attachment from a friend, chances are good that both your e-mail address and his e-mail address are on an infected computer somewhere. Six degrees of separation and all that . . .

If you receive an infected message, look at the header to see whether you can tell where it came from. In Outlook, open the message and then choose View⇨Options. A box at the bottom may (or may not!) tell you who really sent the message (as shown in Figure 49-1).

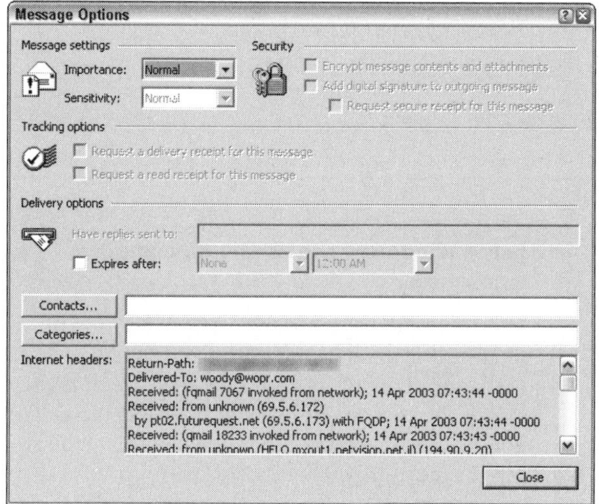

• **Figure 49-1: I blurred the identity of this sender who may have been a victim himself.**

- **If you suddenly see files with two filename extensions scattered around on your computer, beware.** Filenames, such as `kournikova.jpg.vbs` (a VBScript file masquerading as a JPG image file) or `somedoc.txt.exe` (a Windows program that wants to appear to be a text file), should send you running for your antivirus software.

Always, always, always have Windows show you filename extensions. See Technique 20.

- **Your antivirus software suddenly stops working.** If the icon for your antivirus product disappears from the notification area (near the clock), something killed it — and chances are very good that the culprit was a virus.
- **Your Internet connection slows to a crawl.** Even worse than usual.

What to do next

If you think that you're infected, follow these steps in order:

1. **Don't panic.**

   Chances are very good that you're not infected.

2. **Update your antivirus software with the latest signature file from the manufacturer's Web site; then run a full scan of your system.**

   If you don't have an antivirus package installed, run — don't walk — to your nearest computer store and beg for mercy from the PC protection gods.

3. **If your antivirus software doesn't identify the problem, go to the manufacturer's main page and see if it has a warning.**

   Table 49-1 gives the Web addresses for the major antivirus software manufacturers. Note that some sites may have news posted hours before other sites — but it's impossible to tell in advance which will get the story first.

4. **Check** `securityresponse.symantec.com/avcenter/hoax.html` **or** `us.mcafee.com/virusInfo/default.asp?id=hoaxes` **to see if you're the victim of a hoax.**

   Many of the hoaxes floating around these days sound mighty convincing. Save yourself a lot of embarrassment by ensuring that you're not being pulled by the leg.

5. **If you still can't find the source of the problem, follow the instructions on your antivirus software manufacturer's home page to submit a new virus.**

   If you're the first to report a new virus, you're so cutting edge.

6. **Do *not* — repeat — do *not* send messages to all of your friends advising them of the new virus.**

   Messages about a new virus can outnumber infected messages generated by the virus itself — in some cases, causing more havoc than the virus itself. Try not to become part of the problem. Besides, you may be wrong.

Table 49-1: Major Antivirus Software Vendors

Product	Company	Breaking News Web Site
AVG Anti-Virus	GRISoft	www.grisoft.com
F-Secure Antivirus	F-Secure	www.f-secure.com/virus-info
Kaspersky Antivirus	Kaspersky Lab	www.kaspersky.com
McAfee VirusScan	Network Associates	us.mcafee.com/virusInfo/default.asp
Norton AntiVirus	Symantec	securityresponse.symantec.com
Panda Antivirus	Panda	www.pandasecurity.com
Trend PC-cillin	Trend Micro	www.antivirus.com/vinfo

In recent years, I've come to view the mainstream press accounts of virus and malware outbreaks with increasing, uh, skepticism. The antivirus companies are usually slower to post news than the mainstream press, but the information they post tends to be much more reliable. Not infallible, mind you, but better. We also cover security problems at AskWoody.com.

Protecting Yourself — Quickly

Every Windows XP user needs to follow five simple things to guard against viruses, worms, Trojans, and the like:

- **Buy, install, update, and religiously use one of the major antivirus packages listed in Table 49-1 (earlier in this chapter).**

  It doesn't matter which package you use, but you need one.

I recommend AVG Anti-Virus to my penny-pinching friends (of which I seem to have many). It's a solid, frequently updated, easy-to-use program that also happens to be free for private, non-commercial, single home computer use. Go to www.grisoft.com, and look for the AVG Free Edition. Bet you'll be pleasantly surprised.

- **Force Windows to show you filename extensions.**

  Microsoft's decision to have Windows hide filename extensions — the letters at the end of a filename, such as .doc or .vbs — reeks of trying to put the toothpaste back in the tube. It's a dangerous design mistake that you can fix by following the steps in Technique 20.

The important letters in a filename's extension are the ones following the last period. abc.gif.bat is a batch file that runs if you double-click it. Similarly, def.doc.vbs is a VBScript program – not a Word document – that also runs immediately.

- **After you can see filename extensions, watch out for the ones in Table 49-2.**

  If you double-click a file with one of those extensions, it runs immediately, with potentially disastrous results.

Yes, it's true: JPEG files (that is, files with the filename extension .JPG) can include potentially harmful programs. How can picture files turn into malicious programs? Because Microsoft screwed up. Again. Dozens of Microsoft programs mishandle JPG files, and the result can be devastating. You need to patch them all. See www.microsoft.com/security/bulletins/200409_jpeg.mspx for details.

- **Never open or run a file attached to an e-mail message until you (a) contact the person who sent you the message and verify that he or she specifically sent you the file and (b) save the file on your hard drive, update your antivirus software's signature file, and run your antivirus software on the file.**

Infected e-mail attachments are the single most common source of infection at the moment. And it's 100 percent preventable.

Don't rely on the Windows Security Center (shown in Figure 49-2) to tell you if your antivirus software is up to date. Sometimes the Security Center doesn't get the right message from the antivirus software, and sometimes the antivirus software doesn't toss out a warning in time. If you have a file to scan — specifically, a file that is attached to an e-mail message — take the time to update your antivirus software's signature file before you scan the file.

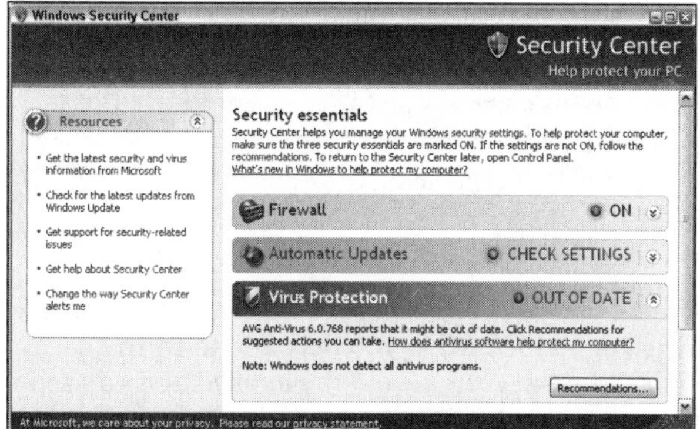

• Figure 49-2: The Windows Security Center doesn't always get the straight story on when an antivirus program is up to date.

- **If you get an e-mail message warning you about a virus, don't forward it.**

  You're only contributing to the problem even if the warning is valid (and it rarely is; see the next section). If the problem sounds dire, find a reference on one of the sites mentioned in Table 49-1 (earlier in this chapter) and then call your friends and tell them to look at the site. That way, they not only get the real story (plus or minus an editorial quirk or three), they also stay informed about new tools to solve the problem.

Follow those five things and you not only help yourself, you help all your coworkers, friends, and colleagues as well.

Table 49-2: Filename Extensions for (Potentially Unsafe) Program Files

.ade	.adp	.asx	.bas	.bat
.chm	.cmd	.com	.cpl	.crt
.exe	.hlp	.hta	.inf	.ins
.isp	.jpg	.js	.jse	.lnk
.mda	.mdb	.mde	.mdt	.mdw
.mdz	.msc	.msi	.msp	.mst
.ops	.pcd	.pif	.prf	.reg
.scf	.scr	.sct	.shb	.shs
.url	.vb	.vbe	.vbs	.wsc
.wsf	.wsh			

Avoiding Hoaxes

Tell me if you've heard this one:

- NEW VIRUS — THIS IS SERIOUS Please take note . . . If you receive an e-mail titled "PLEASE HELP POOR DOG. Win A Holiday" DO NOT OPEN IT ! ! ! It will erase everything on your hard drive. Forward this letter to as many people as you can. This is a new, very malicious virus and not many people know about it. This information was announced yesterday morning from Microsoft; please share it with everyone who might access the Internet.
- WARNING If you receive an e-mail titled "It Takes Guts to Say 'Jesus,' DO NOT OPEN IT. It will erase everything on your hard drive. This information was announced on 21 April by IBM stating that

this is a very dangerous virus, much worse than Melissa, and that there is NO remedy for it at this time.

- PLEASE READ THE MESSAGE BELOW !!!!!!!!!!! Some miscreant is sending e-mail under the title "Good Times" nationwide; if you get anything like this, DON'T DOWNLOAD THE FILE! It has a virus that rewrites your hard drive, obliterating anything on it. Please be careful and forward this mail to anyone you care about.
- URGENT! VIRUS! This information arrived this morning, from Microsoft and Norton. Please send it to everybody you know who accesses the Internet. You may receive an apparently harmless e-mail with a PowerPoint presentation called `Life is beautiful.pps`. If you receive it DO NOT OPEN THE FILE UNDER ANY CIRCUMSTANCES, and delete it immediately. If you open this file, a message will appear on your screen saying: "It is too late now, your life is no longer beautiful," and subsequently you will LOSE EVERYTHING IN YOUR PC. The person who sent it to you will gain access to your name, e-mail, and password.

It continues to amaze me how many people forward messages like that. But every day, hundreds of millions of copies of hoax virus warnings and chain letters clog the Internet.

No, Bill Gates can't keep track of who you send e-mail to — and he certainly won't give you $10 each time you click the Forward button. No, the postal service isn't about to impose a fee for using e-mail. No, you won't have your hard drive erased if you view a message entitled `WTC Survivor`.

Here's how to spot a hoax:

- Unless the message is an official release from a recognized source — say, a Microsoft Security Bulletin, a Symantec Virus Alert, a CERT Advisory, or a news story from AP or Reuters — there's at least a 90 percent chance that you are looking at a hoax.
- If one single exclamation point is in the entire message, or more than one word is in ALL CAPS, or it has more than one or two misspellings, or if it warns in breathless terms about all the data on your disk being destroyed, it's a hoax. Bet on it.
- If the message refers to a legitimate source — say, the Bugtraq news list or Microsoft or Norton — but doesn't quote directly from the source, it's either a hoax or so hopelessly garbled that you don't stand a chance of understanding the real problem.
- Microsoft doesn't distribute files by e-mail. If you get a file attached to a message that purports to be from Microsoft, it isn't. Chances are good you have a hoax message, with a real virus attached.
- If it's too good to be true . . . well, you know the rest of the saying.

Do yourself a favor. If you get junk like this:

- Don't forward it. Forwarding hoaxes does not endear you to most folks. Forwarded hoaxes are indistinguishable from spam. Spam's bad enough without turning it into a cottage industry.
- Check out a site such as Rob Rosenberger's Virus Myths page, `www.vmyths.com`, or CIAC's Hoaxbusters, `hoaxbusters.ciac.org`, and see if you're looking at a known hoax. If you are, write to the person who sent the hoax to you and tell him about it.

Even if you get a real message warning about a real virus, don't forward it. You only add to the damage caused by the virus — and the information you send may be out of date. As I explained in the preceding section, the best way to handle a real warning about a real virus is to find a reliable Web site that's reporting on the infection. Then pick up the phone, call your friends, and tell them about the site. That way you don't add to the volume of e-mail that the virus generates, and you make sure that your friends get the latest, best information from an authoritative source.

That saves your time. It saves their time. And you don't contribute to the volume of e-mail.

Plugging and Unplugging Windows Firewall

Save Time By

- Setting up Windows Firewall for your particular needs
- Poking holes in the Firewall
- Making fast Firewall changes one-click easy

So you have Windows XP Service Pack 2, and Windows Firewall is driving you nuts.

Good. That's what it's supposed to do.

I hate to admit it, but if Windows Firewall doesn't get in your way from time to time, it ain't doing its job.

Windows Firewall isn't a particularly good firewall (see Technique 51 for a look at a much better one). But it comes with Windows XP (at least, with Service Pack 2), and for many people it's good enough. Better the devil ye ken, eh?

My biggest complaint about Windows Firewall has nothing to do with its intrusiveness, its limited feature set, or its very limited coverage in Windows Help. My number-one beef: Microsoft buried the settings so deep that it takes a century to switch back and forth between various Firewall configurations. If you want to open up the Firewall to play a game, or you want to lock down everything before logging onto a public wireless network, the Windows Security Center requires four or five clicks to make it so. When you're done, going back to your "normal" configuration takes another four or five clicks . . . assuming you remember to restore your settings. Assuming you can remember which settings need to be changed. Assuming your clicking finger doesn't fall off in the process.

I figure every Windows user should have a "Lockdown" icon on the desktop — one single button that you can click and have Windows Firewall go into full lockdown. No muss. No fuss. No groping around with a click-click-click-click-click to tell the Firewall "Don't Allow Exceptions."

This technique shows you a never-before-published way to make switching Firewall configurations fast, easy, and safe.

Coping with Windows Firewall

If you have Windows XP Service Pack 2 or later, you have Windows Firewall (see the sidebar, "Getting through Windows Firewall"). Windows Firewall isn't a very capable firewall, as such things go — I talk about a much better one, ZoneAlarm, in Technique 51 — but Windows Firewall plays reasonably well with other firewalls, and you should definitely leave it on all the time.

Getting through Windows Firewall

A firewall is a gatekeeper, protecting your computer from other computers that can reach it. While most people realize that a firewall protects their computer from the big, nasty wide-open abyss commonly known as the Internet, many people don't realize that a firewall has to protect their computer from other computers on the local network, too.

Windows Firewall is a so-called *stateful* firewall. To a first approximation, that means WF keeps track of what goes out of your computer, and only allows stuff back in if it's in response to something that you sent out.

In general, as long as Windows Firewall is working, your computer only responds to three kinds of packets being sent to it:

- Packets that are in response to something you sent out.
- Packets that are sent to a specific program that you put on Windows Firewall's Exceptions list.
- Packets set to specific addresses — called *ports* — that you tell Windows Firewall to ignore.

In addition, you can restrict Windows Firewall to only allow packets coming from other computers on your local network — as is the case, for example, with Windows File and Printer Sharing.

Windows Firewall represents a major shift in the way Windows works, and it's frustrating for network-savvy individuals to adapt. Programs that have worked for the past century or so suddenly stop responding to requests coming from other computers. Believe it or not, that's A Good Thing from a security point of view.

Windows Firewall's job is to keep other computers' stuff from getting into your computer. Unfortunately, in many cases, programs inside your computer need to interact with outside computers to do their job. MSN Messenger (which I discuss in Technique 26) is a good example. When one of your Contacts logs on to MSN Messenger, the network sends you a notice that the Contact is online. That way, MSN Messenger can pop up a little box that says "BillG has just signed in." That notice from the MSN Messenger network has to break through the Windows Firewall, so MSN can pop up its box.

Windows Firewall is smart enough to intercept many programs as they first attempt to reach the outside world, and ask you if you are willing to let the program communicate freely with other programs, both on your local network (if you have one) and on the Internet. In Figure 50-1, for example, MSN Messenger has just started for the first time, and Windows Firewall wants to know if you want to allow it to communicate freely.

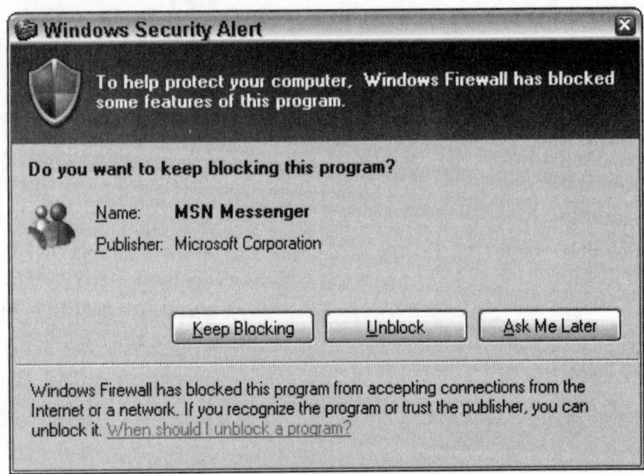

• **Figure 50-1: When MSN Messenger runs for the first time, Windows Firewall asks if you want to allow it to get out.**

If you unblock MSN Messenger, Windows Firewall automatically creates an entry in its Exceptions list that allows MSN Messenger to *receive* messages coming from the outside world. To see how these exceptions work, follow these steps:

1. **Choose Start⇨Control Panel⇨Security Center**

   Windows brings up the Windows Security Center, which I discuss in Technique 49.

2. **At the bottom, click Windows Firewall.**

   You see the Windows Firewall dialog box (see Figure 50-2).

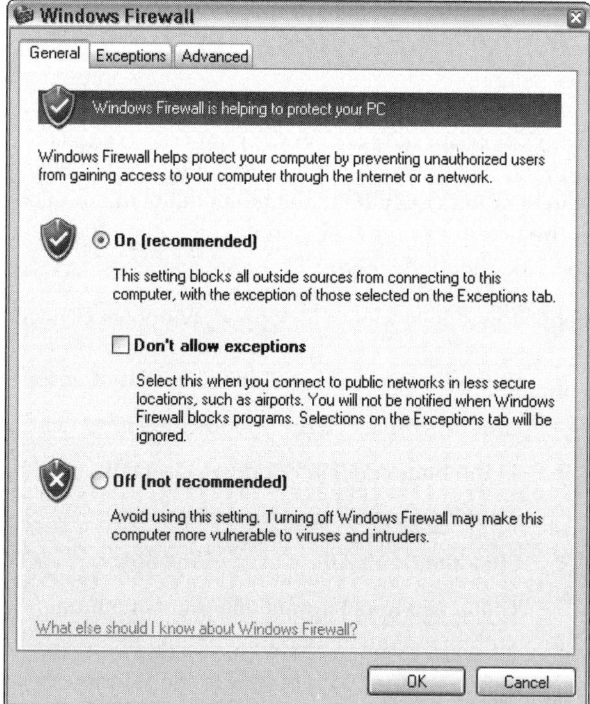

• **Figure 50-2: Control Windows Firewall from this screen.**

3. **Click the Exceptions tab.**

   Windows Firewall shows you all the exceptions — all the programs and/or ports (addresses) that are allowed to receive information sent to your PC (see Figure 50-3).

4. **To see how Windows Firewall identifies exceptions, double-click MSN Messenger.**

If you've never used MSN Messenger, there isn't an entry here. Windows Firewall only sets up the entry if you run MSN Messenger, and specifically choose to unblock it.

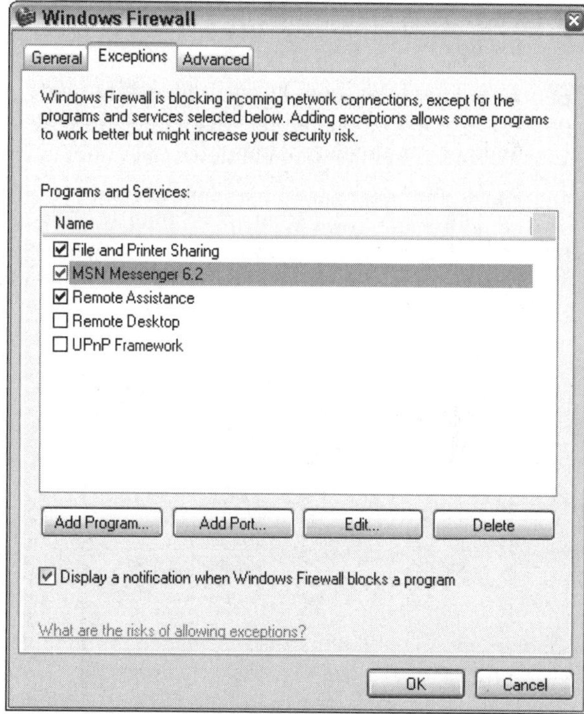

• **Figure 50-3: These exceptions are the only programs and ports that are opened up by Windows Firewall.**

Windows Firewall shows you that it permits incoming data to pass through the firewall, providing it's destined for MSN Messenger (see Figure 50-4).

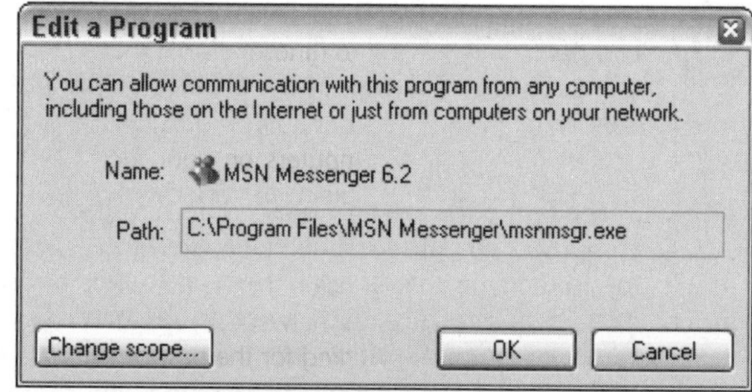

• **Figure 50-4: Individual programs allowed to poke through the Firewall are identified by the program file names.**

5. **Click OK to dismiss the Edit a Program dialog box.**

6. **To see how Windows Firewall identifies ports that are left open, double-click File and Printer Sharing (on the Exceptions tab).**

   File and Printer Sharing uses four ports on your computer, as shown in Figure 50-5. Whereas the MSN Messenger entry in the Exceptions list refers to a specific program, the File and Printer Sharing entry refers to a set of ports.

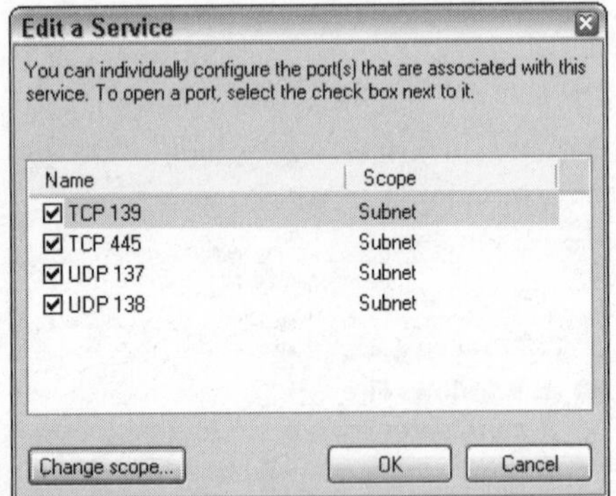

• **Figure 50-5: File and Printer Sharing uses a set of four ports.**

Every exception in the Windows Firewall Exception list covers either a single program, or one or more ports.

If you suddenly find that you can no longer share files or printers residing on a specific computer on your network, make sure that the computer's File and Printer Sharing box is checked.

Those four ports are only opened up for other computers on your local network. Heaven forbid that you should open them up to the Internet at large. If you're curious to see how Windows Firewall restricts access to the local network, click the Change Scope button, and then click Cancel when you have it figured out.

7. **Click OK to dismiss the Edit a Service dialog box, and then click OK to leave Windows Firewall.**

I talk about Windows Firewall settings extensively in *Windows XP All-in-One Desk Reference For Dummies,* 2nd Edition.

Changing Firewall Settings

Every Windows user should be able to lock down Windows Firewall in a New Yawk minute. If you see your ADSL light flickering like a firefly in heat, or if your disk suddenly starts whirring like a tornado is in the box, you're well advised to lock down first, and ask questions later.

Here's the official way to lock down Windows Firewall:

1. **Choose Start⇨Control Panel⇨Security Center.**

   Windows brings up the Windows Security Center.

2. **At the bottom, click Windows Firewall.**

   Windows Firewall appears (refer to Figure 50-2).

3. **Click the Don't Allow Exceptions box.**

   That's Windows Firewall's "lockdown" setting.

4. **Click OK to get out of Windows Firewall, and then click the Close button in the Windows Security Center.**

   That's a whole lotta clickin', especially if you're feeling a bit panicked. In the next section, I show you how to accomplish the same thing with two clicks.

You may need to change your Firewall settings for plenty of other reasons.

In the preceding section, I show you how Windows Firewall pops open a hole for certain programs (such as MSN Messenger) that need to get out. (Or, more accurately, need to allow traffic from the Internet to get in.) If Windows Firewall doesn't pick up a particular program, you have to open a hole manually. In Technique 25, I talk about Shareaza, a scum-free file-sharing program that works remarkably well. When I installed Shareaza shortly after Service Pack 2 hit the streets, it had problems getting through Windows Firewall. (By now those problems are no doubt history.) I consulted the Shareaza Web site and discovered that I needed to add Shareaza to the Windows Firewall Exception list, and that I also needed to open two ports, in order to allow Shareaza to work quickly.

Making ports wide open on the Internet is a risky business. You certainly don't want to leave the ports open for any extended length of time. If you decide to open a port, make sure you follow the instructions in the next section to make it easy and quick to both open and close the hole. And be ever mindful of the fact that exposing your ports leaves you just as vulnerable as anyone running a version of Windows XP without Service Pack 2.

Here's how to manually modify Windows Firewall, first to allow a program to receive data sent to it over the Internet, and second to open up ports directly to the Internet, using Shareaza as an example:

1. **Choose Start⇨Control Panel⇨Security Center. When the Windows Security Center appears, click Windows Firewall down at the bottom.**

   You see Windows Firewall Central (refer to Figure 50-2).

2. **Click the Exceptions tab.**

   Windows Firewall's Exceptions list appears (refer to Figure 50-3).

3. **To put a program like Shareaza on the Windows Firewall Exception list, click the Add Program button.**

   Windows Firewall scans your computer's `\Programs` folder and comes up with a list of possible programs (shown in Figure 50-6).

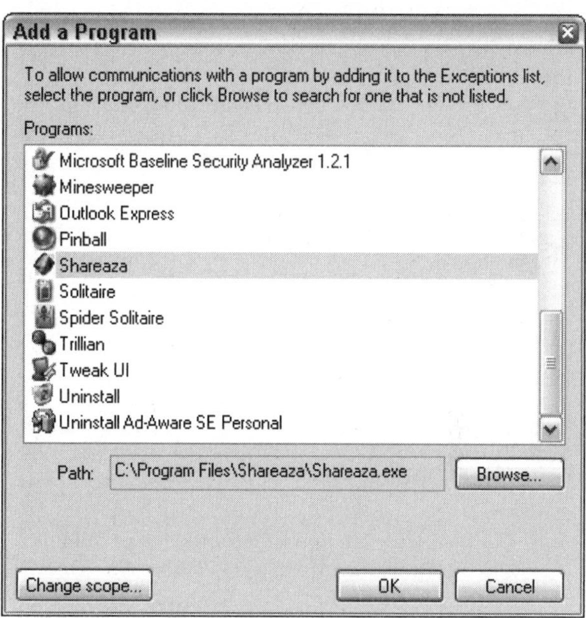

• **Figure 50-6: Windows Firewall constructs a list of likely candidates for the Exceptions list.**

4. **Select the program you want to poke through the firewall. Click Browse to find the program if you don't see it listed. When you're done, click OK.**

   Windows Firewall adds the program to its Exceptions list. The program is allowed to accept incoming data from the Internet.

5. **To add a port to the Exception list, click the Add Port button.**

   Windows Firewall shows you the Add a Port dialog box (see Figure 50-7).

Only add a port to the Exceptions list if a software manufacturer insists — and if you understand the ramifications.

6. **Give the exception a name, and then type the number of the port that you need opened. Choose TCP or UDP to conform to the manufacturer's instructions. Click OK.**

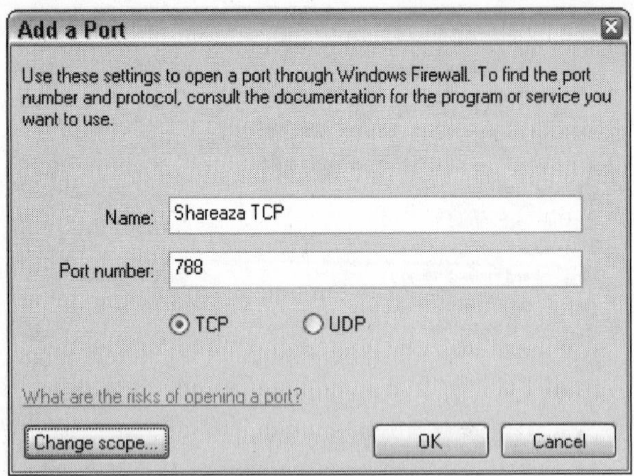

• **Figure 50-7: Opening a port for Shareaza.**

TCP and UDP are two different ways of talking across a port. See *Windows XP All-in-One Desk Reference For Dummies,* 2nd Edition, for details.

When you open a port to the Internet, any creepy-crawly piece of garbage trawling the Net may be able to get into your computer. Only open ports when you absolutely have to, and don't leave them open any longer than necessary. For example, I check the boxes for Shareaza in the Exceptions list only when I need to have those ports open. When I'm not using Shareaza, I uncheck the boxes, thus closing the hole.

My Windows Firewall's Exception list, which includes an exception generated by the instant messaging program Trillian (see Technique 27), looks like Figure 50-8. No, I *don't* leave those ports open all the time.

7. **When you have all your exceptions in line, click OK to get out of Windows Firewall and then close Windows Security Center.**

   Then run, don't walk, to the next section, and get those unnecessary holes plugged.

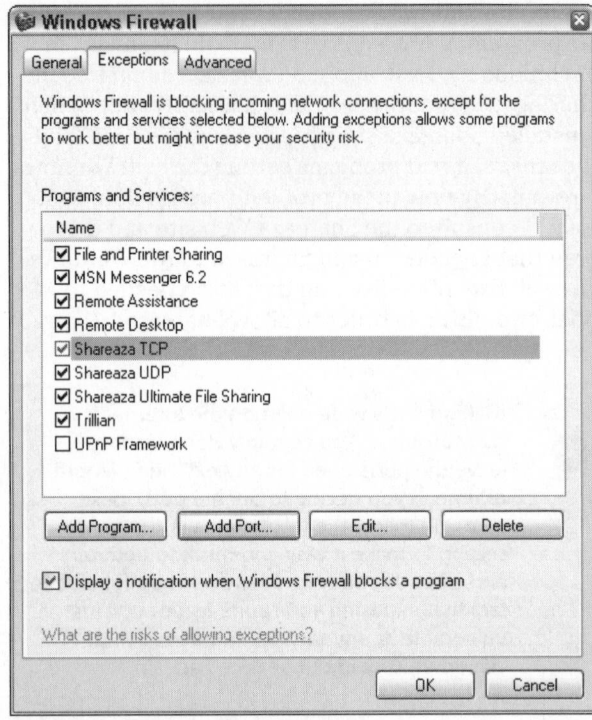

• **Figure 50-8: My Exceptions list.**

Constructing a Firewall Lockdown Icon

In the preceding sections I show you how to make changes to Windows Firewall that can either poke specific holes in the Firewall, or lock it down completely. All those changes have one thing in common: They're incredibly time-consuming (and, I would argue, error-prone). There's a previously undocumented way to get Windows Firewall to make changes quickly and reliably, with just a couple of clicks.

Personally, I have three icons on my Windows desktop that drive Windows Firewall. You may only need two, or you might want more.

I recommend creating icons that perform at least these three actions:

- A **Normal** icon that opens up just enough of Windows Firewall for me to get my everyday work done, and nothing more.
- A **Lockdown** icon that quickly puts Windows Firewall into Don't Allow Exceptions mode, so I can lock down my machine quickly before I log on to a public wireless hot spot, or if I get the willies. When I'm feeling more secure, I click the Normal icon, and life returns to, uh, normal.
- An **Open Wide** icon, which opens up all the ports that I need for things like running the Shareaza file-sharing program. I use this icon sparingly, and only for a short time, when I specifically need to poke unusual holes into the firewall. When I'm done running Open Wide, I click the Normal icon and get back to work.

All the Windows Firewall settings sit in the Registry, and that's the key to making these icons work. Here's what I do on my machine; your situation may be a tad different:

1. **Shut down all your programs, including MSN Messenger or any other instant messaging programs.**

   You may need to right-click the IM program's icon in the notification area next to the clock and choose Exit.

2. **Bring up Windows Firewall: Choose Start⇨Control Panel⇨Security Center; then, at the bottom, click Windows Firewall.**

   You see Windows Firewall's main dialog box (refer to Figure 50-2).

3. **Make any changes you need to put Windows Firewall in a "normal" configuration.**

   In particular, turn off all unnecessary programs on the Exceptions list by unchecking the appropriate boxes. In Figure 50-9, I allow File and Printer Sharing, Remote Assistance, and Trillian, but block everything else.

4. **Click OK to get out of Windows Firewall.**

5. **Choose Start⇨Run, type** regedit **and press Enter.**

   The Registry Editor (see Figure 50-10) comes up.

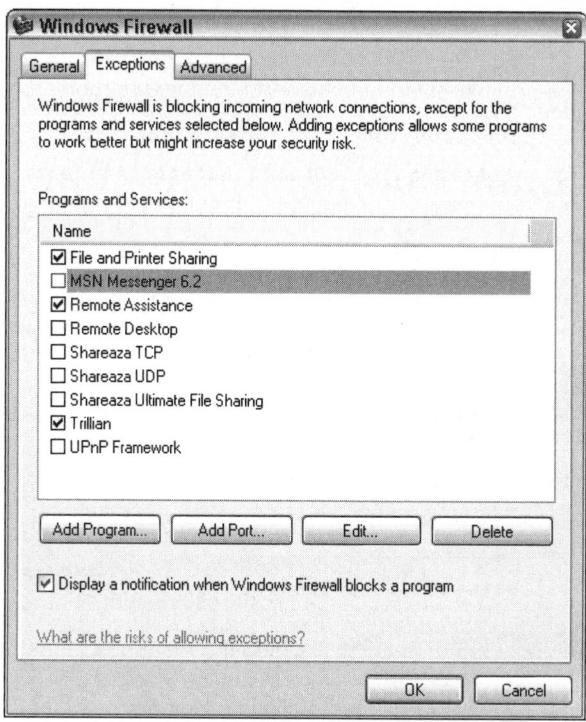

• **Figure 50-9: For the "Normal" icon, only enable the programs and ports that you need to get your work done.**

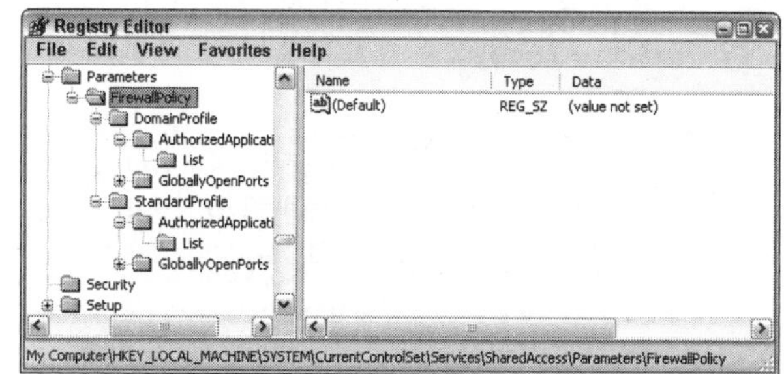

• **Figure 50-10: Windows Firewall settings are stored in this Registry key.**

I talk about the Registry and how to keep it well-fed in Technique 68, and you might find it worthwhile to scan that technique now. Suffice it to say that if you follow these instructions closely, there's nothing to worry about.

6. **On the left, navigate down to** `HKEY_LOCAL_MACHINE\SYSTEM\CurrentControlSet\Services\SharedAccess\Parameters\FirewallPolicy`.

   That's where all your Firewall settings live.

7. **Right-click FirewallPolicy and choose Export.**

   The Registry Editor brings up the Export Registry File dialog box shown in Figure 50-11.

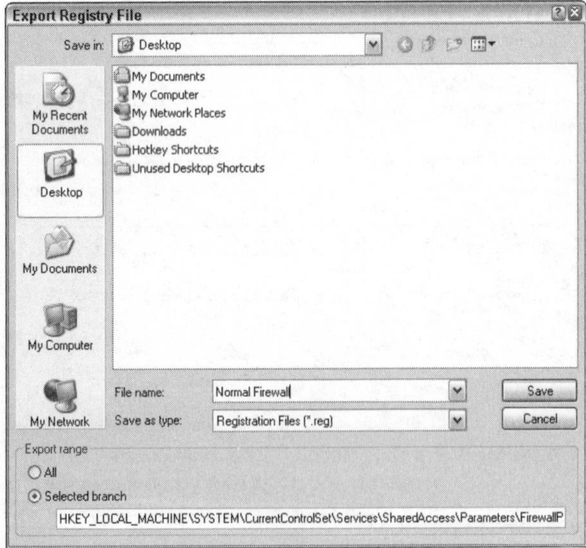

• **Figure 50-11: Create a desktop icon by exporting a Registry key.**

8. **On the left, click Desktop (so your "Normal" icon will go on the Windows desktop). Type a name that's easy to remember in the File Name box, such as** Normal Firewall, **and click Save.**

   The Registry Editor puts an icon called `Normal Firewall.reg` on your Windows desktop.

9. **Choose File⇨Exit to get out of the Registry Editor.**

10. **To create a Lockdown icon on your Windows desktop, follow Steps 1 and 2 to bring up the main Windows Firewall dialog box. Select the Don't Allow Exceptions box, and then click OK to leave Windows Firewall.**

    Windows Firewall makes the change in the Registry, effectively locking down your PC.

11. **Follow Steps 5 through 7 to export the Registry's FirewallPolicy key. Then in Step 8, type a different name, such as** Lock Down, **in the File Name box, and click Save.**

    That puts an icon called `Lock Down.reg` on your Windows desktop.

12. **Choose File⇨Exit to get out of the Registry Editor.**

13. **Repeat Steps 1 and 2, and set up the Windows Firewall so it's wide open.**

Personally, I check all the boxes on the Exceptions list except UPnP Framework. UPnP has been the source of so many problems — including three botched patches from Microsoft — that I simply don't trust it any more. You may own hardware that requires UPnP (the documentation can tell you). If so, you have my condolences.

14. **Click OK to exit Windows Firewall.**

15. **Follow Steps 5 through 7 to export the FirewallPolicy key. In Step 8, type something that will keep you on your toes — I like** Wide Open **— and click Save.**

    You now have an icon called `Wide Open.reg` on your Windows desktop.

16. **Choose File⇨Exit and leave Registry Editor.**

17. **Immediately test your icons by double-clicking the** `Lock Down.reg` **icon. The Registry Editor asks you if you're sure you want to make the changes — yes, of course you do — and it informs you that the changes have been made — yes, you know.**

    If you then bring up Windows Firewall, you see that you're in full lockdown — that Don't Allow Exceptions box is checked.

Hey, maybe Microsoft will figure out how to make Registry changes this quick and easy for the next version of Windows. Whaddya think?

Building a Better Firewall

Save Time By

- Understanding Windows Firewall's shortcomings
- Knowing if you need a better firewall
- Installing and using ZoneAlarm, if you need it

You probably know that a *firewall* watches incoming Internet traffic and makes sure that the bad guys stay out. Windows Firewall, which ships with Windows XP Service Pack 2, does a good job of blocking bad inbound traffic (although the interface makes it harder than it should be — see Technique 50). You may be surprised to know that most firewall programs also block *outgoing* traffic if it looks suspicious. Windows Firewall doesn't. I guess Microsoft ran out of money when they were building Windows Firewall. Something like that.

While it's much more important that you keep the bad guys out, once they've jumped over the fence and infected your machine, it's important to keep them from spreading their offal all across the Internet. If you were infected before you got Service Pack 2 installed, or while you have a momentary lapse in Windows Firewall's protection for whatever reason, your PC may have been turned into a zombie — under the silent control of someone else. Millions of PCs have been subverted. If your firewall doesn't warn you about bad outgoing traffic, you have no way of telling when your PC starts spewing millions of spam messages, or launches a Denial of Service attack on a Web page.

This technique explains why the built-in firewall in Windows XP Service Pack 2 may not be the best choice, how to set up a free-for-personal-use firewall from ZoneAlarm, and how to configure ZoneAlarm quickly and correctly the first time.

Understanding Firewalls

The term *firewall* evokes an image of an impregnable barrier between your computer and the Internet. Alas, in reality, life isn't so simple. A computer firewall is more like a harried cop at a busy intersection than a solid wall.

For the home and small office user, firewalls fall into two broad categories:

- **Hardware firewalls** are built into a box that connects directly to the Internet. Many DSL and cable routers, and Internet address sharing boxes (see Technique 45) include their own built-in firewalls. D-Link and LinkSys both offer good stand-alone hardware firewalls for about $50. They're difficult to update because you have to change the firmware inside the hardware box. Typically, you can change settings on the firewall by using Internet Explorer.
- **Software firewalls** run on the computer that's connected to the Internet. If you have Windows XP Service Pack 2, you're running Windows Firewall. (Unless you've disabled it, anyway.) Windows Firewall does a good job of playing traffic cop with incoming data. But it doesn't even try to catch bad data that's headed out.

Each type of firewall has its pros and cons, as you can see in Table 51-1.

Blocking bad outbound data isn't merely an exercise in good Internet citizenship. It also adds an extra layer of protection for your own home or office network. A firewall that catches malicious outbound packets tells you if your PC has been turned into a zombie, and it's spewing spam or Denial of Service attacks. It also tells you if one PC on your network is trying to infect other PCs, retrieve data from them surreptitiously, or use uninfected PCs to break out to the Internet. Attacks are getting more sophisticated every day. If a piece of malware gets in to a specific PC, you should be very concerned about it getting out.

Every PC should be running a software firewall. In addition, I generally recommend that people use hardware firewalls on small networks, simply because they add an independent layer of protection. To further complicate matters, you may well find that you want to run *two* software firewalls on the same PC. There's nothing wrong with that, particularly if one of the firewalls is Windows Firewall.

TABLE 51-1: PROS AND CONS OF HARDWARE AND SOFTWARE FIREWALLS

Type of Firewall	Pros	Cons
Hardware firewalls	Excellent for keeping intruders from getting into your PC or your local network.	Generally don't do much to monitor outgoing traffic (such as data being transmitted by a Trojan that resides, unbeknownst to you, on your system).
	Easy to use.	Hard to set up.
	Runs fast.	
Software firewalls	Don't weigh anything — a definite plus if you want a firewall for your portable computer when you're on the road.	The kind that monitors outgoing traffic is more difficult to train because they monitor outgoing traffic. You have to tell the firewall which Internet traffic originating on your machine or network is legitimate so that the firewall can block the rest.
	Easier to customize, and usually easier to set up and get working.	Because software firewalls run on your PC, they slow down your PC whenever you're online.
	After they're trained, they're also easy to use.	

What to Look for in a Software Firewall

Software firewalls examine traffic as it leaves your network and goes to the Internet and traffic from the Internet that's being directed to your network. A good firewall can

- **Allow only data into your network that's been requested by someone on your network.** If you ask for a Web page, it appears. But if somebody tries to send something that you didn't request, the unsolicited data gets trashed. The same thing happens on a stand-alone computer: You get only data that you request from the Internet.
- **Ask you if it's okay for a specific program to send out data.** That gives you a chance to clear programs such as Internet Explorer and MSN Messenger that have to send data, but take a look at other programs that may not be so benign. With some firewalls, you can block all outbound traffic from all programs except a handful that you specifically allow (such as Internet Explorer).
- **Block attempts to get at blacklisted Web sites from your network.** If you want to keep everyone on your network from getting at `www.IHateBigCompanies.com`, you can tell the firewall not to allow any information going out that's bound to that site. It can block other types of outbound traffic as well.
- **Make your network (or your computer) *invisible* to the Internet.** Even if somebody knows your IP address, any attempt to get information from that address is met with silence.

Windows Firewall scores high on the first point, and reasonably well on the last point, but doesn't even begin to look at the two in the middle. And there's the rub.

Using Windows Firewall

Windows Firewall comes along for the ride when you install Windows XP Service Pack 2. In general, Windows Firewall just works — you don't have to do anything to it — although you may find yourself in a position where you need to poke a hole in the firewall, particularly if you use software that needs to communicate with other computers on the Internet.

I talk about poking holes in Windows Firewall in Technique 50. A full rundown on using Windows Firewall is in *Windows XP All-in-One Desk Reference For Dummies*, 2nd Edition. And more about firewalls in general is in *Firewalls For Dummies*, 2nd Edition, by Brian Komar, Ronald Beekelaar, and Joern Wettern (Wiley Publishing, Inc.)

If you've never looked at Windows Firewall, it's well worth a few minutes right now to take a look at the high points:

1. **Choose Start➪Control Panel➪Security Center.**

   Windows brings up the Windows Security Center, which I discuss in Technique 49.

2. **At the bottom of the Security Center, click Windows Firewall.**

   Windows Firewall's main dialog box appears (see Figure 51-1). To understand the precise meaning of the three choices, see Table 51-2. Unless you've changed things, Windows Firewall is set On, and it's protecting all your networking connections.

If any of the options in Windows Firewall are grayed out, you aren't permitted to change the settings. Usually that happens when you're connected to a Big Corporate Network, and somebody has decided that you can't be trusted to control your own computer.

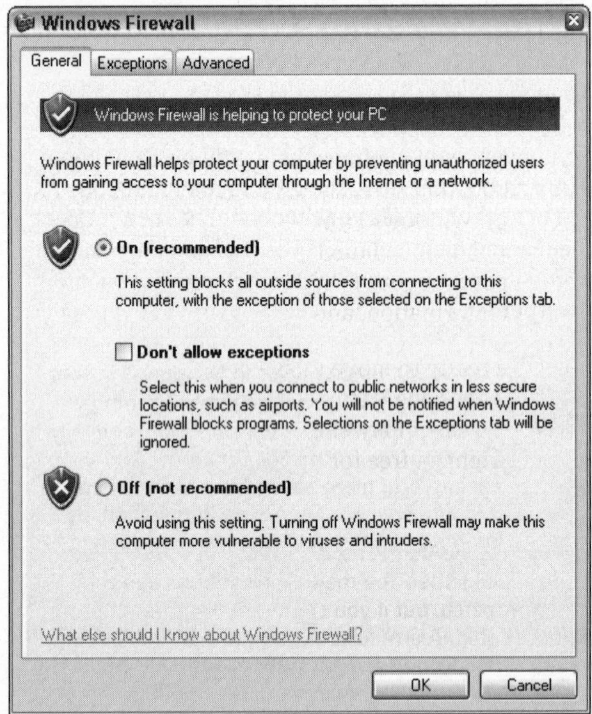

• **Figure 51-1: Windows Firewall's main control point.**

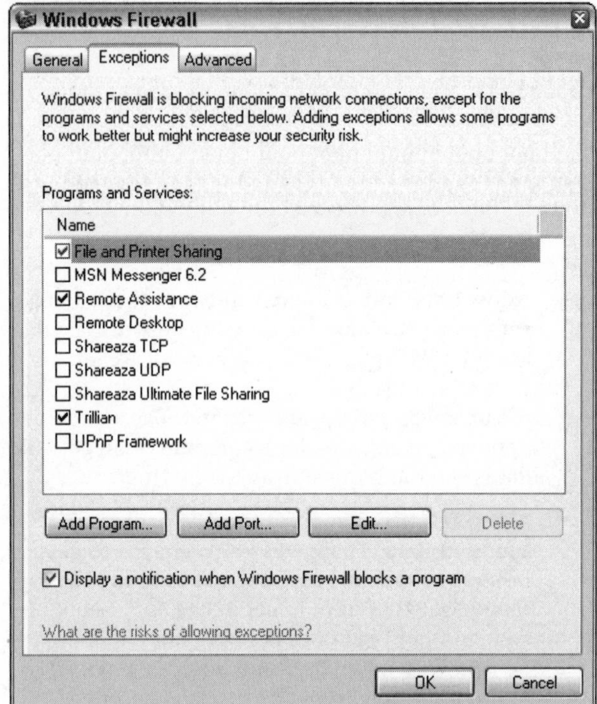

• **Figure 51-2: Exceptions to the stateful firewall rules are listed here.**

3. **Click the Exceptions tab (see Figure 51-2).**

Windows Firewall allows data packets into your machine only if they were sent in response to a specific request originating on your machine (that's the stateful firewall). Exceptions to that

TABLE 51-2: WINDOWS FIREWALL SETTINGS ON THE GENERAL TAB

This setting	Means
On (recommended)	Windows Firewall keeps track of requests for information headed out of the computer (for example, requests to retrieve a Web page, or to download a file) and allows traffic back in only if it can be matched to a specific earlier request. (That's called *stateful monitoring.*) Windows Firewall allows any exceptions detailed on the Exceptions tab (see Technique 50). And it monitors all the networking connections that are checked at the top of the Advanced tab (see Figure 51-3).
Don't Allow Exceptions	Same as On but all the entries on the Exceptions tab are ignored, and every connection gets monitored, regardless of whether or not it's checked on the Advanced tab.
Off (not recommended)	Turns off Windows Firewall.

rule — either programs, or designated *ports* (addresses) — are spelled out on this tab, and you can control which exceptions get enforced by checking or unchecking boxes on this tab. I talk about both kinds of exceptions in Technique 50.

4. **Click the Advanced tab (see Figure 51-3).**

   Make sure that all the boxes in the Network Connection Settings section at the top are checked. If you uncheck a box, Windows Firewall stops monitoring that connection unless you check the Don't Allow Exceptions box on the General tab (refer to Figure 51-1).

5. **Click OK to get out of Windows Firewall.**

No doubt you noticed that absolutely no provision controls outbound data. Windows Firewall doesn't even look at it.

• **Figure 51-3: Make sure all your networking connections are being monitored.**

Installing ZoneAlarm

If you aren't overly worried about infecting other PCs on your network — indeed, if you don't have a network — and you're reasonably sure that your computer isn't currently infected, you may wish to stick with Windows Firewall. That's certainly a reasonable choice, although you should be ever mindful of the fact that your PC could be sending out all sorts of information, and you'd never even know.

If you're ready to move up in the firewall world, I believe that ZoneAlarm is your best choice. It's effective, reasonably easy to install and use, and the price is right — free for individual use. (But there's a charge if you use it for a company.)

ZoneAlarm and Windows Firewall can work together. You may hit an occasional bumpy patch, but if you do, rest assured that the ZoneAlarm folks are most interested in keeping ZoneAlarm compatible with Windows Firewall. ZoneAlarm even shows up in the Windows Security Center firewall status report.

To install ZoneAlarm, follow these steps:

1. **Start Internet Explorer and surf to** `www.zonealarm.com`**.**

   Zone Labs, the company that makes ZoneAlarm, sells a wide variety of products. If you want to buy ZoneAlarm Pro — just $9.95 at this writing, including one year of updates — by all means do so. If you want the free version, you want the product called, simply, ZoneAlarm.

2. **You may have some difficulty finding the free download link, but at this writing, you can download ZoneAlarm by clicking the Download & Buy and then ZoneAlarm links; then click the Free Download button.**

3. **Follow the instructions and download it.**

4. **After you download the file, double-click it.**

   ZoneAlarm then steps you through a very simple setup wizard and has you going in no time.

5. **Click the Select ZoneAlarm Pro radio button in the ZA License Wizard.**

   That gets you kick-started, feeding ZoneAlarm a list of "safe" programs (see Figure 51-4). When you finish the 15-day trial, you can switch back to ZoneAlarm, no problem.

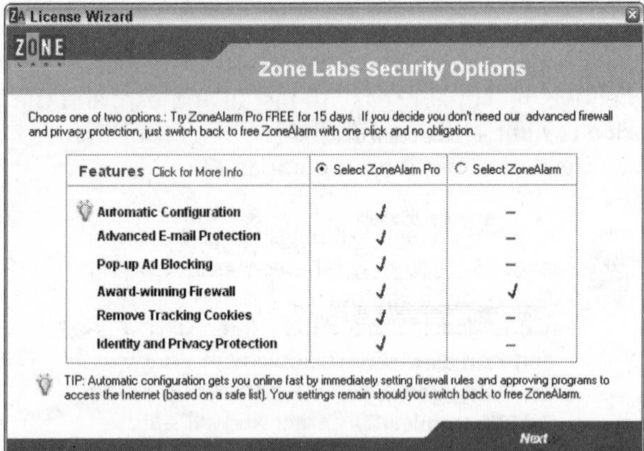

• **Figure 51-4: Install ZoneAlarm Pro to cut down on your setup hassles.**

6. **Finish the setup using Automatic Program AlertAdvisor Settings.**

   ZoneAlarm Pro reboots your machine and takes you through a quick tutorial.

After the tutorial is done, if you have a network, you are taken to a Network Configuration Wizard, which steps you through the process of protecting the PC from the network. Although there are some subtleties, ZoneAlarm is primarily interested in setting up File and Printer Sharing for this computer on the network. In the end, you see ZoneAlarm's main screen (see Figure 51-5).

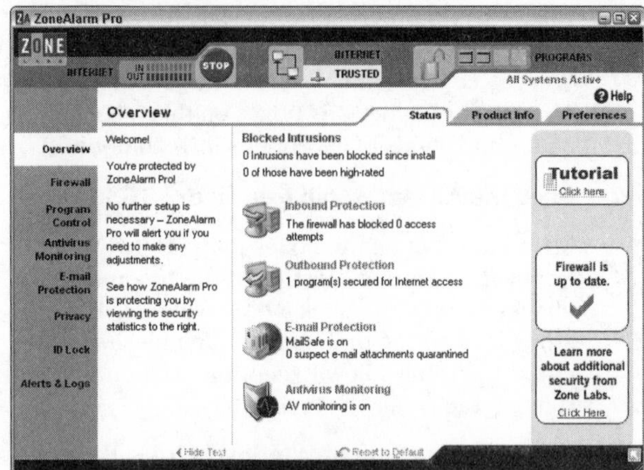

• **Figure 51-5: ZoneAlarm's control screen.**

Honing ZoneAlarm

If you followed the instructions in the preceding section and set up ZoneAlarm Pro with its automatic AlertAdvisor settings, you're ready to run. From time to time, particularly when you start to use the product, you see warnings, such as the one in Figure 51-6. It's easy to get spooked. In the immortal words of Douglas Adams, "DON'T PANIC!"

ZoneAlarm shows two different kinds of alerts:

- **Firewall Alerts** (see Figure 51-6) happen when an attempt occurs to get into your computer. If you see an alert with a red band at the top, however, you may have a problem, and ZoneAlarm has already averted it. When you click OK in a Firewall Alert, you're merely acknowledging that ZoneAlarm has done its job. You aren't changing any settings or reducing the scope of the firewall.
- **Program Alerts** (as shown in Figure 51-7) occur when ZoneAlarm doesn't recognize a program on your network that's trying to connect to the Internet. Internet Explorer is pre-configured as a "good" program. Others — including Outlook — may be allowed to pass through if you chose to

run an automatic configuration in the preceding section. If you click the Allow button in a Program Alert, you're giving your permission for that program to go out to the Internet for as long as the program keeps running.

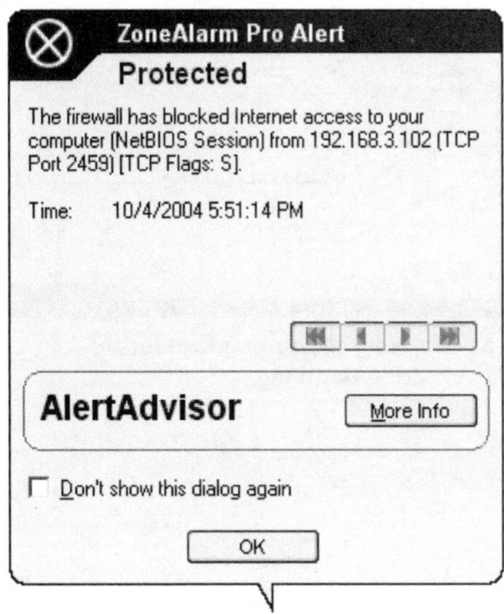

• **Figure 51-6: An alert that another computer is attempting to access this computer directly.**

ZoneLabs has a huge database of programs that may trigger Program Alerts. You can go straight to it by clicking the More Info button on the Alert itself.

When confronted with a Program Alert, if you want that program to contact the Internet just this time, click Yes.

To let that program always connect to the Internet, check the Remember This Setting box.

Click the Deny button if the program is a total unknown, but be alert: If some program you need to use mysteriously stops working, chances are that it's been blocked by your new firewall (per your request).

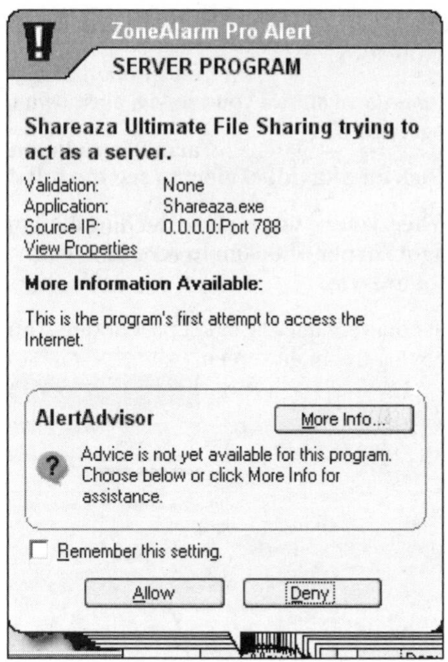

• **Figure 51-7: An alert about a program inside the firewall that's trying to get out — Shareaza, for example.**

You have no automatic way to turn off Program Alerts permanently. Each one requires a Yes or No from you.

Checking the Logs

If you're ever terminally curious about what's been blocked — or if you can't get something to work and you can't figure out why — look at the log:

1. **Double-click the ZA icon in the Windows notification area, down near the clock.**

   ZoneAlarm appears. (Refer to Figure 51-5.)

2. **On the left, click Alerts & Logs.**

   You see the Alerts & Logs dialog box.

3. **Click the Log Viewer tab in the Alerts & Logs dialog box.**

   ZoneAlarm shows you the log, as shown in Figure 51-8.

4. **Click an individual alert to see the full details.**

5. **When you're done, click the X in the upper-right corner of the main screen to exit ZoneAlarm.**

   Of course, ZoneAlarm keeps working. You're just leaving the main screen.

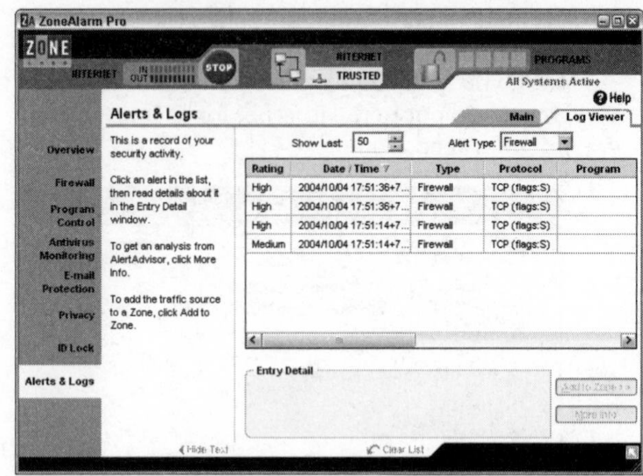

• **Figure 51-8: A very handy interface for the ZoneAlarm log.**

Zapping Scumware

Save Time By

- Recognizing scumware — spyware, adware, hijackers, and other lowlifes
- Installing Spybot-S&D
- Getting the scum out

Scumware's everywhere. Talk about a growth industry.

You have to feel sorry for the folks at Microsoft who deal with the scum. The programmers who wrote the installer for Windows XP Service Pack 2 were livid when they discovered that their final release choked on machines that were running a self-described "permission-based contextual marketing network" called T.V. Media (`www.totalvelocity.com`).

Most people who were running this, uh, contextual marketing network had no idea that the program was installed — and they blamed Microsoft when the Service Pack 2 installer croaked.

Microsoft spent hundreds of millions of dollars on SP2, and this piece of, uh, contextual marketing network software brought the installer to its knees.

And you think *you* have scumware problems.

What Is Scum?

Far as I'm concerned, scumware is in the eyes of the beholder.

To be a leeeetle bit more specific, *scumware* is a generic term for software that slithers into your system, usually as part of a program that you download and install, but occasionally in the guise of an e-mail attachment. Scumware does annoying things — hijacks your Internet Explorer home page, keeps track of the things you type or the pages you visit, or pops up ads while you're trying to work. Some types of scumware even download their own updates automatically, without your permission, or "phone home" and deposit information about you on the scumauthor's computers.

Scumware companies frequently call their products "adware" but that's gilding a jet-black lily. It's true that scumware asks before it installs itself on your computer, but frequently the details are buried in hundreds of lines of dense pseudo-legal mumbo-jumbo.

The most successful company in this business, by far, is an outfit that used to be called Gator, which just changed its name to Claria. Gator also goes by the acrimonious acronym GAIN — for Gator Advertising Information Network. Remember those names. In my book, they're scumware, and if you're ever given an opportunity to download and install a program that's signed by Claria, uh, Gator, er, GAIN, to coin a phrase, just say No. (And you thought I was only cynical about Microsoft.)

Knowing When You've Been Slimed

It's pretty hard to define the term "scum" and, as you might imagine, it's even harder to define the term "scumware". But you can bet that you're looking up the scummy side of the cash cow when:

- Internet Explorer goes bananas: Your home page gets hijacked; IE starts showing you "search" pages that specialize in, uh, barnyard animals with unusual talents; IE suddenly sports a new toolbar; or you get redirected to pages that don't match anything you ever typed.
- You start getting pop-up ads on your desktop and you aren't even using a Web browser, or you get pop-ups that have nothing to do with the site you're visiting. Yes, they often reference barnyard animals with unusual talents.
- You have a firewall that monitors outbound traffic (such as ZoneAlarm; see Technique 51) and it keeps warning you that some program you've never heard of is trying to send data out to the Internet. Moo.

If you think you've stepped in it big time, try running the scan at `www.pcpitstop.com`. It's a good, easy (and free!) place to start.

You should also run Ad-Aware, which I discuss in Technique 53. Ad-Aware's focus lies more with advertising, cookies, and the like — but there's lots and lots of overlap between scummy advertising and, er, scum in general.

Running Spybot-S&D

Every Windows XP user should install and regularly use Spybot-S&D.

Patrick Kolla's Spybot-Search & Destroy rates as the number-one spyware identifier and eliminator. Here's how to get it:

1. **Start Internet Explorer and go to** `www.safer-networking.org`**.**
2. **Click the Download link (which is probably on the left). Then click through to a download site, and download the program.**

   You may get redirected to a different site. You are probably required to click IE's download blocker, and again on a security warning.
3. **Run the downloaded file.**

   Spybot-S&D takes you through a quick, easy installation. When you finish, Spybot launches itself and offers to take a snapshot of the Registry. Go ahead. (Removing some spyware can cause programs to stop working. Spybot-S&D may be able to get those programs working again if it has access to a clean copy of the Registry.) Then Spybot offers to scan for updates. Get them and install them. You end up at the main Spybot-S&D screen (see Figure 52-1).
4. **Click the Search & Destroy icon on the left. Then click Check For Problems (see Figure 52-2).**

   Go get a latte. This can take a while.

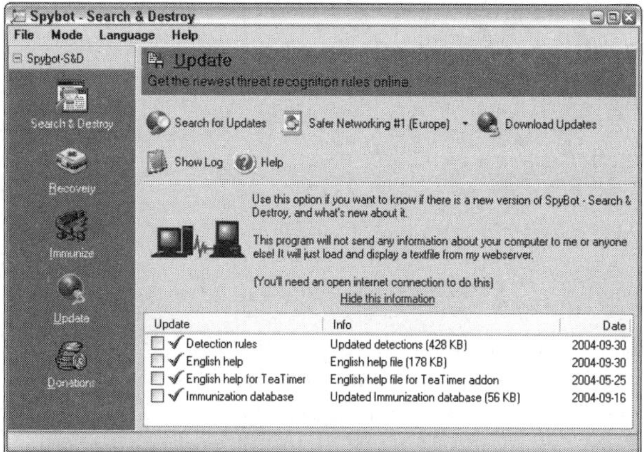

• **Figure 52-1: Spybot-S&D's main screen**

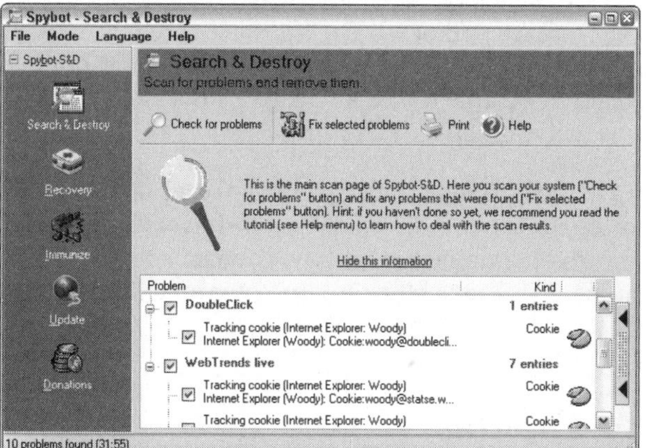

• **Figure 52-2: Spybot-S&D doesn't start until you click Check for Problems.**

5. **When you (and Spybot) come back, all the problem entries are checked. Click Fix Selected Problems.**

   Spybot creates a System Restore Point, and then zaps out the offending entries. The System Restore Point may come in handy in the highly unlikely event that Spybot removes something from your system that you really need. If running Spybot sends everything to Hades in a Handbasket, go through the steps in Technique 64 to bring your old system back.

   In some cases, your piece of scum may launch every time Windows starts, and you may not be able to figure out which program is causing the problem. Spybot can't delete a running program, so you may need to run Spybot in Advanced mode (choose Mode⇨Advanced Mode) and have it scan when you reboot the machine.

6. **Run Spybot every week or two.**

   Make sure you click the Update button to get the latest scummy definitions.

   Patrick asks for a donation if you use the program: money well spent, in my opinion.

Going Beyond Spybot

So you've tried Ad-Aware, you've tried PC Pitstop, and you've tried Spybot-S&D, and you still have problems. Who ya gonna call?

Scumbusters.

Something like that. An excellent discussion of every trick in the scumbusting book is at `www.michaelhorowitz.com/removespyware.html`. Good job, Michael.

Canning Adware and Obnoxious Cookies

Save Time By

- Understanding what cookies can and can't do
- Using Ad-Aware to knock out scumware
- Setting up Internet Explorer to deal with cookies on your terms

Everybody's worried about cookies, of course, but few understand how they work and why they even exist. I find that people have lots of misconceptions about cookies. People lose work — heck, people lose *sleep* — over cookies, when a little bit of plain talk and some simple prevention can reduce your chances of problems to almost zero.

I say "almost zero" because bugs have been discovered in Internet Explorer that pose a real threat to all of us. The bugs allow renegade Web sites to merrily cavort through all the cookies on your PC, even though Web sites aren't supposed to be able to see any cookies but their own. No telling if similar bugs will crop up in the future.

This technique shows you how to fight back against unscrupulous marketing types, using a program called Ad-Aware. It also shows you why most cookies are good for you, demonstrates how you can subvert them, and offers some commonsense, quick steps to protect yourself from the "bad" cookies.

Understanding Cookies

People have wasted more time fretting over cookies than any other Web topic. It's all for naught. Most cookies aren't evil. They aren't even mysterious. But what are they? *Cookies* are simple text files that Web sites place on users' PCs (see Figure 53-1).

• **Figure 53-1: The cookie that was put on my PC by Google (**`www.google.com`**).**

Web sites want to put a cookie on your machine so they can keep track of your online comings and goings. The simplest cookies contain what amounts to a customer number; when you return to the Web site, Internet Explorer delivers the cookie to the site. The Web site's computer can look up your customer number and use that number to figure out all sorts of things. For example, on cnn.com, your customer number tells the CNN computer which regional newsgroup you prefer (U.S., Europe, Asia, and so on). On Amazon.com, your customer number tells the Amazon computer whether you have a shopping basket in the works, or any saved items; Amazon also uses your customer number to look up your buying history and pepper its pages with offerings you may find tantalizing.

Internet Explorer has several cookie settings that are difficult to understand unless you're acquainted with how cookies work in the real world. The following sections step you through the good, the bad, and the ugly, so you can understand what IE settings make sense for you.

In most cases, Web sites stick an identifying number in your cookie. In my Google cookie, shown in Figure 53-1, that number is 4f1d70694c573efa. The number doesn't signify anything. It's just a handy way to keep track of what I've done on the Google Web site. To see what's happening, consider this hypothetical interaction:

1. You start Internet Explorer and go to `www.google.com`.
2. Google asks your computer, "Do you have a Google cookie?"
3. The computer responds, "Yes" and hands over the cookie file.
4. The Google computer looks up the identifying number, 4f1d70694c573efa, and discovers that you have an outstanding order for Froogle (Google's shopping service) pending.

   Actually, I'm the one with the Froogle order, but bear with me.
5. Google sends the computer the standard Google search page, with a little note asking if you want to check on the status of your Froogle order.
6. As you use Google, the Google computer keeps track of what you're doing and adds that information to its database for customer 4f1d70694c573efa.
7. From time to time, for reasons of its own devising, the Google computer may send a new cookie to your computer. Your computer dutifully stores the new cookie, wiping out the old one.

That's how cookies work. Very simple. Nothing to worry about, right? For the most part. But sometimes cookies aren't so simple, or that quaint. The plot thickens.

Gathering information with cookies

Say you surf to `www.billyjoebobsite.com`, and the site puts a cookie on your PC that identifies you as customer 4f1d70694c573efa.

Every time you interact with a Web site, Internet Explorer sends a handful of relatively innocuous information to the Web site:

- **Your IP address:** That's the number that uniquely identifies your computer on the Internet. If you have an always-on Internet connection, such as with a cable modem, or DSL or satellite, your IP address doesn't change. On the other hand, if you have a dial-up Internet connection, your IP address probably changes each time you dial in.
- **The domain name of your Internet service provider:** For example, if your ISP is Earthlink, then the domain name is `earthlink.com`.
- **Your Web browser and version number:** Internet Explorer Version 6, for example.
- **The Web site you just came from:** Commonly called a *referring URL*, this information can be used in somewhat unexpected ways.

All this information can be stored in a database record for a customer number, such as 4f1d70694c573efa.

In the course of running around billyjoebobsite.com, you order *Southern Cooking in a Nutshell* from his online shopping center. You type in your name, address, telephone number, e-mail address, and credit card number.

Bingo.

A cookie is on your computer — one that only billyjoebobsite.com can retrieve — that identifies you as customer 4f1d70694c573efa. Now an entry in the billyjoebobsite.com computer matches 4f1d70694c573efa with a specific name, address, e-mail address, and credit card number. The entry also says you ordered *Southern Cooking in a Nutshell.*

In the normal course of events, the fact that billyjoebobsite.com has your mailing address shouldn't cause you much lost sleep. After all, you're the one who typed your address on its Web page. Chances are good that billyjoebobsite has a security policy that protects you (see Technique 72). No doubt you trusted billyjoebobsite to protect your credit card number when you gave it to them to process your order. The problem comes when billyjoebobsite teams up with a company that isn't quite so scrupulous, and together they start planting spy cookies on your PC.

Passing information with spy cookies

Say that billyjoebobsite.com sells an ad to badadguys.com. That ad appears as a picture — a *banner ad* — on one of the billyjoebobsite.com pages. The folks at badadguys.com pay billyjoebobsite.com to run the banner ad. The ad may be so small you can't even see it. The people at badadguys.com may be selling something — or maybe not. It's entirely possible that badadguys.com pays to have billyjoebobsite.com run the ad, solely so that badadguys.com can harvest information about people who visit the BillyJoeBob site.

Here's how the whole banner ad thing works:

When you surf to the page that contains the banner ad from badadguys.com, the billyjoebobsite.com computer hands over data to the badadguys.com computer, which in turn provides the ad that shows up on the page, on your computer.

Got that? That's the way most banner ads work.

Of course, billyjoebobsite is a conscientious site that doesn't hand out, say, your credit card number. So visiting billyjoebobsite won't send your credit card number to badadguys. Still, as I explain later in this technique, the amount of information badadguys can gather about you and your surfing habits can be considerable.

Because the badadguys.com computer puts an ad on the page, it can stick a cookie on your machine, too — a so-called *third-party cookie*. It's third-party because you didn't go to any badadguys.com Web site: The cookie is brought along to the party when you view the ad on the billyjoebobsite.com Web page.

I tend to use the terms *third-party cookie* and spy cookie interchangeably. Third-party cookies, almost invariably, exist to extract information surreptitiously. They're spies.

To see how this becomes a problem, consider what can happen if the badadguys.com cookie identifies you as, oh, visitor 123456789:

1. You surf to the billyjoebobsite.com page that has the badadguys.com ad on it.
2. The billyjoebobsite.com computer knows that you are customer 4f1d70694c573efa, so the computer looks you up in its database.
3. The billyjoebobsite.com computer contacts the badadguys.com computer and says something like, "My customer number 4f1d70694c573efa just asked for a banner ad. Here's his name, e-mail address, and phone number. I won't give you his credit card number, but he's ordered a copy of *Southern Cooking in a Nutshell* from us, and spent $24.97. Would you send him an ad?"
4. The badadguys.com computer asks your computer if you have a badadguys.com cookie. Your computer says "Yes" and sends the cookie — the third-party (or spy) cookie — to the badadguys.com computer.
5. The badadguys.com computer looks at the cookie, discovers you are badadguys.com visitor number 123456789, *and* that you're billyjoebobsite.com customer 4f1d70694c573efa.

6. The badadguys.com computer puts two and two together and updates its records for visitor 123456789 with your name, address, telephone number, e-mail address, and some information on your shopping habits — all of which are provided, as part of the advertising deal, by billyjoebob site.com.

That's how third-party/spy cookies can be used to transmit information to a central badadguys.com computer.

Combining information with spy cookies

Soon doubleclick.com . . . er, badadguys.com has a big database. The company grows by leaps and bounds. It pays Web sites big bucks to carry their banner ads. Soon every Tom, Dick, Harry, Billy, Joe, and Bob wants to put badadguys.com ads on their Web pages.

Say one day you surf to www.tomdicknharry.com. You don't know it, but the tomdicknharry.com Web site has a banner ad from badadguys.com, too. You sign up for the tomdicknharry.com newsletter, and buy a couple of lavender tortillas from the site.

Click-click-click. The minute you hit a page with a badadguys.com ad on it, the badadguys.com computer is updated with your e-mail address, and the fact that you bought lavender tortillas. Badadguys already knows that you've spent $30 to buy a Southern cooking book. The result: You get more spam — and, no doubt, ads for lavender tortillas.

Even if you don't buy anything or provide any more personally identifiable information, badadguys.com knows who visitor 123456789 is, and it's relatively easy to keep full details of where you've gone and what you've done. Spy cookies make it all possible.

The spy cookie companies are fully aware of the fine line they're treading, and most of them wouldn't dream of asking their "host" sites to pass on credit card numbers or other financial information. But they're still amassing enormous amounts of information, which can be correlated in unexpected ways.

With the proliferation of always-on Internet connections, collating information from spy cookies is much simpler than ever before. Your Internet address – your IP address – goes along for the ride every time you look at a Web page.

Looking for spy cookies on your PC

Are you worried about spy cookies on your PC? Don't be overly concerned: Almost everybody has them, and if the spy cookie cow is already out of the barn, you can't do a whole lot. How's *that* for a mixed metaphor?

If you want to see spy cookies on your machine:

1. **Choose Start⇨My Computer, and navigate to** C:\Documents and Settings*<username>*\Cookies, **where** *<username>* **is your user name.**

   My C:\Documents and Settings\woody\Cookies folder looks like Figure 53-2. It has a lot of small text files — my cookies.

2. **Look for files with the word *ad*, *ads*, or *advertising* in the name. If you're curious, open the ones that look suspicious.**

   There's no need to delete them. In the next section, I show you how to do that automatically.

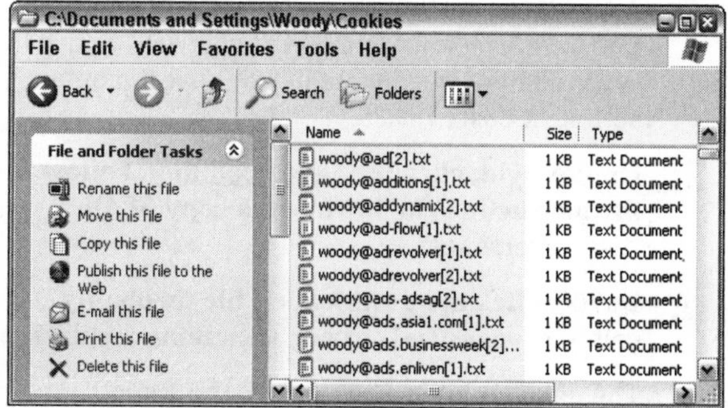

• **Figure 53-2: My cookie collection.**

Zapping Advertising Junk with Ad-Aware

Not all cookies are bad. But the bad ones — spy cookies in particular — can be very irritating. You can end up on spam lists. It's highly unlikely that spy cookies will leave you prone to identity theft, but some personal information could go to a company you've never heard of. Your Web surfing habits could be collated. Not good.

The best, fastest, easiest way to protect yourself is with a two-prong approach. First, install a bad cookie catcher. Second, double-check your Internet Explorer settings to make sure the most irritating cookies don't get through.

The best bad cookie blocker I've found is a product from Lavasoft called Ad-Aware Standard Edition. It's free for noncommercial use. I run it every week. Amazing what it can find.

Here's how to get it going:

1. **Start Internet Explorer and go to `www.lavasoft.nu`.**

   Note the `.nu`.

2. **In the Software category on the left, click the Ad-Aware Personal link.**

   That takes you to the explanation page for Ad-Aware Personal Edition. Ad-Aware Personal is free for non-commercial use. If you want to use it in a commercial, educational, or governmental setting, it costs $39.95.

3. **On the right, click the Download link. Follow the instructions to download a copy of Ad-Aware Personal.**

4. **Double-click the downloaded file (probably called `aawpersonal.exe` or something similar).**

   The installer takes you through the steps.

Make sure you tell Ad-Aware to Update Definition File Now when you install it. Ad-Aware doesn't automatically update its definition file unless you give your permission.

5. **Ad-Aware looks for the latest definition file (see Figure 53-3). Click Connect. If a new reference file is available, click OK. Click Finish.**

   Wait while the reference file is updated. You return to the main screen.

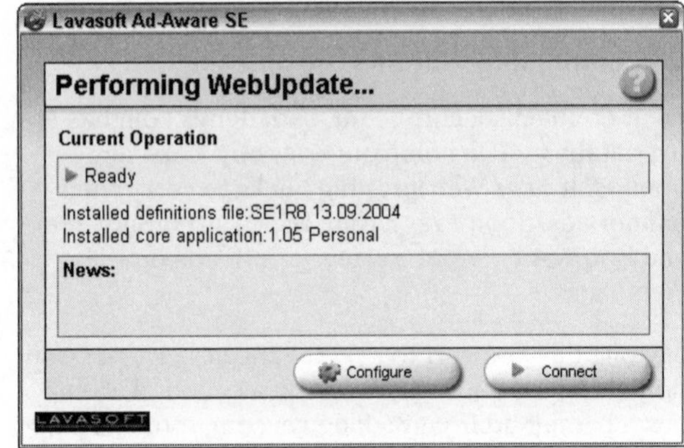

• **Figure 53-3: Ad-Aware looks for the latest definition file.**

6. **Click the Scan Now button.**

   Ad-Aware performs an in-depth scan (see Figure 53-4). Go get a cup of coffee.

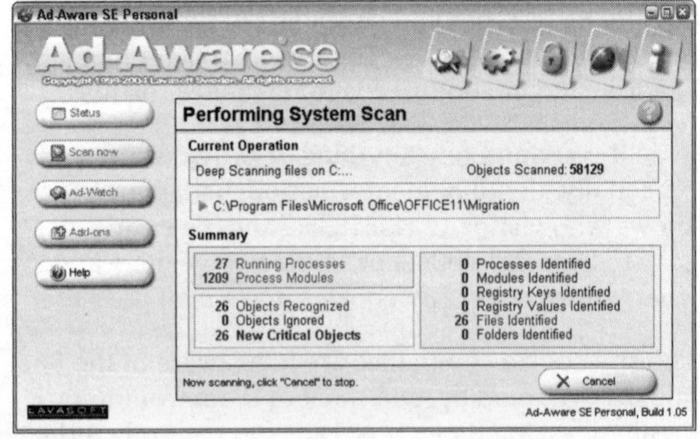

• **Figure 53-4: An Ad-Aware scan in progress.**

When the scan finishes, you hear a rather rude sound, and the Scanning Results dialog box shows you how many ornery critters have been uncovered.

7. Right-click the box in front of the first Object listed and choose Select All Objects.

That puts a check mark in front of each scummy object Ad-Aware has found (see Figure 53-5).

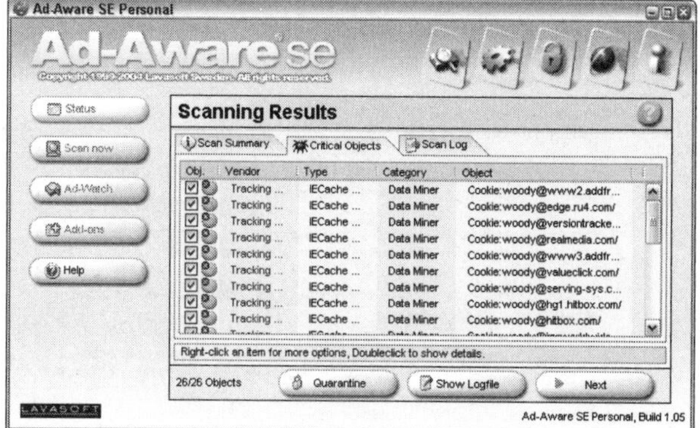

• **Figure 53-5: Select all the junk that Ad-Aware finds.**

8. Scroll through the list of Critical Objects, and see if any stand out as potentially legitimate. If you think one of the entries might be something you want to keep, double-click it and read Ad-Aware's synopsis (see Figure 53-6). Click the Close or To Clipboard button when you're done to go back to the Scanning Results list.

In many cases, you're given an opportunity to link to specific information on Ad-Aware's Web site. If you have any doubt at all, check it out.

9. In the unlikely event that you see something that obviously should be saved, uncheck the box in front of it.

10. Click the Quarantine button.

Ad-Aware prompts you for a filename where it can store the Quarantined entries. It copies all the items you've checked into the Quarantine file, and then returns to the main screen.

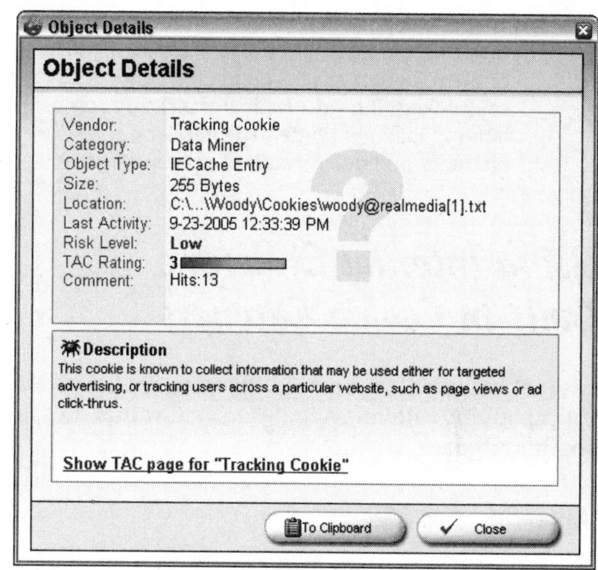

• **Figure 53-6: Double-click an entry to see the details. In this case, RealMedia dumped a ton of scummy cookies on my machine.**

The Quarantine file can come in handy if you suddenly discover that Ad-Aware has removed something that you need in order to keep a program (or Web site) working. If an Ad-Aware scan zaps something it shouldn't have, click Open Quarantine List on the main Ad-Aware page, and restore the offending entry.

11. Click Next.

Ad-Aware deletes all the quarantined files, and then returns to the Status page, ready to run again.

12. Click the Close (X) button to leave Ad-Aware.

In the past, I've advised people to avoid using Ad-Watch, the sprightly offspring of Ad-Aware that watches in the background and warns you when spy cookies are being, uh, deposited on your computer. I had a lot of stability problems with earlier versions. With Ad-Aware SE, though, Lavasoft seems to have solved the earlier difficulties. If you're willing to spring $39.95 to upgrade to the fully licensed version of Ad-Aware (which includes Ad-Watch), you will probably find Ad-Watch a worthy addition to your scum-fighting repertoire. Granted, most of the notices revolve around fairly innocuous spy cookies. But Ad-Watch also picks up some Internet Explorer home page hijacking attempts, and other insults to your intelligence.

Using Internet Explorer's Built-In Cookie Catchers

Internet Explorer has a straightforward cookie catching capability, with one Achilles heel: It works on the honor system.

Understanding P3P

All major Web sites and most smaller ones have a formalized, published policy on gathering personal data and giving it away (or, more likely, selling it). Individual sites may collect individually identifiable data, such as your IP address or your name. They may limit themselves to more general data. They may hold onto the data and never share any of it. They may immediately broadcast any information you give them to the slimiest spammers on the planet. The formal privacy policy statement explains all.

Fortunately, the statements are in a standard form: The *Platform for Privacy Preferences* (or P3P) privacy policy relies on standardized building blocks to let a Web site tell you precisely what it intends to do with your data.

Most importantly, both humans and Internet Explorer can read a P3P policy. To see a P3P policy:

1. **Start Internet Explorer.**
2. **Navigate to the site whose privacy policy interests you.**
3. **Choose View⇨Privacy Report.**

   Internet Explorer shows you a list of all the Web sites that provide pieces of the current Web page. For example www.zdnet.com lists 96 separate Web sites. Windowsmedia.com lists several dozen.

4. **To look at a P3P privacy report for one of the Web sites, click the site name and then click Summary.**
5. **If one of the policies interests you, click it.**

   Figure 53-7, for example, shows you the kind of information WindowsMedia.com gathers about you and sends to Microsoft's vast database, every time you use Windows Media Player.

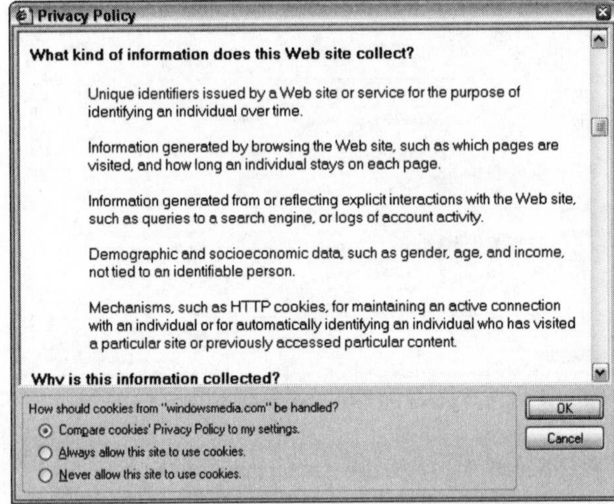

• Figure 53-7: WindowsMedia.com tells you that it's collecting all sorts of information about you.

6. **When you're done, click OK and then click Close.**

   Internet Explorer can read and automatically interpret the P3P privacy policy for each site.

Here's the trick. A Web site can post a P3P policy and not live up to it. There's no computer-based enforcement. If a company fails to live up to its P3P obligations — if it sells your e-mail address, for example, when the P3P statements says it doesn't — the organization can be taken to court. In the meantime, though, the P3P statement stands, and there's precious little anyone can do about it.

Details about P3P are at `www.w3.org/p3p`.

Setting Internet Explorer's cookie policy

Internet Explorer's cookie settings rely on a site's P3P policies to describe precisely what it does with your data. You tell IE how much privacy you want to maintain, and IE adjusts its cookie blocking accordingly.

To check your cookie settings

1. **Start Internet Explorer.**
2. **Choose Tools⇨Internet Options⇨Privacy.**

   IE brings up the Internet Options dialog box.

3. **Slide the bar up or down to change the cookie rejection policy. (If you don't have a slider bar, you're using custom settings, so click the Advanced button and modify each individual component.)**

   See Table 53-1 for a little help translating the settings into English. Keep in mind the discussion at the beginning of this technique: Most cookies are good; you only want to keep out the bad ones (and you have Ad-Aware to help if something gets through). I use the Medium setting, and suggest that you do, too. It seems to block almost all the bad cookies, and let through almost all the good ones.

4. **When you're done, click OK.**

   Your new cookie-rejection policy takes effect immediately.

If you want the full details on Internet Explorer's cookie settings, look at `www.p3ptoolbox.org/guide/appendix.shtml`. It's heavy reading.

TABLE 53-1: TRANSLATING COOKIE SETTINGS INTO ENGLISH

When the Privacy Tab Says This	It Means This
Blocks third-party cookies that do not have a compact privacy policy	Before IE accepts a cookie, it checks to see whether the cookie came from the Web page that you're viewing, or from a Web site that contributed to the page (see the discussion of spy cookies earlier in this technique). If the cookie came from a different Web site, IE goes to that Web site and checks for a P3P policy. If there is no P3P policy, the cookie isn't saved on your computer.
Blocks third-party cookies that use personally identifiable information without your implicit consent	Before IE accepts a cookie, it looks to see where the cookie came from. If it's a third-party (spy) cookie, IE checks the P3P policy from the cookie's site. If that P3P policy says (1) the site doesn't collect personally identifiable information, or (2) the site collects that information, but won't release it unless you give your implicit permission, then IE saves the cookie on your computer.
Restricts first-party cookies that use personally identifiable information without implicit consent	Before IE accepts a cookie that comes from the Web site you're looking at, it checks to see if the P3P policy for that site says (1) the site doesn't collect personally identifiable information, or (2) the site collects that information, but won't release it unless you give your implicit permission. If either of these conditions is true, then IE saves the cookie on your computer.

Checking Your Security Perimeter

Save Time By

- Running automated checks to see if your firewall is working
- Finding and plugging holes (before someone else plugs them for you)
- Using common sense to increase your network security

I just got a call from an old friend who seems to frequently bump into very interesting security problems. My friend was helping a guy set up a home/small office network — and a good one. It had Windows XP on all the machines, XP Professional on the server, Internet Connection Sharing — the whole nine yards.

That evening, the guy's adolescent daughter was startled to see a message pop up on her PC, filled with venomous, sexually explicit epithets, directed at her, personally. Whoever was responsible for the lessons in vulgar vernacular also transmitted a couple of compromising pictures.

On closer examination, we found that the pictures were fakes and that the attacker was probably known to the family and was hiding behind a newly created, virtually untraceable free e-mail account.

In a situation like this, do you need to check your security perimeter? Oh yes, indeed.

Approaching Your Security Perimeter

If you've followed the steps in Techniques 49 through 53, your computer is all ready for anything the world (or at least the Internet) can throw at it.

Right?

Well, yes and no.

The fact is that you'll never be completely prepared for everything. New threats are surfacing every day. Some of them use old methods that your existing security settings should be able to withstand. Some of them come from out of the blue.

That's why it's important to check your PC and check the way that you run your network. It's important not because you'll be 100 percent certain that no intruder can ever appear, but because there's a good chance you can do a better job with the tools at hand.

Running Steve Gibson's ShieldsUp!

Steve Gibson (`www.grc.com`) has been protecting PCs since hard drives were powered by little fuzzy chipmunks running in circles. He used to stand next to banks of hard drives and yell, at periodic intervals, "Spin left! Spin right!"

Sorry. Couldn't resist.

Steve's ShieldsUp! is widely considered to be the granddaddy of all firewall tests. Yes, more probing tests are available. But none of them match the easy-to-use style and no-nonsense explanations of ShieldsUp!.

Besides, it's free.

You should run ShieldsUp! when you install a new firewall and every time you make a major change to your firewall.

To run ShieldsUp!

1. **Start Internet Explorer and go to `grc.com`. Click the ShieldsUp! icon.**
2. **Scroll down the page a bit (Steve always has some interesting projects going), and click the ShieldsUp! link.**
3. **If you use a dial-up modem**
   - **Download the Free IP Agent (see Figure 54-1).**
   - **Double-click it and run it.**
   - **Click Test My Shields, and skip to Step 5.**

   The IP Agent presents you with a dialog box like the one in Figure 54-2.
4. **If you're connected to the Internet via a DSL or cable modem, or using Internet Connection Sharing, scroll farther down the page (see Figure 54-3) and click the File Sharing button.**

Shields UP! quickly checks the SECURITY of *YOUR* computer's connection to the Internet.

For the most reliable results you are invited to use our FREE IP Agent:

192.168.15.96

The ShieldsUP! tests depend upon accurately determining your computer's Internet Protocol (IP) address. If your IP address is incorrectly determined the **wrong machine will be mistakenly tested.** In addition, computers with multiple network connections — like a modem **and** a network adapter — can have more than one IP address. And machines with only one IP address can have it effectively "hidden" or "masqueraded" if the connection passes through any sort of firewall, proxy server, or other buffering agent.

IP Agent easily manages all such complications. **It determines your machine's current IP address — or addresses** — then contacts this ShieldsUP! website for you. If your machine had a single IP address you'll

• Figure 54-1: Take Steve up on his offer to run the free IP Agent if you have a dial-up Internet connection.

• Figure 54-2: Use the IP Agent only if you're connected to the Internet via a dial-up modem.

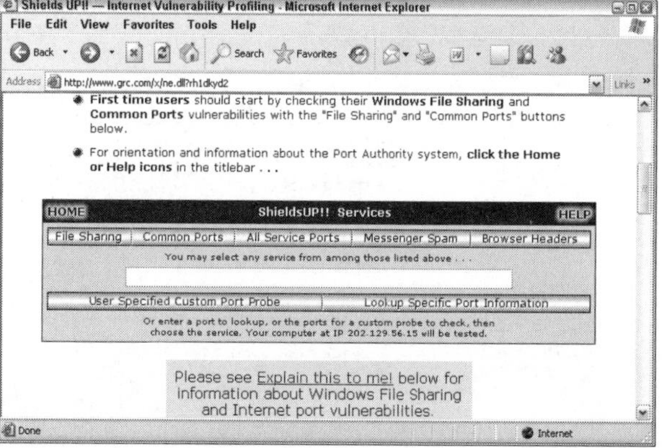

• Figure 54-3: Start by checking your File Sharing settings.

5. A report appears on your screen (see Figure 54-4). Heed it well.

6. Scroll further down the page and click the Common Ports button.

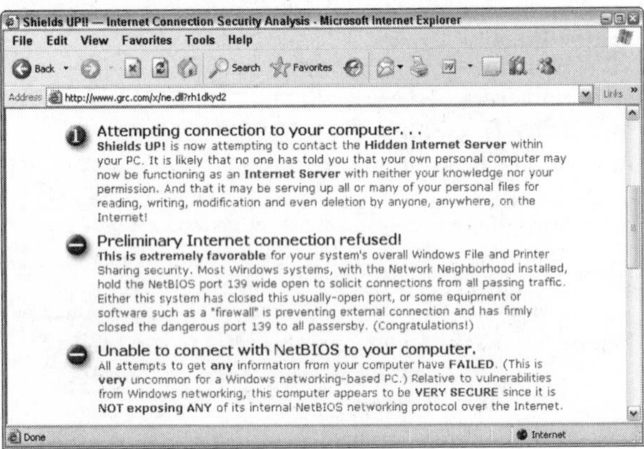

• **Figure 54-4: A clean bill of health.**

You get a second report that discusses port blocking (see Figure 54-5). If the Common Ports test tells you that an important port is open, you need to reconfigure your firewall to block it. The precise method varies depending on what kind of firewall you're using. If you're using Windows Firewall, from Service Pack 2, check Technique 50. If you have a hardware firewall (such as on a DSL router), you may have to dig into the guts of the box.

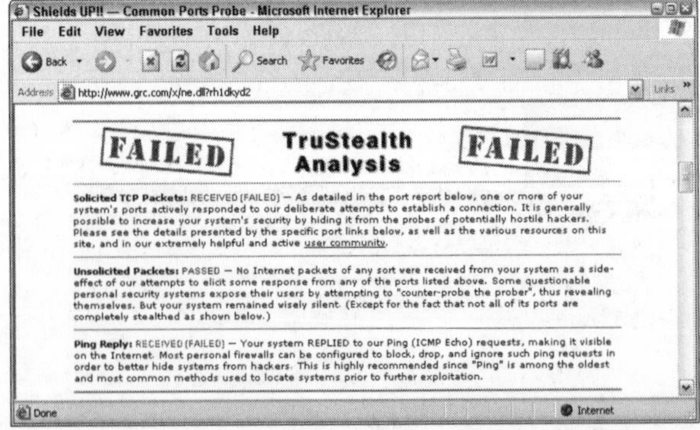

• **Figure 54-5: If the prober can't tell whether a program is "listening" to a specific port, that's very good.**

Few computers have all their ports blocked. In particular, experts disagree about the importance of port 80 being open.

Just a word or two about ports

At the risk of oversimplifying, a *port* is a lot like a telephone extension number. If you want to talk to somebody in a big office, you pick up the phone and dial the office's main number. (That's more-or-less analogous to the computer's IP address; see Technique 45.) After you connect to the switchboard, you need to dial the person's extension. Similarly, after you connect to a computer on the Internet, you have to connect to one of the programs inside the computer.

Each program listens to a specific port or group of ports. So if your PC connects to port 80 on the computer with an IP address of `208.215.179.139`, you end up talking to the Web server (which listens to port 80) on `www.dummies.com` (which is at `208.215.179.139`). Any rogue cracker on the Internet who tries to get into your machine has to go through a port. The Common Ports test (refer to Figure 54-5) "calls" all 65,535 ports on your PC (or on your router, if you have one) and tells you whether any of them are vulnerable to an outside attack.

Running Microsoft's Baseline Security Analyzer

Microsoft has a tool that examines your system to see if any important security patches are missing or if any obvious security exposures are hanging in the wind. Whereas Steve Gibson's ShieldsUp! probes from the Internet in (see "Running Steve Gibson's ShieldsUp!" earlier in this technique), the Microsoft Baseline Security Analyzer looks from the inside out.

The Baseline Security Analyzer goes through your Windows XP machine and checks most of its major components for missing security patches, gaping security holes, and little nit-picking things that you probably never knew existed (or didn't exist, as the case may be).

To run the Baseline Security Analyzer

1. **Start Internet Explorer and go to** `www.microsoft.com/technet/security/tools/mbsahome.mspx`**.**

Make sure that you get a version of the MBSA compatible with your version of Windows. In particular, if you have Windows XP Service Pack 2, you need version 1.2.1 or later.

2. **Follow the instructions to download the MBSA file.**

3. **When the download is complete, double-click the icon and follow the wizard to install the program.**

4. **Double-click the icon to start MBSA.**

   You see the main screen shown in Figure 54-6.

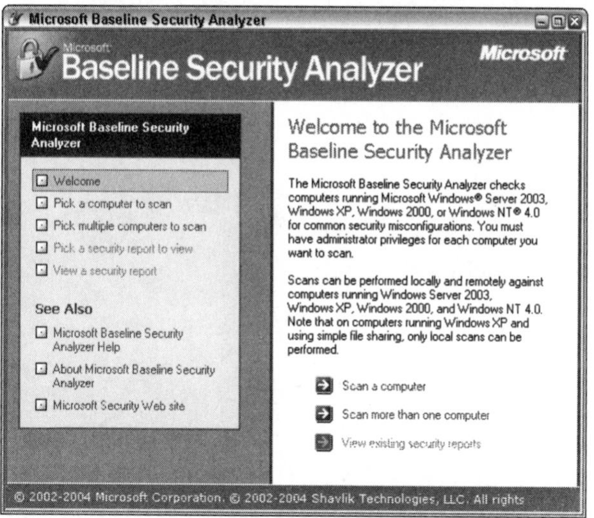

• **Figure 54-6: Microsoft's Baseline Security Analyzer starts here.**

5. **Click Scan a Computer and then click Start Scan.**

   MSBA produces a very detailed report of potential security exposures (see Figure 54-7).

6. **Review the report for real vulnerabilities.**

   For example, the report for my production machine (see Figure 54-7) identified several vulnerabilities that I don't consider to be problems: Having more than two administrators on an XP Home PC, for example, isn't going to cause me any heartburn. And I don't care to enable automatic updates, thank you very much (see Technique 55). Still, the report is worthwhile, and you should consider any exposures it identifies. If you need tips about the source of the problem or possible solutions, click the How To Correct This link.

MBSA leaves a lot to be desired because of its infuriatingly convoluted terminology. But it's a powerful self-help utility that every Windows XP user should stick in his or her bag of tricks.

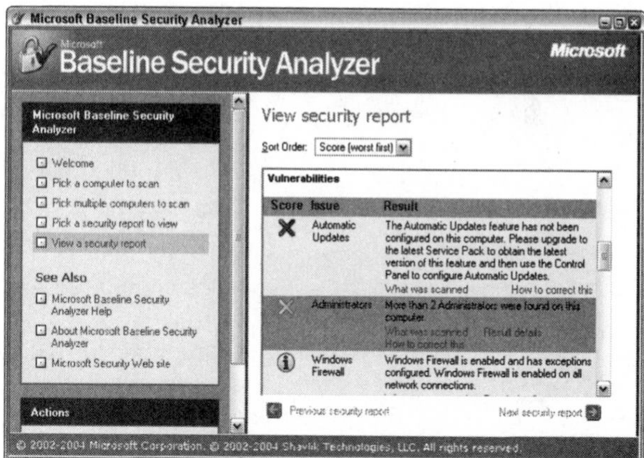

• **Figure 54-7: The MBSA report gives you much insight — but may err on the side of too much security.**

Part IX

Keeping Your PC Alive

The 5th Wave
By Rich Tennant
Maintenance is chagrined to find out the squeak in Clark's disk drive is really a whistle in Clark's nose.
RICHTENNANT

Updating Windows on Your Own Terms

Save Time By

- Dealing with the Security Center's automatic update biases
- Knowing when to update — and how
- Protecting yourself against bad updates

Any large computer program has bugs. Heck, any *small* computer program has bugs. When a program gets as large as Windows — Microsoft claims Windows XP contains 50 million lines of code — the bugs start stacking up like planes at O'Hare in a snowstorm.

Microsoft releases dozens of updates each year. Some of the updates fix bugs that make Windows crash. Many of the updates plug security holes. Most of the updates come in the form of *patches:* Fixes to an individual Windows program that wasn't working right. Some of the patches are small. Most are big — and Windows XP Service Release 2, which contained hundreds of patches, was tantamount to an entirely new version of Windows XP.

You wouldn't need to worry about keeping Windows XP up to date with the latest patches if it weren't for one unavoidable fact: The bad guys are watching. You can bet that some cretin out there, somewhere, will take advantage of one of the patched security holes, and come up with a virus or worm that exploits the hole. If you haven't installed the latest patch to plug the hole in Windows XP, your computer is vulnerable to the cretin's creations.

The only possible way you have to keep up with the latest security patches is Windows Update. I swear by Windows Update, but you have to use it properly.

What happens if something goes wrong and Microsoft's latest update causes yet more problems? It's happened many times before and it'll happen again. Indeed, as I write this, fully 20 percent of the security patches Microsoft has released so far this year caused major problems on a significant number of PCs.

This technique includes ways to protect yourself against the updates themselves. *Caveat updator!*

Reining In Windows Update

When you install Windows XP Service Pack 2, or when you first start a new PC that's running Service Pack 2 or later, Windows greets you with one of the most biased questions in all of computer-dumb, er, -dom. Windows asks if you want to "Help protect my PC by turning on Automatic Updates now" or "Not right now" (see Figure 55-1).

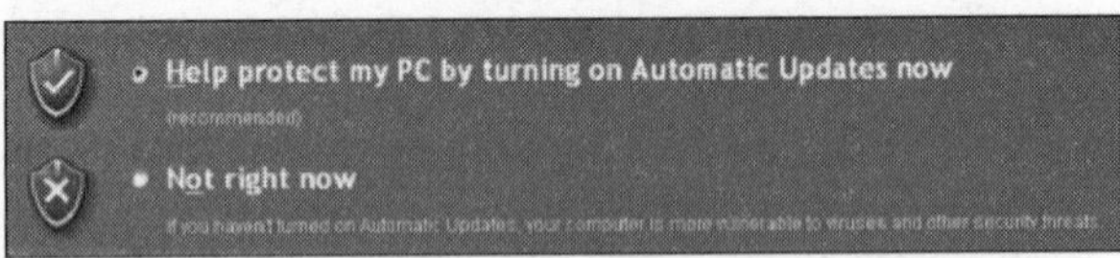

• **Figure 55-1: A truly loaded question.**

Moreover, when you look at your Windows Update setting in the Windows Security Center (choose Start➪Control Panel➪Security Center), you're only given the option of turning on Automatic Updates (see Figure 55-2). If you click the banner that says "Check Settings," the Security Center doesn't do anything at all. You have to dig deep to get at the more reasonable options, as I explain later in this technique.

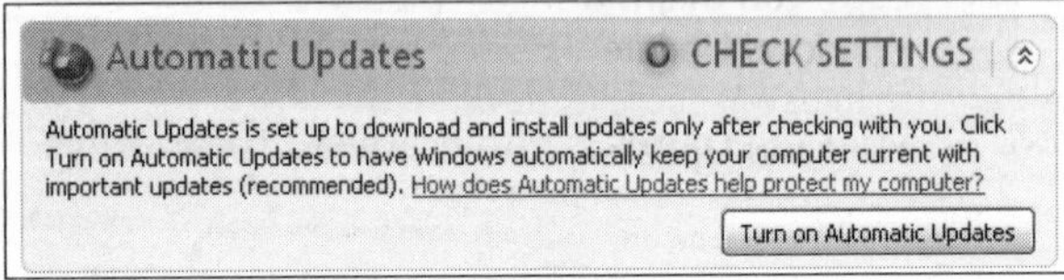

• **Figure 55-2: The only option available: Turn on Automatic Updates.**

Microsoft wants you to turn on Automatic Updates. Heck, most Windows gurus suggest that you turn on Automatic Updates. One of those gurus says that it's better for Microsoft to automatically install its software on your PC than to leave your system wide open for some malicious kid to install *his* software on your PC.

He's got a good point.

Still, I disagree. I believe that Microsoft has proven conclusively that it can't be trusted to produce reliable security fixes. If Microsoft distributes an automatic patch that's so badly flawed that thousands or tens of thousands of PCs suddenly stop working, the people with those PCs won't have the slightest idea that the culprit was a bad patch from Redmond. In my opinion, savvy Windows users should let the Automatic Update service advise them when new patches are available — but they should wait to apply those patches until there's enough real-world experience with the patches to make sure they solve more problems than they create.

I believe in this so strongly that I've devoted a section of my AskWoody.com Web site to tracking Microsoft patches, advising people on whether (or if!) patches should be applied, and how to avoid or work around the problems, even if the solutions involve non-Microsoft products.

It's one of those dammed-if-you-do-dammed-if-you-don't situations that salmon seem to encounter every year (if you'll pardon another fishy metaphor). On the one hand, if you apply Microsoft's patches as soon as they're available, there's a chance that your PC gets all screwed up. On the other hand, if you *don't* install the patches, some cretin who learned about a security hole when a patch was issued could come along and blast you with a worm. In my experience, at least at this point, your chances of getting clobbered by a bad patch are higher than your chances of getting zapped with a worm. So it makes sense to avoid applying Windows updates until you know that they're solid.

Your first big step in taking control of Windows Update is to turn off Automatic Updates, and instead have Windows merely inform you when updates are available:

1. **Choose Start➪Control Panel➪Security Center.**

   Windows XP displays the Windows Security Center, as shown in Figure 55-3.

2. **In the Manage Security Settings For area at the bottom, click Automatic Updates.**

   The Automatic Updates dialog box appears (see Figure 55-4).

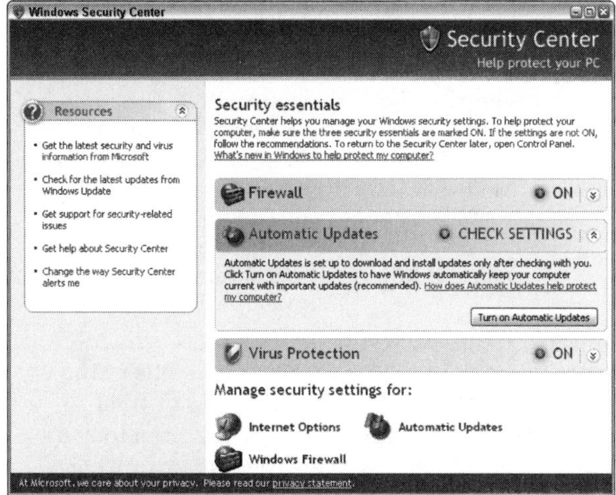

• **Figure 55-3: The Windows Security Center.**

3. **Consider the ramifications of each of the settings, as I explain in Table 55-1. Choose the entry that works best for you.**
4. **Click OK.**

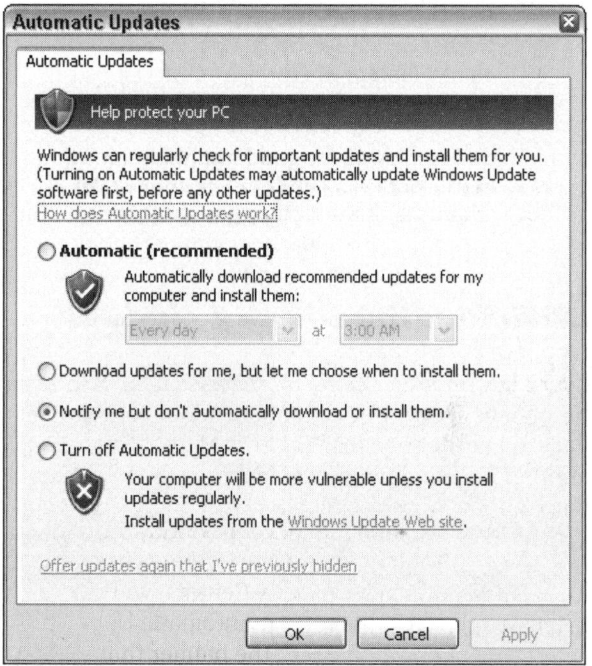

• **Figure 55-4: Turn on Automatic Notification here.**

Microsoft updates Windows Update so often that you need a scorecard to keep the versions straight. This bit is a brain-twister, but if you don't turn on Automatic Updating, Windows can't update Windows Update *itself* until you specifically give your permission.

To avoid an endless loop of chickens and eggs, you might want to log on to the Windows Update Web site, `windowsupdate.microsoft.com`**, from time to time and allow Windows Update to install patches to itself.**

TABLE 55-1: AUTOMATIC UPDATE SETTINGS

Setting	Timesaving Recommendation
Automatic (recommended)	Only use this setting if you trust Microsoft to deliver patches that won't clobber your system. This is a good choice if you don't have time to stay on top of the latest updates — because never patching is the worst choice of all.
Download, don't install	A reasonable choice if you have a slow Internet connection, or you don't want to tie it up with downloads while you're working. The only downside comes when Microsoft re-issues a patch, effectively creating a "version 2.0" patch or a patch of a patch. In that case, you have an extra, useless file hanging around.
Notify, don't download	Your best choice if you have a fast Internet connection. Wait until the patch seems to be working (watch AskWoody.com) and when the coast is clear, go for it.
Turn Off Automatic Updates	The worst of all possible worlds. Avoid it.

Microsoft officially releases new security patches on the second Tuesday of every month. (Except when, uh, it doesn't.) If you hear of a security patch coming out on any date other than the second Tuesday of the month, chances are good that Microsoft has heard about somebody attempting to take advantage of the security hole.

Downloading the Big Updates

Every few months, Microsoft releases a big Windows XP update. There was a giant download for Service Pack 1, another one for Windows Media Player 9, another for Windows Movie Maker 2, then Service Pack 2, then Windows Media Player 10. . . well, you get the idea. You find out about the big updates from the press, or from the Windows Update pop-up in your notification area (next to the clock on the taskbar) that says updates are available.

If you have just one PC that needs updating, you can simply click the notification bubble and follow the instructions to apply the download to the PC that needs it.

If you have more than one PC, downloading the same update file over and over again is a huge, time-consuming chore. For those of you who have unlimited broadband access and enjoy lightning-fast 100MB downloads, I applaud your resourcefulness. Literally. For the rest of us, the idea of downloading a 270MB file four times for four different machines is a bit daunting, to say the least. (Windows XP Service Pack 2 weighed in at 270MB; Service Pack 1, by contrast, ran a sprightly 138MB. On a 56K dial-up modem it would take about a year to download one of the big service packs, if you lasted that long.)

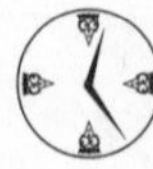

You can't post the updates on the Web for other people to download, but you can hand them around. Microsoft always sells the big updates for the price of shipping and handling for the CD, but it can take weeks for the update to arrive in the mail. There's nothing wrong with downloading say, the Service Pack 2 update, and burning it on a CD. Then you can give copies to your friends (housewarming present?). You also can download one copy of Windows Media Player 10 and update all the computers on your small office network from that single copy. Microsoft's big service packs and product updates are always free.

Automatic Update works by running a "sniffer" program on your PC, to see what versions of the software you have installed. If you don't want to permit Microsoft's update sniffer program to run on your PC, download and save the updates this way — big ones or little ones. You have to keep track of the patches manually, but no sniffer ever phones home with a list of your hardware and software.

Fortunately, you can download the big updates as a single file and save them on your PC, so you can use the saved file multiple times. It isn't worth the effort to find and download small updates — ones that can be downloaded in a few minutes. If you aren't concerned about Microsoft's Windows Update sniffer (and I'm not), let Windows Update do the work of finding and keeping those little ones in line (Windows Update keeps a great list of available updates, even if you don't install them; see the next section). The way to save a whole bunch of Internet time is to look for updates that take 30 minutes or more to download.

To see if a particular update is available for download in its own file:

1. **Choose Start⇨All Programs⇨Windows Update.**

   Windows sends you to the Windows Update Web site (see Figure 55-5).

2. **On the left, click Administrator Options.**
3. **Click the Windows Update Catalog link.**

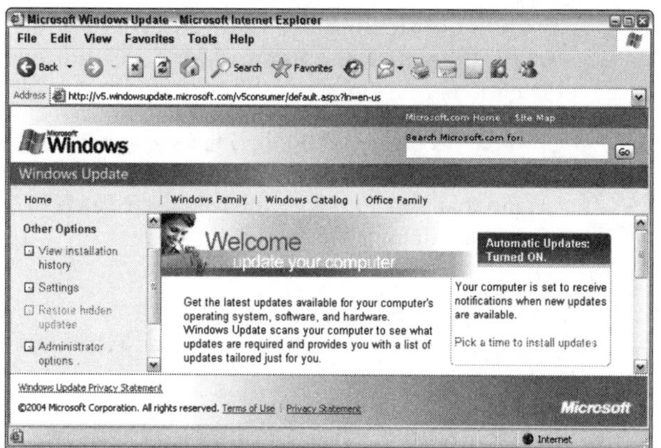

• **Figure 55-5: In spite of what the Windows Update Web site says, I do *not* have Automatic Updates turned on.**

Internet Explorer takes you to the catalog page (see Figure 55-6).

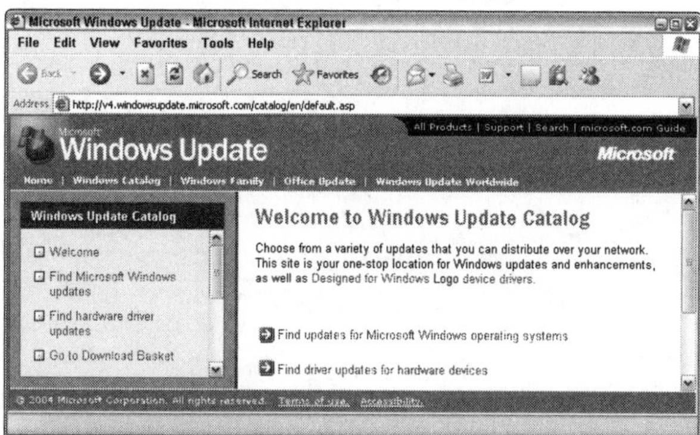

• **Figure 55-6: The main page of the Windows Update Catalog.**

4. **Click the Find Updates for Microsoft Windows Operating Systems link.**

   The Windows Update Catalog lets you select your operating system.

5. **Choose Windows XP (and whatever service pack you may have), and then click the Search button.**

   The Windows Update Catalog finds all available updates for Windows XP (see Figure 55-7).

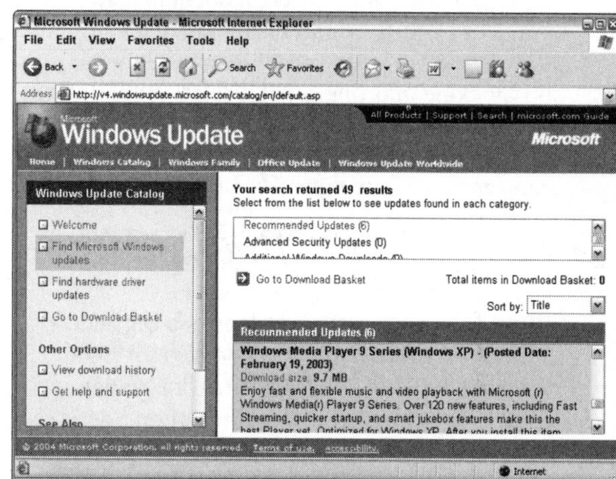

• **Figure 55-7: All available updates are listed.**

6. **Carefully select the update(s) by clicking the Add button for each update you want to download.**

   You're here to download the big updates that have to be applied to multiple computers. Completely ignore updates that don't apply to the computers in your care. For example, if you already have Media Player 10, you have no need for an update to Media Player 9.

7. **When you have the update(s) you want, click the Go to Download Basket link.**

   The Windows Update Catalog takes you to the download basket.

8. **Click the Browse button and move to a location on your computer for the downloads. Then click the Download Now button.**

   Windows responds with one of its insufferable End User License Agreements.

9. **After you read and understand the License Agreement, nod, nod, wink, wink, click the Accept button.**

You may need to click to allow pop-ups. (In fact, as this book went to press, clicking to allow pop-ups also knocked out the Windows Update site, and you had to go back and download all over again.) If the situation gets overwhelming, click the pop-up blocking Information Bar in Internet Explorer and choose Temporarily Allow Pop-ups. Windows downloads the updates, sooner or later, and then returns you to the Windows Update Catalog.

In fact, Windows creates a new hierarchy of folders where you asked to put the update: `WU\Software\en\com_microsoft.windowsxp\86WinXP` and then a folder underneath for each specific download. You'll find the update somewhere. Just keep drilling down.

10. **Click the Close (X) button to exit the Windows Update Catalog, and then run your updates.**

Checking for Small Updates

Although there are powerful reasons for manually downloading just one copy of the big updates, the small ones are far too numerous for most carbon-based life forms to keep track of. As long as you don't mind running Microsoft's Windows Update sniffer program, it's easy to deal with those little updates by letting Windows Automatic Update take care of them.

Follow these steps to do a mini update:

1. **If you receive a notification, such as the one in Figure 55-8, or one saying that new updates are ready for download, you can click the icon and follow the wizard.**

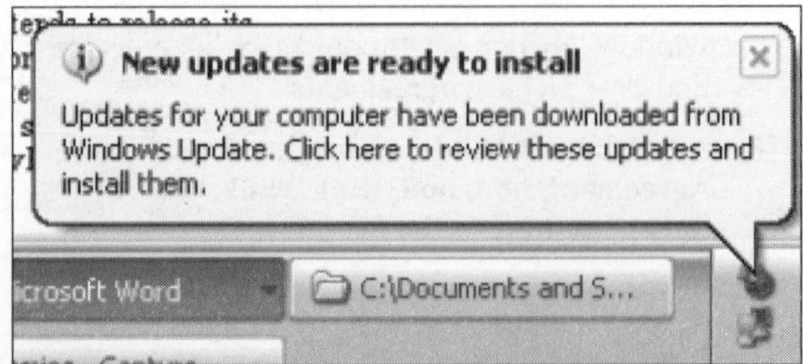

• **Figure 55-8: Windows is ready — but are you?**

2. **Click the notification area icon to bring up the wizard; then click the Remind Me Later button and choose In 3 Days.**

Three days gives you enough time to see if the patch is more trouble than it's worth. I recommend that you start with the Microsoft Patch Reliability Ratings at `www.AskWoody.com`.

3. **If you decide that you want to install the update, choose Start⇨All Programs⇨Windows Update.**

   Internet Explorer takes you to the Windows Update site (refer to Figure 55-5).

4. **Scroll down and click the Custom Install link.**

   Windows Update comes back with notification about how many updates it has available for your particular PC (see Figure 55-9).

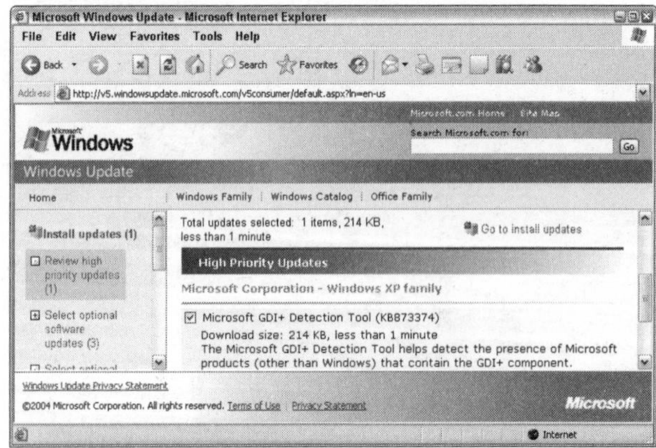

• **Figure 55-9: Windows Update found 1 high priority update, and 3 optional updates.**

5. **Uncheck the boxes next to any patches that you don't want to apply. Then click Go To Install Updates.**

The patch shown in Figure 55-9 is a particularly fitting example. Microsoft came under a lot of well-deserved fire for this particular patch (associated with Microsoft's MS04-048 Security Bulletin) because it didn't solve the problem it was supposed to address. The SANS Institute came up with a much better alternative. We covered the controversy at AskWoody.com.

6. **Double-check the proposed updates carefully, and uncheck the boxes next to any items you don't want.**

   The list that Windows Update offers is far from infallible. I was once advised to install Service Pack 1 on a machine that already had Service Pack 1. I've seen device drivers on the list that I wouldn't touch with a ten-foot pole (see Technique 58 for the skinny on device drivers). Use your discretion — and your brain.

7. **When you're ready, click Install. Follow the instructions to install the updates you've accepted.**

   You may need to install some updates separately, possibly with your PC rebooting. In those cases, make sure you come back to Windows Update after each update gets installed.

Retrieving and Installing a Declined Update

What if you turn down an Automatic Update, and later wonder whether maybe you should've accepted?

No problem. Just follow these steps to get that update:

1. **Choose Start⇨Control Panel⇨Security Center. At the bottom click Automatic Updates.**

   If you have declined any updates in the past, the bottom line, which says Offer Updates Again That I've Previously Hidden, is no longer grayed out.

2. **Click the Offer Updates Again button.**

   Windows XP asks if you want to restore the declined updates (see Figure 55-10).

3. **Click Yes, and then click OK.**

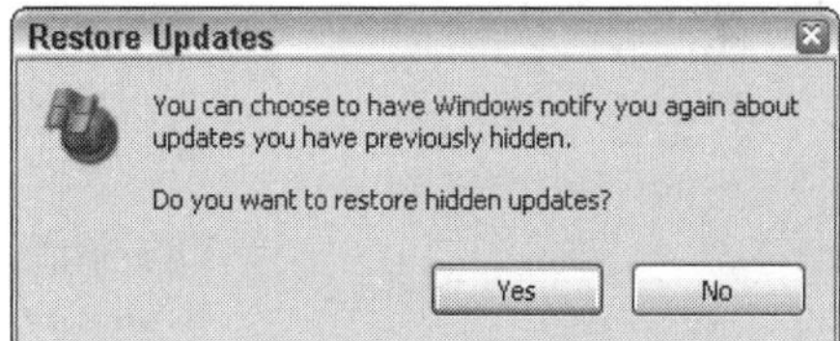

• **Figure 55-10: Tell Automatic Update that you made a mistake and want to look again.**

The next time Windows Update scans for updates, it treats the ones you have declined as new and offers them to you again.

Technique 56

Running Disk Chores While You Sleep

Save Time By

- Having Windows Scheduler clean your disks, even if you aren't around
- Setting up Scheduler so you can use it with other periodic chores

If you've ever tried to use the Windows Scheduler, you probably discovered that it's incredibly easy — a wizard handles all the niggling details — and after you've set it up, you can forget about it.

Right?

Wrong.

One little problem. Bet you didn't know that you have to run Scheduler from an account that has a password on it. If you tell Scheduler to run using an account that doesn't have a password, nothing runs — and you're never notified of the fact.

This technique shows you how to set up an account that works with Scheduler (if you don't have one already), and then it steps you through the method for scheduling automatic disk cleanup runs. As a nifty bonus, by following the steps in this technique, you do everything necessary to quickly set up Scheduler to run any other program automatically.

And *that's* a timesaver that works.

Setting Up an Account for Scheduler

You have to run Scheduler from an account with a password. Even more bedeviling: The password you type into Scheduler when you first schedule a task has to be valid *when the scheduled task runs*. If you change your password, *bang,* all of a sudden your old scheduled tasks don't work anymore — and you aren't notified of that fact, unless you look in a very obscure place. To make your scheduled tasks work again, you have to go through the whole scheduling procedure all over again — run through the steps for every scheduled program — specifying your new password.

If you don't have an account with a password, you have to set one up. If you have an account with a password that never expires, you're in good shape (but then, the security mavens would ask, what good is the password?). If you have an account with a password that expires, and you're very careful to make your new password identical to your old password every time it expires, that works with Scheduler, too (but those security mavens will howl!). All in all, the password restrictions in Scheduler force you to consider whether it's more important to have a secure password or to be able to schedule jobs to run automatically. You can't have both.

Bet they didn't tell you that in Windows class, did they?

If you have an account with a password that you use every day, *and* that password hasn't expired (or doesn't expire, as is usually the case in Windows XP Home Edition), *and* when the password expires you always make the new password identical to the old password, then you can use that account to run Scheduler. Skip to the section, "Running Disk Cleanup Manually."

Creating a new Scheduler account

I figure about 90 percent of you are still with me. Good.

In the remainder of this section, I show you how to set up a dummy account (if you'll pardon the expression) whose only purpose in life is to allow you to use the Scheduler. You need the dummy account, set up with a password that never expires, to run the Scheduler. You don't want to use your regular account for Scheduler because that prevents you from ever selecting a new password. Besides, if you're tricky, you can hide the dummy account where most people wouldn't know how to find it.

If you're attached to a Big Corporate Network, you may be able to run Scheduler with an account that's recognized on the server. Give it a try on your system and verify that everything works before you rely on Scheduler to perform as advertised.

Microsoft has confirmed that Scheduler's refusal to run tasks "is a problem" (see `support.microsoft.com/default.aspx?scid=kb;en-us;311119`), but Microsoft offers no long-term solution. Security concerns boxed Scheduler into a tight corner. This technique gives you a way to escape the box.

I have detailed instructions for setting up accounts in Technique 47, but here are the bare bones of what you need to set up a functional account just for running Scheduler:

1. **Make sure you're logged on with an Administrator account.**
2. **Choose Start⇨Control Panel⇨User Accounts.**

   Windows shows you the Pick a Task dialog box.
3. **Click Create a New Account.**

   You see the Name the New Account dialog box (see Figure 56-1).

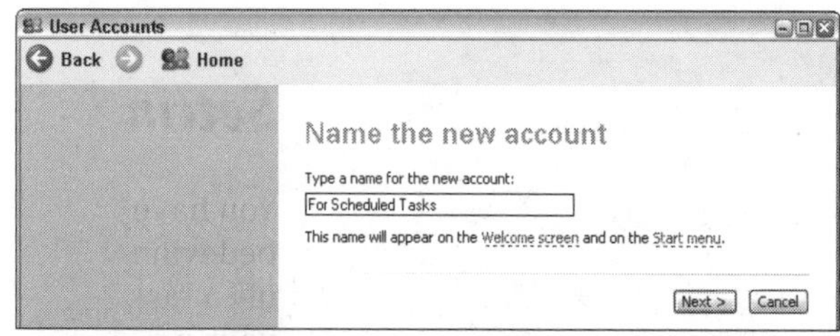

• **Figure 56-1: Give the new account a name.**

4. **In the Type a Name for the New Account box, enter something that won't be easily mistaken for a regular account, such as *For Scheduled Tasks*. Click Next.**

5. In the Pick an Account Type dialog box, click Computer Administrator (see Figure 56-2), and then click the Create Account button.

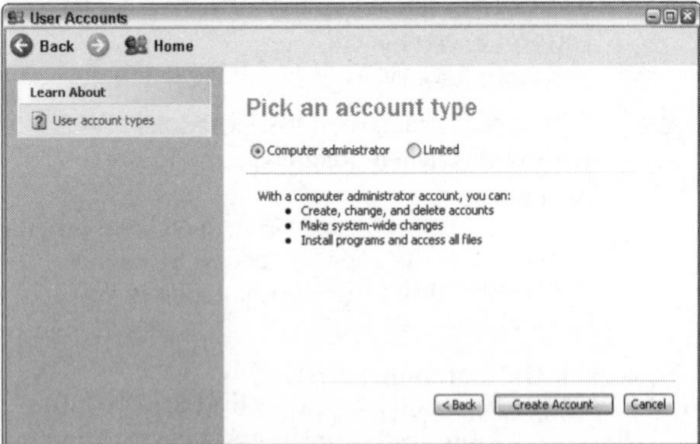

• **Figure 56-2: Almost all scheduled tasks require an Administrator account.**

6. Back in the Pick a Task dialog box (see Figure 56-3), click the For Scheduled Tasks account.

You see the What Do You Want to Change about For Scheduled Tasks's Account dialog box.

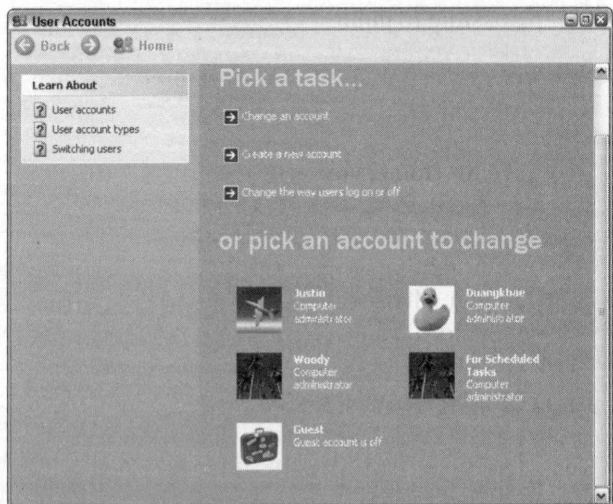

• **Figure 56-3: Now edit the new For Scheduled Tasks account.**

7. Click Create a Password.

8. In the Type a New Password text box, type a password that you can easily remember. Then type it again.

You need this password every time you use the Windows Scheduler.

9. Click the Create Password button; then click the Close button (X) to get out of the User Accounts application.

Don't worry about the hint. In spite of what the dialog box says, only the most determined (and knowledgeable) cracker will ever see it.

This is a real password on a real Administrator account, so you need to take some care in assigning it. See Technique 9 for good advice on choosing strong passwords.

Ensuring that your password doesn't expire in Windows XP Professional

Now that you have a dummy account set up with a password, you need to make sure the password doesn't expire. If the password expires, the Scheduler won't run until you change it — and if you change the password to anything but the old password, you have to modify every single scheduled task. By hand. It ain't pretty.

Windows XP Professional has a nifty interface that allows you to quickly and easily make your password immortal. Finding the interface is another story. Windows XP Home, on the other hand, only offers an obscure, completely half-seat-of-the-pants approach.

If you're using Windows XP Professional, and your network administrator hasn't blocked your ability to determine your password's destiny, follow these steps to immortalize your password:

1. **Choose Start⇨Control Panel⇨Performance and Maintenance⇨Administrative Tools⇨ Local Security Policy.**

   The Local Security Settings window appears (see Figure 56-4).

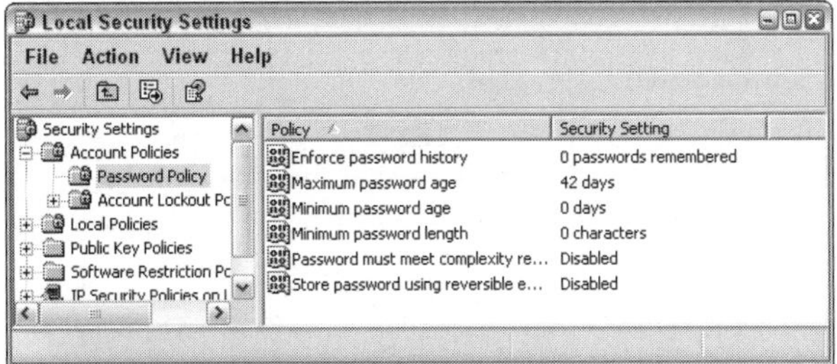

• **Figure 56-4: Security settings are only accessible on Windows XP Professional machines.**

2. **On the left, choose Security Settings⇨Account Policies⇨Password Policy.**
3. **On the right, if the Maximum Password Age says anything but Unlimited, right-click Maximum Password Age and choose Properties.**

   You see the Maximum Password Age Properties dialog box, shown in Figure 56-5.

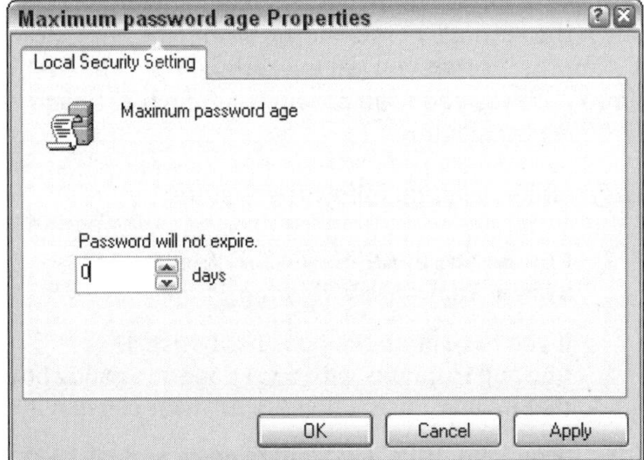

• **Figure 56-5: Set the time limit for passwords here.**

If you can't set the Maximum Password Age at this point, it's almost undoubtedly because your computer is hooked into a network and your network administrator doesn't allow it. Talk to your administrator and see whether he or she can be swayed by the need for a permanent password for a Windows Scheduler account.

4. **Click the Password Expires In text box and type a zero:**

   ```
   0
   ```

   The caption on the box immediately changes to `Password Will Not Expire`.
5. **Click OK and then choose File⇨Exit to get out of the Local Security Settings window.**

   At this point, all the passwords on this machine are immortal. Guard them well.

Ensuring that your password doesn't expire in Windows XP Home

If you're using Windows XP Home, your password probably doesn't expire. I say "probably" because it may be possible to jimmy things around internally so passwords do expire — unfortunately, no documentation (official or otherwise) settles the question once and for all.

If you have XP Home, you may want to go in and make sure the password can never expire, no matter what. If you want to try the procedure I describe in the previous section, go ahead, but it's completely useless to you. Microsoft doesn't include any console support for passwords in XP Home; however, you're not totally out of luck. You can tinker with the settings directly by following these steps:

1. **Choose Start⇨All Programs⇨Accessories⇨ Command Prompt.**
2. **Type** net accounts **and press Enter.**

   You see the current status of your PC's password policies, as shown in Figure 56-6.

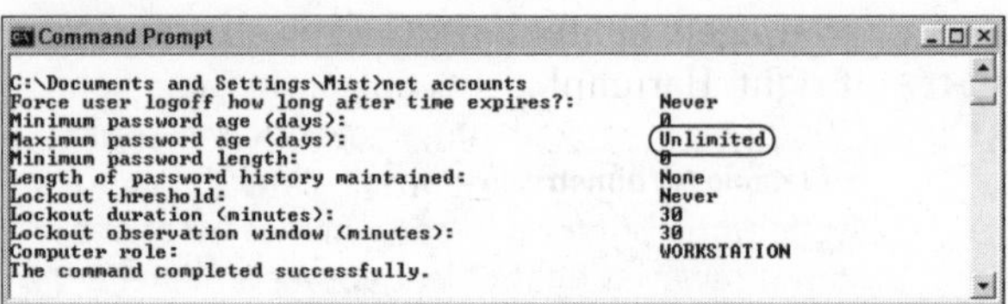

• **Figure 56-6: The only way to get at password settings in XP Home is through the command line.**

3. **If the Maximum Password Days entry is anything other than Unlimited, type** net accounts /maxpwage:unlimited **and press Enter.**

4. **Click the Close (X) button to close the Command Prompt window.**

   Now that's what I call "user-friendly."

Hiding your dummy Scheduler account

If you set up a For Scheduled Tasks account, you can effectively hide it so that you don't keep bumping into it — and so anyone casually using your machine or watching you use it won't know that it's there.

1. **Download and install TweakUI.**

   For full details, check out Technique 5.

2. **Choose Start➪All Programs➪PowerToys for Windows XP➪TweakUI.**

   The TweakUI About screen appears.

3. **On the left, click Logon.**

   TweakUI offers to hide individual accounts on your machine (see Figure 56-7).

4. **Uncheck the Show "For Scheduled Tasks" on Welcome Screen box.**

5. **Click OK.**

   All done.

If you ever need to monkey with the For Scheduled Tasks account – and you shouldn't – the easiest way to get to the account is to make it appear on-screen again by using this TweakUI dialog box.

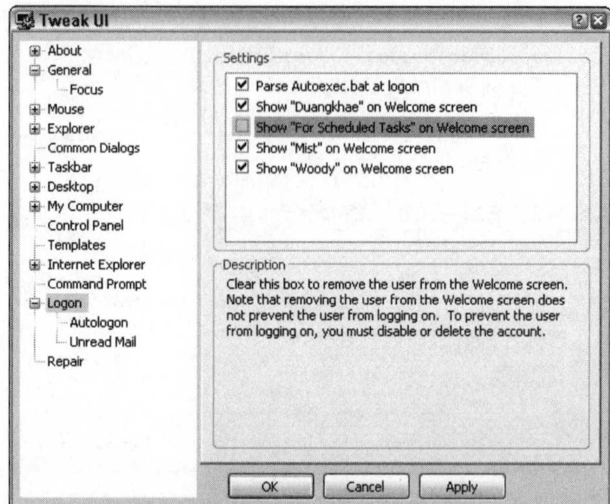

• **Figure 56-7: Remove the account from the welcome screen so snoops don't know about it.**

Running Disk Cleanup Manually

If you want to schedule regular automatic runs of Disk Cleanup, it's important that you run it manually the first time. Disk Cleanup settings are *sticky* — after you set them, they stay in place until you manually change them. By running Disk Cleanup manually once, the settings persist in the automatic runs. So it's important that you get everything right the first time — unless you want to waste a bunch of time resetting them later.

To run Disk Cleanup, follow these steps:

1. **Choose Start➪All Programs➪Accessories➪System Tools➪Disk Cleanup.**

   If you have more than one hard drive, Disk Cleanup responds with a very Spartan dialog box that invites you to choose a drive for cleaning.

2. **Select the drive you want to clean and click OK.**

There doesn't appear to be any way to automatically clean more than one drive, so make sure you select the drive letter that gets the heaviest use.

Disk Cleanup spends an inordinate amount of time scanning the drive and then offers you a smorgasbord of file types to delete (see Figure 56-8). (For a tricky way to speed up the scan, see Technique 68.)

3. **Choose the kinds of files you want to clean; then click OK.**

   Generally, I use the guidelines in Table 56-1.

4. **Disk Cleanup asks whether you want to perform these actions. Click OK.**

   Unless it's been a long time since you cleaned your hard drive, or if you've chosen to compress a horrendous bunch of old files, the cleanup shouldn't take more than a minute or two.

If Disk Cleanup went as you expected, don't touch anything. The settings will be used when you automatically run Disk Cleanup in the future.

On the other hand, if you don't like what happened — if Disk Cleanup took away some files that you want to keep (for example, temporary Internet files), or if it missed some files that should've been tossed (say, Debug dump files), start all over again at Step 1 and keep doing it until you get it right. Harumph.

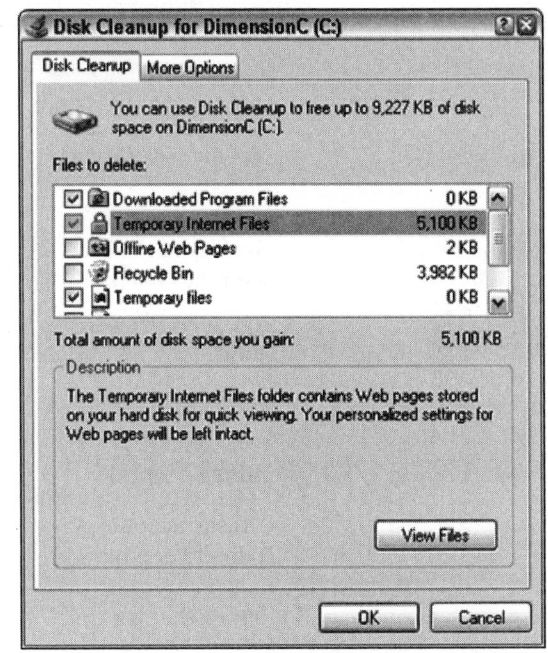

• **Figure 56-8: Types of files that Disk Cleanup can clean.**

TABLE 56-1: CHOOSING WHICH FILES TO CLEAN

Type of File	Contains	Recommendation
Downloaded Program Files	ActiveX controls and Java applets. (These used to be called OLE files, and will soon be called .NET controls and applets.) Typically these are small programs downloaded from the Internet. They work with "custom" applications: games, Web file viewers, and the like.	Give 'em the heave-ho (that is, delete them).
Temporary Internet Files	Cached pictures.	Say, "Hasta la vista, baby," and delete them.
Offline Web Pages	Pages that are downloaded automatically so that you can see them without being connected to the Internet.	Keep 'em exactly as they are.
Recycle Bin	Files in your Recycle Bin.	Never delete Recycle Bin files automatically. If you're ready to get rid of your old files, delete the files manually, one by one.

(continued)

Table 56-1 *(continued)*

Type of File	Contains	Recommendation
Temporary Remote Desktop Files	Pictures used for Remote Desktop.	Zap 'em.
Temporary Files	Anything in a Temp folder.	Delete 'em.
Web Client/Publisher Temporary Files	Obscure files.	Delete 'em.
Compress Old Files	Only available on NTFS-formatted hard drives. If a file is more than 50 days old, Windows offers to use NTFS's compression routine on it.	Marginal space gain, potential heavy hit on performance. Don't do it. Keep these files at their regular, uncompressed size.

Scheduling Automatic Cleanups

If you have an account with a password (preferably a password that doesn't change), and you've run Disk Cleanup at least once, you're ready to set up the Windows Scheduler to run Disk Cleanup on a regular basis.

To schedule Disk Cleanups

1. **Choose Start⇨All Programs⇨Accessories⇨System Tools⇨Scheduled Tasks.**

   Windows Explorer — yes, plain old everyday Explorer — appears on the screen, with the Scheduled Tasks folder open.

2. **Double-click the Add Scheduled Task icon.**

   The Scheduled Task Wizard appears.

3. **Click Next.**

   The Scheduled Task Wizard presents a list of all the programs on your Start menu (see Figure 56-9).

4. **You can schedule any of them, or click the Browse button and choose from any program on your computer. But almost everybody wants to run Disk Cleanup in the middle of the night. Spybot is another good choice for the late-night treatment. (Almost all antivirus programs schedule themselves.)**

5. **Click Disk Cleanup and click Next.**

   The wizard asks you how frequently you want to perform the task.

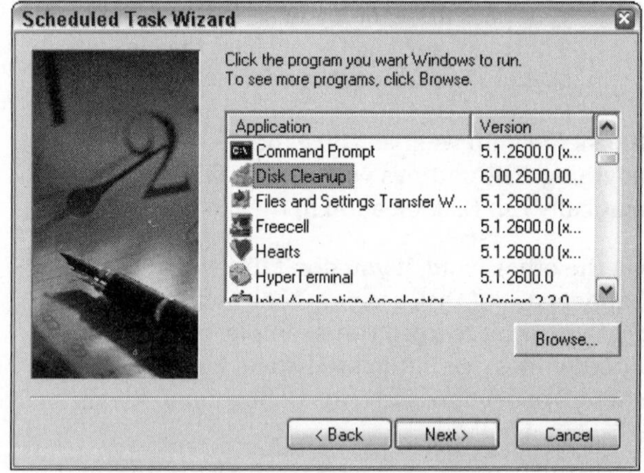

• **Figure 56-9: The Windows Scheduler runs any program on your computer, at the time(s) you specify.**

6. **If you want to run Disk Cleanup once a week (that's what I do), select the Weekly option and click Next.**

   The wizard lets you pick the time and days that it runs (see Figure 56-10).

7. **Set Disk Cleanup to run at 2:00 a.m. on Mondays — or any other time that you figure the PC will be on, but you won't be using it. Click Next.**

Whether you should leave your PC on all the time or turn it off is a personal religious issue that you should resolve with your spiritual advisors. Suffice it to say that I leave my PCs on all the time — or most of the time, anyway. However, I acknowledge that there are plenty of sound reasons for not doing so.

• Figure 56-10: Set the schedule.

The wizard comes up with the key dialog box — the one where you have to enter a user name and password (see Figure 56-11).

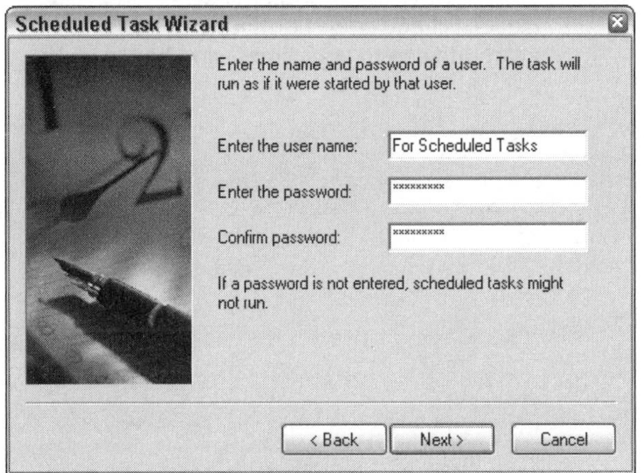

• Figure 56-11: The user name and password are *not* verified when you enter them.

That little note at the bottom of Figure 56-11 is hogwash, so don't waste time believing that you have a chance if you don't enter a password. You *must* use a user name and password that are valid at the time the Scheduler runs the program. Otherwise, the program won't run. Period. No maybe about it.

8. **Enter a user name and password that will be valid *at the time the scheduled task runs.* (The user account doesn't have to be logged on when the scheduled task runs — it only needs to be valid on the computer, and the passwords need to match.) Ideally, you followed the steps earlier in this technique to create an account called For Scheduled Tasks with a password that never expires. Click Next.**

   The task has been scheduled, and you're advised of that fact.

Windows doesn't check whether you entered the user name and password correctly, so take extra care when you type them in. If you make a typo, Scheduler simply doesn't run. If you're typo-prone or just curious, see the next section, "Checking Up on Scheduler."

9. **Click Finish.**

   If you're curious, choose Start➪All Programs➪Accessories➪System Tools➪Scheduled Tasks. You can see your new task in the Scheduled Tasks folder (see Figure 56-12).

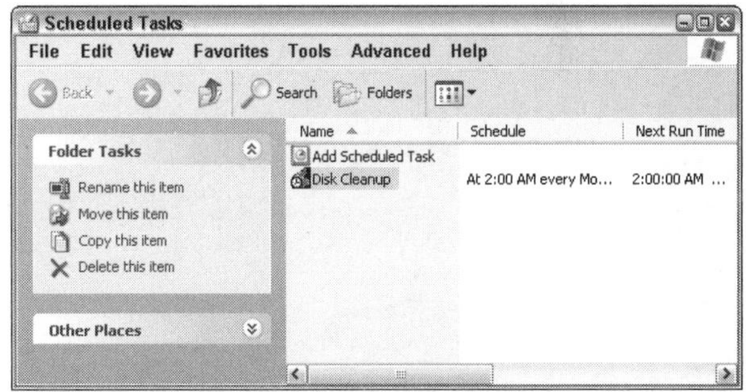

• Figure 56-12: The new task is ready to run.

Checking Up on Scheduler

At times, you may wonder if your scheduled tasks ever run. In fact, I have gone for months thinking that my scheduled tasks were running fine, when password problems kept them from running at all.

A small column is on the right edge when Explorer shows you the Scheduled Tasks folder. It tells you the last time the task was run — but there's no detail, no indication at all of why things went wrong.

If you ever want to know the full story about your tasks and what they are (or, more likely, aren't) doing, follow these steps:

1. **Choose Start⇨All Programs⇨Accessories⇨System Tools⇨Scheduled Tasks.**

   The Scheduled Tasks folder opens (refer to Figure 56-12).

2. **Choose Advanced⇨View Log.**

   Notepad shows up (!) with the Windows Scheduler log file, a very retro text file called `SchedLgU.txt` (see Figure 56-13).

```
SchedLgU.Txt - Notepad
File  Edit  Format  View  Help
"Disk Cleanup.job" (cleanmgr.exe)
        Finished 10/24/2005 2:02:48 AM
        Result: The task completed with an exit code of (0).
[ ***** Most recent entry is above this line ***** ]
```

• Figure 56-13: The Scheduler log file.

   Unfortunately, Windows Scheduler doesn't put its latest entry at the top or bottom of the log file. Instead, it keeps the log's size fixed, adds entries until it gets to the bottom of the file, and then starts again at the top.

3. **To find the latest entry, choose Edit⇨Find and search for ***** (five asterisks).**

   The asterisks take you to the log of the most recent activity. If Scheduler completed successfully, you see an indication (`The task completed with an exit code of (0).`) in the log file.

4. **Choose File⇨Exit to close Notepad, and then choose File⇨Close to exit Scheduled Tasks.**

It's important to realize that Windows Scheduler – as flawed as it is – can launch any program, any time, on a schedule that you can readily adapt. If you set up an account to get around the restrictions (such as the For Scheduled Tasks account I mention in this technique), Scheduler is enormously powerful and a key addition to your timesaving bag o' tricks.

Keeping Your Hard Drive in Shape

Save Time By

- Scanning for hard drive problems before they happen
- Making Check Disk and Scheduler work together
- Defragging your hard drive automatically

I got a message from one of my newsletter subscribers that goes like this:

"Woody, I'm having intermittent troubles with my computer showing that stupid Blue Screen of Death. The blue screen STOP message includes a cryptic description that's written in some indecipherable dialect of English. I think. I looked it up in the Knowledge Base and was told that to 'determine the possible cause, you must properly interpret the error message. If both the first and third parameters are zero, then the four parameters are defined as. . .' and it goes downhill from there. When I try the procedure that's listed, it doesn't help. Now I can't even get my computer to start. What next?"

The short answer is that you can try a couple of things — but they all involve a little luck and a lot of persistence. The best answer is to solve the problem before it starts. And that's what this technique is all about.

Scanning Your Hard Drive

In Technique 5, I talk about running Disk Cleanup and the Windows Defragmenter to get rid of unnecessary files and reorganize existing files so that Windows can run faster.

In Technique 56, I give you the lowdown on running Disk Cleanup automatically.

In this section, I show you how to run Check Disk, the low-level disk maintenance program that comes with Windows. In the next section, I take you through the process of setting up Windows Scheduler to run Check Disk automatically, while you sleep.

In general, Check Disk reads data from your hard drive and looks for errors. A full run of Check Disk reads every single bit of data on your hard drive and verifies that all the locations (also called *sectors*) on the disk are still alive and well.

Before you set up Check Disk, you should know what your options are. Check out Table 57-1 for specifics.

To run Check Disk

1. **Choose Start⇨My Computer.**
2. **Right-click the drive you want to check and choose Properties⇨Tools.**

   You see the Properties dialog box shown in Figure 57-1.

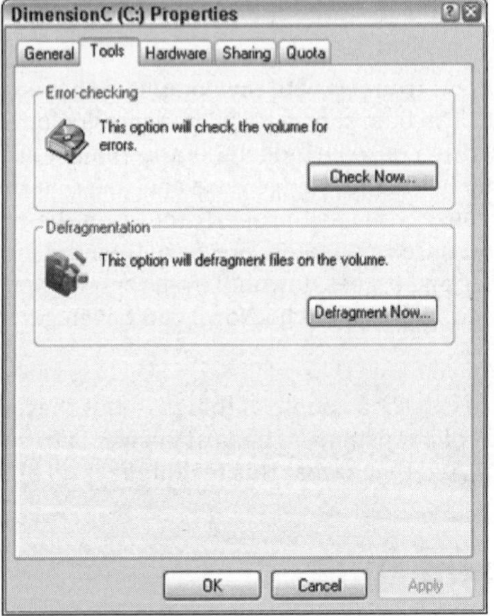

• **Figure 57-1: Check Disk is in here.**

3. **Click Check Now.**

   Don't worry. Windows doesn't really check right now. Instead, it shows you the Check Disk dialog box (see Figure 57-2).

   The choices listed in the Check Disk dialog box aren't very accurate. For the straight story, refer to Table 57-1.

4. **Check both boxes and click Start.**

   If you choose to Automatically Fix File System Errors and any file on the disk is open, you almost always get the message shown in Figure 57-3. You always have a file open if you're trying to scan the drive that has the operating system (typically C:).

• **Figure 57-2: How much do you want to check?**

I've only hit one situation where a check disk went through without rebooting the computer – when I checked a FAT32 disk that didn't have Windows on it. It's quite unusual to have Check Disk run while Windows is chugging away.

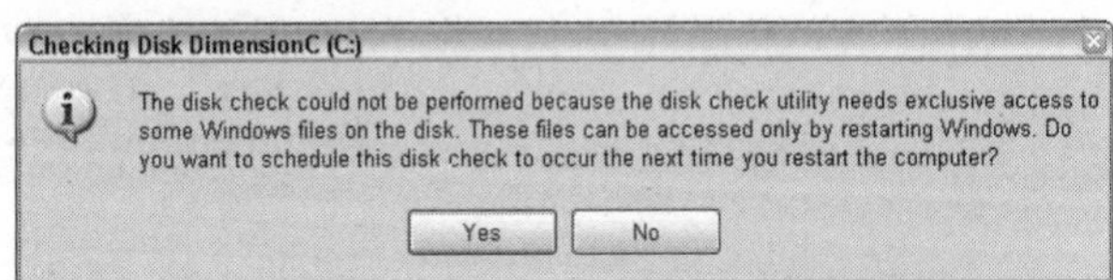

• **Figure 57-3: You see this message if a file is open on a disk while Check Disk tries to do its job.**

5. **Click Yes and restart your computer.**

   When your computer comes up for air — immediately after the Windows XP start screen appears — Check Disk kicks in and performs a full check.

   If Check Disk doesn't find any problems, Windows resumes its normal startup routine and shows you the welcome screen. If Check Disk does hit a problem, it slaps a message up on-screen — *so many bytes found in so many bad sectors* (possibly a notification of lost files) — and waits for you to look at it and click OK.

Table 57-1: Check Disk Options

If This Box Is Checked	Check Disk Does This	Recommendation
Neither (as in, neither of the two boxes is checked)	Scans for internal inconsistencies in the file tables and bad spots on the disk. Check Disk doesn't fix anything, but reports the results of the scan to you.	Choose this option if you've just installed some new hardware (say, a new disk controller) or software that interacts directly with the disk, and you think the problem might be with the new hardware or software.
Automatically Fix File System Errors	Scans the drive and repairs the internal inconsistencies.	Choose this option if you don't ever expect to try to recover the bad data, or if you're so low on disk space that you don't have enough room to store copies of the bad sectors.
Scan for and Attempt Recovery of Bad Sectors	Scans the drive and sticks data from bad sectors in separate recovery files. You may be able to dig into the recovered sectors and retrieve some of the data, but it's a laborious task — and more often than not these bad clusters are useless temporary scraps left behind when something crashes.	Choose this option if there's any chance you might try to recover bad data. I use this option most of the time.

Running Check Disk once a week or so is a good idea.

Running Check Disk Automatically

You'd think that Check Disk would be an ideal candidate for the Windows Scheduler (which I describe in Technique 56), and you'd be right. You'd also think that it would be easy to hook Check Disk into the Scheduler so that it could run automatically from time to time. Ah, there you'd be wrong.

Check Disk is an ornery son of a gun. The only way you can get it to run on your main drive (usually C:) is by shutting down Windows entirely, and even *that* takes using a trick or two in Scheduler.

To complicate matters, unlike Disk Clean, the settings in Check Disk aren't *sticky* — when you change the settings, they don't hang around for the next time you run it.

Setting up Check Disk to run automatically from the Windows Scheduler is a three-step process:

1. **Set up Scheduler to run, using an account with a password that never changes.**

   If you haven't yet set up a hidden For Scheduled Tasks account with a permanent password, follow the steps in Technique 56.

2. **Write a small program that restarts your computer and runs Check Disk.**

   (I promise it's easy!)

3. **Get Scheduler to run the program.**

   Because the program restarts your computer, it's a good idea to run Scheduler in the middle of the night when you're sure you won't be around.

Creating a program to restart Windows and run Check Disk

The first thing you need to do is set up Scheduler so that it automatically runs Check Disk. After you accomplish this task, it's on to Step 2 — creating the short program that automates Check Disk's processes even more.

To create the three-line program that restarts Windows and then runs Check Disk:

1. **Choose Start⇨My Computer.**
2. **Double-click the C: drive and then double-click Program Files.**

   If you haven't yet followed the steps in Technique 20, Windows warns you about all those dangerous files inside your computer (see Figure 57-4). Ho-hum — this warning is not one you need to mind.

These files are hidden.

This folder contains files that keep your system working properly. You should not modify its contents.

Show the contents of this folder

• **Figure 57-4: Just don't delete anything while you're here.**

3. **Click Show the Contents of This Folder.**
4. **Right-click an empty location inside the Program Files folder and choose New⇨Text Document.**

   Windows creates a new document called `New Text Document.txt`.

5. **Immediately type** Restart and Chkdsk.bat **and press Enter.**

If you can't get the file renamed properly, right-click `New Text Document.txt`, choose Rename, and type **Restart and Chkdsk.bat**.

   Windows warns you about changing filename extensions.

6. **Click Yes.**

   You now have an empty text file called `Restart and Chkdsk.bat` in your Program Files folder.

7. **Right-click** `Restart and Chkdsk.bat` **and click Edit.**

   Notepad opens the file.

8. **Type this three-line program into Notepad.**

```
echo y > y.txt
chkdsk /r < y.txt
shutdown -r
```

   See Figure 57-5 for an exact listing.

It's important that you put spaces in all the right places, and that you don't press Enter except at the end of the first and second lines.

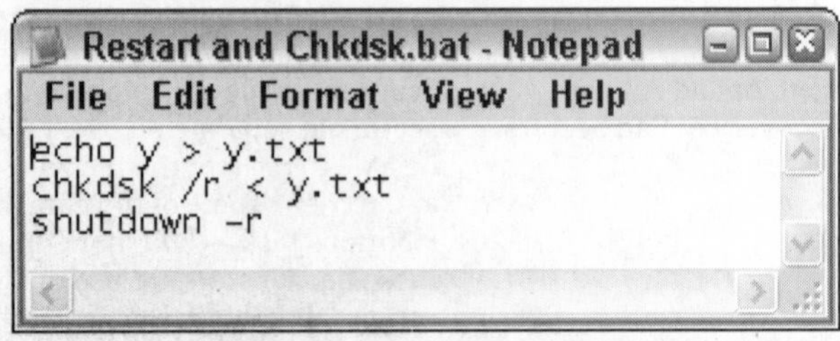

• **Figure 57-5: The three-line program that sets** `Chkdsk` **to run when Windows boots and then restarts Windows.**

9. **Choose File⇨Exit to leave Notepad. Be sure you save the changes.**

This program is short and sweet, but it's also abrupt. Best to test it before putting it in the Windows Scheduler.

10. **Leave Explorer running with the Program Files folder visible, but shut down all other programs.**
11. **Double-click the** `Restart and Chkdsk.bat` **file. Stand back.**

    If the program works right, you see a black box appear on-screen for a moment or two, with a warning that Windows can't lock the current drive.

12. **Don't do anything!**

    The System Shutdown dialog box appears. See Technique 6.

    When your PC comes back, a soothing, light-blue screen appears; you're politely informed that `A Disk Check Has Been Scheduled`.

13. **You have ten seconds to press any key to bypass the check — and I suggest you do precisely that if you don't want to run the scan right now.**

After a Check Disk run has started, the only way to stop it is to turn off your PC, and I *don't* recommend that you cut the power while Windows is looking at the innards of your drives.

Getting Scheduler to run your program

After you have the `Restart and Chkdsk.bat` program working, and you've been through Technique 56 to set up a Windows Scheduler account, you're ready to hitch the two together.

Follow these steps to do just that:

1. **Choose Start⇨All Programs⇨Accessories⇨ System Tools⇨Scheduled Tasks.**

   Windows Explorer appears on-screen, with the Scheduled Tasks folder open (see Figure 57-6).

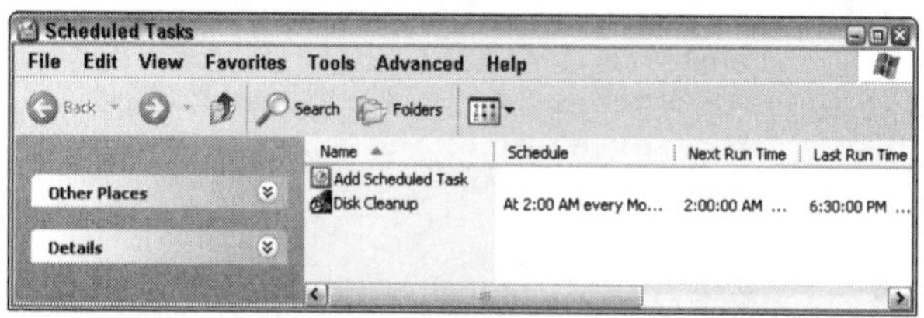

• Figure 57-6: The Windows Scheduler as it appears after you schedule Disk Cleanup.

2. **Double-click Add Scheduled Task.**

   The Scheduled Task Wizard appears.

3. **Click Next.**

   The Scheduled Task Wizard presents a list of all the programs on your Start menu.

4. **Click Browse. Using the drop-down list at the top, navigate to** `C:\Program Files`**.**

5. **Select** `Restart and Chkdsk.bat` **and then click Open.**

   The wizard continues, asking how often you want to perform the task.

6. **If you want to run Check Disk once a week (that's what I do), select the Weekly radio button and click Next.**

   The wizard lets you pick the time and days that it runs.

   I set Check Disk to run at 2:30 a.m. on Mondays, which is 30 minutes after my scheduled run of Disk Cleanup (see Technique 56).

7. **Pick a time that's good for you and click Next.**

Keep in mind that your computer will be rebooting, and it'll be basically out to lunch for a couple of hours after Check Disk starts.

   The wizard asks you to enter a user name and password.

Scheduler does not check your user name or password when you enter them — so make sure you get them right!

8. **Enter a user name and password that will be valid *when the scheduled task runs* and click Next. (Note that the user name doesn't have to be logged on at the time the scheduled task springs to life. But the user name has to be valid on that PC, and the password has to match whatever password is currently assigned to the user.)**

   Ideally, you followed the steps in Technique 56 to create an account called For Scheduled Tasks with a password that never expires.

   Windows confirms that the task is scheduled.

9. **Click Finish.**

   You can see your new task in the Scheduled Tasks folder (see Figure 57-7).

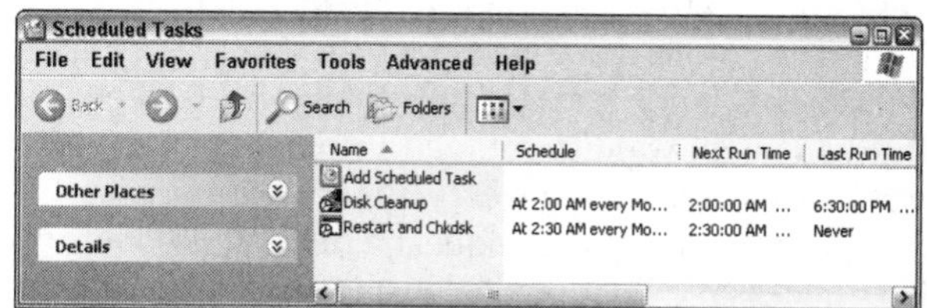

• Figure 57-7: The new task is ready to run.

If you have more than one disk drive, I recommend that you schedule Check Disk runs for the drives on separate nights. If you try to run two on the same night, there's a fair chance the second one won't ever run because the first one takes too long.

To set up a second Check Disk session, make separate `.bat` files with different names for each of your hard drives. The only difference between the files is this line:

```
chkdsk d: /r < y.txt
```

where you substitute `d:` with the drive letter for the drive you want to check. For example, to check your F: drive, use the following `.bat` file:

```
echo y > y.txt
chkdsk f: /r < y.txt
shutdown -r
```

If you wonder whether your tasks are running, choose Advanced⇨View Log and scan for the string *****. Details are in Technique 56.

Running Defrag Automatically

Compared to Check Disk, setting up Windows Scheduler to defragment your hard drive is a breeze.

In Technique 5, I talk about Disk Defragmenter, explain why you need to defrag drives from time to time, and step you through a manual defrag. It's very, very unusual that Windows XP needs to defrag a hard drive more than once in a blue moon, because Windows is much smarter now than it used to be. But you might want to run one automatically every week or so. Also, don't worry about wasting your computer's time. If you request a defrag and one isn't necessary, Windows XP just ignores the request.

The procedure is very similar to the one in the preceding section, so I go through it quickly:

1. **If you haven't yet followed the instructions in Technique 56, make sure Scheduler is set up and working right.**
2. **Choose Start⇨My Computer, double-click the C: drive, and then double-click Program Files.**
3. **Right-click an empty location inside the Program Files folder and choose New⇨Text Document.**
4. **Immediately type** Defragc.bat **and press Enter.**
5. **Windows warns you about changing filename extensions. Click Yes.**
6. **Right-click** `Defragc.bat` **and click Edit.**
7. **Type this simple, one-line program into Notepad:**
   `defrag c:`

Usually, Windows doesn't run a full defrag if the files on the drive occupy more than 85 percent of the available space on the drive. (Defragging can be very time consuming if there isn't a lot of free space.) If you want to force Windows to run a defrag even if files take up more than 85 percent of the space, use this line: `defrag c: -f`.

8. **Choose File⇨Exit to leave Notepad. Be sure you save the changes.**
9. **Choose Start⇨All Programs⇨Accessories⇨System Tools⇨Scheduled Tasks.**
10. **Double-click Add Scheduled Task.**
11. **Click Next.**
12. **Click Browse. Using the drop-down list at the top, navigate to** `C:\Program Files`.
13. **Select** `Defragc.bat` **and then click Open.**
14. **If you want to run a defrag once a week, select the Weekly radio button and click Next.**

    I run a defrag at 2:00 a.m. on Tuesdays, the day after I run Check Disk.
15. **Pick a time that's good for you and click Next.**

16. **Enter a user name and password that will be valid *at the time the scheduled task runs.* Click Next.**

See Technique 56 to find out how to create an account called For Scheduled Tasks with a password that never expires.

17. **Click Finish.**

You can see your new task in the Scheduled Tasks folder (see Figure 57-8).

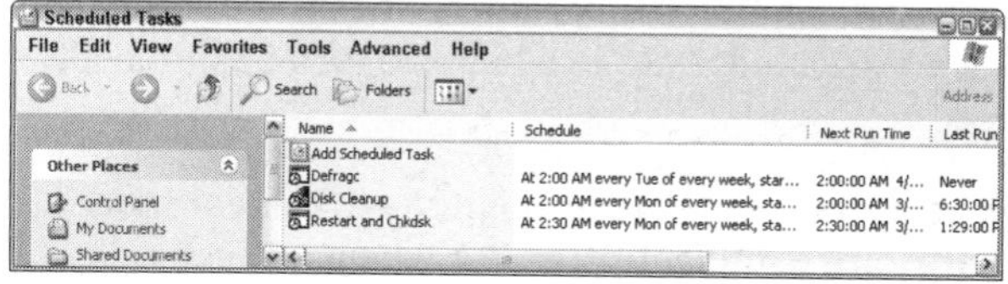

• **Figure 57-8: The new task is ready to run.**

If you have more than one disk drive, run defrags for each hard drive on different nights. To do that, make separate `.bat` files with different names for each of your hard drives. The only difference between the files is this line: `defrag d:` where you substitute d: with the drive letter for the drive you want checked. Rocket science.

Microsoft didn't make the defrag program. It comes from a company called Executive Software International. ESI has a more powerful version, called Diskeeper, available at `www.diskeeper.com`. Among other things, the ESI version includes its own scheduler, has in-depth scanning and reporting capabilities, and can run repeated reads and writes, to see whether there's any way to make a marginal sector go bad.

Updating Drivers Safely

Save Time By

- Choosing your driver updates wisely
- Protecting yourself before the update
- Rolling back quickly when a driver goes bad

Over the years, Windows *device drivers* — those little programs that sit between Windows and the hardware attached to your computer — have instigated more crashes and lock-ups than all other causes combined.

Many times, Windows gets a bad rap even though the drivers are the responsibility of the hardware manufacturers. But when a driver locks up Windows, people get mad at Microsoft because their machines don't work.

If you get in the middle of an expectorating contest — and I have, several times — you see the hardware manufacturer pointing fingers at Microsoft for lousy documentation, and Microsoft firing back at driver programmers who just don't get it. In every instance I've seen, both sides are right, both sides are wrong, and we users get stuck in the middle.

This technique shows you how to fend for yourself and stay out of the fray.

Understanding Drivers

Ya can't live with 'em and ya can't live without 'em.

Device drivers (or drivers for short) serve as the go-betweens on your PC, taking whatever Windows dishes out and delivering it to your device — whether it's a printer, network card, keyboard, video card, USB hub, thermometer (don't laugh), camera, telephone, three-dimensional cutting board, or carrier pigeon. Conversely, if your device needs to do something — "Hey, he pressed the Z key on the keyboard!" — the driver bears the brunt of taking the news to Windows.

Drivers can be enormously complex. And when they don't work right, they can cause all sorts of grief (see Figure 58-1).

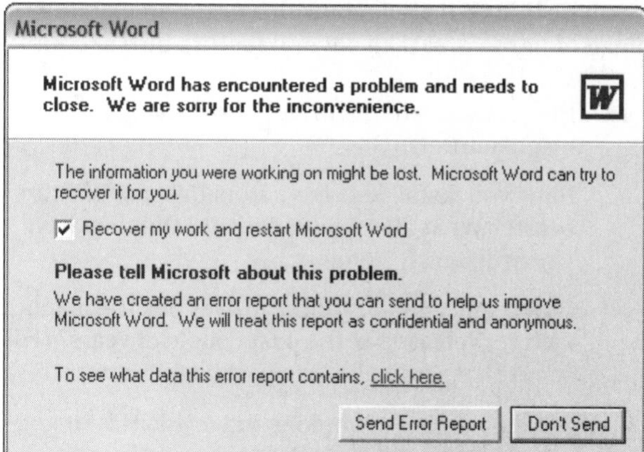

• Figure 58-1: Pardon the inconvenience, but we've, uh, *encountered* this little problem.

At one point, Microsoft figured that *more than half* of the crashes and unexplained freezes in Windows were the direct result of bad drivers. In other words, if a driver hasn't crashed your system yet, it's only a matter of time.

Here's the real rub with driver crashes: You never know where or when they might occur. The same driver problem could lead to the messages in both Figures 58-1 and 58-2 — in completely different applications, under entirely different circumstances.

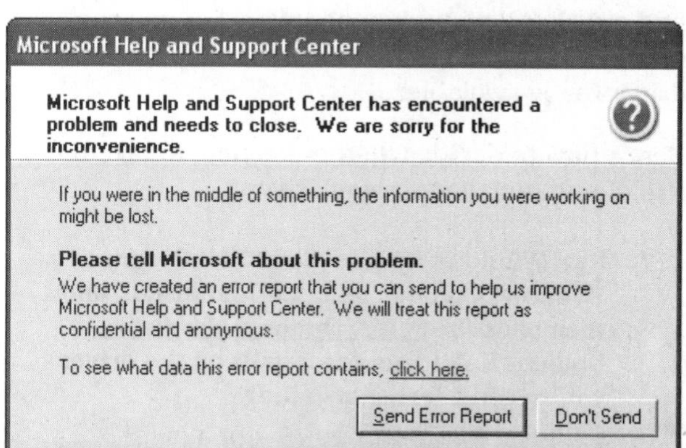

• Figure 58-2: Even Windows Help gets the blues.

Thanks largely to the automatically generated "phone home" error reports, the number of driver crashes has decreased, relatively, in recent months. (Specifically, Microsoft now has the ammunition to pummel driver writers with hard evidence.) But bad drivers still get out — every day, it seems.

If you don't want to send Microsoft logs of your crashes, follow the steps in Technique 5 in the section on disabling automatic error reporting.

Personally, I only send crash reports like this to Microsoft if I'm using a relatively new driver. I figure that older drivers have already generated zillions of reports – and it'd take more time and hassle to send the report than it's worth.

Choosing Your Drivers Wisely

If you're installing new hardware, you have to get a driver to go with it. Fair enough. Install the hardware. Turn on your PC, and the Found New Hardware Wizard takes you through the necessary steps. This is a worry-free process.

But if you hear from a friend or see on the Web that your hardware manufacturer has a new driver for a piece of hardware that you own, you should think long and hard before installing that new driver.

New Windows XP drivers typically come from two sources: Windows Update or the hardware manufacturer's site. I have found – and installed, and come to regret installing – very bad drivers from both sources.

Reasons (Some good, some bad) for changing drivers

I know of just two good reasons for changing drivers:

- **Your current driver doesn't work right.** For example, your video driver may show skips and streaks on the screen, or you may buy a new game that requires you to update your video driver.

- **Your current driver is unstable.** The instabilities may manifest themselves in many ways. For example, if you experience any of the following, your current driver is unstable:
  - If you move your mouse one certain way, it doesn't work anymore.
  - You move your cordless keyboard away from your PC to clean it. When you move it back, what you type on the keys doesn't appear on-screen.
  - Every time you try to play a DVD, Windows Media Player freezes.

If your driver ain't broke, don't fix it.

Contrariwise, I know many bad reasons for changing drivers:

- **The new one is faster.** No driver is ever *that* much faster.
- **The new one has improved features.** Do you really need 'em?
- **The guy at the computer shop recommended it.** Has he honestly installed it on his machine and lived with it?
- **Hey, it's brand new, and it has to be *great*, right?** *Not.*

Evaluating driver reliability

Ultimately, only you can decide if you really want to roll the dice with a new driver. Keep in mind that downloading, installing, living with, and ultimately uninstalling a flakey driver takes a lot of time. Only very rarely do people save more time with a new driver than they lost with the old one.

That said, if the problems with your current driver are bad enough, a change may be warranted — even if installing and troubleshooting the new driver does take a lot of time.

If you decide to install a new driver for an existing piece of hardware, take several factors into account:

- How reliable are the drivers from this manufacturer?

  Have you installed drivers from this manufacturer before? What about your friends? Did they have any problems?
- How many versions of this driver has the manufacturer released in the past couple of years? (For some, that should be "the past couple of weeks?")

If the number of versions and revisions is strikingly high, I say steer clear.

- Are other customers reporting problems with this specific driver?

Do an online search for the driver name and specific version number. You should get a good sense of the driver's reliability based on the number of angry reports you find.

Here's a real-world example to help you evaluate a driver candidate's reliability. Say your video driver has some problems — it doesn't scroll right, and characters get streaked from time to time. You're a savvy Windows XP user, so you've been periodically checking Windows Update (see Technique 55) to find out about new driver software. For months you've received a notification about a new video driver that's available.

Here's how to decide whether it's time to take the risk of updating your buggy driver:

1. **Run Windows Update (Start⇨All Programs⇨Windows Update), click Custom Install, and then click the Select Optional Hardware Updates link to get the details on the driver you're considering installing.**

   For example, in Figure 58-3, NVIDIA has a new driver available.

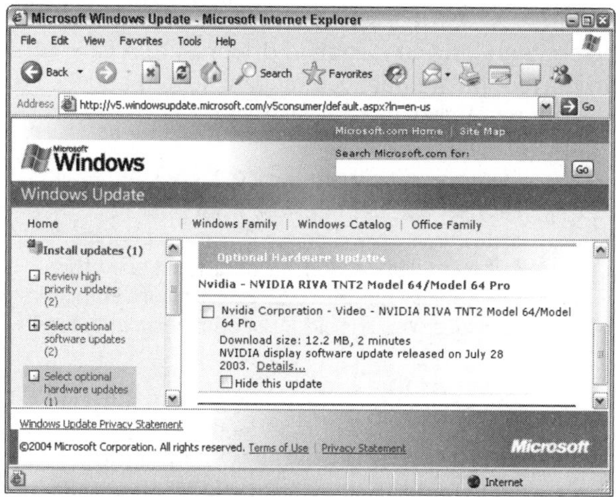

• **Figure 58-3: NVIDIA's latest driver, according to Windows Update.**

2. Click the Details link.

The report tells you when the driver was released. For example, the driver in Figure 58-4 was released on July 28, 2003. Hard to believe, but if true, that's a good sign — it means that the current version of the driver has stood the test of time. On the other hand, Windows Update says the driver was last published on July 28, 2004, precisely one year later.

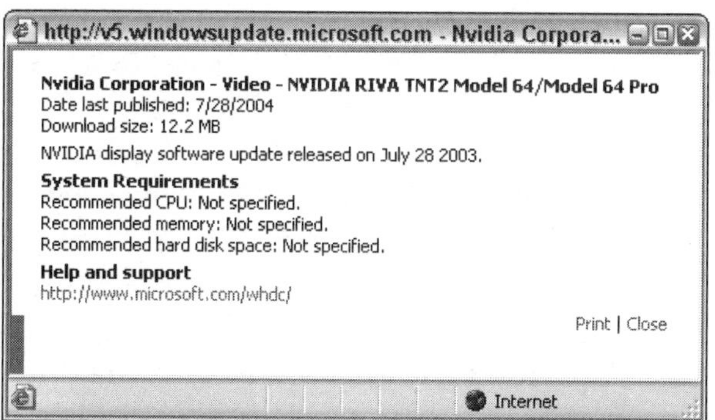

• **Figure 58-4: This driver's old — and, thus, likely to be more stable.**

Something's screwy here. When I saw that date discrepancy, red lights started flashing and sirens wailed. Figuratively, of course.

3. Search for information about the driver.

For example, I use the Google Toolbar (see Technique 24 for more about Google) to search Internet newsgroups for information about drivers. When I searched for information and reviews of the latest NVIDIA driver, I found lots of complaints about the driver's stability.

A driver that's certified by Microsoft is called a *signed driver*, or one that has passed Windows Hardware Quality Labs (WHQL) testing.

4. Check the manufacturer's site.

When I checked NVIDIA's Web site (see Figure 58-5), the only Windows XP driver I could find was version number 61.77. Imagine — this is the 77th revision of driver version 61! Kinda makes you feel warm and fuzzy, doesn't it? This one was released on July 27, 2004. Is Microsoft's July 28, 2003 driver a completely different animal? Or is it just older? There's no information anywhere I can find to resolve the discrepancy.

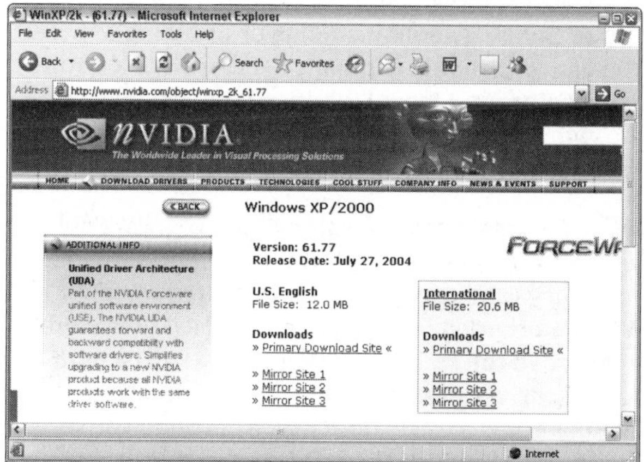

• **Figure 58-5: The driver information on NVIDIA's Web site doesn't match Microsoft's description.**

When you go hunting for drivers, you'll encounter the same problem, perhaps in a slightly different guise. Guaranteed.

If you ever install a driver that has had this many versions and revisions, you are playing with fire. Any company that can't get it right in a few tries probably has some issues. Forget about it. Life's too short.

5. **Install the driver if you dare.**

   There's no way on earth I'll install the driver from the NVIDIA site. But with great fear and trepidation (and a willingness to offer my system and sanity as a sacrifice for this book), I decided to install the possibly older, presumably more stable, Windows Update NVIDIA driver dated July 28, 2003.

   I detail the precise method in the next section.

Updating a Driver

In Technique 64, I talk about setting System Restore Points, so that you can roll back Windows to a previous state. System Restore Points are *vital* when you're thinking about installing or updating a driver. You can and should manually set a System Restore Point before you install a driver. I quickly take you through the steps in this section, or you can refer to Technique 64 for all the details.

Microsoft has a driver certification program that reviews drivers to see if they function properly. It's a voluntary (and expensive) service conducted by the Windows Hardware Quality Labs (WHQL) that aim to improve the stability of Windows XP drivers. If a specific driver passes muster, Microsoft allows the manufacturer to distribute it as a certified (or so-called *signed*) driver. *Unsigned* drivers trigger warning messages when they're installed. Signed drivers install with a couple of clicks.

Windows XP always sets a System Restore Point before installing an unsigned driver — that is, a driver that hasn't been specifically tested and blessed by Microsoft's WHQL team.

Unfortunately, Windows XP doesn't automatically set a System Restore Point prior to installing a signed driver. Call me a Luddite, but even with WHQL certification, I want the extra safety net that a System Restore Point provides. You should insist on having one, too.

As I explain in the following section, "Rolling Back a Bad Driver," most kinds of drivers can be *rolled back* like they were never installed. Printer drivers aren't afforded that protection. If you install a printer driver, you absolutely must have a System Restore Point – and it's safest to create one yourself.

Here's how to safely update a driver, using the NVIDIA video driver described in the preceding section as a real-world example:

1. **Choose Start⇨All Programs⇨Accessories⇨System Tools⇨System Restore.**

   The System Restore Wizard appears.

2. **Click the Create a Restore Point option, and then click Next.**

   The wizard asks for a name for the Restore Point, as shown in Figure 58-6.

3. **Type a name that will make sense to you a week from now to identify the Restore Point, and then click the Create button.**

   The wizard takes a while to create the Restore Point, and then notifies you that it's complete.

4. **Click Close (X) to exit the System Restore Wizard.**

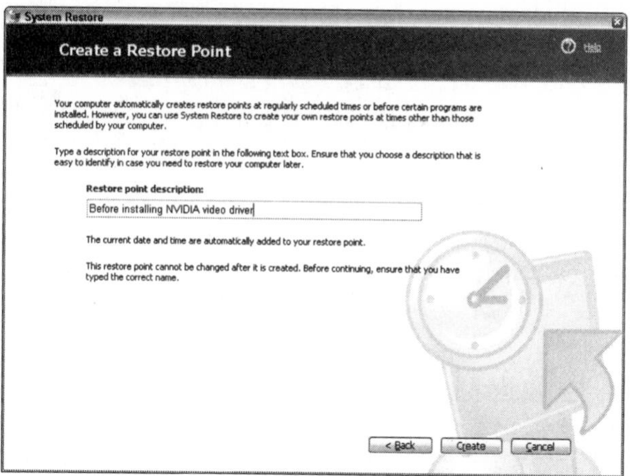

• **Figure 58-6: Type in a name that you'll remember.**

5. **On the Windows Update site (refer to Figure 58-3), click the box next to the driver you want to install, and then click the Go To Install Updates link (see Figure 58-7).**

I suggest installing driver updates all by themselves, one at a time, so that you can trap any problems as quickly as possible.

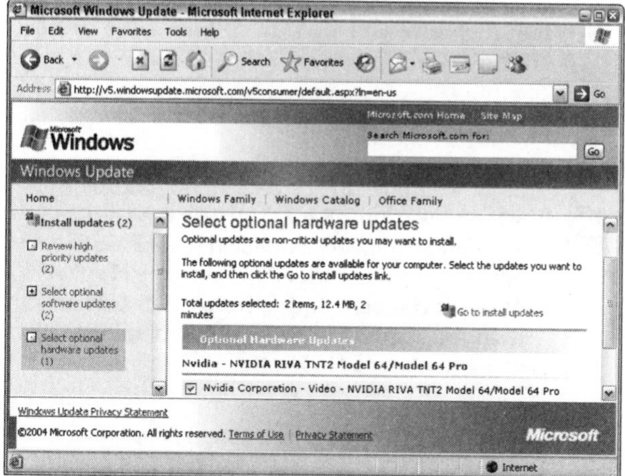

• **Figure 58-7: Check the box(es) next to any drivers you want to install, and then click Go To Install Updates.**

6. **Click the Install button.**

   Downloading a big driver can take a long time, even over a fast Internet connection. Relax.

   The installer kicks in immediately after the download finishes. You may be asked to restart Windows.

7. **Test, test, test.**

   If the driver has a problem, you want to find out about it now, not three weeks from now.

Rolling Back a Bad Driver

So your driver doesn't work worth beans, your system locks up every time you stare at the screen too hard, and even Notepad crashes with astounding frequency.

Time to get rid of that new driver.

In Windows XP, first try to roll back the driver all by itself. *Rolling back* a driver involves getting rid of that new driver and going back to the good old days when you used the previous driver, which crashed Notepad only occasionally. Rolling back an individual driver is quick and almost always effective.

If rolling back the driver doesn't work, don't fuss with it. Go through the System Restore Wizard and move back to the Restore Point you took just before you installed the driver. I talk about that extensively in Technique 64. (Note that you can't roll back a driver by using the Control Panel's Add or Remove Programs applet.)

Here's how to roll back a driver:

1. **Choose Start➪My Computer. Right-click My Computer and choose Properties.**

   The System Properties dialog box appears.

2. **Click the Hardware tab, and then click the Device Manager button.**

   The Device Manager appears, as shown in Figure 58-8. This is a window to the heart and soul of your hardware.

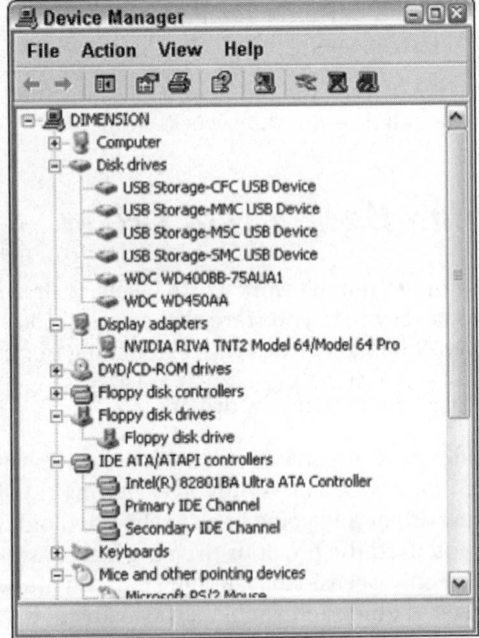

• **Figure 58-8: The Device Manager holds all the hardware secrets.**

3. **Right-click the device that has the offending driver and choose Properties⇨Driver.**

   For example, I chose the NVIDIA RIVA TNT2 device and got the Properties dialog box shown in Figure 58-9.

4. **To roll back the driver — get rid of the current one, and use the older one instead — click the Roll Back Driver button.**

   Windows asks if you're sure.

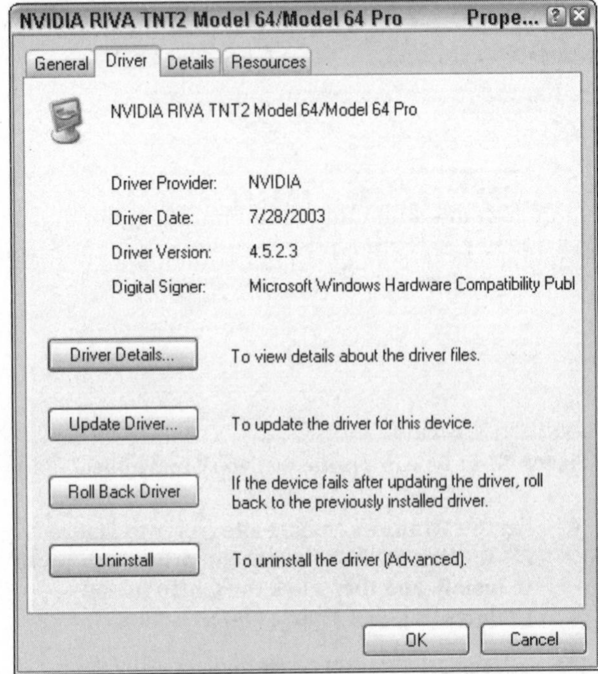

• **Figure 58-9: Properties for the video card with the updated driver.**

5. **If you're sure you want to roll back the driver, click Yes.**

   Sooner or later, the original driver appears (see Figure 58-10).

In this example, the driver dated 5/3/2002 is listed as version 2.9.4.2. The new driver, dated 7/28/2003, appears as version 4.5.2.3. So in a little more than fourteen months, the NVIDIA TNT2 driver went through two major version changes, and dozens (hundreds?) of minor version changes. Hoooo boy.

6. **Click the Close (X) button to exit the Device Manager.**

• Figure 58-10: Out with the new driver, in with the old.

Unfortunately, Windows XP doesn't allow you to roll back printer drivers. If you get a bad printer driver, you have to go to the Restore Point that you created before installing the new printer driver.

Just in case you're curious . . . I went back and re-installed the updated NVIDIA driver, number 4.5.2.3, and it works like a champ. I'm even considering installing the newer one on the NVIDIA Web site.

Some people never learn, eh?

Running Periodic Maintenance

Save Time By

- Buying all the supplies you need in one fell swoop
- Cleaning on schedule
- Using common tools to get the job done

Ever lost ten minutes looking at a special can of computer monitor cleaner, wondering if you really need it? Ever open your computer to discover three inches of caked-on gunk clogging the air inlets?

Maintenance is a pain. It takes time, and you know if you let your teenager (or the housekeeper) try to clean something, it'll take you a half hour to go back and fix it. Still, it has to be done. Otherwise, the inside of your computer will remind you with a bout of spontaneous combustion, and your mouse will start smelling like a dead rodent.

This technique takes you — quickly! — through the steps necessary to keep your beast alive.

Making Your Maintenance Shopping List

Everything you need to keep your PC in tip-top shape is listed in the following list.

- Cotton swabs (Q-Tips or something similar)
- Little balls of cotton
- Paper towels (good, thick ones — the kind that don't fall apart)
- Rubbing alcohol (isopropyl alcohol, or isopropanol — they're all the same thing)
- Glass cleaner (Windex or something similar)
- Diskette (just any old floppy diskette that's lying around)
- Stamp collector's 6-inch round-tip stamp tongs (see the section, "Pulling out a stuck diskette," later in this technique) — nope, tweezers and needle-nose pliers don't work as well, unless they're very long and thin
- Compressed air
- Small pocketknife

- A small computer tool kit with screws, screwdrivers, jumpers, and all those little things that seem to get swallowed whenever you open the case.
- CD lens cleaner (looks like a CD, but cleans the CD/DVD lens)

Make a copy of this list and run through it the next time you go shopping.

Weekly Cleaning

If you're thinking of cleaning each component of your computer, one by one, you're working too hard. Instead, use each cleaning tool once and move from component to component in cleaning phases.

Set up your computer-cleaning schedule to coincide with your regular house cleaning. That way you kill two — or five or ten — birds with one stone.

Here's an overview of your weekly cleaning drill:

1. Vacuum
2. Dust
3. Clean monitor screens
4. Ungunk the mouse
5. Check the floppy drive

I discuss each of these tasks in more detail in the following sections.

Vacuuming strategies

Haul out your vacuum cleaner. (You do that to clean your office anyway, right?) Using the smallest attachment you can find — one of those crevice cleaners works great — vacuum the living daylights out of the following computer components:

- **Keyboard:** Unplug the keyboard. Turn it upside down and shake it. Look for loose keys that might be consumed by the vacuum cleaner. If the keys are all hooked on, vacuum every nook and cranny. Turn the keyboard upside down again and repeat once or twice. Finally, shoot compressed air into all the corners and then vacuum again.
- **Monitor:** If you have a traditional big monitor, turn it off. Vacuum all those holes in the case to get rid of the dust. Bonus points if you can get at the dust inside. You lose all points, and may go literally down in flames, if anything is obstructing the flow of air into and out of the casing. No, don't open up the casing. Sheesh. You could get electrocuted. (LCD/flat panel monitors don't need vacuuming.)
- **The computer itself:** Shut down Windows and turn off the power. Then vacuum every single place you can reach. Use your hand to block the largest air intakes so you get maximum suck where you need it most. Finally, stick your finger in the diskette drive, push the little flap back or up (depending on the kind of drive), and vacuum like crazy.
- **Peripherals:** Turn off your printer, scanner, modem, DSL box, UPS, power distribution bar, network hub, external drives, and everything else, and vacuum, vacuum, vacuum.

I've tried using many variations on the small vacuum cleaner, but I haven't found anything that works as well as a plain, small, everyday household canister vacuum cleaner with a crevice tool.

Dusting tips

After you vacuum, pull out a cleaning rag and wipe off the plastic case on your computer, the back of the monitor, printer, the outside of your scanner, the tray on your CD drive that holds the CDs, and any other plastic that's literally sitting around gathering dust. Don't use any cleaners. If some gunk is stuck to a piece of hardware, use a little water and rub *gently.* If it's still stuck, add a bit of soap and rub *gently.*

If it's still stuck, get a universal solvent like Goo Gone (`www.magicamerican.com/googone.shtml`) and go for it. Yeah, I know you aren't supposed to use solvents on plastic cases. But if you're trying to get off tape residue, you don't have much choice. If you use a solvent, make sure you're in a well-ventilated area, and make sure your Aunt Mildred doesn't haul out a cigarette while you're in the middle of cleaning.

Cleaning screens

How you clean your screen depends on whether you're using an old-fashioned, full-sized, TV-style monitor or have a flat screen. The working end of a monitor is glass. The panel of an LCD screen is a special kind of plastic. They aren't the same, and they don't clean the same:

Never touch a monitor — a traditional monitor, LCD flat screen, or portable screen — with your finger. Cleaning the smudgy oils in human skin isn't always easy.

- **To clean a glass screen:** Spray or pour a small amount of plain, old, everyday glass cleaner onto a good-quality paper towel.

  Don't spray the screen; the cleaner can fall into the electronics. Gently rub down the screen; then rub the glass with a dry piece of paper towel.

I know, I know. You're supposed to use a lint-free cloth to clean a screen. Poppycock. I've been using paper towels for years, and I've never seen a scratch yet. In fact, I seem to get the best results with old newspapers. But I don't have the guts to say that in a big book like this. Heh heh heh.

- **To clean a flat-panel screen, including the screen on a laptop:** Put a bit of rubbing alcohol (isopropanol) on a ball of cotton. Rub very gently, following quickly with a clean ball of cotton. That's how the manufacturers clean the displays as they leave the assembly line.

On the other hand, I *have* scratched an LCD screen with a paper towel. Use cotton. And don't use a commercial screen wipe unless it specifically says that it works with an LCD. I like to use alcohol preps, which you can buy for a pittance at any medical supply store.

- **To clean a scanner:** Scanner beds are glass, just like monitors, and you clean them the same way. But you have to be excruciatingly careful not to let any of the glass cleaner leak over the edges. After the cleaner has dried on the underside of the bed, it takes a screwdriver and a lot of patience to clean things up.

Ungunking the mouse

Nothing drives me nuts faster than a jumping mouse.

Cleaning a mouse involves four steps:

1. **Clean the mouse pad.**

   People tend to overlook this vital first step. If your mouse gets dirty, where does the dirt come from? D'oh. Slick, shiny pads are best cleaned with your fingernails. (You can wash them if you must.) Bumpy mouse pads only need a shake. And if you use your desktop for a mousepad — yech. You eat there, don't you?

2. **Clean the gliders.**

   The gliders are those little plastic things on the bottom of the mouse that the mouse moves around on. Use your fingernails. If a recessed area is around the gliders, clean the gunk out of there with a toothpick or a knife.

3. **Clean the working part.**

   If you have a roller mouse, unplug it first.

   Flip it over, open the cover, and take out the ball.

   Wipe off the ball with a paper towel and a little bit of water.

   Set it aside to dry.

Inside the cavity, use a small knife to scrape the big crud off the metal and plastic rollers (the Microsoft IntelliMouse has two metal rollers and one plastic).

No need to scrape hard because the rubbing alcohol picks up anything that remains.

Flip the mouse over and pop it against the base of your hand to get the big junk out. Then clean all the rollers with cotton swabs, each dipped in rubbing alcohol. Make sure you rotate the rollers. Blow everything out, reassemble, and you're back in business.

If you have an optical mouse, use rubbing alcohol and a cotton swab or cotton ball to clean the eye.

4. **If you have a wireless mouse, check the signal.**

   Each manufacturer is different, but to check the batteries in a Microsoft mouse, choose Start➪Control Panel➪Printers and Other Hardware➪Mouse, and then click the Wireless tab. You see icons for battery status and for signal strength. If the batteries are shot, replace them with cheap NiCads. If the signal strength seems poor, move the base around.

I have a fancy, expensive Microsoft wireless, optical mouse, and I hated it. Why? It kept clicking those weird side-keys (Microsoft calls them "thumb" keys) for me, even when my fingers were miles away. So when I was working on a Web page and moved my mouse up and to the left, CLICK!, the mouse told Internet Explorer I wanted to go back to the previous Web page. I thought the mouse must've been dirty — even when it was new — so I spent ages trying to clean it. Nope. Ultimately, I disabled the thumb keys using the mouse dialog box, and now I can tolerate the mouse. Barely.

Checking the floppy drive

You can buy a floppy cleaning kit if you really want to, but few people use floppies frequently enough these days to accumulate much build-up on the recording heads.

Instead, floppies usually die from neglect. Air gets sucked into the PC through the floppy opening, dust builds up, and sooner or later you can't put a diskette in or take it out.

That's why I recommend that you simply stick an old diskette in the floppy drive every week, make sure you can read it (Start➪My Computer➪3½ Floppy), and then take the diskette out.

If your diskette gets stuck, see the advice on recalcitrant floppies at the end of this technique.

Monthly Cleaning

If you keep up with the weekly cleaning, my recommended monthly cleaning comes easy:

1. **Clean the CD/DVD lens.**

   You need a special lens cleaner for this, but you can buy one at almost any electronics place and many grocery stores. It's just a regular CD with a brush (or brushes) attached to the shiny side.

Some manufacturers would have you believe that there's a difference between CD cleaners and DVD cleaners. If there is, I sure can't figure it out. Save yourself some time and money, and just get a cheap CD cleaner.

2. **Clean the keys on your keyboard.**

   I use my keyboard hard. If you do, too, I suggest you remove the gunk from around the keys once a month. To do so, start with a handful of cotton swabs. Unplug the keyboard (or turn off your laptop, if you're cleaning a laptop). Slowly, carefully, dip a swab in a little bit of rubbing alcohol. Clean around the keys.

Cleaning the keys is tricky (and time-consuming) because you don't want to spill any rubbing alcohol down into the innards of the keyboard. But keeping the keys clean does prevent big globs of hair and dirt from falling into the keyboard, which makes it well worth the effort.

3. **Clean the inside of your printer.**

   Every printer is different. Check the manufacturer's Web site for details.

Fixing Components As Needed

Here's what you need to know about fixing the other parts of your PC.

Cleaning CDs

If a CD won't work and you have a CD cleaning kit handy, you have it made.

But what if you don't have a cleaning kit handy? Here's what I do:

Take your CD into the shower with you. Use a little bit of hand soap, lathered in your hands, lightly applied to the shiny side of the CD. When you get out of the shower, use a soft, clean towel and wipe the shiny side from the middle of the CD toward the outside. If you don't have a soft towel, dry your hands and use toilet paper.

Works like a champ — on eyeglasses, too.

Recovering from spilled coffee or soda

Have you ever spilled a latte on your keyboard? Yech. What a mess.

If you have a run-of-the-mill cheap keyboard, and it stops working after you anoint it, throw it away. Isn't worth the effort.

But if you have a good keyboard — good keyboards are worth their weight in gold — here's how to try to bring it back to life:

1. **Don't panic.**
2. **Disconnect the keyboard.**
3. **Turn the keyboard upside down. Let it sit that way for a few hours.**
4. **Take the screws off the back of the keyboard and pop off as much of the plastic as you can — but *leave the keys attached.***

   Taking them off is an absolute last resort.

5. **Using a washcloth that's been slightly moistened, clean up as much of the spilled junk as you can.**
6. **Pull out a handful of cotton swabs and, using rubbing alcohol, dig into the nooks and crannies.**
7. **Reassemble the keyboard and give it a go.**

If you can't get the keyboard to work, you may have to resort to pulling off all the keys. Here's how:

1. **Take a snapshot of the keyboard, or write down the location of all the keys.**

   It can save your hide. No kidding.

2. **Take the screws off the back and pull off as much plastic as you can.**

   The less plastic, the easier it is to remove keys.

3. **Remove each key cap carefully by pulling it straight up.**

   Use extreme caution when taking off the spacebar, the Enter key, and any oversized keys. Frequently, these keys have a spring or a lever that can't be bent.

4. **Clean the electronic contacts with cotton swabs lightly dipped in rubbing alcohol.**

   You don't want to get them wet.

5. **Clean the key caps in the kitchen sink and dry them thoroughly.**
6. **Carefully put the key caps back on the way you took them off.**

   I know. It's much easier said than done.
7. **Test the keys before you put the plastic back on.**

   Almost always, you'll find one that doesn't feel right. Figure out what's wrong with it before the plastic gets wrapped around it.
8. **Put the plastic back on and try it out.**

The general procedure for a laptop is more drastic — but your chances of bringing a laptop back to life are slim indeed:

1. **Turn the laptop off.**

   If it's plugged into the wall, unplug it.
2. **Turn it upside down — quickly — and pour off as much of the liquid as you can.**
3. **If you spilled anything but water into the laptop, take an amount of fresh water equal to the amount you spilled and pour it right on top of the original spill.**

   You need to rinse off the sugar, coffee, hops . . . whatever.
4. **Turn it upside down again and pour off everything.**
5. **If it's easy to take off the case, do so. If not, don't sweat it.**
6. **Set the portable, upside down, on a couple of stacks of books or magazines.**

   Make sure air can get all around it.
7. **If you have air conditioning, turn it on. (AC lowers the humidity in the room.) If you have a fan, aim it toward the laptop. If you have a hair dryer with a "No Heat" setting, blow it into every ventilation slot.**
8. **Let it dry for at least 24 hours.**
9. **Reassemble it, turn it on, and pray.**

Remember that coffee can't get into your hard drive, at least not very easily, so even if you lose your portable, you almost certainly haven't lost your data. Unless your portable decided to go for a swim in the pool, of course. That could have a deleterious effect on your hard drive's life expectancy.

Pulling out a stuck diskette

As your floppy drive gets older, it starts eating diskettes. The cause of the problem isn't the drive, per se. The real problem is the piece of metal on the diskette that slides away, revealing the recording surface. If your drive gets a bit dirty, it probably has a hard time putting that slider back in place — and that's why the diskette won't come out.

There's a tool that's absolutely perfect for pulling stuck diskettes out of sticky drives. It's called a *stamp tong.* Any kid with a stamp collection can show you one: Philatelists use tongs so they don't leave dirt and oil from their fingers on their stamps. A good picture of one is at `www.globalstamps.com/tongs.htm`.

When a diskette gets stuck, you have to work the stamp tong down into the drive deep enough to release the pressure on the metal slider:

1. **Shut down Windows and turn off the computer.**
2. **Push open the drive cover with your finger.**
3. **Work the stamp tong back and forth until you feel the diskette ease out.**

How to find a stamp tong? Walk into any stamp shop (or most hobby shops) and ask for a round-tip 6-inch stamp tong. It should set you back about five bucks. Cheap insurance.

Pulling out a stuck CD

While getting a diskette out of a floppy drive is hard, removing a stuck CD is almost always very easy:

1. **Shut down Windows and turn off the computer.**
2. **Take a paper clip and unbend it.**
3. **Stick the tip of the paper clip in the little hole at the front of the CD drive.**

   No, I'm not talking about the speaker jack. There's a little hole that's just big enough for a paper clip. Look harder.

   That's all it takes.

Making Backups — Fast

Save Time By

- Knowing what Windows XP Home can — and can't — do
- Creating copies of your essential files in case something goes wrong
- Getting Windows XP to automatically create backups

Have you ever lost a hard drive? I sure have. Several times. When I had good backups, bringing my life and business back only took a day or two. Once I lost a hard drive in the middle of a book — and my last backup was a week old. It took almost a week to recover.

Hard drives are mechanical devices. They get old. They break down. Nothing you can do will change that.

You need to figure out how much data you can afford to lose — and then you need to spend some time figuring out how to get it backed up.

Windows XP comes with a decent backup program, although XP Home users have to go out and find it. XP Professional includes automatic restore features that let you bring back an entire dead drive — even if it's your C: drive — with surprisingly little hassle. XP Home users, however, have to jump through some extra hoops and take extra precautions with backups.

In this technique, I show you how to measure out that crucial ounce of prevention — quickly.

Personally, I use a program called ZipBackup (`www.zipbackup.com`) for my daily backups and Norton Ghost for occasional full-disk image copies. If you can justify the price — $29.95 for ZipBackup, with a free 30-day trial; Ghost runs $69.95 — there's no need to jump through Windows' hoops.

Understanding XP Home's Backup Limitations

When Microsoft made its first announcement about Windows XP Professional and Windows XP Home, the Folks in Charge had to come up with some ways to distinguish the Professional from the Home Edition — ways that would justify the $100-or-so price differential.

They came up with a great idea: They decided to put their fancy automated backup and restore program (which Microsoft bought from a company called Veritas) into XP Professional, but leave it out of XP Home.

Oy! Did the offal hit the fan. Journalists everywhere (including me, I must confess) bemoaned the fact that XP Home users wouldn't have a backup program, fer heaven's sake. Home and small office users need backup just as much as everybody else.

Microsoft, much to its credit, changed its corporate mind. In the end, Windows XP Home got a backup and restore program — a stripped-down version of the Veritas program — but it was stuck on the CD at the last minute.

That's not the end of the story. Some PC manufacturers forgot to include the backup program on their XP Home machines. It isn't even on the System Restore Disks or hidden on the hard drive somewhere. If you fall into that boat, your best bet is to yell really loudly at your hardware manufacturer; then borrow an original Windows XP Home Edition CD from a friend.

Automated System Recovery

The Windows XP Professional version of the backup program includes *Automated System Recovery (ASR)*. With ASR, you can reformat or replace your C: drive, boot from the Windows XP Professional CD, and completely restore your system to the point of your last backup. (It isn't easy, but it's possible: Search in Windows Help and Support for **ASR** to get the gory details.)

In Windows XP Home, the backup program doesn't include ASR. If your C: drive dies and you buy a new one, or if you reformat your C: drive for whatever reason, you can restore all your data files — but that's about it. Your Windows settings are gone. You can't restore your Registry settings, so you have to reinstall all your programs. Most (if not all) of your passwords are lost, too.

The real situation is a bit dicier than that. In fact, on some Windows XP Home machines (I'm told) ASR *does* work. Microsoft is mum on which systems work and which don't, but you can see all the news they see fit to print at `support.microsoft.com/?kbid=302700`.

Automated System Recovery is not the same as a System Restore Point (see Technique 64). System Restore can help you roll back really bad Windows changes — the bits and pieces of Windows that get gummed up can be reset to their original state. The backup and restore methods I describe in this technique refer to data files and/or entire drives, and they're commonly used when you mess up a file beyond recognition, or an entire hard drive collapses.

What to do about backup limitations

If you use Windows XP Home Edition, you have two choices when it comes to restoring your hard drive in the event of a crash:

- Resign yourself to the fact that if your C: drive crashes, you may have to reinstall all your programs, and reconstructing your system is going to be hairy.
- Buy a good disk-imaging package, such as Norton Ghost (`www.symantec.com/sabu/ghost/ghost_personal/`), and run it regularly.

Windows XP Professional users, on the other hand, can feel pretty (but not completely) comfortable that ASR can restore an entire hard drive.

Manually installing the backup program

If you have Windows XP Home, you have to manually install the Veritas backup/restore program:

1. **Put the Windows XP Home CD in your CD drive.**

   Windows shows you its installation splash screen in Figure 60-1.

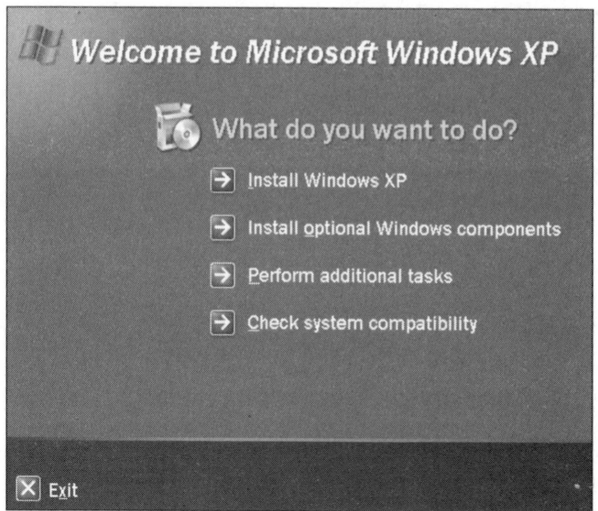

• **Figure 60-1: Where do you want to go today?**

2. **Click the Perform Additional Tasks link.**

   The Windows CD gives you more options.

3. **Click the Browse This CD link.**

   Windows Explorer kicks in, and (finally!) lets you look at the contents of the CD.

4. **Double-click to VALUEADD⇨MSFT⇨NTBACKUP, and then double-click the `Ntbackup.msi` file.**

   The installer takes off in a blink of an eye.

5. **Exit out of the installer.**

   You return to Windows.

Creating a Backup

Windows XP backup backs up everything on your hard drive: data files, programs, settings, even Windows itself. It essentially creates a clone of your hard drive, optionally compresses all the files, and sticks them on a backup medium of your choice. In the best of circumstances, you have enough room on a different hard drive (perhaps a hard drive connected to your network, or a removable hard drive) to copy your cloned drive quickly. In the worst of circumstances, you may need to copy to tape. Many people only make backups of part of their hard drives — say, data files only, or the contents of their My Documents folder — and burn the backup on a CD.

Most music (MP3 or WMA), picture (JPG or GIF), and video files are already compressed. Using the compression option in Windows Backup doesn't hurt, but it's a waste of time and won't save much, if any, space on the backup media. Generally, it's better to just copy these files to a backup media. It stops the main backup file from getting too large, and separate files are easier to find and retrieve later. Music, pictures, and video are all good candidates for writing to a CD or DVD.

When you want to make a backup:

1. **Choose Start⇨All Programs⇨Accessories⇨System Tools⇨Backup.**

   The Backup or Restore Wizard appears.

If you have XP Professional, and you want to create System Restore Disks for ASR, you must click the Advanced Mode link at this point. Then, from the Welcome tab, click Automated System Recovery Wizard. If you're on a Big Corporate Network, check with your network administrator first to make sure you don't mess up any settings that have been put in place for you.

2. **Click Next.**

   The wizard asks whether you want to back up or restore (see Figure 60-2).

3. **Click the Backup Files and Settings option, and then click Next.**

   The wizard needs to know what you want to back up, as shown in Figure 60-3. If you're not entirely sure, a safe bet is the first choice — My Documents and Settings gets the most critical data, including your e-mail messages.

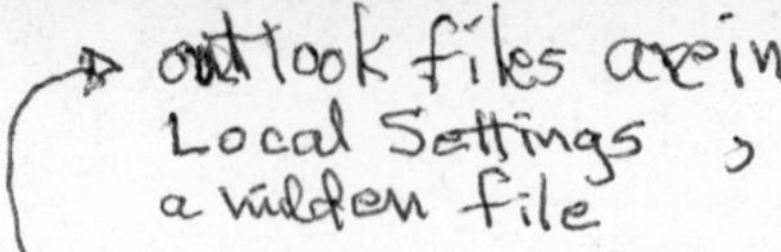

outlook files are in
Local Settings,
a hidden file

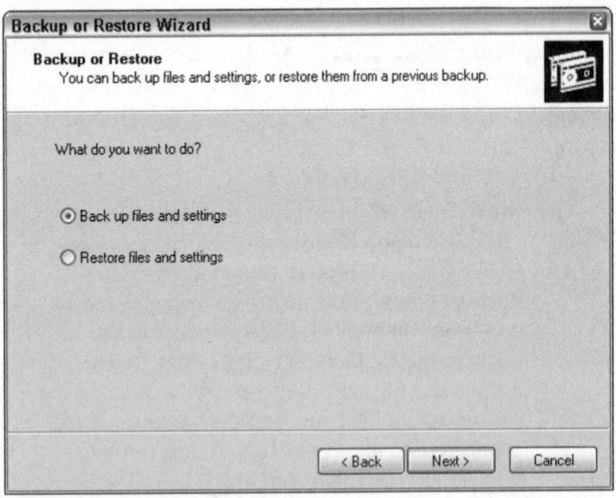

• **Figure 60-2: Back up or restore?**

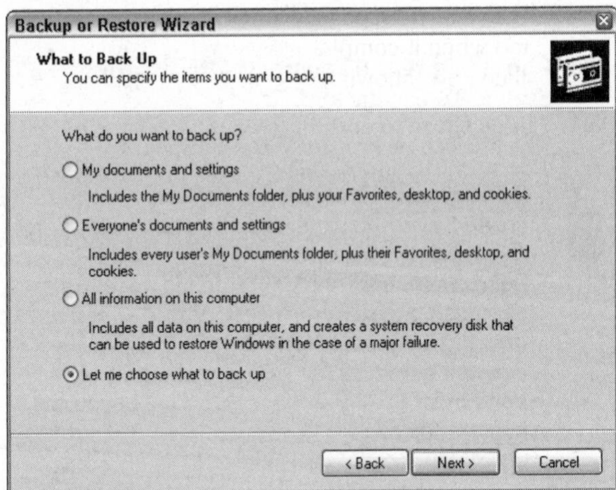

• **Figure 60-3: What do you want to back up?**

4. **Choose what you want to back up, and then click Next.**

   If you pick the Let Me Choose What to Back Up option, you need to be aware of a rather obscure setting in the next wizard step. Underneath My Computer (see Figure 60-4), the System State option includes your boot files and Registry files. This option is a good one to have in the event of a catastrophic failure.

cl pick c:\ Documents and Settings and System State

If you choose your own files, be very aware of the fact that neither Outlook nor Outlook Express stores e-mail messages in the My Documents folder.

The wizard asks for a location to place the backup.

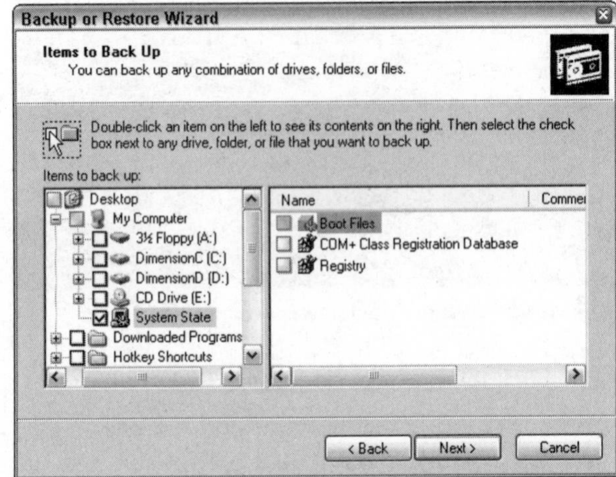

• **Figure 60-4: If you decide to choose your own files, be aware of this odd choice under My Computer.**

5. **Click Browse, and then navigate to a location suitable for the backup (see Figure 60-5). Click Save.**

   The Backup or Recovery Wizard puts all the backed up data in one big, compressed `.bkf` file. Several, uh, design limitations of the wizard point to its roots as a tape backup program (see the sidebar, "Backup alternatives").

If you want to keep your backups on CD, you need to put the `.bkf` file somewhere on a hard drive, let the wizard do its thing, and then manually copy the `.bkf` file to your CD-RW (or DVD-RW) drive. Unfortunately, there's no way to break up a `.bkf` file, so make sure you don't select too much data to back up at once. An example: Say you back up a My Documents and Settings folder and the resulting `.bkf` file is 600MB big. (That's a big file, but if you have a lot of electronic photographs or music files — or a ton of spam in Outlook, or a lot of temporary

In Outlook, Tools → Options → Maintenance tab → Store folder. This gives the path to the hidden folder where messages are stored. Page 1017 of Windows XP Inside Out tells how to set up for My Messages under My Documents. See the NT Notebook
3 July 2005

Internet files — it isn't out of the question.) After you create the .bkf file, you drag it to your CD-RW drive, work your way through the CD Writing Wizard (see Technique 41), and burn the .bkf file to CD. Works like a champ: You can restore the files and they work just like the originals. But if your My Documents and Settings folder is so big that the resulting .bkf file weighs in at 900MB, that file won't fit on a CD. You have to make two backups, each of which fit on a CD. Or you can buy a DVD writer.

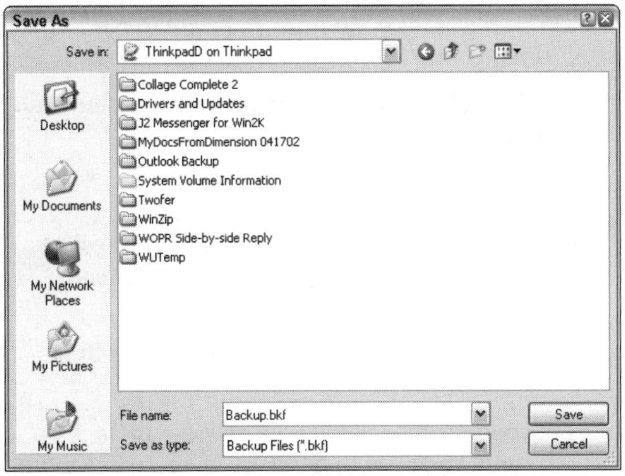

Save As
Save in: ThinkpadD on Thinkpad
Desktop
My Documents
My Network Places
My Pictures
My Music
Collage Complete 2
Drivers and Updates
J2 Messenger for Win2K
MyDocsFromDimension 041702
Outlook Backup
System Volume Information
Twofer
WinZip
WOPR Side-by-side Reply
WUTemp
File name: Backup.bkf
Save as type: Backup Files (*.bkf)
Save
Cancel

• **Figure 60-5: Choose a destination for the backup.**

The Backup or Restore Wizard returns, as shown in Figure 60-6.

6. **Type a good name for the backup — something descriptive, so you can figure out what you were trying to back up, if worse comes to worst — and then click Next.**

   The Backup or Restore Wizard now has all the information it needs and shows you a summary.

7. **Click Finish.**

   Depending on how much data you chose, this may be a good time to grab a latte.

   The wizard starts backing up the data, using a sophisticated technique called *shadowing* — essentially taking a snapshot of files that may change in the course of the backup.

Backup or Restore Wizard
Backup Type, Destination, and Name
Your files and settings are stored in the destination you specify.
Select the backup type:
File
Choose a place to save your backup:
\\Thinkpad\ThinkpadD\
Browse...
Type a name for this backup:
Docs and Settings Backup 2003 10 20
< Back
Next >
Cancel

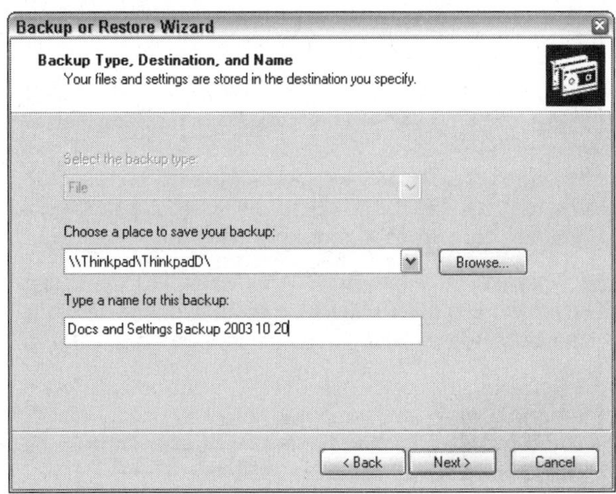

• **Figure 60-6: Location and name.**

   The wizard keeps you posted on its progress, and when it completes the backup, you see the dialog box shown in Figure 60-7.

8. **Click Close to end the wizard.**

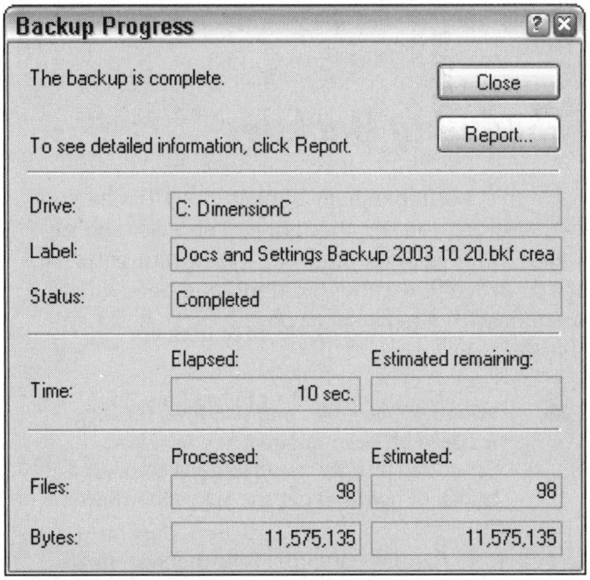

Backup Progress
The backup is complete.
Close
To see detailed information, click Report.
Report...
Drive: C: DimensionC
Label: Docs and Settings Backup 2003 10 20.bkf crea
Status: Completed
Elapsed:
Estimated remaining:
Time: 10 sec.
Processed:
Estimated:
Files: 98 98
Bytes: 11,575,135 11,575,135

• **Figure 60-7: Summary.**

Backup alternatives

A few years ago, it looked like everyone would have to install a tape drive to make backups. These days, few people bother with tape drives because they're expensive, slow, and often unreliable. Far too often, people have relied on backup tapes, only to find them useless. Unless you're running a big server, tape drives are not worth the trouble.

So what are the alternatives? A writeable CD (or better, DVD) gives you space to back up documents, but probably not enough room to copy an entire drive onto a single disc.

If a home or small office network has room, you can place the backup from one computer on another computer(s). This is fast and easy access, but not much good if the whole building burns down (perish the thought!).

A cheap and fast alternative is a second, portable hard drive. These plug into your computer via the USB or FireWire port and appear as another hard drive. Usually, no special software or drivers are required. You simply copy files and backups to the portable hard drive. When you're done, unplug the hard drive and take it away for safekeeping. You can buy simple sealed units with a hard drive and connection cables from any major retailer. Or get a shell with just the case and cables to use with any bare hard drive you have handy.

Scheduling Backups

You can schedule regular backups as often as you want. Before you try, though, you should read my admonitions in Technique 56. If you want your backups to proceed without incident, you need a user account with a permanent password that doesn't change.

Windows Scheduler and Windows security squared off head-to-head, and Windows Scheduler lost. You have to jump through a bunch of hoops to get the Scheduler to work.

To schedule regular backups, follow these steps:

1. **Choose Start⇨All Programs⇨Accessories⇨System Tools⇨Backup.**

   The Backup or Restore Wizard appears.

   If you have XP Professional, and you want to create System Restore Disks for ASR, you must click the Advanced Mode link at this point. Then, from the Welcome tab, click Automated System Recovery Wizard. If you're on a Big Corporate Network, check with your network administrator first to make sure you don't mess up any settings that have been put in place for you.

2. **Click Next.**

   The wizard asks whether you want to back up or restore.

3. **Click the Backup Files and Settings option, and then click Next.**

   The wizard needs to know what you want to back up. If you're not entirely sure, a safe bet is the first choice — My Documents and Settings gets the most critical data, including your e-mail messages.

4. **Choose what you want to back up, and then click Next.**

   If you pick the Let Me Choose What to Back Up option, you need to be aware of a rather obscure setting in the next wizard step. Underneath My Computer, the System State box includes your boot files and Registry files. This option is a good one to have in the event of a catastrophic failure.

   The wizard asks for a location to place the backup.

5. **Click Browse, navigate to a location suitable for the backup, and then click Save.**

   The Backup or Recovery Wizard puts all of the backed up data in one big, compressed `.bkf` file.

   The Backup or Restore Wizard returns.

6. **Type a good name for the backup — something descriptive, so you can figure out what you were trying to back up, if worse comes to worst. Click Next.**

   The Backup or Restore Wizard has all the information it needs.

7. **Click the Advanced button.**

The wizard presents you with a series of options, none of which are particularly useful for most people.

8. **Click Next until you arrive at When to Back Up, as shown in Figure 60-8.**

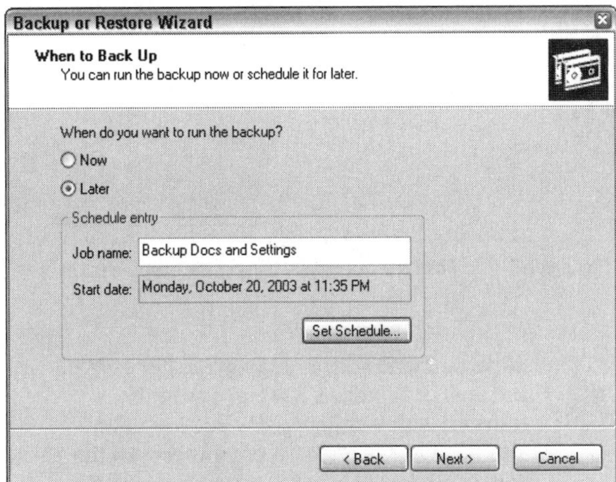

• Figure 60-8: Use this step to schedule backups.

9. **Select the Later option, and then click the Set Schedule button.**

You see the Schedule Job dialog box, as shown in Figure 60-9.

10. **Set the scheduling options you want, and then click OK.**

You return to the When to Backup dialog box, as shown in Figure 60-8.

11. **Click Next.**

The wizard has you enter a user account and password (see Figure 60-10). Refer to Technique 56, and make sure you use a valid Administrator account with a password that will work *when the backup runs*.

12. **Enter an ID and password, and then click OK.**

A dialog box appears.

13. **Click Finish.**

• Figure 60-9: A wide variety of scheduling options are available.

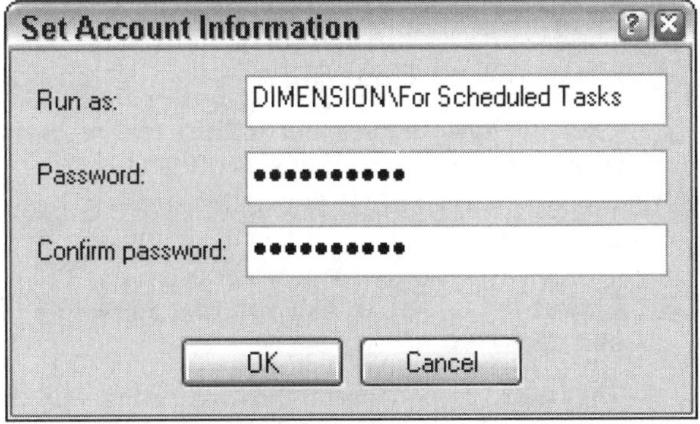

• Figure 60-10: The ID and password must work whenever the backup is scheduled to run.

Depending on how much data you chose, this may be a good time to grab a latte.

When the backup is complete, a dialog box appears (refer to Figure 60-7).

14. **Click Close to end the wizard.**

With a scheduled backup to a removable media (tape, CD-R, and so on), it's up to you to ensure that a blank tape or CD is ready when the backup starts.

Restoring a Backup

Restoring a backup is considerably simpler than creating one.

If you have to restore an entire drive, make sure the new drive has the same formatting as the one you backed up. You can lose important file attributes if you restore NTFS files to an FAT drive or even an NTFS drive made with Windows NT 4.

Follow these steps:

1. **Choose Start⇨All Programs⇨Accessories⇨System Tools⇨Backup.**

   The Backup or Restore Wizard appears.

2. **Click Next.**

   The wizard asks whether you want to back up or restore (refer to Figure 60-2).

3. **Click the Restore Files and Settings option, and then click Next.**

   The wizard responds with a list of all the folders that are available on the left (see Figure 60-11).

4. **Choose the folders or files you wish to restore, and click Next.**

   The wizard responds with the Completing Backup or Restore Wizard dialog box.

5. **Click Finish.**

   This might be a good time to fetch a cup o' something warm. When the Restore is done, you see a summary.

6. **Click Close.**

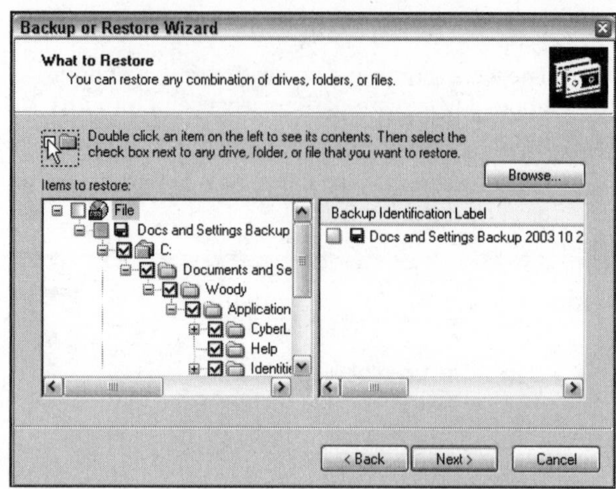

• **Figure 60-11: Folders available for restore appear on the left.**

Backups made with Windows 95, 98, or Me versions of Windows Backup cannot be restored with Windows XP's Backup utility. You have to restore on a computer with the earlier version of Windows installed, and then copy the files to the Windows XP computer.

Alternatives to Windows Backup

Running Windows Backup gives you a single compressed `.bkf` file. You have no choice. That's fine for tape backup (see the "Backup alternatives" sidebar), but it's a pain in the neck if you have a large backup that you want to burn onto a CD or two or ten: CDs are limited to 600 to 700MB of data, and even DVDs max out around 4.7GB — smaller than most home offices' hard drives.

It's hard to generalize, but consider my (admittedly atypical) system. My Documents and Settings folder, the folder that holds all of my data, weighs in at 1.3GB. Even compressed, it won't fit on a CD. My

Documents, on the other hand, is only 350MB — which is no problem at all for a CD. The biggest hog? A hidden folder called Local Settings, which contains my Outlook files (300MB) and temporary Internet files (400MB). The solution for me is to skip all of my temporary Internet files when creating a backup. If I do that, the resulting `.bkf` file is well within the size limitations for a CD.

There are alternatives to consider:

- **Create a backup by simply copying the files to a writeable CD or DVD using XP's internal CD-R support.** You get no compression, but finding and selecting a document is easy if you want to recover it. You don't need to run the Backup or Restore Wizard to backup or restore. All you do is copy.
- **Make backups of the files into a compressed format like ZIP or RAR.** As mentioned at the beginning of this technique, I've been using ZipBackup for years, and it's great. You can choose the maximum size of a single compressed file and, when that limit is reached, you get a second, "follow on" file, then a third, then a fourth. This gives you backup files that can each fit onto a single CD.
- **Choose one of the many backup programs on the market.** Most of them run rings around Windows XP's backup. Norton Ghost is the best of the bunch, and you get an exact image of your hard drive. Veritas Backup Exec (`www.veritas.com`) will look familiar to Windows XP users, because the Windows XP backup system is based on an old version of Veritas. Backup NOW! is an excellent alternative (`www.ntibackupnow.com`), especially if you back up to CD.

Requesting Remote Assistance

Save Time By

- Having a friend take over your machine — via the Internet — while you watch
- Using timesaving Remote Assistance features
- Knowing when to give up on Remote Assistance — it doesn't always work

When Remote Assistance works, it's great. Say you're chatting with a friend in Windows Messenger, and she really wants to know how to set up Windows XP to show filename extensions. (Smart lady.) You could type, type, type, and take her through all the steps. But that's slow and boring. Far better: She clicks Ask for Remote Assistance. You accept. All of a sudden, you're working on her computer while she watches.

And she can terminate the session at any time by pressing the Escape key.

Nothing is faster or better than watching while your problems get solved. If you have a knowledgeable friend who can spare a few minutes – even if your friend lives halfway around the world – and you're both using Windows XP, you have all you need to solve the problem and find out how the solution goes, so you don't need to bug your friend in the future.

Unfortunately, Remote Assistance doesn't work all the time — and there are sound technical reasons why. I talk about those in this technique at the very beginning, so you don't get your hopes up too high.

But if you ever wanted to save time, Remote Assistance does it in spades.

Using Remote Assistance Wisely — Quickly

Remote Assistance (RA) rates as one of the best timesaving features of Windows XP. Instead of dwelling on when to use RA (answer: almost any time you can!), RA really doesn't work in these cases:

- **If you have a problem that crashes Windows.** As soon as your system crashes, RA goes down with it, and your friend is disconnected. In order to get RA working again, you have to go through the entire cycle of inviting her to help, accepting the invitation, and so on (see "Requesting Remote Assistance" later in this technique).

- **If you have a problem with a video driver.** Chances are very good that any "artifacts" you see on your screen — weird lines or shading or streaks that appear and disappear mysteriously — won't show up on your helper's screen.
- **If you have an intermittent problem.** If you can't reliably replicate your problem, you're only wasting your friend's time. To make matters worse, some problems that occur reliably when RA is not running, suddenly clear themselves up when you have an RA connection going. Blame gamma rays and sunspots.

In most other situations, if you can get RA to work, it's a tremendous timesaver.

Coping with Remote Assistance Limitations

Here's what you need to run Remote Assistance:

- Both you and your friend must be running Windows XP.
- If the person requesting assistance has a dial-up connection, he has to stay connected continuously from the time the invitation goes out until the Remote Assistance session ends.
- If you or your friend are running Windows Firewall, set it to allow Remote Assistance to poke through the firewall.

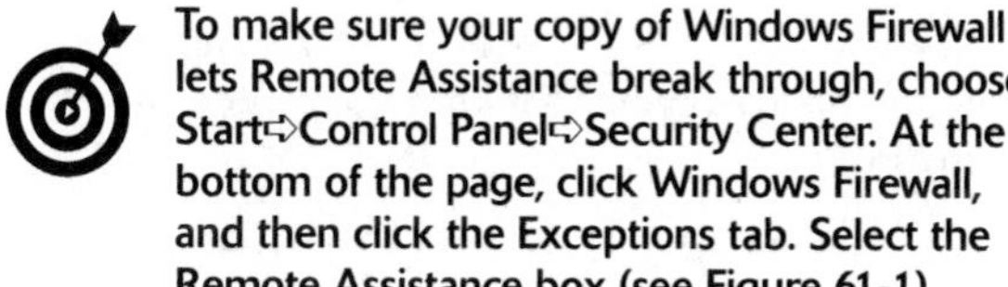

To make sure your copy of Windows Firewall lets Remote Assistance break through, choose Start⇨Control Panel⇨Security Center. At the bottom of the page, click Windows Firewall, and then click the Exceptions tab. Select the Remote Assistance box (see Figure 61-1).

- If you or your friend have a firewall other than Windows Firewall, it must allow the Remote Assistance program (called `sessmgr.exe`) to communicate with computers beyond the firewall, or it cannot block port 3389.

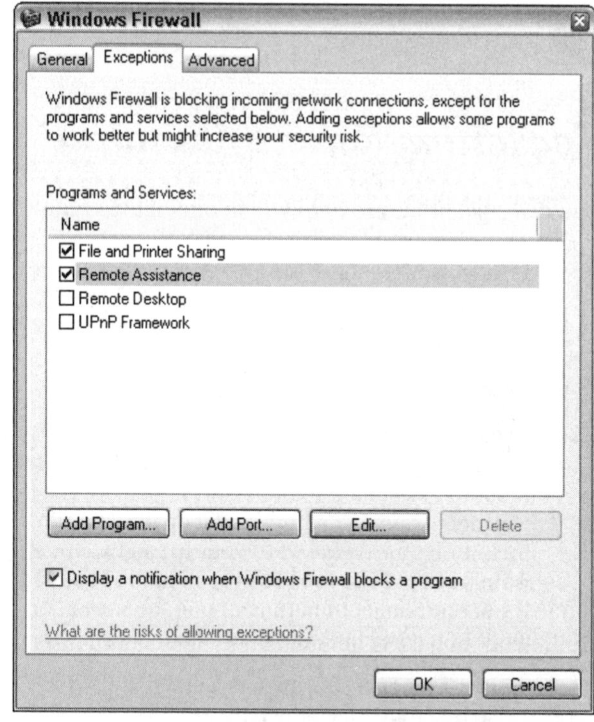

• **Figure 61-1: Windows Firewall must be set to allow Remote Assistance to poke through.**

Remote Assistance may or may not work with home and small office DSL and cable modems. It generally does not work if either you or your friend is running the free version of ZoneAlarm (see Technique 51), although you can configure the for-pay version of ZoneAlarm to allow `sessmgr.exe` to get through, or open up port 3389. Nothing is magical about port 3389. It's just the hard-coded port that RA always uses to communicate between two PCs. See Technique 50 for details on ports.

As more and more small offices and homes use fast Internet connections with DSL and cable modems, and the number of firewalls increases, the chances of being able to get Remote Assistance to work have sadly decreased. The problem isn't fast connections — RA works very well indeed over a fast Internet connection. The problem is the proliferation of firewalls. Most firewalls block port 3389.

Don't get your hopes up until you get Remote Assistance to work.

Requesting Remote Assistance

You can ask a friend to help you in one of three ways:

- **Windows Messenger (or MSN Messenger):** This is the easiest option for communicating your need for Remote Assistance. All you have to do is start a conversation with your friend, click a couple of buttons, and Remote Assistance kicks in.
- **Send e-mail:** You send an e-mail message. Your friend clicks a link in the e-mail message, and the Remote Assistance session starts. This approach is problematic if you have a dial-up modem. The invitation that you send to your friend by e-mail is only valid for as long as you remain connected. If you disconnect from the Internet for any reason, when you come back on, the invitation won't work.
- **Send a file:** This approach is a real pain in the neck, but sometimes the only way that works — particularly if your friend is on AOL (where the "hot link" in the e-mail invitation may not work). You create a file that contains an invitation for Remote Assistance. You then send the file to your friend — perhaps attached to an e-mail message, but you can also send it over a local network, or even on a floppy disk. Your friend double-clicks the file, and the Remote Assistance session starts.

Sending a Remote Assistance SOS Using IM

To ask for help via Windows (or MSN) Messenger

1. **Log on to Windows (or MSN) Messenger.**

   If you don't yet have a Messenger account, be sure to follow the timesaving and privacy protecting approach detailed in Technique 26.

2. **Initiate a conversation with the person who will help you (or who you're going to help).**

   In Figure 61-2, I'm having a conversation with Justin, and I suggest that he let me connect to his computer.

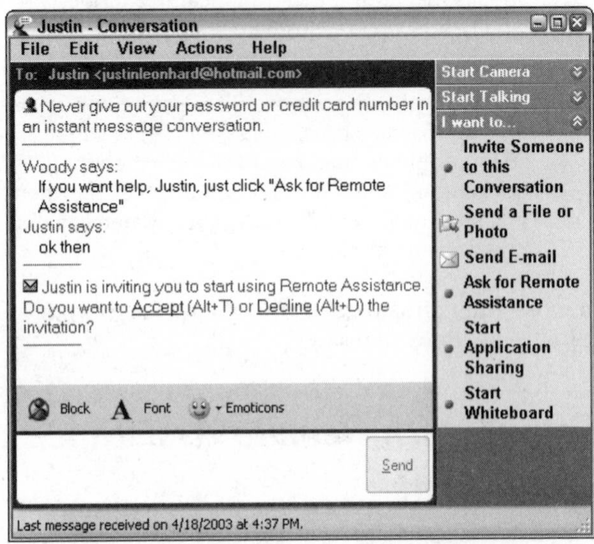

• Figure 61-2: Start a conversation with your helper.

3. **When the person asking for help (the *novice*) is ready to let the other person (the *expert*) see his computer, the novice clicks Ask for Remote Assistance, on the right side of the Messenger window.**

   The novice always initiates the Remote Assistance session.

4. **The expert presses Alt+T to signify that he or she is ready to start the Remote Assistance session.**

   In Figure 61-3, I press Alt+T and Messenger responds by saying that I have accepted the invitation.

   The machines try to connect to each other, as shown in Figure 61-4.

   The novice's machine requests permission to get the assistance session going (see Figure 61-5).

   At every point in this conversation, the novice has complete control.

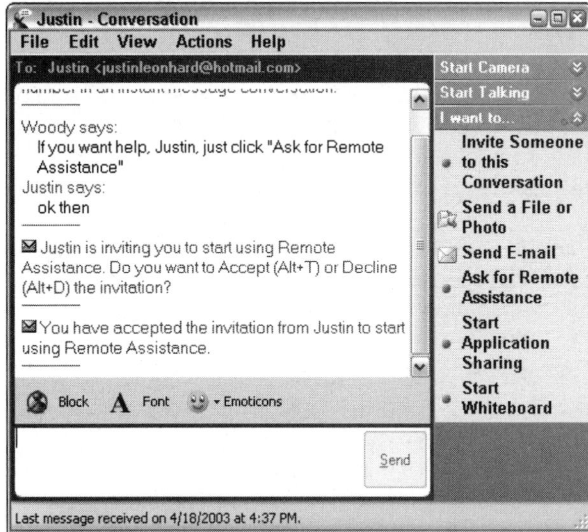

• **Figure 61-3: The novice initiates the Remote Assistance session, and the expert must accept.**

• **Figure 61-4: My PC starts the connection with Justin's PC.**

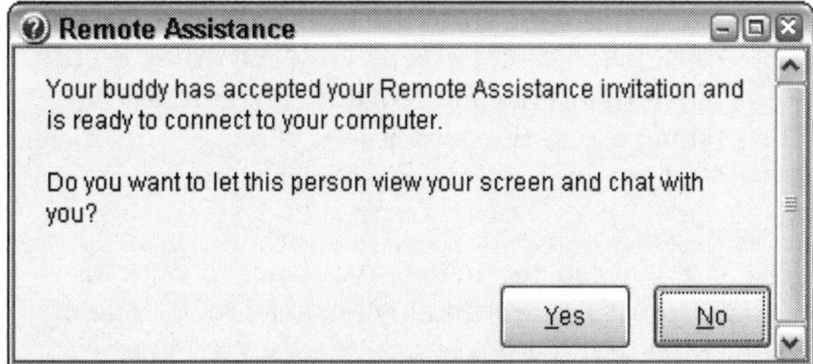

• **Figure 61-5: The novice must again give permission for the session to start.**

5. The novice clicks Yes to initiate the Remote Assistance session.

Although the connection may take a while to get through, ultimately the novice sees the notice in Figure 61-6, and the expert sees the novice's desktop.

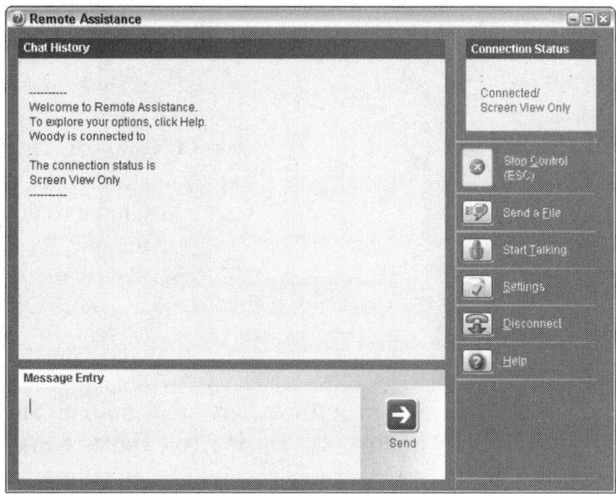

• **Figure 61-6: The warning that the novice sees when the expert is looking over his shoulder.**

6. In the normal course of events, the expert clicks the Take Control button in the upper-left corner of the Remote Assistance window.

7. In order to start the Remote Assistance session, the novice must give permission for the expert to take control.

If the novice gives permission, the expert sees the dialog box shown in Figure 61-7, and then the novice's desktop, as shown in Figure 61-8.

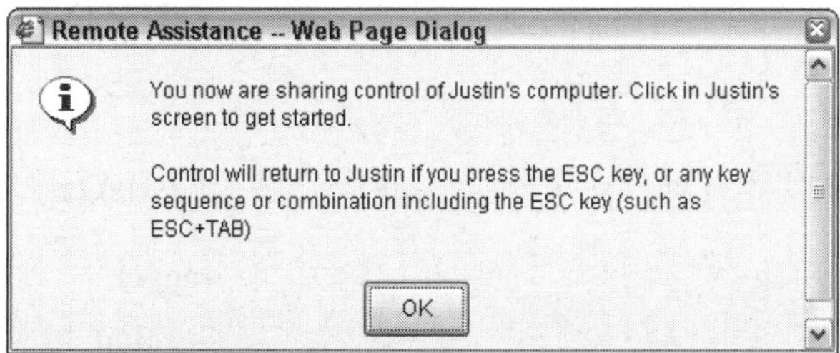

• **Figure 61-7: The expert receives notification that the session is under way.**

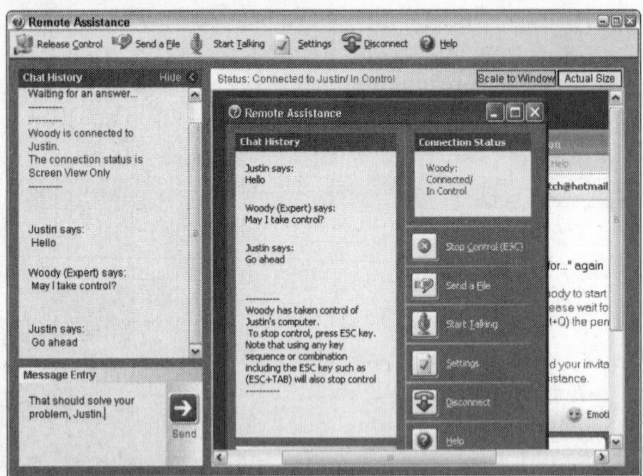

• **Figure 61-8: The expert can see the novice's desktop.**

8. **Either the novice or the expert can terminate the session by pressing the Esc key (see Figure 61-9).**

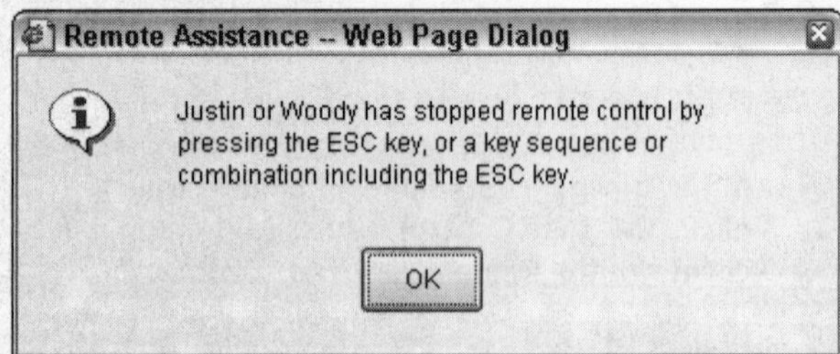

• **Figure 61-9: Pressing Esc breaks the connection.**

If you want to ask for help by e-mail or by sending a file, look at *Windows XP All-in-One Desk Reference For Dummies* (published by Wiley).

Fine-Tuning Remote Assistance

If you can get it to work, Remote Assistance is one of the best timesaving features in Windows XP. It does have some limitations, though. A few points worth noting:

- Remote Assistance is a one-way street. The expert can see the novice's computer, but the novice has absolutely no way to see the expert's computer. So if you're the expert, you don't need to worry about the novice snooping around your machine.
- Remote Assistance exposes everything to the expert. The expert can even make changes to the Registry. That means you should never invite anyone but a highly trusted friend to help you with Remote Assistance — during a Remote Assistance session, your expert can to anything you can do. If you don't understand what's happening, don't hesitate to press the Escape key.
- Even with a fast connection, Remote Assistance is slow as molasses. You can speed things up considerably by having a solid color as your desktop background. To do so, right-click an empty spot on the desktop, choose Properties⇨Desktop, and in the Background box, choose None.
- Both the novice and the expert can control the same mouse pointer and can press keys simultaneously: If the novice and expert both start typing at the same time, the keys they type appear on-screen, interspersed with each other. If both move their mice at the same time, there's no telling where the cursor goes. If one of you doesn't back off, pandemonium results.

If you can get Remote Assistance to work for you, it's an enormously powerful tool — one of the best reasons to use Windows XP, in my opinion.

Getting Help Fast

Save Time By

- Using Windows Help and Support the smart way
- Creating shortcuts to Help topics — and sending them to friends
- Finding real answers to really vexing questions

Many people get to Windows XP's Help and Support Center, type a keyword, click a bunch of links, and come away frustrated. In some cases, that's because the Help and Support Center leaves much to be desired (all those old, inaccurate bits of recycled Windows 98 advice can really get frustrating, eh?). But in many cases, you probably feel frustrated because the Help and Support Center doesn't work like the rest of Windows. Help and Support has plenty of tools, but they're hard to find. Besides, when you're sitting in the Help and Support Center, you want help about something that's going wrong — not help about Help, if you know what I mean.

Take a few minutes to figure out how to handle Help, and you can use your newfound knowledge to save yourself loads of time. This technique shows you how. Quickly.

The Help and Support Center isn't the only game in town — particularly when you're trying to fix something, and you can't get past the ol' Microsoft Party Line. Fortunately, some non-Microsoft options are worth turning to. In this technique, I show you some of those, too.

Exploring the Help and Support Center

Think of Windows XP's Help and Support Center as Internet Explorer, but with all the things that make IE easy to use taken away. That's how I think of it, anyway.

Searching for Help rarely goes as easily as you might think. The other day I wanted to find out how to use Windows XP's multimedia editing capabilities to combine two movie clips. Here's how my search for Help went:

1. **Choose Start⇨Help and Support Center.**

   The Help and Support Center main window appears, as shown in Figure 62-1. Your main page may look a little different because some hardware manufacturers jimmy the main Help page to add references to their own sites.

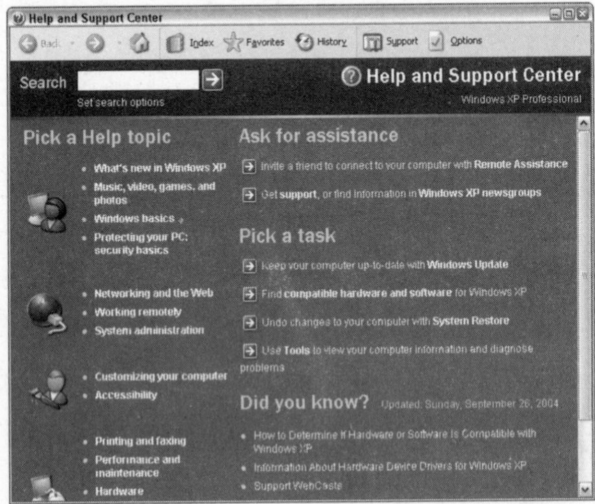

• **Figure 62-1: HSC's main window.**

2. **Type your search topic in the Search box and press Enter.**

   In this example, I typed **combine movie clips** and pressed Enter.

   Help searches the list of predefined keywords in its Help articles to come up with the links under Suggested Topics.

   Then it searches all the text in all its Help articles to arrive at the entries under Full-Text Search Matches.

   Finally, it reaches out to the Knowledge Base to return the articles mentioned under Microsoft Knowledge Base.

   If Help doesn't find anything (and it didn't for my movie clip search), it tells you it found 0 search results.

If you want to save time using the search options, I suggest that you use the Suggested Topics search. This search option works very quickly because Help only has to scan its index (on the other hand, you also can just as easily do this yourself, as I explain in Step 3). The Full-Text Match search goes much slower because Help scans for matches on all the words that you typed in the Search box, and then for individual words in the Search box. The Microsoft Knowledge Base search can take years, and it's most likely to turn up obscure articles, frequently bearing little resemblance to what you seek.

3. **If you strike out doing a standard search, look at the index. Click the Index icon up at the top of the screen.**

   Help brings up its index, which is a bit like the index in a book.

4. **Type the search topic you're looking for.**

   In this example, I typed **movi**, and the index moves down to the movie entries (see Figure 62-2).

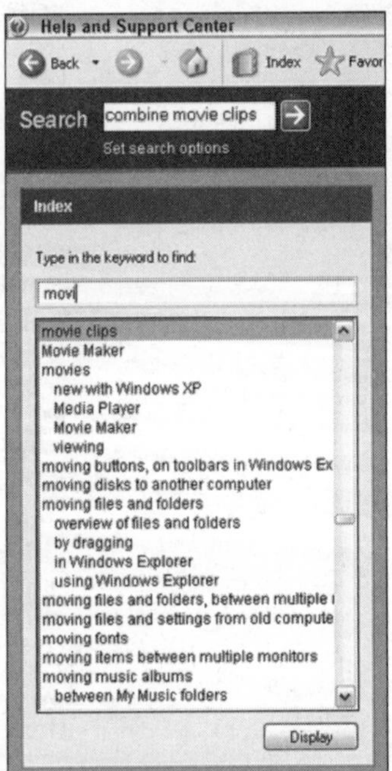

• **Figure 62-2: The index follows along as you type.**

5. **Select the index topic that is closest to the one that you're searching for information about.**

   In this example, I selected Movie Maker, and the Windows Help and Support Center responds with a blurb about Movie Maker.

6. **If Windows Help and Support Center doesn't have an answer, you may have to try looking inside the Help systems for individual Windows programs.**

   In this example, the Windows Movie Maker blurb isn't any help, so I dug into Windows Movie Maker's help. With Movie Maker open, I chose Help➪Help Topics➪Search, typed **combine** in the Search For box, and pressed Enter. I selected the To Combine Contiguous Clips entry, and I was finally (finally!) rewarded with the explanation.

Unless Microsoft has a special article that covers precisely the problem you want to solve, you really have to hunt to find answers to questions in the Windows Help and Support Center! Sometimes you can dig into individual applications — as I did in this example with Windows Movie Maker. Sometimes you're left dangling with no help in sight.

Using Help Effectively

Here's what you need to know about Windows XP's Help and Support Center:

- **The Search box only looks for keywords.** "Natural language" questions confuse it. For example, if you search for **install scanner**, the Install a Scanner or Digital Camera task appears as the first choice. If you type **How do I install a scanner?**, the Install a Scanner or Digital Camera task doesn't even show up.
- **Frequently, Help ignores what you type.** Sometimes you can use the search modifying terms that Microsoft documents in the Help and Support Center (see Figure 62-3), but I've had lots of problems with them.
- **The Search engine is buggy.** For example, if you search for **clip not movie**, the first hit in Suggested Topics doesn't include either of the terms **clip** or **movie**, and the first four hits from the Knowledge Base contain both **clip** and **movie**. Unfortunately, I don't know any way to work around the bugs in the Search engine.
- **You can't search for a specific word or phrase inside a Help article.** In other words, you can't use an Internet Explorer-like Edit➪Find function.

If you want to search for something inside a Help article, select the article, copy it and paste it into, say, Notepad or Word, and use that program to search the pasted-in text.

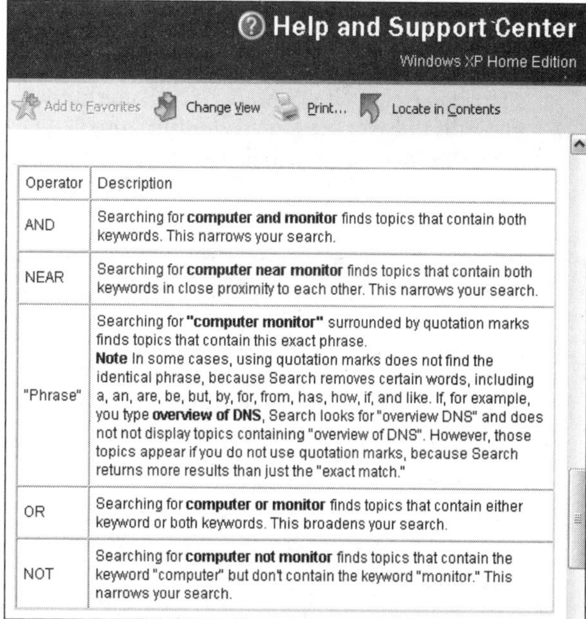

Operator	Description
AND	Searching for **computer and monitor** finds topics that contain both keywords. This narrows your search.
NEAR	Searching for **computer near monitor** finds topics that contain both keywords in close proximity to each other. This narrows your search.
"Phrase"	Searching for **"computer monitor"** surrounded by quotation marks finds topics that contain this exact phrase. **Note** In some cases, using quotation marks does not find the identical phrase, because Search removes certain words, including a, an, are, be, but, by, for, from, has, how, if, and like. If, for example, you type **overview of DNS**, Search looks for "overview DNS" and does not not display topics containing "overview of DNS". However, those topics appear if you do not use quotation marks, because Search returns more results than just the "exact match."
OR	Searching for **computer or monitor** finds topics that contain either keyword or both keywords. This broadens your search.
NOT	Searching for **computer not monitor** finds topics that contain the keyword "computer" but don't contain the keyword "monitor." This narrows your search.

• **Figure 62-3: Sometimes these modifiers work. Many times they don't.**

- **Help always highlights search terms in found Help articles — any word you type in the Search box appears in the Help article with a gray background.** Most people find this really aggravating. To turn off this function, click the Options icon on the main Help toolbar, choose Set Search Options, and uncheck the Turn On Search Highlight box.
- **Help's Table of Contents can be very useful — if you can figure out how to get to it!** Start by searching for a topic. After you find it (see Figure 62-4), click the Locate in Contents button. You're taken to the appropriate place in the (hidden!) Help Table of Contents (see Figure 62-5). From there, you may be able to get at related items of interest.

To get out of the Table of Contents, click the Back button on the main Help screen.

- **Help's Favorites feature (which doesn't hold a candle to Internet Explorer's) can come in handy — if you only have a few Favorites.** Otherwise, it's truly lame. When you find an article in Help that you want to bookmark, click the Add to Favorites icon (refer to Figure 62-4). To see a list of all your bookmarked Favorites, click the Favorites icon at the top of the Help window.

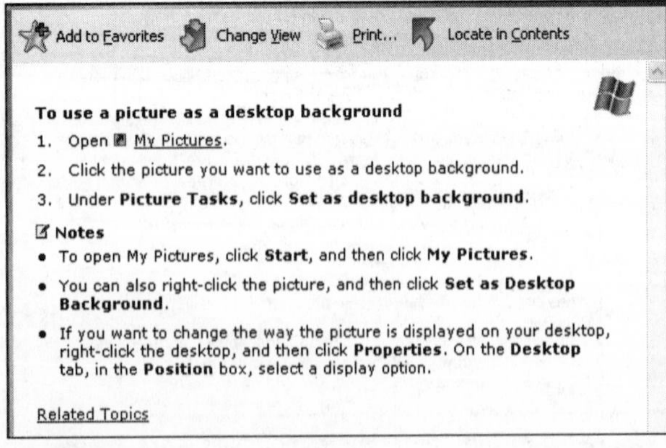

• **Figure 62-4: Locate in Contents.**

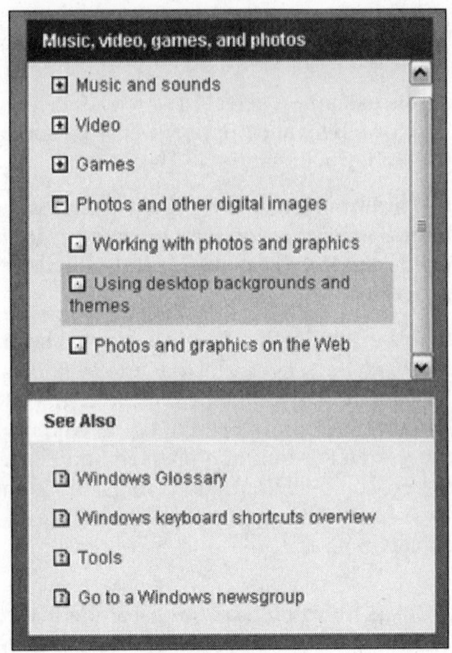

• **Figure 62-5: You can only get into the Table of Contents via this circuitous method.**

Getting to Help Sections — Quickly

Creating a shortcut to a specific Help article is easy. You can put the shortcut on your desktop, or you can e-mail the shortcut to another user. If your friend double-clicks the shortcut, Help comes up looking at the precise article that you chose.

E-mailing a shortcut is particularly useful because it's very, *very* hard to tell another Windows XP user how to get to a specific Help article.

To create a shortcut to a help topic on the desktop, follow these steps:

1. **Choose Start⇨Help and Support.**
2. **Navigate to the Help article.**

3. Right-click in the body of the Help article and choose Properties.

Help shows you the Properties dialog box for that particular Help article. (See Figure 62-6).

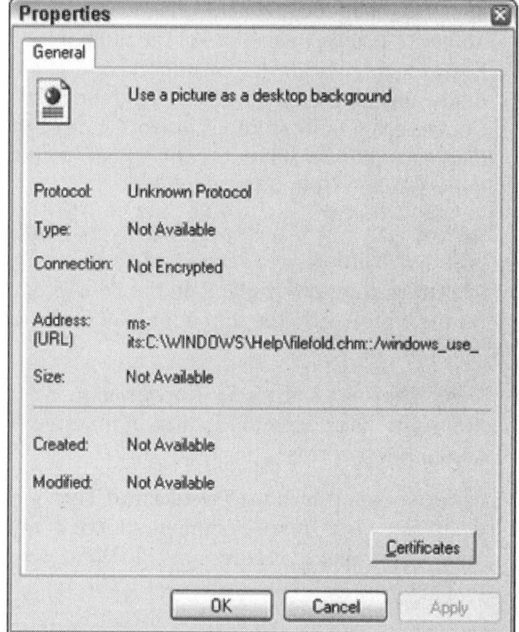

• **Figure 62-6: A Properties dialog box for a Help article.**

4. Click inside the Address (URL) section, press Ctrl+A to select the entire address of the Help article, and then press Ctrl+C to copy it to the Clipboard.

Copying the address may be a bit difficult because the addresses tend to be quite long — so long that you can't see them in their entirety.

5. Click the Cancel button to get out of the Properties dialog box.

6. Choose Start⇨My Computer, and in Windows Explorer, work your way down to `C:\Windows\PCHEALTH\HELPCTR\Binaries`**.**

Windows Explorer looks like Figure 62-7.

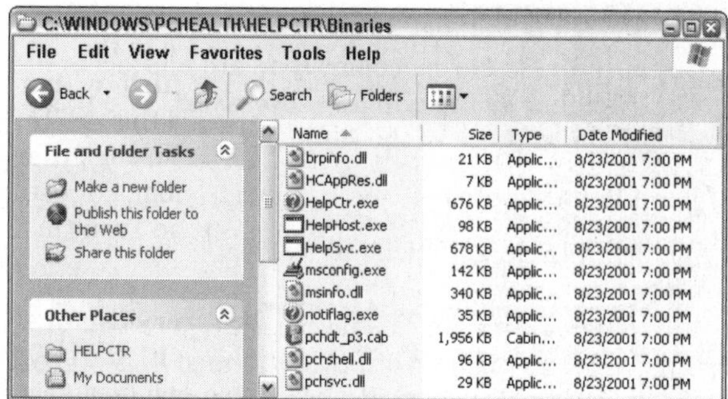

• **Figure 62-7: Navigate to** `HelpCtr.exe`**.**

7. Right-click `HelpCtr.exe` **and choose Send To⇨Desktop (create Shortcut). Click the Close button to exit Windows Explorer.**

Your Windows desktop has a new `Shortcut to HelpCtr.exe` icon.

8. Right-click the new shortcut on the desktop and choose Properties.

You see the Properties dialog box in Figure 62-8.

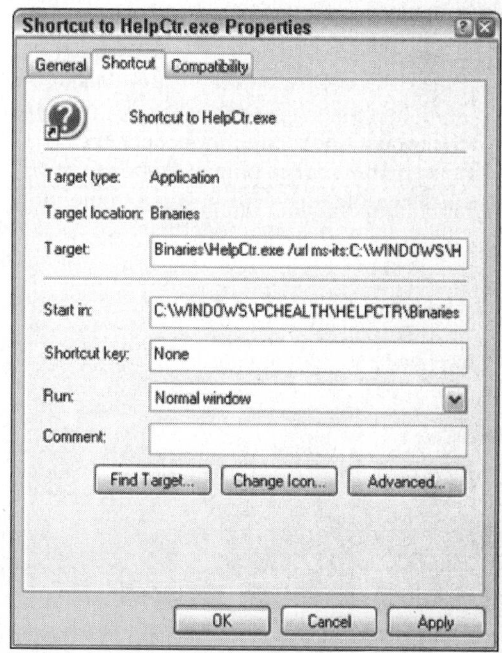

• **Figure 62-8: Change the shortcut to point to the Help article.**

9. **Press the End key to go to the end of the Target box, press the spacebar, type** /url **and press the spacebar again, and then press Ctrl+V to paste in the address of the Help article.**

10. **Click OK.**

11. **Double-click the icon to test it.**

    You go directly to the Help article.

    You can rename the shortcut, e-mail it, and even copy it into a Word document. Double-clicking the shortcut on any Windows XP computer brings up the precise Help topic you chose.

Using Other Help Sources

What if the Help and Support Center falls short on help and support?

Of course, I believe the first two resources you should turn to for Windows XP help should be this book and *Windows XP All-in-One Desk Reference For Dummies*. But then, I'm a bit biased.

Other sources of accurate, free information:

- **Microsoft's Knowledge Base,** `support.microsoft.com`**:** The ultimate repository of the Microsoft Party Line — but a tremendous source of information, nonetheless.
- `www.AskWoody.com`**, of course:** All-volunteer, all the time, with some of the nicest people on the Web. We can't answer every question we get, but we sure do try!
- **Brian Livingston's WindowsSecrets Newsletter,** `www.WindowsSecrets.com`**:** Brian has an uncanny ability to track down some of the most important issues facing Windows consumers, and offer many alternatives that most of us overlook. Contributing Editors Paul Thurrott (one of the leading Windows activists) and, ahem, yours truly, pitch in from time to time.
- `www.neowin.net`**:** An extraordinarily insightful group of Windows reporters and enthusiasts, who have repeatedly changed the course of computing. Frequently the first source of important Windows news.
- **Kelly Theriot's Kelly's XP Korner,** `www.kellys-korner-xp.com/xp.htm`**:** A massive compilation of tips.
- **Doug Knox's Windows Tweaks and Tips,** `www.dougknox.com`**:** The pre-eminent source of quick, short programs that solve specific Windows problems.

All these sites do an outstanding job, and they're all free.

Part X

Fast (Nearly Painless) Disaster Recovery

"I saw the flames when they started, too. I just thought it was part of the exhibit."

Getting Your PC to Boot When It Doesn't Want To

Save Time By

- Finding out what options you have — before you tear your hair out
- Trying Safe Mode to see if you can fix relatively minor problems
- Hauling out the Big Guns: Recovery Console

Sooner or later it happens to every system: Windows goes to that big bit bucket in the sky.

You may have trouble starting Windows. Maybe the computer goes through its normal memory check and lists the hard drives and then . . . nothing. Maybe the Windows splash screen appears, with its rolling beads, and then everything goes dark. Maybe your system boots okay and runs for a while, and then it dies mysteriously.

If you can get your system to boot into Windows, but every so often your screen goes blank and Windows is out to lunch, try running the System File Checker. SFC looks at all the system files on your PC and makes sure they're intact.

Sometimes you need to get into Safe Mode — Windows' analog to the Twilight Zone, where some things work and others don't. Sometimes, Safe Mode comes to you. No matter how you get there, you want to get out — quickly.

Those of you who feel adept at the command line may want to get into the Windows Recovery Console some day. That's where clones of the old, familiar, Windows Me-and-earlier commands live. You can mess up your system with one bad keystroke. Or you can breathe new life into an ailing system. Ya pays yer money, and ya takes yer chances.

If you can't get anything to work and you need a boot disk, look at Technique 67. If you want to roll back your system to a previous state, try Technique 64. But if you want to fix what's going on right now, this technique is for you.

Running the System File Checker

If your computer starts normally, but shuts down or hangs unexpectedly, consider running the System File Checker (SFC). An SFC run is particularly valuable if the screen just goes blank from time to time, and you can't get it back. Running SFC is also a good idea if Windows itself freezes periodically: Your mouse won't move, the keyboard gets locked up, and even the old standby Ctrl+Alt+Del doesn't work anymore.

If you're having problems with an individual program locking up — say, Internet Explorer works for a while and then suddenly freezes, or Outlook tells you that it's quitting — don't even bother with SFC. It's a waste of time. You need to fix the program that's gone bad, and SFC doesn't even touch programs — it works with Windows system files only.

Windows XP is quite protective of its crown jewels, but nonetheless, sometimes system-wide files do get clobbered. Hardware problems, particularly a hard drive that's misbehaving, can corrupt system files. Sometimes installers sneak past Windows XP's protective layers and replace good system files with dubious versions of their own choosing. System File Checker verifies that you have Microsoft-blessed versions of the system files running.

You must have an Administrator account in order to run System File Checker. To set one up, see Technique 47.

If you want to make sure that your system files are all kosher:

1. **Put your Windows XP CD in the CD drive.**

   This CD contains the full version of Windows XP. If you bought a computer with Windows XP preinstalled, you probably have a backup CD. Use that CD. If you didn't get a backup CD with your new computer, call the manufacturer and complain loudly.

2. **Close any installation screen(s) that appear automatically.**

3. **Choose Start⇨All Programs⇨Accessories⇨Command Prompt.**

   The Windows XP command prompt appears. You are forgiven if you think of this as the old DOS command line. It isn't, really, but it sure acts like the old graybeard.

4. **At the command prompt, type** sfc /scannow **and press Enter.**

   See Figure 63-1.

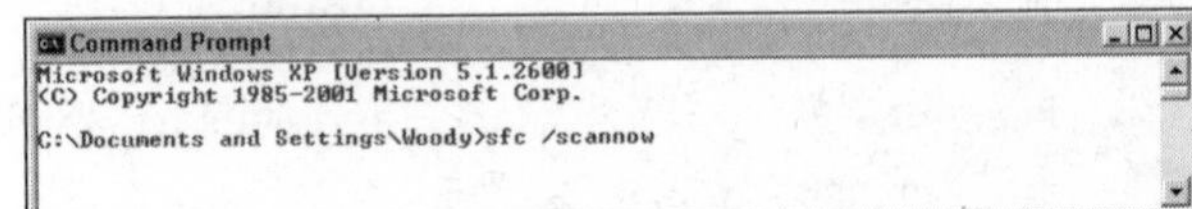

• **Figure 63-1: Start System File Checker only from the command line.**

   The System File Checker starts its scan (see Figure 63-2). This process is painstaking and can take 15 minutes or more, particularly if you have more than a few bad files.

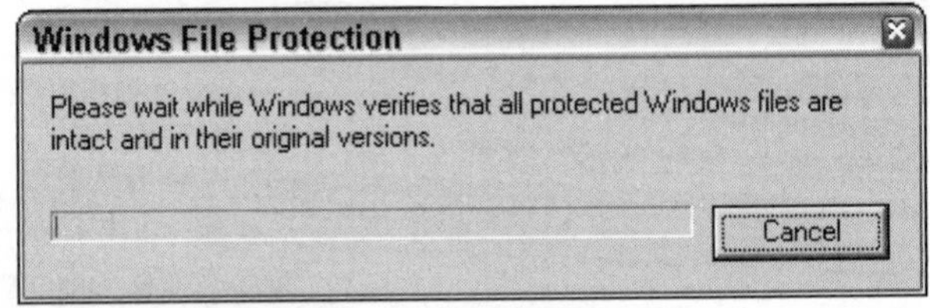

• **Figure 63-2: SFC keeps you apprised of its progress.**

   If System File Checker doesn't find any corrupt files, it exits without saying anything. If it does find corrupt files, it asks for your permission, and then automatically pulls good copies from the Windows XP CD.

5. **Close the command prompt.**

I always run SFC with great fear and trepidation, anticipating that it pulls old versions of files from the CD, when Windows XP should be running with the latest files – particularly with the massive changes in Service Pack 2. So far, knock on wood, I haven't encountered any problems with SFC.

System File Checker has a bunch of command line options that aren't documented correctly in many places. See Table 63-1 for details.

Falling Back to Safe Mode

Windows XP's Safe Mode is a minimally functional version of Windows designed to give you enough power to go in and fix a problem — if you can figure out what the problem might be. Safe Mode strips away all the fun stuff: You get a very limited video driver, minimal keyboard and mouse support, and access to most system programs. You don't get your printer, or your scanner, or your USB ports; there's no sound support or any other fancy stuff that may be causing problems. You can choose whether you want your network to be available or not.

You can get into Safe Mode in two ways: You can go through the steps in this section and force Windows into Safe Mode; or Windows can put itself into Safe Mode after a particularly traumatic attempt to boot. Usually that happens because Windows encounters a problem that's big enough to cause your entire system to be unstable. In my experience, it's very unusual for Windows to go into Safe Mode all by itself, unless you've just installed some particularly inhospitable hardware. When you try to boot immediately after installing the unfriendly hardware, the new hardware makes a grab for something Windows won't give up, the two tussle for a nanosecond, and then Windows blows the whistle and falls back into Safe Mode.

When Windows XP goes into Safe Mode, whether of its own volition or because you pushed it, here's what happens:

- None of your startup programs run.
- Only the critical Windows XP services start.
- Most of your fancy hardware won't work. Forget about USB and FireWire. Yes, if you have a USB keyboard and/or mouse, they probably get the axe, too.

Table 63-1: Important System File Check Parameters

This Parameter	Does This	Use This Command If
`/scannow`	Performs a full scan.	You are running SFC for the first time.
`/scanonce`	Performs a full scan the next time you boot your PC. Better be ready with the Windows XP CD, or have a copy of it on your hard drive somewhere.	You ran SFC once with `/scannow`, didn't find anything, but you still believe that you have a corrupt system file.
`/scanboot`	Sets up the System File Checker so that it does a full scan every time you boot your PC. Again, you better have your CD handy.	Rarely used because it's an intrusive, time-consuming pain in the neck.
`/cancel` or `/revert`	Cancels the `/scanboot` setting.	If you run `sfc /scanboot` and then change your mind (some would say "come to your senses").
`/quiet`	Allows the System File Checker to replace corrupt files without asking permission.	Not recommended unless you want to leave SFC alone while it does the work.

Because Windows XP without a keyboard or mouse is about as useless as a car without a steering wheel, you may need to plug an old-fashioned PS/2 keyboard and mouse into your machine to get any work done.

- Even your video driver (frequently the source of major problems!) gets shoved aside, replaced by Windows XP's nice, safe, lowest-common-denominator video driver.

Safe Mode doesn't solve your problems — that crucial step is up to you. But it gives you a level playing field so that you can track down malfunctioning pieces without the interference of all the highfallutin' applications and hardware you might have installed on your machine.

- **Use the methods in Technique 64 to restore Windows to an earlier point:** If you aren't sure what happened, but you know darn good and well *when* it happened, this is the easiest, fastest way to get things going again.
- **Use the Help and Support Center (Start⇨Help and Support):** If you have a hunch about what may be wrong with Windows XP, this might be a good place to go to check and see if Microsoft has a tutorial for you, or maybe even a troubleshooter.
- **Use the methods in Technique 11 to keep auto-starting programs at bay:** If you're having trouble, running as few programs as possible is a smart idea. Each additional program adds one more possible source of problems.
- **Use the Registry Editor (Start⇨Run, type** regedit**, and press Enter):** If you know exactly how to cure what ails you (perhaps from information in this book, or in the Microsoft Knowledge Base), `regedit` is alive and well in Safe Mode.

Using Safe Mode of your own volition

To use Safe Mode, follow these steps:

1. **Reboot your computer.**
2. **Immediately after you see the message that your hard drive is alive, press and hold down the F8 key on your keyboard.**

   Windows XP shows you the Advanced Boot Options screen, as shown in Figure 63-3. If you have a network card, Safe Mode with Networking is one of the options.

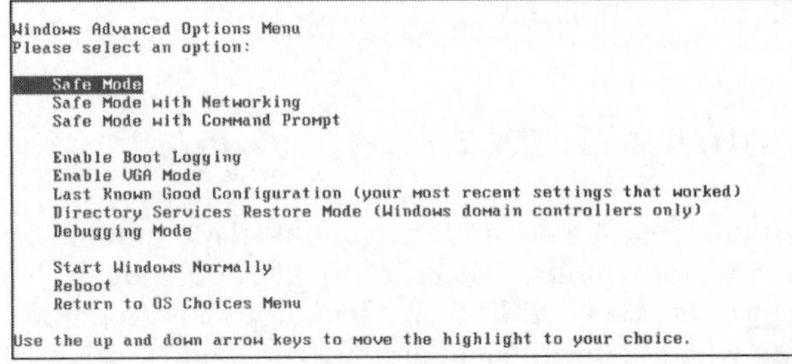

• Figure 63-3: Press and hold F8 during boot-up, and you get these options.

3. **If you're sure that networking on your PC is working fine, push the down arrow to choose Safe Mode with Networking. Otherwise, leave the highlight on Safe Mode. Press Enter.**

   If you're using the Windows welcome screen, the welcome screen appears with the Administrator account being the only account available on it. If you aren't using the Windows welcome screen, you get the old-fashioned Windows logon screen.

4. **Log on as Administrator.**

   If you're using the Windows welcome screen, click Administrator. If you aren't using the Windows welcome screen, type **Administrator** in the User Name box.

5. **Give the Administrator password.**

   If you're using Windows XP Home Edition, the Administrator account does not have a password. Leave the password box empty and click the right arrow (or press Enter) to log on. If you are using Windows XP Professional Edition, you established the Administrator account's password when you set up Windows. Type it in the password box and press Enter or click the right arrow (if you're using the Windows XP welcome screen) or press Enter (if you're using the old-fashioned Windows logon screen).

Windows XP boots into Safe Mode, as shown in Figure 63-4. It's a bit, uh, difficult to miss.

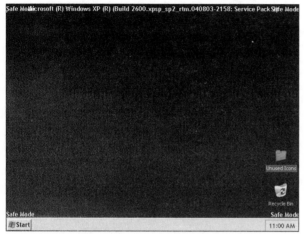

• **Figure 63-4: Safe Mode has "Safe Mode" written all over it.**

6. **Click Start.**

   The Start Menu appears (see Figure 63-5). Windows is starting to look familiar again.

7. **If you're having troubles with video — Windows XP boots to a completely blank or utterly distorted screen, for example — try right-clicking an empty spot on the desktop and choosing Properties⇨Settings.**

   You see the video settings, as shown in Figure 63-6. In some cases, merely adjusting the Screen Resolution or Color Quality setting may solve the problem.

8. **If you can't figure out where to start, choose Start⇨Control Panel⇨Performance and Maintenance⇨System.**

   Windows XP shows you the System Properties dialog box, as shown in Figure 63-7.

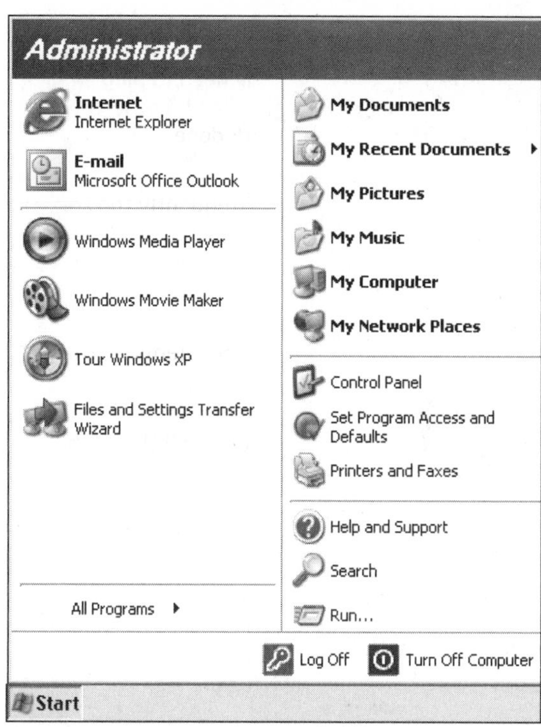

• **Figure 63-5: A familiar Start menu.**

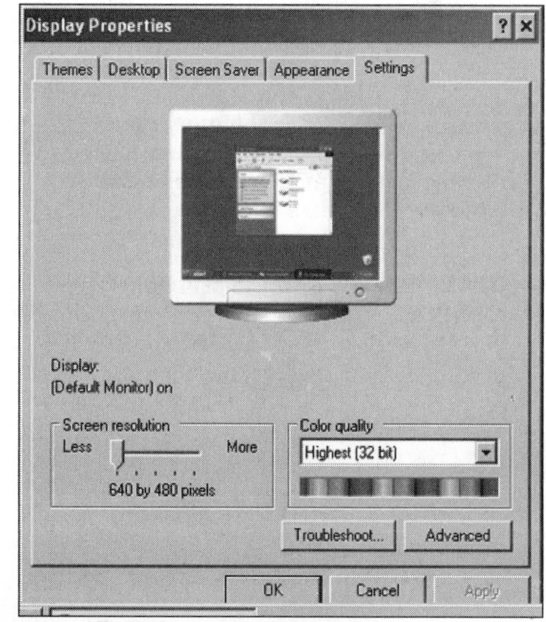

• **Figure 63-6: Adjust video settings here.**

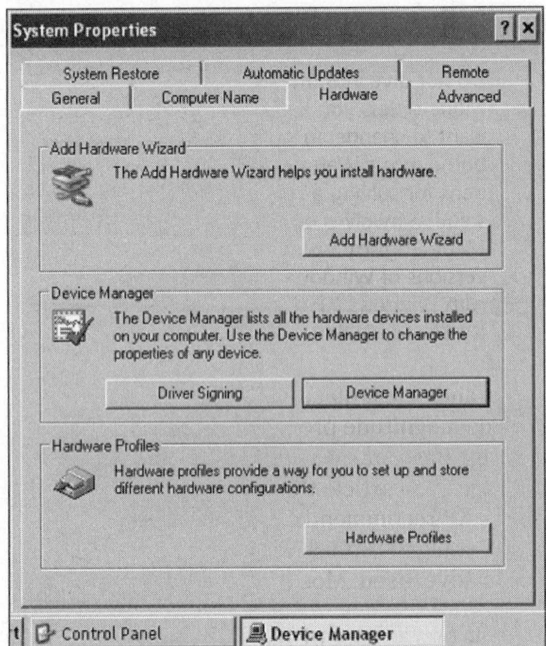

• **Figure 63-7: A good place to start your search for other problems.**

9. **Click the Device Manager button.**

   The Device Manager (see Figure 63-8) may have a warning (!) or (?) sign, or other indication of a problem. Double-check any hardware that's misbehaving.

The next sections give you more Windows-saving ideas for making changes in Safe Mode.

10. **When you're done with Safe Mode and you want to see if your changes made a difference, choose Start⇨Turn Off Computer⇨Restart.**

11. **If you see the options screen again (refer to Figure 63-3), choose Start Windows Normally.**

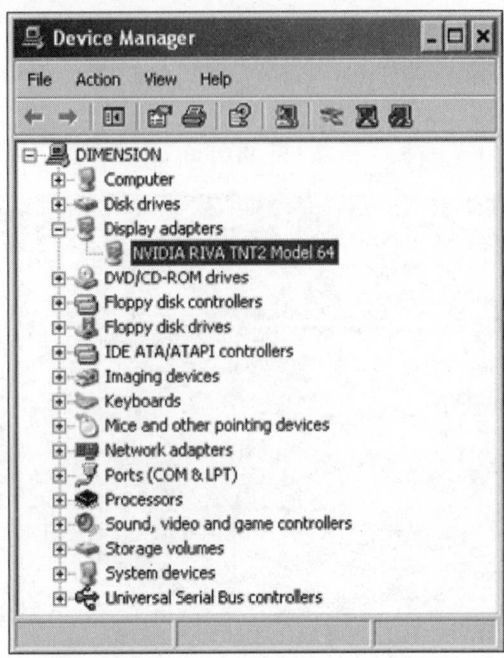

• **Figure 63-8: The mother lode of hardware information.**

Using System Restore in Safe Mode

The Last Known Good Configuration option in the Advanced Boot Options screen (refer to Figure 63-3) simply runs a System Restore, using the last System Restore point. (Whether that's a "good" point or not is open to question.)

There are good reasons for avoiding the Last Known Good Configuration option and for working directly with System Restore, even if you have to dig into System Restore while in Safe Mode. The primary stumbling point: If you use the Last Known Good Configuration option, the currently screwed-up state of Windows is set as a System Restore Point, so if you try to use the Last Known Good Configuration option a second time, you return to the current messed-up state.

Sound complicated? It is.

System Restore is a cult unto its own. I talk about it extensively in Technique 64.

Using Help and Support in Safe Mode

Windows Help and Support can be useful in Safe Mode, primarily for the hardware troubleshooters. The troubleshooters aren't infallible, and they have a nasty way of "going circular" (if you follow a particular course of action long enough, the troubleshooter returns to the point where it started). But they're an excellent place to look for Safe Mode solutions.

If you have a second PC running Windows XP, or you have a friend with a portable that uses Windows XP, it's almost always easier and faster to go into the Help and Support Center on the second PC. Why? Because you can keep the Help article up while you're trying to make repairs.

To see a list of all the Help and Support Center's troubleshooters, follow these steps:

1. **Choose Start⇨Help and Support.**
2. **In the Search box, type** troubleshooter, **and then press Enter.**
3. **On the left, click Full-Text Search Matches.**
4. **Click the List of Troubleshooters link.**

Using smart techniques to keep the system running at minimal levels

If you've just installed a program and suddenly find yourself booting to Safe Mode, chances are good an auto-starting program decided to play "Pin the Tail on Windows." Windows doesn't play well with others. If it doesn't like what another program is doing while it's trying to boot, it goes into Safe Mode.

See Technique 11 for an extensive list of approaches to knocking out auto-starting programs.

Using the Registry in Safe Mode

Do not dive into the Registry while in Safe Mode unless you know precisely what you want to change and why. Sometimes you'll bump into a Web page that gives you instructions for solving a problem like yours, and the solution involves editing the Registry. Be wary. Many Registry hacks were written for earlier versions of Windows, and they just don't work with Windows XP — particularly not Windows XP Service Pack 2.

The best and safest place to look for solutions to Safe Mode-magnitude problems is the Microsoft Knowledge Base, at `support.microsoft.com`. If a Knowledge Base article that's specifically written for Windows XP recommends that you edit your Registry, you can be fairly certain that the change works as advertised. Most of the time.

For details on working with your Registry, see Technique 68.

Using Recovery Console

If you can't get Windows to start, or if the trip through Safe Mode and running the System File Checker leave Windows crashing, you have one last resort before you seriously consider reformatting your hard drive: Windows XP's Recovery Console.

Do not use the Windows Recovery Console unless you know, in advance, *exactly* what you want to do. You might want to follow a suggestion in Microsoft's Knowledge Base to restore a file. You might need to use Recovery Console to dislodge a virus, following the recommendations from one of the major antivirus companies. Recovery Console can even come in handy when you have to forcibly evict a driver, following the recommendations of your hardware manufacturer. But in every case, you should have your course of action planned before you haul out the Recovery Console's big guns.

The Recovery Console is a powerful (and thus dangerous) tool. If you've whiled away a few hours (days, weeks) playing with DOS trying to fix a Windows Me/98/98 SE machine, you'll feel right at home with Recovery Console. If you blanche at the thought of rewriting your master boot record (or if you don't know what a master boot record is), it's better to hire (or bribe) someone who has suffered the slings and arrows of outrageous Windows fortune.

The Microsoft Knowledge Base has many discussions of how to put the Windows XP Recovery Console on your boot menu. Don't bother reading these discussions. If you use the Recovery Console more than a few times, you're doing something very wrong. It's easy enough to bring up the Recovery Console from the installation CD on the few occasions when you need it.

To use Windows XP's Recovery Console

1. **Put your Windows XP CD in the CD drive.**

   You need to boot from the Windows XP CD. This CD contains the full version of Windows XP. If you bought a computer with Windows XP preinstalled, you probably have a backup CD or a "repair" CD. Use that CD, if you can boot from it. If you didn't get a backup CD with your new computer, or you can't boot from it, call the manufacturer and get very angry.

2. **Restart your computer.**

   You probably have your PC set up to boot from CD, but if you don't, you may have to play around with BIOS settings inside the PC to get it to boot. The manual that came with your PC can tell you how. Good luck.

   Eventually you see the Windows XP Setup screen, as shown in Figure 63-9.

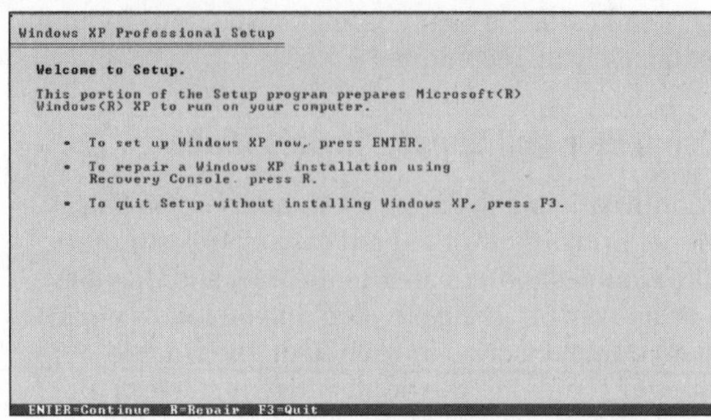

• **Figure 63-9: The easiest way to the Recovery Console.**

3. **Press the R key.**

   The setup routine asks which system you want to run Recovery Console on, as shown in Figure 63-10. If you have a single-boot system (that is, a PC with only one operating system on it), the Windows XP directory is listed as 1. If you have a multiboot system, each operating system has a number.

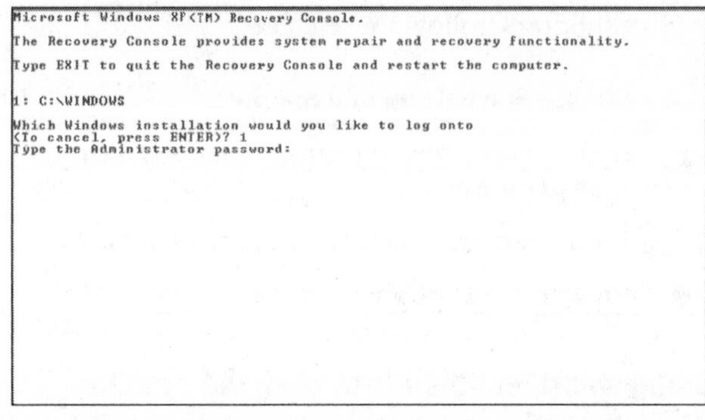

• **Figure 63-10: You must log on with the Administrator account.**

4. **Type the number for the operating system you want to run Recovery Console.**

   This number is almost always 1.

   The Recovery Console asks for the Administrator account's password.

This is the password for the account called "Administrator" (see Technique 47). If you're using XP Professional, you typed this password when you first installed Windows XP (although you may have changed it since then). If you're using XP Home, the Administrator account has no password.

5. **If you are using XP Professional, type the password for the Administrator account. If you are using XP Home, press Enter.**

   Windows Recovery Console responds with something that looks just like an old-fashioned DOS command prompt:

   ```
   C:\WINDOWS>
   ```

6. **Use any of the commands listed in Table 63-2.**

   You should be following instructions — from the Microsoft Knowledge Base, from an antivirus software manufacturer, from a hardware manufacturer, or some other very reputable source. This isn't a place to experiment with commands and/or concepts you've never dealt with before.

If you need help on any command, type help followed by the command. For example, to get help on using the `attrib` command, type **help attrib**. You're presented with a list of all the arguments that you can use with the `attrib` command, and what those arguments mean. See Figure 63-11.

```
Command Prompt
C:\>help attrib
Displays or changes file attributes.

ATTRIB [+R | -R] [+A | -A ] [+S | -S] [+H | -H] [drive:][path][filename]
       [/S [/D]]

  +   Sets an attribute.
  -   Clears an attribute.
  R   Read-only file attribute.
  A   Archive file attribute.
  S   System file attribute.
  H   Hidden file attribute.
  [drive:][path][filename]
      Specifies a file or files for attrib to process.
  /S  Processes matching files in the current folder
      and all subfolders.
  /D  Processes folders as well.
```

• Figure 63-11: Get help by typing Help and the command.

7. **When you finish, type**

   ```
   exit
   ```

   Windows XP reboots, and with any luck, you're back in normal Windows XP momentarily.

You can find a complete list of commands at `support.microsoft.com/?kbid=314058`.

Table 63-2: Commands Available in Windows XP's Recovery Console

This Command	Does This	Example/Use This Command . . .
`attrib`	Changes file and directory attributes (read-only, archive, system, hidden).	If you have to manipulate a hidden or read-only file.
`batch`	Runs a text file. `batch C:\myprog.bat` runs the commands in `myprog.bat`.	To run a long list of commands that you'd rather not type.
`cd`	Changes the folder.	To move up or down one level in the folder hierarchy.
`chdsk`	Runs `chkdsk.exe` (see Technique 57).	If you absolutely need to run Check Disk with nothing else going.
`copy`	Copies one file (no wildcards). Automatically uncompresses files stored on the Windows XP distribution CD.	To copy a file from the Windows XP installation CD into a Windows folder (sometimes used to fix clobbered system files).

(continued)

Table 63-2 *(continued)*

This Command	Does This	Example/Use This Command . . .
`del`	Deletes one file.	To delete a bad file, for example, a virus program that can't be dislodged any other way.
`dir`	Displays a list of files and subfolders.	To see what files and folders are available.
`disable`	Disables a Windows system service or driver.	To turn off a service that may be causing problems.
`diskpart`	Manages partitions. (Think `FDISK`.)	When you're reformatting a hard drive.
`enable`	The opposite of disable.	To start a system service, presumably after you've fixed it.
`exit`	Leaves the Recovery Console and reboots.	When you're done.
`expand`	Decompresses one compressed file (typically from the Windows XP CD).	Rarely used, because `copy` can find the file.
`fixboot`	Creates a new boot sector on the system partition.	During the process of reformatting a hard drive.
`fixmbr`	Writes a new master boot record (which is the tiny program located in a reserved area on your hard drive that Windows uses to load itself).	To overwrite the master boot record, typically because a virus has infected it, but possibly because you messed up the installation of a multiboot system.
`format`	Formats a disk.	To perform the key step in reformatting a hard drive.
`help`	Lists commands and parameters.	See Figure 63-11.
`listsvc`	Shows all available system services and drivers.	To find out which services are running. Can be used to run down viruses.
`md`	Creates a new folder.	When you need a new folder.
`rd`	Deletes a folder.	To get rid of a folder.
`ren`	Renames a file.	Possibly as part of the process of disabling a virus.
`type`	Displays a text file.	To look inside text files.

Restoring Your System after Calamitous Change

Save Time By

- Making a System Restore Point before you install something new
- Rolling back immediately with System Restore
- Using the Last Known Good Configuration option in a Windows boot

Ever get the feeling that Windows was about to head down the tubes, in a hurry? *Before* you get to that point, you should make a Restore Point. That way, after your system has gone to Hades in a handbasket, you can use System Restore to bring it back to its original upright position.

Or something like that.

Finding out how to create System Restore Points takes only a few minutes. If you create a Restore Point before you install an unknown piece of software — oh, I won't mention KaZaA by name — then you have everything you need to quickly, easily, wipe all vestiges of KaZaA from your system. If you don't make a System Restore Point, oh man, are you in for a wild ride.

This technique can save you all sorts of time.

You may have read that Windows XP Home Edition doesn't support System Restore. 'Tain't so. Windows System Restore works fine with XP Home. XP Professional users get Automatic System Restore, but unless you're connected to a Big Corporate Network, you probably don't want to go to the hassle of wrangling with ASR. Normal ol' Windows System Restore more than suffices.

This technique shows you how to use System Restore.

Understanding System Restore's Limitations

Let me just make one thing clear, right off the bat. Windows XP's System Restore *is not a backup program.* It doesn't back up your spreadsheets, keep track of your e-mail, or create automatic copies of all those Word documents you have lying around.

Rather, System Restore takes snapshots of Windows XP that include copies of key system files, all the Registry, various settings for each user — basically everything that's necessary to roll back Windows to a previous point in time *except for* your data. And it doesn't back up your programs, either. Just Windows.

You have to make your own backups, thank you very much. Technique 60 shows you how.

Windows automatically creates snapshots — called *Restore Points* — on these occasions:

- When you install an application (if the installer is a recent one and behaves properly by notifying Windows).
- When you install a Windows update, patch, or service pack.
- When you install an unsigned driver. (For more about unsigned drivers — programs that make hardware work, which haven't been approved by Microsoft — see Technique 58.)
- When you manually create a Restore Point.
- Just before you restore an old Restore Point (so you can, in effect, undo the undo if need be).
- Every 24 hours if you keep your computer on all the time, or when you turn your computer on and it's been more than 24 hours since the last Restore Point. Windows XP waits until there hasn't been any activity on the machine for a while before creating a Restore Point.

When you restore a Restore Point, only Windows gets restored. That can lead to some mighty confounding behavior.

Say you install a program that you think might be unstable. You create a Restore Point before you install it. The program bombs and takes your system along with it, so you roll back to the Restore Point. Windows won't know that the program was ever installed — but the program's files are still on your hard drive. If you accidentally try to open one of these files before you have reinstalled the program, there's no telling what might happen. A good guess: Windows chokes on the file, forcing you to reboot.

Creating a Restore Point

Say you have a copy of Uncle Billy Joe Bob's Blaster Beta, and you're about to install it. You know Billy Joe Bob doesn't have a real installer package — one that properly notifies Windows that it's about to install a program and give Windows a chance to create a Restore Point automatically. It's time for you to ponder your immediate future.

Maybe the Blaster Beta won't do anything bad to your system. Maybe it will. Maybe it has a good installer. Maybe it doesn't.

When in doubt, run a Restore Point before you install new software or hardware. It's a quick, easy ounce of prevention.

To manually create a Restore Point, follow these steps:

1. **Choose Start⇨All Programs⇨Accessories⇨System Tools⇨System Restore.**

   The System Restore Wizard appears, as shown in Figure 64-1.

2. **Click the Create a Restore Point option, and then click Next.**

   The wizard wants a name for the Restore Point, shown in Figure 64-2, so you can figure out when it was made.

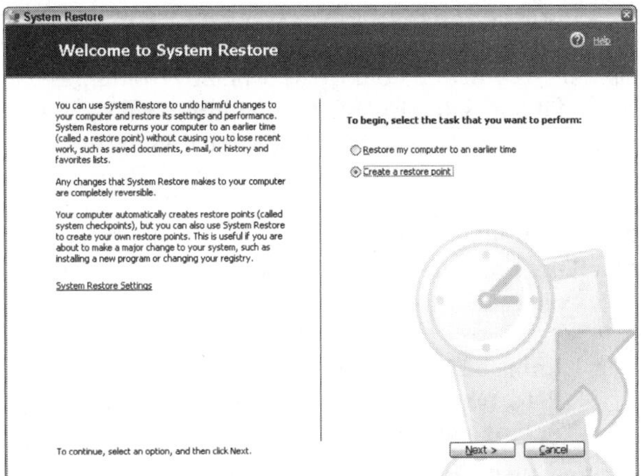

• **Figure 64-1: The System Restore Wizard also creates Restore Points.**

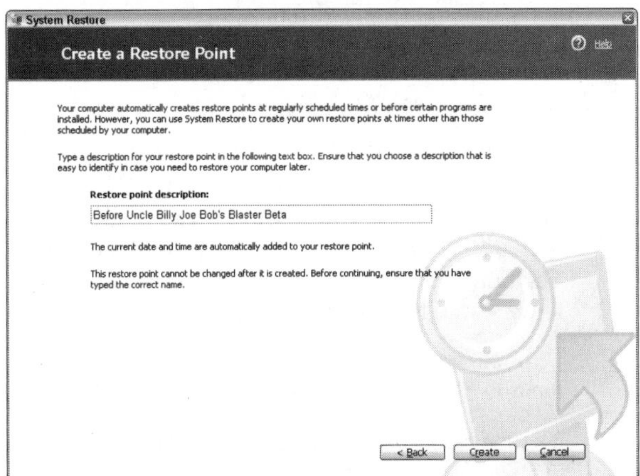

• **Figure 64-2: Use a name that you can identify with.**

3. **Give the Restore Point a name that you will understand a day or a week from today, and then click the Create button.**

   "System Restore Point May 2" doesn't cut it as a good Restore Point name. Why? Because Windows automatically saves the date and time with the Restore Point. Instead use a name such as Before Uncle Billy Joe Bob's Blaster Beta.

   The wizard takes a while to gather all the pertinent data, but when it's done, you see the report in Figure 64-3.

4. **Click the Close button.**

Windows XP saves your Restore Points for 90 days, or until the wizard runs out of space. It's hard to imagine why you would want a Restore Point that's, say, 73 days old, but if you need it, Windows has it.

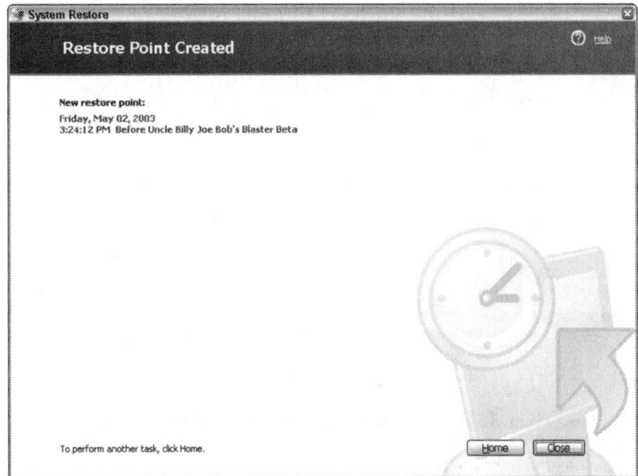

• **Figure 64-3: Your official confirmation that the wizard completed its task.**

Restoring to a Restore Point — Quickly

So something has gone terribly wrong with your system, and you want to get Windows back to the way it was a day ago (or, if you installed Uncle Bill Joe Bob's Blaster Beta, maybe just a few seconds ago).

The exact method you use for restoring Windows depends on how badly Windows is hurting.

If Windows isn't running and won't start

If you can't get Windows to start, don't fret. You can restore Windows to the last Restore Point by following these steps:

1. **Reboot your computer.**

   Every PC goes through its self-test a little differently, but typically you see a counter as the PC tests its memory, and then you see notices about keyboard and mouse drivers, and then you see a notice about your hard drives. (Assuming these don't flash by so fast you see only a blur.)

2. **Immediately after you see the message that your hard drive is alive, press F8 and hold it down.**

   Windows XP shows you the Advanced Boot Options screen, as shown in Figure 64-4.

```
Windows Advanced Options Menu
Please select an option:

    Safe Mode
    Safe Mode with Networking
    Safe Mode with Command Prompt

    Enable Boot Logging
    Enable VGA Mode
    Last Known Good Configuration (your most recent settings that worked)
    Directory Services Restore Mode (Windows domain controllers only)
    Debugging Mode

    Start Windows Normally
    Reboot
    Return to OS Choices Menu

Use the up and down arrow keys to move the highlight to your choice.
```

• Figure 64-4: The fast way to restore Windows to the most recent Restore Point.

3. **Use the down arrow to highlight Last Known Good Configuration (Your Most Recent Settings That Worked).**

4. **Press Enter.**

   The Last Known Good Configuration choice simply runs Windows System Restore using the last Restore Point, and then boots normally.

Windows automatically makes a Restore Point when you restore — so if you run through these steps twice in a row (without setting a new Restore Point), the second time you use Last Known Good Configuration, you get your original (presumably bad!) Restore Point.

If Windows runs

As long as you can coax Windows into running — even if it's in Safe Mode (see Technique 63) — you can restore to any Restore Point created in the past 90 days.

If you're rolling back Windows specifically because of a flaky program, start by uninstalling the program. Follow these steps:

1. **Choose Start➪Control Panel➪Add or Remove Programs, select the program, and click the Remove button.**

If the program has a halfway decent uninstaller (not all of them do), this simple step gets rid of most of the program files and other gross pieces of the program.

2. **If you're rolling back Windows because of a bad driver, see Technique 58.**

   Usually, there's no need to roll back all of Windows because of a bad driver. On the other hand, sometimes you want to make really, really sure you get rid of all the pieces, so if you follow Technique 58 and it doesn't solve all your problems, come back here to Step 3.

3. **Choose Start➪All Programs➪Accessories➪System Tools➪System Restore.**

   The System Restore Wizard appears.

4. **Click the Restore My Computer to an Earlier Time option, and then click Next.**

   The wizard lets you scroll through a calendar full of Restore Points.

5. **Choose the Restore Point that will cause the least disruption but still get the job done, and then click Next.**

   The System Restore Wizard tells you to save and shut down everything.

6. **Close any open programs, and then click Next.**

The wizard performs the restore, and then immediately shuts down Windows and restarts. When Windows comes back, it tells you that it has been restored.

7. **If you want to undo the restore, choose Start⇨All Programs⇨Accessories⇨System Tools⇨System Restore.**

   The wizard adds an option to undo, as shown in Figure 64-5.

8. **To undo, click the Undo My Last Restoration option, click Next, and follow the wizard.**

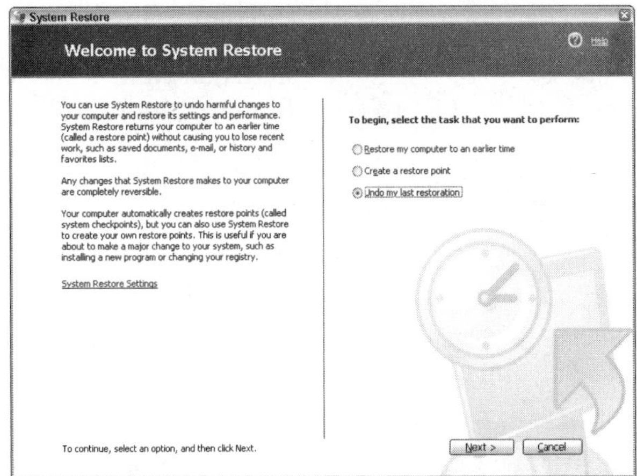

• **Figure 64-5: Undoing a restore is very easy.**

Recovering a Lost Password

Save Time By

- Setting up a password reset disk *now* — before you need it
- Using a password reset disk quickly and correctly
- Figuring out what to do if you lost your password and don't have a reset disk

There's a downside to creating good, strong passwords. What if you forget yours?

If your PC is connected to a Big Corporate Network (in Microsoft speak, a *domain*), you can use the password reset disk I discuss in this technique to get on to your PC — but you can't log on to the network. Should you require files, printers, or anything else on the network, you have to rouse the network administrator and get her to change your password. Then you have to log on to the network and change your password once again. It's a pain in the posterior, but there's no alternative. That's how BCNs work.

If you have a peer-to-peer network (a *workgroup* in Microsoft speak), or a stand-alone PC, the situation isn't nearly as dire – providing that you're prepared. This technique's password reset disk can have you going in seconds. A few minutes spent creating a password reset disk can save you hours of hassle and pain.

Technique 9 shows you how to make passwords that withstand concerted, knowledgeable attempts to break them.

This technique shows you how to break them. Or at least, how to set things up ahead of time so you can break them. It's easy, if you know how.

Creating a Password Reset Disk

The minute you turn on password protection for an account, you should create a password reset disk for that account. Why? Because any administrator who can get on your PC can switch your password — and you can do nothing about it!

As I describe in Technique 47, unless you're attached to a Big Corporate Network, or you've taken specific steps to rein them in, every user on your Windows XP system has Administrator privileges. That means anybody can change your password, anytime — even accidentally.

Unless you're using a Big Corporate Network, a password reset disk is a defensive maneuver. It guards you against the slings and arrows of others who use your PC.

The password reset disk has two severe limitations:

- Windows XP forces you to use specific kinds of removable drives when you create the password reset disk and when you use it. In my experience, you can use a floppy disk, a USB-connected flash drive, or other type of drive connected via a USB port (including a SmartCard reader), and even (believe it or not) a camera attached to your PC.

I have had no luck at all using CD-R or CD-RW drives, or other kinds of removable media. Once upon a time, every PC had a floppy drive, and Microsoft assumed that your password reset disk would naturally be a floppy diskette. Times change. Microsoft hasn't kept up. If your PC doesn't have a floppy drive, and you don't own a USB floppy or flash drive, consider plugging in your camera. Most of the time it works. Really.

- If you are on a Novell Netware network, you can create a password reset disk — but you can't use it. Netware doesn't have a feature that allows you to use the password reset disk, even if you only want to get onto your own PC.

Follow these steps to make a password reset disk:

1. **Choose Start⇨Control Panel⇨User Accounts.**
2. **Click your account.**

   The User Accounts applet asks what you want to change (see Figure 65-1).

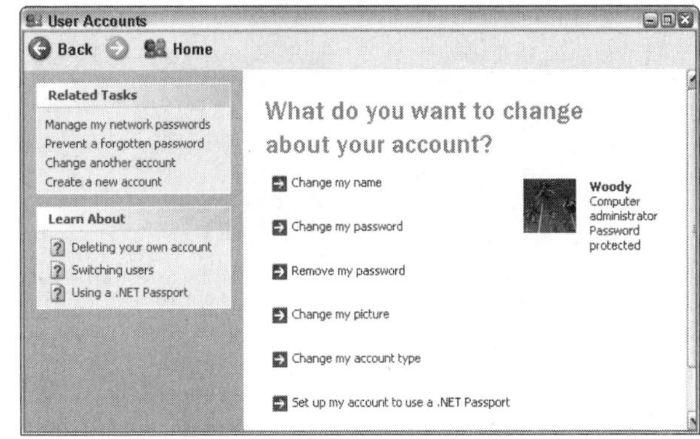

• **Figure 65-1: Start the Password Reset Disk Wizard here.**

3. **In the Related Tasks section, double-click Prevent a Forgotten Password.**

   The Forgotten Password Wizard starts, as shown in Figure 65-2.

• **Figure 65-2: The Forgotten Password Wizard steps you through creating a password reset disk.**

4. **Click Next.**

   The wizard asks for a drive, as shown in Figure 65-3. In fact, you can create a password reset disk on various kinds of removable drives, including flash drives or Flash Memory cards, but the most common is a simple floppy.

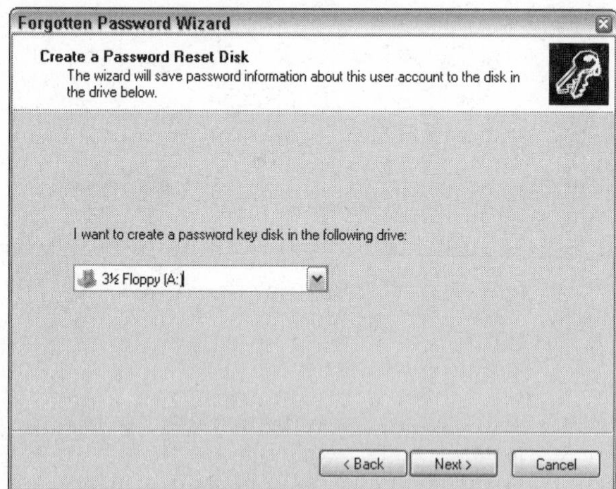

• **Figure 65-3: A "password key disk" is a password reset disk.**

5. **Choose the drive you want to use for the password reset disk, and then click Next.**

   The wizard asks for the current password, as shown in Figure 65-4.

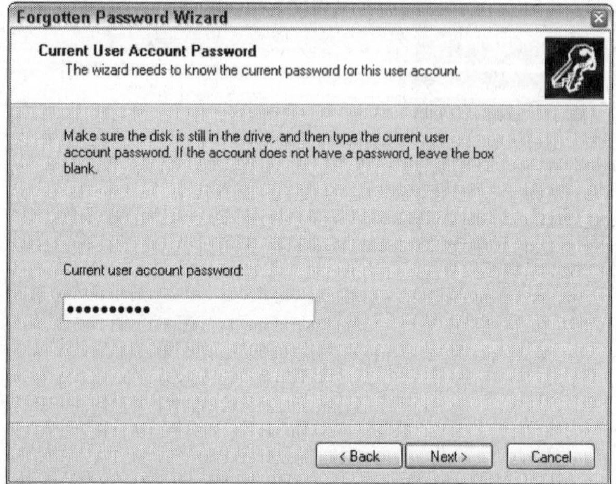

• **Figure 65-4: You must supply the password in order to create the disk.**

6. **Type the password for the account, and then click Next.**

   The wizard puts a small file called `userkey.psw` on the disk, and then displays the final screen.

7. **Click the Finish button.**

Although Microsoft likes to make it sound like there's something magical about the password reset disk, in fact there isn't. The `userkey.psw` file holds the information that unlocks the account. You can copy `userkey.psw` onto any disk at all and use it to log in to this particular PC with this particular account. On the other hand, if you use the wizard a second time to create a second password reset disk (in fact, a second `userkey.psw`), the original password reset disk (`userkey.psw`) doesn't work anymore.

No matter how many times you change your password, the last password reset disk (actually, the last version of `userkey.psw`) created for that account still works. There's no reason to update the disk when you change your password.

8. **Store the disk — specifically, the file `userkey.psw` — in a safe place. Anyone who gets the file can log on to your PC without knowing your password.**

Using Your Password Reset Disk

So the sad day has come — you can't remember your password. That's okay. Happens to everybody — except the folks who write their passwords with permanent markers on the front of their screens. But those people have other problems.

You know you've reached that sad state of affairs when the welcome screen greets you with the dour message shown in Figure 65-5.

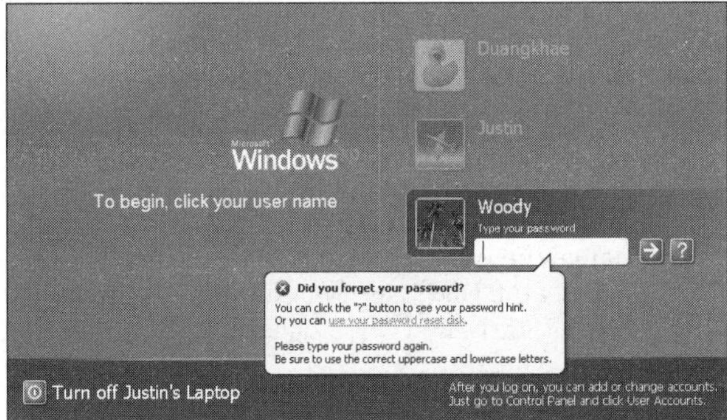

• Figure 65-5: You *did* remember to make a password reset disk, didn't you?

If you have your password reset disk handy, here's how to use it:

1. **Click the Use Your Password Reset Disk link on the welcome screen.**

   The Password Reset Wizard appears.

2. **Click Next.**

   The wizard wants to know where to find your password reset disk.

3. **Choose the removable drive that contains** `userkey.psw` **(probably your floppy drive, with the password reset disk in it, but you have other alternatives). Click Next.**

   The wizard asks you to provide a new password (see Figure 65-6).

4. **Give the wizard a new password and hint for this account. Click Next.**

   The wizard reaches into Windows XP and changes the password for this particular user. It doesn't matter what the old password was, this new password now takes effect.

5. **Click the Finish button, and then log on with the new password you specified.**

   It's quite remarkable, but the password isn't stored on the password reset disk (nor is it in `userkey.psw`).

• Figure 65-6: Type a new password for this account.

Getting Around Your Own Password

So what do you do if you forget your password, you don't have a network administrator to bail you out, and you didn't create a password reset disk?

In short, you have to go in with a different account and change your password.

If you forget your password, don't have a password reset disk, and you're using the NTFS file system and its Encrypted File System (described in Technique 8), *don't attempt anything listed here* — if you succeed in changing the password, you clobber all those encrypted files. (Encrypted File System corresponds to the Make This Folder Private option I discuss in Technique 48.) If you bought your computer with Windows XP installed, chances are good it has NTFS. If you made the My Documents folder inaccessible to other people, you're using EFS, and you should not undertake any of these steps.

Some companies claim to have software that opens up those encrypted files — `www.sunbelt-software.com` is among them — but it's far from a sure thing. Spend some time on the Internet and keep trying.

If your folders are *not* marked as Private (see Technique 48), try the following steps to get your account back in order.

Log on with a different Administrator account and change your password. This step really is as simple as it sounds. If you don't believe me, I describe the process in Technique 47. When you change your account's password, you lose any other passwords that Internet Explorer has stored for you, as well as some other stored passwords — so you may have to provide your password again the next time you check out of Amazon.com, and you have to come up with your dial-up Internet account password, if you have one. But that's usually a small price to pay.

If there is no other Administrator account, you have to log on to the account named Administrator and change your account's password.

Windows XP goes to great lengths to hide it, but there's probably an account called Administrator enabled on your system. You typed a password for that account when you installed Windows XP Pro, even if you have no recollection of doing so.

If Windows has a password for the account called Administrator and you can't remember it or don't know it, you are in for some interesting times. The best alternative I've seen is to reinstall Windows XP from the original Windows XP Installation CD: Reinstalling gives you an opportunity to provide a new Administrator password without completely wiping out Windows. For instructions on performing a reinstallation, see `www.microsoft.com/windowsxp/using/helpandsupport/learnmore/tips/doug92.mspx`.

Here's how to log on to the Administrator account if you're running Windows XP Pro:

1. **If you use the welcome screen, first disable Fast User Switching.**

   Choose Start➪Control Panel➪User Accounts➪Change the Way Users Log On or Off, and uncheck the Fast User Switching check box. Log off (Start➪Log Off➪Log Off).

   The Windows welcome screen appears.

2. **Hold down Ctrl and Alt, and press Del twice.**

   The old-fashioned Windows 2000 logon screen appears.

3. **In the User Name text box, type Administrator. In the Password text box, type the password and click OK.**

   From that point, it's easy to go into User Accounts (Start➪Control Panel➪User Accounts) and change your own account's password.

If there is no other Administrator account with Windows XP Home Edition, you have a blank password for the account called Administrator. You need to change it to a real password. Follow these steps to do so:

The only way to change the real password is in Safe Mode. I describe Safe Mode in Technique 63.

1. **Follow the instructions in Technique 63 to go into Safe Mode. When you see the welcome screen, click Administrator.**

2. **Choose Start➪Control Panel➪User Accounts.**

   You see a modified User Accounts dialog box, as shown in Figure 65-7.

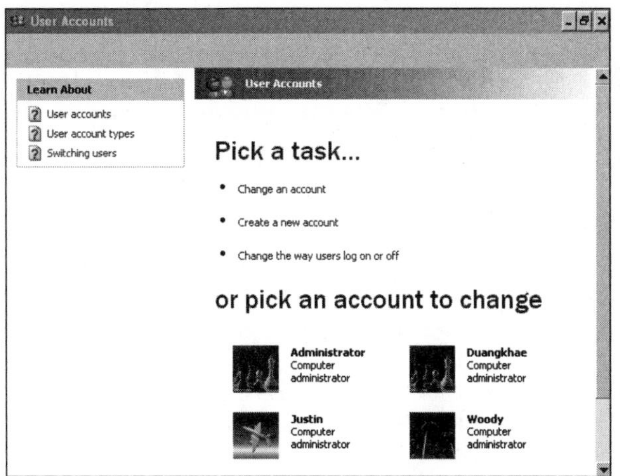

• Figure 65-7: The User Accounts window in Safe Mode.

3. **Click Administrator, and then click Create a Password to give the account a real password.**

4. **Get out of Safe Mode by choosing Start➪Log Off Computer➪Restart.**

5. **If you use the welcome screen, first disable Fast User Switching**

   Choose Start➪Control Panel➪User Accounts➪Change the Way Users Log On or Off, and uncheck the Fast User Switching check box. Log off (Start➪Log Off➪Log Off).

   The Windows welcome screen appears.

6. **Hold down Ctrl and Alt, and press Del twice.**

   The old-fashioned Windows 2000 logon screen appears.

7. **In the User Name text box, type Administrator. In the Password text box, type the password and click OK.**

   From that point, it's easy to go into User Accounts (Start➪Control Panel➪User Accounts) and change your own account's password.

   Good luck.

Surviving the Blue Screen of Death

Save Time By

- Knowing when to laugh and when to panic
- Using common sense to nail — and solve — the problem
- Getting back online quickly, with a minimum of headaches

```
A problem has been detected and windows has been shut down to
prevent damage to your computer.

The problem seems to be caused by the following file: NTLDR

PAGE_FAULT_IN_NONPAGED_AREA

If this is the first time you've seen this stop error screen,
restart your computer. If this screen appears again, follow
these steps:

Log on to Windows using the Administrator account. Oops.
Wait a second. I guess you can't log on to Windows, can you?
Hmmm. Man, I dunno what to do. Dig out a copy of Windows XP
Timesaving Techniques For Dummies, and see if Technique 66
solves your problem.

Technical information:

*** STOP: 0x00000050 (0xF7AC0640, 0xc0000034, 0x00000000,
   0x00000000)
```

Anyone who has used Windows XP for a long time, particularly on an older PC, has undoubtedly encountered a Windows STOP message — more formally known as a *Blue Screen of Death* or BSOD, as shown in Figure 66-1. The BSOD dates all the way back to Windows 2.0. Some wags inside Microsoft went as far as to declare that Windows XP Professional didn't have BSODs anymore. What fools these mortals be . . . .

If you follow the instructions on-screen and restart your machine, the BSOD might go away. For a day or two. Then again, it might not.

The BSOD is Windows XP's way of saying, "I give up!" Your PC simply freezes, leaving behind this blue screen as an only marginally decipherable legacy. You can't do a thing except restart your PC.

If it *will* restart.

```
A problem has been detected and windows has been shut down to prevent damage
to your computer.

If this is the first time you've seen this stop error screen,
restart your computer. If this screen appears again, follow
these steps:

Check for viruses on your computer. Remove any newly installed
hard drives or hard drive controllers. Check your hard drive
to make sure it is properly configured and terminated.
Run CHKDSK /F to check for hard drive corruption, and then
restart your computer.

Technical information:

*** STOP: 0x0000007B (0xF7AC0640, 0xc0000034,0x00000000,0x00000000)
```

• **Figure 66-1: A typical BSOD. Sounds scary, doesn't it?**

This technique takes you through the leading causes of BSODs and helps you quickly identify what might be going wrong. It includes a bunch of school-of-hard-knocks advice for getting your machine up and working fast — or for putting your errant hardware out of its misery — without consuming days, weeks, or months of your time.

A crash by any other name

Everyone — absolutely everyone — refers to a STOP error as a Blue Screen of Death, or BSOD. But sometimes the official documentation tries to put a little spin on the ugly side. You can find references in Microsoft's documentation to "STOP errors," "kernel errors," "system faults," or "bug checks" (although the latter term is rapidly falling out of favor). All these phrases mean the same thing.

There are more than 250 *documented* BSOD errors. There are countless others, but they simply aren't documented. Even the ones that *are* documented bear explanations so obtuse that they bring tears to the eyes of the most hardened, experienced, knowledgeable Windows fanatics. No, you aren't going crazy. Yes, these BSOD people do talk funny. Their native language is Geek.

Encountering a Blue Screen of Death

Windows can roll over and cry *Uncle* for any number of reasons. In my experience, most common BSODs fall into these categories:

- **Symptom:** Windows says it can't read key system information from the hard drive.

  Likely cause: The main hard drive (or at least a piece of it) is going bad. Usually this is because the drive has a bad spot, or because the drive's about to, uh, byte the dust.

- **Symptom:** Windows says it can't read key system information from main memory.

  Likely cause: Usually a memory card is going flaky. Maybe a memory chip isn't seated right, or a cockroach has taken up residence on a chip.

A secondary symptom of a memory issue is that your PC may also run physically hot. In some cases if a memory card isn't connecting correctly, it can get so hot your PC shuts itself down.

- **Symptom:** Windows says that a program needs something from another program, but can't find it.

  Likely cause: DLL hell. *DLL hell* is the awful event in which constantly changing system files can prevent programs from talking to each other in the way they need to. It transforms Windows' version of Three Card Monty into a rousing round of 52 Card Pickup. Usually DLL hell triggers warning messages and unexpected system crashes. But if core system files get screwed up, a BSOD can result.

- **Symptom:** Windows says something about a driver error or an adapter problem.

  Likely cause: Your drivers aren't getting along, either with Windows, or with each other. Maybe you recently installed some weird piece of hardware with an old pre-XP driver. Did you install a whiz-bang video adapter with a "made for XP" driver that doesn't work worth beans? Been there, done that.

- **Symptom:** Windows says something about your IDE controller or NIC.

  Likely cause: Some other piece of hardware (IDE controller, network interface card) has intermittent problems. These can be extraordinarily difficult to trace down and solve. Heat is a prime suspect.

Starting with Common-Sense Approaches

As soon as the shock wears off from seeing your first BSOD, you might be tempted to fight back — go into Microsoft's Knowledge Base or look on the Internet at large for a solution. Relax. Some BSODs clear themselves up, if you simply follow the instructions and restart your computer. Others don't, and if you take some simple, common-sense steps when the first BSOD hits, you can save yourself a ton of frantic time down the road.

If you get a BSOD, follow these steps:

1. **Eliminate the obvious problems.**

   If you just installed a new piece of hardware or a new driver (perhaps by using Windows Update and not checking carefully enough!), get rid of it. You can roll back a driver using the steps in Technique 58 (if you set a System Restore Point). If you just plugged a USB device into your PC, unplug it and return it to the vendor. If you just started playing a CD, clean your CD drive (see Technique 59). And so on.

2. **Write down the STOP 0x000000?? error number (if there is one), along with any information in plain English that may appear.**

   BSODs vary greatly in their ability to communicate in plain English, as shown in Figure 66-2. Usually all you need is the error number, but it doesn't hurt to have more.

A problem has been detected and windows has been shut down to prevent damage to your computer.

The problem seems to be caused by the following file: winacusb.sys

PAGE_FAULT_IN_NONPAGED_AREA

If this is the first time you've seen this stop error screen, restart your computer. If this screen appears again, follow these steps:

• Figure 66-2: Stellar information from a computer experiencing a USB power overload.

3. **Turn off your computer, wait a minute or two, and then turn it back on.**

4. **If you get another BSOD — either immediately, or up to a week or so later — something's wrong and you need to fix it.**

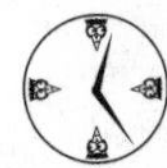

The error number and symptoms may be the same as your earlier BSOD, or they may be quite different. In either case, don't waste time thinking that the BSODs are unrelated, and certainly don't search for solutions to two problems. BSODs are unusual. Having two different BSODs stemming from two different problems in the course of a week or so is very unlikely. Most likely, you're seeing two different symptoms of the same problem.

5. **Back up everything on your hard drive.**

   Refer to Technique 60. Prepare for the possibility — some would say the likelihood — that a vital piece of hardware is going to give out, and you may be down for a while.

6. **Cool your system down.**

   Heat really does a number on all sorts of components. If nothing else, get a room fan and train it directly on the PC.

7. **Don't turn off your PC unless you absolutely have to.**

   I'm not sure why, but I have the worst problems trying to restart my PC after it's been off for several hours. Thermal contraction, most likely.

8. **Update your antivirus software and run it.**

   Certain *boot sector viruses* can cause BSODs, although I've never seen one in action. Boot sector viruses are quite unusual these days.

9. **Run Check Disk several times by turning to Technique 57 and following the instructions in the first section.**

   Not all BSODs tell you to run `CHKDSK` (as in Figure 66-1), but many do. It never hurts.

10. **If you continue to have BSODs, turn off your computer, remove the memory cards, clean the contacts that plug into the connector (check with the manufacturer, but a clean gum eraser usually works fine), and put them back in.**

    Sometimes it helps to swap the memory cards.

11. **If you still have BSODs, it's time to try to figure out specifically what's causing them.**

    Move on to the next section.

Digging into Specific Errors

BSODs always have a STOP code. It's the long number that starts 0x0000 . . ., usually listed at the end of the message. In addition, some marginally legible English language may be in the description, such as IRQL_NOT_LESS_OR_EQUAL. Emphasis on the term *marginally*.

Computer jocks aren't about to copy down all the 0s in the STOP codes, so they're always abbreviated. 0x0000000A, for example, becomes 0x0A. 0x0000007F becomes 0x7F.

I list the most common BSOD errors, and their possible causes and solutions.

Microsoft Knowledge Base (KB) articles are referenced by number. For example, KB article 314063 is available at `support.microsoft.com/?kbid=314063`. You can find detailed discussions of all these BSOD errors in a Windows XP Resource Kit article, which is available (free!) online at `www.microsoft.com/technet/prodtechnol/winxppro/reskit/prmd_stp_tnvo.asp`. Yes, the same information applies to both Windows XP Professional and Windows XP Home.

While I'm on the topic, you did realize that the entire Windows XP Resource Kit is available online, didn't you? No need to shell out $60 for the book. Just drop by `www.microsoft.com/resources/documentation/Windows/XP/all/reskit/en-us/Default.asp`, any ol' time.

TABLE 66-1: A TIMESAVING REFERENCE FOR THE BLUE SCREEN OF DEATH

Code	Description	KB	Possible Cause
0x0A	IRQL_NOT_LESS_OR_EQUAL	314063	Usually happens when a bad driver tries to get at memory locations where it isn't allowed.
0x1E	KMODE_EXCEPTION_NOT_HANDLED	183169	Bad machine code instruction, probably from a screwed-up driver.
0x23	FAT_FILE_SYSTEM	290182	You probably have a FAT hard drive that's ready to go.
0x24	NTFS_FILE_SYSTEM	228888	Your NTFS drive may be on its last legs.

(continued)

TABLE 66-1 *(continued)*

Code	Description	KB	Possible Cause
0x2E	DATA_BUS_ERROR	218132	Memory parity error.
0x3F	NO_MORE_SYSTEM_PTES	256004	Some program is doing a lot of input/output.
0x50	PAGE_FAULT_IN_NONPAGED_AREA	183169	Lots of possible causes, including bad memory cards.
0x77	KERNEL_STACK_INPAGE_ERROR	315266	Your hard drive probably has a bad sector.
0x79	MISMATCHED_HAL	310064	Can happen if you changed your PC's ACPI power management settings.
0x7A	KERNEL_DATA_INPAGE_ERROR	315266	Your hard drive probably has a bad sector.
0x7B	INACCESSIBLE_BOOT_DEVICE	324103	Bad disk controller.
0x7E	SYSTEM_THREAD_EXCEPTION_ NOT_HANDLED	327863, 321637	Trying to run a USB device too fast, or using a particular kind of Creative Labs SoundBlaster.
0x7F	UNEXPECTED_KERNEL_MODE_TRAP	137539	Bad memory or *overclocking* (trying to run your computer faster than it's supposed to).
0x9F	DRIVER_POWER_STATE_FAILURE	315249	Trouble going into or out of Standby or Hibernate mode.
0xBE	ATTEMPTED_WRITE_TO_READONLY_ MEMORY	315252	Bad driver.
0xC1	SPECIAL_POOL_DETECTED_MEMORY_ CORRUPTION	315252	Bad driver.
0xC2	BAD_POOL_CALLER	265879	Bad driver.
0xCE	DRIVER_UNLOADED_WITHOUT_ CANCELLING_PENDING_OPERATIONS	310899	Bad driver.
0xD1	DRIVER_IRQL_NOT_LESS_OR_EQUAL	316208	Bad driver.
0xD8	DRIVER_USED_EXCESSIVE_PTES	256004	Bad driver.
0xEA	THREAD_STUCK_IN_DEVICE_DRIVER	293078	Bad driver.
0xED	UNMOUNTABLE_BOOT_VOLUME	297185	Wrong IDE cable for your fast hard drives.
0xF2	HARDWARE_INTERRUPT_STORM	290101	Devices fighting over the same IRQ.
0xC0000135	UNABLE_TO_LOCATE_DLL	318159	Corrupt Registry (see Technique 64).
0xC0000218	UNKNOWN_HARD_ERROR	307545	Corrupt Registry (see Technique 64).
0xC000021A	STATUS_SYSTEM_PROCESS_TERMINATED	318666	Buffer overrun in Internet Explorer, or your network administrator messed up file permissions.
0xC0000221	STATUS_IMAGE_CHECKSUM_MISMATCH	315241	Damaged driver.

Technique 67: Creating a Startup Disk

Save Time By

- Demanding a Windows XP CD when you buy a new computer
- Creating a Windows XP startup disk that bypasses key system files
- Making an old DOS startup disk work on your system

If you grew up in the Windows Me/98 world, you know the importance of having an emergency boot disk — a floppy disk that you could stick in the drive, click Restart, and bring your computer back to life. Heck, those older versions of Windows stepped you through a complicated procedure for creating a two-disk set that could help you cure whatever ailed Windows. And back then, *puh*-lenty ailed Windows.

When Microsoft released Windows XP, there was no provision whatsoever for a boot disk. "Let them eat cake!" came the cry from the Windows executives. Or words to that effect. If your PC wouldn't boot from the CD, you couldn't even install Windows. There was a little check box in the disk formatting dialog box that claimed it would create a boot disk — but the generated floppy amounted to little more than a cruel joke. Yes, it would boot your PC. No, you couldn't do anything much when you booted.

Microsoft now allows you to download a six-disk collection that really does let you boot from your floppy drive — but only so you can install Windows XP from CD, nothing more. The idea: If your PC won't boot from CD (perhaps the computer refuses to make the CD drive the "boot drive"), you can still boot from a floppy disk — but only if you immediately install or repair Windows. No, you can't boot from a floppy disk and then run Windows from the CD.

Every Windows user needs a way to get his machine running if the copy of Windows on the hard drive goes bananas. If you prepare for the problem now, you can save yourself hours or days of hassle, down the road.

This technique shows you how to make your machine start, no matter what ails Windows.

Getting the CD You Deserve

Rant /ON.

When you buy a new PC, you should get a Windows XP recovery CD to go with it.

That CD should

- Boot all by itself — when you stick the CD in your CD drive and restart, your computer can boot from that CD and allow you to install or repair Windows XP.
- Include all the Windows XP files — so when you've booted your PC, you can reinstall Windows or make fresh copies of any munged files on your hard drive.

If your friendly computer maker says that you don't need a recovery CD, tell 'em to take a hike.

If they tell you all the recovery files are on the hard drive, ask 'em what you're supposed to do if your hard drive dies — by far the most likely reason why you need a recovery CD in the first place.

If they tell you Microsoft is forcing them to refrain from distributing recovery CDs, laugh and take your business elsewhere.

Even if the company proffering all this nonsense goes by the name of HP.

When you buy a new PC, you pay for a copy of Windows XP. Make sure that you get your copy on a CD – one that you can hold onto and store away in case you ever need it. If you bought a new PC and didn't get a CD, you were conned. Contact the company and complain loudly. More and more customers are getting the CD they deserve – even after they pay for their PCs – but only if they bellyache enough.

'Nuff said.

Rant /OFF.

Creating a Boot File Bypass Disk

Once in a very blue moon, the part of your hard drive that holds Windows XP's initial programs — the *master boot record* (or MBR, as it's called) — will give up the ghost. Occasionally, one of three crucial system files — `NTLDR`, `boot.ini`, or `Ntdetect.com` — can disappear. These maladies have several symptoms, but the most common occurs when you try to start your PC and you get a text message, such as one of the following:

```
Missing operating system.
Error loading operating system.
Invalid partition table.
NTLDR is missing.
A disk read error occurred.
NTLDR is compressed.
```

Your MBR or the key boot files can get scrambled in any number of creative ways:

- A particularly stupid virus tries to overwrite the MBR and doesn't do it right.
- You (or, ahem, someone else using your machine) delete a key file, such as `NTLDR` or `boot.ini`.
- That part of your hard drive decides it doesn't want to work today.

You can create a disk that bypasses Windows XP's MBR and the key startup files. That disk can come in handy if the MBR doesn't work, or if (for any number of reasons) your PC refuses to boot directly from the hard drive. The big advantage to a boot file bypass disk: If it works, when you finally get your machine going again, everything should work just fine. You have access to all your files on all your drives, all your hardware should be chugging away, and you can scramble around madly backing up your files in anticipation of the possibility you have to replace your hard drive.

If you get to the point that you need this disk, your machine probably won't start, so you may have to use a friend's Windows XP machine to make the disk. There's no guarantee that a boot file bypass disk generated on one machine will work on another, but I haven't hit any problems, as long as neither machine is set up to boot to multiple operating systems, and you aren't using SCSI drives. Your friend must be running the same version of Windows XP that you're using — XP Home or XP Professional — although it doesn't matter if you both have the same Service Packs installed.

The steps here create a floppy disk that will boot your PC, bypassing the key files on your hard drive. If you don't have a floppy drive, and you're getting error messages, your only real choice is to reinstall Windows, wiping out the old copies of those key files entirely. For instructions on performing a reinstallation, see `www.microsoft.com/windowsxp/using/helpandsupport/learnmore/tips/doug92.mspx`.

To make a boot file bypass disk

1. **Put a diskette in the floppy drive.**

   Everything on the disk will be overwritten.

2. **Choose Start➪My Computer, right-click the floppy drive (probably A:), and choose Format.**

   Windows XP's Format dialog box appears, as shown in Figure 67-1.

3. **Type a volume label for the disk, if you wish, and then click Start.**

4. **When the format is complete, click OK, and then click Close.**

• **Figure 67-1: Format the disk under Windows XP.**

5. **Back in Windows Explorer, double-click the C: drive (or wherever you installed Windows XP).**

6. **Make sure that Windows Explorer shows you all your files: Choose Tools➪Folder Options➪View, click Show Hidden Folders, and uncheck the Hide Extensions for Known File Types and Hide Protected Operating System Files (Recommended) check boxes. Click OK.**

7. **Under the C: drive, right-click the `boot.ini` file, and then choose Send To➪3½ Floppy (A:), as shown in Figure 67-2.**

8. **Right-click the `NTLDR` file and choose Send To➪3½ Floppy (A:).**

9. **Right-click the `Ntdetect.com` file and choose Send To➪3½ Floppy (A:).**

10. **Look for a `Bootsect.dos` file here in the root of the C: drive. You probably don't have one, but if you do, right-click it and choose Send To➪3½ Floppy (A:).**

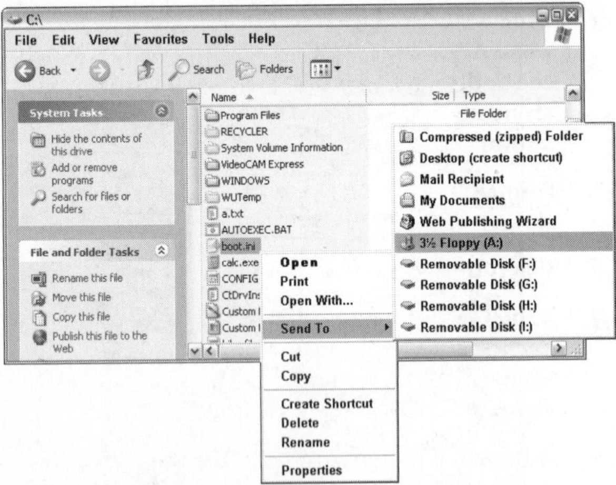

• **Figure 67-2: Send a copy of** `boot.ini` **to the newly formatted floppy.**

11. **Look for a** `Ntbootdd.sys` **file here in the root of the C: drive. You probably don't have one, but if you do, right-click it and choose Send To➪3½ Floppy (A:).**

12. **Close Windows Explorer.**

The disk you just created should be able to boot your PC, providing that the hard drive is working and only your MBR or the key files are clobbered.

Using DOS Boot Disks — If You Can

So where's the beef? Why can't you just slap an old DOS or Windows Me (or 98 or 98SE or 95 or 3.1) boot disk in your floppy and have your PC fire up DOS — or whatever your particular flavor of Windows uses to call its DOS persona?

The problem: NTFS — the NT File System. I talk about NTFS in Technique 48.

DOS, Windows Me, Windows 98, and all their old, carefully crafted boot disks aren't smart enough to see an NTFS drive. They work only with the old-fashioned FAT32 hard drive format. If you have an NTFS drive (and you probably do if you bought your PC with Windows XP preinstalled), you can boot to DOS till the cows come home, but unless you have some way of seeing NTFS drives, you can't do much.

On the other hand, if all your hard drives are formatted as FAT32 drives, any old DOS boot disk works.

If you bought a new PC with Windows XP preinstalled, your drives almost undoubtedly use NTFS. If you installed Windows XP on a PC, you may or may not have NTFS drives.

Do you have NTFS or FAT32 drives?

To see if a particular drive is NTFS or FAT32:

1. Choose Start➪My Computer.
2. Right-click the drive in question and choose Properties.

   You see the drive type listed as the File System, as shown in the following figure.

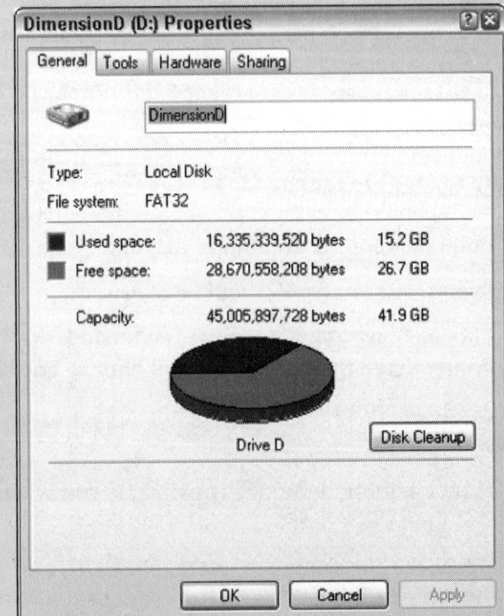

If you have any NTFS drives, when you boot from a DOS boot disk, you won't see any data on them. Chances are good you won't get much of your hardware to work, either, because most modern hardware relies on drivers that don't work with DOS. That said, if you have FAT32 drives, you may be able to use a DOS boot disk to pull the, uh, FAT out of the fryer, if Windows refuses to start. Here's how to make a DOS boot disk:

1. **Put a disk in your floppy drive.**

   Everything on the disk will be overwritten.

2. **Choose Start⇨My Computer, right-click the floppy drive (probably A:), and click Format.**

   Windows XP's Format dialog box appears, as shown in Figure 67-3.

For reasons known to only a few people in Redmond, you can't format a disk and make it an MS-DOS Startup disk at the same time. You have to take each step, one at a time.

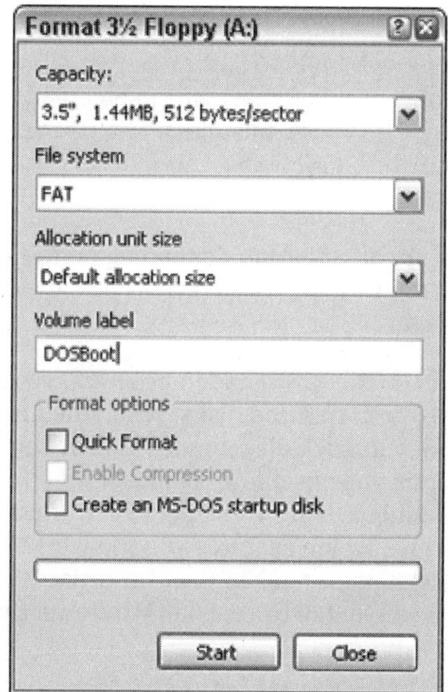

• **Figure 67-3: If the disk isn't formatted, you must format it first.**

3. **Type a volume label for the boot disk, if you wish. If you know the disk is already formatted, check the Quick Format check box. (If you aren't sure, leave it unchecked.) Click the Start button.**

   Formatting a blank disk from scratch is painfully slow.

4. **When the formatting finishes, click OK.**

5. **If the Quick Format check box is checked, uncheck it. Check the Create an MS-DOS Startup Disk check box, as shown in Figure 67-4. Click the Start button.**

   Windows XP transfers a handful of DOS files to the disk.

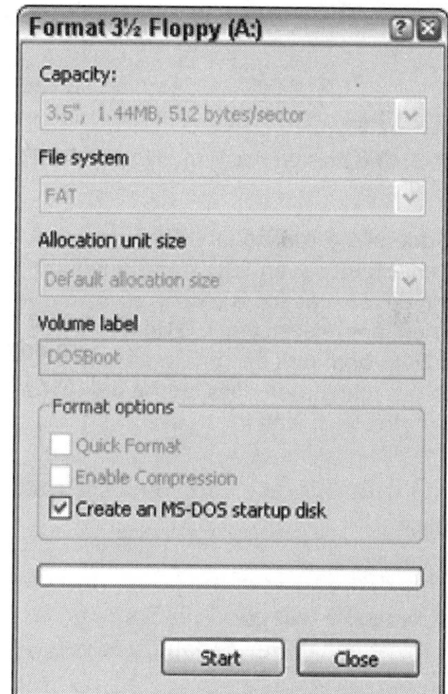

• **Figure 67-4: Creating an MS-DOS startup disk.**

6. **When the format is complete, click OK, and then click Close.**

If you have ever used the Windows Me, 98, or earlier boot disks, you may be surprised — shocked — to see what Windows XP has put on this disk (see Figure 67-5). It's a minimally capable disk, which just barely boots, and absolutely nothing more. All sorts of files that you normally expect to go on a boot disk (and, in fact, are placed on the Windows Me boot disk) aren't even here.

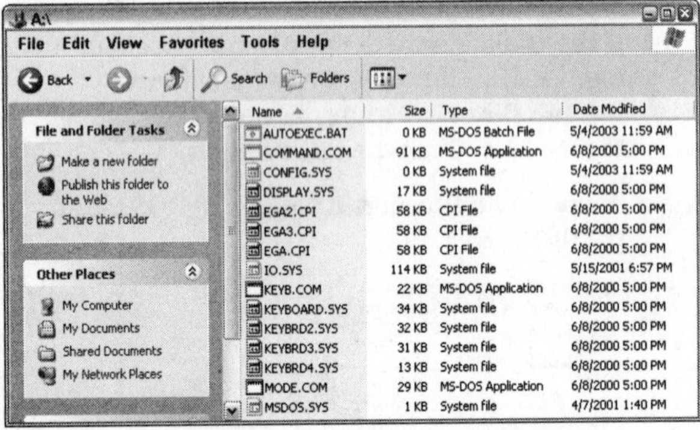

• Figure 67-5: The files on the Windows XP DOS boot disk.

None of the traditional DOS commands go on the disk (not even `FDISK` or `SMARTDRV`). The `autoexec.bat` file is empty, as is `config.sys`. There aren't even any CD drivers. If you create a DOS boot disk using Windows XP, you need to put many more files on the disk before you can do much with it.

Try booting with this disk and you'll see that it does work — barely.

Think of this disk as a starting point, not a finished product. There are two good places to go to help flesh it out with whatever capabilities you need:

- To get into your NTFS drives (if you have any), you need a free program called NTFS Reader for DOS at `www.ntfs.com/products.htm`. I wouldn't bet the farm on it, but it may solve some sticky problems.
- You can find a huge collection of DOS (and Windows Me) utilities for boot disks at `www.bootdisk.com`.

Creating Windows XP Setup Disks

The third type of "boot disk" that may come in handy has nothing to do with examining your computer in case of an emergency. The so-called Windows XP Setup Disks have only one purpose: They let you install Windows from a CD, even if your PC can't boot from a CD.

That's important because Windows XP, straight out of the box, can be installed only on PCs that can be rigged to boot from their CD drives.

Quite some time after Windows XP was originally released, Microsoft softened its approach to CD booting and released a set of six disks that allow you to start your computer from floppy disk so that you can *then* install Windows XP from CD.

Some people call these disks "boot diskettes," but they aren't, really. They won't let you do anything except start your computer and install Windows XP from a CD. If you think you have a set of Windows XP boot disks — which is to say, disks that allow you to boot your machine and perform emergency maintenance — you're mistaken. The last version of Windows with functioning boot disks was Windows Me.

The disks are all different, depending on the version of XP you're installing, the Service Pack level, and the language.

When you run the downloaded program, you have to provide six preformatted disks. When the disks are assembled, you stick disk number one in your floppy drive, restart your machine, keep feeding it diskettes, and ultimately you get to the Windows XP setup routine, which requires you to insert the Windows installation CD in your CD drive. At that point, you can install or reinstall Windows. But you can't run Windows.

Details are at `support.microsoft.com/?kbid=310994`.

Part XI

The Scary (Or Fun!) Stuff

"I'm not saying anything. All I know is that since it's been there Windows has been running 50% faster."

Changing the Registry without Getting Burned

Save Time By

- Getting in and out of the Registry without breaking anything
- Knowing when tweaking the Registry is a waste of time (Answer: usually)
- Making a few changes . . . just for practice, right?

The Registry is a big, dark spooky place full of peril and hidden pitfalls. Kind of like, oh, Form 1040. If you aren't very, very careful, you can bring Windows crashing down, and you'll never get it to work again — ever. Click once in the wrong place, and your machine freezes so tight you have to send it back to Boise.

At least, that's what some people think. Personally, I think of the Registry as a big time sink. But scary? Naw.

Sure, you have to be careful, but if you don't go around changing everything in sight, you can dive into the Registry and come back unscathed.

This technique shows you how.

Don't Mess with This?

The Registry is Windows' central repository for all sorts of different settings — the name of your keyboard driver, the size of your desktop, the location of the program that plays MP3 files, and tens of thousands more.

Nobody understands the Registry. Not completely, anyway. Nobody has ever pulled together a complete description of what all those settings mean. The items are infuriatingly inconsistent, generally entirely undocumented, and stored away in a very nearly random order.

But these items control Windows.

Once upon a time, you had to be able to edit the Registry if you ever hoped to get Windows working efficiently. (Indeed, I would argue, working at all.) Those times have passed. Nowadays, you probably want to go into the Registry for one of three reasons:

- You read on the Internet that if you change some Registry setting, your copy of Windows works better or faster or both.
- You have a specific problem that Microsoft says can be fixed only by manually changing a Registry setting. Unfortunately, this type of

Registry editing is on the upswing. The MS Knowledge Base is packed with articles that require changes to the Registry.

- You have a specific problem that Microsoft *doesn't* talk about, but experts know it can be fixed by changing Registry settings anyway. For example, a lot of Registry tweaks force Windows to bypass (what I believe are) senseless security restrictions in Outlook. My favorite quick Registry tweak, which I detail in this technique, involves setting the NumLock key on or off whenever you start your machine. (The NumLock key, which appears on full-size keyboards, controls whether the number pad keys are interpreted as numbers or as directional arrow keys.) There are many others.

No matter how much you feel the temptation, it's never a good idea to go into the Registry to "fix" something if you don't know precisely what needs fixing and how. Changing Registry settings willy-nilly to try to fix random problems only lands you in hot water.

Understanding the Registry

The worst part of the Registry isn't the Registry itself — it's the lousy terminology. The Windows Registry has grown up in a hodge-podge way, and terms that (arguably) made some sense back in the days of Windows 3.1 don't mean bologna now. But we're stuck with them.

Historically, Microsoft has put absolutely no emphasis on maintaining consistency inside the Registry. It's kind of like a teenager's closet: You never know what you'll find in there, and any resemblance to organization is entirely coincidental.

The Windows Registry may look like a file or a database, but it's really a conglomeration of many different pieces, drawn from several places. You can change some of the entries, but other entries are completely off limits: Your PC generates them, internally, and you can't do anything to modify them.

The Registry is organized by keys, much as your disk is organized in folders. Just as a folder may have other folders and files inside, Registry keys may have other keys and values inside. Just as Windows Explorer helps you move from a higher-level folder down to a lower-level folder, and down and down before you finally find the file you want, the Registry Editor helps you move from a higher-level key down to a lower-level key, and down and down until you get to the value you seek.

The Registry has five main keys, called *high level keys*. Confusingly, in different places in Microsoft's documentation (I told you the terminology was bad, eh?) they're also called *root keys* and/or *predefined keys*. Those five main keys have very long names (see Table 68-1), but the common abbreviations are HKCR, HKCU, HKLM, HKU and HKCC. I use those abbreviations in this technique, rather than the long names, because almost all documentation about the Registry refers to the abbreviations.

Just as you can add or delete folders in Windows Explorer, you can add or delete keys in the Registry Editor. When you delete a folder in Explorer, you delete all the files and folders inside the folder. When you delete a key in the Registry Editor, you delete all the keys and values inside the key.

That's where the similarities end. You can move a folder in Explorer, but you can't move a key in the Registry Editor. And when you delete a key in the Registry Editor, there's no Recycle Bin sitting there helping you recover from your mistakes. After you delete a key, it's gone — for good.

Almost all the changes you make to the Registry involve modifying values: changing, adding, or deleting values (although once in a very blue moon you may need to add a key). Each value in the Registry has a name and data.

For example, in Figure 68-1, the HKCC\Software\Fonts key contains five values. (The HKCC\Software\Fonts key controls which fonts Windows XP uses when it's displaying system-level commands.) The name of the second value is `FIXEDFON.FON`, and its data is `vgafix.fon`.

Table 68-1: Windows XP's High Level Keys

Abbreviation	Means	What It Does	What This Means to You
HKCR	HKEY_CLASSES_ROOT	Associates filename extensions (such as `.doc` or `.exe`) with the actions Windows is supposed to take when, for example, you double-click a file. Also associates types of objects (folders, drives) with actions Windows takes when you double-click them.	If you double-click an MP3 file and the wrong program shows up, something is messed up in this Registry key. Don't try to fix the key directly. Use Windows Explorer's File Name Associations dialog box (see Technique 20).
HKCU	HKEY_CURRENT_USER	Controls many settings for the currently logged-on user, from the user's name to his or her desktop background, and tens of thousands of additional Windows entries.	You can make very detailed changes to your Windows desktop by editing entries in this key.
HKLM	HKEY_LOCAL_MACHINE	Thousands of settings that apply to all users, no matter who is logged on to the PC at any given moment.	Program settings for all users frequently go in here.
HKU	HKEY_USERS	A collection of all the HKCU entries for everyone who has ever logged on to the PC, in addition to a special entry called .DEFAULT, which is copied when a new user gets added.	This is where you can change desktop settings for all users.
HKCC	HKEY_CURRENT_CONFIG	A tiny key that describes the current hardware configuration, and a few basic system settings.	You can change only a few of these settings, primarily the ones associated with basic system functions.

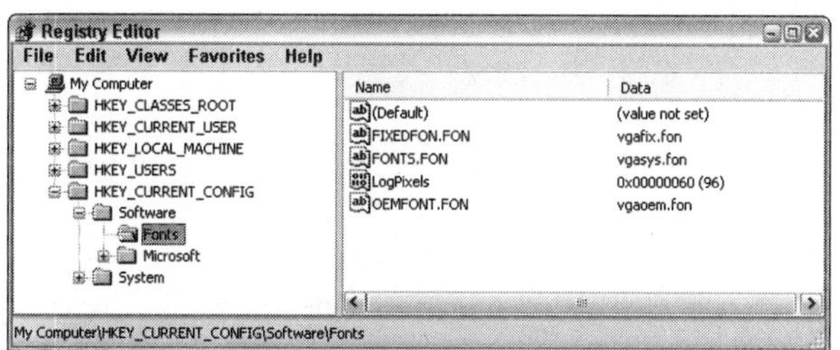

• **Figure 68-1: Inside the HKCC\Software\Fonts key.**

All this would be academic, if it weren't for the fact that when you create a new value, or change a value, you have to be sure that you use the right data type for the value's data. If the value's data is supposed to be a number, and you type in a bunch of characters, you can mess up everything — even, in very rare cases if you're working with a truly critical key, freeze Windows so tight you have to reinstall it.

That's why it's very important that you follow instructions for changing the Registry quite precisely.

Table 68-2 shows you the three most common types of value data that you encounter in the Registry. Make sure you stick to the type of data that the value requires.

The really confounding fact is that the programmers who set up Registry entries usually don't give a fiddler's fig about data types; programmers frequently put strings in *binary values*, for example. The problem comes when you want to change a value by hand. When that happens, you need to conform to the way the programmer set up things originally. Otherwise, the program won't understand what you've done — and may start having conniption fits.

Table 68-2: Common Registry Data Types

Type	Description	Using This Info to Save Time
String	Characters — letters, numbers, weird characters.	Anything you can type on the keyboard is fair game. This is the best kind of key because it's hard to mess up!
DWORD	A "double word" 32-bit (4-byte) integer between 0 and 4,294,967,295 in decimal (or hex 00 00 00 00 to FF FF FF FF). When Registry programmers know they're going to need a small integer, they usually use DWORDs because they're easy to program.	When you type in DWORD data, use only these characters: `0 1 2 3 4 5 6 7 8 9 A B C D E F` You don't really need to understand that an `A` is ten in hexadecimal, but it doesn't hurt. Heh heh heh.
Binary	Similar to DWORD, but Binary can be any number of bytes long. Throughout the Registry, many strings are stored as Binary data.	In many cases, you have to be very, very careful when you change Binary data so that you don't change its length. Follow your instructions precisely and keep track of the Binary data's length.

In certain rare instances (such as the odd editing necessary to add line breaks in the logon screen, described in Technique 8), you have to work with the Binary data that sits behind strings. There's rarely any good reason for it. Be very careful when editing the Binary numbers behind strings. It's easy to add or lose one number — and throw off the whole string.

Backing Up Data the Registry Way

Before you start spelunking through your Registry, you need to back it up. I recommend that you perform not one but *two* separate backups:

- **Create a System Restore Point.** That way, if the wheels fall off and you crash Windows utterly and completely, you can restore the Registry to the point you were at before you started fiddling around (or use the Last Known Good Configuration option on the system boot menu, if you can't get Windows to boot). For details about setting a System Restore Point, see Technique 64.
- **Back up the Registry key(s) that you expect to change.** That's what this section is about.

If Windows heads south, you save yourself a lot of time if you have decent backups at hand.

The Registry can store keys and values in many different ways, but you really need to be concerned about only two:

- `.reg` **file:** A text file that contains Registry entries. You can pick a Registry key and have the Registry Editor copy into a text file all the keys and values contained in that particular key. The text file is called a `.reg` file.

  You keep the `.reg` file as a backup. Restoring from the backup is easy: When you double-click the `.reg` file, entries in the file overwrite corresponding entries in the Registry. So if you save a `.reg` file as a backup for a key, mess up something in the key, and then double-click the `.reg` file, your mistakes get overwritten with the original entries. Very simple.
- **Hive:** A bunch of Registry entries stored as a binary file. (Don't be intimidated: A *hive* is just a bunch of keys under a single key. It's roughly analogous to a folder.) I don't recommend that you use hives, because you can't make changes to them by hand, but in some ways, they're better than `.reg` files. If you are curious about hives, though, a discussion about referencing hives is at `http://support.microsoft.com/?kbid=199190`.

I step you through a real-world example, creating a `.reg` file as a backup for my favorite quick Registry tweak, in the last section of this technique.

Making Changes Safely

Here's the general approach to making safe changes in the Registry:

1. **Create a System Restore Point (see Technique 64).**
2. **Back up the key that you're going to change to a `.reg` file (see the preceding section).**
3. **Make the changes.**
4. **If necessary, force Windows to recognize those changes.**

   Generally, the most reliable way to do that is to log off and then log back on again.
5. **Test the changes.**

   Depending on the kind of change you made, this step can be quite straightforward or very difficult. For example, testing to see whether a Registry tweak speeds up your Internet connection could be iffy at best. On the other hand, testing to see whether a modified desktop setting (say, a new color for your menus) worked could be as simple as looking at your desktop.
6. **If the change didn't do what you wanted it to do, restore the Registry by double-clicking the `.reg` file that you saved.**
7. **If something goes very, very wrong, follow the steps in Technique 64 to restore your system to the System Restore Point.**

Running My Favorite Quick Registry Tweak

There are very, very few worthwhile Registry tweaks that TweakUI *doesn't* handle faster, easier, and more reliably.

Let me say that a different way.

If you want to tweak your Registry settings based on something you read in a magazine or a book, or you saw a trick posted on the Internet — chances are very good that TweakUI can do what you want with a couple of clicks. Check out Technique 5 for details on TweakUI.

That said, I know of a good, quick timesaving Registry change that TweakUI doesn't handle.

Does your computer have a NumLock key? If you have a full-size keyboard, chances are good that the NumLock key sits above the 7 over on the number pad — to the right of the main keyboard. When the NumLock key is "on", the keys on the number pad act like numbers. When the NumLock key is "off", the keys on the number pad usually turn into directional arrow keys, possibly with Home/End/PgUp/PgDown on the four corners.

In theory, the status of each user's NumLock key is "sticky" — when you log off or turn off your computer, WinXP is supposed to remember how you left your NumLock key and reinstate the setting when you log back on. In some cases that's great. But there are two potential problems:

- Sometimes Windows XP doesn't remember correctly.

Okay, okay. Maybe *I* don't remember correctly. At least, something or someone comes along and changes my NumLock key, and when I restart Windows, it doesn't come back the way I remember setting it. Hey, I've got more important things to think about.

- The NumLock key is set "off" when the PC starts. (Because nobody has logged on yet, Windows doesn't have a NumLock setting to remember, eh?) If you have passwords on your accounts, you might think that you can type numbers on the number pad, but you can't. At least, some of the time.

In my particular case, I'm just too darn lazy to want to deal with it. I always want Windows to come up with the NumLock key "on" — no matter what happened in a previous lifetime.

Telling Windows that you always want it to start with the NumLock key "on" is easy — all it takes is a little trip to the Registry. Here's an extra-cautious first-timer's approach to editing your Registry:

1. **Go through Technique 64 and set a System Restore point.**

   This is the extra-cautious part. Yes, I'm telling you to put on your training wheels. If you have a System Restore Point, even if you change every scary setting in the Registry and your whole world comes crashing down, all you have to do is run a System Restore (or boot with the Last Known Good Configuration), and your old Registry returns.

2. **Choose Start⇨Run, type** regedit **and press Enter.**

   The Registry Editor appears.

3. **On the left side, double-click down the tree until you get to HKEY_USERS\.Default\Control Panel\Keyboard.**

   Your screen looks like Figure 68-2.

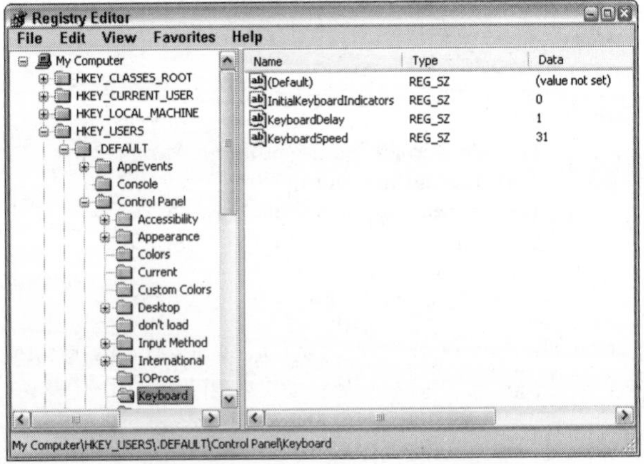

• **Figure 68-2: Navigate to the "Default" settings for all users.**

4. **Click once on Keyboard, on the left, and then choose File⇨Export. Give your** `.reg` **backup file a name (say,** `Original Keyboard Settings for Default User`**) and click Save.**

   If you don't like this change, you can double-click that `.reg` file any time and return the HKEY_USERS\.Default\Control Panel\Keyboard Registry entries to their original state.

5. **On the right, in the Name column, double-click InitialKeyboardIndicators.**

   The Registry Editor brings up an Edit String dialog box (see Figure 68-3).

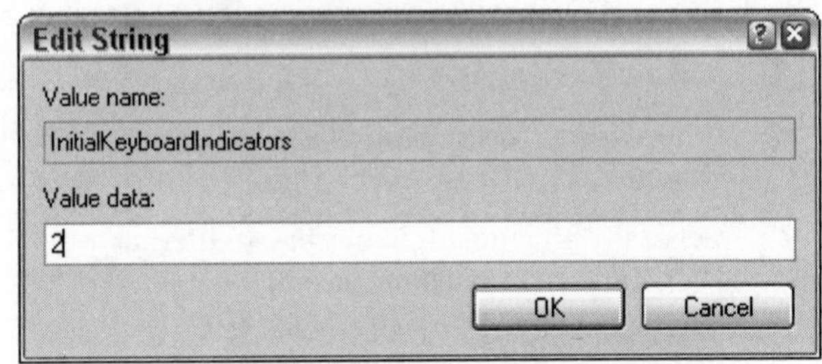

• **Figure 68-3: Change InitialKeyboardIndicators to 2.**

6. **In the Value Data box, type** 2 **and click OK.**

   With that value data changed to 2, Windows knows to turn on the NumLock key every time it starts.

7. **If you want to force Windows to turn the NumLock key on every time you log on to the computer, navigate to HKEY_CURRENT_USER\Control Panel\Keyboard.**

8. **Click once on Keyboard, on the left, and then choose File⇨Export. Give this** `.reg` **backup file a name (say,** `Original Keyboard Settings for Me`**) and click Save.**

9. **Double-click InitialKeyboardIndicators, change the Value Data to 2, and click OK.**

10. **Choose File⇨Exit.**

    You return to Windows. Next time you start your machine, or the next time you log on, the NumLock key is forced "on."

If you ever change your mind about Windows' NumLock key on startup, double-click the `Original Keyboard Settings for Default User.reg` file, and that Registry key is stored. Similarly, if you want to change your own settings back, double-click the `Original Keyboard Settings for Me.reg` file.

That's the long, boring, safe way to make Registry changes. Once you're familiar with the Editor, you'll probably dispense with running a System Restore Point, but you should always take a moment to export a `.reg` file before you make any changes.

There's a shorthand for all of the work you just did. If you ever wanted to feel way cool, try the jargon. I can normally summarize the ten steps as: Yo, dude. Change HKU\.Default\Control Panel\Keyboard\InitialKeyboardIndicators and HKCU\Control Panel\Keyboard\InitialKeyboardIndicators to 2.

Updating Windows' Registered Owner

Save Time By

- Finding out what name your computer is registered to
- Updating Windows' Registered Owner and Registered Company

So you just finished reading Technique 68 and you want to try a Registry change that won't get you tied up in knots. Have I got a tweak for you.

When you first installed Windows, or when you fired up your PC as soon as you got it out of the box, the installer asked you for your name and your organization's name. Did you get it right? Has it changed since then?

Yeah, me, too.

This short technique takes you through the simple steps to change the Registry so Windows thinks it belongs to the person and organization *you* choose. Whether you feed Windows the real thing — well, that's up to you.

Seeing Who Owns Your PC

Every Windows XP PC has a registered owner and a registered organization. Confusingly, these settings have nothing to do with whether you, uh, registered Windows or not. (I talk about registering your copy of Windows — actually, I warn you not to do it — in Technique 2.)

Your computer's registered owner and registered organization come from information that you typed into the Windows installer. Chances are good that was so long ago you've forgotten that you ever did it.

The easiest way to see Windows' official registered owner and organization is to

1. **Click Start.**
2. **Right-click My Computer.**
3. **Choose Properties.**

   Windows shows you the System Properties dialog box in Figure 69-1. You can read the owner and organization underneath the Registered To line.

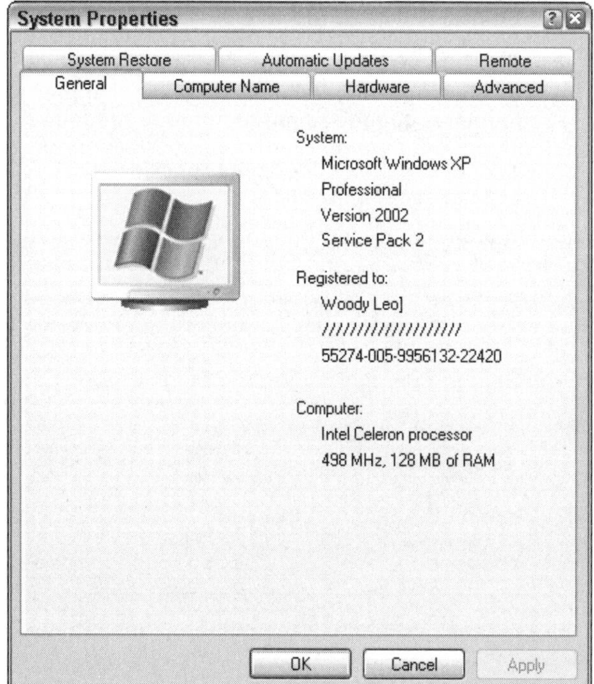

• **Figure 69-1: My completely screwed-up registered owner and organization settings.**

If your registered owner and organization are wrong, don't feel too bad. I'd guess that half of all the PCs in the world are working just fine with incorrect owners and organizations.

The biggest problem with an incorrect owner and organization? Other programs frequently pick up the names when they get installed, so you either have to over-type the name and organization when you install new programs — or you simply live with being identified as **Woody Leo]**. Hey, I've been called worse.

Changing the Owner and Organization

It just so happens that changing the registered owner and organization takes just a minute or two, providing you're willing to dive into the Windows Registry.

The first rule of editing the Registry: Don't do it unless you have to. TweakUI (which I talk about in Technique 5) handles a wide range of changes, and almost always eliminates the need to dig into the Registry. Surprisingly, though, TweakUI doesn't let you change the registered owner or organization. Thus, a quick dip in the Registry is warranted.

To change the registered owner and organization

1. **Choose Start⇨Run, type** regedit **and press Enter.**

   The Windows Registry Editor appears (shown in Figure 69-2).

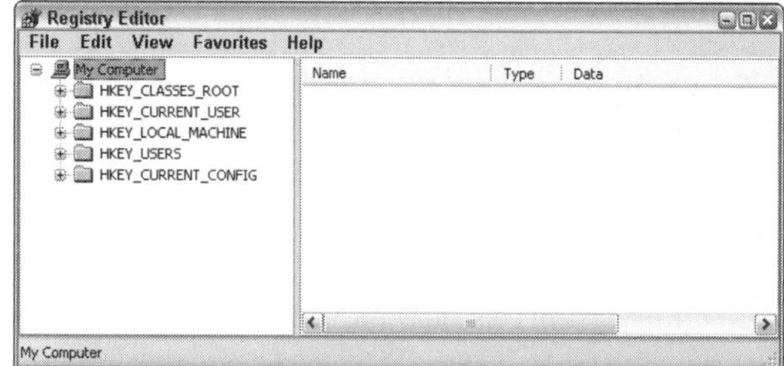

• **Figure 69-2: The Registry Editor in all its glory.**

2. **On the left side, under My Computer, double-click and navigate all the way down to HKEY_LOCAL_MACHINE\SOFTWARE\Microsoft\Windows NT\CurrentVersion (see Figure 69-3).**

   Yes, I know that you aren't running Windows NT. Some Registry settings are in really weird places.

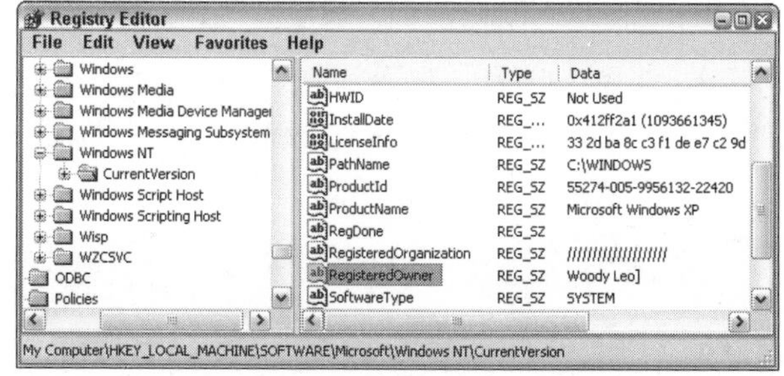

• **Figure 69-3: The Registry key that contains the registered owner and organization.**

3. **On the left, make sure you click CurrentVersion. Then on the right, scroll down to RegisteredOwner and double-click it.**

   An Edit String dialog box appears (see Figure 69-4).

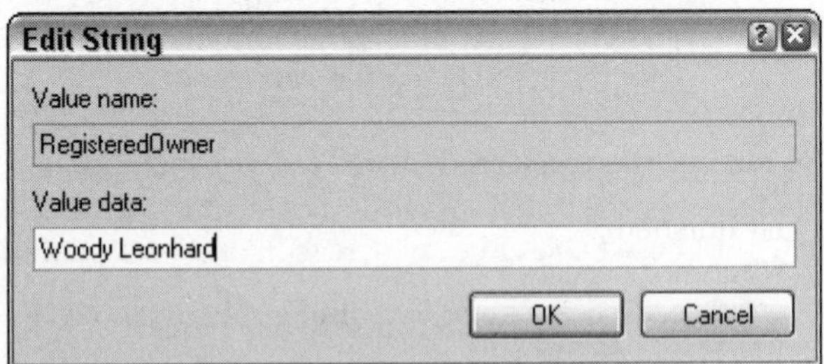

• **Figure 69-4: The registered owner appears here.**

4. **In the Value Data box, type the name you want to use for the registered owner. Then click OK.**

   The Registry gets updated with the value you typed.

5. **On the right, double-click RegisteredOrganization.**

   Again, you see an Edit String dialog box.

6. **In the Value Data box, type the name you want to appear for the registered organization. Then click OK.**

   Yes, you can claim that this copy of Windows XP is registered to Microsoft Corp. Or the Central Intelligence Agency. Or SMERSH.

7. **Choose File⇨Exit to leave the Registry Editor.**

8. **Check to make sure your changes are correct by clicking Start, right-clicking My Computer, and choosing Properties.**

   Your new, improved System Properties box appears (see Figure 69-5).

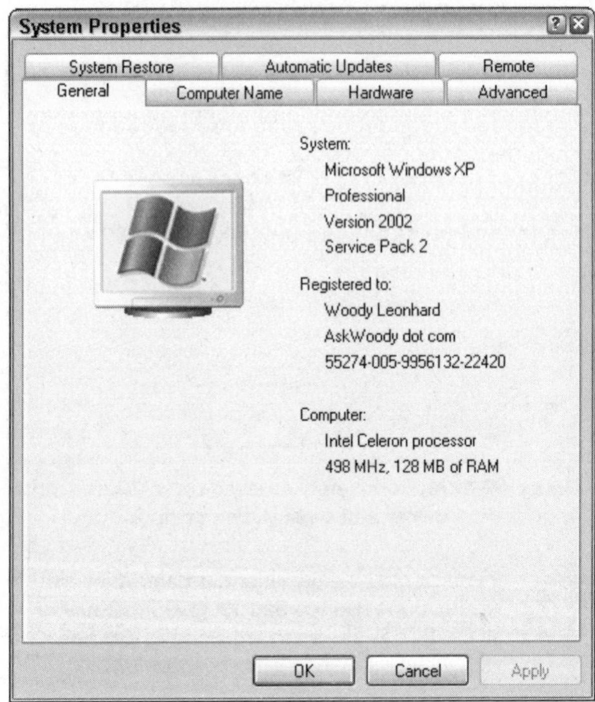

• **Figure 69-5: Now that's more like it.**

Speeding Up Scanning for Squishable Files

Save Time By

- Changing the Registry quickly and easily
- Telling Windows how to speed up disk cleanup by ignoring squishable files

No doubt you've just finished Techniques 68 and 69, and you're ready for a somewhat more complex Registry tweak.

Good. This one's my favorite because it's straightforward and quick — and if you ever have Windows run through its Disk Cleanup routine, making this one simple Registry change saves you eons of time.

There are very few worthwhile Registry changes that TweakUI doesn't handle. (I talk about TweakUI extensively in Technique 5.) If you want to change your Registry settings based on a trick you saw posted on the Internet, or written up in a book or magazine, first check to make sure that TweakUI can't handle it. This is one of few worthwhile changes that TweakUI can't touch.

Scanning for Squishers

Windows XP has a remarkably thorough Disk Cleanup routine that helps you recover space on any disk. Here's how it goes:

1. **Choose Start⇨My Computer, right-click a hard drive, and choose Properties.**

   The Properties dialog box appears, as shown in Figure 70-1.

2. **Click the Disk Cleanup button.**

   I discuss this topic in Technique 56. Windows examines the contents of the disk to see how much space can be saved (see Figure 70-2).

   Windows actually checks every file on the hard drive and sees how much space you can save by compressing files.

Unfortunately, the "Scanning: Compress Old Files" activity can take ages.

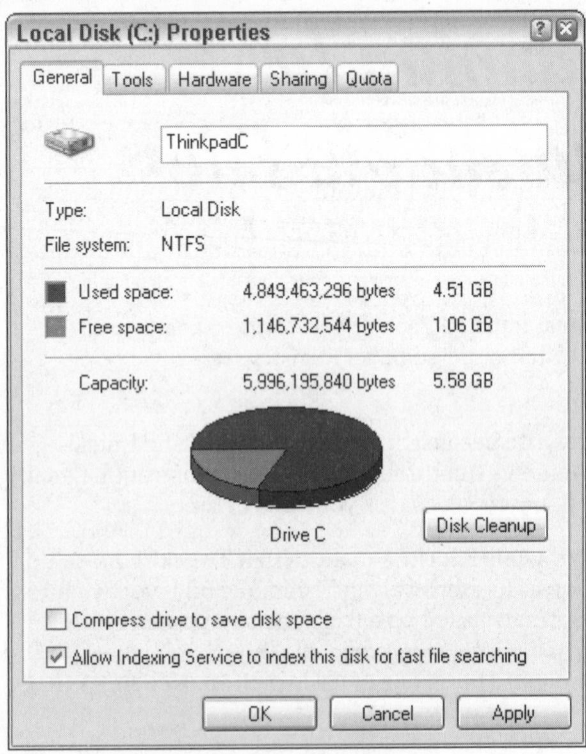

• **Figure 70-1: A hard drive's properties.**

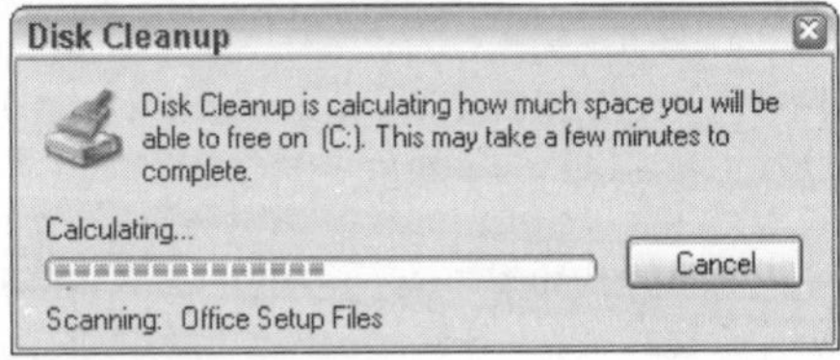

• **Figure 70-2: Scanning and scanning and scanning.**

With hard drives as cheap as they are nowadays, why compress a whole drive?

Speeding Up the Scan

You can set a Registry entry to turn off the scan for potentially squishable files. Here's how to set it:

1. **Choose Start⇨Run, type** regedit, **and press Enter.**

   The Registry Editor appears.

2. **In the Registry Editor, double-click the left side down to HKEY_LOCAL_MACHINE\ SOFTWARE⇨Microsoft⇨Windows⇨ CurrentVersion⇨Explorer⇨VolumeCaches⇨ Compress Old Files.**

   Yes, that's the name of the key (see Figure 70-3). Don't blame me.

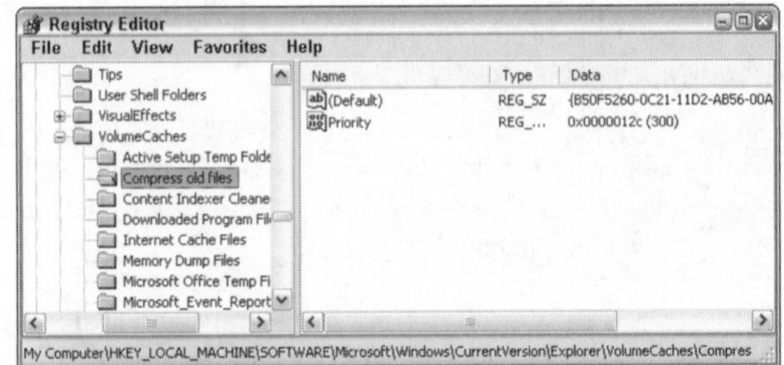

• **Figure 70-3: The offending value.**

3. **Click once on Compress Old Files, and then choose File⇨Export.**

   This is a how you back up a key to a `.reg` file (see Figure 70-4).

4. **In the Export Range area at the bottom, make sure that the Selected Branch option is selected, with HKEY_LOCAL_MACHINE\ SOFTWARE\ . . . and so on in the text box underneath the option.**

5. **Navigate to a location for the backup (in Figure 70-4, I put it on the desktop). In the Save as Type drop-down list, choose Registration Files (`*.reg`). Type a name for the `.reg` file and click Save.**

It's unlikely that you'll ever want to change the key back, but if you ever change your mind, double-click this `.reg` file and this part of the Registry gets restored to its former settings. You never know.

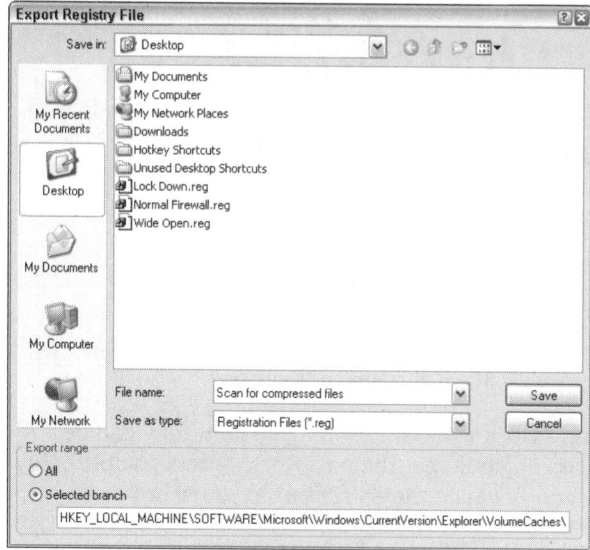

• **Figure 70-4: Export this small key as a `.reg` file.**

After exporting the key, return to the Registry Editor.

6. **In the Registry Editor, double-click (Default).**

   (Default) is a valid value name, just like any other. You see the Edit String dialog box, as shown in Figure 70-5, without a value name.

7. **Delete the stuff in the Value Data text box and click OK.**

   The Registry Editor looks like Figure 70-6.

8. **Choose File⇨Exit to close the Registry Editor.**

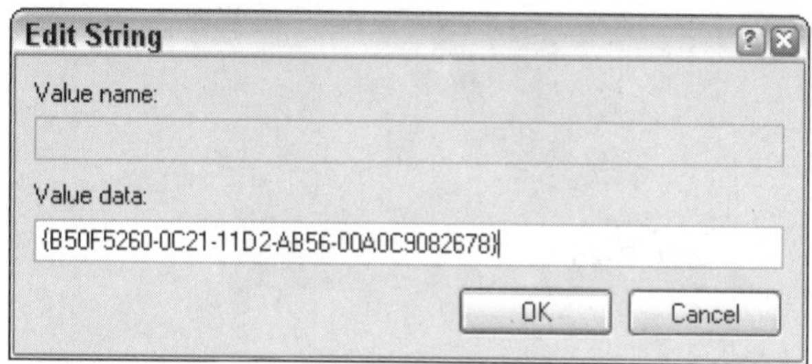

• **Figure 70-5: Delete the value data.**

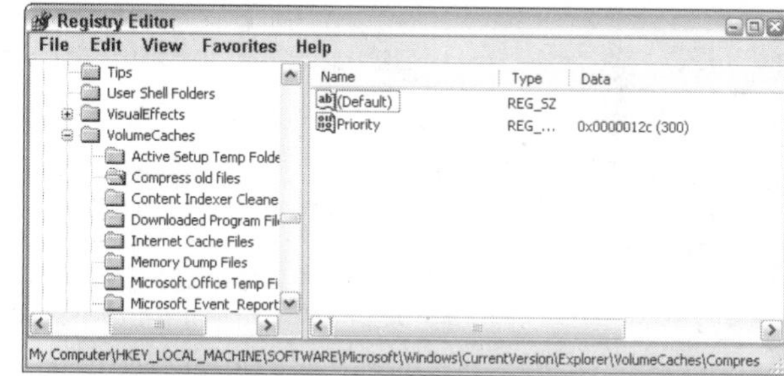

• **Figure 70-6: A clean (Default) value.**

9. **Hold onto your hat. Choose Start⇨My Computer, right-click a hard drive, choose Properties, and then click the Disk Cleanup button.**

   I bet the Disk Cleanup scan runs in one-tenth the time it took before. Slick, huh?

10. **If you change your mind and you really, really want Disk Cleanup to run like a slug, er, to scan for files to compress, just double-click the `.reg` file you created in Step 5.**

    The Registry reverts to its former entry, and Disk Cleanup falls back into the Stone Age.

Using Program Compatibility Modes

Save Time By

- Scanning your system for old programs that might cause problems
- Making your old programs work — quickly
- Installing old programs when the installer doesn't work

If you have a trusted, old, dog-eared copy of Norton Anti-Virus for Windows 98, throw it away. And that classic disc with Steve Gibson's ScanRite for Windows 95? Give it the heave-ho, too.

Old system utilities don't work with Windows XP. In fact, they can be downright dangerous. If you could get them to work — and you probably can't — there's a very good chance they'll scramble your hard drive.

Ah, but Commander Keen? Now there's a trooper. Old games, like old accounting programs, never die. They just keep eating into your productivity.

This technique shows you how to make your old programs work with Windows XP.

Scanning for Program Compatibility

Most application programs that worked in Windows 98, 98 Second Edition, Me, NT, or 2000 can work with Windows XP. Windows XP has an amazingly high tolerance for the odd behavior of games, word processors, databases, all sorts of communication programs, accounting programs, weird printing utilities, timers, and the myriad of diverse programs that helped make the computer industry what it is today.

On the other hand, most utilities — disk scanners, defragmenters, backup programs, antivirus products, firewalls, tune up packs, and the like — that aren't already compatible with Windows XP have to be built from the ground up to become Windows XP–compliant. If you try to run them, even in Windows XP's special compatibility mode, you have a chance of breaking something.

Every commercial program available on store shelves today works with Windows XP. Most programs that you download from the Internet also work with Windows XP, although some older programs (primarily games and commercial products that aren't being sold anymore) may have problems.

A *compatibility mode* is just a collection of smoke and mirrors that makes programs believe they're running under an older version of Windows (or even DOS). Running in compatibility mode doesn't necessarily protect your PC. Mostly, it deceives the programs.

Windows XP has a wizard that gathers the names of programs on your computer and lets you test out various compatibility mode settings with each. To run the compatibility wizard, follow these steps:

1. **Choose Start⇨All Programs⇨Accessories⇨Program Compatibility Wizard.**

   The Program Compatibility Wizard appears, as shown in Figure 71-1.

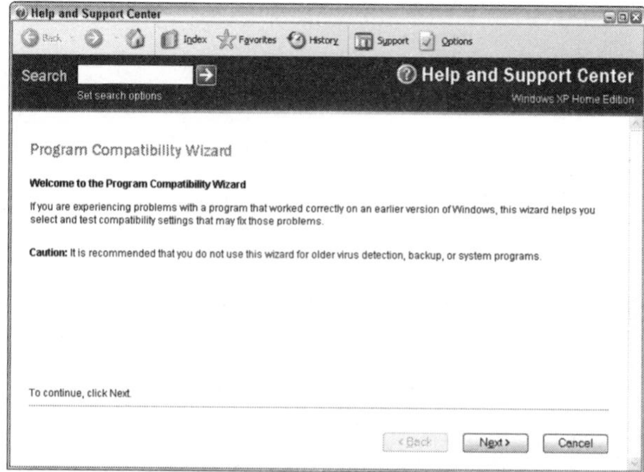

• **Figure 71-1: Windows XP's Compatibility Wizard.**

2. **Click Next.**

   The wizard wants to know whether it should scan your computer and create a list of programs, or if you have a specific CD or program that you want to use.

3. **If you have trouble with one specific program, select the I Want to Locate the Program Manually option. Otherwise, select the I Want to Choose from a List of Programs option. Click Next.**

   The wizard assembles a list of programs (see Figure 71-2).

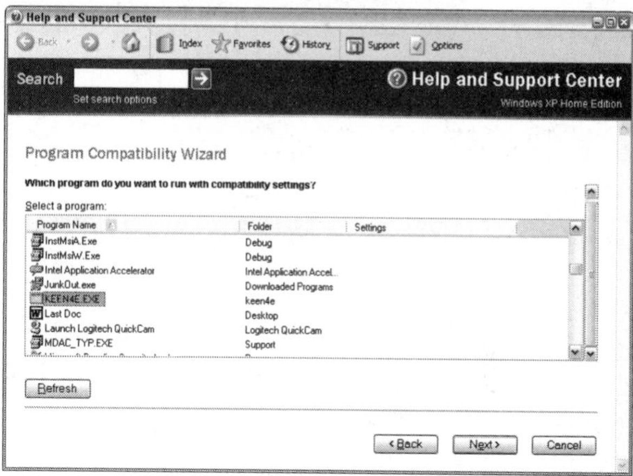

• **Figure 71-2: The wizard's list doesn't seem to conform to any particular rules.**

The wizard doesn't find all the programs on your PC. I couldn't get it to scan my D: drive, and it missed several obvious candidates for compatibility mode on my C: drive. If you have a problem with a specific program, choose it — don't rely on the wizard to be very wizardly.

4. **Choose a program for compatibility mode testing.**

   In Figure 71-2, I chose Commander Keen 4. (Ever wonder what Id Software made before Quake and Doom?)

5. **Click Next.**

   The wizard wants to know which version of Windows it should trick the program into "seeing," as shown in Figure 71-3.

6. **Choose the version of Windows that you want to test, and then click Next.**

   The wizard allows you to trick the application into thinking that it only has a very limited number of colors available on-screen, as shown in Figure 71-4.

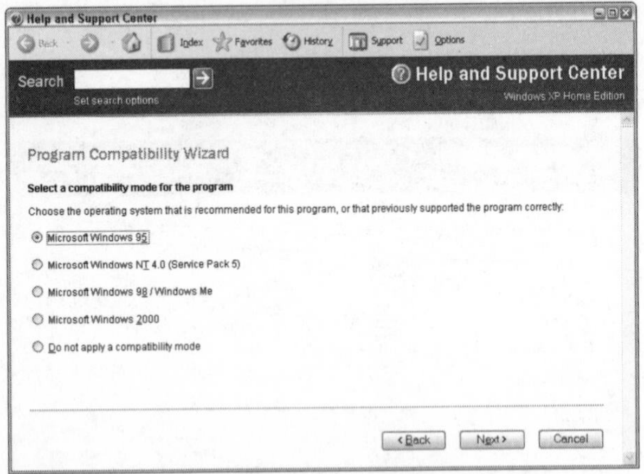

• **Figure 71-3: Pick a Windows compatibility version.**

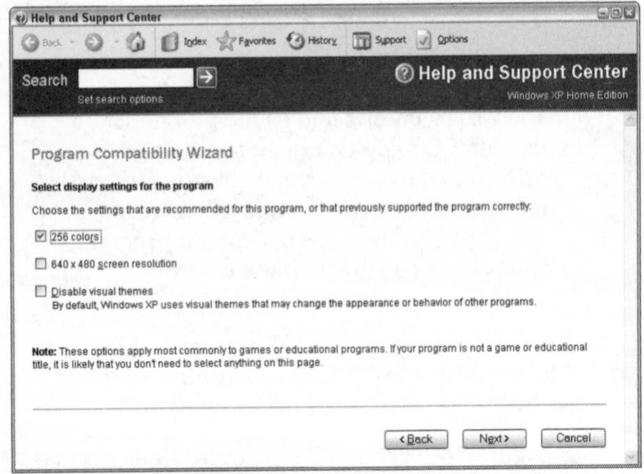

• **Figure 71-4: Sometimes color depth is a crucial compatibility factor — older programs get confused when they can use too many colors.**

7. **If you think color might be a problem, choose a limit to the number of colors in the compatibility mode, and click Next.**

   The wizard displays the settings you chose.

8. **Click Next.**

   Windows launches the program in compatibility mode. It's up to you to see whether the program works right.

   When you exit the program, you go back to the wizard, as shown in Figure 71-5.

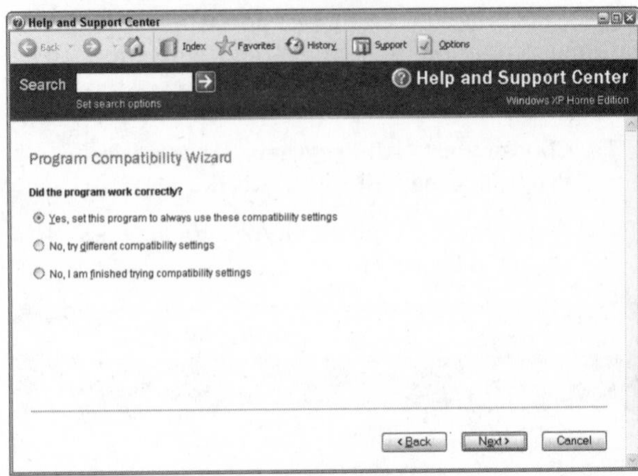

• **Figure 71-5: The wizard wants to know whether it should store the compatibility settings.**

9. **If the program worked correctly, click Next. If not, select one of the No options.**

   The wizard asks whether you want to send the settings that you just put together to Microsoft.

10. **Click the No button, and then click Next.**

    You see a typical wizard Finish screen.

11. **Click Finish.**

    Although the wizard doesn't tell you, in fact it has made changes to the compatibility settings for this particular program (see Figure 71-6). See the next section for details.

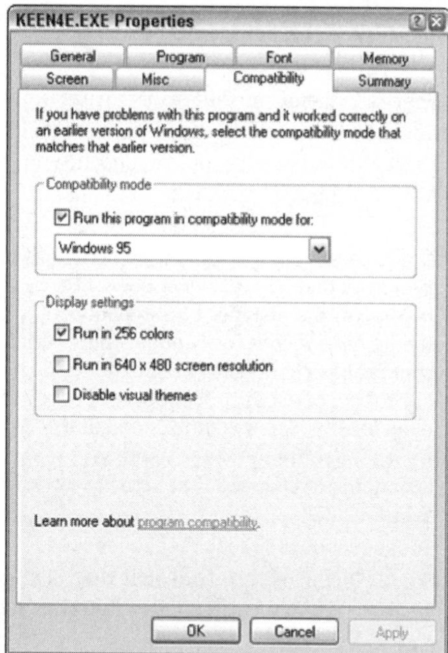

• Figure 71-6: Compatibility settings generated by the wizard for Commander Keen 4.

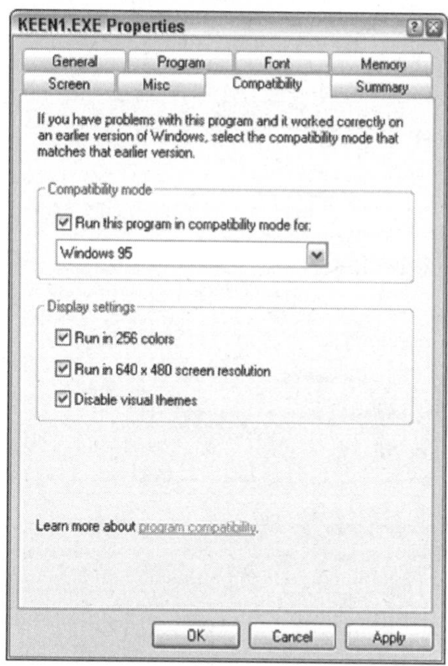

• Figure 71-7: Commander Keen's compatibility.

Setting Compatibility Modes

Although you can use the Program Compatibility Wizard to set up compatibility modes, in many cases going in and making the changes manually is just simpler. In fact, the wizard won't even handle several settings.

Here's how to go it alone:

1. **Choose Start⇨My Computer and navigate to the program that you want to run in compatibility mode.**
2. **Right-click the program and choose Properties⇨Compatibility.**

   In Figure 71-7, you see the compatibility settings for the original Commander Keen 1 (vintage 1990).
3. **Change compatibility settings to match the kinds of hardware and software that were available when the program was released.**

   In Figure 71-7, I used the most retro settings available: Windows 95 (the oldest operating system offered), VGA mode (256 colors at 640 x 480), and disabling the fancy Windows XP visual themes.
4. **Click the Memory tab. If the program requires old-fashioned EMS, XMS, XMS/HMA, or DPMI memory, or if it needs to run in protected main memory, make the appropriate adjustments to your settings.**

   Many people overlook the fact that you have to set up special memory settings independently of the other compatibility settings. (See Figure 71-8.) In fact, even the Program Compatibility Wizard ignores this crucial information. If your program requires any of these complex, obsolete ways of addressing memory, the program's documentation lists that fact.

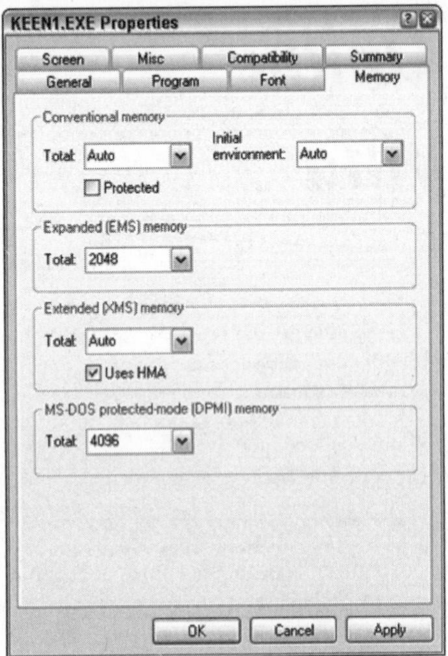

• **Figure 71-8: Ancient (and confusing!) memory settings go here.**

5. **Click OK and run the program.**
6. **If the program still won't run, go back to Step 1 and try tweaking the settings.**
7. **If you experience memory violations, and you can't get the settings in Step 4 to work right, go on to the Internet and use Google (`www.google.com`) to search for the name of the program, plus one of the types of memory.**

   For example, search for **Commander Keen XMS**. If the program requires an oddball memory setting, you'll probably find it on the Web.

If your old program is on a CD, your settings aren't saved. You have to go in and adjust the settings using these steps every time you run the program. Copy the program to a convenient place on your hard drive. When you do that, the settings are stored and take effect every time you run the program.

Installing the Retro Way

I've seen reports from people on the Internet who are having trouble installing older programs. In many cases, the problem is that the *installer* needs to run in Program Compatibility Mode.

Some of the old installers make changes to Windows that fly under Windows XP's radar. If you run the installer under Windows XP, the installer thinks it's running under DOS, so it makes changes to `autoexec.bat` and `config.sys` — which Windows XP doesn't even look at. On the other hand, if the installer thinks it's running under Windows NT 4, it may make changes that actually work in Windows XP.

If you have an old program that just doesn't work under Windows XP, try running the installer in compatibility mode. Here's how:

1. **Choose Start⇨My Computer and navigate to the installer.**

   Old installers were invariably called `install.exe` or `setup.exe`. Come to think of it, *new* installers are invariably called . . . oh, never mind.

2. **Right-click `install.exe` or `setup.exe` and choose Properties⇨Compatibility.**
3. **If you've never run the installer in program compatibility mode before, choose Windows NT 4.0 (Service Pack 5) from the drop-down list in the Compatibility Mode area.**
4. **Click OK and run the installer.**

   If that doesn't work — either the installer doesn't run, or the program itself doesn't work right — go back and, in Step 3, try running in Windows 95 compatibility mode.

   Good luck! Commander Keen awaits.

Fast, Easy, and Safe Online Shopping

Save Time By

- Finding what you want — fast
- Ordering with full confidence
- Using eBay the right way

One hundred billion bucks. That's about how much consumers will spend while using the Internet this year. It's a staggering number — but barring some extraordinary calamity, it's going to keep on growing.

You already know why people shop online — it's fast, it's easy, and you don't need to find a parking spot. If you look in the right places, comparing prices can take just a click or two. Although you rarely find the absolute-lowest price for most consumer products online, particularly after you pay for shipping, you come pretty darn close.

And you won't waste an hour driving to the mall and back.

Sure, online shopping has its problems. You can't feel the fabric. You can't try on the pants to see if they bag in the butt. You can't hand your kids a five dollar bill and tell 'em to buy the biggest ice cream cone they've ever seen.

But when it comes to saving time, online shopping can't be beat.

Searching Reliable E-Tailers

Whether you want a genuine first edition signed Hemingway or an almost-certainly-fake, signed *Lincoln in Dalivision,* you find much of what you want — and much more of what you don't want — on the Web.

If you've been on the Web for any time at all, no doubt you've bookmarked dozens of places that deserve your hard-earned dollars or Euros or yen or shekels or baht.

In this section, I offer you three lists of sites that I think every online shopper should check at least once. This isn't a scientific list or a paid advertisement (which is more than can be said for advertising on some search engines!). It's a quick rundown of good places to shop if you're in the mood to save some time.

Table 72-1 lists the retailers that I have used for years. They're reliable, the sites are put together so that you can get in and out quickly, and they don't sock you with hidden charges or time-wasting games.

When I want to look for bargains, I go to these two sites:

- **Overstock.com** (`www.overstock.com`)**:** Discounted name-brand products in more than a hundred categories — electronics, home, clothes, jewelry, and sports.
- **Eddie Bauer Outlet** (`www.eddiebaueroutlet.com`)**:** An online version of its outlet stores.

The sites are a bit harder to negotiate than the ones in Table 72-1, but that's at least partially attributable to the fact that the merchandise changes constantly.

Here are the sites I use when I know what I want and I'm looking for the best price:

- **mySimon** (`www.mysimon.com`)**:** Compare prices from dozens of online retailers. Strong on electronics, computer parts, books, office supplies, clothes, and the like, but not as thorough as it once was.
- **PriceGrabber** (`www.pricegrabber.com`)**:** Fast comparisons on cameras, computer products, video games, and DVDs.
- **BizRate** (`www.bizrate.com`)**:** Compares prices for computer equipment, cameras, clothes, travel, office supplies, toys, and much more.
- **Froogle** (`froogle.google.com`)**:** The new kid on the chopping, er, shopping block lists just about everything, but I found that other sites linked to places with slightly lower prices.

If you aren't sure where to look for a product, you should try:

- **The Google shotgun approach:** Type a description of the product into the Google Search box and press Enter.

Table 72-1: All-Time Favorite Shopping Sites

Address	Company	Description
`www.amazon.com`	Amazon	The original online bookstore now features toys, clothes, electronics, and software.
`www.bn.com`	Barnes & Noble	Giving Amazon a run for the money and staying focused on books.
`www.cooking.com`	Cooking.com	Absolutely everything a cook could ever want. Shipping is available only to the U.S., territories, APO addresses, and Canada, undoubtedly because people who live outside the U.S. don't like to eat.
`www.landsend.com`	Lands' End	One of the first, and still one of the best. Clothes, shoes, luggage, and more.
`www.llbean.com`	L.L. Bean	Great clothes, legendary shoes, outdoor gear, and still the best return policy on the planet.
`www.oldnavy.com`	Old Navy	You call 'em generic. I call 'em cool. Cheap, too.
`www.rei.com`	REI	Long-time favorite with innovative outdoor products. Includes a tab for REI-Outlet.com.
`www.wonderfullywacky.com`	Baron Bob Gifts	If you want an Airzooka gun or a Talking Trash Teddy Bear — well, you get the idea.

- **The Yahoo! indexed approach:** Go to `shopping.yahoo.com` and drill down to the product you want.

Paying It Safe

Every major retail site nowadays has adopted the shopping-cart approach. Most online retailers enable you to store information on their Web sites — credit card number, shipping address, and the like — to make it easier for you make repeated purchases.

If you want to save something in your shopping cart, you almost always have to enable cookies on your computer. That's how the retailer's computer keeps track of who you are and what you're buying. For more about cookies, see Technique 53.

Choosing a payment method

When you shop online, you're generally offered a number of ways to pay:

- **Credit card:** By far the most flexible and safest option for you (also one of the most problematic sources of income for the retailer).
- **Debit card:** If you have an ATM card or check card in which the full amount of a purchase is deducted from your bank account as soon as you buy something, it's a debit card. In the U.S., a debit card purchase is not protected nearly as well as a credit card purchase. Outside the U.S., laws and/or card company policies vary.
- **PayPal or similar third-party payment:** A very efficient means of paying, with an established conflict resolution method (if you have a PayPal account, see item 15 of the User Agreement at `https://www.paypal.com/row/cgi-bin/webscr?cmd=p/gen/ua/ua`), but you don't have anything close to the kind of protection given to credit card charges.
- **E-money or micropayments:** Although the first wave of companies died in the dot-dom bust, there's been a tiny resurgence of interest. These accounts and/or cards generally reflect some sort of prepaid, stored value. You pay with e-money, and the amount is debited from your card or account.

Getting what you pay for

You should treat a business transaction on the Internet the same way you would treat any other business transaction — only more so.

Before you order a product or service, follow these steps:

1. **Retrieve and save precise details about the product.**

   At the very least, you need a model number and a description of the product. Surf to the page that describes what you're ordering; then print or save the page. To save the page, choose File➪Save, and in the Save as Type drop-down list, choose Web Archive, Single File (`*.mht`) (see Figure 72-1). That saves the page and all the pictures on it in a single file.

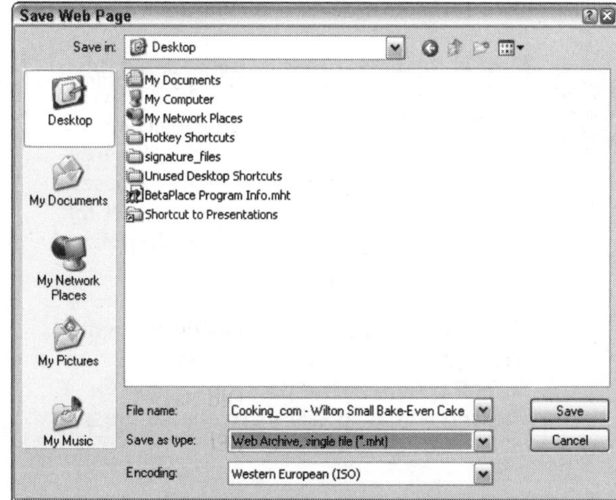

• **Figure 72-1: Save an entire page, including all its pictures, by using the Web Archive, Single File option.**

2. **Find the company's refund and return policies and save them.**

   Again, print or save the appropriate page as a Web Archive, Single File (`*.mht`).

3. **Get the e-mail address or phone number of the customer service people.**

   Print it or save it. You know the drill.

4. **Get something in writing about the expected delivery date.**

   There should be an explicit statement about delivery somewhere during the checkout process. Make sure that you save (or print) the page with that information.

5. **Make sure that you know how much you will be charged.**

   If the final on-screen bill doesn't include shipping and handling, you only have yourself to blame if your product arrives in the back of a Rolls, hand-delivered by a big football star — and you're billed for the privilege.

6. **Print or save the order page.**

   Every legitimate retail site e-mails you a receipt. But even under the best of circumstances, sometimes things go awry.

Most of the time, a specific transaction number is associated with the order. Make sure you have a record of it. Also, many sites send separate e-mail confirmations when the order is placed, and when it's shipped. Keep those, too. And if you receive a tracking number for UPS, FedEx, or some other carrier (Amazon, among many others, includes a tracking number in the shipment notification), take a moment and visit the Web site to ensure the package is headed in the right direction. Several times, I've had packages bound for Thailand end up in Taiwan, or ones addressed to Australia go to Austria.

When everything arrives as expected and your credit card (or debit card, PayPal account, e-account, or whatever) is charged correctly, you can breathe a sigh of relief. In fact, in my experience, the vast majority of online purchases work just as well as their meatspace analogs. But whether you're clicking online or standing at a checkout counter, it's a whole lot easier to prepare for any eventuality before a disaster strikes.

Using reputable Web sites

So how do you know if a specific Web site is on the up-and-up?

The short answer: You never really know for sure. Here are a few pointers:

- If the Web site has the same name as a store chain you know and trust, you should expect that the policies and services online will be at least as good as what you would receive in person, in the store.
- If you have any doubt at all about a Web site's credibility, check the Better Business Bureau's online site, `www.bbbonline.com`. The Better Business Bureau isn't infallible, it only covers the United States, and it doesn't have entries for every Web shop, but the 15,000-or-so businesses listed in its directory have gone to extraordinary lengths to ensure that their customers are treated fairly.
- If you aren't dealing with a big-name chain, and the Web site isn't in the BBB's list, you have to rely on your own devices. You might be able to find out how long the company has been in business. You can scan the Google newsgroups for the company's name. You can look at the site and see if it's well designed: A poorly designed site is a dead tip-off for a company that doesn't care. You can track down a customer service number, and call and ask about the company's return policy, product warranties, shipping costs, and so on. More than anything, though, if you start to get second thoughts about dealing with a specific Web site, insist on using a credit card.

Spend the time up front to save time down the line. When you're sure of a business's reliability, you can shop without fear and save time. Remember that the first rule of buying online is *caveat emptor* – and that a fool and his money soon go separate ways.

On the technical side, you should only send out your credit card or other personal information if the Web site requesting it uses something called the Secured Sockets Layer. You don't need to remember that arcane name. But you should remember to look for the locked (padlock) symbol at the bottom of the Internet Explorer screen (see Figure 72-2).

• Figure 72-2: Check for a padlock in the lower-right corner of your screen when you're shopping online.

The locked symbol signifies that it's very, very, very difficult for someone to eavesdrop on your conversation with the Web site. Yes, holes have been discovered in SSL. No, nobody has lost any money because of them.

Handling credit card fraud

If someone steals your credit card and the card was issued in the United States, the Fair Credit Billing Act and the Electronic Fund Transfer Act basically protect you from any charges in excess of $50.

If someone steals your credit card *number*, as opposed to the card itself, and the card was issued in the United States, your liability for unauthorized charges is zero.

You should call your bank immediately if you find that your card has been stolen, of course.

The situation with U.S.-issued debit cards is different. If your debit card is lost or stolen, you're liable for up to $50 if you report the card stolen to the bank within 48 hours. If you wait longer, you could be on the hook for more; and if you don't report a lost card within 60 days of receiving a statement with a bogus charge on it, you may be held liable for the entire amount in your account.

There don't appear to be any laws about stolen debit card numbers. Call your bank and find out your liability if your debit card number (and not the card itself) is stolen.

Laws and credit card company procedures vary in different countries, but many places have laws that are even tougher than those in the United States, and many U.S.-based credit card companies try to match the parent companies' policies overseas.

If you pay for something online with a U.S.-issued debit card or credit card, and if any of these things happen

- You don't receive the goods or service
- You receive something that differs from what was promised
- You were billed for an amount that isn't right

you must immediately write to the credit or debit card company.

It pays to follow through on online fraud — even if you only lose five or ten dollars. Some of the most successful online con men (and women) bilk thousands of customers out of small amounts of money. When you make the effort to correct even small problems, you save time for everyone.

Here's what you need to do:

1. **Make a reasonable effort to resolve the problem with the vendor.**

   Conduct all conversations in writing — e-mail or snail mail — and keep copies of everything. Don't let the negotiating go on for more than a couple of weeks.

2. **If the vendor won't make good on the product or service, write to the credit or debit card company.**

   Theoretically, you're supposed to wait for the bill to come through; but in the case of a debit card, in particular, handling the problem immediately is best — don't wait for your statement. In any case, make sure that your letter arrives at the credit or debit card company within 60 days of when the contested bill was sent to you.

3. **Send the letter certified mail, return receipt requested.**

   Keep the return receipt when it comes back.

4. **Use the address on your credit or debit card statement for billing inquiries or billing disputes.**

   If you write to the payment address, you'll never hear a thing.

5. **In the letter, include your name, address, telephone number, account number, brief (and I do mean brief) description of the dispute, the amount that's in question, your e-mail address, and copies of everything you can find.**

   Make your first shot across the bow overwhelming — not by whining on, page after page, but by presenting the facts clearly and succinctly and supporting what you say with incontrovertible documentation. Ask that the credit card or debit card company contact you by e-mail.

6. **Make copies of everything you're about to send.**

   Keep the whole package stapled together so you can refer to it later.

If you do all of those things, the law is on your side.

There are no laws, at this point, for stored value e-money or micropayment accounts.

If someone takes your money and disappears without supplying the goods you purchased, you have two chances of seeing that money again: slim and none. But if you're smart enough to use a credit card, the credit card company gets the short end of the stick.

It tickles me when people say they're concerned that someone will steal their credit card number when they order something over the Internet. The fact is that you're far more likely to have your number stolen by a clerk in a store or someone rummaging through a trash can. The largest (known) heist of credit card numbers to date came from a computer hacker who broke into the computers at a credit card processing company. The incident had absolutely nothing to do with online shopping.

Keeping private information private

Many a failing dot-com in the past five years has discovered that its most valuable asset is its mailing list. As the bubble burst, strapped companies scrambled for negotiable assets. Many a "private" mailing list ended up on the list of assets, right next to manicured office parks and used office chairs.

Never give out any personal information to anyone unless it's absolutely necessary. That's good advice both on and off the computer. Yes, you have to give out your e-mail address if you order online, and you may have to divulge your telephone number. But the site selling you a printer doesn't need to know your job title or annual income — much less your level of education.

Every Web site that asks for information from you better have a detailed *Platform for Privacy Preferences* (or P3P) privacy statement. The minute you're asked for any personal information — even if it's just to sign up for an account — you should ensure that you can tolerate the company's stated privacy policy. To see the privacy statement, follow these steps:

1. **In Internet Explorer, choose View⇨Privacy Report.**

The Web site divulges all the sites that contribute to the current page (as shown in Figure 72-3).

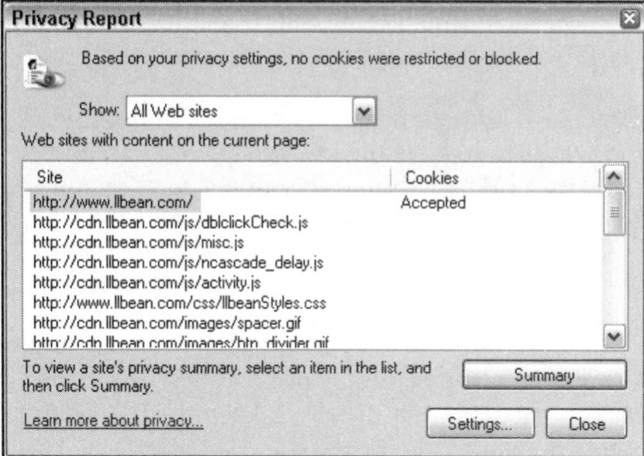

• Figure 72-3: Every Web site that contributes something to the current page — pictures or text — appears in this privacy report.

2. **Click the main site; then click the Summary button.**

   In Figure 72-3, I clicked `www.llbean.com`, and then clicked Summary. The L.L. Bean site responded with its privacy report, part of which is shown in Figure 72-4.

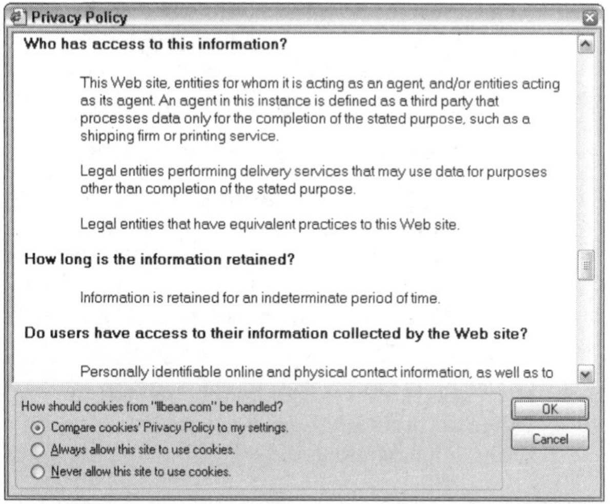

• Figure 72-4: Automated privacy reports can be complex, but good retail sites keep things simple.

Not all companies participate in P3P privacy reporting. Amazon.com, for example, has a comparatively simple privacy statement — basically, it won't sell your information — and that's it. No P3P entry. No automation. Just a straightforward statement.

3. **Click OK and then click Close.**

If you aren't comfortable with a site's stated privacy policy, pass it by. Plenty of alternatives are on the Web.

Remember that the privacy statement is a promise made by the company behind the site. There's no independent way to verify if the company is, for example, selling your e-mail address or demographic information. Independent review organizations, such as `www.bbbonline.com` and `www.truste.com`, react to specific complaints about companies, but they don't monitor for privacy statement compliance. Only trust the privacy statement if you trust the company behind it.

Complaining Effectively

Got a beef? Did somebody rip you off online? The Federal Trade Commission wants to hear about it. Really.

Go to `https://rn.ftc.gov/dod/wsolcq$.startup?Z_ORG_CODE=PU01` and fill out the form.

You'll hear back, I bet.

Mastering eBay

So many people use eBay these days that it's worthwhile understanding some of the more arcane bits and pieces of the eBay way.

When you look at an item for sale, a large amount of information about the seller is encoded in some cute icons and staccato notices.

Look for these entries:

- **The number after the seller's name:** The number indicates the seller's *feedback rating.* Feedback is the lifeblood of eBay, and it's what keeps the venue making money while other online retailers and auction venues go belly up. The feedback rating tells you the net number of positive comments that have been submitted about a particular seller. A high number is a good sign, particularly when you realize that the seller gets 1 point for a positive review, 0 points for a so-so review, and -1 for a negative review. (The star icon following the number is a color-coded repeat of the number.)

Don't just go by the feedback rating shown by the seller's name; it only reflects the *net positive* rating (that is, the total number of positives, minus any negative feedback). Click the number to find out the *total* number of feedback submissions. For example, it's possible for someone to have a feedback rating of 500, which ain't a shabby feedback rating. But if you click the number, you may find that the seller has received several neutral comments (which don't have any effect on the total rating), or negative feedback comments (which decrease the total shown by the seller's name). If you're interested in getting a quick look at how to use eBay to shop for bargains, check out *eBay Bargain Shopping For Dummies* by Marsha Collier (Wiley Publishing, Inc.).

- **A Power Seller icon:** eBay recognizes its best sellers — ones who sell a lot, remain committed to the eBay rules, and get excellent feedback — with the Power Seller icon.
- **A Shades icon:** The icon looks like a pair of sunglasses. It means that the person hasn't been using eBay long enough to have established a reputation through feedback. Maybe they're new. If an eBay seller changes his or her ID, the new ID gets a shades icon for the next 30 days. Although the shades icon doesn't mean anything, uh, shady is going on, there's usually a good reason why a member would change his or her ID — and frequently it's because of sketchy feedback.

eBay has a large staff that keeps track of problems and works to resolve the inevitable conflicts that go along with running the world's largest auction house. Before you bid, you should take a look at `pages.ebay.com/help/confidence/programs-investigations.html` and make sure that you feel comfortable with the safety net that eBay has in place.

Although eBay may or may not be responsible for various aspects of its offerings, keep the following points in mind:

- **eBay is not responsible for the item itself.** If you buy a used washing machine and it falls apart the day you install it, eBay is not at fault.
- **Every bid is a legal and binding contract between you and the seller.** If you have any questions about the item on offer, you should e-mail the seller and ask. Don't place a bid until you are absolutely sure about every detail of the product, its quality, shipping, insurance, and so on. If you don't ask questions before you place your bid, and you get something that matches the description but it wasn't what you were expecting, that isn't fraud — it's lack of due diligence on your part.
- **Beware of anything that's too good to be true.**
- **Con men (and women) work eBay, too.** If someone takes your money and runs, you have very little recourse unless you used a credit card. By the time you get to the point where you're asking eBay to investigate, you might as well kiss your money goodbye.
- **eBay says it has enough people on staff to police all their auctions.** If you were in eBay's shoes, what would you say?

Caveat biddor.

Index

Symbols and Numbers

A

B

C

D

G

H

I

J

K

L

M

N

O

P

Q

R

T

W

X

Z

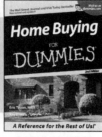

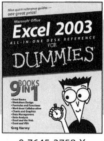

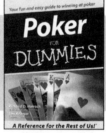

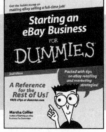

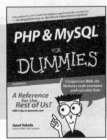

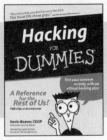